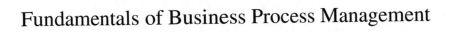

Fundamentals of Business Process Management

Marlon Dumas • Marcello La Rosa •
Jan Mendling • Hajo A. Reijers

Fundamentals of Business Process Management

Second Edition

 Springer

Marlon Dumas
Institute of Computer Science
University of Tartu
Tartu, Estonia

Marcello La Rosa
School of Computing and Information
  Systems
The University of Melbourne
Melbourne, Australia

Jan Mendling
Institute for Information Business
Vienna University of Economics
  and Business
Vienna, Austria

Hajo A. Reijers
Department of Computer Sciences
Vrije Universiteit Amsterdam
Amsterdam, The Netherlands

ISBN 978-3-662-58585-6   ISBN 978-3-662-56509-4   (eBook)
https://doi.org/10.1007/978-3-662-56509-4

Printed on acid-free paper

This Springer imprint is published by the registered company Springer-Verlag GmbH, DE part of Springer Nature.
The registered company address is: Heidelberger Platz 3, 14197 Berlin, Germany

To Inga and Maia – Marlon
To Chiara, Lorenzo, and Valerio – Marcello
To Stefanie – Jan
To Maddy, Timon, and Mayu – Hajo

Foreword

Business processes represent one of the core assets of organisations for many reasons. They have direct impact on the attractiveness of products and services, influence customer experiences and ultimately revenue in case of corporations. Processes orchestrate corporate resources to fulfil these external demands and therefore are a key factor determining the cost-to-serve and operational efficiency. In particular, they determine tasks, jobs, and responsibilities and by this, shape the future work of every employee and machine along a business process. Processes are the arterial system within organisations and in inter-organizational supply networks. Consequently, any process failure can bring corporate life and the entire process ecosystem to a standstill. Processes determine the potential and speed of an organization to adapt to new circumstances and to comply with a fast-growing number of legislative requirements.

However, unlike other corporate assets such as products, services, workforce, brand, physical or monetary assets, the significance of business processes had not been appreciated for a long period. Despite the fact that processes are the lifeblood of an organization, they did not develop the status of a primary citizen in boardroom discussions and managerial decision-making processes until the very end of the twentieth century.

The growing demands for globalization, integration, standardization, innovation, agility, and operational efficiency, coupled with the opportunities raised by digital technologies, have finally increased the appetite for reflecting on and ultimately improving existing as well as designing entire new business processes.

In response, a comprehensive body of tools, techniques, methods, and entire methodologies to support all stages of the business process lifecycle has emerged over the past two decades. It is called Business Process Management (BPM), and it consolidates a plethora of tools and approaches coming from diverse disciplines, including Industrial Engineering, Operations Management, Quality Management, Human Capital Management, Corporate Governance, Computer Science, and Information Systems Engineering.

"Fundamentals of Business Process Management" takes on the challenge of distilling the current landscape of BPM methods and tools succinctly and pedagogically. It brings meaningful order and consistency into approaches that often have been developed, discussed, and deployed in isolation. It derives its merits from its firm foundation in the latest applied BPM research. Relying on scientifically sound practices means capitalizing on evidence rather than depending on confidence. This clearly differentiates this much-needed publication from many of its predecessors. In particular, it gives BPM the credibility that a still growing discipline requires.

The book itself is also a compelling showcase for the importance of a new class of processes, i.e. internationally distributed, complex, and flexible business processes. In this case, it is the process of jointly writing a book involving four authors in four different countries. The team has addressed this challenge brilliantly and the outcome is an impressive compilation of the individual strengths of each author grounded in a shared understanding of the essential BPM fundamentals and a common passion for the topic.

It has been no surprise that the first edition of the book had a tremendous uptake and gained rapid adoption worldwide. The hundreds of institutions that have adopted the book in their teaching, and the tens of thousands of students and professionals who have taken the Massive Open Online Course (MOOC) developed on the basis of this book, are a testimony of both the growing demand for BPM education and the technical and pedagogical value of the book.

As the field evolves and matures, a second updated and extended edition is most welcome. The second edition significantly expands the reach of the first one with a more in-depth coverage of process architecture, process discovery, process innovation, process analytics, BPM strategic alignment, and governance, all of which are essential ingredients in a sustainable BPM program.

I have no doubts that this second edition will contribute to shaping the toolset, and even more the mindset, of the current and future generations of BPM professionals. The book will continue to be the standard reference for everyone who is keen to learn more about and to embrace the fascinating discipline of Business Process Management.

Brisbane, Australia   Michael Rosemann
February 2018

Preface

Almost 5 years ago, we decided to join forces and deliver a textbook on Business Process Management (BPM). Since then, BPM has grown more important than ever. Businesses around the world are carrying out BPM initiatives with the aim to outperform their competitors or meet the demands of regulatory authorities. At the same time, a lively academic community is pushing the boundaries of the discipline: computer scientists, management scientists, and engineers add new elements to its repertoire, which are eagerly being picked up by practitioners. We felt that having a textbook available that organizes the broad spectrum of the topic would help us teaching at our institutions about the fascinating concepts, methods, and technologies behind BPM. What is more, we hoped that a textbook on BPM would also enable a broader audience beyond the students in our own classrooms to learn about its marvels.

When the first edition of the book hit the shelves in early 2013, it became clear to us that our textbook met an unsaturated demand. The book quickly became the basis for BPM courses at around 200 universities across the continents. Lecturers around the world reached out to us to discuss the material and a community of BPM educators evolved from these interactions. We traveled to various institutions ourselves to deliver guest lectures on the basis of the book and, from time to time, also stepped into the corporate world to preach the BPM gospel. The demand was such that we were compelled to produce a Massive Open Online Course (MOOC) based on the textbook, which brought together over 7,500 participants in its first delivery and over 25,000 in total after several deliveries. In a sense, our mission seemed to be accomplished. But then again, we knew it was not.

After all, BPM is a cross-disciplinary field that is continuously evolving. The boundaries of what we previously saw as the fundamentals of the discipline have moved in the five years since the first edition of our book appeared. On the positive side, we could see the emergence of new methods, the evolvement of important standards, and a maturation of BPM technology. However, we also saw how difficult some organizations found it to successfully apply BPM, as accentuated by a number of failed BPM projects. In other words, it was time to carry out a major update to our book to reflect on such developments and insights. The result of our efforts in this direction is this second edition.

Compared to the first edition of the book, the new edition incorporates a range of extensions and improvements. The highlights are as follows:

- The roots of BPM are more thoroughly discussed, in particular the relationship with the concept of Adam Smith's division of labor;
- Major rework took place to better illustrate the design of a process architecture and the way performance measures can be integrated in such an architecture;
- We extended our treatment of process modeling with the modeling standards CMMN and DMN;
- We enhanced the coverage of process discovery and modeling methods;
- To the wide range of process analysis techniques already present in the first edition, we added waste analysis, stakeholder analysis, capacity analysis, and the critical path method;
- The treatment of redesign methods has been vastly expanded with a range of methods, both old and new, that were not covered in the previous edition;
- A new chapter has been added to provide an overview of both domain-specific (ERP, CRM) and domain-agnostic process-aware information systems;
- The overview of process monitoring techniques has been substantially revised and enhanced to incorporate recent developments in the field of process mining;
- A new chapter has been added to introduce BPM as an enterprise capability. This chapter expands the scope of the book to encompass topics such as the strategic alignment and governance of BPM initiatives.

Some things have not changed. Every chapter of the textbook still contains a number of elaborated examples and exercises. Some of these exercises are spread throughout the chapter and are intended to help the reader to incrementally put into action, via concrete scenarios, concepts and techniques exposed in the chapter. These "in-chapter" exercises are paired with sample solutions at the end of the chapter. In addition, every chapter closes with a number of further exercises for which no solution is provided. Instructors may wish to use these latter exercises for assignments. We are happy to announce that through the various extensions, over 40 additional examples and exercises have become part of this second edition.

The reader will also note that most chapters contain "highlighted boxes" that provide complementary insights into a specific topic, some of them brand new in comparison to the first edition. These boxes are tangential to the flow of the book and may be skipped by readers who wish to concentrate on the essential concepts. Similarly, every chapter closes with a "Further Readings" section that provides external pointers for readers wishing to deepen their understanding of a specific topic. These sections have been updated to include the most recent developments in the various areas.

What is also still around is our website, which has the primary aim to collect course materials: http://fundamentals-of-bpm.org. This website includes slides, lecture recordings, sample exams, links to related resources, and additional exercises. The interested reader can also find in the website a list of institutions where the book is used in class. There is an active community of instructors who have adopted the book and who regularly share their insights via a message forum. New instructors who adopt this book in their classes can request to be added to this community. By joining the community, instructors get access to a wealth of instructors-only material.

This book draws from the work of many of our colleagues in the BPM field. We would like to thank Han van der Aa, Wil van der Aalst, Adriano Augusto, Thomas Baier, Saimir Bala, Wasana Bandara, Alistair Barros, Anne Baumgraß, Boualem Benatallah, Jan vom Brocke, Cristina Cabanillas, Fabio Casati, Raffaele Conforti, Claudio Di Ciccio, Gero Decker, Remco Dijkman, Boudewijn van Dongen, Dirk Fahland, Avigdor Gal, Paul Harmon, Arthur ter Hofstede, Henrik Leopold, Fabrizio Maria Maggi, Monika Malinova, Fredrik Milani, Michael zur Muehlen, Markus Nüttgens, Fabian Pittke, Johannes Prescher, Artem Polyvyanyy, Manfred Reichert, Jan Recker, Stefanie Rinderle-Ma, Michael Rosemann, Stefan Schönig, Matthias Schrepfer, Priya Seetharaman, Sergey Smirnov, Andreas Solti, Lucinéia Heloisa Thom, Peter Trkman, Irene Vanderfeesten, Barbara Weber, Ingo Weber, Matthias Weidlich, Mathias Weske, and J. Leon Zhao, who all provided constructive feedback on drafts of earlier versions of this book or inspired us in other ways while we were writing it. Last but not least, we are grateful to the numerous instructors and students who reported errata in the first edition of the book and who made useful suggestions. Our thanks, in particular, go to Ahmad Alturki, Anis Charfi, Dave Chaterjee, Manfred Jeusfeld, Worarat Krathu, Ann Majchrzak, Shane Tomblin, Phoebe Tsai, Inge van de Weerd, and Chris Zimmer.

Tartu, Estonia	Marlon Dumas
Melbourne, Australia	Marcello La Rosa
Vienna, Austria	Jan Mendling
Amsterdam, The Netherlands	Hajo A. Reijers
February 2018	

Contents

1 Introduction to Business Process Management 1
  1.1 Processes Everywhere 1
  1.2 Ingredients of a Business Process 3
  1.3 Origins and History of BPM 8
      1.3.1 The Functional Organization 8
      1.3.2 The Birth of Process Thinking 11
      1.3.3 The Rise and Fall of BPR 13
  1.4 The BPM Lifecycle 16
  1.5 Recap 27
  1.6 Solutions to Exercises 28
  1.7 Further Exercises 30
  1.8 Further Readings 32

2 Process Identification 35
  2.1 The Context of Process Identification 35
  2.2 Definition of the Process Architecture 41
      2.2.1 Process Categories 41
      2.2.2 Relationships Between Processes 42
      2.2.3 Reuse of Reference Models 45
      2.2.4 Process Landscape Model 48
      2.2.5 The Example of SAP's Process Architecture 55
  2.3 Process Selection 56
      2.3.1 Selection Criteria 56
      2.3.2 Process Performance Measures 59
      2.3.3 Process Portfolio 64
  2.4 Recap 65
  2.5 Solutions to Exercises 66
  2.6 Further Exercises 69
  2.7 Further Readings 72

3   Essential Process Modeling 75
3.1   First Steps with BPMN 75
3.2   Branching and Merging... 79
         3.2.1   Exclusive Decisions 80
         3.2.2   Parallel Execution 82
         3.2.3   Inclusive Decisions.. 86
         3.2.4   Rework and Repetition 90
3.3   Business Objects 93
3.4   Resources.. 96
3.5   Process Decomposition 102
3.6   Process Model Reuse 105
3.7   Recap 107
3.8   Solutions to Exercises 108
3.9   Further Exercises.. 112
3.10   Further Readings 114

4   Advanced Process Modeling.. 117
4.1   More on Rework and Repetition 117
         4.1.1   Parallel Repetition... 119
         4.1.2   Uncontrolled Repetition 122
4.2   Handling Events 123
         4.2.1   Message Events 123
         4.2.2   Temporal Events.. 124
         4.2.3   Racing Events 126
4.3   Handling Exceptions.. 129
         4.3.1   Process Abortion 129
         4.3.2   Internal Exceptions....................................... 130
         4.3.3   External Exceptions 132
         4.3.4   Activity Timeouts 133
         4.3.5   Non-Interrupting Events and Complex Exceptions...... 133
         4.3.6   Event Sub-processes 135
         4.3.7   Activity Compensation.................................... 136
         4.3.8   Summary 138
4.4   Processes and Business Rules 138
4.5   Recap 139
4.6   Solutions to Exercises 140
4.7   Further Exercises.. 149
4.8   Further Readings 157

5   Process Discovery 159
5.1   The Setting of Process Discovery 159
         5.1.1   Process Analyst Versus Domain Expert................. 160
         5.1.2   Three Process Discovery Challenges.................... 162
5.2   Process Discovery Methods 165
         5.2.1   Evidence-Based Discovery 165
         5.2.2   Interview-Based Discovery 168

	5.2.3	Workshop-Based Discovery	172
	5.2.4	Strengths and Weaknesses	175
5.3	Process Modeling Method		177
	5.3.1	Step 1: Identify the Process Boundaries	178
	5.3.2	Step 2: Identify Activities and Events	178
	5.3.3	Step 3: Identify Resources and Their Handoffs	179
	5.3.4	Step 4: Identify the Control Flow	180
	5.3.5	Step 5: Identify Additional Elements	182
	5.3.6	Summary	182
5.4	Process Model Quality Assurance		183
	5.4.1	Syntactic Quality and Verification	183
	5.4.2	Semantic Quality and Validation	187
	5.4.3	Pragmatic Quality and Certification	189
	5.4.4	Modeling Guidelines and Conventions	192
5.5	Recap		194
5.6	Solutions to Exercises		195
5.7	Further Exercises		205
5.8	Further Readings		211
6	**Qualitative Process Analysis**		213
6.1	Value-Added Analysis		213
6.2	Waste Analysis		218
	6.2.1	Move	219
	6.2.2	Hold	221
	6.2.3	Overdo	222
6.3	Stakeholder Analysis and Issue Documentation		224
	6.3.1	Stakeholder Analysis	225
	6.3.2	Issue Register	229
	6.3.3	Pareto Analysis and PICK Charts	232
6.4	Root Cause Analysis		236
	6.4.1	Cause-Effect Diagrams	236
	6.4.2	Why-Why Diagrams	241
6.5	Recap		244
6.6	Solutions to Exercises		244
6.7	Further Exercises		249
6.8	Further Readings		253
7	**Quantitative Process Analysis**		255
7.1	Flow Analysis		255
	7.1.1	Calculating Cycle Time Using Flow Analysis	256
	7.1.2	Cycle Time Efficiency	261
	7.1.3	Critical Path Method	263
	7.1.4	Little's Law	266
	7.1.5	Capacity and Bottlenecks	267
	7.1.6	Flow Analysis for Cost	271
	7.1.7	Limitations of Flow Analysis	272

7.2   Queues... 273
        7.2.1   Basics of Queueing Theory 274
        7.2.2   M/M/1 and M/M/c Models 276
        7.2.3   Limitations of Basic Queueing Theory.............. 279
7.3   Simulation.. 279
        7.3.1   Anatomy of a Process Simulation 279
        7.3.2   Input for Process Simulation..................... 280
        7.3.3   Simulation Tools 286
        7.3.4   A Word of Caution 287
7.4   Recap 288
7.5   Solutions to Exercises 288
7.6   Further Exercises... 291
7.7   Further Readings 295

8   Process Redesign... 297
8.1   The Essence of Process Redesign 297
        8.1.1   Product Versus Process Innovation 298
        8.1.2   Redesign Concepts 300
        8.1.3   The Devil's Quadrangle........................... 303
        8.1.4   Approaches to Redesign 304
        8.1.5   The Redesign Orbit 306
8.2   Transactional Methods..................................... 307
        8.2.1   Overview of Transactional Methods 308
        8.2.2   7FE... 312
        8.2.3   Heuristic Process Redesign 315
8.3   Transformational Methods 319
        8.3.1   Overview of Transformational Methods 319
        8.3.2   Business Process Reengineering 323
        8.3.3   Product-Based Design 325
8.4   Recap 329
8.5   Solutions to Exercises 330
8.6   Further Exercises... 333
8.7   Further Readings 338

9   Process-Aware Information Systems 341
9.1   Types of Process-Aware Information Systems 341
        9.1.1   Domain-Specific Process-Aware Information
                 Systems 342
        9.1.2   Business Process Management Systems 344
        9.1.3   Architecture of a BPMS 347
        9.1.4   The Case of ACNS 353
9.2   Advantages of Introducing a BPMS 355
        9.2.1   Workload Reduction 355
        9.2.2   Flexible System Integration...................... 356
        9.2.3   Execution Transparency 358
        9.2.4   Rule Enforcement 359

9.3 Challenges of Introducing a BPMS 360
    9.3.1 Technical Challenges.. 360
    9.3.2 Organizational Challenges 362
9.4 Recap 365
9.5 Solutions to Exercises 365
9.6 Further Exercises... 367
9.7 Further Readings 368

10 Process Implementation with Executable Models 371
10.1 Identify the Automation Boundaries 372
10.2 Review Manual Tasks.. 375
10.3 Complete the Process Model 378
10.4 Bring the Process Model to an Adequate Granularity Level...... 381
    10.4.1 Task Decomposition 381
    10.4.2 Decomposition of Ad Hoc Sub-Processes with
            CMMN 382
    10.4.3 Task Aggregation... 384
10.5 Specify Execution Properties...................................... 384
    10.5.1 Variables, Messages, Signals, Errors, and Their
            Data Types 386
    10.5.2 Data Mappings 388
    10.5.3 Service Tasks 389
    10.5.4 Send and Receive Tasks, Message and Signal Events ... 390
    10.5.5 Script Tasks 391
    10.5.6 User Tasks 391
    10.5.7 Task, Event, and Sequence Flow Expressions 394
    10.5.8 Implementing Rules with DMN 394
    10.5.9 Other BPMS-Specific Properties 396
10.6 The Last Mile 399
10.7 Recap 400
10.8 Solutions to Exercises 400
10.9 Further Exercises... 408
10.10 Further Readings 411

11 Process Monitoring 413
11.1 The Context of Process Monitoring 413
11.2 Process Performance Dashboards 415
    11.2.1 Operational Dashboards 415
    11.2.2 Tactical Dashboards...................................... 416
    11.2.3 Strategic Dashboards..................................... 418
    11.2.4 Tools for Dashboard Creation 419
11.3 Introduction to Process Mining 419
    11.3.1 Process Mining Techniques.............................. 420
    11.3.2 Event Logs.. 421
11.4 Automated Process Discovery...................................... 427
    11.4.1 Dependency Graphs 428

	11.4.2	The α-Algorithm	432
	11.4.3	Robust Process Discovery	436
	11.4.4	Quality Measures for Automated Process Discovery	439
11.5		Process Performance Mining	442
	11.5.1	Time Dimension	442
	11.5.2	Cost Dimension	447
	11.5.3	Quality Dimension	448
	11.5.4	Flexibility Dimension	450
11.6		Conformance Checking	451
	11.6.1	Conformance of Control Flow	452
	11.6.2	Conformance of Data and Resources	457
11.7		Variants Analysis	458
11.8		Putting It All Together: Process Mining in Practice	461
11.9		Recap	463
11.10		Solutions to Exercises	464
11.11		Further Exercises	470
11.12		Further Readings	472

12   BPM as an Enterprise Capability 475

12.1		Barriers to BPM Success	476
12.2		The Six Success Factors of BPM Maturity	477
	12.2.1	Strategic Alignment	480
	12.2.2	Governance	484
	12.2.3	People	486
	12.2.4	Culture	488
12.3		Measuring Process Maturity and BPM Maturity	490
12.4		Recap	495
12.5		Solutions to Exercises	495
12.6		Further Exercises	498
12.7		Further Readings	499

A   Redesign Heuristics 501

A.1	Customer Heuristics	501
A.2	Business Process Operation Heuristics	502
A.3	Business Process Behavior Heuristics	503
A.4	Organization Heuristics	503
A.5	Information Heuristics	505
A.6	Technology Heuristics	505
A.7	External Environment Heuristics	506

References 509

Index 519

List of Figures

Fig. 1.1   Ingredients of a business process 6
Fig. 1.2   How the process moved out of focus through the ages 9
Fig. 1.3   Purchasing process at Ford at the initial stage 12
Fig. 1.4   Purchasing process at Ford after redesign 12
Fig. 1.5   Job functions of a manager responsible for a process (a.k.a.
            process owner), based on Rummler & Brache [153] 16
Fig. 1.6   Process model for the initial fragment of the equipment
            rental process 19
Fig. 1.7   The BPM lifecycle 23

Fig. 2.1   The balanced scorecard by Kaplan & Norton 36
Fig. 2.2   Example of process categories of a production company 42
Fig. 2.3   Value chain models for sequence, decomposition, and
            specialization 43
Fig. 2.4   A process architecture with three levels 44
Fig. 2.5   The process architecture of British Telecom and its
            different levels. © British Telecommunications (2005) 45
Fig. 2.6   Process landscape model of Vienna's public transport
            operator Wiener Linien [168] 48
Fig. 2.7   Process profile of BuildIT's procure-to-pay process,
            adapted from [190] 52
Fig. 2.8   Process landscape model of BuildIT 54
Fig. 2.9   The SAP process map describing the process landscape of
            the company [139] 55
Fig. 2.10   Example of balanced scorecards with the cascading
            definition and measurement of various process performance
            measures 63
Fig. 2.11   Process portfolio of a financial institution 64
Fig. 2.12   Process portfolio of a university 68

Fig. 3.1   The model of a simple order-to-cash process 76
Fig. 3.2   Progress of three instances of the order-to-cash process 77

Fig. 3.3   The Solomon R. Guggenheim building in New York (**a**),
            its timber miniature (**b**) and its blueprint (**c**) 78
Fig. 3.4   An example of the use of XOR gateways 81
Fig. 3.5   An example of the use of AND gateways 82
Fig. 3.6   A more elaborated version of the order-to-cash process
            diagram 83
Fig. 3.7   A variant of the order-to-cash process with two different
            triggers 84
Fig. 3.8   Modeling an inclusive decision: first trial 86
Fig. 3.9   Modeling an inclusive decision: second trial 87
Fig. 3.10   Modeling an inclusive decision with the OR gateway 88
Fig. 3.11   What type should the join gateway have such that instances
            of this process can complete correctly? 88
Fig. 3.12   The order-to-cash process model with product
            manufacturing 90
Fig. 3.13   A process model for addressing ministerial correspondence 91
Fig. 3.14   The order-to-cash example with data objects and data stores 94
Fig. 3.15   The order-to-cash example with resource information 98
Fig. 3.16   Collaboration diagram between a seller, a customer, and
            two suppliers 100
Fig. 3.17   Identifying sub-processes in the order-to-cash process of
            Figure 3.12 103
Fig. 3.18   A simplified version of the order-to-cash process after
            hiding the content of its sub-processes 104
Fig. 3.19   A process model for disbursing home loans, laid down over
            three hierarchical levels via the use of sub-processes 105
Fig. 3.20   The process model for disbursing student loans invokes
            the same model for signing loans used by the process for
            disbursing home loans, via a call activity 106
Fig. 4.1   The process model for addressing ministerial
            correspondence of Figure 3.13 simplified using a loop
            activity 118
Fig. 4.2   An example of unstructured cycle 118
Fig. 4.3   Obtaining quotes from five suppliers 119
Fig. 4.4   Obtaining quotes from a number of suppliers determined
            on-the-fly 120
Fig. 4.5   Using a multi-instance pool to represent multiple suppliers 121
Fig. 4.6   Using an ad hoc sub-process to model uncontrolled
            repetition 122
Fig. 4.7   Replacing activities that only send or receive messages (**a**)
            with message events (**b**) 124
Fig. 4.8   Using timer events to drive the various activities of a
            business process 125
Fig. 4.9   A race condition between an incoming message and a timer 126

Fig. 4.10   Matching an internal choice in one party with an
             event-based choice in the other party 127
Fig. 4.11   An example of collaboration that can deadlock if the
             decision is made for "already registered" 128
Fig. 4.12   Using an event-based gateway to fix the problem of a
             potential deadlock in the collaboration of Figure 4.11 128
Fig. 4.13   A collaboration diagram between a customer, a travel
             agency, and an airline 130
Fig. 4.14   Using a terminate event to signal abnormal process
             termination 131
Fig. 4.15   Error events model internal exceptions 131
Fig. 4.16   Boundary events catch external events that can occur
             during an activity 132
Fig. 4.17   Non-interrupting boundary events catch external events
             that occur during an activity and trigger a parallel
             procedure without interrupting the enclosing activity 133
Fig. 4.18   Non-interrupting events can be used in combination
             with signal events to model complex exception handling
             scenarios 134
Fig. 4.19   Event sub-processes can be used in place of boundary
             events and to catch events thrown from outside the scope
             of a particular sub-process 135
Fig. 4.20   Compensating for the shipment and for the payment 137
Fig. 4.21   A replenishment order is triggered every time the stock
             levels drop below a threshold 139

Fig. 5.1   Organization chart of the Office of the DVC (Student
             Affairs) 168
Fig. 5.2   Extract of the UML class diagram of the student admission
             system 168
Fig. 5.3   Organizational policies for student admission 169
Fig. 5.4   Phases of the interview method 169
Fig. 5.5   The activities and events of the order-to-cash process 179
Fig. 5.6   The activities and events of the order-to-cash process
             assigned to lanes 179
Fig. 5.7   The handoff of work between the seller, the customer, and
             the supplier 180
Fig. 5.8   The control flow of the order-to-cash process 181
Fig. 5.9   Process model quality aspects and assurance activities........... 183
Fig. 5.10   A structurally incorrect process model 184
Fig. 5.11   Common behavioral anomalies in block structures............... 185
Fig. 5.12   A process model with a deadlock (**a**) and one with
             a livelock (**b**).. 186
Fig. 5.13   A process model with lack of synchronization (**a**) and one
             with a dead activity (**b**)...................................... 186

Fig. 5.14   A process model for fulfilling special orders...................... 187
Fig. 5.15   An unstructured process model (**a**) and its structured
             counterpart (**b**). *Acknowledgement* This example is taken
             from [40]... 190
Fig. 5.16   Extract of the order-to-cash process model: with bad layout
             (**a**), with good layout (**b**) 191
Fig. 5.17   A process model for cost planning. *Acknowledgement* This
             example is taken from [87] 191
Fig. 5.18   A process model for handling complaints, as found in
             practice 193
Fig. 5.19   The process model for fulfilling special orders,
             syntactically and semantically correct, and of high
             pragmatic quality 204
Fig. 5.20   The reworked complaint handling process model 204
Fig. 5.21   A process model 208
Fig. 5.22   A process model for loan risk assessment 208
Fig. 5.23   A process model for damage compensation........................ 209
Fig. 5.24   A process model for handling motor claims 209
Fig. 5.25   A process model for handling claims.............................. 210
Fig. 5.26   A process model for organizing professional training
             courses 210
Fig. 5.27   A sales campaign process model 211

Fig. 6.1   Process model for the initial fragment of the equipment
             rental process 215
Fig. 6.2   Fragment of the equipment rental process from creation of
             rental request up to creation of the PO 220
Fig. 6.3   Pareto chart for excessive equipment rental expenditure 234
Fig. 6.4   PICK chart visualizing the payoff and difficulty of
             addressing each issue 235
Fig. 6.5   Template of a cause-effect diagram based on the 6 M's 239
Fig. 6.6   Cause-effect diagram for issue "Equipment rejected at
             delivery".. 240
Fig. 6.7   Template of a why-why diagram 242
Fig. 6.8   Pareto chart of causal factors of issue "Equipment not
             available when needed" 248

Fig. 7.1   Fully sequential process model (durations of tasks in hours
             are shown between brackets) 256
Fig. 7.2   Process model with XOR-block 256
Fig. 7.3   XOR-block pattern 257
Fig. 7.4   Process model with AND-block 258
Fig. 7.5   AND-block pattern 258
Fig. 7.6   Credit application process 258
Fig. 7.7   Example of a rework block 259
Fig. 7.8   Rework pattern 260

Fig. 7.9   Situation where a fragment (task) that is reworked at most
              once 260
Fig. 7.10   Credit application process with rework 261
Fig. 7.11   Credit application process without XOR gateways 264
Fig. 7.12   Process model of a call center 270
Fig. 7.13   Structure of an M/M/1 or M/M/c system, input parameters
              and computable parameters 277
Fig. 7.14   Histograms produced by simulating the credit application
              process with BIMP 284
Fig. 7.15   Cetera's claim-to-resolution process 285
Fig. 7.16   Request for handling a request for quote at MetalWorks 293
Fig. 7.17   Mortgage process model 294

Fig. 8.1   The waves of product and process innovation 298
Fig. 8.2   The Devil's Quadrangle 304
Fig. 8.3   The Redesign Orbit: A spectrum of business process
              redesign methods 306
Fig. 8.4   A selection of redesign heuristics 317
Fig. 8.5   The Process Model Canvas 321
Fig. 8.6   The NESTT room 322
Fig. 8.7   A sample product data model 328
Fig. 8.8   The intake process model 336

Fig. 9.1   The spectrum of BPMS types...................................... 346
Fig. 9.2   The architecture of a BPMS 348
Fig. 9.3   The process modeling tool of Bonita BPM 349
Fig. 9.4   The worklist handler of Camunda BPM............................ 350
Fig. 9.5   The monitoring tool of Perceptive 351
Fig. 9.6   Model of the claims handling process at ANCS 353

Fig. 10.1   The order-to-cash model that we want to automate 373
Fig. 10.2   Admission process: the initial (a) and final (c) assessments
              can be automated in a BPMS; the assessment by the
              committee (b) is a manual process outside the scope of the
              BPMS 376
Fig. 10.3   The order-to-cash model of Figure 10.1, completed with
              control-flow and data-flow aspects relevant for automation 380
Fig. 10.4   The sales process of a B2B service provider 381
Fig. 10.5   Excerpt of an order-to-cash process model (from
              out-of-stock product to product provided) captured in CMMN ... 383
Fig. 10.6   Structure of the BPMN format 386
Fig. 10.7   The XSD describing the purchase order (a) and one of its
              instances (b) 387
Fig. 10.8   Example of a decision table for loan applications 395
Fig. 10.9   Another decision table 396
Fig. 10.10   Loan application process with task markers 401

Fig. 10.11   The automated prescription fulfillment process.................... 403
Fig. 10.12   Completed version of the loan application model 405
Fig. 10.13   The model for the sales process of a B2B service provider,
             completed with missing control-flow and data relevant for
             execution 406
Fig. 10.14   FixComp's process model for handling complaints 409
Fig. 10.15   Claims handling process model.................................... 409

Fig. 11.1   Example of operational dashboard produced by Bizagi's
             BAM component 416
Fig. 11.2   Cycle time histogram of cases completed during a 1-year
             period 417
Fig. 11.3   Categories of process mining techniques and their inputs
             and output 420
Fig. 11.4   Example of an event log for the order-to-cash process 423
Fig. 11.5   Metamodel of the XES format 424
Fig. 11.6   Example of a file in the XES format 425
Fig. 11.7   Definition of a workflow log 427
Fig. 11.8   Event log and corresponding dependency graph.................. 428
Fig. 11.9   Example of a full dependency graph and an abstracted
             version thereof. (a) Full dependency graph. (b) Filtered
             dependency graph 430
Fig. 11.10   Simple control flow patterns 433
Fig. 11.11   Footprint represented as a matrix of the
             workflow log $L = [\langle a, b, g, h, j, k, i, l \rangle,$
             $\langle a, c, d, e, f, g, j, h, i, k, l \rangle]$ 435
Fig. 11.12   Process model constructed by the α-algorithm from log
             $L = [\langle a, b, g, h, j, k, i, l \rangle, \langle a, c, d, e, f, g, j, h, i, k, l \rangle]$ 437
Fig. 11.13   Examples of two short loops, (b) and (c), that cannot be
             distinguished from model (a) by the α-algorithm 437
Fig. 11.14   Models discovered from a sample log using three discovery
             techniques. (a) Heuristics miner (ProM v6). (b) Inductive
             miner (ProM v6). (c) Structured heuristics miner (Apromore).... 441
Fig. 11.15   Dotted chart of log data 443
Fig. 11.16   Example of timeline chart 444
Fig. 11.17   Performance view of the BPI Challenge 2017 event log in
             Disco 445
Fig. 11.18   Handoff view of the Sepsis event log in myInvenio 446
Fig. 11.19   BPMN model with a token on the start event for replaying
             the case $\langle a, b, g, i, j, k, l \rangle$ 453
Fig. 11.20   Replaying the non-conforming case $\langle a, b, i, j, k, l \rangle$ 455
Fig. 11.21   Result of replaying cases in the process model 456
Fig. 11.22   Visualization of a model-log discrepancy in Apromore 457

Fig. 11.23   Operational dashboard for pharmacy prescription process.
             (a) Segmented bar chart of unfulfilled prescriptions. (b)
             Bar chart of demand (required processing time) vs. capacity 465
Fig. 11.24   Process model constructed by the α-algorithm 468
Fig. 11.25   Model discovered by the inductive miner from the Sepsis log 468
Fig. 11.26   Model discovered by Apromore's split miner from the
             Sepsis log 468

Fig. 12.1   The BPM Maturity Model, adapted from [33, 150] 479
Fig. 12.2   Patterns of BPM maturity 492
Fig. 12.3   Example of BPM maturity assessment for an insurance
             company 493

List of Tables

Table 2.1   Level 1 and Level 2 of the APQC Process Classification
Framework 47

Table 5.1   Relative strengths and weaknesses of process discovery
methods 175

Table 5.2   Summary of strengths and weaknesses per discovery method..... 176

Table 6.1   Classification of steps in the equipment rental process 217

Table 6.2   Issue register of equipment rental process 231

Table 7.1   Cycle times for credit application process 259

Table 7.2   Processing times for credit application process 262

Table 7.3   Task cycle times and processing times for ministerial
enquiry process 263

Table 7.4   Analysis of cycle times in white-collar processes [21] 263

Table 7.5   Cost calculation table for credit application process 272

Table A.1   Performance dimensions for the redesign heuristics 507

List of Acronyms

6 M	Machine, Method, Material, Man, Measurement, Milieu
4 P	Policies, Procedures, People, Plant/Equipment
7PMG	Seven Process Modeling Guidelines
ABC	Activity-Based Costing
ACM	Adaptive Case Management
API	Application Programming Interface
APQC	American Productivity and Quality Center
ATAMO	And Then, A Miracle Occurs
B2B	Business-to-Business
BAM	Business Activity Monitoring
BOM	Bill-of-Material
BPA	Business Process Analysis
BPE	Business Process Excellence
BPEL	Web Service Business Process Execution Language
BPM	Business Process Management
BPMN	Business Process Model & Notation
BPMS	Business Process Management System
BPR	Business Process Reengineering
BTO	Build-To-Order
BVA	Business Value-Adding
CEO	Chief Executive Officer
CEP	Complex Event Processing
CFO	Chief Financial Officer
CIO	Chief Information Officer
CMMI	Capability Maturity Model Integrated
CMMN	Case Management Model and Notation
CNC	Coefficient of Network Connectivity
COO	Chief Operations Officer
CPIO	Chief Process and Innovation Officer
CPM	Critical Path Method
CPN	Colored Petri Net

CPO	Chief Process Officer
CRM	Customer Relationship Management
CSV	Comma Separated Values
CT	Cycle Time
CTC	Cost-To-Company
CTE	Cycle Time Efficiency
DBMS	Database Management System
DCOR	Design Chain Operations Reference (product design)
DES	Discrete-Event Simulation
DMN	Decision Model and Notation
DMR	Department of Main Roads
DMS	Document Management System
DRG	Decision Requirements Graph
DUR	Drug Utilization Review
DVS	Deputy Vice Chancellor
EDI	Electronic Data Interchange
EF	Early Finish
EHS	Environmental Health and Safety
EPA	Environment Protection Agency
EPC	Event-driven Process Chain
ERP	Enterprise Resource Planning
ES	Early Start
eTOM	Enhanced Telecom Operations Map
FIFO	First-In-First-Out
HR	Human Resources
IDEF3	Integrated Definition for Process Description Capture Method
ISP	Internet Service Provider
IT	Information Technology
ITIL	Information Technology Infrastructure Library
JSON	JavaScript Object Notation
KM	Knowledge Management
KPI	Key Performance Indicator
LF	Late Finish
LS	Late Start
NESTT	Navigate, Expand, Strengthen, and Tune/Take-off
NRW	Department of Natural Resources and Water
NVA	Non-Value-Adding
OASIS	Organization for the Advancement of Structured Information Standards
OMG	Object Management Group
OS	Operating System
PAIS	Process-Aware Information System
PCG	Productivity Consulting Group
PCF	Process Classification Framework
PD	Product Development

PDCA	Plan-Do-Check-Act
PDF	Portable Document Format
PICK	Possible, Implement, Challenge, Kill
PLM	Product Lifecycle Management
PMBOK	Project Management Body of Knowledge
PO	Purchase Order
POS	Point-of-Sale
PPI	Process Performance Indicator
PPM	Process Performance Measurement
PRINCE2	Projects in Controlled Environments
RBAC	Role-based Access Control
REST	Representational State Transfer
RFID	Radio-Frequency Identification
RFQ	Request for Quote
ROI	Return-On-Investment
RPA	Robotic Process Automation
RPH	Reference Process House
SCAMPI	Standard CMMI Appraisal Method for Process Improvement
SCM	Supply Chain Management
SCOR	Supply Chain Operations Reference Model
S-FEEL	Simple Friendly Enough Expression Language
SIPEX	Siemens Processes for Excellence
Smart eDA	Smart Electronic Development Assessment System
SOA	Service-Oriented Architecture
SPICE	Software Process Improvement and Capability Determination
STP	Straight-Through-Processing
TCT	Theoretical Cycle Time
TOC	Theory of Constraints
TPS	Toyota Production System
TQM	Total Quality Management
UIMS	User Interface Management System
UEL	Universal Expression Language
UML	Unified Modeling Language
UML AD	UML Activity Diagram
URI	Uniform Resource Identifier
VA	Value-Adding
VCH	Value Creation Hierarchy
VCS	Value Creation System
VOS	Voice of the Customer
VRM	Value Reference Model
WIP	Work-In-Process
WfMC	Workflow Management Coalition
WfMS	Workflow Management System
WS-BPEL	Web Service Business Process Execution Language
WSDL	Web Service Definition Language

XES	Extensible Event Stream
XML	Extensible Markup Language
XPATH	XML Path Language
XSD	XML Schema Definition
YAWL	Yet Another Workflow Language

Chapter 1
Introduction to Business Process Management

> *Ab ovo usque ad mala.*
> Horace (65 BCE–8 BCE)

Business Process Management (BPM) is the art and science of overseeing how work is performed in an organization to ensure consistent outcomes and to take advantage of improvement opportunities. In this context, the term "improvement" may take different meanings depending on the objectives of the organization. Typical examples of improvement objectives include reducing costs, reducing execution times, and reducing error rates, but also gaining competitive advantage through innovation. Improvement initiatives may be one-off or of a continuous nature; they may be incremental or radical. Importantly, BPM is not about improving the way individual activities are performed. Rather, it is about managing entire chains of events, activities, and decisions that ultimately add value to the organization, and its customers. These chains of events, activities, and decisions are called *processes*.

In this chapter, we introduce the essential concepts behind BPM. We start with a description of typical processes that are found in contemporary organizations. Next, we discuss the basic ingredients of a business process and provide a definition of business process and BPM. In order to place BPM in a broader perspective, we then provide a historical overview of the BPM discipline. Finally, we discuss how a BPM initiative in an organization typically unfolds. This discussion leads us to the definition of a BPM lifecycle, around which the book is structured.

1.1 Processes Everywhere

Each organization—be it a governmental agency, a non-profit organization, or an enterprise—has to manage a number of processes. Typical examples of processes that can be found in most organizations include:

- *Order-to-cash*. This is a type of process performed by a vendor, which starts when a customer submits an order to purchase a product or a service and ends

© Springer-Verlag GmbH Germany, part of Springer Nature 2018
M. Dumas et al., *Fundamentals of Business Process Management*,
https://doi.org/10.1007/978-3-662-56509-4_1

when the product or service in question has been delivered to the customer and the customer has made the corresponding payment. An order-to-cash process encompasses activities related to purchase order verification, shipment (for physical products), delivery, invoicing, payment receipt, and acknowledgment.

- *Quote-to-order*. This type of process typically precedes an order-to-cash process. It starts from the point when a supplier receives a Request for Quote (RFQ) from a customer and ends when the customer in question places a purchase order based on the received quote. The order-to-cash process takes the relay from that point on. The combination of a quote-to-order and the corresponding order-to-cash process is called a *quote-to-cash* process.

- *Procure-to-pay*. This type of process starts when someone in an organization determines that a given product or service needs to be purchased. It ends when the product or service has been delivered and paid for. A procure-to-pay process includes activities such as obtaining quotes, approving the purchase, selecting a supplier, issuing a purchase order, receiving the goods (or consuming the service), and paying the invoice. A procure-to-pay process can be seen as the counterpart of the quote-to-cash process in the context of business-to-business interactions. For every procure-to-pay process there is a corresponding quote-to-cash process on the supplier's side.

- *Issue-to-resolution*. This type of process starts when a customer raises a problem or issue, such as a complaint related to a defect in a product or an issue encountered when consuming a service. The process continues until the customer, the supplier, or preferably both of them agree that the issue has been resolved. A variant of this process can be found in insurance companies that have to deal with insurance claims. This variant is called *claim-to-resolution*.

- *Application-to-approval*. This type of process starts when someone applies for a benefit or privilege and ends when the benefit or privilege in question is either granted or denied. This type of process is common in government agencies, for example when citizens apply for building permits or when entrepreneurs apply for business licenses (e.g., to open a restaurant). Another process that falls into this category is the admissions process in a university, which starts when a student applies for admission into a degree program. Yet another example is the process for approval of vacation or special leave requests in a company.

As the above examples illustrate, business processes are what companies do whenever they deliver a service or a product to customers. The way processes are designed and performed affects both the *quality of service* that customers perceive and the *efficiency* with which services are delivered. An organization can outperform another organization offering similar kinds of service if it has better processes and executes them better. This is true not only for customer-facing processes, but also for internal processes such as the procure-to-pay process, which is performed for the purpose of fulfilling an internal need.

As we go along in this book, we will use a concrete example of a procure-to-pay process for renting construction equipment, as described below.

Example 1.1 Equipment rental at BuildIT.

BuildIT is a construction company specialized in public works, such as roads, bridges, pipelines, tunnels and railroads. Within BuildIT, it often happens that engineers working at a construction site (called *site engineers*) need a piece of equipment, such as a truck, an excavator, a bulldozer, a water pump, etc. BuildIT owns very little equipment and instead it rents most of its equipment from specialized suppliers.

The existing business process for renting equipment goes as follows. When site engineers need to rent a piece of equipment, they fill in a form called "Equipment Rental Request" and send this request by email to one of the clerks at the company's depot. The clerk at the depot receives the request and, after consulting the catalogs of the equipment suppliers, selects the most cost-effective equipment that complies with the request. Next, the clerk checks the availability of the selected equipment with the supplier via phone or email. Sometimes the selected option is not available. In these cases, the clerk has to select an alternative piece of equipment and check its availability with the corresponding supplier.

After finding a suitable and available piece of equipment, the clerk adds the details of the selected equipment to the rental request. Each rental request has to be approved by a works engineer, who also works at the depot. In some cases, the works engineer rejects the equipment rental request. Some rejections lead to the cancelation of the request, i.e., no equipment is rented at all. Other rejections are resolved by replacing the selected equipment with another equipment—such as a cheaper piece of equipment or a more appropriate piece of equipment for the job. In this latter case, the clerk needs to lodge another availability request.

When a works engineer approves a rental request, the clerk sends a confirmation to the supplier. This confirmation includes a Purchase Order (PO) for renting the equipment. The PO is produced by BuildIT's financial information system using information entered by the clerk. The clerk also records the equipment rental in a spreadsheet that is used to monitor all ongoing equipment rentals.

In the meantime, the site engineer may decide that the equipment is no longer needed. In this case, the engineer asks the clerk to cancel the request for renting the equipment.

In due time, the supplier delivers the rented equipment to the construction site. The site engineer then inspects the equipment. If everything is in order, the site engineer accepts the engagement and the equipment is put into use. In some cases, the equipment is sent back because it does not comply with the requirements of the site engineer. In this case, the site engineer has to start the rental process all over again.

When the rental period expires, the supplier comes to pick up the equipment. Sometimes, the site engineer asks for an extension of the rental period by contacting the supplier via email or phone 1 to 2 days before pick-up. The supplier may accept or reject this request.

A few days after the equipment is picked up, the equipment's supplier sends an invoice to the clerk by email. At this point, the clerk asks the site engineer to confirm that the equipment was indeed rented for the period indicated in the invoice. The clerk also checks if the rental prices indicated in the invoice are in accordance with those in the PO. After these checks, the clerk forwards the invoice to the financial department. The financial department eventually pays the invoice.

□

1.2   Ingredients of a Business Process

The BuildIT example in the previous section shows that a business process encompasses a number of *events* and *activities*. Events correspond to things that happen atomically, which means that they have no duration. The arrival of a piece of equipment at a construction site is an event. This event may trigger the execution of a series of activities. For example, when a piece of equipment arrives, the site engineer inspects it. This inspection is an activity, in the sense that it takes time.

When an activity is rather simple and can be seen as one single unit of work, we call it a *task*. For example, if the equipment inspection is simple—e.g., just checking that the equipment received corresponds to what was ordered—we can say that the equipment inspection is a task. If on the other hand the equipment inspection involves several checks—such as checking that the equipment fulfills the specification included in the purchase order, checking that the equipment is in working order, and checking the equipment comes with all the required accessories and safety devices—we will call it an activity instead of a task. In other words, the term task refers to a fine-grained unit of work performed by a single process participant, while the term activity is used to refer to both fine-grained or coarse-grained units of work.

In addition to events and activities, a typical process includes *decision points*, that is, points in time when a decision is made that affects the way the process is executed. For example, as a result of the inspection, the site engineer may decide that the equipment should be returned or that the equipment should be accepted. This decision affects what happens later in the process.

A process also involves:

- *Actors*, including human actors, organizations, or software systems acting on behalf of human actors or organizations.
- *Physical objects*, such as equipment, materials, products, paper documents.
- *Informational objects*, such as electronic documents and electronic records.

For example, the equipment rental process involves three human actors (clerk, site engineer, and works engineer) and two organizational actors (BuildIT and the equipment supplier). The process also involves a physical object (the rented equipment), electronic documents (equipment rental requests, POs, invoices), and electronic records (equipment engagement records maintained in a spreadsheet).

Actors can be internal or external. The internal actors are those who operate inside the organization where the process is executed. These actors are called *process participants*. In the example at hand, the clerk, the site engineer, and the works engineer are process participants. On the other hand, external actors operate outside the organization where the process is executed. For example the equipment supplier is an external actor (a.k.a. *business party*).

Finally, the execution of a process leads to one or several *outcomes*. For example, the equipment rental process leads to a piece of equipment being used by BuildIT, as well as a payment being made to the equipment's supplier. Ideally, an outcome should deliver value to the actors involved in the process, which in this example are BuildIT and the supplier. In some cases, this value is not achieved or is only partially achieved. For example, when a piece of equipment is returned, no value is gained, neither by BuildIT nor by the supplier. This corresponds to a *negative outcome*, as opposed to a *positive outcome* that delivers value to the actors involved.

Among the actors involved in a process, the one who consumes the output is called the *customer*. In the above process, the customer is the site engineer, since it is the site engineer who puts the rented equipment to use. It is also the site engineer who is dissatisfied if the outcome of the process is unsatisfactory (negative outcome) or if the execution of the process is delayed. In this example, the customer is an employee of the organization (internal customer). In other processes, such as an order-to-cash process, the customer is external to the organization. Sometimes, there are multiple customers in a process. For example, in a process for selling a house, there is a buyer, a seller, a real estate agent, one or multiple mortgage providers, and at least one notary. The outcome of the process is a sales transaction. This outcome provides value both to the buyer who gets the house and to the seller who monetizes the house. Therefore, both the buyer and the seller are customers in this process, while the remaining actors provide various services.

Exercise 1.1 Consider the following process for the admission of international graduate students at a university.

In order to apply for admission, students first fill in an online form. Online applications are recorded in an information system to which all staff members involved in the admissions process have access. After a student has submitted the online form, a PDF document is generated and the student is requested to download it, sign it, and send it by post together with the required documents, which include:

- certified copies of previous degree and academic transcripts,
- results of English language test,
- curriculum vitae,
- two reference letters.

When these documents are received by the admissions office, an officer checks the completeness of the documents. If any document is missing, an email is sent to the student. The student has to send the missing documents by post. Assuming the application is complete, the admissions office sends the certified copies of the degrees to an academic recognition agency, which checks the degrees and gives an assessment of their validity and equivalence in terms of local education standards. This agency requires that all documents be sent to it by post, and that all documents be certified copies of the originals. The agency sends back its assessment to the university by post as well. Assuming the degree verification is successful, the English language test results are then checked online by an officer at the admissions office. If the validity of the English language test results cannot be verified, the application is rejected (such notifications of rejection are sent by email).

Once all documents of a given student have been validated, the admissions office forwards these documents by internal mail to the corresponding academic committee responsible for deciding whether to offer admission or not. The committee makes its decision based on the academic degrees and transcripts, the CV, and the reference letters. The committee meets once every three months to examine all applications that are ready for academic assessment at the time of the meeting.

At the end of the committee meeting, the chair of the committee notifies the admissions office of the selection outcomes. This notification includes a list of admitted and rejected candidates. A few days later, the admissions office notifies the outcome to each candidate via email. Additionally, successful candidates are sent a confirmation letter by post.

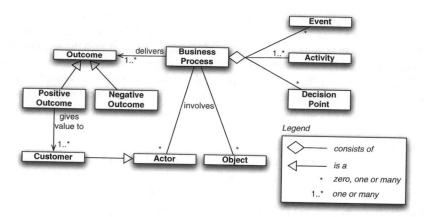

Fig. 1.1 Ingredients of a business process

With respect to the above process, consider the following questions:

1. Who are the actors in this process?
2. Which actors can be considered as customers in this process?
3. What value does the process deliver to its customers?
4. What are the possible outcomes of this process?

In light of the above, we define a business process as *a collection of inter-related events, activities, and decision points that involve a number of actors and objects, which collectively lead to an outcome that is of value to at least one customer.* Figure 1.1 depicts the ingredients of this definition and their relations.

Armed with this definition of a business process, we define BPM as *a body of methods, techniques, and tools to identify, discover, analyze, redesign, execute, and monitor business processes in order to optimize their performance.* This definition reflects the fact that business processes are the focal point of BPM. It also reflects the fact that BPM involves different phases and activities in the lifecycle of business processes, as we will discuss later in this chapter.

Other disciplines besides BPM deal with business processes in different ways, as explained in the box "Related Disciplines". One of the features commonly associated with BPM is its emphasis on the use of process models throughout the lifecycle of business processes. Accordingly, two chapters of this book are dedicated to process modeling and almost all other chapters use process models in some way. In any case, while it is useful to know that multiple disciplines share the aim of improving business processes, we should remain pragmatic and not pitch one discipline against the other as if they were competitors. Instead, we should embrace any technique that helps us to improve business processes, whether or not this technique is perceived as being part of the BPM discipline (in the strict sense) and regardless of whether or not it uses process models.

RELATED DISCIPLINES

BPM is by no means the only discipline that is concerned with improving the operational performance of organizations. Below, we briefly introduce some related disciplines and identify key relations and differences between these disciplines and BPM.

Total Quality Management (TQM) is an approach that both historically preceded and inspired BPM. The focus of TQM is on continuously improving and sustaining the quality of products, and by extension also of services. In this way, it is similar to BPM in its emphasis on the necessity of *ongoing* improvement efforts. But where TQM puts the emphasis on the products and services themselves, the view behind BPM is that the quality of products and services can best be achieved by focusing on the improvement of the processes that create these products and deliver these services. It should be admitted that this view is somewhat controversial, as contemporary TQM adepts would rather see BPM as one of the various practices that are commonly found within a TQM program. Not so much a theoretical distinction but an empirical one is that applications of TQM are primarily found in manufacturing domains—where the products are tangible—while BPM is more oriented to service organizations.

Operations Management is a field concerned with managing the *physical* and *technical* functions of a firm or organization, particularly those relating to production and manufacturing. Probability theory, queuing theory, decision analysis, mathematical modeling, and simulation are all important techniques for optimizing the efficiency of operations from this perspective. As will be discussed in Chapter 7, such techniques are also useful in the context of BPM initiatives. What is rather different between operations management and BPM is that operations management is generally concerned with controlling an existing process without necessarily changing it, while BPM is often concerned with making changes to an existing process in order to improve it.

Lean is a management discipline that originates from the manufacturing industry, in particular from the *Toyota Production System*. One of the main principles of Lean is the *elimination of waste*, i.e., activities that do not add value to the customer as we will discuss in Chapter 6. The customer orientation of Lean is similar to that of BPM and many of the principles behind Lean have been absorbed by BPM. In that sense, BPM can be seen as a more encompassing discipline than Lean. Another difference is that BPM puts more emphasis on the use of information technology as a tool to improve business processes and to make them more consistent and repeatable.

(continued)

Six Sigma is another set of practices that originate from manufacturing, in particular from engineering and production practices at Motorola. The main characteristic of Six Sigma is its focus on the minimization of defects (errors). Six Sigma places a strong emphasis on measuring the output of processes or activities, especially in terms of quality. Six Sigma encourages managers to systematically compare the effects of improvement initiatives on the outputs. In practice, Six Sigma is not necessarily applied alone, but in conjunction with other approaches. In particular, a popular approach is to blend the philosophy of Lean with the techniques of Six Sigma, leading to an approach known as *Lean Six Sigma*. Nowadays, many of the techniques of Six Sigma are commonly applied in BPM as well. In Chapter 6, we will introduce a few business process analysis techniques that are shared by Six Sigma and BPM.

In summary, we can say that BPM inherits from the continuous improvement philosophy of TQM, embraces the principles and techniques of operations management, Lean and Six Sigma, and combines them with the capabilities offered by modern information technology, in order to optimally align business processes with the performance objectives of an organization.

1.3 Origins and History of BPM

Below, we look into the drivers of the BPM discipline from a historical perspective. We start with the emergence of functional organizations, continue with the introduction of process thinking, and conclude with the innovations and failures of business process reengineering. This discussion gives us the basis for the definition of the BPM lifecycle we provide afterwards.

1.3.1 The Functional Organization

The key idea of BPM is to focus on processes when organizing and managing work in an organization. This idea may seem intuitive and straightforward at first glance. Indeed, if one is concerned with the quality of a particular product or service and the speed of its delivery to a customer, why not consider the very steps that are necessary to produce it? Yet, it took several evolutionary steps before this idea became an integral part of the work structures of organizations. Figure 1.2 provides an overview of some historical developments relevant to BPM.

In prehistoric times, humans mostly supported themselves or the small groups they lived in by producing their own food, tools, and other items. In such early

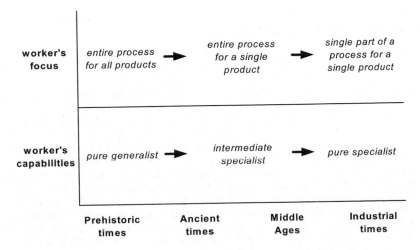

Fig. 1.2 How the process moved out of focus through the ages

societies, the consumers and producers of a given good were often the same persons. In industrial terms, we can say that people in that time carried out their own production processes. As a result, they had knowledge of how to produce many different things. In other words, they were generalists.

In ancient times, in parallel with the rise of cities and city states, this work structure based on generalists started to evolve towards what can be characterized as an *intermediate level of specialism*. People started to specialize in the art of delivering one specific type of goods, such as pottery, or providing one particular type of service, such as lodging for travelers. This widespread development towards a higher level of specialism of the workforce culminated in the guilds of the craftsmen during the Middle Ages. These guilds were essentially groups of merchants and artisans concerned with the same economic activity, such as barbers, shoemakers, masons, surgeons, and sculptors. Workers in this time would have a good understanding of the entire process they were involved in, but knew little about the processes that produced the goods or services they obtained from others.

This higher degree of specialization of the medieval worker shifted further towards a form of pure specialization during the Industrial Revolution. A witness of these developments was Adam Smith (1723–1790), Scottish economist and philosopher, who is best known for his book "An inquiry into the nature and causes of the wealth of nations".[1] Among others, this book discusses the *division of labor* that is used by a manufacturing company for producing pins. While Smith emphasizes division of labor, it is actually the design of the process (what he calls

---

[1] Full book available at http://www.econlib.org/library/Smith/smWN.html.

combination) that contributes to the good performance of the manufacturer. Smith explains the process of pin-making as follows:

> One man draws out the wire, another straights it, a third cuts it, a fourth points it, a fifth grinds it at the top for receiving the head; to make the head requires two or three distinct operations; to put it on, is a peculiar business, to whiten the pins is another; it is even a trade by itself to put them into the paper; and the important business of making a pin is, in this manner, divided into about eighteen distinct operations, which, in some manufactories, are all performed by distinct hands, though in others the same man will sometimes perform two or three of them. I have seen a small manufactory of this kind where ten men only were employed, and where some of them consequently performed two or three distinct operations. [...] Those ten persons, therefore, could make among them upwards of forty-eight thousand pins in a day. Each person, therefore, making a tenth part of forty-eight thousand pins, might be considered as making four thousand eight hundred pins in a day. But if they had all wrought separately and independently, and without any of them having been educated to this peculiar business, they certainly could not each of them have made twenty, perhaps not one pin in a day; that is, certainly, not the two hundred and fortieth, perhaps not the four thousand eight hundredth part of what they are at present capable of performing, in consequence of a proper division and combination of their different operations.

In the second half of the nineteenth century towards the First World War, many of such small manufacturers had grown to become major factories. A name that is inseparably linked with these developments is that of Frederick W. Taylor (1856–1915), who proposed a set of principles known as *scientific management*.[2] A key element in Taylor's approach is an extreme form of labor division and work analysis. By meticulously studying labor activities, such as the individual steps that were required to handle pig iron in steel mills, Taylor developed very specific work instructions for workers. Workers would only be involved with carrying out one of the many steps in the production process. Not only in industry, but also in administrative settings, such as government organizations, the concept of division of labor became the most dominant form of organizing work. The upshot of this development was that workers became pure specialists who were concerned with only a single part of one business process.

A side effect of the ideas of Taylor and his contemporaries was the emergence of an altogether new class of professionals—the class of *managers*. After all, someone needed to oversee the productivity of groups of workers concerned with the same part of a production process. Managers were responsible for pinning down the productivity goals for individual workers and making sure that such goals were met. In contrast to the masters of the medieval guilds, who could only attain such a rank on the basis of a masterpiece produced by themselves, managers are not necessarily experts in carrying out the job they oversee. Their main interest is to optimize how a job is done with the resources under their supervision.

After the emergence of managers, organizations became structured along the principles of labor division. A next and obvious challenge arose then: How to differentiate between the responsibilities of all these managers? The solution was to create functional units in which people with a similar focus on part of the production

---

[2] An excerpt of Taylor's book, "The Principles of Scientific Management", is available at http:// sourcebooks.fordham.edu/mod/1911taylor.asp.

process were grouped together. These units were overseen by managers with different responsibilities. Moreover, the units and their managers were structured hierarchically. For example, groups are placed under departments, departments are placed under business units, etc. What we see here is the root of the functional units, which are still familiar to us today when we think about organizations: purchasing, sales, warehousing, finance, marketing, human resource management, etc.

The *functional organization* that emerged from the mindset of the Second Industrial Revolution, dominated the corporate landscape for the greatest part of the nineteenth and twentieth centuries. Towards the end of the 1980s, however, major American companies such as IBM, Ford, and Bell Atlantic (now Verizon) came to realize that their emphasis on functional optimization was creating inefficiencies in their operations that were affecting their competitiveness. Costly projects that introduced new IT systems or reorganized work within a functional department with the aim of improving its efficiency, were not notably helping these companies to become more competitive. It seemed as if customers remained oblivious to these efforts and continued to take their business elsewhere, for example to Japanese competitors.

1.3.2 The Birth of Process Thinking

One of the breakthrough events for the development of BPM was Ford's acquisition of a big financial stake in Mazda during the 1980s. When visiting Mazda's plants, one of the things that Ford executives noticed was that units within Mazda seemed considerably understaffed in comparison with comparable units within Ford, yet operated normally. A famous case study illustrating this phenomenon, first narrated by Michael Hammer [59] and subsequently analyzed by many others, deals with Ford's purchasing process. This inspired what became known as Business Process Reengineering (BPR), which Hammer and Champy define as "the fundamental rethinking and radical redesign of business processes to achieve dramatic improvements in critical, contemporary measures of performance, such as cost, quality, service, and speed."

Figure 1.3 depicts the way purchasing was done within Ford at the time. Every purchase that Ford would make needed to go through the purchasing department. On deciding that a particular quantity of products indeed had to be purchased, this department sent out an order to the vendor in question. It would also send a copy of that order to accounts payable. When the vendor followed up, the ordered goods would be delivered at Ford's receiving warehouse. Along with the goods came a shipping notice, which was passed on to accounts payable. The vendor would also send out an invoice to accounts payable directly.

Against this background, it becomes clear that the main task of accounts payable was to check the consistency between three documents (purchase order copy, shipping notice, and invoice), each document consisting of roughly 14 data items (type of product, quantity, price, etc.). Not surprisingly, numerous discrepancies

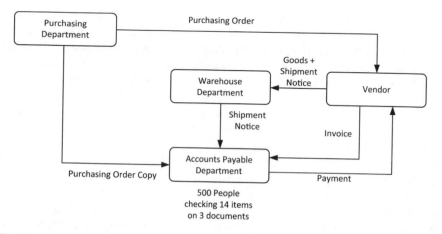

Fig. 1.3 Purchasing process at Ford at the initial stage

were discovered every day and sorting out these discrepancies occupied several hundred people within Ford. By contrast, at Mazda only five people worked in this department (as opposed to 500 people at Ford), while Mazda was not 100 times smaller than Ford in any relevant measure. Fundamentally, the problem is that Ford was detecting and resolving discrepancies one by one, while Mazda instead was avoiding the discrepancies in the first place. After a more detailed comparison with Mazda, Ford carried out several changes in its own purchasing process, which led to the redesigned process depicted in Figure 1.4.

First of all, a central database was developed to store information on purchases. This database was used by the purchasing department to store all the information on purchase orders. This database replaced one of the original paper streams. Secondly, new computer terminals were installed at the warehouse department which gave

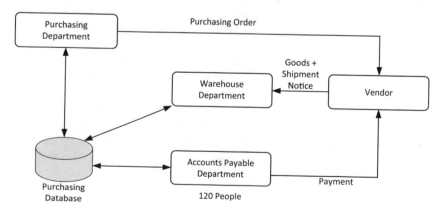

Fig. 1.4 Purchasing process at Ford after redesign

direct access to that database. When goods arrived, the warehouse personnel could immediately check whether the delivery actually matched what was originally purchased. If this was not the case, the goods were simply not accepted: This put the onus on the vendor to ensure that what was delivered was exactly what was requested. In cases where a match was found between the delivered goods and the recorded purchase order, the acceptance of the goods was registered. So, the only thing left to do for accounts payable was to pay what was agreed upon in the original purchase order. Following this new set-up, Ford managed to bring down their workforce in accounts payable from roughly 500 people down to 120 people—a 76% reduction.

Exercise 1.2 Consider the purchasing process at Ford.

1. Who are the actors in this process?
2. Which actors can be considered as customers in this process?
3. What value does the process deliver to its customers?
4. What are the possible outcomes of this process?

A key element in this case study is that a problematic performance issue (i.e., an excessive amount of time and resources spent on checking documents in accounts payable) is approached by considering an entire process. In this case, the accounts payable department plays an important role in the overall purchasing process, but the process also involves tasks by staff at the purchasing department and at the warehouse, and by the vendor. Regardless of these barriers, changes are made across the process and these changes are multi-pronged: They include informational changes (information exchanges), technological changes (database, terminals), and structural changes (checks, policies).

This characteristic view on how to look at organizational performance was put forward in a seminal article by Tom Davenport and James Short [31]. This article urged managers to look at *entire, end-to-end processes* when trying to improve the operations of their business, instead of looking at one particular task or business function. The article discussed various cases where indeed this particular approach proved to be successful. In the same paper, the important role of IT was emphasized as an enabler to come up with a redesign of existing business processes. Indeed, when looking at the Ford-Mazda example it would seem difficult to change the traditional procedure without the specific qualities of IT, which in general allows access to information in a way that is independent of time and place.

1.3.3   The Rise and Fall of BPR

The work by Davenport and Short, as well as that of others, chiefly Michael Hammer, triggered the emergence and widespread adoption of a management concept that was referred to as *Business Process Redesign* or *Business Process Reengineering*, often conveniently abbreviated as *BPR*. Numerous white papers, articles, and books appeared on the topic throughout the 1990s and companies throughout the world assembled BPR teams to review and redesign their processes.

The enthusiasm for BPR faded away by the late 1990s. Many companies terminated their BPR projects and stopped supporting further BPR initiatives. What had happened? In a retrospective analysis, a number of factors can be distinguished:

1. Concept misuse: In some organizations, just about every change program or improvement project was labeled BPR, even when business processes were not the core of these projects. During the 1990s, many corporations initiated considerable reductions of their workforce (downsizing) which, since they were often packaged as process redesign projects, triggered intense resentment among operational staff and middle management against BPR. After all, it was not at all clear that operational improvement was really driving such initiatives.
2. Over-radicalism: Some early proponents of BPR, including Hammer, empha- sized from the very start that redesign had to be radical, in the sense that a new design for a business process had to overhaul the way the process was initially organized. A telling indication is one of Hammer's early papers on this subject which bore the subtitle: "Don't Automate, Obliterate". While a radical approach may be justified in some situations, it is clear that many other situations require a much more gradual (incremental) approach.
3. Support immaturity: Even in projects that were process-centered from the start and took a more gradual approach to improving the business process in question, people ran into the problem that the necessary tools and technologies to implement such a new design were not available or insufficiently powerful. One particular issue centered around the fact that much logic on how processes had to unfold was hard-coded in the supporting IT applications of the time. Understandably, people grew frustrated when they noted that their efforts on redesigning a process were thwarted by a rigid infrastructure.

Subsequently, two key events revived some of the ideas behind BPR and laid the foundation for the emergence of BPM. First of all, empirical studies appeared, showing that organizations that were process-oriented—that is, organizations that sought to improve processes as a basis for gaining efficiency and satisfying their customers—factually did better than non-process-oriented organizations. While the initial BPR gurus provided compelling case studies, such as the one on Ford-Mazda, it remained unclear to many whether these were exceptions rather than the rule. In one of the first empirical studies on this topic, Kevin McCormack [107] investigated a sample of 100 US manufacturing organizations. He found that process-oriented organizations showed better overall performance, tended to have a better *esprit de corps* in the workplace, and suffered less from inter-functional conflicts. Follow-up studies confirmed this picture, which gave renewed credibility to process thinking.

A second important development was technological in nature. Different types of IT systems emerged, most notably Enterprise Resource Planning (ERP) systems and Workflow Management Systems (WfMSs). ERP systems are essentially systems that store all data related to the business operations of a company in a consistent manner, so that all stakeholders who need access to these data can gain such access. This idea of a single shared and centralized database enables the optimization of information usage and information exchanges, which is a key enabler of process improvement (see Chapter 8).[3] WfMSs, on the other hand, are systems that distribute work to various actors in a company on the basis of process models. By doing so, a WfMS makes it easier to implement changes to business processes (e.g., to change the order in which steps are performed). Indeed, the changes made in the process model can be put into execution with relative ease, as compared to the situation where the rules for executing the process are hard-coded inside complex software systems and buried inside tens of thousands of lines of code. Also, a WfMS very closely supports the idea of working in a process-centered manner.

Originally, WfMSs were concerned mainly with routing work between human actors. Later on, these systems were gradually extended with modules to monitor and analyze the execution of business processes. In parallel, the emergence of Web services made it easier to connect a WfMS with other systems, in particular ERP systems. As WfMSs became more sophisticated and better integrated with other enterprise systems, they became known as Business Process Management Systems (BPMSs).

BPMSs are just one type of IT tool that supports the implementation and execution of business processes. There are many others, including ERP systems, Customer Relationship Management (CRM) systems, and Document Management Systems (DMSs). These tools are known under the umbrella term of Process-Aware Information Systems (PAISs). Chapter 9 will discuss the functionality of PAISs in general and of BPMSs in particular. How business processes can be implemented using process models and a BPMS is the focus of Chapter 10.

The above historical view suggests that BPM is a revival of BPR, as indeed BPM adopts the process-centered view on organizations. Some caution is due, though, when BPR and BPM are equated. The relation is much better understood on the basis of Figure 1.5.

This figure shows that a manager that is responsible for a business process—also called the *process owner*—is concerned with planning and organizing the process on the one hand and monitoring the process on the other. The figure allows us to explain the differences in *scope* between BPR and BPM. While both approaches take the business process as a starting point, BPR is primarily concerned with planning and organizing the process. By contrast, BPM provides concepts, methods, techniques, and tools that cover all aspects of managing a process—to plan, organize, and monitor it—as well as its actual execution. In other words, BPR should be seen as a subset of techniques that can be used in the context of BPM.

---

[3]In reality, ERP systems are much more than a shared database. They also incorporate numerous modules to support typical functions of an organization such as accounting, inventory management, production planning, logistics, etc. However, from the perspective of process improvement, the shared database concept behind ERP systems is a major enabler.

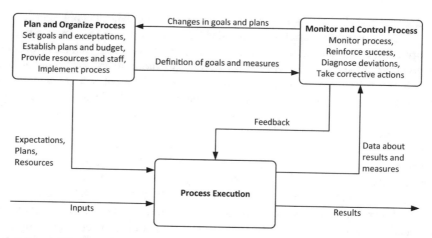

Fig. 1.5 Job functions of a manager responsible for a process (a.k.a. process owner), based on Rummler & Brache [153]

This discussion highlights that BPM encompasses the entire lifecycle of business processes. Accordingly, the next section provides an overview of the concepts, methods, techniques, and tools that compose the BPM discipline through the lens of the *BPM lifecycle*. This lens provides a structured view of how a given process can be managed.

1.4   The BPM Lifecycle

In general, the first question that a team embarking on a BPM initiative needs to clarify is: Which business processes do we aim to improve? Right at the outset and before the possibility of applying BPM is put on the table, there will probably already be an idea of what operational problems the team has to address and which business processes are posing those operational problems. In other words, the team will not start from scratch. For example, if the problem is that site engineers complain that their job is being hampered by difficulties in securing construction equipment when needed, it is clear that this problem should be addressed by looking at the equipment rental process. Still, one has to delimit this process in more precise terms. In particular, one has to answer questions such as: Does the process start right from the moment when rental suppliers are selected? Does it end when the rented equipment is delivered to the construction site? Or does it end when the equipment is returned? Or does it continue until the fee for equipment rental has been paid to the supplier?

These questions might be easy or hard to answer depending on how much *process thinking* has taken place in the organization beforehand. If the organization has engaged in BPM initiatives before, it is likely that an inventory of business processes is available and that the scope of these processes has been defined, at least to some extent. In organizations that have not engaged in BPM before, the BPM team has to start by at least identifying the processes that are relevant to the problem on the table, delimiting the scope of these processes, and identifying relations between these processes. This initial phase of a BPM initiative is termed *process identification*. This phase leads to a so-called *process architecture*: a collection of inter-linked processes covering the bulk of the work that an organization performs in order to achieve its mission in a sustainable manner.

In general, the purpose of engaging in a BPM initiative is to ensure that the business processes covered by the BPM initiative lead to consistently positive outcomes and deliver maximum value to the organization in servicing its clients. Measuring the *value* delivered by a process is a crucial step in BPM. As renowned software engineer Tom DeMarco once famously put it: "You can't control what you can't measure". So, before starting to analyze any process in detail, it is important to clearly define the *process performance measures* (also called *process performance metrics*) that will be used to determine whether a process is in good shape or in bad shape. Typical process performance measures relate to cost, time, quality, and flexibility.

Cost-related measures are a recurrent class of performance measures in the context of BPM. For example, coming back to the equipment rental process, a possible performance measure is the total cost of all equipment rented by BuildIT per time interval (e.g., per month). Another broad and recurrent class of measures are those related to time. An example is the average amount of time elapsed between the moment an equipment rental request is submitted by a site engineer and the delivery of the equipment to the construction site. This measure is generally called *cycle time*. A third class of recurrent measures are those related to quality, specifically error rates. Error rate is the percentage of times that an execution of the process ends up in a negative outcome. In the case of the equipment rental process, one such measure is the number of pieces of equipment returned because they are unsuitable, or due to defects in the delivered equipment. Finally, flexibility measures capture the extent to which the performance of a process is maintained under changing or abnormal conditions, for example when a works engineer resigns suddenly or when a supplier goes bankrupt.

The identification of performance measures (and associated performance objectives) is crucial in any BPM initiative. This identification is generally seen as part of the process identification phase, although in some cases it may be postponed until later phases.

Exercise 1.3 Consider the student admission process described in Exercise 1.1 (page 5). Taking the perspective of the customer, identify at least two performance measures that can be attached to this process.

Once a BPM team has identified which processes they are dealing with and which performance measures should be used, the next phase for the team is to understand the business process in detail. We call this phase *process discovery*. Typically, one of the outcomes of this phase is one or several *as-is* process models. These as-is process models reflect the understanding that people in the organization have about how work is done. Process models are meant to facilitate communication between stakeholders involved in a BPM initiative. Therefore, they have to be easy to understand. In principle, we could model a business process by means of textual descriptions, like the textual description in Example 1.1. However, such textual descriptions are cumbersome to read and easy to misinterpret because of the ambiguity inherent in free-form text. This is why it is common practice to use diagrams in order to model business processes. Diagrams allow us to more easily comprehend the process. Also, if a diagram is made using a modeling language that is understood by all stakeholders, there is less room for any misunderstanding. Note that these diagrams may still be complemented with textual descriptions. In fact, it is common to see analysts documenting a process using a combination of diagrams and text.

There are many languages for modeling business processes diagrammatically. Perhaps one of the oldest are *flowcharts*. In their most basic form, flowcharts consist of rectangles, which represent activities, and diamonds, which represent points in the process where a decision is made. More generally, we can say that regardless of the specific notation used, a diagrammatic process model typically consists of two types of nodes: activity nodes and control nodes. Activity nodes describe units of work that may be performed by humans or software applications, or a combination thereof. Control nodes capture the flow of execution between activities. Although not all process modeling languages support it, a third important type of element in process models are event nodes. An event node tells us that something may or must happen, within the process or in the environment of the process, that requires a reaction, like for example the arrival of a message from a customer requesting the cancelation of purchase order. Other types of nodes may appear in a process model, but we can say that activity nodes, event nodes, and control nodes are the most basic ones.

Several extensions of flowcharts exist, such as cross-organizational flowcharts. Here, the flowchart is divided into so-called *swimlanes*, which denote different organizational units (e.g., different departments in a company). If you are familiar with the Unified Modeling Language (UML), you have probably come across *UML Activity Diagrams*. At their core, UML Activity Diagrams are cross-organizational flowcharts. However, UML Activity Diagrams go beyond basic cross-organizational flowcharts by providing symbols to capture data objects, signals, and parallelism among other aspects. Yet another language for process modeling are *Event-driven Process Chains (EPCs)*. EPCs have some similarities with flowcharts but they differ from flowcharts in that they treat events as first-class citizens. Other languages used for process modeling include *data-flow diagrams* and *Integrated DEFinition for Process Description Capture Method (IDEF3)*.

It would be mind-boggling to learn all these languages. Fortunately, nowadays there is a widely-used standard for process modeling, namely the Business Process Model and Notation (BPMN). The latest version of BPMN is BPMN 2.0.2. It was released as a standard by the Object Management Group (OMG) in December 2013. In BPMN, activities are represented as rounded rectangles. Control nodes (called

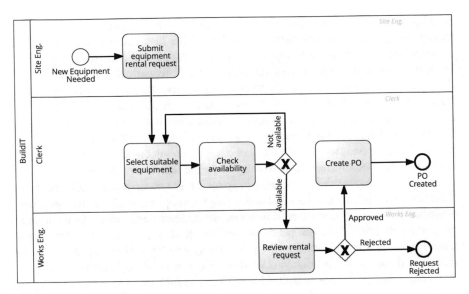

Fig. 1.6 Process model for the initial fragment of the equipment rental process

gateways) are represented using diamond shapes. Activities and control nodes are connected by means of arcs (called sequence flows) that determine the order in which the process is executed. Figure 1.6 contains a model of an initial fragment of the equipment rental process, up to the point where the works engineer accepts or rejects the equipment rental request. This process model shows two decision points. In the first one, the process takes one of two paths depending on whether the equipment is available or not. In the second, the equipment rental request is either approved or rejected. The model also shows the process participants involved in this fragment of the process, namely the site engineer, the clerk, and the works engineer. Each of these participants is shown as a separate *lane*, which contains the activities performed by the participant in question.

The process model in Figure 1.6 is minimalistic. At best, it can serve to give to an external person a summary of what happens in this process. Generally, a process model needs to have more details to be useful. Which additional details should be included in a process model depends on its purpose. Some process models are intended to serve as documentation for new employees. In this case, additional text annotations may be added to the process model to clarify the meaning of certain activities or events. Other times, process models are intended to be analyzed quantitatively, for example in order to calculate performance measures. If so, further details may be required such as how much time each task takes on average. Finally, some process models are intended to be deployed into a BPMS to coordinate the execution of the process (see Section 1.3.3). In this latter case, the model should contain details about the inputs and outputs of the process and of each of its tasks.

Once we have understood the as-is process in detail, the next step is to identify and analyze the issues in this process. One potential issue in BuildIT's equipment rental process is that the cycle time is too high. As a result, site engineers do not manage to get the required equipment on time. This may cause delays in various construction tasks, which may ripple down into delays in the construction projects. In order to analyze these issues, an analyst needs to collect information about the time spent in each task of the process. Moreover, the analyst needs to gather information regarding the amount of rework that takes place in the process. Here, rework means that one or several tasks are repeated because something went wrong. For example, when the clerk identifies a suitable piece of equipment in a supplier's catalog, but later finds out that the piece of equipment is not available on the required dates, the clerk might need to search again for an alternative piece of equipment from another supplier. Valuable time is spent by the clerk going back and forth between consulting the catalogs and contacting the suppliers to check the equipment availability. In order to analyze this issue, the analyst needs to find out in what percentage of cases the clerk needs to identify an alternative piece of equipment (rework). Given this information, the analyst may employ various techniques to be discussed throughout this book to track down the causes of long cycle times.

Another potential issue in BuildIT's equipment rental process is that sometimes the equipment delivered at the construction site is unsuitable. The site engineer then has to reject it—an example of a negative outcome. To analyze this issue, an analyst needs to find out how often such negative outcomes occur. Furthermore, the analyst needs to find out why these negative outcomes are happening; in other words, where do things go wrong in the first place. Sometimes, a negative outcome might stem from miscommunication, for example between the site engineer and the clerk. On other occasions, it might come from inaccurate data (e.g., errors in the description of the equipment) or from an error on the supplier's side. By identifying, classifying, and understanding the main causes of such negative outcomes, the analyst can ultimately find ways of eliminating or minimizing them. The identification and assessment of issues and opportunities for process improvement is called the *process analysis* phase.

We observe that the two issues discussed above are tightly related to performance measures. For example, the first issue above is tied to cycle time and waiting time, both of which are typical performance measures of a process. Similarly, the second issue is tied to the percentage of equipment rejections, which is essentially an error rate—another typical performance measure. Thus, assessing the issues of a process often goes hand-in-hand with measuring the current state of the process with respect to certain performance measures.

Exercise 1.4 Consider again the student admission process described in Exercise 1.1 (page 5). Taking the perspective of the customer, think of at least two issues that this process might have.

Once issues in a process have been analyzed and possibly quantified, the next phase is to identify and analyze potential remedies for these issues. At this point, the analyst will consider multiple possible options for addressing a problem. In doing so, the analyst needs to keep in mind that a change in a process to address one issue may potentially cause other issues down the road. For example, in order to speed up the equipment rental process, one might think of removing the approval steps involving the works engineer. If pushed to the extreme, however, this change would mean that the rented equipment might sometimes not be optimal since the works engineer viewpoint is not taken into account. The works engineer has a global view on the construction projects and may be able to propose alternative ways of addressing the equipment needs of a construction project in a more effective manner.

Changing a process is not as easy as it sounds. People are used to working in a certain way and are often inclined to resist changes. Furthermore, if the change implies modifying the information systems underpinning the process, the change may be costly or may require changes not only in the organization that coordinates the process, but also in other organizations. For example, we could eliminate rework in the equipment rental process if the suppliers provided an online interface allowing clerks to easily retrieve all the available pieces of equipment that can be used for a given job. However, this change in the process would require that the suppliers change their information system, so that their system exposes up-to-date equipment availability information to BuildIT. This change is, at least partially, outside the control of BuildIT. Assuming that suppliers would be able to make such changes, a more radical solution would be to provide mobile devices to the site engineers, so that they can consult the equipment catalog (including availability information) anytime and anywhere. In this way, the clerk would not need to be involved in the process during the equipment search phase. Whether or not this more radical change is viable would require an in-depth analysis of the cost of changing the process in this way versus the benefits that such change would provide.

Exercise 1.5 Given the issues in the student admission process identified in Exercise 1.4 (page 20), what possible changes do you think could be made to this process in order to address these issues?

Armed with an understanding of the issues in a process and a candidate set of potential remedies, analysts can propose a redesigned version of the process. This *to-be* process design is the main output of the *process redesign phase*. Here, it is important to keep in mind that analysis and redesign are intricately related. There may be multiple redesign options. Each of these options needs to be analyzed, so that an informed choice can be made as to which option is preferable.

Once redesigned, the necessary changes in the ways of working and the IT systems of the organization should be implemented so that the to-be process can eventually be put into execution. This phase is called *process implementation*. In the case of the equipment rental process, the process implementation phase would involve putting in place an information system to record and to track equipment rental requests, POs associated with approved requests, and invoices associated with these POs. Deploying such an information system means more than deploying a new IT system. It also entails getting the process participants to embrace the new system and training them so that they perform their work in the spirit of the redesigned process.

More generally, process implementation involves two complementary facets: *organizational change management* and *process automation*. Organizational change management refers to the set of activities required to change the way of working of all participants involved in the process. These activities include:

- Explaining the changes to the process participants to the point that they understand both what changes are being introduced and why these changes are beneficial to the company.
- Putting in place a change management plan so that stakeholders know when the changes will come into effect and what transitional arrangements will be employed to address problems during the transition to the to-be process.
- Training users to the new way of working and monitoring the changes in order to ensure a smooth transition to the to-be process.

Process automation, on the other hand, involves the configuration or implementation of an IT system (or the re-configuration of an existing IT system) to support the to-be process. This IT system should support process participants in the performance of the tasks of the process. This may include assigning tasks to process participants, helping process participants to prioritize their work, providing process participants with the information they need to perform a task, and performing automated cross-checks and other automated tasks where possible. There are several ways to implement such an IT system. This book focuses on one particular approach, which consists of extending the to-be process model obtained from the process redesign phase in order to make it executable by a BPMS.

Over time, adjustments may be required in the implemented business process when it does not meet expectations any longer. To this end, the process needs to be monitored. Analysts ought to scrutinize the data collected by monitoring the process in order to identify needed adjustments. These activities are encompassed by the *process monitoring* phase. Lack of continuous monitoring and improvement of a process leads to degradation. As Hammer once put it: "every good process eventually becomes a bad process", unless continuously adapted and improved to keep up with the ever-changing landscape of customer needs, technology and competition. This is why the BPM lifecycle should be seen as circular: the output of the monitoring phase feeds back into the discovery, analysis, and redesign phases.

To sum up, we can view BPM as a continuous cycle comprising the following phases (see Figure 1.7):

- *Process identification.* In this phase, a business problem is posed. Processes relevant to the problem being addressed are identified, delimited, and inter-related. The outcome of process identification is a new or updated process architecture, which provides an overall picture of the processes in an organization and their relationships. This architecture is then used to select which process or set thereof to manage through the remaining phases of the lifecycle. Typically, process identification is done in parallel with performance measure identification.
- *Process discovery* (also called *as-is process modeling*). Here, the current state of each of the relevant processes is documented, typically in the form of one or several as-is process models.
- *Process analysis.* In this phase, issues associated with the as-is process are identified, documented, and whenever possible quantified using performance

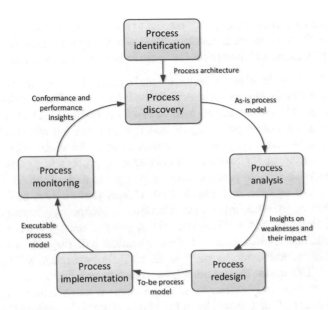

Fig. 1.7 The BPM lifecycle

measures. The output of this phase is a structured collection of issues. These issues are prioritized based on their potential impact and the estimated effort required to resolve them.

- *Process redesign* (also called *process improvement*). The goal of this phase is to identify changes to the process that would help to address the issues identified in the previous phase and allow the organization to meet its performance objectives. To this end, multiple change options are analyzed and compared in terms of the chosen performance measures. Hence, process redesign and process analysis go hand-in-hand: As new change options are proposed, they are analyzed using process analysis techniques. Eventually, the most promising change options are retained and combined into a redesigned process. The output of this phase is typically a to-be process model.

- *Process implementation*. In this phase, the changes required to move from the as-is process to the to-be process are prepared and performed. Process implementation covers two aspects: organizational change management and automation. Organizational change management refers to the set of activities required to change the way of working of all participants involved in the process. Process automation refers to the development and deployment of IT systems (or enhanced versions of existing IT systems) that support the to-be process. In this book, our focus with respect to process implementation is on automation. We will only briefly touch upon change management, which is a field on its own.

- *Process monitoring*. Once the redesigned process is running, relevant data are collected and analyzed to determine how well the process is performing with respect to its performance measures and performance objectives. Bottlenecks, recurrent errors, or deviations with respect to the intended behavior are identified and corrective actions are undertaken. New issues may then arise, in the same or in other processes, which requires the cycle to be repeated on a continuous basis.

The BPM lifecycle also helps us to understand the role of technology in BPM. Technology in general, and especially Information Technology (IT), is a key instrument to improve business processes. Not surprisingly, IT specialists such as system engineers often play a significant role in BPM initiatives. However, to achieve maximum efficacy, system engineers need to be aware that technology is just one instrument for managing and executing processes. System engineers need to work together with process analysts in order to understand what issues are affecting a given process, and how to best address these issues, be it by means of automation or by other means. As a renowned technology businessman, Bill Gates, once famously put it: "The first rule in any technology used in a business is that automation applied to an efficient operation will magnify the efficiency. The second is that automation applied to an inefficient operation will magnify the inefficiency". This means that learning how to design and improve processes—and not only how to build an IT system to automate a narrow part of a business process— is a fundamental skill that should be in the hands of any IT graduate. Reciprocally, business graduates need to understand how technology, and particularly IT, can be used to optimize the execution of business processes. This book aims at bridging these two viewpoints by presenting an integrated viewpoint covering the whole BPM lifecycle.

A complementary viewpoint on the BPM lifecycle is given by the box "Stakeholders in the BPM lifecycle". This box summarizes the roles in a company that are directly or indirectly involved in BPM initiatives.[4] The list of roles described in the box highlights the fact that BPM is inter-disciplinary. A typical BPM initiative involves managers at different levels in the organization, administrative and field workers (called process participants in the box), business and system analysts, and IT teams. Accordingly, the book aims at giving a balanced view of techniques both from management science and IT, as they pertain to BPM.

STAKEHOLDERS IN THE BPM LIFECYCLE

Many stakeholders are involved in a business process throughout its lifecycle [93]. Among them we distinguish the following individuals and groups.

- **Management Team.** Depending on how the management of a company is organized, one might find the following positions. The *Chief Executive Officer* (CEO) is responsible for the overall business success of the company. The *Chief Operations Officer* (COO) is responsible for defining the way operations are set up. In some companies, the COO is also responsible

(continued)

---

[4]The role of the customer is not listed in the box as this role has been discussed previously.

for process performance, while in other companies there is a dedicated executive position of *Chief Process Officer* (CPO) [78] or *Chief Process and Innovation Officer* (CPIO) for this purpose. The *Chief Information Officer* (CIO) is responsible for the efficient and effective operation of the information system infrastructure. In some organizations, process redesign projects are driven by the CIO. The *Chief Financial Officer* (CFO) is responsible for the overall financial performance of the company. The CFO may also be responsible for certain business processes, particularly those that have a direct impact on financial performance. Other management positions that have a stake in the lifecycle of processes include the *Human Resources (HR) director*. The HR director plays a key role in processes that involve significant numbers of process participants. In any case, the management team is responsible for overseeing all processes, initiating process redesign initiatives, and providing resources and strategic guidance to stakeholders involved in all phases of the BPM lifecycle.

- **Process Owners.** A process owner is responsible for the efficient and effective operation of a given process. As discussed in the context of Figure 1.5, a process owner is responsible on the one hand for planning and organizing, and on the other hand for monitoring the process. In the planning and organizing role, the process owner is responsible for defining performance measures and objectives as well as initiating and leading improvement projects related to their process. The process owner is also responsible for securing resources so that the process runs smoothly on a daily basis. In their monitoring role, process owners are responsible for ensuring that the performance objectives of the process are met, and for taking corrective actions in case these objectives are not met. Process owners also provide guidance to process participants on how to resolve exceptions and errors that occur during the execution of the process. Thus, the process owner is involved in process modeling, analysis, redesign, implementation, and monitoring. Note that the same individual could well be responsible for multiple processes. For example, in a small company, a single manager might be responsible both for the company's order-to-cash process and for the after-sales customer service process.

- **Process Participants.** Process participants are human actors who perform the activities of a business process on a day-to-day basis. They conduct routine work according to the standards and guidelines of the company. Process participants are coordinated by the process owner, who is responsible for dealing with non-routine aspects of the process. Process participants are also involved as domain experts during process discovery and process analysis. They support redesign activities and implementation efforts.

- **Process Analysts.** Process analysts conduct process identification, discovery (in particular modeling), analysis, and redesign activities. They

(continued)

coordinate process implementation as well as process monitoring. They report to management and process owners and closely interact with process participants. Process analysts typically have one of two backgrounds. Process analysts concerned with organizational requirements, performance, and change management have a business background, while those concerned with process automation have an IT background.

- **Process Methodologist.** The process methodologist provides expert knowledge and advice to process analysts on the choice of suitable methods, techniques and software tools to use in each phase of the BPM lifecycle. This role is also in charge of coordinating the technical training on BPM for the process analysts. The process methodologist is typically available only in large-scale BPM initiatives.

- **System Engineers.** System engineers are involved in process redesign and implementation. They interact with process analysts to capture system requirements. They translate requirements into a system design and are responsible for the implementation, testing and deployment of this system. System engineers also liaise with the process owner and process participants to ensure that the developed system supports their work effectively. Oftentimes, system implementation, testing and deployment are outsourced to external providers, in which case the system engineering team will at least partially consist of contractors.

- **BPM Group** (also called *BPM Center of Excellence*). Large organizations that have been engaged in BPM for several years possess a wealth of valuable knowledge on how to plan and execute BPM projects as well as substantial amounts of process documentation. The BPM group is responsible for preserving this knowledge and documentation and ensuring that they are used to meet the organization's strategic goals. Specifically, the BPM group is responsible for maintaining the process architecture, prioritizing process redesign projects, giving support to the process owners and process analysts, and ensuring that the process documentation is maintained in a consistent manner and that the process monitoring systems are working effectively. In other words, the BPM group is responsible for maintaining a BPM culture and aligning the BPM efforts with the strategic goals of the organization. Not all organizations have a dedicated BPM group. BPM groups are most common in large organizations with several years of BPM experience.

The BPM lifecycle encompasses a range of methods and tools to identify processes and to manage individual processes. While these methods and tools are important, the success of BPM in an organization depends on many other factors beyond their scope. As mentioned in the box "Stakeholders in the BPM lifecycle", it is important to ensure that BPM initiatives are aligned with the strategic goals of the organization (*strategic alignment*). It is also important that the roles and responsibilities in BPM initiatives and the associated decision-making processes are clearly defined, and that measurement systems, guidelines, and conventions are in place to ensure that BPM initiatives are conducted in a consistent manner (*governance*). It is further important that process participants are engaged in and informed of the BPM initiatives that affect their processes and that managers and analysts who engage in such initiatives have the necessary skills. Last but not least, it is important to develop an organizational culture that is responsive to process change and embraces process thinking. In other words, the role that an organization's *people* and *culture* play for the success of BPM should not be underestimated. In sum, for BPM to be sustainably successful, an organization has to treat BPM as an enterprise capability, at the same level as other organizational management capabilities such as risk management and performance management.

In the rest of the book, we will dive consecutively into each of the phases of the BPM lifecycle. Chapter 2 deals with the process identification phase. Chapters 3–4 provide an introduction to process modeling, which serves as background for subsequent phases in the BPM lifecycle. Chapter 5 deals with the process discovery phase. Chapters 6–7 present a number of process analysis techniques. We classify these techniques into qualitative (Chapter 6) and quantitative ones (Chapter 7). A quantitative technique focuses on performance measures, while a qualitative technique involves human judgement, for example in order to classify tasks or issues according to subjective criteria. Next, Chapter 8 gives an overview of process redesign methods. Chapters 9–10 deal with the process implementation phase. Chapter 9 introduces different types of PAISs. Meanwhile, Chapter 10 shows concretely how to use a process model to drive the implementation of a process using one specific type of PAIS, namely a BPMS. Chapter 11 introduces a range of techniques for process monitoring, thus closing the BPM lifecycle. Finally, Chapter 12 discusses the question of how to make BPM sustainably successful by treating it as an enterprise capability and assessing this capability using a maturity model.

1.5 Recap

We retain from this chapter that a process is a collection of events, activities, and decisions that collectively lead to an outcome that brings value to an organization's customers. Every organization has processes. Understanding and managing these processes in order to ensure that they consistently produce value is a key ingredient for the effectiveness and competitiveness of organizations.

If we wanted to capture BPM in a nutshell, we would say that BPM is a body of principles, methods, and tools to discover, analyze, redesign, implement, and monitor business processes. We have also seen that process models and performance measures are foundational pillars for managing processes. It is on top of them that much of the art and science of BPM builds. The provided definition encompasses the main phases of the BPM lifecycle and the various related disciplines that complement BPM, such as Lean, Six Sigma, and Total Quality Management. The aim of this chapter was to give a "sneak peek" of the activities and stakeholders involved in each of the phases of the BPM lifecycle. The rest of the book aims to shed light on many of the principles and methods that are used in each of these phases.

1.6 Solutions to Exercises

Solution 1.1

1. Admissions officer, applicant, academic recognition agency, and academic committee. The admissions office as an organizational unit can also be recognized as a separate actor.
2. The applicant.
3. One can argue that the *value* that the process provides to the applicant is the assessment of the application and the subsequent decision to accept or reject. In this case, the process delivers value whether the applicant is accepted or rejected, provided that the application is processed in due order. Another viewpoint would be to say that the process only gives value to the applicant if the application is accepted, and not if it is rejected. Arguments can be put forward in favor of either of these two viewpoints.
4. Applicant rejected due to incomplete documents; Applicant rejected due to English language test results; Applicant rejected due to assessment of academic recognition agency; Applicant rejected due to academic committee decision; Applicant accepted. A more in-depth analysis could reveal other possible outcomes such as "Application withdrawn by applicant" or "Applicant conditionally accepted subject to providing additional documents". However, there are not enough elements in the description of the process to determine if these latter outcomes are possible.

Solution 1.2

1. The unit with a purchasing need, the purchasing department, the vendor, the warehouse, and the accounts payable department.
2. The unit with a purchasing need.
3. The *value* that the process provides to the unit with a purchasing need is the timely, accurate, and cost-efficient provision of a particular purchasing item. In this case, the process delivers value if the purchasing need is fulfilled by means of a timely, accurate, and cost-efficient shipment of a vendor, accompanied by a timely and accurate payment.

4. The shipment of goods can be accepted if accurate, leading to a corresponding payment, or they can be rejected if the amount or type of shipment is not correct.

Solution 1.3 Possible measures include:

1. Average time between the moment an application is received and the moment it is accepted or rejected (cycle time). Note that if the university advertises a pre-defined deadline for notifying acceptance/rejection, an alternative performance measure would be the percentage of times that this deadline is met.
2. Percentage of applications rejected due to incomplete documents. Here we could distinguish between two variants of this measure: one that counts all cases where applications are initially rejected due to incomplete documents, and another one that counts the number of cases where applications are rejected due to incomplete documents and where the applicant does not resubmit the completed application, for example because the deadline for applications has expired before the applicant gathers the required documents.
3. Percentage of applications rejected due to expired, invalid, or low English language test results.
4. Percentage of applications rejected due to advice from academic recognition.
5. Percentage of accepted applications.

Note that the cost incurred by the university per application is not a measure that is relevant from the perspective of the applicant, but it may be relevant from the perspective of the university.

Solution 1.4 Possible issues include:

1. Long execution times.
2. Inconvenience of gathering and submitting all required documents.
3. Potentially: mishandled applications due to handoffs of paper documents between process participants.

Solution 1.5 To reduce cycle time as well as mishandled applications, applications could be shared in electronic format between admissions office and academic committee. To reduce the amount of preparation required to submit an application, applications could be evaluated in two stages. The first stage would involve purely electronically submitted documents (e.g., scanned copies instead of physical copies). Only applicants accepted by the academic committee would then need to go through the process of submitting certified copies of degrees by post for verification by the academic recognition agency.

1.7   Further Exercises

Exercise 1.6 Consider the following process at a pharmacy.

Customers drop off their prescriptions either in the drive-through counter or in the front counter of the pharmacy. Customers can request that their prescription be filled immediately. In this case, they have to wait between 15 min and 1 h depending on the current workload. However, most customers are not willing to wait that long, so they opt to nominate a pick-up time at a later point during the day. Generally, customers drop their prescriptions in the morning before going to work (or at lunchtime) and they come back to pick up the drugs after work, typically between 5 p.m. and 6 p.m. When a prescription is dropped off, a technician asks the customer for the pick-up time and puts the prescription in a box labeled with the hour preceding the pick-up time. For example, if the customer asks to have the prescription be ready at 5 p.m., the technician will drop it in the box with the label 4 p.m. (there is one box for each hour of the day).

Every hour, one of the pharmacy technicians picks up the prescriptions due to be filled in the current hour. The technician then enters the details of each prescription (e.g., doctor details, patient details and medication details) into the pharmacy system. As soon as the details of a prescription are entered, the pharmacy system performs an automated check called *Drug Utilization Review* (DUR). This check is meant to determine if the prescription contains any drugs that may be incompatible with other drugs that had been dispensed to the same customer in the past, or drugs that may be inappropriate for the customer taking into account the customer data maintained in the system (e.g., age).

Any alarms raised during the automated DUR are reviewed by a pharmacist who performs a more thorough check. In some cases, the pharmacist even has to call the doctor who issued the prescription in order to confirm it.

After the DUR, the system performs an insurance check in order to determine whether the customer's insurance policy will pay for part or for the whole cost of the drugs. In most cases, the output of this check is that the insurance company will only pay for a certain percentage of the costs, while the customer has to pay for the remaining part (also called the *co-payment*). The rules for determining how much the insurance company will pay and how much the customer has to pay are very complicated. Every insurance company has different rules. In some cases, the insurance policy does not cover one or several drugs in a prescription, but the drug in question can be replaced by another drug that is covered by the insurance policy. When such cases are detected, the pharmacist generally calls the doctor and potentially also the patient to determine if it is possible to perform the drug replacement. Once the prescription passes the insurance check, it is assigned to a technician who collects the drugs from the shelves and puts them in a bag with the prescription stapled to it. After the technician has filled a given prescription, the bag is passed to the pharmacist who double-checks that the prescription has been filled correctly. After this quality check, the pharmacist seals the bag and puts it in the pick-up area. When a customer arrives to pick up a prescription, a technician retrieves the prescription and asks the customer for payment in case the drugs in the prescription are not fully covered by the customer's insurance.

With respect to the above process, consider the following questions:

1. What type of process is the above one: order-to-cash, procure-to-pay, application-to-approval, or issue-to-resolution?
2. Who are the actors in this process?
3. Who are the customers?
4. What are the tasks of this process?
5. What value does the process deliver to its customers?

6. What are the possible outcomes of this process?
7. Taking the perspective of the customer, what performance measures can be attached to this process?
8. What potential issues do you foresee this process might have? What information would you need to collect in order to analyze these issues?
9. What possible changes do you think could be made to this process in order to address the above issues?

Acknowledgement This exercise is inspired by [106].

Exercise 1.7 Consider the following process at a company of 800 employees in the early 1990s.

Almost any employee at the company can initiate a purchase request by filling in a form. The purchase request includes information about the goods to be purchased, the quantity, the desired delivery date, and the approximate cost. The employee can nominate a specific vendor. Employees often request quotes from vendors in order to get the required information. Completing the entire form can take a few days as the employee often does not have the required data. The quote is attached to the purchase request. This completed request is signed by two supervisors. One supervisor has to provide a financial approval, while the other supervisor has to approve the necessity of the purchase and its conformance with the company's policy (e.g., if purchasing a software tool, is it compatible with the company's standard IT operating environment?). Collecting the signatures from the two supervisors takes on average 5 days. If it is urgent, the employee can hand-deliver the form, otherwise it is circulated via internal mail. A rejected purchase request is returned to the employee. Sometimes, the employee makes minor modifications and resubmits the purchase request. Once a purchase request is approved, it is returned to the initiator of the request. The employee forwards the form to the purchasing department. Employees often make a copy of the form for their own record, in case the form gets lost. The purchasing department checks the completeness of the purchase request and returns it to the employee if it is incomplete. The purchasing department then enters the approved request into the company's enterprise system. If the employee has not nominated any vendors, a clerk at the Purchasing Department selects one based on the quotes attached to the purchase requisition, or based on the list of vendors (also called *master vendor list*) available in the company's enterprise system.
Sometimes, the quote attached to the request has expired in the meantime. In this case, an updated quote is requested from the corresponding vendor. Other times, the vendor who submitted the quote is not recorded in the company's enterprise system. In this case, the purchasing department should give preference to other vendors who are registered in the enterprise system. If no such vendors are available or if the registered vendors offer higher prices than the one in the submitted quote, the purchasing department can add the new vendor into the enterprise system.
When a vendor is selected, the enterprise system automatically generates a purchase order. The purchase order is sent to the vendor by fax. A copy of the purchase order is sent to the accounts payable office. This office, part of the financial department, uses an accounting system that is not integrated with the enterprise system, where purchase orders are stored. The goods are always delivered to the goods receipt department. When goods are received, a clerk at this department selects the corresponding purchase order in the enterprise system. The clerk checks the quantity and quality, and generates a document called goods receipt form from the purchase order stored in the enterprise system. The goods are forwarded to the employee who initiated the purchase requisition. A print-out of the goods receipt form is sent to the accounts payable office. If there are any issues with the goods, they are returned

to the vendor and a note is sent to the purchasing department and to the accounts payable office for archival.

The vendor eventually sends the invoice directly to the accounts payable office. A clerk at this office compares the purchase order, the goods receipt and the invoice. This latter task is called three-way matching. Three-way matching is time-consuming because the clerk needs to carefully investigate each discrepancy. The payment process takes so long that the company often misses the deadline for invoice payment and has to pay a penalty.

At the end, the clerk triggers the bank transfer and sends a payment notice to the vendor. Some vendors explicitly indicate in their invoice the bank account number to which the transfer should be made. It happens that the bank account number and name indicated in the invoice differ from the one recorded in the vendor database. Sometimes payments bounce back, in which case the vendor is contacted by phone, email or postal mail. If new bank details are given, the transfer is attempted again. If the issue is still not resolved, the accounts payable office has to contact again the vendor in order to trace the cause of the bounced payment.

1. What type of process is the above one: order-to-cash, procure-to-pay, application-to-approval, or issue-to-resolution?
2. Who are the actors in this process? Who are the customers?
3. What are the tasks of this process?
4. What value does the process deliver to its customers?
5. What are the possible outcomes of this process?
6. Taking the perspective of the customer, what performance measures can be attached to this process?
7. What potential issues do you foresee this process might have? What information would you need to collect in order to analyze these issues?
8. What possible changes do you think could be made to this process in order to address the above issues?

Acknowledgment This exercise is adapted from a similar exercise developed by Michael Rosemann, Queensland University of Technology.

Exercise 1.8 Consider the phases of the BPM lifecycle. Which of these phases are not included in a business process re-engineering project?

1.8 Further Readings

Rummler is one of the pioneers of process thinking as an approach to address the shortcomings of purely functional organizations. His work on process thinking was popularized by a book co-authored with Brache: "Improving Performance: How to Manage the White Space on the Organizational Chart" [153]. A paper published two decades later by Rummler & Ramias [154] gives a summary of Rummler's method for structuring organizations around processes.

Two key articles that popularized process thinking as a management concept are those of Hammer [59] and Davenport & Short [31], which were discussed in this chapter. While Rummler's work deals broadly with structuring organizations based on processes, Hammer and Davenport & Short focus on how to redesign individual business processes to improve their performance.

A comprehensive and consolidated treatment of BPM from a business management perspective is provided by Harmon in his book [65]. Harmon's book presents the so-called BPTrends method for BPM. Harmon is also editor of the BPTrends newsletter and portal[5] which features numerous articles and resources related to BPM. A good overview of the field is also provided in books by Becker et al. [17] and by Rosemann & vom Brocke [186, 187].

As mentioned in this chapter, BPM is related to several other fields, including TQM and Six Sigma. Elzinga et al. [43] discuss the relation between BPM and TQM, while the application of Six Sigma techniques to BPM is discussed by Harmon [65, Chapter 12], Laguna & Marklund [85, Chapter 2], and Conger [28].

---

[5]http://www.bptrends.com.

Chapter 2
Process Identification

Process identification refers to those management activities that aim to systematically define the set of business processes of an organization and establish clear criteria for selecting specific processes for improvement. The output of process identification is a *process architecture*, which represents the processes and their interrelations. This process architecture serves as a framework for defining the priorities and the scope of process modeling and redesign projects.

In this chapter, we start by discussing the context of process identification. Then, we present a method for process identification that is based on two steps: process architecture definition and process selection. The definition step is concerned with listing an initial set of processes and their overall architecture. The selection step considers suitable criteria for defining priorities of these processes using a portfolio.

2.1 The Context of Process Identification

In order to understand the importance of process identification, we have to look at the strategic context of an organization. Few organizations have the resources required to model all their processes in detail, to rigorously analyze and redesign each of them, to deploy automation technology for each of these processes, and finally to continuously monitor the performance of these processes in detail. And even if such resources were available, it would not be cost-effective to spend them in this way. BPM is not for free. Like any other investment, investments in BPM have to pay off. Thus, it is imperative for organizations engaged in BPM to focus their attention on a relevant subset of processes.

Some processes need to receive priority because they are of strategic importance to an organization's survival. Mintzberg defines *business strategy* as an organizational perspective on setting and meeting business goals. Typically, it can be

© Springer-Verlag GmbH Germany, part of Springer Nature 2018
M. Dumas et al., *Fundamentals of Business Process Management*,
https://doi.org/10.1007/978-3-662-56509-4_2

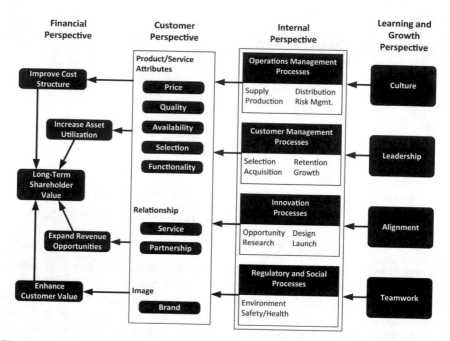

Fig. 2.1 The balanced scorecard by Kaplan & Norton

assumed that a business strategy exists and can be taken into account for process identification. Strategy can be operationalized in different ways. One prominent option is to define business goals using the structure of a *balanced scorecard*.

Figure 2.1 shows the logic of the balanced scorecard using the *strategy map* notation of Kaplan & Norton [73]. The explicit representation of the strategy in such a way is also often referred to as the *business model* of a company. Long-term shareholder value is assumed as a generic and overarching corporate goal in this setting. In the *financial* perspective, this goal is broken down into the four sub-goals of improving the cost structure, increasing asset utilization, expanding revenue opportunities, and enhancing customer value. These financial goals are presumably influenced by factors of the *customer* perspective. The concept of a customer value proposition posits that the product and service-related attributes of price, quality, availability, selection and functionality, service and partner relationships, as well as brand image are valued by customers. For instance, a company used to selling books in shops and now making them available on Amazon could improve its customer value proposition, because it becomes easier to order (availability). The customer perspective is influenced by the *internal* perspective as defined by processes of operations management, customer management, innovation, and regulatory compliance. This means that, for example, offering cheap books as a product-related proposition should be consistent with cheap production processes on the operations management level. The capability of setting up efficient and effective processes in the internal perspective is ultimately influenced by human capital, information capital, and organizational capital in the *learning and growth* perspective. The balanced scorecard underlines the importance of business processes for implementing the business strategy. Business processes build on human, information, and organization capital and provide the basis for the customer value proposition, which will eventually result in financial success. This means, implementing the strategy requires transparency of business processes and their contribution to strategic goals.

Exercise 2.1 Consider the construction company BuildIT and its procure-to-pay process that is described on page 3. To which category in the internal perspective of Figure 2.1 does this process belong? How does it influence different aspects of the customer perspective? How is it shaped by aspects of the learning and growth perspective?

The strategic importance is just one consideration for looking at processes. For example, two processes can be of equal strategic importance, but only one of them might show striking problems, which should be resolved for the sake of all involved stakeholders. In order to trace problems of processes, we need to understand how processes are related to other perspectives of an organization. The balanced scorecard emphasizes the causal relationship between different goals of an organization. In contrast, the *enterprise architecture* describes the structural dependencies between different perspectives of the organization. Different frameworks are used for describing enterprise architectures, among others *The Open Group Architecture Framework* (TOGAF)[1] and the *Zachman Framework*.[2] The latter framework defines the following perspectives:

- The *organizational* perspective describing the actors, roles, and organizational structure by use of *organization charts*,
- the *product* perspective defining the products and services an organization offers along with their relationships by use of *product and service catalogs*,
- the *business process* perspective described using a *process architecture*,
- the *data* perspective including the informational entities and their relationships as described by a *data model*,
- the *application* perspective describing the different pieces of software with their dependencies by use of an *application model*, and
- the *technical infrastructure*, often with an emphasis on computer hardware and communication networks, as described by an *infrastructure model*.

The point of an enterprise architecture is that business processes play a central role for integrating these different perspectives of the enterprise. The importance of business processes is emphasized by Scheer's ARIS framework that places processes at the center. An enterprise architecture does not only describe these perspectives separately, but it also defines their connections. If systematically documented, a manager might use enterprise architecture documentation to answer

---

[1] http://www.opengroup.org/subjectareas/enterprise/togaf.

[2] https://www.zachman.com/about-the-zachman-framework.

the following questions: To which process does the downtime of an online service relate and which IT system supports activities in the process that might be affected by the downtime?

Exercise 2.2 Consider again the construction company BuildIT and its procure-to-pay process described on page 3. Which aspects in the organizational, product, data, application, and technical infrastructure perspectives have to be described to understand this process?

The reason for conducting process identification is that an organization should focus on those processes that either create value of strategic relevance or that have substantial problems (or both). This makes process identification an ongoing task, because processes *inside* an organization are subject to the dynamics of time and change. Specific processes may be problematic at one point, but once the issues have been identified and resolved, it is time to shift the focus to other processes. For example, an insurance company suffering from customer dissatisfaction will naturally tend to focus on its customer-oriented processes, for instance its claims handling process. Once this process has improved and customer satisfaction is again within the desired range, the emphasis might move to its risk assessment processes, which are important for the long-term viability and competitiveness of the company.

But there are also dynamics *outside* in the environment of organizations. What may be processes that are of strategic importance to an organization at some point may grow less important as time elapses. Market demands may change and new regulations or the introduction of new products may limit what was once a profitable business activity. For example, the arrival of new competitors offering discount insurance policies through Web-based channels may push an established company to redesign its insurance sales processes to make them leaner, faster and accessible from the Web.

Example 2.1 Changes of the strategic relevance of certain processes are often slow, but they can be drastic. Consider the German company Mannesmann. Mannesmann was established in the last decade of the nineteenth century as a producer of steel pipes. In the twentieth century, Mannesmann expanded into various industries, among others into producing trucks. In 1990, Mannesmann set up a business division for telecommunications after the liberalization of the German telecommunications market. Its cellular network D2 Mannesmann soon became the major competitor of Deutsche Telekom. In 2000, after a thrilling takeover battle, Mannesmann was acquired by the British company Vodafone for € 190 billion. The story of Mannesmann illustrates that the strategic importance of different processes may drastically change over a longer period of time. Therefore, process identification can never be a one-time activity. For more on the history of Mannesmann, see the Wikipedia entry.[3]   □

---

[3]https://en.wikipedia.org/wiki/Mannesmann.

To address the imperative of focusing on a subset of key processes, the management team, process analysts, and process owners need to have answers to the following two questions: (i) what processes are executed in the organization? and (ii) which ones should the organization focus on? In other words, an organization engaged in a BPM initiative needs to maintain a map of its processes as well as clear criteria for determining which processes have the highest priority. The box on the "Process Checklist" helps to identify what is a process when answering these two questions.

PROCESS CHECKLIST

It may not be easy to decide on what to consider as a business process. A chunk of work that is frequently repeated might not be a business process on its own. To prevent poor scoping decisions, it is useful to consider the following *process checklist*:

Is it a process at all?   Not everything we can observe in a business context is a process. A department, for example, is not a process. Neither is a manager or email. For any *proper* process it must be possible to identify the *main action*, which is applied to a *category of cases*. For example, we can identify the business process *approve—leave requests*. Note how this name is of the form *verb + noun*. We can also test how appropriate the name is by considering whether the process outcome is of the form *noun + past participle*. For our example, completed cases are indeed *leave requests* that have been *approved*.

Can the process be controlled?   Something that is ongoing or active may resemble a process, while it is not. A proper way of looking at business processes is to see them as a repetitive series of events and activities to execute individually observable *cases*. In an insurance business process, cases may be the applications for healthcare coverage that flow through the process. Each application is clearly distinguishable from another. Without a clear case notion, process management is not feasible. Consider how difficult it would be to identify cases for false process candidates like *Human Resource Management* or *Strategy*. Also, without any sense of repetition, a group of business activities may better qualify as a *project* than as a business process. A case in point would be the Mars Orbiter Mission, which is a unique endeavor—not a business process, considering the currently scarce space trips to Mars.

Is the process important enough to manage?   Some processes do not even reach the minimum threshold to be considered as such. Clear indications for at least a modest importance of a process are that: (a) there is a customer who is willing to pay for its outcomes, (b) the organization that carries out the process would—in principle—be willing to pay another

(continued)

party for taking over, or (c) there is a legal, mandatory framework that compels an organization to execute it. If none of these apply, the business process may be safely disregarded.

Is the scope of the process not too big?   Care should be taken that the activities that are considered to be within the scope of the process really contribute to its purpose. A good check for this is to determine whether there is a 1:1 relation between the event that initiates the process and each of the activities that are thought to be in scope. For example, let us consider a candidate make-to-order process like *manufacture bikes*. Even though it is important to *clean the work floor* for a bike factory, such an activity does not relate on a 1:1 basis to a bike manufacturing order. Rather, cleaning may take place periodically, such as at the end of the day. In other words, cleaning the work floor should not be part of this process (but it may be part of another process of course).

Is the scope of the process not too small?   One can sometimes come across *micro* business processes, which are not worth managing as processes at all. A rule of thumb is that for something to be a business process, there should be at least three different actors—*excluding* the customer—involved. If there are no handoffs between multiple actors or systems, there is little that can be improved using BPM methods.

We have seen in Chapter 1 that there is a range of stakeholders involved in the management and execution of a business process. Generally, only a handful of such stakeholders have a full overview of all the business processes in an organization. Yet, it is precisely this insight that is required in order to identify the subset of processes that need to be closely managed or improved. Capturing this knowledge and keeping it up-to-date is the aim of process identification.

More specifically, process identification is concerned with two steps: definition of the process architecture and selection of processes. The first step to *define a process architecture* (also called designation) has the objective to gain an understanding of the processes an organization is involved in as well as their interrelationships. The second step of *selecting processes* aims to develop a prioritization of processes for the BPM activities (discovery, analysis, redesign, implementation, monitoring, etc). Note that *neither* of these two steps is concerned with the development of process models. Indeed, process identification is not even concerned with a single process. It always takes the overall set of processes into account. Therefore, it is sometimes called *multi-process management*. The set of all processes is also referred to as a *process portfolio*.

2.2 Definition of the Process Architecture

The aim of a process architecture is to provide a representation of the processes that exist in an organization. The definition of a process architecture has to face the complexity of the whole organization. In order to approach this complexity in a systematic way, we first differentiate categories of processes. Second, we describe different relationships between processes that are important for a process architecture. Third, we present a method for defining the process landscape as a top-level representation of the process architecture.

2.2.1 Process Categories

If an organization is at the very start of becoming a process-centered organization, the first difficult task it faces is to come up with a meaningful enumeration of its existing processes. One difficulty here arises from the hierarchical nature of business processes: different criteria can be considered for determining which chains of operations can be seen as forming an independent business process and which ones are seen as being part of another process. There are various views on how to categorize business processes. Some of these support the idea that there are actually *very few* processes within any organization. For example, some researchers have argued for the existence of only two processes: managing the product line and managing the order cycle. Others identify three major processes: developing new products, delivering products to customers, and managing customer relationships.

One of the most influential categorization schemes is Porter's Value Chain model. It originally distinguished two categories of processes: core processes (called primary activities) and support processes (support activities). Management processes were added as a third category.

Core processes cover the essential value creation of a company, that is the production of goods and services for which customers pay. These include design and development, manufacturing, marketing and sales, delivery, after-sales, and direct procurement (i.e., sourcing required for the making of products or the delivery of services).

Support processes enable the execution of these core processes. These include indirect procurement (i.e., sourcing of hardware, furniture, stationery, etc.), human resource management, information technology management, accounting, financial management, and legal services.

Management processes provide directions, rules, and practices for the core and support processes. These include strategic planning, budgeting, compliance and risk management, as well as investors, suppliers, and partners management.

The distinction of core, support, and management processes is of strategic importance to a company.

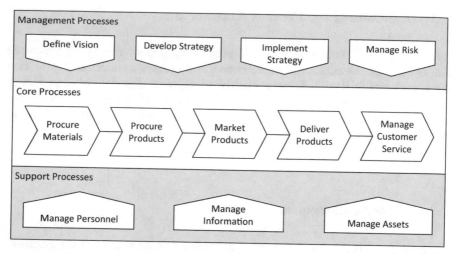

Fig. 2.2 Example of process categories of a production company

Figure 2.2 shows the example of a production company and a high-level representation of its processes. We will later call this type of representation a *process landscape model*, which describes the most abstract view of the process architecture. The example uses three categories for grouping the business processes according to their strategic importance. The core processes include the direct procurement of materials, produce products, market products, deliver products, and manage customer service. These core processes are supported by processes to manage personnel, information, and assets. Management processes include the definition of a vision, the development and implementation of the corporate strategy, and the management of risk.

Visual representations like the one in Figure 2.2 are often used in organizations to summarize the major processes in a compact and readable manner. The symbol used for core processes is called chevron and modeling processes as a sequence of sub-processes shown as chevrons is often called *value-chain modeling*. For a better visual distinction, support processes can be shown with upwards pointing blocks and management processes with downwards pointing blocks.

Exercise 2.3 What are core, support, and management processes of a university?

2.2.2 Relationships Between Processes

For a process architecture, we can distinguish three types of relationships between processes: sequence, decomposition, and specialization.

Sequence: This relationship describes that there is a logical sequence between two processes. Sequence is also referred to as a horizontal relationship. For

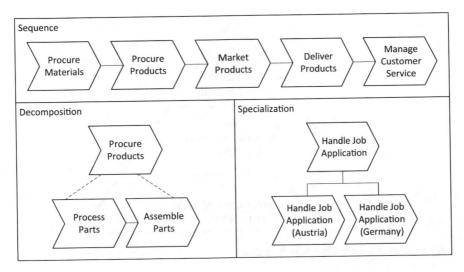

Fig. 2.3 Value chain models for sequence, decomposition, and specialization

instance, processes can be in a consumer-producer relationship. This means that one process provides an output that the other process takes as an input. In Chapter 1, we distinguished the quote-to-order and the order-to-cash processes. The output of the first one (the order) is the input to the second one. Also the example of Figure 2.3 shows that the core processes are in a sequential relationship from Procure Materials to Produce Products, Market Products, Deliver Products, and eventually Manage Customer Service. The object that is passed between the sequential processes characterizes the relationship.

Decomposition: This relationship describes that there is a decomposition in which one specific process is described in more detail in one or more sub-processes. Decomposition is also referred to as a vertical or hierarchical relation-ship. For instance, the Produce Products process of Figure 2.3 can be described in more detail including the different activities that have to be executed to bring it to a successful completion. Decomposition is often used as the primary relationship that defines the structure of the process architecture. Figure 2.4 illustrates this idea: at the most abstract level of the process architecture, we define a process landscape like the one above. Each element of this process landscape model is decomposed into a more detailed process on the next level.

Specialization: This relationship describes that there exist several variants of a generic process. For instance, there might be a generic process for handling job applications in a multi-national company. Since there are different legal constraints on this process in different countries, there will be, for example, one variant of this process for Austria and one for Germany (see Figure 2.3). Variants are not only defined for different legal contexts, but also for different categories of products or services and for different types of customers or suppliers. Our production company offers different products, and naturally the production

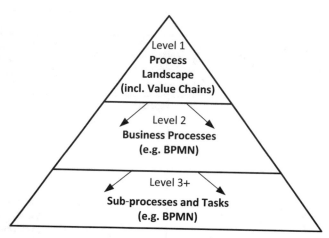

Fig. 2.4 A process architecture with three levels

process for these products varies. All of these different production variants refer to the single "Procure Products" element in Figure 2.3.

Value chains can be systematically described by the help of these relationships. To this end, we can first identify generic processes and then ask ourselves of which sequences they are composed. For example, consider an organization that has a generic process called order management. Its value chain includes order booking, billing, shipment, and delivery. Among each other, these processes are related in a sequential way. With respect to the generic order management process, they are decompositions. Furthermore, we call billing an upstream process of shipment: for the same order, the bill is sent out usually *before* the ordered goods are shipped. In the same way, shipment can be considered a downstream process of billing.

Exercise 2.4 At this point, we discussed sequence, decomposition, and specialization relations between business processes. Can you think of other types of relations that are useful to distinguish between processes?
Hint. Think about the purpose of identifying the relations between business processes.

The definition of a process architecture often proceeds in a top-down fashion, as illustrated by the pyramid in Figure 2.4. The starting point is the process landscape on Level 1 that shows the value chains of the company. Level 2 provides a decomposition for each business process of the value chains. Level 3 provides a further decomposition down to sub-processes and tasks. The arrows in the figure indicate these decompositions.

Question Should a process architecture have three levels like in Figure 2.4, or more, or maybe less?

First, it has to be noted that a level should be defined with respect to a specific purpose. This has often the implication that modeling concepts are tailored or

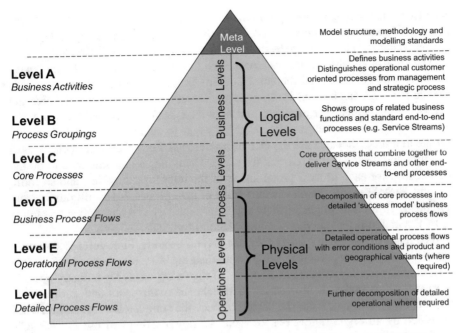

Fig. 2.5 The process architecture of British Telecom and its different levels . © British Telecommunications (2005)

utilized to specifically address this purpose. For example, Figure 2.4 emphasizes that processes on Level 1 are often modeled as so-called value chains while processes on Levels 2 and 3 are modeled with BPMN. Second, the different requirements for a process architecture depend on the overall approach to business process management. Figure 2.5 shows the example of the process architecture as defined by British Telecom in 2005. Here, six levels were defined down to a detailed operational level. Note that organizations will often define their own terms for these levels. For example, the term "Core Process" as used by British Telecom for processes on Level C is related, but not identical to the definition by Porter.

2.2.3   Reuse of Reference Models

Often, process analysts find it difficult to identify processes of an organization and the levels of a process architecture. It might be helpful to use reference models as an aid. These reference models are developed by a range of industry consortia, non-profit associations, government research programs, and academia. The best-known examples are the *Information Technology Infrastructure Library* (ITIL) by

AXELOS,[4] the *Supply Chain Operations Reference Model* (SCOR) by APICS,[5] the *Process Classification Framework* (PCF) by the American Productivity and Quality Center (APQC),[6] and the *Performance Framework* by Rummler & Brache.[7]

The excerpt in Table 2.1 shows Level 1 and Level 2 of APQC's PCF four levels: the categories (in bold) and the corresponding process groups. Reference models standardize what can be seen as different processes, with unique characteristics and delivering distinguishable products, and how their performance can be measured. For example, when a company like BuildIT wants to create a process architecture for the first time, they can use the PCF as a reference. First, they would check each category and decide if it is relevant for them. Then, they would continue to do the same check for each process group inside of the relevant categories, and so forth. Second, BuildIT would double-check if some of their processes are still missing and add them. Third, they might partially adjust terminology and replace generic terms of PCF with terms that are more common within BuildIT.

The reuse of reference models provides several benefits. First, reference models can serve as a starting point to develop a classification of major process areas. In this way, they directly support the identification of regulatory or highly industry-specific processes. This makes it also easier to benchmark with peers and competitors. Second, reference models may be useful to check the completeness of the processes identified by an organization. For example, an organization can use the APQC's PCF to inventory the processes they use, flag those they do not use, and add its own unique processes. Third, reference models provide a standardized vocabulary that is useful for labeling processes. In fact, terms may not always be precisely defined when process identification is conducted for the first time in an organization. Different stakeholders may use heterogeneous terminology. Homonyms and synonyms pose a challenge in this context. For example, what is called "acquisition" in one part of the organization may be called "market survey" in another (synonym). At the same time, the term "implementation" may represent different activities: one may represent the implementation of software, while the other represents the implementation of new regulations in the organization (homonym). Apart from being aware of the various terms that are being used, an intricate understanding of the operations of an organization is important to sort these issues out. Reference models like APQC's PCF can help us to avoid terminological issues right from the start. Note that there are several more specialized versions of the PCF, for example, for automotive, for banking, and for retail.

Exercise 2.5 Which APQC categories on Level 1 are relevant for a construction company like BuildIT?

---

[4]https://www.axelos.com/best-practice-solutions/itil.

[5]http://www.apics.org/.

[6]https://www.apqc.org/pcf.

[7]https://www.rummlerbrache.com.

Table 2.1 Level 1 and Level 2 of the APQC Process Classification Framework

1.0 Develop Vision and Strategy
1.1 Define the business concept and long-term vision
1.2 Develop business strategy
1.3 Execute and measure strategic initiatives

2.0 Develop and Manage Products and Services
2.1 Govern and manage product and service development program
2.2 Generate and define new product and service ideas
2.3 Develop products and services

3.0 Market and Sell Products and Services
3.1 Understand markets, customers, and capabilities
3.2 Develop marketing strategy
3.3 Develop and manage marketing plans
3.4 Develop sales strategy
3.5 Develop and manage sales plans

4.0 Deliver Physical Products
4.1 Plan for and align supply chain resources
4.2 Procure materials and services
4.3 Produce, manufacture, and deliver product
4.4 Manage logistics and warehousing

5.0 Deliver Services
5.1 Establish service delivery governance and strategies
5.2 Manage service delivery resources
5.3 Deliver service to customer

6.0 Manage Customer Service
6.1 Develop customer care and customer service strategy
6.2 Plan and manage customer service contacts
6.3 Service products after sales
6.4 Manage product recalls and regulatory audits
6.5 Evaluate customer service operations and customer satisfaction

7.0 Develop and Manage Human Capital
7.1 Develop and manage human resources planning, policies, and strategies
7.2 Recruit, source, and select employees
7.3 Develop and counsel employees
7.4 Manage employee relations
7.5 Reward and retain employees
7.6 Redeploy and retire employees
7.7 Manage employee information and analytics
7.8 Manage employee communication
7.9 Deliver employee communications

8.0 Manage Information Technology (IT)
8.1 Manage the business of information technology

8.2 Develop and manage IT customer relationships
8.3 Develop and implement security, privacy, and data protection controls
8.4 Manage enterprise information
8.5 Develop and maintain information technology solutions
8.6 Deploy information technology solutions
8.7 Deliver and support information technology services

9.0 Manage Financial Resources
9.1 Perform planning and management accounting
9.2 Perform revenue accounting
9.3 Perform general accounting and reporting
9.4 Manage fixed-asset project accounting
9.5 Process payroll
9.6 Process accounts payable and expense reimbursements
9.7 Manage treasury operations
9.8 Manage internal controls
9.9 Manage taxes
9.10 Manage international funds/consolidation
9.11 Perform global trade services

10.0 Acquire, Construct, and Manage Assets
10.1 Plan and acquire assets
10.2 Design and construct productive assets
10.3 Maintain productive assets
10.4 Dispose of assets

11.0 Manage Enterprise Risk, Compliance, Remediation and Resiliency
11.1 Manage enterprise risk
11.2 Manage compliance
11.3 Manage remediation efforts
11.4 Manage business resiliency

12.0 Manage External Relationships
12.1 Build investor relationships
12.2 Manage government and industry relationships
12.3 Manage relations with board of directors
12.4 Manage legal and ethical issues
12.5 Manage public relations program

13.0 Develop and Manage Business Capabilities
13.1 Manage business processes
13.2 Manage portfolio, program, and project
13.3 Manage quality
13.4 Manage change
13.5 Develop and manage enterprise-wide knowledge management (KM) capability
13.6 Measure and benchmark
13.7 Manage environmental health and safety (EHS)

2.2.4 *Process Landscape Model*

The model of the process architecture that covers the processes on Level 1 is known as the *process landscape model* or simply the process architecture for Level 1. It shows the core processes on a very abstract level. Each of the elements of the process landscape model points to one or more detailed business processes on Level 2.

The definition of a process landscape model is the most important challenge for the definition of the process architecture. The process architecture on Level 1 has to be understandable by all major stakeholders in the first place. As a rule of thumb, it should be compact, showing no more than 20 business processes of an organization. Further, it has to be sufficiently complete such that all employees of the organization can relate their daily work to it, and accept it as a consensual description of the company. Therefore, it is important to define the process architecture in a systematic way, with a specific focus on the derivation of the process landscape model.

Figure 2.6 shows the example of a process map of Vienna's public transport operator Wiener Linien. We see that the categories of core processes, support processes, and management processes were used. It is interesting to note that the core processes are subdivided into different end-to-end processes: manage customer relationship, operate vehicles, transport customer, and provide infrastructure. Visually, these are shown as *process groups*. Organizations often have more than one end-to-end process, such that different sequences are shown in the process landscape's category of core processes.

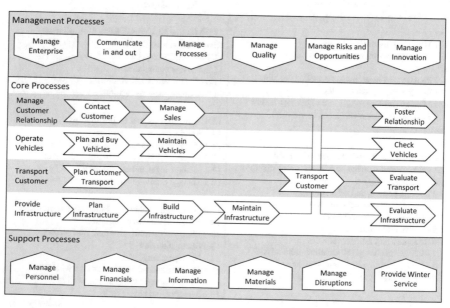

Fig. 2.6 Process landscape model of Vienna's public transport operator Wiener Linien [168]

The definition of a process landscape model requires the involvement of major stakeholders of the organization, either using interviews or, preferably, using a workshop setting. The contributions of the stakeholders are required in order to establish the legitimacy of the resulting model. For this reason, it is important that all senior executives are involved.

Once the commitment of the stakeholders is secured, there are several steps that help us to define the process landscape model in a systematic way. We present these steps as a sequence, but note that in practice there will be jumps back and forth with iterations.

1. **Clarify terminology:** The key terms to be used in the process landscape model should be defined. Often, there exists already an organizational glossary, which can be used as a reference. Reference models are also useful to support this step. The definition helps to make sure that all stakeholders have a consistent understanding of the process landscape model to be defined.

2. **Identify end-to-end processes:** End-to-end processes are those processes that interface with customers and suppliers of the organization. The goods and services that an organization provides to customers or procures from suppliers are a good starting point for this identification, since they are explicitly defined in most organizations. Several properties help us to distinguish end-to-end processes, including:

   - Product type: This property identifies types of products that are produced in a similar way. For instance, at this abstract level, an automotive company might distinguish cars from trucks.
   - Service type: This property identifies types of services that are produced in a similar way. For instance, a software vendor might distinguish purchased software from software-as-a-service.
   - Channel: this property represents the channels through which the organization interacts with its customers. For example, an insurance company might separate its Internet offerings from its offerings via intermediary banks.
   - Customer type: This property represents the types of customer that the organization deals with. A bank might, for instance, distinguish wealth customers, private banking customers, and retail customers.

   The identification of end-to-end processes combines an *external view of what* the provisions of the organization are from the view of the customer, and an *internal view of how* these are created. The selection of the listed properties should be driven by the idea to only define separate end-to-end processes when their internal behavior is substantially different. Those end-to-end processes that are shown on the process landscape model represent the value chains of the organization.

3. **For each end-to-end process, identify its sequential processes:** For this step, it is important to identify the internal, intermediate outcomes of an end-to-end

process. There are different perspectives that help setting the boundaries of these processes:

- Product lifecycle: The lifecycle of a product or service includes different states, which can be used to subdivide an end-to-end process. For instance, a plant construction company typically first submits a quote, then sets up the contract, designs the plant in collaboration with the customer, produces its building blocks, delivers and constructs the plant on premise, writes the invoice, and provides maintenance services.
- Customer relationship: There are also typical stages that a customer relationship goes through. First, leads are generated, then a contract is sealed and services provided. For these, invoices are written. The contract might be changed and eventually terminated.
- Supply chain: Along the supply chain, materials are procured, which are used to produce products. These are checked for quality assurance and delivered to customers.
- Transaction stages: There are different stages that transactions typically go through from initiation to negotiation, execution, and acceptance. Consider, for instance, buying clothes at a fashion retailer. First, interest in the products is generated (initiation). Advisory services in the shop have to be provided to the customers, such that they can make a good decision (negotiation). Taking the clothes to the point of sale marks execution. The payment completes the transaction (acceptance).
- Change of business objects: If there are different business objects, the process should be split up into respective business processes. For instance, the transition from a quote to a contract or from an order to a payment mark the boundaries of different processes. A change of multiplicity is a specific condition for splitting up; for example, when several job applications lead to one hiring.
- Separation: Different stages of a process can also be defined by a temporal, spatial, logical, or other type of separation. Often, these separations define handoffs, and major handoffs are suitable points to distinguish sequential processes.

The identification of business processes is closely connected with the internal view of an end-to-end process. It is also referred to as the identification of internal functions, because there typically exist functional units in the organization like divisions or departments that are responsible for particular business processes.

4. **For each business process, identify its major management and support processes:** The question for this step is what is required in order to execute the previously identified processes. Typical support processes, as also shown in Figure 2.6, are management of personnel, financials, information, and materials. Note, however, that these support processes can be core processes if they are an integral part of the business model. For a staff-borrowing company, personnel management is a core process. However, management processes are usually generic.

5. **Decompose and specialize business processes:** Each of the business processes of the process landscape should be further subdivided into an abstract process on Level 2 of the process architecture. Also further subdivision to Level 3 might be appropriate until processes are identified that can be managed autonomously by a single process owner. There are different considerations when this subdivision should stop:

- Manageability: The smaller the number of the identified processes, the bigger their individual scope is. In other words, if only a small number of processes is identified, then each of these will cover numerous operations. This makes their management more difficult. Among others, the involvement of a large number of staff in a single process will make communication more difficult and improvement projects more complex.
- Impact: A subdivision into only a few large processes will increase the impact of their management. The more operations are considered to be part of a process, the easier it will become, for example, to spot opportunities for efficiency gains by rooting out redundant work. Also risks arising from compliance violations might be considered as having an impact.

6. **Compile process profile:** Each of the identified processes should not only be modeled, but also described using a process profile. This process profile supports the definition of the boundaries of the process, its vision and process performance indicators, its resources, and its process owner. Figure 2.7 shows an example of a process profile of BuildIT's procure-to-pay process.

7. **Check completeness and consistency:** These checks should build on the following inputs. First, reference models can be used to check whether all major processes that are relevant for the organization are included. Reference models can also help us to check the consistency of the terminology. Second, it should be checked whether all processes can be associated with functional units of the organization chart and the other way around.

Example 2.2 We already know BuildIT from the descriptions of its procure-to-pay process in Example 1.1 on page 3. The following passage describes the company from a more general perspective. With this information, we will construct its process landscape model.

> The overall end-to-end process of BuildIT starts with a customer demand and ends with the expiry of the warranty of construction works. The business development department is responsible for identifying customer demands and public tenders. Together with the pre-sales engineering department, they select projects for which BuildIT prepares bids. Bids that are approved lead to contract negotiations. Once contracts are signed, the contract is transferred to execution. Contract execution starts with the project initiation, which includes engineering, design, and planning. What follows then are the actual construction works. The procure-to-pay process that we already know from Example 1.1 also belongs to these initiation procedures. Once the construction works are finished, the construction site is commissioned to the customer. What can still follow are corrective works to meet warranty obligations.

Name of Process: Procure-to-Pay	
Vision: The objective of the procurement process is to secure that the entire range of external products and services becomes available on time and is at the required level of quality.	
Process Owner: Chief Financial Officer (CFO)	
Customer of process: • Requesting unit	**Expectation of customer:** • Timely, economic and complete provision
Outcome: Delivered products or provided services for the requested unit	
Trigger: Need is identified	
First activity: Submit Request ..... **Last activity:** Create Purchase Order	
Interfaces inbound: Plan-to-Procure **Interfaces outbound:** Construct-to-Complete	

Required resources:
• Human resources:
  Site Engineer, Clerk, Works Engineer
• Information, documents, know-how:
  procurement guidelines, supplier rating, framework contract
• Work environment, materials, infrastructure:
  Procurement information system	

Process Performance Measures: • Cycle Time • Operational Costs • Error Rate	

Fig. 2.7 Process profile of BuildIT's procure-to-pay process, adapted from [190]

We proceed with our seven-step design method as follows:

1. Clarify terminology: The decision was made to design the process landscape model based on APCQ. Accordingly, APQC's terms are adopted for management and support processes. The APCQ Categories 1–3 plus 13 were also found relevant for management processes and 7–12 for support processes. Instead of "products and services", BuildIT only refers to "services". The core processes in the end-to-end value chain are replaced by the more specific descriptions of the construction business from above.

2. Identify end-to-end processes: The end-to-end process starts with the identification of the customer demand and ends when the warranty expires. We might want to differentiate different types of construction works, but the text does not provide us information in this direction.
3. For each end-to-end process, identify its sequential processes: The end-to-end process includes the following business processes. They reflect the product lifecycle of the construction work, organized in the two groups "Contract Acquisition" and "Contract Execution":

   - Demand-to-Selection,
   - Selection-to-Bid,
   - Approval-to-Contract,
   - Contract-to-Plan,
   - Plan-to-Completion,
   - Completion-to-Expiry.

4. For each business process, identify its major management and support processes: Here, we rely on the APQC categories 1–3 and 7–13. The names are slightly shortened.
5. Decompose and specialize business processes: Here, we only decompose the planning process as an example. It can be subdivided into several business processes including: plan-to-procure and procure-to-pay, plan-to-deliver and deliver-to-pay for ordering construction materials, and plan-to-schedule for assigning workers to construction sites.
6. Compile process profile: BuildIT defines process profiles for each process on Level 2. The procure-to-pay process belongs to the set of these processes. We have shown the process profile of this process in Figure 2.7.
7. Check completeness and consistency: Finally, we have to check if all major departments of BuildIT are represented. The result is shown in Figure 2.8.

                                                                                       □

Exercise 2.6 Create a process landscape model for a university by applying the seven steps described in this section. Use the APQC Process Classification Framework as an aid.

To balance the advantages and disadvantages of a large process scope, Davenport suggests that it may be useful to identify both *broad* and *narrow* processes. Broad processes are identified in those areas where an organization feels it is important to completely overhaul the existing operations at some point, for example because of fierce competitive forces. For example, an organization may have found out that its procurement costs are overly high compared to its competitors. Accordingly, it selects procurement as a broad process, which covers all of the services and products the company acquires from other parties. By contrast, narrow processes are not targeted for major overhauls; they need to be actively monitored and are subjected to continuous fine-tuning and updating. A narrow process may be, for example, how the same company deals with improvement suggestions of employees.

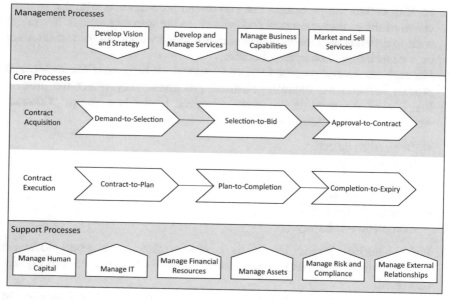

Fig. 2.8 Process landscape model of BuildIT

Exercise 2.7 Explain how the trade-off between impact and manageability works out for broad and narrow processes, respectively.

Any enumeration of business processes should strive for a reasonably detailed outcome, which needs to be aligned with the organization's specific goals of process management. For most organizations, as a rule of thumb, this will boil down to a couple of dozen business processes. Very large and diversified organizations might be better off with identifying a couple of hundred processes. As an example, consider the multinational software vendor SAP that has identified one thousand different business processes. Each of these business processes is assigned to a process owner, who oversees the performance of the process and monitors the achievement of its objectives in terms of profitability, compliance, and accountability. Detailed process models are kept up-to-date, both as a means for documenting planned changes to any process and for satisfying the requirements of reporting. By contrast, for a small medical clinic in The Netherlands, which employs medical specialists, nurses, and administrative staff, 10 different treatment processes have been identified. A few of these have been mapped in the form of process models and are now in the process of being automated with a business process management system. For all other processes, it is sufficient to be aware of the distinctive treatment options they can provide to different patient categories.

Finally, it is worth emphasizing again with respect to the design of the process architecture that processes change over time, deliberately or not. Above, we have discussed the changes of Mannesmann's business focus in the past. Change naturally implies that process identification is a continuous pursuit. There are organizations that have defined governance procedures to continuously update their process architecture. In case such procedures are not in place, a process architecture may well be usable for a period of time (e.g., 2–3 years) and should then be revised.

Clearly, given the extent and depth of a process architecture, coming up with a comprehensive architecture is hardly achieved in one go. Practically, this can be done by applying incremental extensions and updates as part of each new BPM project, especially as far as the hierarchical perspective of the process architecture is concerned. For example, a project to manage the claims handling process of an insurance company will use the process architecture to determine which support and management processes should also be considered. Then, as the project is executed and sub-processes and individual activities within the claims handling process are discovered, this information is used to update the process architecture.

2.2.5 The Example of SAP's Process Architecture

SAP is one of the largest software vendors worldwide. Its ambition is to help its customers to streamline their processes, such that they are able to predict customer trends based on live data. SAP also has an internal unit that is responsible for business process management, organizing the processes in which more than 87,000 employees of SAP work.[8]

Figure 2.9 shows the model of Level 1 of SAP's process architecture. It distinguishes ten major processes: two in the category management processes, three

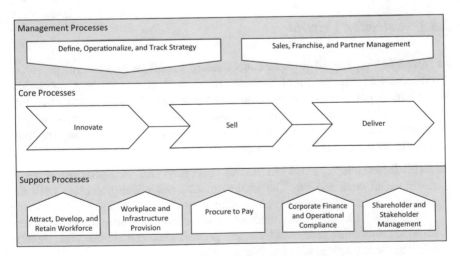

Fig. 2.9 The SAP process map describing the process landscape of the company [139]

---

[8]http://www.sap.com/corporate/en/company.html (accessed in Nov. 2017).

core processes, and five support processes. The core processes Innovate, Sell, and Deliver are part of an overarching end-to-end process. To a certain extent, it is inspired by the product lifecycle view of innovating, selling, and delivering software solutions. An important aspect of SAP's process architecture is that it defines three levels. Those processes on Level 1 shown in Figure 2.9 are subdivided into more detailed processes on Level 2 and Level 3 using the same value-chain notation with chevron symbols as used for the sequence of core processes [139]. For example, there is a sub-process on Level 2 called Order-to-Cash that belongs to the Sell process. This is further refined on Level 3. As a result, there are roughly 1,000 processes on Level 3. A process is only specified on this level if it generates more than € 1 million cost or returns, if it is relevant to compliance, or if it directly supports a core process. All text labels of the process architecture are in line with company terminology.

2.3 Process Selection

The aim of process selection is to define criteria for assessing the performance of the identified business processes. This task builds on the observation that business processes differ in terms of their importance and maturity. In order to define a solid basis for process selection, process performance measures should be considered in combination with general criteria. The advantage of process performance measures is that they can be used to plot the set of processes as a process portfolio.

2.3.1 Selection Criteria

As stated before, not all processes are equally important and not all processes can receive the same amount of attention. BPM involves commitment, ownership, investment in performance improvement and redesign. Therefore, processes that create loss or risk can be considered for consolidation, decommissioning, or outright elimination. Various criteria have been proposed to steer this evaluation. The most commonly used ones are the following:

Strategic Importance: This criterion is concerned with assessing the strategic relevance of each process. The goal is to find out which processes have the greatest impact on the strategic goals of an organization, for example considering profitability, uniqueness, or contribution to competitive advantages. It makes sense to select those processes for active process management that most directly relate to the strategic goals of an organization.

Health: This criterion aims to render a high-level judgement of the health of each process. The question here is to determine which processes are in the deepest trouble. These processes are the ones that may profit the most from BPM initiatives.

Feasibility: For each process, it should be determined how susceptible it is to BPM initiatives, either incidental or on a continuous basis. Most notably, culture and politics involved in a particular process may be obstacles to achieving results from such initiatives. In general, BPM should focus on those processes where it is reasonable to achieve benefits.

All of these criteria assume that there is certain information available. For example, to assess the *strategic importance* of a process it is of utmost importance that an organization has an idea of its strategic course. Sometimes, it is sufficient if such strategic considerations are defined at an abstract level, but often this is additionally justified by a business case. For example, an increasing number of organizations are exploiting the strategic benefit of being able to change the products they provide according to the demands of customers. Zara, the Spanish clothing retailer, is a prime example of an organization that follows a measure-and-react strategy. It sends out agents to shopping malls to see what people already wear for determining the styles, fabrics, and colors of the products it wants to deliver. Such an organization may look with specific interest at the production and logistic business processes that are best able to support this strategy.

Similarly, to determine the *health* of a business process, an organization needs information. Here, we do encounter a chicken-and-egg problem. Many organizations that are not working in a process-centered way do not have a good, quantitative insight into the performance of their individual processes. One of the BPM initiatives that such an organization may be after would exactly be to put the systems and procedures in place to collect the data that is needed for a performance assessment of its processes. In such cases, an organization will need to use more qualitative approaches to determine which of its processes do not perform well, for example depending on the impressions that management or process participants have about the efficiency or effectiveness of the various processes. Another approach would be to rely on customer evaluations, either gathered by surveys or spontaneously delivered in the form of complaints.

The criterion of *feasibility* needs attention, too. It has become common practice for organizations to undergo a continuous stream of programs to improve their performance in one dimension or the other. Consider Philips, the multi-national electronics company. It has gone through an intermittent range of improvement programs since the 1980s to boost its performance. The same phenomenon can now be observed within many telecommunication and utility organizations. Since the profitability of products may change sharply from 1 year to the other, this requires continuous changes to product and service portfolios as well as market priorities. In such a volatile setting, it may happen that managers and process participants become tired or outright hostile towards new initiatives. This kind of situation is not a good starting point for BPM initiatives. After all, like other organizational measures, such initiatives also depend on the cooperation and good intentions of those directly involved. While we will not deal with the subject of change management in much detail in this textbook, it is important to realize that political sensitivities within an organization may have an effect on the success rate of process management efforts too.

Exercise 2.8 Consider again the procure-to-pay process of BuildIT (page 3) and the admission process of a university (page 5) as described in Chapter 1. Discuss their strategic importance, their health, and the feasibility of a potential improvement to these processes.

Question Given all the discussed criteria, does an assessment of the importance, health, and feasibility always point us to the same processes to actively manage?

No, there is no guarantee for that. It may very well be that a strategically important process is also the process that can be expected to be the most difficult one to manage, simply because so many earlier improvement efforts have already failed. An organization may not have a choice in such a situation. If a strategic process cannot be improved, this may turn out to be fatal for an organization as a whole. Think of a situation where the process to come up with new products creates much turmoil and conflicts within an organization: If the issues cannot be sorted out, the company may stop functioning quickly. In other settings, it may be more important to gain credibility with process management activities first. This can be accomplished by first focusing on problematic processes of milder strategic importance but where there is a great desire to change. If successful, an improvement project at such a place may give credibility to the BPM initiative. These are not choices that can be easily prescribed without taking the specific context into consideration. The various evaluation outcomes should be balanced to reach a list of those processes that should receive priority over others.

Question Should all processes that are unhealthy, of strategic importance, and feasible to manage be subjected to BPM?

The general answer to this question is that for most organizations this is not doable. Recall again that BPM consumes resources. Even when there is a clear incentive to, for example, redesign various existing business processes, most organizations lack sufficient resources—people, funds, and time—to do so. Only the largest organizations are able to support more than a handful of BPM projects at the same time. A good example is IBM, an organization known to have process improvement projects going on within all its existing business processes on a continuous basis. Another caveat of carrying out many simultaneous BPM efforts is that these will create coordination complexity. Remember that processes may be linked to each other in various respects, such that measures taken for one process should be synchronized with those taken for others.

Davenport emphasizes that many companies focus on a small set of critical business processes in order to gain experience with innovation initiatives; each successful initiative can then become a model for future efforts [30].

2.3.2 Process Performance Measures

For many BPM-related management activities, we need a precise measurement of the health of a business process. In this context, we distinguish generic performance dimensions and specific performance measures. Often, four generic dimensions of process performance measures are distinguished: time, cost, quality, and flexibility. Any company would ideally like to make its processes faster, cheaper, and better. This simple observation leads us already to identifying three *process performance dimensions*: time, cost, and quality. A fourth dimension gets involved in the equation once we consider the issue of change. A process might perform extremely well under normal circumstances, but then perform poorly in other perhaps equally or more important circumstances. For example, Van der Aalst et al. [178] report the story of a business process for handling claims at an Australian insurance company. Under normal, everyday conditions, the process performed to the entire satisfaction of all managers concerned (including the process owner). However, Australia is prone to storms and some of these storms cause damages to different types of properties (e.g., houses and cars), leading to numerous claims being lodged in a short period of time. The call center agents and backoffice workers involved in the process were literally over-flooded with claims and the performance of the process degraded—precisely at the time when the customers were most sensitive to this performance. What was needed was not to make the process faster, cheaper, or better during normal periods. Rather, there was a need to make the process more flexible to sudden changes in the amount of claims. This observation leads us to the identification of a fourth dimension of process performance, namely flexibility.

Each of the four performance dimensions mentioned above (time, cost, quality, and flexibility) can be refined into a number of *process performance measures* (also called *key performance indicators* or *KPIs*). A process performance measure is a quantity that can be unambiguously determined for a given business process—assuming that the data to calculate this performance measure is available.

For example, there are several types of cost such as cost of production, cost of delivery, or cost of human resources. Each of these types of cost can be further refined into specific performance measures. To do so, one needs to select an aggregation function, such as count, average, variance, percentile, minimum, maximum, or ratios of these aggregation functions. A specific example of a cost performance measure is the average delivery cost per item.

Below, we briefly discuss each of the four dimensions and how they are typically refined into specific performance measures.

Time: Often the first performance dimension that comes to mind when analyzing processes is time. Specifically, a very common performance measure for processes is *cycle time* (also called *throughput time*). Cycle time is the time that it takes to handle one case from start to end. Process selection is often driven by the ambition to reduce cycle time, and there are many different ways of further specifying this aim. For example, one can aim at a reduction of the average cycle time or the maximal cycle time. It is also possible to focus on the ability to meet cycle times that are agreed upon with a client. Yet another way of looking at cycle time is to focus on its variation, which is notably behind approaches like Six Sigma (see Chapter 1). Other aspects of the time dimension come into view when we consider the components of cycle time, namely:

- *Processing time* (also called *service time*): the time that resources, such as process participants or software applications invoked by the process, spend on actually handling the case.
- *Waiting time*: the time that a case spends in idle mode. Waiting time includes *queueing time*—waiting time due to the fact that no resources are available to handle the case—and other waiting time, for example because synchronization must take place with another process, with other activities, or because an input is expected from a customer or from another external party.

Cost: Another common performance dimension when analyzing and redesigning a business process has a financial nature. While we refer to cost here, it would also have been possible to put the emphasis on turnover, yield, or revenue. Obviously, a yield increase may have the same effect on an organization's profit as a decrease of cost. However, process redesign is more often associated with reducing cost. There are different perspectives on cost. In the first place, it is possible to distinguish between fixed and variable cost. Fixed costs are overhead costs which are (nearly) not affected by the intensity of processing. Typical fixed costs follow from the use of infrastructure and the maintenance of software systems. Variable costs are positively correlated with some variable quantity, such as the level of sales, the number of purchased goods, the number of new hires, etc. A cost notion which is closely related to productivity is *operational cost*. Operational costs can be directly related to the outputs of a business process. A substantial part of operational cost is usually labor cost, the cost related to human resources in producing a good or delivering a service. Within process redesign efforts, it is very common to focus on reducing operation cost, particularly labor cost. The automation of tasks is often seen as an alternative for labor. Obviously, although automation may reduce labor cost, it may cause incidental cost involved with developing the respective application and fixed maintenance cost for the lifetime of the application.

Quality: The quality of a business process can be viewed from at least two different angles: from the client's side and from the process participant's perspective. This is also known as the distinction between external quality and internal quality. The *external quality* can be measured as the client's satisfaction with either the product or the process. Satisfaction with the product can be expressed as the extent to which a client feels that the specifications or expectations are met by the delivered product. *Service level agreements* (SLAs) precisely specify what is to be expected. On the other hand, a client's satisfaction concerns the way how the process is executed. A typical issue is the amount, relevance, quality, and timeliness of the information that a client receives during execution on the progress being made. Various specific measures are used to capture customer satisfaction:

- *Churn rate*: In particular for processes that interface with the customer over the Internet, it is important to know how many customers do not complete their interaction successfully. Such processes with customer interactions are also called *customer journeys*. The churn rate is calculated by dividing this amount by the number of all interactions.
- *Net promoter score*: This measure is often defined in a range from 1 to 10, and captures how far customers would be willing to recommend a product or service. Specifically for services, it is directly connected with the business process behind it.

On the other hand, the *internal quality* of a business process relates to the process participants' viewpoint. Typical internal quality concerns are: the level that a process participant feels in control of the work performed, the level of variation experienced, and whether working within the context of the business process is felt as challenging. It is interesting to note that there are various direct relations between quality and other dimensions. For example, the external process quality is often measured in terms of time, e.g., the average cycle time or the percentage of cases where deadlines are missed. In this book, we make the choice that whenever a performance measure refers to time, it is classified under the time dimension even if the measure is also related to quality.

Flexibility: The criterion that is least noted to measure the effect of process redesign is the flexibility of a business process. Flexibility can be defined in general terms as the ability to react to changes. These changes may concern various parts of the business process, for example:

- The ability of resources to execute different tasks within a business process setting;
- The ability of a business process as a whole to handle various cases and changing workloads;
- The ability of the management to change the structure and allocation rules;
- The organization's ability to change the structure and responsiveness of the business process to wishes of the market and business partners.

Another way of approaching the performance dimension of flexibility is to distinguish between runtime and build-time flexibility. *Runtime flexibility* concerns the opportunities to handle changes and variations while executing a specific business process. *Build-time flexibility* concerns the possibility to change the business process structure. It is increasingly important to distinguish the flexibility of a business process from the other dimensions.

Example 2.3 Let us consider the following scenario.

A restaurant has recently lost many customers due to poor customer service. The management team has decided to address this issue first of all by focusing on the delivery of meals. The team gathered data by asking customers about how quickly they liked to receive their meals and what they considered as an acceptable wait. The data suggested that half of the customers would prefer their meals to be served in 15 min or less. All customers agreed that a waiting time of 30 min or more is unacceptable.

In this scenario, it appears that the most relevant performance dimension is time, specifically serving time. One objective that we can distill from the scenario is to completely avoid waiting times above 30 min. In other words, the percentage of customers served in less than 30 min should be as close as possible to 100%. Thus, the percentage of customers served in less than 30 min is a relevant performance measure. Another threshold mentioned in the scenario is 15 min. There is a choice between aiming to have an average meal serving time below 15 min or again, minimizing the number of meals served above 15 min. In other words, there is a choice between two performance measures: average meal delivery time or percentage of customers served in 15 min. □

This example illustrates that the definition of process performance measures is tightly connected with the definition of *performance objectives*. In this respect, one possible method for deriving performance measures for a given process is the following:

1. Formulate performance objectives of the process at a high level, in the form of a desirable state that the process should ideally reach, e.g., customers should be served in less than 30 min.
2. For each performance objective, identify the relevant performance dimension(s) and aggregation function(s), and from there, define one or more performance measures for the objective in question, e.g., the percentage of customers served in less than 30 min. Let us call this measure ST_{30}.
3. Define a more refined objective based on this performance measure, such as $ST_{30} \geq 99\%$.

During the redesign and implementation phases, a possible additional step is to attach a timeframe to the refined performance objective. For example, one can state that the above performance objective should be achieved in 12 months time. A performance objective with a timeframe associated to it is usually called a *performance target*. At the end of the chosen timeframe, one can assess to what extent the redesigned process has attained its targets.

Exercise 2.9 Consider the following summary of issues reported in a travel agency.

A travel agency has recently lost several medium-sized and large corporate customers due to complaints about poor customer service. The management team of the travel agency decided to appoint a team of analysts to address this problem. The team gathered data by conducting interviews and surveys with current and past corporate customers and also by gathering customer feedback data that the travel agency has recorded over time. About 2% of customers complained about errors that had been made in their bookings. In one occasion, a customer had requested a change to a flight booking. The travel agent wrote an email to the customer suggesting that the change had been made and attached a modified travel itinerary. However, it later turned out that the modified booking had not been confirmed in the flight reservation system. As a result, the customer was not allowed to board the flight and this led to a series of severe inconveniences for the customer. Similar problems had occurred when booking a flight initially: the customer had asked for certain dates, but the flight tickets had been issued for different dates. Additionally, customers complained of the long times it took to get responses to their requests for quotes and itineraries. In most cases, employees of the travel agency replied to requests for quotes within 2–4 working hours, but in the case of some complicated itinerary requests (about 10% of the requests), it took them up to 2 days. Finally, about 5% of customers also complained that the travel agents did not find the best flight connections and prices for them. These customers essentially stated that they had found better itineraries and prices on the Web by searching by themselves.

1. Which business processes should the travel agency select for improvement?
2. For each of the business processes you identified above, indicate which performance measure the travel agency should improve.

All the specific process performance measures related to the dimensions of time, cost, quality, and flexibility can be further aggregated in order to obtain a single measure of process health. Such an aggregated measure must be defined for each business process separately, because processes differ in terms of their vision and performance objectives. The health then captures to what extent these objectives have been achieved.

Balanced scorecards can be used for this purpose. Figure 2.10 shows an example of balanced scorecard for three processes of a utility company. For each process, the balanced scorecard provides a hierarchy of process performance measures over four layers of granularity: from detailed process performance measures (Layers 3 and 4) up to key process performance areas (Layer 1). By populating the measures at the lowest level with concrete measurements and aggregating the results, one can obtain a single health measure for each business process.

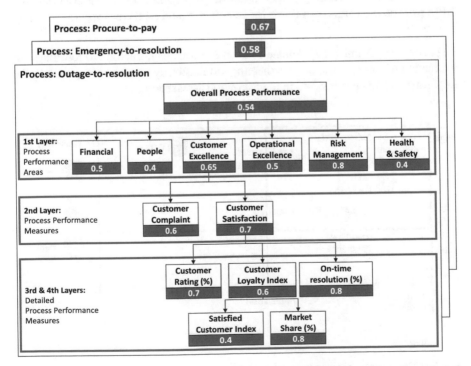

Fig. 2.10 Example of balanced scorecards with the cascading definition and measurement of various process performance measures

2.3.3 Process Portfolio

The term *process portfolio* refers to the set of all processes in general, and more specifically to their visualization by the help of different criteria. Process selection builds on the three criteria of importance, health, and feasibility. The strategic importance of each process can be assessed by senior managers in reference to the organization's strategy. Health can be quantified by calculating the difference between the objectives and actual values for the major process performance measures of each process. Feasibility requires an assessment by the process owner. In this way, we get numeric values for each of the three criteria for each process, such that the process portfolio can be plotted as shown in Figure 2.11.

Process selection should prioritize processes in the left upper quadrant, but also take feasibility into account. A detailed business case might further substantiate the feasibility assessment. Not too many processes should be selected for improvement for two reasons. First, as discussed, the temporal and financial resources of improvement teams are typically limited. Second, having too many improvement projects running leads to complexity of coordination, since processes are often interrelated. Davenport also suggests not to tackle for first the process that is the most strategically important and the least healthy, because you will have high chances of failure. Rather, we should start with a small number of projects and learn from these. Accordingly, with reference to Figure 2.11, if this was our first BPM project, the natural candidate for selection would be the process for handling payments.

Exercise 2.10 A university defined four core processes in relation to teaching. An evaluation of strategic importance, health, and feasibility using a survey among the department chairs has resulted in the following assessment:

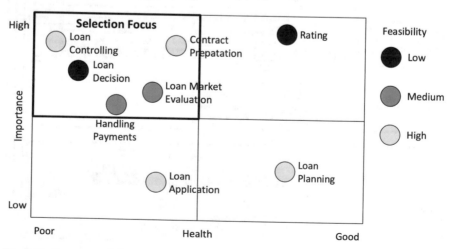

Fig. 2.11 Process portfolio of a financial institution

- Develop and Manage Study Programs: Importance 90%, Health 90%, Feasibility 40%.
- Market Study Programs: Importance 75%, Health 80%, Feasibility 60%.
- Schedule Courses: Importance 95%, Health 30%, Feasibility 50%.
- Deliver Courses: Importance 95%, Health 70%, Feasibility 30%.
- Manage Student Services: Importance 85%, Health 50%, Feasibility 40%.
- Manage Facilities: Importance 40%, Health 35%, Feasibility 70%.

Draw a process portfolio and suggest one process to be selected for process improvement. Justify your choice.

We have already emphasized that it is not feasible to have too many BPM projects at the same time, and that a BPM initiative should try to create success stories in the beginning. What is *really* happening in some organizations is that widespread efforts are made to at least *model* all important business processes at an abstract level, delaying the decision to make the step to more advanced BPM efforts (e.g., process redesign or automation). The idea is that process models are a cornerstone of any further BPM effort in any case and that their existence will help us to better understand where improvements can be gained. Creating a model of a process leads to the valuable insight of how that process works at all, and can provide a good basis for small improvements that can easily be implemented. On the downside, such an approach bears the risk that major improvements are missed and stakeholders create a feeling of a lack of return for the efforts. It should be stressed here, too, that the actual modeling of business processes is not an element of the process identification stage. Also, making a specific process subject to discovery, but not further through to analysis and redesign, will not provide improvements of the process and, therefore, it will fail to deliver the benefits that BPM promises.

2.4   Recap

In this chapter, we discussed the process identification phase of the BPM lifecycle. First, we distinguished the two steps of process architecture definition and process selection. The step of process architecture definition aims at enumerating the major processes within an organization, as well as determining the boundaries between those processes. An insight into the major processes that are carried out in an organization is important before setting up any BPM activity.

A process architecture defines the relationship between the different processes. Often, different levels of detail are distinguished. We discussed a seven-step method for the definition of a process architecture including the process landscape model.

The step of process selection is concerned with prioritizing processes before conducting discovery, analysis, and redesign. It is a good practice to base priorities upon the importance of processes, their health, and the feasibility of improvements. These three criteria can be assessed by process owners or they can be grounded on process performance measures and objectives. The most common performance dimensions are time, cost, quality, and flexibility. Process portfolios help in the selection of processes for improvement by visualizing the most important criteria for improvement. Those processes that have been selected become the subject of the remaining phases of the BPM lifecycle.

2.5 Solutions to Exercises

Solution 2.1 The procure-to-pay process belongs to the operations management processes. The way it is organized has an impact on the customer perspective. If it is not working well, this causes problems with availability and quality. Customers might be less willing to pay a high price and to extend the partnership. Altogether, these problems would also translate into a bad brand image. The procure-to-pay process is influenced by how well the process owner takes leadership of the management responsibility and how well the process is aligned with strategic goals. Problems are less likely to occur if there is good teamwork of the process participants and a general organization culture of getting problems solved.

Solution 2.2 In the organizational perspective, the process builds on the three roles site engineer, office clerk, and works engineer. Organization charts can be used to describe to which departments they belong. The product perspective captures which products and services BuildIT provides. These can be various types of construction work. A service catalog can be used to specify these services systematically. Different data fields are used to process a request between the different roles involved, such as "available" or "approved". A data model can be used to define the elements of the data perspective. The application landscape of BuildIT includes an email system and a financial information system. The overall application landscape can be described using an application model. The technical infrastructure encompasses the computer hardware and the construction machinery of BuildIT. It can be described using an infrastructure model.

Solution 2.3 The management processes of a university relate to vision and strategy. The core processes are typically centered around research and teaching. Regarding research, there are processes in place for producing research results and potentially for commercializing research results. Regarding teaching, there are processes for managing the study programs, for scheduling courses each semester, for managing student enrollments in courses, and many other processes covering the entire lifecycle of a student. There are also support processes for personnel administration, information technology management, and infrastructure management.

Solution 2.4 Organizations wish to accomplish certain *goals*. Processes are a means to achieve these goals. A relation that, therefore, may be important is how processes are related to one another in the sense that they contribute to the same or related goals. Other, context-specific relations may be important for organizations as well. Consider how it may be important for an organization to know on which *technologies* their processes are based; if a particular technology becomes obsolete, such an organization knows which processes are affected. A similar line of reasoning can be taken for geographic areas, regulations, etc.

Solution 2.5 In general, all of the Level 1 categories of APQC's Process Classification Framework are relevant. Categories 1–3 and 13 are related to BuildIT's management processes. BuildIT's construction operations relate to categories 4–6; however, they might be too generic to capture the construction business. Categories 7–12 refer to support processes of BuildIT. Although BuildIT tries to minimize ownership of construction machinery, they still need to manage and handle these assets, which is related to category 10.

Solution 2.6 We use the seven steps of designing a process landscape model.

1. Clarify terminology: We make use of APQC where possible.
2. Identify end-to-end processes: We refine the APQC Categories 4–6 as follows: Deliver Research Outcomes, Deliver Teaching Services, Manage Student Services.
3. For each end-to-end process, identify its sequential processes:

   - Deliver Research Outcomes: We identify the sequential business processes using the product lifecycle. These are Plan Research, Conduct Research, Report Research.
   - Deliver Teaching Services: We take inspiration from the supply chain phases. The processes are Prepare Materials, Deliver Course, Grade Students, Check Quality.
   - Manage Student Services: We consider the customer relationship. The sequence is Generate Leads, Grant Admission, Collect Credits, Graduate.

4. For each business process, identify its major management and support processes: Management processes are Develop Vision and Strategy, Develop and Manage Study Programs, Market and Sell Study Programs, and Manage Business Capabilities. Support processes are Manage Human Capital, Manage IT, Manage Financial Resources, Manage Assets, Manage Risk and Compliance, and Manage External Relationships.
5. Decompose and specialize business processes: The core processes should be further decomposed.
6. Compile process profiles: All processes should be described with a profile.
7. Check completeness and consistency: All major departments must be represented.

Solution 2.7 Explain how the trade-off between impact and manageability works out for broad and narrow processes, respectively. A broad process has by definition a large scope. Managing it actively can potentially have a large impact on an organization's performance. The flip side is that it is more difficult to actively manage such a broad process and the improvement projects that are related to it. For a narrow process, this is exactly the other way around: given its smaller scope, it is more easily managed but it will probably have a lesser impact on an organization's performance as a whole.

Solution 2.8 The procure-to-pay process of BuildIT has an internal customer, and is therefore of secondary importance. The description in Chapter 1 points to several problems, but it is also explicitly defined who does what. Therefore, we can rate its health as medium. An improvement seems feasible, because there is only a small number of process participants involved.

The admission process is of major importance, because it is the process that brings students into the university. The description in Chapter 1 points to several problems, but it is also explicitly defined who does what. An improvement is more difficult to achieve, because there are many parties involved at different stages.

Solution 2.9   There are at least two business processes that need improvement: the quote-to-booking process—which starts from the moment a quote is received to the moment that a booking is made—and the process for modifying bookings.

The quote-to-book process needs to be improved with respect to cycle time, and with respect to error rate. The booking modification process needs improvement with respect to error rate.

Solution 2.10   The process portfolio can be plotted as shown in Figure 2.12. It is recommended to select the Schedule Courses process for improvement.

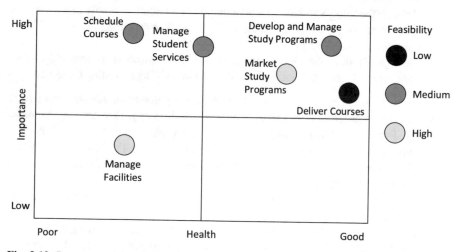

Fig. 2.12 Process portfolio of a university

2.6   Further Exercises

Exercise 2.11 Consider the university and its admission process that is described on page 5. To which category of processes in the internal perspective of Figure 2.1 does it belong? How does it influence different aspects of the customer perspective, how is it shaped by aspects of the learning and growth perspective?

Exercise 2.12 Consider the following organization.

The University of West Holland provides education and services to its students. This starts with admission of students to the university. When regular students, i.e., students who come from a Dutch high-school, send in their admission form, they are registered by the admissions office. Subsequently, their eligibility to study in a certain program is checked based on the information that the student provided on the admission form. For students who arrive from another school, such as a polytechnic, the previous study that the student took, according to his admission form, must be examined in detail. Polytechnic students can either come to the university after completing 1 year of courses (propedeuse) or after receiving a polytechnic diploma. Students from universities in other countries are also accepted. Also for them, the studies that they took previously must be examined in detail. When students are considered eligible and the courses that they have already followed (if applicable) check out, they are enrolled at the university, which involves sending a letter that they are accepted and entering the details of their enrollment in the information system of the university. Once enrolled, the students eventually start their respective study program, e.g., law, medicine, or industrial engineering.

After the students are enrolled, they can take courses or do projects and they can use the services that are provided by the university, which include: language training and sports facilities. Projects are done on an individual basis by a student together with a lecturer. The university recognizes part-time students who do their studies while they are working in a company. These students typically do projects of a more practical nature, and hence the processes for monitoring the progress of these students are not the same as the processes for monitoring the progress of regular students.

Design a process architecture as follows:

1. Identify the end-to-end processes that should appear in the process landscape model,
2. Identify the business processes of each end-to-end process,
3. For each business process, identify its major management and support processes.

Exercise 2.13 Consider the following organization.

A consultancy firm provides consultancy, outsourcing and interim management services. The firm considers acquisition of projects as part of those services. Acquisition can be done both for existing clients and for new clients, because it concerns acquisition of projects rather than clients. Acquisition is typically started at 'networking events' by partners of the consultancy firm. It is handled according to a fixed procedure, but no standard document is used. When a client shows interest in a consultancy service, an intake is done with the client. To maintain a long-term relationship with clients as much as possible, the firm will always try to establish a framework contract with new clients during the intake. For existing clients a framework contract does not have to be established. As another form of relationship management, regular meetings are held with existing clients. During these meetings the client's organization is discussed with the client. This enables the client to decide whether additional work should be done to further improve the organization. At the same time this enables the firm to bring in additional assignments. The intake and the regular meetings happen according to the same form, on which an inventory of the client's wishes can be made.

For consultancy and outsourcing services, a project team must be created directly after a project assignment was given to the consultancy firm. After a project team is created, there is a kick-off meeting with the client and after the kick-off meeting, the project is executed. The kick-off meeting is the same for each type of project, but the way in which the project is executed differs largely per type of service. At the end of the project there always is an evaluation meeting with the client as a means of quality control. The creation of the project team, the kick-off meeting, the execution of the project and the evaluation of the project happen according to a project plan.

The consultancy company has a services department, which takes care of market research for the consultants, manages the leasing of cars and provides secretarial services.

Design a process architecture as follows:

1. Identify the end-to-end processes that should appear in the process landscape model,
2. Identify the business processes of each end-to-end process,
3. For each business process, identify its major management and support processes.

Exercise 2.14 Consider the following organization.

RentIT is an equipment rental company providing a wide range of construction equipment on demand, all the way from minor equipment items such as water pumps and drillers, to major equipment such as bulldozers, crawl dozers and cranes.

RentIT receives orders mainly from construction companies, with which it maintains long-term relations. To maintain these relations, sales representatives meet periodically with existing customers to understand their upcoming demand for construction equipment, to find ways of better satisfying their needs, and to negotiate special deals and discounts.

The main process at RentIT is the order-to-cash process, which starts when a new Purchase Order (PO) is received via its information system. The PO specifies the equipment to be rented and the rental period, among other details.

When a Purchase Order (PO) is received, a sales representative at RentIT checks the PO and the availability of the equipment requested in the PO. This may lead to one of three outcomes: (i) the PO is accepted; (ii) the PO is rejected and accordingly the customer is informed and the case is closed; or (iii) a question is sent to the customer. In the latter case, the customer should provide a response within 3 days. If the customer does not respond within this time, a reminder is sent by RentIT's information system, and if the customer has not responded 3 days after the reminder, the PO is canceled. When a customer responds to a question, the sales rep can accept the PO, reject it, or ask another question to the customer; in this latter case, the above 3-day delays for sending reminders and for canceling the PO are applied again.

Once the PO has been accepted, RentIT's information system marks the corresponding equipment item(s) as busy for the duration of the rental. The system also automatically schedules the delivery and pick-up of the equipment from/to the warehouse where the equipment is located. Deliveries and pick-ups are outsourced to an external logistics company.

A customer can send a request to cancel a PO, in which case the equipment is freed up and the delivery is canceled. A cancelation request must be received before the equipment is dispatched from RentIT's warehouse. Once the equipment has been dispatched (i.e., it has left RentIT's warehouse), it is no longer possible to accept the customer's cancelation request.

On the due date, the logistics company picks up the equipment from RentIT's warehouse and delivers it to the construction site. At the site, an engineer of the construction company (called a site engineer) checks the equipment together with the logistics agent. In general the delivery is accepted. Occasionally though, the site engineer rejects the delivery. There can be two reasons for rejection: (i) because of an error of the customer or because the customer changed its mind; or (ii) because of a defect in the delivered equipment or an error attributable to RentIT. In the former case, an invoice equivalent to the cost of 1 day of rental is sent to the customer and the payment procedure described below takes place. In the latter case, the sales rep is alerted by RentIT's information system. The sales rep contacts the customer immediately to negotiate an alternative arrangement. This may lead either to cancelling the PO, or scheduling a new delivery as soon as possible.

Normally, the equipment is picked up on the end date indicated in the PO. It may happen however that the customer asks for an extension to the deadline by sending an updated purchase order (also known as a PO update). When a PO update asking for a deadline extension request is received, the sales rep checks if it is possible to grant the extension. If so, the deadline extension is recorded in RentIT's information system. If an extension is not possible, the deadline remains unchanged. In both cases, the customer is informed.

Once the equipment has been picked up, RentIT issues an invoice for the amount indicated in the latest version of the PO. Invoices should be paid 14 days after they are issued. If payment has not been received within this time, a payment reminder is sent to the customer. If no payment has been received 14 days after the invoice was sent, the invoice is put on debt collection.

It may happen that the customer disagrees with an invoice. In this case, the sales rep contacts the customer, and amends the invoice if required. This leads to an amended invoice being issued. The customer has 14 days to pay after an amended invoice is issued (after which the same process as above for payment reminder and putting into debt collection is followed).

When an invoice falls into debt collection, the sales rep tries to negotiate a special repayment agreement with the customer. Generally, this leads to a repayment within a few weeks. In very extreme cases where the debt is still outstanding after two months of the invoice due date, the invoice is sold to a debt collection agency. The equipment that RentIT holds is stored in one of several warehouses. Every piece of equipment undergoes periodic maintenance. When an equipment is due for maintenance, a repairs and maintenance supplier comes to pick it up (there are several such service suppliers for different types of equipment). The same supplier delivers the equipment once the maintenance is completed. The same applies when a piece of equipment breaks. In some cases, the equipment breaks while it is located at a customer's premises. In this case, the repairs service supplier picks up the broken equipment from the customer's site, or in some cases, it performs an on-site repair. If the equipment becomes unavailable while it is in use by a customer, the sales rep dispatches an alternative piece of equipment to the customer site. If this is not possible, the original purchase order is updated accordingly, in such a way that the customer is only billed for the days the equipment was in use. The sales rep might apply a special discount in case an equipment breaks while in use.

RentIT needs to handle inbound invoices from repair service providers and logistics providers in addition to invoices arising from indirect procurement. RentIT also needs to make recurrent payments for equipment leasing. In order to optimize cash flow, RentIT does not actually own the equipment it rents out but it rather sources it via equipment lessors. The Chief Financial Officer (CFO) and his team are responsible for strategic sourcing of equipment, which involves planning new equipment acquisitions, retirement of older or broken equipment and negotiation of terms with the equipment lessors. The CFO and his team are also responsible for financial planning and budgeting, financial monitoring, approval of major expenses, and compilation of the quarterly and annual financial reports. On the other hand, the team of the Chief Operations Officer (COO) oversees the management of the warehouses, human resources, IT systems, office facilities, and relations with logistics service providers and repairs and maintenance service suppliers.

Finally, the Sales and Marketing Director oversees all sales representatives, and together with her team, she oversees all activities related to marketing, acquisition of new customers, and strategic development of relations with the large customers.

Design a process architecture as follows:

1. Identify the end-to-end processes that should appear in the process landscape model,
2. Identify the business processes of each end-to-end process,
3. For each business process, identify its major management and support processes.

2.7 Further Readings

One of the first authors to shed light on the importance of process identification is Davenport [30], while a similar perspective is offered by Hammer & Champy [62]. Sharp & McDermott [161] give practical advice on exploring the process landscape. Another practical book covering process architecture design is that of Ould [124]. One of the questions left open by these books is to what extent it pays off to identify and delineate processes in a company-specific manner as opposed to adopting standardized reference models for this purpose.

Dijkman [38] provides a survey of popular process architecture approaches. One of the findings is that practitioners tend to apply a mix of styles to derive process architectures and that no single approach is followed systematically. Some research has been conducted in this area in recent years. The works by Frolov et al. [50] and Zur Muehlen et al. [198] emphasize the importance of a hierarchical process architecture. Malinova and Mendling investigate various approaches for high-level modeling of processes and propose an integrated meta-model for process landscape modeling [99]. The same authors find connections between process architecture design quality and BPM success [100]. Various empirical insights into the quality of process landscape models are presented in the PhD thesis of Malinova [97].

Different frameworks have been proposed for capturing the various perspectives of an enterprise architecture, including the previously mentioned TOGAF framework developed by the Open Group. This standardization body also provides a modeling language, namely ArchiMate,[9] to support the modeling of enterprise architectures according to TOGAF. An alternative framework is the Zachman Framework. Originally developed by Zachman in the eighties, this framework has evolved over time and is currently maintained by Zachman International.[10]

The concept of value chain—which generally appears at the top of a process architecture—was popularized by Porter [128]. Related and to some extent complementary to the concept of value chain is the organizational performance framework

---

[9]https://publications.opengroup.org/c179.

[10]https://www.zachman.com/about-the-zachman-framework.

of Rummler & Brache [153]. In this framework, organizations are viewed as systems whose purpose is to produce value within a certain environment, which includes competitors, suppliers, capital markets, labor markets, regulations and other external factors. Rummler & Ramias [154] describe a variant of Rummler & Brache's framework, namely the Value Creation Hierarchy (VCH). In this framework, the system that transforms resources into products or services is called the Value Creation System (VCS). The VCS is decomposed into processing sub-systems, which in turn are decomposed into end-to-end processes and then into sub-processes, tasks and sub-tasks. The VCH thus provides a conceptual framework that goes all the way from the organizational context to the lowest level of a process architecture. Another important framework that uses value chain models is the Architecture of Integrated Information Systems (ARIS) proposed by Scheer [156]. Process models are at the center of it, complemented by different views including the organizational view, the functional view, the data view, and the product view.

The balanced scorecard concept was proposed by Kaplan & Norton in 1992 [73] and quickly gained popularity thereafter as a tool to define organizational strategy and performance measures. Harmon [65] argues that the traditional approach to apply the balanced scorecard leads to a bias towards functional units (i.e., performance measures are defined for company departments). To address this bias, he elaborates an approach to apply the balanced scorecard along the process architecture rather than the functional architecture. Fürstenau [51] gives a more detailed overview of approaches to process performance measurement all the way from the identification of performance measures using the balanced scorecard, to their implementation in the context of IT-enabled processes.

Chapter 3
Essential Process Modeling

Essentially, all models are wrong, but some are useful.
George E.P. Box (1919–)

Business process models are important at various stages of the BPM lifecycle. Before starting to model a process, it is crucial to understand *why* we are modeling it. The models we produce will look quite different depending on the purpose for which we produce them. There are many reasons for modeling a process. The first reason is to understand the process and to share our understanding of the process with the people who are involved with it on a daily basis. Indeed, process participants typically perform quite specialized activities in a process such that they are hardly confronted with its full complexity. Therefore, process models help us to better understand the process and to identify and prevent issues. This step towards a thorough understanding of business processes is the prerequisite to conduct process analysis, redesign, or automation.

In this chapter we will become familiar with the basic ingredients of process modeling using the BPMN language. First, we will describe the essential concepts of process models, namely how process models relate to process instances. Next, we will explain the four main structural blocks of branching and merging in process models. These define exclusive decisions, parallel execution, inclusive decisions, and repetition. We will then show how to model business objects and resources involved in a process. Finally, we will learn how to use sub-processes to reduce the model's complexity, and how to reuse these sub-process models from within different process models.

3.1 First Steps with BPMN

With over 100 symbols, BPMN is a fairly complex language. But as a learner, there is no reason to panic. A handful of those symbols will already allow you to cover many of your modeling needs. Once you have mastered this subset of BPMN, the remaining symbols will naturally come to you with practice. So instead

© Springer-Verlag GmbH Germany, part of Springer Nature 2018
M. Dumas et al., *Fundamentals of Business Process Management*,
https://doi.org/10.1007/978-3-662-56509-4_3

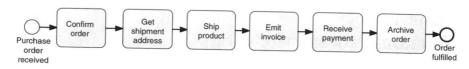

Fig. 3.1 The model of a simple order-to-cash process

of describing each and every BPMN symbol at length, we will learn BPMN by introducing its symbols and concepts gradually, by means of examples.

In this chapter we will become familiar with the core set of symbols provided by BPMN. As stated earlier, a business process involves *events* and *activities*. Events represent things that happen instantaneously (e.g. an invoice has been received) whereas activities represent units of work that have a duration (e.g. an activity to pay an invoice). Also, we recall that in a process, events and activities are logically related. The most elementary form of relation is that of *sequence*, which implies that one event or activity A is followed by another event or activity B. Accordingly, the three most basic concepts of BPMN are events, activities, and arcs. Events are represented by circles, activities by rounded rectangles, and arcs (called *sequence flows* in BPMN) are represented by arrows with a full arrow-head.

Example 3.1 Figure 3.1 shows a simple sequence of activities modeling an order-to-cash process in BPMN. This process starts whenever a purchase order has been received from a customer. The first activity that is carried out is confirming the order. Next, the shipment address is received so that the product can be shipped to the customer. Afterwards, the invoice is emitted and once the payment is received the order is archived, thus completing the process. □

From the example above we notice that the two events are depicted with two slightly different symbols. We use circles with a thin border to capture start events and circles with a thick border to capture end events. Start and end events have an important role in a process model: the start event indicates when *instances* of the process start whereas the end event indicates when instances complete. For example, a new instance of the order-to-cash process is triggered whenever a purchase order is received, and completes when the order is fulfilled. Let us imagine that the order-to-cash process is carried out at a seller's organization. Every day this organization will run a number of instances of this process, each instance being independent of the others. Once a process instance has been spawned, we use the notion of *token* to identify the progress (or *state*) of that instance. Tokens are created at the start event and flow throughout the process model until they are destroyed in an end event. We depict tokens as colored dots on top of a process model. For example Figure 3.2 shows the state of three instances of the order-to-cash process: one instance has just started (black token on the start event), another is at the stage of shipping the product (red token on activity "Ship product"), and the third one has received the payment and is about to start archiving the order (green token in the sequence flow between "Receive payment" and "Archive order").

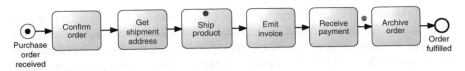

Fig. 3.2   Progress of three instances of the order-to-cash process

While it is natural to give a name (also called *label*) to each activity, we should not forget to give labels to events as well. For example, giving a name to each start event allows us to communicate what can trigger the creation of a new instance of the process. Similarly, giving a label to the end event allows us to communicate what conditions hold when an instance of the process completes, i.e. what the outcome of the process is.

We recommend the following *naming conventions*. For activities, the label should begin with a verb in the imperative form followed by a noun referring to a business object, e.g. "Approve order". The noun may be preceded by an adjective, e.g. "Issue driver license", and the verb may be followed by an adverbial clause to explain how the action is being done, e.g. "Renew driver license via offline agencies". However, we will try to avoid long labels as this may hamper the readability of the model. As a rule of thumb, we will avoid labels with more than five words excluding prepositions and conjunctions. Articles are typically avoided to shorten labels. For events, the label should begin with a noun (again, this would typically be a business object) and end with a past participle, e.g. "Invoice emitted". The past participle is a verb form indicating that something has just happened. Similarly to activity labels, the noun may be prefixed by an adjective, e.g. "Urgent order sent". We capitalize the first word of activity and event labels.

General verbs like "to make", "to do", "to perform", or "to conduct" should be replaced with meaningful verbs that capture the specifics of the activity being performed or the event occurring. Words like "process" or "order" are also ambiguous in terms of their part of speech. Both can be used as a verb ("to process", "to order") and as a noun ("a process", "an order"). We recommend using such words consistently, only in one part of speech, e.g. "order" always as a noun.

To name a process model we should use a noun, potentially preceded by an adjective, e.g. "loan origination", "order fulfillment", or "claim handling" process. This label can be obtained by nominalizing the verb describing the main action of a business process, e.g. "fulfill order" (the main action) becomes "order fulfillment" (the process label). Nouns in hyphenated form like "order-to-cash" and "procure-to-pay" indicating the sequence of main actions in the process, are also possible.

We do not capitalize the first word of process names, e.g. the "order-to-cash" process. By following such naming conventions we will keep our models more consistent, make them easier to understand for communication purposes and increase their reusability.

The example in Figure 3.1 represents one possible way of modeling the order-to-cash process. However, we could have produced a quite different process model. For example, we could have neglected certain activities or expanded on certain others, depending on the specific intent of our modeling. The box "Mapping, Abstraction, and Purpose of a Model" reflects on the properties that underpin a model and relates these to the specific case of process models.

MAPPING, ABSTRACTION, AND PURPOSE OF A MODEL

A model is characterized by three properties: mapping, abstraction, and purpose. First, a model implies a *mapping* of a real-world phenomenon—the modeling subject. For example, a residential building to be constructed could be modeled via a timber miniature. Second, a model only documents relevant aspects of the subject, i.e. it *abstracts* from certain details that are irrelevant. The timber model of the building clearly abstracts from the materials the building will be constructed from. Third, a model serves a particular *purpose*, which determines the aspects of reality to omit when creating a model. Without a specific purpose, we would have no indication on what to omit. Consider the timber model again. It serves the purpose of illustrating how the building will look. Thus, it neglects aspects that are irrelevant for judging the appearance, like the electrical system of the building. So we can say that a model is a means to abstract from a given subject with the intent of capturing specific aspects of the subject.

  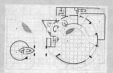

Fig. 3.3 The Solomon R. Guggenheim building in New York (**a**), its timber miniature (**b**) and its blueprint (**c**)[1]

A way to determine the purpose of a model is to understand the *target audience* of the model. In the case of the timber model, the target audience could be a prospective buyer of the building. Thus, it is important to focus on the appearance of the building, rather than on the technicalities of the construction. On the other hand, the timber model would be of little use to an engineer who has to design the electrical system. In this case, a blueprint of the building would be more appropriate.

(continued)

---

[1]Figure 3.3b: © 2010, Bree Industries; Figure 3.3c: used by permission of planetclaire.org.

Thus, when modeling a business process, we need to keep in mind the specific purpose and target audience for which we are creating the model. There are two main purposes for process modeling: *organizational design* and *application system design*. Process models for organizational design are *conceptual* in nature. These conceptual models are built by process analysts and used to facilitate understanding and communication during the discovery phase of the BPM lifecycle. They are also used as a basis for process analysis and redesign. As such, these models need to be intuitive enough to be comprehended by the various stakeholders involved in the BPM lifecycle, including managers, process owners, business analysts, and process participants. Because of this requirement, conceptual process models should not contain IT-related implementation details such as definitions of data types, data mappings, or system interfaces.

In contrast, process models for application system design are *IT-oriented*. They are produced by technical stakeholders such as system engineers, solution architects, or software developers for the purpose of process automation. They contain implementation details in order to be used as blueprints for software development or to be deployed in a BPMS. These models are called *executable* process models.

In this and in the next two chapters we will deal with conceptual process models. In Chapter 10 we will show how to turn conceptual process models into executable ones.

3.2 Branching and Merging

Activities and events may not necessarily be performed sequentially. For example, in the context of a claim handling process, the approval and the rejection of a claim are two activities which exclude each other. This means that an instance of this process will perform either of these activities. When two or more activities are alternative to each other, we say they are *mutually exclusive*.

Coming back to our claim handling process, once the claim has been approved, the claimant is notified and the disbursement is made. Notification and disbursement are two activities which are typically performed by two different business units, hence they are independent of each other and as such they do not need to be performed in sequence: they can be performed in parallel, i.e. at the same time. When two or more activities are not interdependent, they are *concurrent*.

To model these behaviors we need to introduce the notion of a *gateway*, which has a diamond shape in the BPMN notation. The term *gateway* implies that there is a gating mechanism that either allows or disallows passage of tokens through the gateway. As tokens arrive at a gateway, they can be merged together on input, or split apart on output depending on the gateway type. Accordingly, we distinguish between split and join gateways. A *split* gateway represents a point where the process flow diverges while a *join* gateway represents a point where the process flow converges. Split gateways have one incoming sequence flow and multiple outgoing sequence flows (representing the branches that diverge), while join gateways have multiple incoming sequence flows (representing the branches to be merged) and one outgoing sequence flow.

Let us now see how examples like the above ones can be modeled with gateways.

3.2.1 Exclusive Decisions

To model the relation between two or more alternative activities, like in the case of the approval or rejection of a claim, we use an *exclusive (XOR) split*. We use an *XOR-join* to merge two or more alternative branches that may have previously been forked with an XOR-split. An XOR gateway is indicated with an empty diamond or with a diamond marked with an "X". From now on, we will always use the "X" marker.

Example 3.2 Let us consider the following invoice checking process.

> As soon as an invoice is received from a customer, it needs to be checked for mismatches. The check may result in any of the following three options: (i) there are no mismatches, in which case the invoice is posted; (ii) there are mismatches but these can be corrected, in which case the invoice is resent to the customer; and (iii) there are mismatches but these cannot be corrected, in which case the invoice is blocked. Once one of these three activities is performed the invoice is parked and the process completes.

To model this process we start with a decision activity, namely "Check invoice for mismatches" following a start event "Invoice received". A *decision activity* is an activity that leads to different outcomes. In our example, this activity results in three possible outcomes, which are mutually exclusive; so we need to use an XOR-split after this activity to fork the flow into three branches. Accordingly, three sequence flows will emanate from this gateway, one towards activity "Post invoice", performed if there are no mismatches, another one towards "Re-send invoice to customer", performed if mismatches exist but can be corrected, and a third flow towards "Block invoice", performed if mismatches exist which cannot be corrected (see Figure 3.4). From a token perspective, an XOR-split routes the token coming from its incoming branch towards one of its outgoing branches, i.e. only one outgoing branch can be taken.

When using an XOR-split, make sure each outgoing sequence flow is annotated with a label capturing the condition upon which that specific branch is taken. Moreover, always use mutually exclusive conditions, i.e. only one of them can be true every time the XOR-split is reached by a token. This is the characteristic of the XOR-split gateway. In our example an invoice can either be correct, or contain

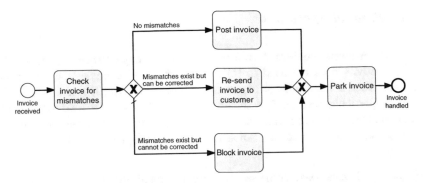

Fig. 3.4 An example of the use of XOR gateways

mismatches that can be fixed, or mismatches that cannot be fixed: only one of these conditions is true per invoice received.

In Figure 3.4 the flow labeled "mismatches exist but cannot be corrected" is marked with an oblique cut. This notation is optional and is used to indicate the *default flow*, i.e. the flow that will be taken by the token coming from the XOR-split in case the conditions attached to all the other outgoing flows evaluate to false. Since this arc has the meaning of *otherwise*, it can be left unlabeled. However, for readability purposes, we will generally attach a label to the default flow anyway.

Once either of the three alternative activities has been executed, we merge the flow back in order to execute activity "Park invoice" which is common to all three cases. For this we use an XOR-join. This particular gateway acts as a *passthrough*, meaning that it waits for a token to arrive from one of its input arcs and as soon as it receives the token, it sends it to the output arc. In other words, with an XOR-join we proceed whenever an incoming branch has completed.

Coming back to our example, we complete the process model with an end event "Invoice handled". Make sure to always complete a process model with an end event, even if it is obvious how the process would complete.   □

Exercise 3.1 Model the following fragment of a business process for assessing loan applications (loan origination process).

> Once a loan application has been approved by the loan provider, an acceptance pack is prepared and sent to the customer. The acceptance pack includes a repayment schedule which the customer needs to agree upon by sending the signed documents back to the loan provider. The latter then verifies the repayment agreement: if the applicant disagreed with the repayment schedule, the loan provider cancels the application; if the applicant agreed, the loan provider approves the application. In either case, the process completes with the loan provider notifying the applicant of the application status.

3.2.2 *Parallel Execution*

When two or more activities do not have any order dependencies on each other (i.e. one activity does not need to follow the other, nor excludes the other) they can be executed concurrently, or *in parallel*. The *parallel (AND) gateway* is used to model this particular relation. Specifically, we use an *AND-split* to model the parallel execution of two or more branches, and an *AND-join* to synchronize the execution of two or more parallel branches. An AND gateway is depicted as a diamond with a "+" mark.

Example 3.3 Let us consider the security check at an airport.

> Once the boarding pass has been received, passengers proceed to the security check. Here they need to pass the personal security screening and the luggage screening. Afterwards, they can proceed to the departure level.

This process consists of four activities. It starts with activity "Proceed to security check" and finishes with activity "Proceed to departure level". These two activities have a clear order dependency: a passenger can only go to the departure level after undergoing the required security checks. After the first activity, and before the last one, we need to perform two activities which can be executed in any order, i.e. which do not depend on each other: "Pass personal security screening" and "Pass luggage screening". To model this situation we use an AND-split linking activity "Proceed to security check" with the two screening activities, and an AND-join linking the two screening activities with activity "Proceed to departure level" (see Figure 3.5).

The AND-split *splits* the token coming from activity "Proceed to security check" into two tokens. Each of these tokens independently flows through one of the two branches. This means that when we reach an AND-split, we take all outgoing branches (note that an AND-split may have more than two outgoing arcs). As we said before, a token is used to indicate the state of a given instance. When multiple tokens of the same color are distributed across a process model, e.g. as a result of executing an AND-split, they collectively represent the state of an instance. For example, if a token is on the arc emitting from activity "Pass luggage screening"

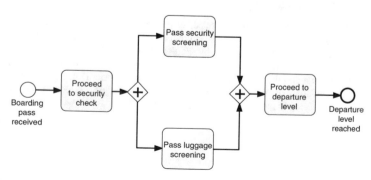

Fig. 3.5 An example of the use of AND gateways

and another token of the same color is on the arc incident to activity "Pass personal security screening", this indicates an instance of the security check process where a passenger has just passed the luggage screening but not yet started the personal security screening. □

The AND-join of our example waits for a token to arrive from each of the two incoming arcs, and once they are all available, it *merges* the tokens back into one. The single token is then sent to activity "Proceed to departure level". This means that we proceed when all incoming branches have completed (note again that an AND-join may have more than two incoming arcs). This behavior of waiting for a number of tokens to arrive and then merging the tokens into one is called *synchronization*.

Example 3.4 Let us extend the order-to-cash example of Figure 3.1 (see page 76) by assuming that a purchase order is only confirmed if the product is in stock, otherwise the process completes by rejecting the order. If the order is confirmed, the shipment address is received and the requested product is shipped *while* the invoice is emitted and the payment is received. Afterwards, the order is archived and the process completes.

The resulting model is shown in Figure 3.6. Let us make a couple of remarks. First, this model has two activities that are mutually exclusive: "Confirm order" and "Reject order", thus we preceded them with an XOR-split (remember to put an activity before an XOR-split to allow the decision to be taken, such as a check like in this case, or an approval). Second, the two sequences "Get shipment address"-"Ship product" and "Emit invoice"-"Receive payment" can be performed independently of each other, so we put them in a block between an AND-split and an AND-join. In fact, these two sets of activities are typically handled by different resources within a seller's organization, like a sales clerk for the shipment and a financial officer for the invoice, and thus can be executed in parallel (note the word "meantime" in the process description, which indicates that two or more activities can be performed at the same time). □

Let us compare this new version of the order-to-cash process with that in Figure 3.1 in terms of events. The new version features two end events while the first

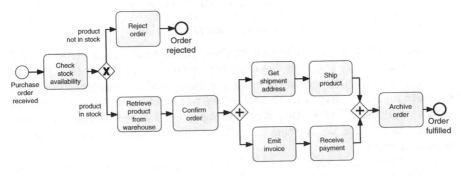

Fig. 3.6 A more elaborated version of the order-to-cash process diagram

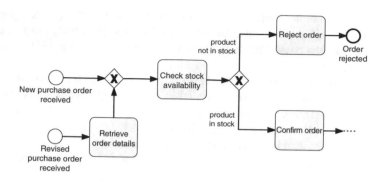

Fig. 3.7 A variant of the order-to-cash process with two different triggers

version features one end event. In a BPMN model we can have multiple end events, each capturing a different outcome of the process (e.g. balance paid vs. arrears processed, order approved vs. order rejected). BPMN adopts the so-called *implicit termination* semantics, meaning that a process instance completes only when each token flowing in the model reaches an end event. Similarly, we can have multiple start events in a BPMN model, each event capturing a different trigger to start a process instance. For example, we may start our order-to-cash process either when a new purchase order is received or when a revised order is resubmitted. If a revised order is resubmitted, we retrieve the order details from the orders database, and then continue with the rest of the process. This variant of the order-to-cash model is shown in Figure 3.7. An instance of this process is triggered by the first event that occurs.

Exercise 3.2 Model the following fragment of a business process for assessing loan applications.

> A loan application is approved if it passes two checks: (i) the applicant's loan risk assessment, done automatically by a system, and (ii) the appraisal of the property for which the loan has been asked, carried out by a property appraiser. The risk assessment requires a credit history check on the applicant, which is performed by a financial officer. Once both the loan risk assessment and the property appraisal have been performed, a loan officer can assess the applicant's eligibility. If the applicant is not eligible, the application is rejected, otherwise the acceptance pack is prepared and sent to the applicant.

There are two cases when a gateway can be omitted. An XOR-join can be omitted before an activity or event. In this case, the incoming arcs to the XOR-join are directly connected to the activity or event. An example of this shorthand notation is shown in Figure 1.6 (page 19), where there are two incident arcs to activity "Select suitable equipment". An AND-split can also be omitted when it follows an activity or event. In this case, the outgoing arcs of the AND-split emanate directly from the activity or event.

Now that we have seen the main elements of BPMN, you may want to start practicing by using a modeling tool. An overview of such tools is given in the following box.

BUSINESS PROCESS MODELING TOOLS
There are various tools for creating business process models, including:[2]

Pen & Paper: This approach is suitable for an initial sketch. However, it is not suitable for systematic knowledge sharing across an organization.

Haptic: Haptic tools, i.e. tools that rely on physical objects, are used to make the modeling experience interactive, for example in the context of workshops. Examples of such tools are Post-its or sticky notes that can be put on brown paper or whiteboards. There are also tool boxes with plastic and magnetic BPMN elements as well as interactive touchscreen tables. One of the advantages of these tools is that they stimulate the engagement of process stakeholders.

Single-user: Single-user tools can be general-purpose or specialized process modeling tools. A *general-purpose* drawing tool that is commonly used to sketch BPMN models is Microsoft Visio,[3] which offers a BPMN stencil. However, in tools such as Visio it is only possible to export the model as a drawing (e.g. in JPEG or PDF), rather than into an interchange format (e.g. XML or JSON) that can later be imported into another tool. This problem is solved by *specialized* business process modeling tools. Examples are Bizagi Modeler,[4] BOC Group's ADONIS:CE,[5] Software AG's ARIS Express,[6] and Camunda Modeler,[7] which support BPMN natively. However, standalone tools have the disadvantage that they hardly allow the joint design and management of business processes across a company.

Multi-tenant: Multi-tenant tools are available to multiple users, typically within the same organization. They provide a shared repository in which models can be stored and organized. These tools support model-sharing and collaborative process modeling among their users, and are available on-premises or on the cloud. Examples are BOC Group's ADONIS NP,[8] IBM BlueWorks Live,[9] Software AG's ARIS,[10] and Signavio Process

(continued)

---

[2]A list of BPMN tools is maintained on Wikipedia: https://en.wikipedia.org/wiki/Comparison_of_Business_Process_Modeling_Notation_tools.

[3]https://products.office.com/visio.

[4]https://www.bizagi.com/modeler.

[5]http://en.adonis-community.com.

[6]http://www.ariscommunity.com/aris-express.

[7]https://camunda.org/download/modeler.

[8]https://www.boc-group.com/adonis.

[9]https://www.blueworkslive.com.

[10]http://www.softwareag.com/aris.

Manager[11] (the latter is the tool that we used to create the models in this book). An open-source alternative to these commercial tools is the process analytics platform Apromore.[12]

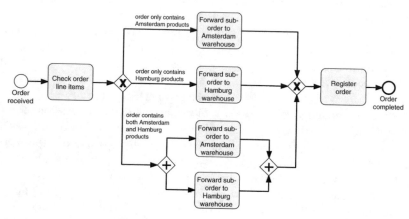

Fig. 3.8 Modeling an inclusive decision: first trial

3.2.3 Inclusive Decisions

Sometimes we may need to take one *or more* branches after a decision activity.

Example 3.5 Consider the following order distribution process.

A company has two warehouses that store different products: Amsterdam and Hamburg. When an order is received, it is distributed across these warehouses: if some of the relevant products are maintained in Amsterdam, a sub-order is sent there; likewise, if some relevant products are maintained in Hamburg, a sub-order is sent there. Afterwards, the order is registered and the process completes.

Can we model the above scenario using a combination of AND and XOR gateways? The answer is yes. However there are some problems. Figures 3.8 and 3.9 show two possible solutions. In the first one, we use an XOR-split with three alternative branches: one taken if the order only contains Amsterdam products (where the sub-order is forwarded to the Amsterdam warehouse), another taken if the order only contains Hamburg products (similarly, in this branch the sub-order is forwarded to the Hamburg warehouse), and a third branch to be taken in

---

[11]https://www.signavio.com.

[12]http://apromore.org.

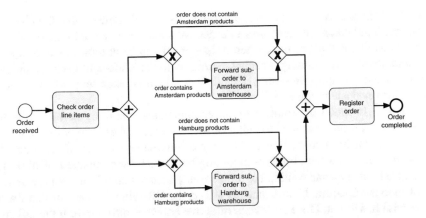

Fig. 3.9 Modeling an inclusive decision: second trial

case the order contains products from both warehouses (in which case sub-orders are forwarded to both warehouses). These three branches converge in an XOR-join which leads to the registration of the order.

While this model captures our scenario correctly, the resulting diagram is somewhat convoluted, since we need to duplicate the two activities that forward sub-orders to the respective warehouses twice. And if we had more than two warehouses, the number of duplicated activities would increase. For example, if we had three warehouses, we would need an XOR-split with seven outgoing branches, and each activity would need to be duplicated four times. Clearly this solution is not scalable.

In the second solution we use an AND-split with two outgoing arcs, each of which leads to an XOR-split with two alternative branches. One is taken if the order contains Amsterdam (Hamburg) products, in which case an activity is performed to forward the sub-order to the respective warehouse; the other branch is taken if the order does not contain any Amsterdam (Hamburg) products, in which case nothing is done until the XOR-join, which merges the two branches back. Then an AND-join merges the two parallel branches coming out of the AND-split and the process completes by registering the order.

What is the problem with this second solution? The example scenario allows three cases: the products are in Amsterdam only, in Hamburg only, or in both warehouses, while this solution allows one more case, i.e. when the products are in neither of the warehouses. This case occurs when the two empty branches of the two XOR-splits are taken, which results in doing nothing between activity "Check order line items" and activity "Register order". Thus this solution, despite being more compact than the first one, is incorrect.

To model situations where a decision may lead to one or more options being taken at the same time, we need to use an *inclusive (OR) split gateway* . An *OR-split* is similar to the XOR-split, but the conditions on its outgoing branches do not need to be mutually exclusive, i.e. more than one of them can be true at the same time. When we encounter an OR-split, we thus take one or more branches depending on which conditions are true. In terms of token semantics, this means that the OR-split takes the input token and generates a number of tokens equivalent to the number of output conditions that are true, where this number can be at least one and at most the total number of outgoing branches. Similarly to the XOR-split gateway, an OR-split can also be equipped with a default flow, which is taken only when all other conditions evaluate to false.

Figure 3.10 shows the solution to our example using the OR gateway. After the sub-order has been forwarded to either of the two warehouses or to both, we use an *OR-join* to synchronize the flow and continue with the registration of the order. An OR-join proceeds when all *active* incoming branches have completed. Waiting for an active branch means waiting for an incoming branch that will ultimately deliver a token to the OR-join. If the branch is active, the OR-join will wait for that token, otherwise it will not. Once all tokens of active branches have arrived, the OR-join synchronizes these tokens into one (similarly to what an AND-join does) and sends that token to its output arc. We call this behavior *synchronizing merge* as opposed to the simple merge of the XOR-join and the synchronization of the AND-join. □

Let us delve into the concept of an active branch. Consider the model in Figure 3.11, which features a join gateway with undefined type (the one grayed

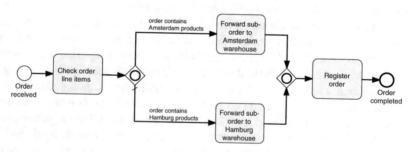

Fig. 3.10 Modeling an inclusive decision with the OR gateway

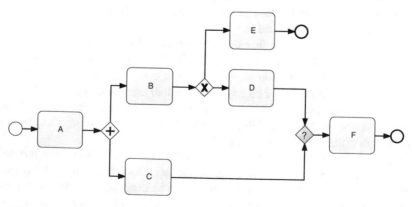

Fig. 3.11 What type should the join gateway have such that instances of this process can complete correctly?

out with a question mark). What type should we assign to this join? Let us try an AND-join to match the preceding AND-split. We recall that an AND-join waits for a token to arrive from each incoming branch. While the token from the branch with activity "C" will always arrive, the token from the branch with activities "B" and "D" may not arrive if this is routed to "E" by the XOR-split. So if activity "D" is not executed, the AND-join will wait indefinitely for that token, with the consequence that the process instance will not be able to progress any further. This behavioral anomaly is called *deadlock* and should be avoided.

Let us try an XOR-join. We recall that the XOR-join works as a passthrough by forwarding to its output branch each token that arrives through one of its input branches. In our example this means that we may execute activity "F" once or twice, depending whether the preceding XOR-split routes the token to "E" (in this case "F" is executed once) or to "D" ("F" is executed twice). While this solution may work, we have the problem that we do not know whether activity "F" will be executed once or twice, and we may actually not want to execute it twice. Moreover, if this is the case, we would signal that the process has completed twice, since the end event following "F" will receive two tokens. And this, again, is something we want to avoid. This behavioural anomaly is called *lack of synchronization*.

The only join type left to try is the OR-join. An OR-join will wait for all incoming active branches to complete. If the XOR-split routes control to "E", the OR-join will not wait for a token from the branch bearing activity "D", since this will never arrive. Thus, it will proceed once the token from activity "C" arrives. On the other hand, if the XOR-split routes control to "D", the OR-join will wait for a token to also arrive from this branch, and once both tokens have arrived, it will merge them into one and send this token out, so that "F" can be executed once and the process can complete normally.

Question When should we use an OR-join?

Since the OR-join semantics is sophisticated, the presence of this element in a model may confuse the reader. Thus, we suggest to use it only when it is strictly required. Clearly, it is easy to see that an OR-join must be used whenever we need to synchronize control from a preceding OR-split. Similarly, we should use an AND-join to synchronize control from a preceding AND-split and an XOR-join to merge a set of branches that are mutually exclusive. In other cases the model will not have a lean structure like the examples in Figures 3.8 or 3.10, where the model is made up of nested blocks each delimited by a split and a join of the same type. The model may rather look like that in Figure 3.11, where there can be entry points into, or exit points from a block-structure. In these cases play the token game to understand the correct join type. Start with an XOR-join, next try an AND-join and if both gateways lead to incorrect models use the OR-join which will work for sure.

Now that we have learned the three core gateways, let us use them to extend the order-to-cash process. Assume that if the product is not in stock, it can be manufactured. In this way, an order can never be rejected.

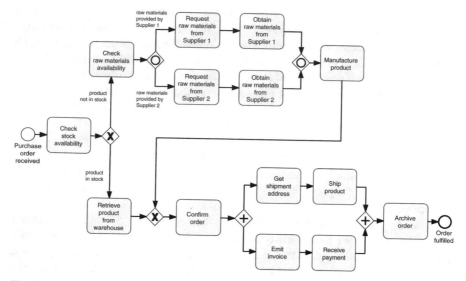

Fig. 3.12 The order-to-cash process model with product manufacturing

Example 3.6 Let us extend the order-to-cash process with the possibility of manufacturing products that are not in stock.

> If the product requested is not in stock, it needs to be manufactured before the order handling
> can continue. To manufacture a product, the required raw materials have to be ordered. Two
> preferred suppliers provide different types of raw materials. Depending on the product to
> be manufactured, raw materials may be ordered from either Supplier 1 or Supplier 2, or
> from both. Once the raw materials are available, the product can be manufactured and the
> order can be confirmed. On the other hand, if the product is in stock, it is retrieved from the
> warehouse before confirming the order. In either case, the process continues normally.

The model for this process is shown in Figure 3.12.   □

Exercise 3.3 Model the following fragment of a business process for assessing loan
applications.

> A loan application may be coupled with a home insurance which is offered at discounted
> prices. The applicants may express their interest in a home insurance plan at the time of
> submitting their loan application to the loan provider. Based on this information, if the
> loan application is approved, the loan provider may either only send an acceptance pack
> to the applicant, or also send a home insurance quote. The process then continues with the
> verification of the repayment agreement.

3.2.4 Rework and Repetition

So far we have seen structures that are linear, i.e. each activity is performed at most
once. However, sometimes we may require to repeat one or several activities, for
instance because of a failed check.

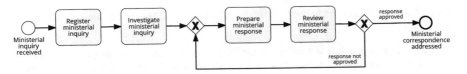

Fig. 3.13 A process model for addressing ministerial correspondence

Example 3.7 Let us consider this process for addressing ministerial correspondence.

> In the treasury minister's office, once a ministerial inquiry has been received, it is first registered into the system. Then the inquiry is investigated so that a ministerial response can be prepared. The finalization of a response includes the preparation of the response itself by the cabinet officer and the review of the response by the principal registrar. If the registrar does not approve the response, the latter needs to be prepared again by the cabinet officer for review. The process finishes only once the response has been approved.

To model rework or repetition we first need to identify the activities, or more in general the fragment of the process, that can be repeated. In our example this consists of the sequence of activities "Prepare ministerial response" and "Review ministerial response". Let us call this our *repetition block*. The property of a repetition block is that the last of its activities must be a decision activity. In fact, this will allow us to decide whether to go back before the repetition block starts, so that this can be repeated, or to continue with the rest of the process. As such, this decision activity should have two outcomes. In our example the decision activity is "Review ministerial response" and its outcomes are: "response approved" (in this case we continue with the process) and "response not approved" (we go back). To model these two outcomes, we use an XOR-split with two outgoing branches: one which allows us to continue with the rest of the process (in our example, this is simply the end event "Ministerial correspondence addressed"), the other which goes back to before activity "Prepare ministerial response". We use an XOR-join to reconnect this branch to the point of the process model just before the repetition block. The model for our example is illustrated in Figure 3.13.   □

Question Why do we need to merge the loopback branch of a repetition block with an XOR-join?

The reason for using an XOR-join is that this gateway has a very simple semantics: it moves any token it receives in its input arc to its output arc, which is what we need in this case. In fact, if we merged the loopback branch with the rest of the model using an AND-join we would deadlock since this gateway would try to synchronize the two incoming branches when we know that only one of them can be active at a time: if we were looping we would receive the token from the loopback branch; otherwise we would receive it from the other branch indicating that we are entering the repetition block for the first time. An OR-join would work but is an overkill since we know that only one branch will be active at a time.

Exercise 3.4 Model the following fragment of a business process for assessing loan applications.

Once a loan application is received by the loan provider, and before proceeding with its assessment, the application itself needs to be checked for completeness. If the application is incomplete, it is returned to the applicant, so that they can fill out the missing information and send it back to the loan provider. This process is repeated until the application is found complete.

We have learned how to combine activities, events and gateways to model basic business processes. For each such element we have shown its graphical representation and the rules for combining it with other modeling elements. We have also explained the behavior of each element in terms of token movement rules. All these aspects fall under the term *components of a modeling language*. If you want to know more about this topic, you can read the box "Components of a Modeling Language".

COMPONENTS OF A MODELING LANGUAGE

A *modeling language*, as any other language, consists of four aspects: vocabulary, syntax, semantics, and notation. The *vocabulary* provides the set of modeling elements of the language. The *syntax* describes a set of rules to govern how these elements can be combined. The *semantics* bind these elements, including their textual descriptions, to a precise meaning. The *notation* defines a set of graphical symbols for the visualization of the elements. In the case of the BPMN language, the BPMN vocabulary includes activities, events, gateways, and sequence flows. An example of a syntactic rule is that start events only have outgoing sequence flows whereas end events only have incoming sequence flows. Another one is that each element should be on a path from a start to an end event, i.e. there should not be disconnected nodes or dangling arcs. The BPMN semantics describes the meaning of each of the elements in the vocabulary, as well as the overall meaning of the business process captured by the model. For example, activities model something actively performed during the business process, while XOR gateways model exclusive decisions and simple merging points. By considering the meaning of all the elements in a given model, we can infer the meaning of the underlying business process. For instance, our model in Figure 3.12 describes an order-to-cash process that starts with the receipt of a purchase order which is then checked against stock levels: if the product is in stock, it is directly retrieved from the warehouse, otherwise the product needs to be manufactured, and so on. Finally, examples of the BPMN notation are the labeled rounded boxes to depict activities and the circles with a thin border to depict start events. We will talk more about BPMN syntax and semantics in Chapter 5.

3.3 Business Objects

As described in Chapter 2, a business process relates to different organizational aspects such as functions, business objects, humans, and software systems. These aspects are captured by different process modeling perspectives. So far we have seen the *functional perspective*, which indicates what activities should happen in the process, and the *control-flow perspective*, which indicates when activities and events should occur. Another important perspective that we ought to consider when modeling business processes is the *object perspective*, also called the *data perspective*. The object perspective indicates which business objects, also known as artifacts (e.g. documents, files, material) are required to perform an activity, and which ones are produced as a result of performing an activity.

Let us enrich the order-to-cash process of Example 3.6 with business objects. Let us start by identifying the objects that each activity requires in order to be executed, and those that each activity creates as a result of its execution. For example, the first activity of the order-to-cash process is "Check stock availability". This requires a purchase order as input to check whether or not the ordered product is in stock. This object is also required by activity "Check raw materials availability" should the product be manufactured. Business objects like "Purchase order" are called *data objects* in BPMN. Data objects represent information and material flowing in and out of activities; they can be physical objects carrying information such as a paper invoice or material such as a product, or electronic objects such as an email or an invoice on PDF. We depict them as a document with the upper-right corner folded over, and link them to activities with a dotted arrow with an open arrowhead (called *data association* in BPMN). Figure 3.14 shows the data objects involved in the order-to-cash process model.

We use the direction of the data association to establish whether a data object is an input or output for a given activity. An incoming association, like the one used from the purchase order to the activity "Check stock availability", indicates that the purchase order is an input object for this activity; an outgoing association, like the one used from activity "Obtain raw materials from Supplier 1" to raw materials, indicates that raw materials is an output object for this activity. To avoid cluttering the diagram with data associations that cross sequence flows, we may repeat a data object multiple times within the same process model. However, all occurrences of a given object do conceptually refer to the same artifact. For example, in Figure 3.14 "Purchase order" is repeated twice as input to "Check stock availability" and to "Confirm order" since these two activities are far away from each other in terms of model layout.

Often the output from an activity coincides with the input to a subsequent activity. For example, once raw materials have been obtained, these are used by activity "Manufacture product" to create a product. The product in turn is packaged and sent to the customer by activity "Ship product". Effectively, data objects allow us to model the flow of information or material between process activities. Bear in mind, however, that data objects and their associations with activities cannot replace the

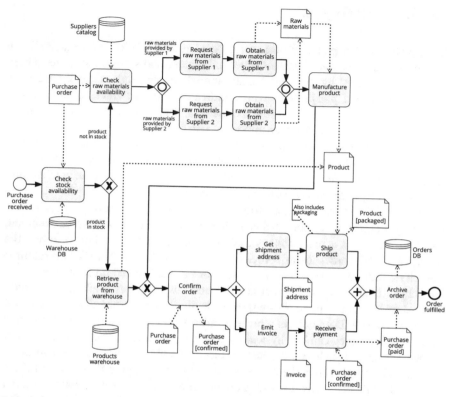

Fig. 3.14 The order-to-cash example with data objects and data stores

sequence flow. In other words, even if an object is passed from an activity A to an activity B, we still need to model the sequence flow from A to B. A shorthand notation for passing an object from an activity to the next is by directly connecting the data object to the sequence flow between two consecutive activities via an undirected association. See for example the shipment address being passed from activity "Get shipment address" to activity "Ship product", which is a shorthand for indicating that shipment address is an output of "Get shipment address" and an input to "Ship product".

Sometimes we may need to represent the *state* of a data object. For instance, in Figure 3.14 activity "Confirm order" takes a purchase order as input and returns a "confirmed" purchase order as output: input and output objects are the same, but the object's state has changed to "confirmed". Similarly, activity "Receive payment" takes as input a "confirmed" purchase order and transforms it into a "paid" purchase order. An object can go through a number of states, e.g. an invoice is first "opened", then "approved" or "rejected", and finally "archived". Indicating data objects' states is optional: we can do so by appending the name of the state between square brackets to a data object's label, e.g. "Purchase Order [confirmed]", "Product [packaged]".

A *data store* is a place containing data objects that need to be persisted beyond the duration of a process instance, e.g. a database for electronic objects or a filing cabinet for physical ones. Process activities can extract/store data objects from/to data stores. For example, in Figure 3.14, activity "Check stock availability" retrieves the stock level for the ordered product from the warehouse database, which contains stock level information for the various products. In this case, effectively what is being extracted is information—the stock level—which may be represented as an electronic data object, though this is not very common on conceptual models such as our order-to-cash example, where this data object is simply omitted. Similarly, activity "Check raw materials availability" consults the suppliers catalog to check which supplier to contact. Continuing with our order-to-cash example, activity "Retrieve product from warehouse" is used to retrieve a physical data object—the product—from the products warehouse. The products warehouse, the suppliers catalog, and the warehouse database are examples of data stores used as input to activities. An example of data store employed as output is the orders database, which is used by activity "Archive order" to store the confirmed purchase order. In this way, the order just archived will be available for other business processes within the same organization, e.g. for a business process that handles requests for product returns. Data stores are represented as an empty cylinder (the typical database symbol) with a triple upper border. Similarly to data objects, they are connected to activities via data associations.

Question Do data objects affect the token flow?

Input data objects are required for an activity to be executed. Even if a token is available on the incoming arc of that activity, the latter cannot be executed until all input data objects are also available. A data object is available if it has been created as a result of completing a preceding activity (whose output was the data object itself), or because it is an input to the whole process (like purchase order). Output data objects only affect the token flow indirectly, i.e. when they are used by subsequent activities.

Exercise 3.5 Is there any missing data object or data store in the example of Figure 3.14 (page 94)?

Question Do we always need to model data objects?

Data objects help the reader understand the flow of information and material from one activity to the other. However, the price to pay is an increased complexity of the diagram. Thus, we suggest using them only when they are needed for a specific purpose, for example when we later want to use the process model to communicate with an IT application development team in order to automate the process (cf. Chapter 10).

There are cases in which we may need to provide additional information to the process model reader, for the sake of improving the understanding of the model. For example, in the order-to-cash process we may want to specify that activity "Ship product" includes the packaging of the product. Also, we may want to clarify what business rule is followed behind the choice of raw materials from suppliers. Such additional information can be provided via *text annotations*. An annotation is depicted as an open-ended rectangle encapsulating the text of the annotation, and is linked to a process modeling element via a dotted line (called *association*)—see Figure 3.14 for an example. Text annotations do not bear any semantics, thus they do not affect the flow of tokens through the process model.

Exercise 3.6 Put together the four fragments of the loan assessment process that you created in Exercises 3.1–3.4.
Hint. Look at the labels of the start and end events to understand the order dependencies among the various fragments. Then extend the resulting model by adding all the required business objects. Moreover, attach annotations to specify the business rules behind (i) checking an application completeness, (ii) assessing an application eligibility, and (iii) verifying a repayment agreement.

3.4 Resources

A further aspect we need to consider when modeling business processes is the *resource perspective*. This perspective, also called the *organizational perspective*, indicates who or what performs which activity. *Resource* is a generic term to refer to anyone or anything involved in the performance of a process activity. A resource can be:

- A *process participant*, i.e. an individual person like the employee John Smith,
- A *software system*, for example a server or a software application,
- A piece of *equipment*, such as a printer or a manufacturing plant.

We distinguish between *active resources*, i.e. resources that can autonomously perform an activity, and *passive resources*, i.e. resources that are merely involved in the performance of an activity. For example, a photocopier is used by a participant to make a copy of a document, but it is the participant who performs the photocopying activity. So, the photocopier is a passive resource while the participant is an active resource. A bulldozer is another example of a passive resource since it is the driver who performs the activity in which the bulldozer is used. The resource perspective of a process is interested in active resources, so from now on with the term "resource" we refer to an "active resource".

Frequently, in a process model we do not explicitly refer to one resource at a time, like for example an employee John Smith, but instead we refer to a group of resources that are interchangeable in the sense that any member of the group can perform a given activity. Such groups are called *resource classes*. Examples are a whole organization, an organizational unit or a role.[13]

---

[13]In BPMN the term "participant" is used in a broad sense as a synonym of resource class, though in this book we do not adopt this definition.

Example 3.8 Let us examine the resources involved in our order-to-cash example.

The order-to-cash process is carried out by a seller's organization which includes two departments: the sales department and the warehouse & distribution department. The purchase order received by warehouse & distribution is checked against the stock. This operation is carried out automatically by the ERP system of warehouse & distribution, which queries the warehouse database. If the product is in stock, it is retrieved from the warehouse before the sales department confirms the order. Next, the sales department emits an invoice and waits for the payment, while the product is shipped from within warehouse & distribution. The process completes with the order archival in the sales department. If the product is not in stock, the ERP system within warehouse & distribution checks the raw materials availability by accessing the suppliers catalog. Once the raw materials have been obtained the warehouse & distribution department takes care of manufacturing the product. The process completes with the purchase order being confirmed and archived by the sales department.

BPMN provides two constructs to model resource aspects: *pools* and *lanes*. Pools are generally used to model resource classes, lanes are used to partition a pool into sub-classes or single resources. There are no constraints as to what specific resource type a pool or a lane should model. We would typically use a pool to model a *business party* like a whole organization such as the seller in our example, and a lane to model a department, unit, team, software system, or equipment within that organization. In our example, we partition the Seller pool into two lanes: one for the Warehouse & Distribution department, the other for the sales department.

Lanes can be nested within each other in multiple levels. For example, if we need to model both a department and the roles within that department, we can use one outer lane for the department, and one inner lane for each role. In the order-to-cash example we nest a lane within Warehouse & Distribution to represent the ERP System within that department.

Pools and lanes are depicted as rectangles within which we can place activities, events, gateways and data objects. Typically, we model these rectangles horizontally, though modeling them vertically is also possible. The name of the pool or lane is shown vertically on the left-hand side of a horizontal rectangle (or horizontally if the pool or lane is vertical); for pools, and for lanes containing nested lanes, the name is enclosed in a band. Figure 3.15 shows the revised order-to-cash example with resource aspects.

It is important to place an activity within the right lane. For example, we placed activity "Check stock availability" under the ERP System lane of Warehouse & Distribution to indicate that this activity is carried out automatically by the ERP system of that department. It is also important to place events properly within lanes. In our example we put event "Purchase order received" under the ERP system lane to indicate that the process starts within the ERP system of Warehouse & Distribution, while we put the event "Order fulfilled" under the Sales pool to indicate that the process completes in the sales department. It is not relevant where data objects are put, as they depend on the activities they are linked to. As per gateways, we need to place those modeling (X)OR-splits under the same lane as the preceding decision activity has been put in. On the other hand, it is irrelevant where we place an AND-split and all join gateways, since these elements are passive in the sense that they behave according to their context. □

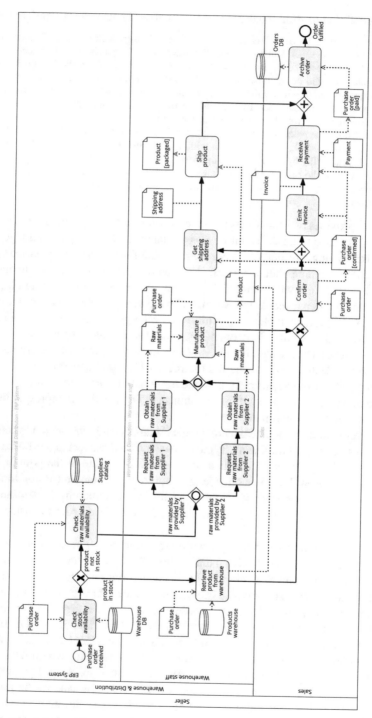

Fig. 3.15 The order-to-cash example with resource information

We may organize lanes within a pool in a matrix when we need to model complex organizational structures. For example, if we have an organization where roles span different departments, we may use horizontal lanes to model the various departments and vertical lanes to model the roles within these departments. Bear in mind however that in BPMN each activity can be performed by one resource only. Thus, if an activity sits in the intersection of a horizontal lane with a vertical lane, it will be performed by the resource that fulfills the characteristics of both lanes, e.g. a resource that has that role and belongs to that department.

Exercise 3.7 Extend the business process for assessing loan applications that you created in Exercise 3.6 on page 96 by considering the following resource aspects.

> The process for assessing loan applications is executed by four roles within the loan provider: a financial officer takes care of checking the applicant's credit history; a property appraiser is responsible for appraising the property; an insurance sales representative sends the home insurance quote to the applicant if this is required. All other activities are performed by the loan officer who is the main point of contact with the applicant.

Often there is more than one business party participating in the same business process. For example, in the order-to-cash process there are four parties: the seller, the customer and the two suppliers. When we model business parties that are independent from one another, we represent them as pools. In our example, we can thus use one pool for the customer, one for the seller and one for each supplier. Each of these pools will contain the activities, events, gateways and data objects that model the specific portion of the business process occurring at that organization. Or to put it differently, each pool will model the same business process from the perspective of a specific organization. For example, the event "Purchase order received", which sits in the sales pool, will have a corresponding activity "Submit purchase order" occurring in the customer pool. Similarly, activity "Ship product" from sales will have a counterpart activity "Receive product" in the customer pool. So, how can we model the interactions among the pools of two collaborating organizations? We cannot use the sequence flow to connect activities that belong to different pools since the sequence flow cannot cross the boundary of a pool. For this, we need to use a specific element called *message flow*.

A message flow represents the flow of information between two separate resource classes (pools). It is depicted as a dashed line that starts with an empty circle and ends with an empty arrowhead, and bears a label indicating the content of the message, e.g. a fax, a purchase order, but also a letter or a phone call. That is, the message flow models any type of communication between two organizations, no matter if this is electronic like sending a purchase order via email or transmitting a fax, or manual like making a phone call or handing over a letter on paper. And despite its name, a message flow may also be used to capture an exchange of materials between organizations, such as for example the delivery of physical products.

Figure 3.16 shows the complete order-to-cash process model including the pools for the customer and the two suppliers. Here we can see that message flows are labelled with the piece of information they carry, e.g. "Raw materials" or "Shipment address". An incoming message flow may lead to the creation of a data object

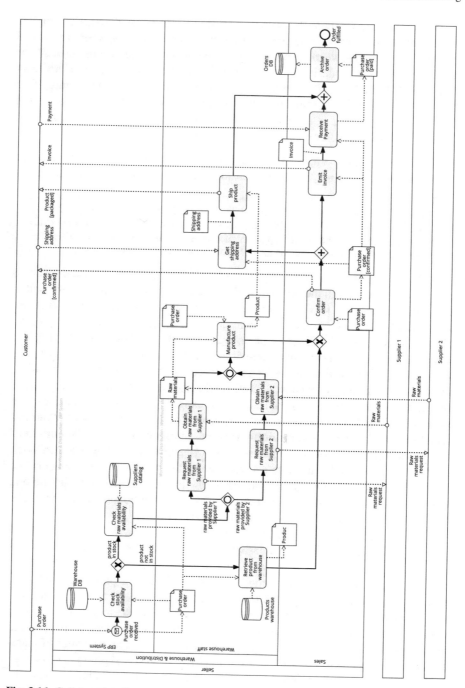

Fig. 3.16 Collaboration diagram between a seller, a customer, and two suppliers

by the activity that receives the message. For example, the message flow "Raw materials" is received by activity "Obtain raw materials from Supplier 1" which then creates the data object "Raw materials". This is also the case of the purchase order, which is generated by the start event "Purchase order received" from the content of the incoming message flow. We do not need to create a data object for each incoming message flow, only when the information carried by the message is needed elsewhere in the process. In our case, "Raw materials" is consumed by activity "Manufacture product" so we need to represent it as a data object. Similarly, we do not need to explicitly represent the data object that goes into an outgoing message if this data object is not needed elsewhere in the process. For example, activity "Emit invoice" generates an invoice which is sent to the customer, but there is no data object "Invoice" since this is not consumed by any activity in the Seller pool.

A BPMN diagram that features two or more pools is called *collaboration diagram*. Figure 3.16 shows different uses of a pool in a collaboration diagram. A pool like that for the seller is called *private process*, or *white box* pool, since it shows how the seller organization participates in the order-to-cash process in terms of activities, events, gateways and data objects. On the contrary, a pool like that for the customer and the two suppliers is called *public process*, or *black box* pool, since it hides how these organizations actually participate in the order-to-cash process. In order to save space, we can represent a black box with a *collapsed pool*, which is an empty rectangle bearing the name of the pool in the middle.

Question Black box or white box?

Modeling a pool as a white box or as a black box is a matter of relevance. When working on a collaboration diagram, an organization may decide whether or not to expose their internal behavior depending on the requirements of the project at hand. For example, if we are modeling the order-to-cash process from the seller's perspective, it may be relevant to expose the business process of the seller only, but not that of the customer and the suppliers. That is, the internal behavior of the customer and that of the suppliers are not relevant for the sake of understanding how the seller should fulfill purchase orders, and as such they can be hidden. On the other hand, if we need to improve the way the seller fulfills purchase orders, we may also want to know what it takes for a supplier to provide raw materials, as a delay in the provision of raw materials will slow down the product manufacturing at the seller's side. In this case, we should also represent the suppliers using white box pools.

The type of pool affects the way we use the message flow to connect to the pool. Accordingly, a message flow may cross the boundary of a white box pool and connect directly to an activity or event within that pool, like the purchase order message which is connected to the start event in the seller pool. On the other hand, since a black box pool is empty, message flows must stop at the boundary or emanate from the boundary of a black box pool. Bear in mind that a message flow is only used to connect two pools and never to connect two activities within the same pool. For that, we use a sequence flow.

An activity that is the source of a message—such as "Emit invoice" in the Seller pool—is called a *send activity*. The message is sent upon completion of the activity's execution. On the other hand, an activity that receives a message—such as "Get shipping address"—is a *receive activity*. The execution of such an activity will not start until the incoming message is available. An activity can act as both a receive and a send activity when it has both an incoming and outgoing message flow, e.g. "Make payment". The execution of this activity will start when both the control-flow token and the incoming message are available. Upon completion of the activity, a control-flow token will be put on the output arc and the outgoing message will be sent out. Finally, when a message flow is incident to a start event like "Purchase order received", we need to mark this event with a light envelope (see Figure 3.16). This event type is called *message event*. A message event can be linked to an output data object in order to store the content of the incoming message. We will learn more about events in the next chapter.

Exercise 3.8 Extend the model of Exercise 3.7 by representing the interactions between the loan provider and the applicant.

In the order-to-cash example we used pools to represent business parties and lanes to represent the departments and systems within the sales organization. This is because we wanted to focus on the interactions between the seller, the customer and the two suppliers. As mentioned before, this is the typical use for pools and lanes. However, since BPMN does not prescribe what specific resource types should be associated with pools and lanes, we may use these elements differently. For example, if the focus is on the interactions between the departments of an organization, we can model each department with a pool, and use lanes to partition the departments, e.g. in units or roles. In any case, we should avoid using pools and lanes to capture participants by their names since individuals tend to change frequently within an organization; rather, we should use the participant's role, e.g. financial officer. On the other hand, we can use pools and lanes to represent a software system, e.g. an ERP system, since such systems are used for long periods of time.

3.5 Process Decomposition

As we tackle more complex business processes, we will undoubtedly produce larger models, i.e. models with many elements, and this will hamper the overall model understandability. Take the order-to-cash process model in Figure 3.12 (page 90). While the process at hand is still relatively simple, this model already contains 14 activities, six gateways and two events. And as we enrich it with data objects, resources and message flows, the model gets larger and so harder to understand (compare Figures 3.16 with 3.12). So, how can we tackle the problem of increasing model complexity? To improve understandability, we can simplify the model by hiding certain parts within a *sub-process*. A sub-process represents a self-contained, composite activity that can be broken down into smaller units of work. Conversely, an atomic activity, also called *task*, is an activity capturing a unit of work that cannot be further broken down.

To use a sub-process, we first need to identify groups of related activities, i.e. those activities which together achieve a particular goal or generate a particular

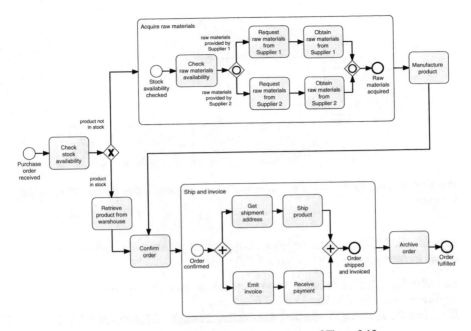

Fig. 3.17   Identifying sub-processes in the order-to-cash process of Figure 3.12

outcome. In our order-to-cash example, we can see that the activities "Check raw materials availability" and "Purchase raw materials from Supplier 1(2)", lead together to the acquisition of raw materials. Thus these activities, and their connecting gateways, can be encapsulated in a sub-process. In other words, they can be seen as the internal steps of a macro-activity called "Acquire raw materials". Similarly, the two parallel branches for shipping and invoicing the order can be grouped under another sub-process activity called "Ship and invoice". Figure 3.17 illustrates the resulting model, where the above activities have been enclosed in two sub-process activities. We represent such activities with a large rounded box which encloses the internal steps. As we can observe from Figure 3.17, we also added a start event and an end event inside each sub-process activity, to explicitly indicate when the sub-process starts and completes.

Recall that our initial objective was to improve understandability. Once we have identified the boundaries of the sub-processes, we can simplify the model, and thus improve its readability, by hiding the content of its sub-processes, as shown in Figure 3.18. This is done by replacing the macro-activity representing the sub-process with a standard-size activity. We indicate that this activity hides a sub-process by marking it with a small square with a plus sign (+) inside (as if we could expand the content of that activity by pressing the plus button). This operation is called collapsing a sub-process. By collapsing a sub-process we reduce the total number of activities (the order-to-cash process has only six activities now), thus improving the model readability. In BPMN, a sub-process which hides its internal

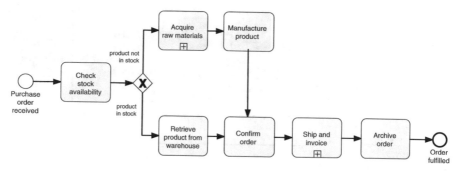

Fig. 3.18 A simplified version of the order-to-cash process after hiding the content of its sub-processes

steps is called *collapsed sub-process*, as opposed to an *expanded sub-process* which shows its internal steps (as in Figure 3.17).

Exercise 3.9 Identify suitable sub-processes in the process for assessing loan applications modeled in Exercise 3.6 (page 96).
Hint. Use the building blocks that you created throughout Exercises 3.1–3.4.

Collapsing a sub-process does not imply losing its content. The sub-process is still there, just defined at an abstraction level below. In fact, we can nest sub-processes in multiple levels, so as to decompose a process model hierarchically. An example is shown in Figure 3.19, which models a business process for disbursing home loans. In the first level we identified two sub-processes: one for checking the applicant's liability, the other for signing the loan. In the second level, we factored out the scheduling of the loan disbursement within the process for signing loans into a separate sub-process.

As we go down the hierarchical decomposition of a process model, we can add more details. For example, we may establish a convention that at the top level we only model core business activities, at the second level we add decision points, and so on all the way down to modeling exceptions and details that are only relevant for process automation.

Question When should we decompose a process model into sub-processes?

We should use sub-processes whenever a model becomes so large that it becomes hard to understand. While it is hard to precisely define when a process model is "too large", since understandability is subjective, it has been shown that using more than approximately 30 flow objects (i.e. activities, events, gateways) leads to an increased probability of making mistakes in a process model (e.g. introducing behavioral issues). Thus, we suggest using as few elements as possible per each process model level. As a rule of thumb, we suggest to decompose a process model into multiple ones if the model has more than 30 flow objects.

Reducing the size of a process model, for example by collapsing its sub-processes, is one of the most effective ways of improving a process model's read-

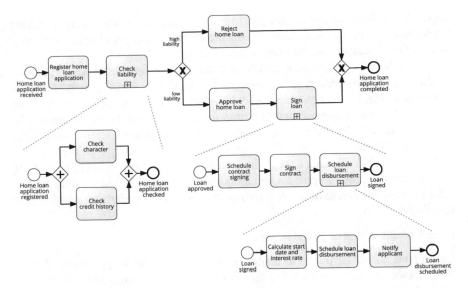

Fig. 3.19 A process model for disbursing home loans, laid down over three hierarchical levels via the use of sub-processes

ability. Other structural aspects that affect the readability include the density of the process model connections, the number of parallel branches, the longest path from a start to an end event, as well as cosmetic aspects such as the layout, the labels style (e.g. always use a verb-noun style), the colors palette, the lines thickness, etc. More information on establishing process modeling guidelines can be found in Chapter 5.

We have shown that we can simplify a process model by first identifying the content of a sub-process, and then hiding this content by collapsing the sub-process activity. Sometimes, we may wish to proceed in the opposite direction, meaning that when modeling a process we already identify activities that can be broken down in smaller steps, but we intentionally under-specify their content. In other words, we do not link the sub-process activity to a process model at a lower level capturing its content (as if by pressing the plus button nothing would happen). The reason for doing this is to tell the reader that some activities are made up of sub-steps, but that disclosing the details of these is not relevant. This could be the case of activity "Ship product" in the order-to-cash example, for which modeling the distinction between its internal steps for packaging and for shipping is not relevant.

3.6 Process Model Reuse

By default a sub-process is embedded within its parent process model, and as such it can only be invoked from within that process model. Often, when modeling a business process we may need to reuse parts of other process models of the same organization. For example, a loan provider may reuse the sub-process for signing loans contained in the home loan disbursement for other types of loans, such as a process for disbursing student loans or motor loans.

In BPMN, we can define the content of a sub-process outside its parent process, by defining the sub-process as a *global* process model. A global process model is a process model that is not embedded within any process model, and as such can be invoked by other process models within the same process model collection. To indicate that the sub-process being invoked is a global process model, we use the collapsed sub-process activity with a thicker border (this activity type is called *call activity* in BPMN). Coming back to the loan disbursement example of Figure 3.19, we can factor out the sub-process for signing loans and define it as a global process model, so that it can also be invoked by a process model for disbursing student loans (see Figure 3.20).

Question Embedded or global sub-process?

Our default choice should be to define sub-processes as global process models so as to maximize their reusability within our process model collection. Supporting processes such as payment, invoicing, HR, printing, are good candidates for being defined as global process models, since they are typically shared by various business processes within an organization. Besides reusability, another advantage of using global process models is that any change made to these models will be automatically propagated to all process models that invoke them. In some cases, however, we may want to keep the changes internal to a specific process. For example, an invoicing process used for corporate orders settlement would typically be different than the invoicing process for private orders. In this case, we should keep two model variants of the invoice sub-process, each embedded within its parent process model: corporate and private order settlement.

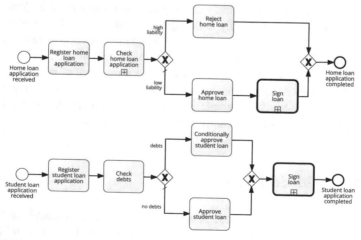

Fig. 3.20 The process model for disbursing student loans invokes the same model for signing loans used by the process for disbursing home loans, via a call activity

Example 3.9 Let us consider the procurement process of a pharmaceutical company.

A pharmaceutical company has different business units within its manufacturing department, each producing a specific type of medicine. For example, there is a business unit looking after inhaled medications, and another one producing vaccines. The various business units make use of a direct procurement process for ordering chemicals, and of an indirect procurement process for ordering spare parts for their equipment.

The direct procurement process depends on the raw materials that are required to produce a specific type of medicine. For example, vaccines typically include adjuvants that help improve the vaccine's effectiveness, which are not contained in inhaled medications. Similarly, inhaled medications contain a chemical propellant to push the medicine out of the inhaler, which is not required for vaccines. Since this procurement process is specific to each business unit, we need to model it as an embedded sub-process within the manufacturing process model of each unit. On the other hand, the process for ordering spare parts to the equipment for synthesizing chemicals can be shared across all units, since all units make use of the same equipment. Thus, we will model this process with a global process model.   □

Before concluding our discussion on sub-processes, we need to point to some syntactical rules for using this element. A sub-process is a regular process model. It should start with at least one start event, and complete with at least one end event. If there are multiple start events, the sub-process will be triggered by the first such an event that occurs. If there are multiple end events, the sub-process will return control to its parent process only when each token flowing in this model reaches an end event. Moreover, we cannot cross the boundary of a sub-process with a sequence flow. To pass control to a sub-process, or receive control from a sub-process, we should always use start and end events. On the other hand, message flows can cross the boundaries of a sub-process to indicate messages that emanate from, or are directed to, internal activities or events of the sub-process.

Exercise 3.10 Identify suitable sub-processes in the process of Exercise 1.7 (page 31). Among these sub-processes, identify those that are specific to this process versus those that can potentially be shared with other processes of the same company.

3.7 Recap

At the end of this chapter, we should be able to understand and produce basic process models in BPMN. A basic BPMN model includes simple activities, events, gateways, data objects, pools, and lanes. Activities capture units of work in a process. Events define the start and end of a process, and signal something that happens during the execution of it. Gateways model exclusive and inclusive decisions, merges, parallelism and synchronization, and repetition.

We studied the difference between process model and process instance. A process model depicts all the possible ways a given business process can be executed, while a process instance captures one specific process execution out of all possible ones. The progress, or state, of a process instance is represented by tokens, which we use to define the behavior of gateways.

We also learned how to use data objects to model the information and material flow between activities and events. A data object captures a physical or an electronic business object required to execute an activity or trigger an event, or that results from the execution of an activity or an event occurrence. Data objects can be stored in a data store like a database or file cabinet such that they can be persisted beyond the process instance where they are created. Further, we saw how pools and lanes can be used to model both human and non-human resources that perform process activities. Pools generally model resource classes while lanes are used to partition pools. The interaction between pools is captured by message flows. Message flows can be attached to the boundary of a pool, should the details of the interaction not be relevant.

Activities, events, gateways, business objects, and resources belong to the main modeling perspectives of a business process. The functional perspective captures the activities that are performed in a business process while the control-flow perspective combines these activities and related events in a given order. The data perspective covers the business objects manipulated in the process while the resource perspective covers the resources that perform the various activities.

Finally, we learned how to structure process models in hierarchical levels via sub-process activities. Sub-processes represent activities that can be broken down in a number of internal steps, as compared to tasks, which capture single units of work. An interesting aspect of sub-processes is that they can be collapsed to hide details. We also discussed how to maximize reuse by defining global sub-processes within a process model collection, and invoking them via call activities. A global sub-process is modeled once and shared by different process models in a repository.

In the next chapter, we will learn how to model complex business processes by delving into the various extensions of the core BPMN elements that we presented here.

3.8 Solutions to Exercises

Solution 3.1

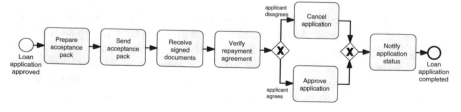

Solution 3.2

Solution 3.3

Solution 3.4

Solution 3.5   Activities "Retrieve product from warehouse" and "Manufacture product" require the purchase order as input, to identify which product to take from the warehouse or to build. Likewise, activities "Get shipment address" and "Emit invoice" require the confirmed purchase order as input, while activity "Receive payment" requires the payment as input, besides the confirmed purchase order. Anything else?

Solution 3.6

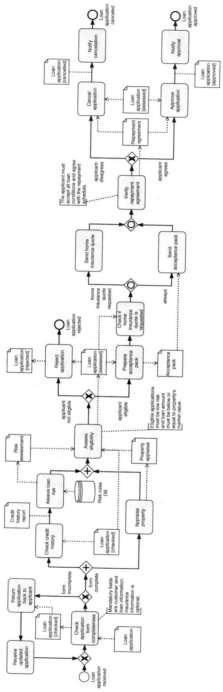

Solution 3.7 See the Loan Provider pool in the model of Solution 3.8.

Solution 3.8

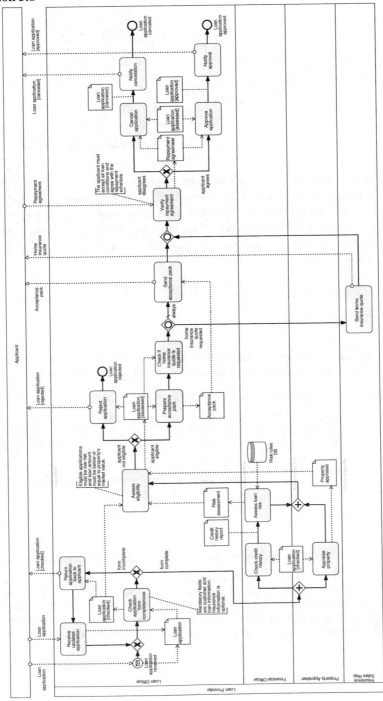

Solution 3.9

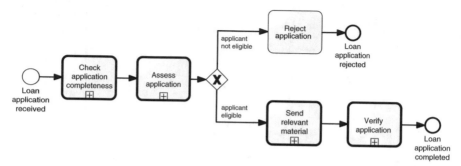

Solution 3.10 Possible sub-processes are "Request purchase", "Issue purchase order", "Receive goods", and "Handle invoice". Of these, "Handle invoice" could be shared with other procure-to-pay processes of the same company, e.g. with that described in Example 1.1 for BuildIT. The first three sub-processes are internal to this procure-to-pay process, because they are specific to the enterprise system that supports this process.

3.9 Further Exercises

Exercise 3.11 What types of splits and joins can we model in a process? Make an example for each of them using the security check at an airport as a scenario.

Exercise 3.12 Describe the following process model as text.

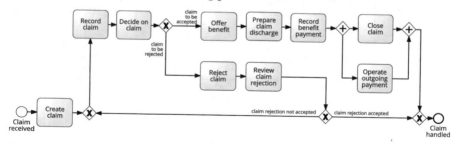

Exercise 3.13 Model the following business process for handling downpayments.

The process for handling downpayments starts when a request for payment has been approved. It involves entering the downpayment request into the system, the automatic subsequent payment, the emission of the direct invoice and the clearance of the vendor line items. The clearing of the vendor line items can result in a debit or credit balance. In case of debit balance, the arrears are processed, otherwise the remaining balance is paid.

Exercise 3.14 Model the following business process for assessing credit risks.

When a new credit request is received, the risk is assessed. If the risk is above a threshold, an advanced risk assessment needs to be carried out, otherwise a simple risk assessment will suffice. Once the assessment has been completed, the customer is notified with the result of the assessment while the disbursement is organized. For simplicity, assume that the result of an assessment is always positive.

Exercise 3.15 Model the following fragment of a business process for insurance claims.

After a claim is registered, it is examined by a claims officer who then writes a settlement recommendation. This recommendation is then checked by a senior claims officer who may mark the claim as "OK" or "Not OK". If the claim is marked as "Not OK", it is sent back to the claims officer and the recommendation is repeated. If the claim is "OK", the claim handling process proceeds.

Exercise 3.16 Model the control flow of the following business process for damage compensation.

If a tenant is evicted because of damages to the premises, a process needs to be started by the tribunal in order to hold a hearing to assess the amount of compensation the tenant owes to the owner of the premises. This process starts when a cashier of the tribunal receives a request for compensation from the owner. The cashier then retrieves the file for those particular premises and checks that the request is both acceptable for filing and compliant with the description of the premises on file. After these checks, the cashier needs to set a hearing date. Setting a hearing date incurs fees to the owner. It may be that the owner has already paid the fees with the request, in which case the cashier allocates a hearing date and the process completes. It may be that additional fees are required, but the owner has already paid also those fees. In this case the cashier generates a receipt for the additional fees and proceeds with allocating the hearing date. Finally, if the owner has not paid the required fees, the cashier produces a fees notice and waits for the owner to pay the fees before reassessing the document compliance.

Exercise 3.17 Extend the model of Exercise 3.16 by adding the business objects involved in this process.

Exercise 3.18 Extend the model of Exercise 3.17 by adding the involved resources. Is there any non-human resource?

Exercise 3.19 Model the following business process. Use gateways and data objects where needed.

In a court each morning the files that have yet to be processed are checked to make sure they are in order for the court hearing that day. If some files are missing a search is initiated, otherwise the files can be physically tracked to the intended location. Once all the files are ready, these are handed to the associate. In the meantime the judge's lawlist is distributed to the relevant people. Afterwards, the directions hearings are conducted.

Exercise 3.20 Model the following business process. Use pools and lanes where needed.

The motor claim handling process starts when a customer submits a claim with the relevant documentation. The notification department at the car insurer checks the documents upon completeness and registers the claim. Next, the Handling department picks up the claim and checks the insurance. Then, an assessment is performed. If the assessment is positive, a garage is phoned to authorize the repairs and the payment is scheduled (in this order). Otherwise, the claim is rejected. In any case (whether the outcome is positive or negative), a letter is sent to the customer and the process is considered to be complete.

Exercise 3.21 Model the following business process. Use pools and lanes where needed.

When a claim is received, a claims officer first checks if the claimant is insured. If not, the claimant is informed that the claim must be rejected by sending an automatic notification via an SAP system. Otherwise, a senior claims officer evaluates the severity of the claim. Based on the outcome (simple or complex claims), the relevant forms are sent to the claimant, again using the SAP system. Once the forms are returned, they are checked for completeness by the claims officer. If the forms provide all relevant details, the claim is registered in the claims management system, and the process ends. Otherwise, the claimant is informed to update the forms via the SAP system. Upon reception of the updated forms, they are checked again by the claims officer to see if the details have been provided.

Exercise 3.22 Create a BPMN model for the process described in Exercise 1.1 (page 5). Make sure to include business objects and annotations where appropriate.

Exercise 3.23

1. Model the prescription fulfillment process described in Exercise 1.6 (page 30). Use sub-processes where required, and nest them appropriately.
2. Is there any sub-process that can potentially be shared with other business processes of the same pharmacy, or of other pharmacies, e.g. as part of a consortium?

3.10   Further Readings

In this chapter we presented the basics of process modeling using BPMN as a language. Other mainstream languages that can be used to model business processes are UML Activity Diagrams (UML ADs), Event-driven Process Chains (EPCs), and Web Services Business Process Execution Language (WS-BPEL). UML ADs are another OMG standard [120]. They are mainly employed in software engineering where they can be used to describe software behavior and can be linked to other UML diagram types, e.g. class diagrams, to generate software code. UML ADs offer a subset of the modeling elements present in BPMN. For example, constructs like the OR-join are not supported. A good overview of this language and its application to business process modeling is provided in [44].

EPCs were initially developed for the design of the SAP R/3 reference process model [29]. They obtained a widespread adoption by various organizations when they became the core modeling language of the ARIS toolset [32, 156]. Later, they were used by other vendors for the design of SAP-independent reference models such as ITIL and SCOR. The EPC language includes modeling elements corresponding to BPMN activities, AND, XOR and OR gateways, untyped events, and data objects. The popularity of EPCs has dropped in the past decade, after the ARIS toolset adopted the BPMN standard as its main process modeling language.

WS-BPEL (BPEL for short) [8] is a language for specifying executable business processes that rely on Web service technology. Unlike BPMN, WS-BPEL does not provide a visual notation, but only an XML syntax. BPEL was relatively popular in the 2000s, however its popularity has dropped in recent times, and it has been largely replaced by BPMN.

Other process modeling languages originate from research efforts. Two of them are Workflow nets and Yet Another Workflow Language (YAWL). Workflow nets [176] are an extension of Petri nets to model business processes. Their syntax is purposefully simple and revolves around two elements: places and transitions. The former roughly correspond to BPMN events, while the latter to BPMN activities.

YAWL is a successor of Workflow nets. YAWL adds several constructs, including OR-joins, multi-instance activities, sub-processes, and cancelation regions. YAWL and its supporting environment are presented in detail in [67].

A comparison of the above languages in terms of their expressiveness along the control-flow, data, and resource perspectives can be found in the Workflow Patterns Initiative website [195]. Over time this initiative has collected a repository of workflow patterns, i.e. recurring process behavior as it has been observed from a thorough analysis of various process modeling languages and supporting tools. Various languages and tools have been compared based on their support for such patterns.

In this chapter we showed how sub-processes can be used to lessen the complexity of a process model by reducing the overall process model *size*. Size is a metric strongly related to the understandability of a process model. Intuitively, the smaller the size, the more understandable is the model. There are other metrics that can be measured from a process model to assess its understandability, for instance the *degree of structuredness*, the *diameter*, and the *coefficient of connectivity*. A comprehensive discussion on process model metrics is available in [108]. The advantages of modularizing process models into sub-processes and automatic techniques for process model modularization are covered in [137], while the correlation between number of flow objects and error probability in process models is studied in [111, 112].

Finally, we discussed the use of global process models to improve reuse within a process model collection. There exist techniques to automatically identify *clones* [39] or *approximate clones* [84] in a collection of process models, i.e. shared process model fragments that are identical or very similar to each other. These fragments offer opportunities for improving reuse as they can be factored out into separate sub-processes defined as global process models, for example, using the technique described in [42].

Chapter 4
Advanced Process Modeling

The sciences do not try to explain, they hardly even try to interpret, they mainly make models.
John von Neumann (1903–1957)

In this chapter we will delve more into how to model complex business processes with BPMN. The constructs presented here build on top of the knowledge acquired in Chapter 3. In particular, we will expand on activities, events, and gateways. We will extend activities to model more sophisticated forms of rework and repetition. We will also discuss more specific types of events, including message events, temporal events, and cancelation. These can be used to model race conditions together with a new type of gateway. Finally, we will also learn how to use events to handle business process exceptions.

4.1 More on Rework and Repetition

In the previous chapter, we described how to model rework and repetition via the XOR gateways. Expanded sub-processes offer an alternative way to model parts of a process that can be repeated. Let us consider again the process for addressing ministerial correspondence of Example 3.7. To make this model simpler, we can take the fragment identified by the XOR-join and the XOR-split (which includes the repetition block and the loopback branch) and replace it with a sub-process containing the activities in the repetition block. To identify that this sub-process may be repeated (if the response is not approved), we mark the sub-process activity with a loop symbol, as shown in Figure 4.1. We can use an annotation to specify the loop condition, e.g., "until response approved".

As for any sub-process, you may decide not to specify the content of a loop sub-process. However if you do specify the content, do not forget to put a decision activity as the last activity inside the sub-process, otherwise there is no way to determine when to repeat the sub-process.

© Springer-Verlag GmbH Germany, part of Springer Nature 2018
M. Dumas et al., *Fundamentals of Business Process Management*,
https://doi.org/10.1007/978-3-662-56509-4_4

Question Loop activity or cycle?

The loop activity is a shorthand notation for a structured cycle, i.e., a repetition block delimited by a single entry point to the cycle and a single exit point from the cycle, like in the example in Figure 4.1. Sometimes there might be more than one entry and exit point, or the entry or exit point might be inside the repetition block. Consider for example the model in Figure 4.2. Here, there is a cycle consisting of activities "Assess application", "Notify rejection", and "Receive customer feedback". This cycle has one entry point and two exit points, and therefore it is unstructured. A cycle with multiple exit points, like this one, cannot be rewritten as a cycle with only one exit point, unless additional conditions are used to specify the situations in which the cycle can be exited.

Exercise 4.1

1. Identify the entry and exit points that delimit the unstructured cycles in the process models shown in Exercise 3.12 (page 112) and in Solution 3.4 (page 109). What are the repetition blocks?
2. Model the business process of Solution 3.4 (page 109) using a loop activity.

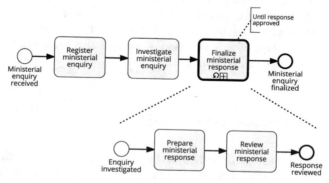

Fig. 4.1 The process model for addressing ministerial correspondence of Figure 3.13 simplified using a loop activity

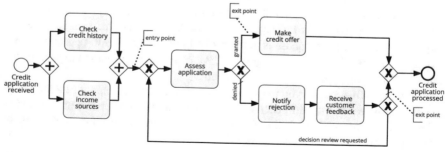

Fig. 4.2 An example of unstructured cycle

4.1.1 Parallel Repetition

The loop activity allows us to capture sequential repetition, meaning that instances of the loop activity are executed one after the other. Sometimes though, we may need to execute multiple instances of the same activity at the same time, like in the following example.

Example 4.1 In a procurement process, a quote is to be obtained from all preferred suppliers. After all quotes are received, they are evaluated and the best quote is selected. A corresponding purchase order is then placed.

Let us assume there are five preferred suppliers. We can use an AND-split to model five tasks in parallel, each to obtain a quote from one supplier, as shown in Figure 4.3. However, there are two issues with this solution. First, the larger the number of suppliers, the larger the resulting model will be, because we need one task per supplier. Second, we need to revise the model every time the number of suppliers changes. In fact, it is often the case in reality that an updated list of suppliers is kept in an organizational database which is queried before contacting the suppliers.

To avoid these problems, BPMN provides a construct called *multi-instance* activity. A multi-instance activity indicates an activity (a task or a sub-process) that is executed multiple times *concurrently*, i.e., potentially in parallel. This construct is useful when the same activity is executed for multiple entities or data items, as for example to request quotes from multiple suppliers (as in our example), to check the availability of each line item in an order separately, to send and gather questionnaires for multiple witnesses in the context of an insurance claim, etc.

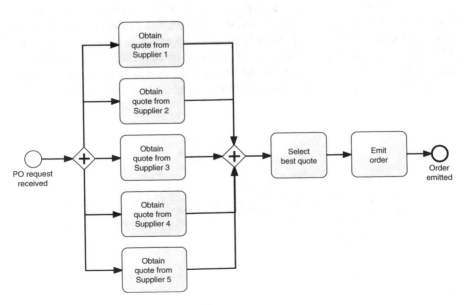

Fig. 4.3 Obtaining quotes from five suppliers

A multi-instance activity is depicted as an activity marked with three small vertical lines at the bottom. Figure 4.4 shows a revised version of the procurement process model in Figure 4.3. Not only is this model smaller, but it can also work with a dynamic list of suppliers, which may change on an instance-by-instance basis. To do so, we added a task to retrieve the list of suppliers and passed this list to a multi-instance task, which contacts the various suppliers. You may have noticed that in this example we have also marked the data object Suppliers list with the multi-instance symbol. This is used to indicate a *collection* of similar data objects, like a list of order items or a list of customers. When a collection is used as input to a multi-instance activity, the number of items in the collection determines the number of activity instances to be created. Alternatively, we can specify the number of instances to be created via an annotation on the multi-instance activity (e.g., "15 suppliers" or "as per suppliers database").

Let us come back to our example. Assume the list of suppliers has become quite large over time, say there are 20 suppliers in the database. As per our organizational policies, however, five quotes from five different suppliers are enough to make a decision. Thus, we do not want to wait for all 20 suppliers to attend to our request for a quote. To do so, we can annotate the multi-instance activity with the minimum number of instances that need to complete before passing control to the outgoing arc (e.g., "complete when 5 quotes obtained" as shown in Figure 4.4). When the multi-instance activity is triggered, 20 tokens are generated, each marking the progress of one of the 20 instances. Then, as soon as the first five instances complete, all the other instances are canceled (the respective tokens are destroyed) and one token is sent to the output arc to signal completion.   □

Let us take the order-to-cash example in Figure 3.18, and expand the content of the sub-process for acquiring raw materials. To make this model more realistic, we can use a multi-instance sub-process in place of the structure delimited by the two OR gateways, assuming that the list of suppliers to be contacted will be determined on the fly from a suppliers database (the updated model is shown in Figure 4.5). By the same principle, we replace the two pools "Supplier 1" and "Supplier 2" with a

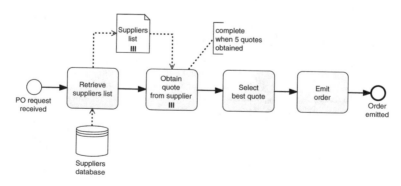

Fig. 4.4 Obtaining quotes from a number of suppliers determined on-the-fly

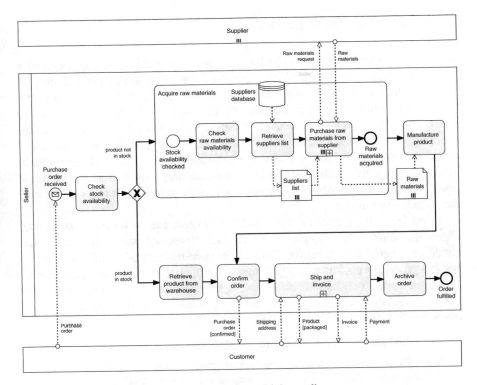

Fig. 4.5 Using a multi-instance pool to represent multiple suppliers

single pool called "Supplier", which we also mark with the multi-instance symbol—
a multi-instance pool represents a set of resource classes or resources having similar
characteristics.

From this figure we note that there are four message flows connected to the sub-
process "Ship and invoice" as a result of collapsing the content of this activity.
The order in which these messages are exchanged is determined by the activities
inside this sub-process that receive and send them. In other words, when it comes
to a collapsed sub-process activity, the message semantics for tasks described in
Section 3.4 is not enforced.

Exercise 4.2 Model the following process fragment.

> After a car accident, a statement is sought from two witnesses out of the five that were
> present in order to lodge the insurance claim. As soon as the first two statements are
> received, the claim can be lodged with the insurance company without waiting for the other
> statements.

4.1.2   Uncontrolled Repetition

Sometimes we may need to model that one or more activities can be repeated a number of times without a specific order until a condition is met. For example, let us assume that the customer of our order-to-cash process needs to inquire about the progress of its order. The customer may do so simply by sending an email to the seller. This may be done any time after the customer has submitted the purchase order and as often as the customer desires. Similarly, the customer may attempt to cancel the order or update the personal details before the order has been fulfilled. These activities are *uncontrolled* in the sense that they may be repeated multiple times with no specific order or not occur at all until a condition is met—in our case the order being fulfilled.

To model a set of uncontrolled activities, we can use an *ad hoc sub-process*. Figure 4.6 shows the example of the customer process, where the completion condition ("until order is fulfilled") has been specified via an annotation. The ad hoc sub-process is marked with a tilde symbol at the bottom of the sub-process box.

A partial order may be established among the activities of an ad hoc sub-process via the sequence flow. However, we cannot represent start and end events in an ad hoc sub-process.

Exercise 4.3 Model the following process snippet.

A typical army recruitment process starts by shortlisting all candidates' applications. Those shortlisted are then called to take the following tests: drug and alcohol, eye, color vision, hearing, blood, urine, weight, fingerprinting, and doctor examination. The color vision can only be done after the eye test, while the doctor examination can only be done after color vision, hearing, blood, urine, and weight have been tested. Moreover, it may be required for some candidates to repeat some of these tests multiple times in order to get a correct assessment, e.g., the blood test may need to be repeated if the candidate has taken too much sugar in the previous 24 h. The candidates who pass all tests are asked to take a mental exam and a physical exam, followed by an interview. Only those who pass all these exams and perform well in the interview can be recruited in the army.

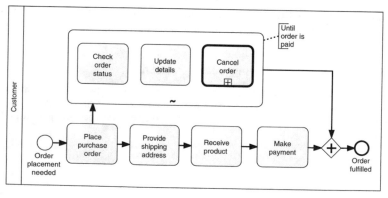

Fig. 4.6 Using an ad hoc sub-process to model uncontrolled repetition

4.2   Handling Events

We have learnt in Chapter 3 that events are used to model something that happens instantaneously in a process. We saw start events, which signal how process instances start (tokens are created), and end events, which signal when process instances complete (tokens are destroyed). When an event occurs during a process, e.g., an order confirmation is received after sending an order out to the customer and before proceeding with the shipment, the event is called *intermediate*. A token remains *trapped* in the incoming sequence flow of an intermediate event until the event occurs. Once the event occurs, the token traverses the event instantaneously, i.e., events cannot retain tokens. An intermediate event is represented as a circle with a double border.

4.2.1   Message Events

In the previous chapter, we showed that we can mark a start event with an empty envelope to specify that new process instances are triggered by the receipt of a message (see Figure 3.16). Besides the start message event, we can also mark an end event and an intermediate event with an envelope to capture the interaction between our process and another party. These types of events are collectively called *message events*. An end message event signals that a process concludes upon sending a message. An intermediate message event signals the receipt of a message or that a message has been sent during the execution of the process. Intermediate and end message events represent an alternative notation to those activities that are solely used to send or receive a message. Take for example activities "Return application to applicant" and "Receive updated application" in Figure 4.7a, which is an extract of the loan assessment model of Solution 3.8. It is more meaningful to replace the former activity with an intermediate send message event and the latter activity with an intermediate receive message event, as illustrated in Figure 4.7b, since these activities do not really represent units of work, but rather the mechanical sending or receiving of a message. An intermediate message event that receives a message is depicted as a start message event, but with a double border. If the intermediate event signals a message being sent, the envelope is dark.

Further, if the send activity is immediately followed by an untyped end event, we can replace this with an end message event, since again, this activity is merely used to send a message after which the process concludes. An end message event is depicted as an end event marked with a darkened envelope. Beware that a start message event is not an alternative notation for an untyped start event followed by a receive activity: these two constructs are not interchangeable. In the former case, process instances start upon the receipt of a specific message; in the latter case, process instances may start at any time, after which the first activity requires a message to be received.

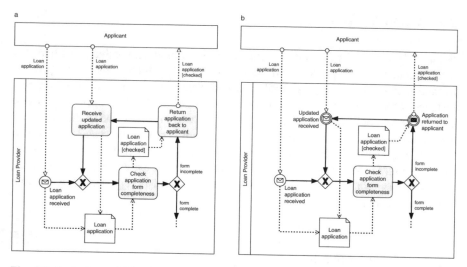

Fig. 4.7 Replacing activities that only send or receive messages (**a**) with message events (**b**)

Question Typed or untyped event?

We suggest specifying the type of an event whenever this is known, since it helps the reader to better understand the process model.

Exercise 4.4 Is there any other activity in the loan assessment model of Solution 3.8 (page 111) that can be replaced by a message event?

In BPMN, events come in two flavors based on the filling of their marker. A marker with no fill, like that on the start message event, denotes a *catching event*, i.e., an event that catches a trigger, typically originating from outside the process. A marker with a dark fill like that on the end message event denotes a *throwing event*, i.e., an event that throws a trigger from within the process. An intermediate message event can be used in both as a catching event (the message is received from another pool) or as a throwing event (the message is sent to another pool).

4.2.2 Temporal Events

Besides the message event, there are other triggers that can be specified for a start event. One of them is the *timer event*. This event type indicates that process instances start upon the occurrence of a specific temporal event, e.g., every Friday morning, every working day of the month, every morning at 7 a.m.

A timer event may also be used as an intermediate event to capture that a temporal interval needs to elapse before the process instance can proceed. To indicate a timer event, we mark the event symbol with a watch inside the circle. Timer events are catching events only since a timer is a trigger outside the control of the process. In other words, the process does not generate the timer, but rather reacts to this.

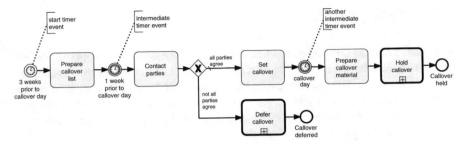

Fig. 4.8 Using timer events to drive the various activities of a business process

Example 4.2 Let us consider the following process at a small claims tribunal.

In a small claims tribunal, callovers occur once a month to set down the matter for the upcoming trials. The process for setting up a callover starts three weeks prior to the callover day with the preparation of the callover list containing information such as contact details of the involved parties and estimated hearing date. One week prior to the callover, the involved parties are contacted to determine if they are all ready to go to trial. If this is the case, the callover is set, otherwise it is deferred to the next available slot. Finally on the callover day, the callover material is prepared and the callover is held.

This process is driven by three temporal events: it starts three weeks prior to the callover date, continues one week prior to the callover date, and concludes on the day of the callover. To model these temporal events we need one start and two intermediate timer events, as shown in Figure 4.8. Let us see how this process works from a token semantics point of view. A token capturing a new instance is generated every time it is three weeks prior to the callover date (we assume this date has been scheduled by another process). Once the first activity "Prepare callover list" has been completed, the token is sent through the incoming arc of the following intermediate timer event, namely "1 week prior to callover day". The event thus becomes *enabled*. The token remains trapped in the incoming arc of this event until the temporal event itself occurs, i.e., only when it is one week prior to the callover day. Once this is the case, the token instantaneously traverses the event symbol and moves to the outgoing arc. This is why events are said to be instantaneous: they cannot retain tokens as opposed to activities, which retain tokens for the duration of their execution (recall that activities consume time). ☐

Exercise 4.5 Model the billing process of an Internet Service Provider (ISP).

The ISP sends an invoice by email to the customer on the first working day of each month (Day 1). On Day 7, the customer has the full outstanding amount automatically debited from its bank account. If an automatic transaction fails for any reason, the customer is notified on Day 8. On Day 9, the transaction that failed on Day 7 is re-attempted. If it fails again, on Day 10 a late fee is charged to the customer's bank account. At this stage, the automatic payment is no longer attempted. On Day 14, the Internet service is suspended until payment is received. If the payment is still outstanding on Day 30, the account is closed and a disconnection fee is applied. A debt-recovery procedure is then started.

4.2.3   Racing Events

A typical scenario encountered when modeling processes with events is the one where two external events *race* against one another. The first of the two events that occurs determines the continuation of the process. For example, after an insurance quote has been sent to a client, the client may reply either with an acceptance message, in which case an insurance contract will be made, or with a rejection, in which case the quote will be discarded.

This race between external events is captured by means of the *event-based exclusive (XOR)* split. An event-based exclusive split is represented by a gateway marked with an empty pentagon enclosed in a double-line circle. Figure 4.9 features an event-based exclusive split. When the execution of the process arrives at this point (in other words, when a token arrives at this gateway), the execution stops until either the message event or the timer event occurs. Whichever event occurs first will determine which way the execution will proceed. If the timer event occurs first, a shipment status inquiry will be initiated and the execution flow will come back to the event-based exclusive gateway. If the message signaling the freight delivery is received first, the execution flow will proceed along the sequence flow that leads to the AND-join.

The difference between the XOR-split, which we saw in Chapter 3, and the event-based XOR-split is that the former models an internal choice that is determined by the outcome of a decision activity, whereas the latter models a choice that is determined by the environment of the process. For this reason, the XOR-split of Chapter 3 is called *data-based XOR-split*, because the branch to be taken is determined based on the evaluation of two or more conditions on data produced by a decision activity. An internal choice is determined by the outcome of a decision activity. Thus, the event-based XOR-split can only be followed by intermediate catching events like a timer or a message event, or by receiving activities. Since the choice is delayed until an event happens, the event-based split is also known as

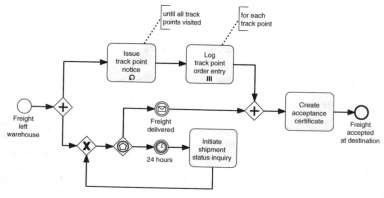

Fig. 4.9   A race condition between an incoming message and a timer

deferred choice. There is no event-based XOR-join, so the branches emanating from an event-based split are merged with a normal XOR-join.

Exercise 4.6 Model the following process.

A restaurant chain submits a purchase order (PO) to replenish its warehouses every Thursday. The restaurant chain's procurement system assumes the receipt of either a "PO Response" or an error message. However, it may also happen that no response is received at all due to system errors or due to delays in handling the PO on the supplier's side. If no response is received by Friday afternoon or if an error message is received, a purchasing officer at the restaurant chain's headquarters should be notified. Otherwise, the PO Response is processed normally.

The event-based XOR-split can be used as the counterpart of an internal decision on a collaborating party. For example, consider Figure 4.10. The choice made from within the client pool to send either an acceptance message or a rejection message to an insurer has to be matched by an event-driven decision on the insurer pool to *react* to the choice made by the client.

Event-based gateways can be used to avoid behavioral anomalies in the communication between pools. Take for example the collaboration diagram of the auctioning service and the seller in Figure 4.11. This collaboration may deadlock if the seller is already registered, because this party will wait for the account creation request message that can never arrive. To fix this issue, we need to allow the seller to receive the creation confirmation message straightaway in case the seller is already registered, as shown in Figure 4.12.

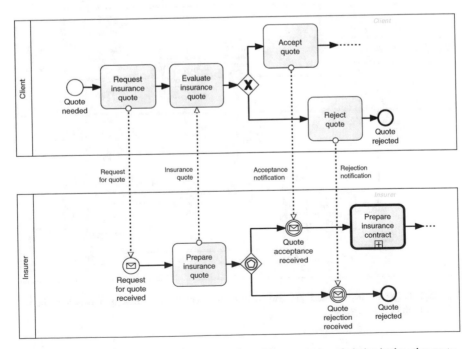

Fig. 4.10 Matching an internal choice in one party with an event-based choice in the other party

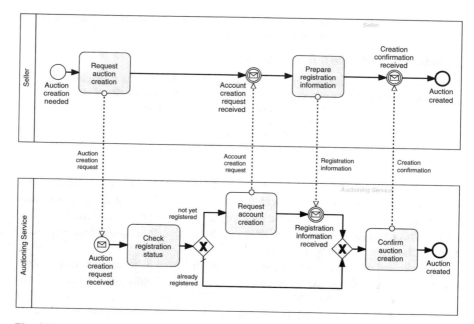

Fig. 4.11 An example of collaboration that can deadlock if the decision is made for "already registered"

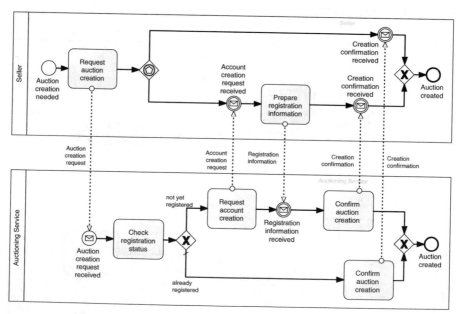

Fig. 4.12 Using an event-based gateway to fix the problem of a potential deadlock in the collaboration of Figure 4.11

When connecting pools with each other via message flows, make sure you check the order of these connections so as to avoid deadlocks. Recall, in particular, that an internal decision of one party needs to be matched by an event-based decision of the other party and that an activity with an outgoing message flow will send that message upon activity completion, whereas an activity with an incoming message flow will wait for that message to start.

4.3 Handling Exceptions

Exceptions are events that deviate a process from its normal course, i.e., from what is commonly known as the "sunny-day" scenario. "Rainy-day" scenarios happen frequently in reality and as such they should be modeled when the objective is to identify all possible causes of problems in a given process. Exceptions include *business faults* such as an out-of-stock or discontinued product and *technology faults* like a database crash, a network outage or a program logic violation. They cause the interruption or abortion of the running process. For example, in case of an out-of-stock product, an order-to-cash process may need to be interrupted to order the product from a supplier, or aborted altogether if the product cannot be supplied within a given timeframe.

Exercise 4.7 Fix the collaboration diagram in Figure 4.13.

Acknowledgment This exercise is partly inspired by [92].

4.3.1 Process Abortion

The simplest way of handling an exception is to abort the running process and signal an abnormal process termination. This can be done by using an *end terminate event* as shown in Figure 4.14. An end terminate event (depicted as an end event marked with a full circle inside) causes the immediate cessation of the process instance at its current level and for any sub-process.

In the example of Figure 4.14—a variant of the home loan that we already saw in Figure 3.19—a home loan is rejected and the process is aborted if the applicant has high debts or high liability. The terminate event destroys all tokens in the process model and in any sub-process. In our example, this is needed to avoid the process to deadlock at the AND-join, since a token may remain trapped before the AND-join if there is high liability and low debts or low liability and high debts.

Observe that if a terminate event is triggered from within a sub-process, it will not cause the abortion of the parent process but only that of the sub-process, i.e., the terminate event is only propagated downwards in a process hierarchy.

Exercise 4.8 Revise the examples presented so far in this chapter by using the terminate event appropriately.

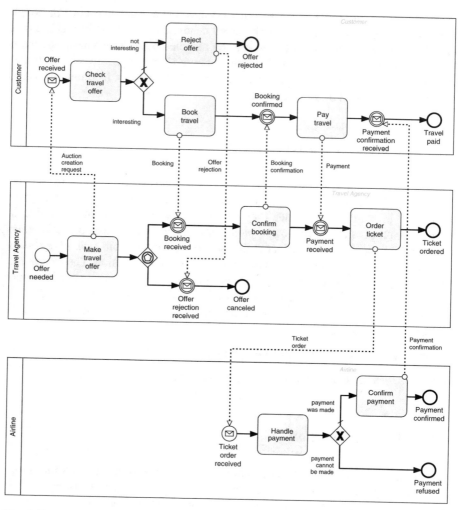

Fig. 4.13 A collaboration diagram between a customer, a travel agency, and an airline

4.3.2 Internal Exceptions

Instead of aborting the whole process, we can handle an exception by interrupting
the specific activity that has caused the exception. Next, we can start a recovery
procedure to bring the process back to a consistent state and continue its execution,
and if this is not possible, only then, abort the process altogether. BPMN provides
the *error event* to capture these types of scenarios. An end error event is used to
interrupt the enclosing sub-process and throw an exception. This exception is then
caught by an intermediate catching error event which is attached to the boundary of
the same sub-process. In turn, this *boundary event* triggers the recovery procedure
through an outgoing branch, which is called *exception flow*.

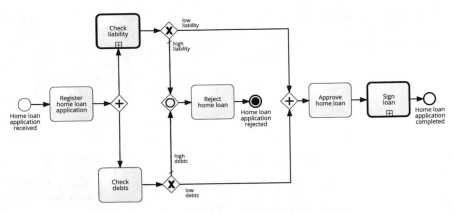

Fig. 4.14 Using a terminate event to signal abnormal process termination

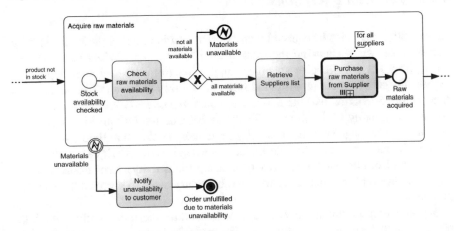

Fig. 4.15 Error events model internal exceptions

The error event is depicted as an event with a lightning marker. Following the BPMN conventions for throwing and catching events, the lightning is empty for the catching intermediate event and full for the end throwing event.

An example of error events is shown in Figure 4.15 in the context of our order-to-cash process. If there is an out-of-stock exception, the acquisition of raw materials is interrupted and a recovery procedure is triggered, which in this case simply consists of a task to notify the customer before aborting the process. In terms of token semantics, upon throwing an end error event, all tokens are removed from the enclosing sub-process (causing its interruption) and one token is sent via the exception flow emanating from the boundary error event. There is no restriction on the modeling elements we can put in the exception flow to model the recovery procedure. Typically, we would complete the exception flow with an end terminate event to abort the process, or wire this flow back to the normal sequence flow if the exception has been properly handled.

Fig. 4.16 Boundary events
catch external events that can
occur during an activity

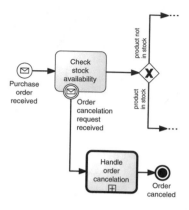

4.3.3 External Exceptions

An exception may also be caused by an external event occurring during an activity. For example, while checking the stock availability for the product in a purchase order, the seller may receive an order cancelation from the customer. Upon this request, the seller should interrupt the stock availability check and handle the order cancelation. Scenarios like the above are called *unsolicited exceptions* since they originate externally to the process. They can be captured by attaching a catching intermediate message event to an activity's boundary as shown in Figure 4.16. From a token semantics, when the intermediate message event is triggered, the token is removed from the enclosing activity, causing the activity interruption, and sent via the exception flow emanating from the boundary event to perform the recovery procedure.

Before using a boundary event we need to identify the *scope* within which the process should be receptive of this event. For example, in the order-to-cash example, order cancelation requests can only be handled during the execution of task "Check stock availability". Thus, the scope for being receptive to this event is made up by this single task. Sometimes the scope should include multiple activities. In these cases, we can encapsulate the interested activities into a sub-process and attach the event to the boundary of the sub-process.

Exercise 4.9 Model the following routine for accessing an Internet bank service.

The routine for logging into an Internet bank account starts once the credentials entered from the user have been retrieved. First, the username is validated. If the username is not valid, the routine is interrupted and the invalid username is logged. If the username is valid, the number of password trials is set to zero. Then, the password is validated. If this is not valid, the counter for the number of trials is incremented and if lower than three, the user is asked to enter the password again, this time together with a CAPTCHA test to increase the security level. If the number of failed attempts reaches three times, the routine is interrupted and the account is frozen. Moreover, the username and password validation may be interrupted should the validation server not be available. Similarly, the server to test the CAPTCHA may not be available at the time of log in. In these cases, the procedure is interrupted after notifying the user to try again later. At any time during the log in routine, the customer may close the web page, resulting in the interruption of the routine.

4.3.4 Activity Timeouts

Another type of exception is the interruption of an activity which is taking too long to complete. To model that an activity must be completed within a given timeframe (e.g., an approval must be completed within 24 h), we can attach an intermediate timer event to the boundary of the activity: the timer is activated when the enclosing activity starts. If it fires before the activity completes, it provokes the interruption of the activity. In other words, a timer event works as a timeout when attached to an activity boundary.

Exercise 4.10 Model the following process fragment.

> Once a wholesale order has been confirmed, the supplier transmits this order to the carrier for the preparation of the transportation quote. In order to prepare the quote, the carrier needs to compute the route plan (including all track points that need to be traversed during the travel) and estimate the trailer usage (e.g., whether it is a full track load, half track load or a single package). By contract, wholesale orders have to be dispatched within 4 days from the receipt of the order. This implies that transportation quotes have to be prepared within 48 h from the receipt of the order to remain within the terms of the contract.

4.3.5 Non-Interrupting Events and Complex Exceptions

There are situations where an external event occurring during an activity should just trigger a procedure without interrupting the activity itself. For example, in the order-to-cash process, the customer may send a request to update its details during the stock availability check. The details should be updated in the customer database without interrupting the stock check. To denote that the boundary event is *non-interrupting*, we use a dashed double border as shown in Figure 4.17.

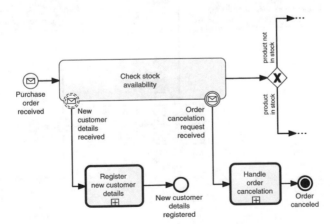

Fig. 4.17 Non-interrupting boundary events catch external events that occur during an activity and trigger a parallel procedure without interrupting the enclosing activity

Exercise 4.11 Extend the process for assessing loan applications from Solution 3.8 (page 111) as follows.

> An applicant who has decided not to combine the loan with a home insurance plan may change its mind any time before the eligibility assessment has been completed. If a request for adding an insurance plan is received during this period, the loan provider will simply update the loan application with this request.

Non-interrupting events can be used to model more complex exception handling scenarios. Consider again the example in Figure 4.15 and assume that the customer sends a request to cancel the order during the acquisition of raw materials. We catch this request with a non-interrupting boundary message event, and first determine the penalty that the customer will need to incur based on the raw materials that have already been ordered. We forward this information to the customer who then may decide within 48 h to either stop the cancelation, in which case nothing is done, or go on with it (see Figure 4.18). In the latter case, we throw an end *signal event*. This event, depicted with a triangle marker, broadcasts a signal defined by the event label. This signal can be caught by all catching signal events bearing the

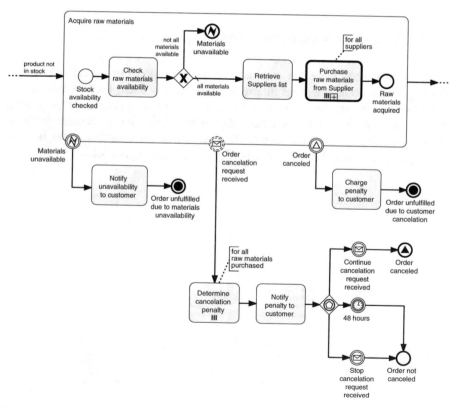

Fig. 4.18 Non-interrupting events can be used in combination with signal events to model complex exception handling scenarios

same label. In our case, we throw an "Order canceled" signal and catch this with a matching intermediate signal event on the boundary of the sub-process for acquiring raw materials. This event causes the enclosing sub-process to be interrupted and then triggers a recovery procedure to charge the customer, after which the process is aborted. We observe that in this scenario the activity interruption is triggered from within the process, but outside the activity itself.

Observe that the signal event is different than the message event, since it has a source but no specific target, whilst a message has both a specific source and a specific target. Like messages, signals may also originate from a process modeled in a separate diagram.

4.3.6   Event Sub-processes

An alternative notation to boundary events is the *event sub-process*. An event sub-process is started by the event, which would otherwise be attached to the boundary of an activity, and encloses the procedure that would be triggered by the boundary event. An important difference with boundary events is that event sub-processes do not need to refer to a specific activity, but can model events that occur during the execution of the whole process. For example, any time during the order-to-cash process the customer may send an inquiry about the order status. To handle this request, which is not specific to a particular activity of this process, we can use an event sub-process as shown in Figure 4.19.

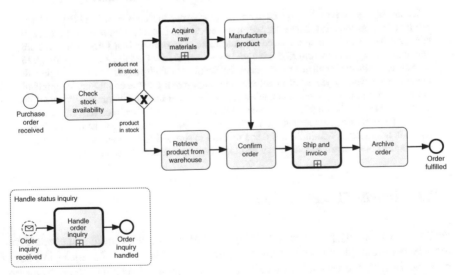

Fig. 4.19 Event sub-processes can be used in place of boundary events and to catch events thrown from outside the scope of a particular sub-process

The event sub-process is depicted within a dotted rectangle with rounded corners, which is placed into an expanded sub-process or into the top-level process. Similarly to boundary events, an event sub-process may or may not interrupt the enclosing process depending on whether its start event is interrupting or not. If its start event is non-interrupting, this is depicted with a dashed (single) border.

All syntactical rules for a sub-process apply to the event sub-process, except for boundary events, which cannot be defined on event sub-processes. For example, the event sub-process can also be represented as a collapsed sub-process. In this case, the start event is depicted on the top-left corner of the collapsed event sub-process rectangle to indicate how this event sub-process is triggered.

Question Event sub-processes or boundary events?

Event sub-processes are self-contained, meaning that they must conclude with an end event. This has the disadvantage that the procedure captured inside an event sub-process cannot be wired back to the rest of the sequence flow. The advantage is that an event sub-process can also be defined as a global process model and thus be reused in other process models of the same organization. Another advantage is that event sub-processes can be defined at the level of an entire process whereas boundary events must refer to a specific activity. Thus, we suggest using event sub-processes when the event that needs to be handled may occur anytime during the process or when we need to capture a reusable procedure. For all other cases, boundary events are more appropriate since the procedure triggered by these events can be wired back to the rest of the flow.

Exercise 4.12 Model the following business process for reimbursing expenses.

> After an expense report is received from an employee, the employee is notified of the receipt of the report. Next, a new account must be created if the employee does not already have one. The report is then reviewed for automatic approval. Amounts under € 1,000 are automatically approved while amounts equal to or over € 1,000 require manual approval. In case of rejection, the employee must receive a rejection notice by email. In case of approval, the reimbursement is deposited directly to the employee's bank account and an approval notice is sent to the employee via email, with the details of the money transfer. At any time during the review, the employee can send a request for amount rectification. In that case the rectification is registered and the report needs to be reviewed again. Moreover, if the report is not handled within 30 days, the process is stopped and the employee receives a cancelation notice email so that he can resubmit the expense report from scratch.

4.3.7 Activity Compensation

As part of a recovery procedure, we may need to *undo* one or more steps that have already been completed, due to an exception that occurred in the enclosing sub-process. In fact, the results of these steps, and possibly their side effects, may no longer be desired and for this reason they should be reversed. This operation is called *compensation* and tries to restore the process to a business state close to the one before starting the sub-process that was interrupted.

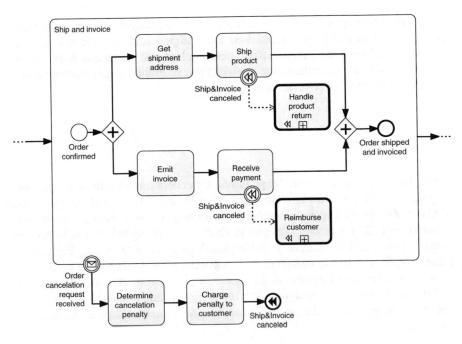

Fig. 4.20 Compensating for the shipment and for the payment

Let us delve into the sub-process for shipment and invoice handling of the order-to-cash example and assume that also this activity can be interrupted upon the receipt of an order cancelation request (see Figure 4.20). After communicating the cancelation penalty to the customer, we need to revert the effects of the shipment and of the payment. Specifically, if the shipment has already been made, we need to handle the product return, whereas if the payment has already been made, we need to reimburse the customer. These compensations can be modeled via a *compensation handler*. A compensation handler is made up of a throwing *compensate event* (an event marked with a rewind symbol), a catching intermediate compensate event, and a compensation activity. The throwing compensate event is used inside the recovery procedure of an exception to start the compensation and can be an intermediate or an end event (in the latter case, the recovery procedure concludes with the compensation). The catching intermediate compensation event is attached to those activities that need to be compensated—in our example "Ship product" and "Receive payment". These boundary events catch the compensation request and trigger a *compensation activity* specific to the activity to be compensated. For example the compensation activity for "Receive payment" is "Reimburse customer". The boundary event is connected to the compensation activity via a dotted arrow with an open arrowhead, called *compensation association* (whose notation is the same as that of the data association). This activity is marked with the compensate symbol to indicate its purpose. It must not have any outgoing flow. In case the compensation procedure is complex, this activity can be a sub-process.

Compensation is only effective if the attached activity has completed. Once all activities that could be compensated are compensated, the process resumes from after the throwing compensation event, unless this is an end event. If the compensation is for the entire process, we can use an event sub-process with a start compensate event in place of the boundary event.

4.3.8   Summary

In this section we saw various ways to handle exceptions in a business process, ranging from simple process abortion to complex error event and compensation handling. Before adding exceptions it is important to understand the sunny-day scenario well. So we recommend you to start by modeling the simple sunny-day scenario first. Then, think of all possible situations that can go wrong. For each of these exceptions, identify what type of exception handling mechanism needs to be used. First, determine the cause of the exception: internal or external. Next, decide if aborting the process is enough or if a recovery procedure needs to be triggered. Finally, evaluate whether the interrupted activity needs to be compensated as part of the recovery procedure.

Exercise 4.13 Modify the model that you created in Exercise 4.12 as follows.

> If the report is not handled within 30 days, the process is stopped, the employee receives a cancelation notice email, and must resubmit the expense report. However, if the reimbursement for the employee's expenses had already been made, a money recall needs to be made to get the money back from the employee before sending the cancelation notice email.

4.4   Processes and Business Rules

A business rule implements an organizational policy or practice. For example, in an online shop, platinum customers have a 20% discount for each purchase above € 250. Business rules can appear in different forms in a process model. We have seen them modeled in a decision activity and in the condition of a flow coming out of an (X)OR-split (see Exercise 3.6 on page 96 for some examples). A third option is to use a dedicated BPMN event called *conditional event*. A conditional event causes the activation of its outgoing flow when the respective business rule is fulfilled. Conditional events, identified by a lined page marker, can be used as start or intermediate catching events, including after an event-based gateway, or they can be attached to an activity boundary. An example of conditional event is shown in Figure 4.21.

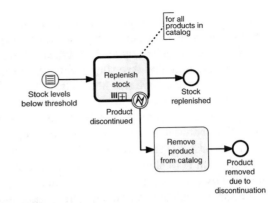

Fig. 4.21 A replenishment order is triggered every time the stock levels drop below a threshold

The difference between an intermediate conditional event and a condition on a flow is that the latter is only tested once, and if it is not satisfied the corresponding flow is not taken (another flow or the default flow will be taken instead). The conditional event, on the other hand, is tested until the associated rule is satisfied. In other words, the token remains trapped before the event until the rule is satisfied.

In the example of Figure 4.21, observe the use of the error event on the boundary of a multi-instance activity. This event only interrupts the activity instance that refers to the particular product being discontinued, i.e., the instance from which the error event is thrown. All other interrupting boundary events, i.e., message, timer, signal and conditional, interrupt all instances of a multi-instance activity.

Chapter 10 will illustrate how business rules can be implemented using decision tables specified using the Decision Model and Notation (DMN) language.

Exercise 4.14 Model the following business process snippet.

In a stock exchange, stock price variations are continuously monitored during the day. A day starts when the opening bell rings and concludes when the closing bell rings. Between the two bells, every time the stock price changes by more than 10%, the entity of the change is first determined. Next, if the change is high, a "high stock price" alert is sent, otherwise a "low stock price" alert is sent.

4.5 Recap

This chapter provided us with the means to model complex business processes. First, we expanded on the topic of rework and repetition. We illustrated how structured loops can be modeled using a loop activity. Furthermore, we presented the multi-instance activity as a way to model an activity that needs to be executed multiple times without knowing the number of occurrences beforehand. We also saw how the concept of multi-instantiation can be related to data collections and extended to pools, and discussed ad hoc sub-processes for capturing unstructured repetition.

Next, we expanded on various types of events. We explained the difference between catching and throwing events and distinguished between start, end, and intermediate events. We saw how message exchange between pools can be framed by message events and how timer events can be used to model temporal triggers to the process or delays during the process. We then showed how to capture racing conditions between external events via the event-based XOR-split.

Afterwards, we showed how to handle exceptions. The simplest way to react to an exception is to abort the process via a terminate end event. Exceptions can be handled by using a catching intermediate event on the boundary of an activity. If the event is caught during the activity's execution, the activity is interrupted and a recovery procedure may be launched. Another type of exception is the activity timeout. This occurs when an activity does not complete within a given timeframe. A boundary event can also be non-interrupting, to model procedures that have to be launched in parallel to an activity's execution. Related to exception handling is the notion of activity compensation. Compensation is required to revert the effects of an activity that has been completed, if these effects are no longer desired due to an exception that has occurred.

We also saw how business rules can be defined in process models via conditional events. A conditional event allows a process instance to start or progress only when the corresponding business rule evaluates to true.

4.6   Solutions to Exercises

Solution 4.1

1. In Exercise 3.12 the repetition block goes from activity "Record claim" to activity "Review claim rejection". The entry point to the cycle is the arc from activity "Create claim" to the subsequent XOR-join. The exit points are the arcs "claim to be accepted" and "claim rejection accepted", the former emanating from within the repetition block.
2. In Solution 3.4 the repetition block is made up of the activities "Check application form completeness", "Return application back to applicant", and "Receive updated application". The entry point to the cycle is the outgoing arc of the XOR-join, while the exit point is the arc "form complete" which emanates from

within the repetition block. To model this cycle with a loop activity, we need to repeat activity "Check application form completeness" outside the loop activity, as shown below.

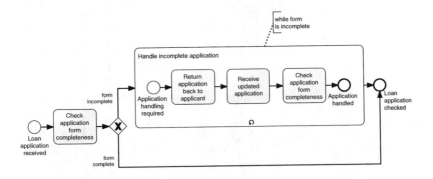

In this case using a loop activity is still advantageous, since we reduce the size of the original model if we collapse the sub-process.

Solution 4.2

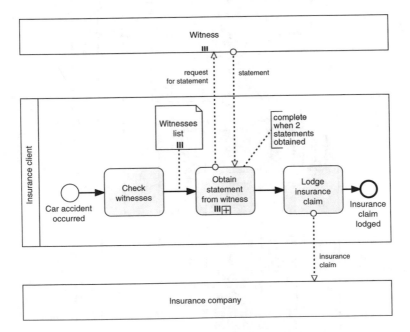

Solution 4.3

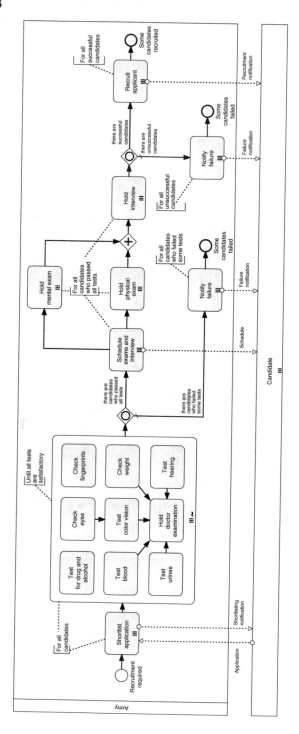

Solution 4.4 The activity "Send acceptance pack" can be replaced by an intermediate send message event; activities "Notify cancelation" and "Notify approval" can
each be replaced by an end message event, thus removing the last XOR-join and the
untyped end event altogether. Note that the activity "Send home insurance quote"
cannot be replaced by a message event since it subsumes the preparation of the
quote. In fact, a more appropriate label for this activity would be "Prepare home
insurance quote". Similarly, we cannot get rid of activity "Reject application" as
this activity changes the status of the application before sending the latter out.

Solution 4.5

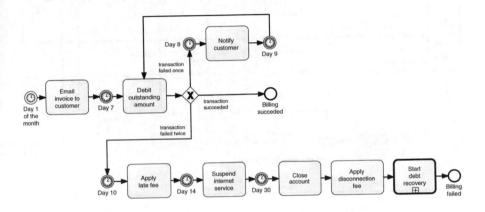

Solution 4.6

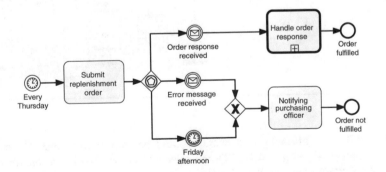

Solution 4.7

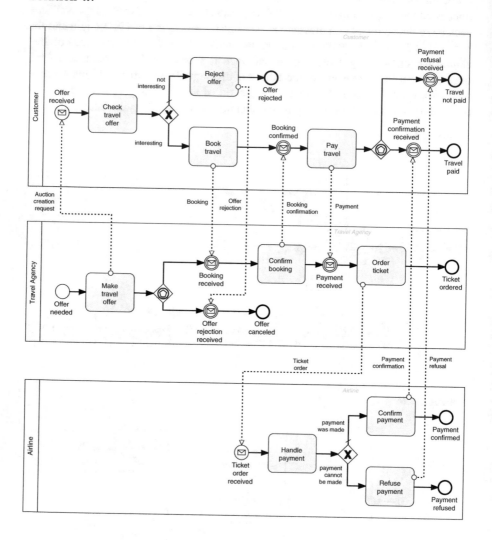

Solution 4.8 The following end events should be terminate events. Figure 4.8: "callover deferred"; Figure 4.10: "Quote rejected" in the client and insurer pools; Figure 4.14: "Offer rejected" in the customer pool, "Offer canceled" in the travel agency pool, and "Payment refused" in the airline pool.

Solution 4.9

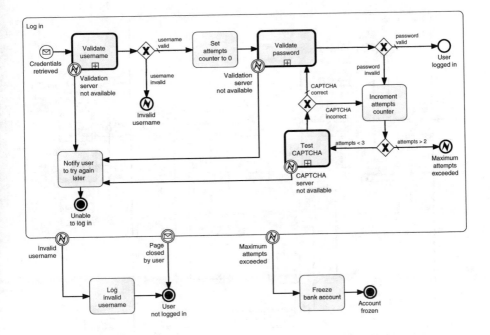

Solution 4.10

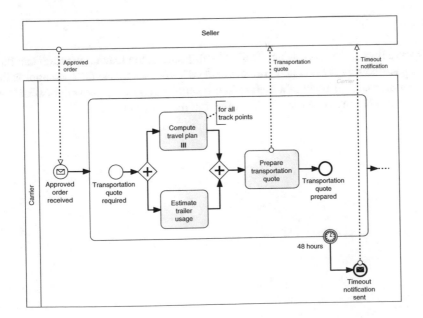

Solution 4.11

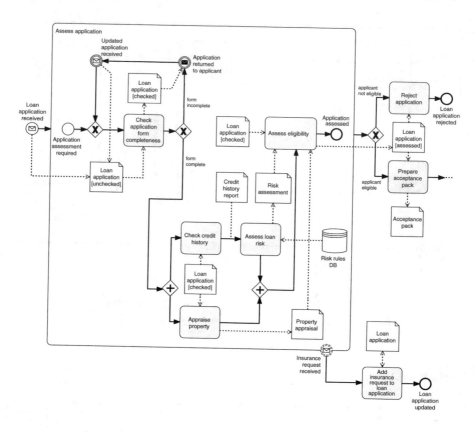

Observe that in the "Assess application" sub-process, the loan application can have two possible states: "checked" or "unchecked". In order to use the loan application in any such state as input of activity "Add insurance request to loan application", we do not specify any state for this data object in the above model.

Solution 4.12

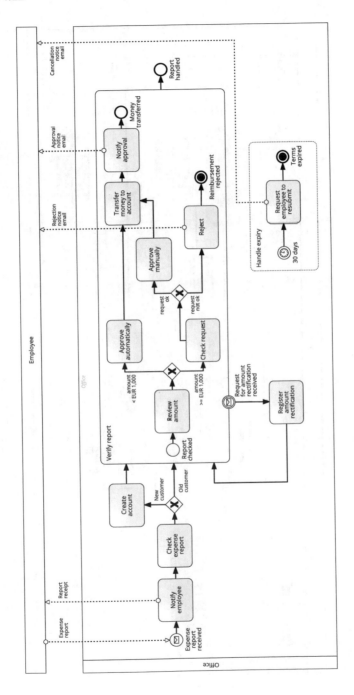

Solution 4.13

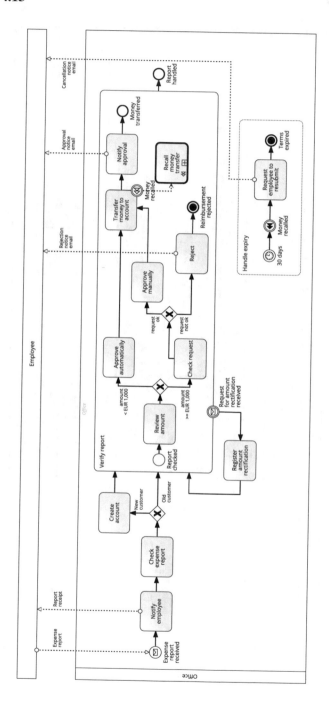

Solution 4.14

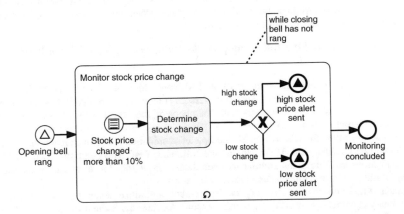

Here, we did not use a boundary event to stop the sub-process for monitoring stock price changes since this way, the sub-process would only stop because of an exception. Rather, we used the loop condition to allow the sub-process to complete normally, i.e., without being interrupted.

4.7   Further Exercises

Exercise 4.15   Model the business process described in Exercise 3.15 (page 113) using a loop activity.

Exercise 4.16   Answer the following questions.

1. What is the limitation of using a loop activity to model repetition instead of using unstructured cycles?
2. What is the requirement for a sub-process to be used as a loop activity?
3. Model the procure-to-pay process described in Example 1.1 (page 3).

Hint. Use the model in Figure 1.6 (page 19) as a starting point for item (3).

Exercise 4.17   Model the following business process.

Mail from the party is collected on a daily basis by the mail processing unit. Within this unit, the mail clerk sorts the unopened mail into the various business areas. The mail is then distributed. When the mail is received by the registry, it is opened and sorted into groups for distribution, and thus registered in a mail register. Afterwards, the assistant registry manager within the registry performs a quality check. If the mail is not compliant, a list of requisitions explaining the reasons for rejection is compiled and sent back to the party. Otherwise, the matter details are captured and provided to the cashier, who takes the applicable fees attached to the mail. At this point, the assistant registry manager puts the receipt and copied documents into an envelope and posts it to the party. Meantime, the cashier captures the party details and prints the physical court file.

Exercise 4.18 Model the following process for selecting Nobel Prize laureates for chemistry.

September: nomination forms are sent out. The Nobel committee sends out confidential forms to around 3,000 people—selected professors at universities around the world, Nobel laureates in physics and chemistry, and members of the Royal Swedish Academy of Sciences, among others.

February: deadline for submission. The completed nomination forms must reach the Nobel Committee no later than 31 January of the following year. The committee screens the nominations and selects the preliminary candidates. About 250–350 names are nominated as several nominators often submit the same name.

March–May: consultation with experts. The Nobel committee sends the list of the preliminary candidates to specially appointed experts for their assessment of the work of the candidates.

June–August: writing of the report. The Nobel committee puts together the report with recommendations to be submitted to the Academy. The report is signed by all members of the committee.

September: committee submits recommendations. The Nobel committee submits its report with recommendations on the final candidates to the members of the Academy. The report is discussed at two meetings of the chemistry section of the Academy.

October: Nobel laureates are chosen. In early October, the Academy selects the Nobel laureates in chemistry through a majority vote. The decision is final and without appeal. The names of the Nobel laureates are then announced.

December: Nobel laureates receive their prize. The Nobel Prize award ceremony takes place on 10 December in Stockholm, where the Nobel laureates receive their Nobel Prize, which consists of a Nobel medal, a diploma, and a document confirming the prize amount.

Acknowledgment This exercise is taken from "Nomination and Selection of Chemistry Laureates", Nobelprize.org. 9 Oct 2017 (http://www.nobelprize.org/nobel_prizes/chemistry/nomination).

Exercise 4.19

1. What is the difference between throwing and catching events?
2. What is the meaning of an event attached to an activity's boundary and what events can be attached to an activity's boundary?
3. What is the difference between the untyped end event and the terminate end event?

Exercise 4.20 What is wrong with the following model?

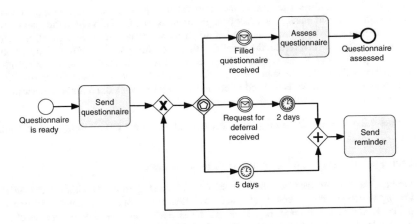

Exercise 4.21 Extend the billing process model in Exercise 4.5 (page 125) as follows.

Any time after the first transaction has failed, the customer may pay the invoice directly to the ISP. If so, the billing process is interrupted and the payment is registered. This direct payment must also cover the late fees based on the number of days passed since Day 7 (the last day to avoid incurring late fees). If the direct payment does not include late fees, the ISP sends a notification to the customer that the fees will be charged in the next invoice, before concluding the process.

Exercise 4.22 What is wrong with the following model?

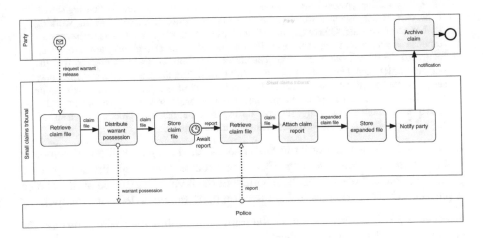

Exercise 4.23 Model the following business process at a supplier.

After a supplier notifies a retailer of the approval of a purchase order, the supplier can receive an order confirmation, an order change, or an order cancelation from the retailer. It may happen that no response is received at all. If no response is received after 48 h, or if an order cancelation is received, the supplier will cancel the order. If an order confirmation is received within 48 h, the supplier will process the order normally. If an order change is received within 48 h, the supplier will update the order and ask again the retailer for confirmation. The retailer is allowed to change an order at most three times. Afterwards, the supplier will automatically cancel the order.

Exercise 4.24 Revise the model in Exercise 3.12 (page 112) by using the terminate event.

Exercise 4.25 Model the following business process.

When a claim is received, it is first registered. After registration, the claim is classified leading to two possible outcomes: simple or complex. If the claim is simple, the insurance policy is checked. For complex claims, both the policy and the damage are checked independently. A possible outcome of the policy check is that the claim is invalid. In this case, any processing is canceled and a letter is sent to the customer. In the case of a complex claim, this implies that the damage checking is canceled if it has not been completed yet. After the check(s), an assessment is performed which may lead to two possible outcomes: positive or negative. If the assessment is positive, the garage is phoned to authorize the repairs and the payment is scheduled (in this order). In any case (whether the outcome is positive or negative), a letter is sent to the customer and the process ends. At any moment after the registration and before the end of the process, the customer may call to modify the details of the claim. If a modification occurs before the payment is scheduled, the claim is classified again (simple or complex) and the process is repeated. If a request to modify the claim is received after the payment is scheduled, the request is rejected.

Exercise 4.26 Model the following business process.

An order handling process starts when an order is received. The order is first registered. If the current date is not a working day, the process waits until the following working day before proceeding. Otherwise, an availability check is performed and a purchase order response is sent back to the customer. If none of the items is available, any processing related to the order must be stopped. Thereafter, the client needs to be notified that the purchase order cannot be further processed. Anytime during the process, the customer may send a purchase order cancel request. When such a request is received, the purchase order handling process is interrupted and the cancelation is processed. The customer may also send a "Customer address change request" during the order handling process. When such a request is received, it is just registered without further action.

Exercise 4.27 Model the order-to-cash process of the equipment rental company described in Exercise 2.14 (page 70). The process starts with the receipt of a purchase order, and ends when the payment of the invoice is received or the invoice is put into debt collection (the debt collection itself should be left out of scope).

Exercise 4.28 Draw a collaboration diagram for the following business process for electronic land development applications.

The Smart Electronic Development Assessment System (Smart eDA) is a Queensland Government initiative aimed to provide an intuitive service for preparing, lodging, and assessing land development applications. The land development business process starts with the receipt of a land development application from an applicant. Upon the receipt of a land development application, the assessment manager interacts with the cadastre to retrieve geographical information on the designated development area. This information is used to get an initial validation of the development proposal from the city council. If the plan is valid, the assessment manager sends the applicant a quote of the costs of processing the application. These costs depend on the type of development plan (for residential or commercial purposes) and on the permit or license that will be required for the plan to be approved. If the applicant accepts the quote, the assessment can start.

The assessment consists of a detailed analysis of the development plan. First, the assessment manager interacts with the Department of Main Roads (DMR) to check for conflicts with planned road development works. If there are conflicts, the application cannot proceed and must be rejected. In this case, the applicant is notified by the assessment manager. The applicant may wish to modify the development plan and resubmit it for assessment. In this case, the process is resumed from where it was interrupted.

If the development plan includes modifications to the natural environment, the assessment manager needs to request a land alteration permit to the Department of Natural Resources and Water (NRW). If the plan is for commercial purposes, additional fees will be applied to obtain this permit. Once the permit is granted, this is sent by NRW directly to the applicant. Likewise, if the designated development area is regulated by special environment protection laws, the assessment manager needs to request an environmental license to the Environmental Protection Agency (EPA). Similarly, once the license is granted, this is sent by EPA directly to the applicant. Once the required permit and/or license have been obtained, the assessment manager notifies the applicant of the final approval.

At any time during this process, the applicant can track the progress of their application by interacting directly with the assessment manager. Moreover, they can cancel the application should they wish to do so. In that case, all involved parties need to be notified and any license or permit needs to be revoked.

Assessment manager, cadastre, DMR, NRW, and EPA are all Queensland Government entities. In particular, NRW and EPA are part of the Department of Environment and Resource Management within the Queensland Government.

Exercise 4.29 Draw a collaboration diagram for the following business process for ordering maintenance activities at Sparks.

The ordering business process starts with the receipt of a request for work order from a customer. Upon the receipt of this request, the ordering department of Sparks estimates the expected usage of supplies, parts and labour and prepares a quote with the estimated total cost for the maintenance activity. If the customer's vehicle is insured, the ordering department interacts with the insurance department to retrieve the details of the customer's insurance plan so that these can be attached to the quote. The ordering department then sends the quote to the customer, who can either accept or reject the quote by notifying the ordering department within 5 days. If the customer accepts the quote, the ordering department contacts the warehouse department to check if the required parts are in stock before scheduling an appointment with the customer. If some parts are not in stock, the ordering department orders the required parts by interacting with a certified reseller and waits for an order confirmation from the reseller to be received within 3 days. If it is not received, the order department orders the parts again from a second reseller. If no reply is received from the second reseller too, the order department notifies the customer that the parts are not available and the process terminates. If the required parts are in stock or have been ordered, the ordering department interacts with an external garage to book a suitably-equipped service bay and a suitably-qualified mechanic to perform the work. A confirmation of the appointment is then sent by the garage to the order department which forwards the confirmation to the customer. The customer has one week to pay Sparks, otherwise the ordering department cancels the work order by sending a cancelation notice to both the service bay and the mechanic that have been booked for this order. If the customer pays in time, the work order is performed.

Exercise 4.30 Draw a collaboration diagram for the following business process at MetalWorks.

A build-to-order (BTO) process, also known as make-to-order process, is an order-to-cash process where the products to be sold are manufactured on the basis of a confirmed purchase order. In other words, the manufacturer does not maintain any ready-to-ship products in their stock. Instead, the products are manufactured on demand when the customer orders them. This approach is used in the context of customized products, such as metallurgical products, where customers often submit orders for products with very specific requirements.

We consider a BTO process at a company called MetalWorks. The process starts when MetalWorks receives a purchase order (PO) from one of its customers. This PO is called the "customer PO". The customer PO may contain one or multiple line items. Each line item refers to a different product.

Upon receiving a customer PO, a sales officer checks the PO to determine if all the line items in the order can be produced within the timeframes indicated in the PO. As a result of this check, the sales officer may either confirm the customer PO or ask the customer to revise the terms of the PO (for example: change the delivery date to a later date). In some extreme cases, the sales officer may reject the PO, but this happens very rarely. If the customer is asked to revise the PO, the BTO process will be put in "stand-by" until the customer submits a revised PO. The sales officer will then check the revised PO and accept it, reject it, or ask again the customer to make further changes. However, the sales officer has been instructed to accept changes to the PO up to three times, after which the PO must be escalated to a senior sales officer, who can either accept the further changes one more time, or reject the PO altogether.

Once a PO is confirmed, the sales officer creates one "work order" for each line item in the customer PO. In other words, one customer PO gives place to multiple work orders (one per line item). The work order is a document that allows employees at MetalWorks to keep track of the manufacturing of a product requested by a customer.

In order to manufacture a product, multiple raw materials are required. Some of these raw materials are maintained in stock in the warehouse of MetalWorks, but others need to be sourced from one or multiple suppliers. Accordingly, each work order is examined by a production engineer. The production engineer determines which raw materials are required in order to fulfill the work order. The production engineer annotates the work order with a list of required raw materials. Each raw material listed in the work order is later checked by a procurement officer. The procurement officer determines whether the required raw material is available in stock or it has to be ordered by accessing the specific catalog for that product line. If the material has to be ordered, the procurement officer consults the suppliers database, selects one or more suitable suppliers for the raw material and sends a request for quote to the selected suppliers. If more than one supplier is identified, the procurement officer selects the best quote out of the first three quotes received from the suppliers (the other quotes, if they arrive, are discarded), and emits a "material PO" for the selected supplier. This material PO is a PO for a raw material and is different from the customer PO. A material PO is a PO sent by MetalWorks to one of its suppliers, whereas a customer PO is a PO received by MetalWorks from one of its customers.

Once all materials required to fulfill a work order are available, the production can start. The responsibility for the production of a work order is assigned to the same production engineer who previously examined the work order. The production engineer is responsible for scheduling the production. Once the product has been manufactured, it is checked by a quality inspector. Sometimes, the quality inspector finds a defect in the product and reports it to the production engineer. The production engineer then decides whether: (i) the product should undergo a minor fix; or (ii) the product should be discarded and manufactured again.

Once the production has completed, the product is shipped to the customer. There is no need to wait until all the line items requested in a customer PO are ready before shipping them. As soon as a product is ready, it can be shipped to the corresponding customer.

At any point in time before the shipment of the product, the customer may send a "cancel order" message for a given PO. When this happens, the sales officer determines if the order can still be canceled, and if so, whether or not the customer should pay a penalty. If the order can be canceled without penalty, all the work related to that order is stopped and the customer is notified that the cancelation has been successful. If the customer needs to pay a penalty, the sales officer first asks the customer if they accept to pay the cancelation penalty. If the customer accepts to pay the cancelation penalty, the order is canceled and all work related to the order is stopped. Otherwise, the work related to the order continues.

Exercise 4.31 Draw a collaboration diagram for the following booking-to-cash process.

Fotof provides photography services in the fields of family photography, personal event photography (e.g. weddings and party photography) and commercial photography (e.g., corporate events). One of the core processes of Fotof is its booking-to-cash process, which goes all the way from the moment a customer makes a booking for a photo shooting session, through the order placement, to the moment the customer pays and obtains the ordered pictures. In the last year, Fotof received 10K orders from commercial customers, and 80K orders from private customers.

The booking-to-cash process starts when a customer makes a booking for a shooting session at a photo studio. A booking can be done via phone or via email addressed directly to a specific photo studio. The request is handled by a customer service representative at the photo studio. Each studio employs two customer service representatives: a senior one, who is also manager of the studio, and a junior one. The customer service representative enters the details of the booking into the photo studio information system.

The booking is assigned to one of the photographers of the studio. After a photo shooting session, the photographer uploads the pictures to a file server. Eventually, a technician cleans up the pictures by deleting duplicates and failed shots. Later the technician edits the remaining shots and arranges them into a photo gallery using a dedicated photo studio software tool. Once the gallery is completed, the customer is notified by email. The notification includes a URL of the gallery.

Customers can view the gallery, select the pictures they wish to order in print (and how many copies) and those they wish to get in digital copy (full resolution). Customers can also annotate a selected picture in order to ask for additional editing (special requests). When placing their order, customers can specify whether they will pickup the printed copies at the studio or have them delivered by post. In the latter case, a shipment fee is added to the order. Once the customer has submitted the order, a technician performs additional editing (if required by the customer). In the case of special requests, the technician may need to communicate with the customer by email or phone to clarify the request and to determine how to fulfill it, and whether the special request will entail an additional fee and how much. If printouts are required, the technician prints them out, puts them in an envelope, and drops them at the studio's counter.

Pictures from a shooting session are kept in the corresponding gallery for up to 30 days (a reminder is sent to the customer 5 days before the expiry date). If a customer has not placed an order past this period, an invoice is sent for the minimum billing amount (see below). Invoices are payable within 7 days of their issue. A customer service representative sends a reminder when an invoice is overdue.

Once the pictures are ready, a customer service representative determines the amount to be invoiced (including additional fees for special requests). The customer service representative then produces an invoice and sends it to the customer. Once the invoice has been paid, the customer service representative packs and sends the printouts for postal delivery (if the customer ordered printouts) and sends a URL to the customer where the customer can find the full-resolution digital pictures they ordered. The matching of incoming payments to invoices is done automatically by an accountancy system (the same system that is used to issue invoices).

Booking or order cancelations can occur in three ways: (i) prior to the shooting session (booking cancelation); (ii) in case of no-show (the customer did not show up to the shooting session and did not reschedule it); or (iii) after the shooting, if the customer does not order any pictures within 30 days. Cancelations prior to the photo shooting session do not incur a fee. Cancelations due to no-shows do not attract a fee if they are in-studio; they attract a fee of € 50 if they are "on location". In case of a no-show, the customer may reschedule the booking to a later day but the no-show fee for on-location shootings is charged to the customer in any case. If a customer does not order any picture after a shooting session, the customer is invoiced a photo shooting fee of € 100 for in-studio sessions (€ 150 for on-location ones).

Exercise 4.32 Draw a collaboration diagram for the following mortgage application process at BestLoans.

The mortgage application process starts with the receipt of a mortgage application from a client. When an application is sent in by the client to the broker, the broker either examines the application, if the amount of the mortgage loan is within the mandate the broker has been given by BestLoans, or forwards the application to BestLoans.

If the application is examined by the broker, the broker must send either a rejection or an approval letter to the client within one week. If the broker sends an approval letter, then it forwards the details of this application to BestLoans so that from there on the client can interact directly with BestLoans for the sake of disbursing the loan. In this case, BestLoans registers the application and sends an acknowledgment to the client.

The broker can only handle a given number of clients at a time. If the broker is not able to reply within one week, the client must contact BestLoans directly. In this case, a reduction on the interest rate is applied should the application be approved.

If BestLoans deals with the application directly, its mortgage department checks the credit of the client with the Bureau of Credit Registration. Moreover, if the loan amount is more than 90% of the total cost of the house being purchased by the client, the mortgage department must request a mortgage insurance offer from the insurance department. After these interactions BestLoans either sends an approval letter or a rejection to the broker, which the broker then forwards to the client (this interaction may also happen directly between the mortgage department and the client if no broker is involved).

After an approval letter has been submitted to the client, the client may either accept or reject the offer by notifying this directly to the mortgage department. If the mortgage department receives an acceptance notification, it writes a deed and sends it to an external notary for signature. The notary sends a copy of the signed deed to the mortgage department. Next, the insurance department starts an insurance contract for the mortgage. Finally, the mortgage department submits a disbursement request to the financial department. When this request has been handled, the financial department notifies the client directly.

Any time during the application process, the client may inquire about the status of the application with the mortgage department or with the broker, depending on which entity is dealing with the client. Moreover, the client may request the cancelation of the application. In this case the mortgage department or the broker computes the application processing fees, which depend on how far the application process is, and communicates these to the client. The client may reply within 2 days with a cancelation confirmation, in which case the process is canceled, or with a cancelation withdrawal, in which case the process continues. If the process has to be canceled, BestLoans may need to first recall the loan (if the disbursement has been done), then annul the insurance contract (if an insurance contract has been drawn), and finally annul the deed (if a deed has been drawn).

4.8   Further Readings

We have seen single-pool business process diagrams as well as multi-pool col-laboration diagrams. There are two other types of diagrams in BPMN, namely *choreography diagrams* and *conversation diagrams*. Choreography diagrams allow us to capture interactions between parties (as opposed to tasks) and the order of these interactions. Conversation diagrams allow us to capture interactions only, without any ordering. Choreography and conversation diagrams in BPMN originate from a language for modeling Web service interactions called Let's Dance [197].

For further information on the BPMN language we point to the BPMN website.[1] This site also provides a link to handy BPMN material including a quick reference guide to all BPMN elements and a comprehensive list of books on the subject. Among the many books dedicated to BPMN, we can cite those by Silver [163], Allweyer [7], and Freund & Rücker [49]. A compact BPMN poster, available in 15 languages can be downloaded from the BPM Offensive Berlin website.[2]

---

[1] http://www.bpmn.org.

[2] http://www.bpmb.de/index.php/BPMNPoster.

Chapter 5
Process Discovery

All truths are easy to understand once they are discovered;
the point is to discover them.
Galileo Galilei (1564–1642)

In the previous two chapters we learned how to create process models. However, our starting point was often a textual description of the process, which is hardly available in practice, at least the first time a model is created for a given business process. There are various methods that we can use to create process models by inferring information about the business processes within an organization, e.g., by interviewing process participants or by observing how they operate in practice. By the same token, it is important to ensure that a model is not only syntactically correct, but that it also accurately reflects the actual business process being modeled. To this end, we need to thoroughly understand the operations of a business process, as well as to possess the modeling skills to represent a business process in a high-quality BPMN model. These two types of skills are hardly unified in the same person. Hence, multiple stakeholders with different and complementary skills are typically involved in the construction of a process model.

In this chapter, we first present the challenges faced by the stakeholders involved in the lead-up to a process model. Then, we discuss methods to facilitate effective communication and information gathering in this setting. Given the information gathered in this way, we show step-by-step how to construct a process model and what quality criteria should be checked before the model can be accepted as an authoritative representation of a business process.

5.1 The Setting of Process Discovery

Process discovery is defined as the act of gathering information about an existing process and organizing it in terms of an as-is process model. This definition emphasizes gathering and organizing information. This means that process discovery is

© Springer-Verlag GmbH Germany, part of Springer Nature 2018
M. Dumas et al., *Fundamentals of Business Process Management*,
https://doi.org/10.1007/978-3-662-56509-4_5

a much broader activity than process modeling. Clearly, modeling is a part of this activity. The problem is though that modeling can only start once enough information has been put together. And indeed, gathering information often proves to be cumbersome and time-consuming in practice. Therefore, we need to first define a setting in which information can be gathered effectively. In order to address these issues, we can describe four tasks of process discovery:

1. Defining the setting: dedicated to assembling a team in a company that will be responsible for working on the process.
2. Gathering information: concerned with building an understanding of the process. Different discovery methods can be used to acquire information on a process.
3. Conducting the modeling task: deals with the actual creation of the process model. A modeling method gives guidance for mapping out the process in a systematic way.
4. Assuring process model quality: aims to guarantee that the resulting process model meets different quality criteria. This task is important for establishing trust in the process model.

Once the setting has been defined, the remaining three tasks are often performed in an iterative manner, i.e., as we gather information about a given process, we create a draft model and assure that this is of good quality. In the following, we discuss the key roles involved in process discovery.

5.1.1 Process Analyst Versus Domain Expert

Two roles are fundamental in a process discovery project: the *process analyst* and the *domain expert*. One or more process analysts are commonly responsible for gathering information about a given business process, and driving the modeling task, under the leadership of the process owner. As such, a process analyst must be familiar with process modeling languages such as BPMN and be skilled at gathering and organizing process-related information. However, process analysts are hardly knowledgeable of all the details of the process in question.

Example 5.1 Let us consider the following two modeling tasks:

- Modeling the process for ordering books through an online bookstore, from the perspective of the customer.
- Modeling the same process from the perspective of the bookstore.

If you have already learned how to model business processes by the help of this book, you should be able to complete the first modeling task above. The reason is that quite likely you will be familiar with this process as you have already ordered a book online, through your preferred bookstore. The case is likely to be different for the second modeling task: you will only be able to complete this task if you have worked for an online bookstore, which is less common.   □

Ultimately, the participation in a business process from behind the scenes, i.e., from the perspective of the company that delivers a service or produces a product via a given process, is what determines whether or not we are intimately familiar with that process. In practice, process analysts are supposed to model business processes which they have experienced neither as process participants nor as customers. So they have to gather an extensive amount of information about the process in order to understand how it works from the inside, by consulting with those who are involved in its performance on a daily basis, i.e., the domain experts.

A domain expert is thus any individual who has an intimate knowledge of how a process or specific tasks within that process are performed. Typically, this is a process participant, but it can also be the process owner or an operational manager who coordinates a team of process participants. External roles such as partners, suppliers, and customers of the process should also be consulted as domain experts, since they can offer a complementary view on the same process, though their knowledge of the process would undoubtedly be confined to their limited exposure to it. On the downside, domain experts are not proficient in process modeling. In some companies, domain experts even refuse to discuss process models, because they do not feel comfortable explaining their involvement in the process before a process model. As a consequence, they often rely on process analysts for organizing their process knowledge in terms of a process model.

Such difference in modeling skills between process analysts and domain experts results from a different exposure to practical modeling and to modeling training. Many companies use training programs to improve the modeling skills of domain experts. Such training is a prerequisite for modeling initiatives where process participants are expected to model their own processes. On the other hand, there are BPM consultancy companies that specialize in particular industry domains such as auditing, finance, or mining. It is an advantage when BPM consultants who also have domain expertise can be assigned to process modeling projects.

It is the task of the *process owner* to secure the commitment and involvement of both analysts and domain experts during the definition of the setting of process discovery. The number and type of process analysts and domain experts to involve depends on the complexity of the process in question. In the rest of this section we will elaborate on this, starting with the three challenges of process discovery.

Exercise 5.1 You are the manager of a consulting company and you need to hire a person for the newly signed BPM project with an online bookstore. Consider the following two profiles; who would you hire as a process analyst?

- Mike Miller has ten years of work experience with an online retailer. He has worked in different teams involved with the order-to-cash process of the online retailer.
- Sara Smith has five years of experience working as a process analyst in the banking sector. She is familiar with two different process modeling languages and with several modeling tools.

5.1.2 Three Process Discovery Challenges

The fact that modeling knowledge and domain knowledge are often available in different persons gives rise to three essential challenges of process discovery, namely fragmented process knowledge, thinking in cases, and lack of familiarity with process modeling languages.

The first challenge of process discovery relates to *fragmented process knowledge*. Business processes are a set of related tasks. Nowadays, however, due to specialization and division of labor, hardly all the tasks of a process will be performed by the same resource. Rather, different tasks will be assigned to different specialized resources. This has the consequence that a process analyst must gather information about a given process by talking with different domain experts who are responsible for the various tasks in the process. Typically, domain experts have an abstract understanding of the overall process and a very detailed understanding of their own tasks. This makes it difficult to puzzle the different views together. In particular, one domain expert might have a different idea about what output has to be expected from an upstream task than the person that actually works on it. Potential conflicts in the provided information have to be resolved. It is also often the case that the rules of the process are not explicitly defined in detail. In those situations, domain experts may operate under diverging assumptions, which may not be consistent with each other. Fragmented process knowledge is one of the reasons why process discovery requires several iterations. Having received input from all relevant domain experts, the process analyst must make proposals for resolving inconsistencies, which again requires feedback from, and eventually approval from, the domain experts, before obtaining the final endorsement from the process owner.

The second challenge stems from the fact that domain experts typically *think of processes on a case level*. Domain experts will find it easy to describe the tasks they conducted for one specific process instance, but they might have problems responding to general questions about how a process works in the general way. Process analysts often get answers like "You cannot really generalize, every case is different" or "We can never do anything exactly in the same way, there are so many special conditions to answer such a question". It is indeed the role of the process analyst to organize and abstract the pieces of information provided by the domain expert in such a way that a systematically defined process model can emerge. Therefore, it is required to formulate questions on specific aspects of the process for the domain experts, e.g., what happens if certain conditions do or do not hold, if a given outcome is achieved, or if certain deadlines are not met. In this way, the process analyst can reverse-engineer the conditions that govern the routing decisions of a business process.

The third challenge of process discovery is a result of the fact that domain experts are typically *not familiar with business process modeling languages*. This observation already gave rise to the distinction between domain experts and process analysts. In this context, the problem is not only that domain experts are hardly trained to create process models themselves, but also that they are not trained to read process models that others have created. This lack of training can encumber the act of seeking feedback on a draft process model. In this situation, it is typically not appropriate to show the model to the domain expert and ask for corrections. Even if domain experts understand the activity labels well, they would often not understand the routing constructs of a modeling language like BPMN. Therefore, the process analyst has to explain the content of a process model in detail, for example by translating the model to natural language. Domain experts will feel at ease in commenting on natural-language explanations of the process, pointing out aspects that need modification or further clarification according to their understanding of the process.

The box "Profile of an Expert Process Analyst" describes what makes a process analyst an expert.

Exercise 5.2 Consider the order-to-cash process of your preferred online bookstore and assume you have access to three internal resources: a customer relationship manager (who handles sales and reclaims), a warehouse worker (who looks after shipments), and a financial officer (who raises invoices and collects payments). As a process analyst, what questions do you need to ask these domain experts to be able to obtain a complete and systematic view of this process?

Hint. Think of the different exposure to this process that the three resources have and of the possible conditions, process outcomes, and exceptions that they may have experienced while executing this process.

PROFILE OF AN EXPERT PROCESS ANALYST

The skills of a process analyst play an important role in process discovery. *Expert* process analysts can be described based on a set of general dispositions, their actual behavior in a BPM project, and in terms of the quality of the process models resulting from their efforts.

Research on expertise in the general area of system analysis and design has found that there are certain personal traits that are likely to be observed in expert process analysts. One of the ways to describe personality is the so-called *Five Factor Model* developed in psychological research. In essence, this model describes five psychological factors, namely *openness* (appreciating art, emotion, and adventure), *conscientiousness* (tendency to self-discipline, achievement, and planning), *extraversion* (being positive, energetic, and seeking company), *agreeableness* (being compassionate and cooperative), and *neuroticism* (being anxious, depressed, and vulnerable). These factors have also been studied regarding their connection with expert analysts. Expert analysts appear to be strong both in terms of conscientiousness and extraversion. Indeed, process discovery projects require the conscientious planning and coordination of interviews or workshops with various domain experts in a limited period of time. Further, process discovery projects are sometimes

(continued)

subject to internal politics within the organization, in situations where the agenda of different process stakeholders is not thoroughly clear, where they might fear losing their position, or even where they have conflicting agendas. In such environments, it is valuable to have an energetic and extraverted process analyst who can create a positive atmosphere for working on the project, and seek compromise between the involved parties, conscious of the interests at stake.

Process discovery in general belongs to the category of ill-defined problems. This means that at the beginning of a process discovery project it might not be very clear which domain experts have to be contacted, what documentation should be utilized, and what agenda the different stakeholders might have in mind. The way expert analysts navigate through a project is strongly influenced by their experience with former projects. Thus, there is a strong difference between the way novices conduct problem understanding and solving and the way expert analysts do. In terms of problem understanding, it has been observed that expert analysts approach a project in terms of what things need to be achieved. Novices lack this clear goal orientation and try to approach things in a bottom-up way. This means, they often start by investigating material that is easily accessible and talk to persons that respond readily. Experts work in a different way. They have an explicit set of triggers and heuristics available from experience with prior projects. They tend to pay specific attention to the following aspects:

- *Getting the right people on board.* If you need to talk to a given process participant, make sure their immediate superior is on board and that the process participant knows that their hierarchy backs their involvement in the process discovery effort.
- *Having a set of working hypotheses on how the process is structured at different levels of detail.* In order to progress with the project, it is important to have a short and precise set of working hypotheses, which you can then validate. Prepare an extensive set of questions and assumptions to be discussed with domain experts, e.g., in interviews or workshops.
- *Identifying patterns in the information provided by domain experts.* These can be used for constructing parts of a process model. Such pieces of information typically refer to specific control-flow structures. For instance, statements about certain activities being alternative, exclusive, or subject to certain conditions often point to the use of XOR gateways. In a similar way, statements about activities being independent from one another, or sometimes being in one or another order, often point to the use of AND gateways. It is often easy for expert analysts to sketch out processes by combining these patterns.

(continued)

- *Paying attention to model quality.* Easy-to-understand models help better engage relevant stakeholders and are also valuable for the analyst throughout the creation of the model itself. Experts also use the right level of abstraction. For example, you should not show a very detailed model to a manager. The importance of layout is apparent from the fact that expert analysts often take a great deal of time in arranging the various model elements neatly, so as to render the model more readable.

5.2 Process Discovery Methods

As we now have an idea of the tasks process analysts have to perform, of their capabilities, and of what limitations they have to keep in mind when interacting with domain experts, we turn to different methods for gathering information about a process. We distinguish three classes of discovery methods, namely evidence-based discovery, interview-based discovery, and workshop-based discovery. They have relative strengths and weaknesses, which we will discuss subsequently.

5.2.1 Evidence-Based Discovery

Various pieces of evidence are typically available for studying how an existing process works. We discuss three evidence-based methods: document analysis, observation, and automated process discovery.

Document analysis: Document analysis exploits the fact that there is usually documentation available that can be related to an existing business process. In the ideal scenario, this can take the form of process descriptions, which are available from previous modeling exercises. Other document types include internal policies, organization charts, employment plans, quality certificate reports, glossaries and handbooks, user forms, data and system models, work instructions, and work profiles. However, there are potential issues with document analysis. First, most of the documentation that is available about the operations of a company is not readily organized in a process-oriented way. Think of an organization chart, for instance. It defines the organizational units and positions, and is helpful to identify a potential set of process stakeholders. For example, in case of our online bookstore, it might reveal that the sales department, the logistics department, and the financial department are likely to be involved in the order-to-cash process. Second, the level of granularity of the documentation might not be appropriate. While an organization chart draws rather an abstract picture of a company, there are often many documents that summarize parts of a process on a too fine-grained level. Many companies document detailed work instructions for tasks, and work profiles for positions. These are typically too detailed for modeling a business process at a conceptual level. So we may need to abstract from, or refine, the information found in these documents, to get the required information to model our business process. Third, many of the documents are only partially trustworthy. For a process discovery project, it is important to identify how a process works in reality. Many documents do not necessarily capture reality. Some of them are outdated and some state how things should work idealistically (normative documents), and not how people actually do their work. The advantage of document analysis is that a process analyst can use the available documentation to get familiar with certain parts of a process and its environment, and also to formulate hypotheses. This method is helpful before talking to domain experts. On the downside, an analyst has to keep in mind that documents do not necessarily reflect the reality of the process.

Observation: If we use observation as a method of discovery, we directly follow the processing of individual cases in order to get an understanding of how the process works. As a process analyst, we can either play the active role of a customer of the process or the passive role of an observer. As part of the *active customer role*, we trigger the execution of a process and record the steps that are executed and the set of choices that are offered. For instance, in the case of our online bookstore, we can create a new book order and keep track of which activities are performed at the side of the retailer. This provides a good understanding of the boundaries of the process and its essential milestones. However, we will only see those parts of the process that require interaction with the customer. All back-office processing remains a black box. The role of a *passive observer* is more appropriate for understanding the end-to-end process, but it requires access to the people and sites where the process is being performed. Usually, such access needs the approval of the managers and supervisors of the corresponding teams, and not all sites can be accessed (think of an offshore oil platform). Furthermore, there might be a potential issue with people acting differently, because they are aware of being observed. People usually change their behavior under observation in such a way that they work faster and more diligently. This is important to remember when execution times have to be estimated, and possible exceptions to the normal process flow have to be identified, as part of the modeling task. However, discovery based on observation has the advantage that it reveals how a process is conducted in reality as of today, which is in contrast to document analysis that typically captures the past.

Automated process discovery: *Automated process discovery* is a method that uses *event logs*, i.e. process execution data stored by common enterprise systems available in an organization, to automatically discover a model of the business process that is supported by these systems. Think for example of a claims management system in an insurance company. This system does not necessarily have an explicit definition of the claims handling process it supports by means of a process model. With automated process discovery, though, it is possible to automatically extract a model of this process even if the process is hard-coded in the system. The advantage of this method is threefold. First, event logs capture the actual execution of business processes, so we obtain an objective representation of the process, as opposed to relying on our understanding of it as a result of observing the process directly or consulting with domain experts. Second, event logs often record a rich set of process-related information beyond the tasks that have been performed, including for example task timestamps and the resources that executed these tasks. We can use this input to enrich our models with performance information such as activity durations and frequencies, or by discovering alternative views of the process, e.g., the social network of how process resources interact with each other. Third, this method is not limited by the confines of a given enterprise system, so it can be used to reconstruct end-to-end processes that span different systems, which would be hard to do by accessing each system in isolation. Consider for example the meter-to-cash process of a utility company from the moment a customer's service consumption is measured to the time the customer is billed. This process may be supported by two different systems: an ERP system to handle the measurement and a CRM system for the billing part. By creating a unified event log from process execution data out of these two systems, it would be possible to trace the entire meter-to-cash process, hence going beyond the boundaries of individual systems. A limitation is that event logs are not always available, and when they are, they sometimes only record some tasks in the process and not others (i.e., there are gaps in the log), or contain noise and other logging errors. Also, depending on the granularity in which process information has been logged, the resulting models may be too low-level and so hard to understand. We will introduce concrete techniques for automated process discovery and further discuss advantages and limitations within the process monitoring phase in Section 11.4.

Exercise 5.3 As a process analyst working for the University of Newtown, you have been engaged by Mark Johnson, the process owner of the student admission process, in a project that aims at improving this process. In order to model the as-is process, you start by collecting relevant information about this process. The available documentation includes the organization chart of the Office of the Deputy Vice-Chancellor (DVC)[1] for Student Affairs where Mark's team sits, the UML class diagram of the student admission system which supports this process, and a set of relevant organizational policies that you extract from the university's Web pages. These documents are reported in Figures 5.1, 5.2, 5.3.

Based on this documentation, formulate initial hypotheses on how the student admission process works. Next, identify the relevant domain experts to interview and their supervisors whom you should seek approval from.

---

[1]The Deputy Vice-Chancellor is one of the most senior academic positions at a college or university. Depending on the country, this position is variously called Vice-President, Vice-Rector, or Provost.

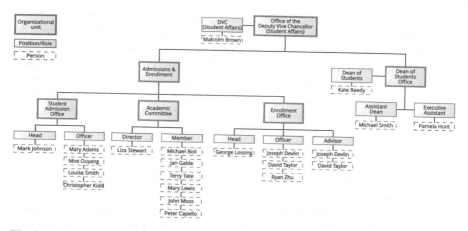

Fig. 5.1 Organization chart of the Office of the DVC (Student Affairs)

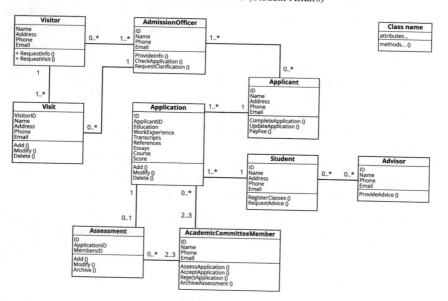

Fig. 5.2 Extract of the UML class diagram of the student admission system

5.2.2 Interview-Based Discovery

Interview-based discovery aims at interviewing domain experts to inquire about how a process is executed. Figure 5.4 illustrates the typical phases of the interview method. First, those involved in the process of interest are approached for an initial interview. We mentioned that process knowledge tends to be fragmented due to specialization and division of labor (first discovery challenge). For this reason, we need to interview multiple domain experts. Since at the time of the interviews we

- *An applicant is admitted if:*
  - *their prior education is consistent with the study area of the selected course*
  - *the submitted essay is not plagiarized and is of good quality*
  - *the score of the prior degree is at least 70 out of 100 (standard 100-point scale)*
  - *the two reference letters are satisfactory.*

- *Successful applicants must accept the offer within four weeks from notification.*

Fig. 5.3 Organizational policies for student admission

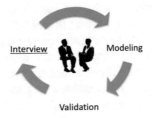

Fig. 5.4 Phases of the interview method

may not yet grasp the details of the involvement of different domain experts in the process, it may be required to discover the process step-by-step, and as we learn the latter, plan interviews with additional people.

We can use two strategies for conducting an interview: (i) starting from the process outcomes (e.g., an order being fulfilled), we work our way *backwards* until we reach the process triggers (e.g., the receipt of a purchase order); or (ii) starting from the triggers, we proceed *forward* until we reach the process outcomes. Conducting interviews in a forward manner enables us to elicit process knowledge from the interviewee by naturally following the flow of processing in the order of how it unfolds. This is particularly helpful for understanding which decisions are taken at which stage. Following the process backward can also be helpful. For example, some domain experts may find it easy to identify the possible outcomes of a process or of an activity (e.g., an order fulfilled or rejected), and from that retrieve what is required to get to that outcome by traversing the process backward (e.g., the payment and the delivery notice are needed for an order to be fulfilled). Both strategies, downstream and upstream, are important when interviewing domain experts. With each interviewee, it must be clarified what input is expected from prior upstream activities, what decisions are taken, what is produced as output of their activities, and to what resource it is then forwarded.

When conducting an interview, it is more effective to balance between a structured and a free-form interview approach. For example, considering a 1-h interview, one may spend the first 45 min to go through a list of predefined questions to validate current hypotheses (structured part), and use the remaining 15 min to let the interviewee discuss any concern or aspect of the process they believe to be relevant (free-form part). *Free-form* interviews have the advantage of enabling domain experts to discuss the process at a level of detail that they find appropriate, which may lead to uncovering certain aspects of the process previously disregarded. *Structured* interviews, in contrast, allow us to validate our hypotheses but may create in the interviewee a feeling of running through a checklist, with the effect of holding back important information one is not explicitly asked about. In fact, a recurrent pitfall is that when asked how a given process or activity is performed, the interviewee tends to describe the normal way of processing. Thus, exceptions tend to be neglected. In other words, the interview ends up covering only the "sunny-day" scenario. One way to prevent this pitfall is to explicitly ask questions about the "rainy-day" scenarios. For example, one may ask: "How did you handle your most difficult customer?", "What was the most difficult case you worked on?", "What happens if the customer does not reply on time?". To formulate these questions, it is handy to think of the possible exceptions that may arise in a process (internal, external, or activity timeouts) and of their nature (business vs. technology fault). This can help to uncover exceptions and more generally process variants that while not necessarily frequent have a sufficient impact on the process to be worth documenting. For example, in an order-to-cash process, one may ask a sales officer what happens if the ordered items are out-of-stock (internal business exception), or if the customer decides to cancel the order (external business exception), or if the ERP system that checks stock levels is unresponsive (internal technology exception).

Coming back to the phases in Figure 5.4, after an initial interview, we can construct a process model offline (second phase), based on our interview notes or recordings. Due to domain experts thinking on a case level (second discovery challenge), we must be able to abstract information on individual cases from the interviewees, in order to construct meaningful process models. Once the model has been created, we need to validate it with the domain experts (third phase) to make sure that it correctly reflects their view (we will talk more about validation later in this chapter). To validate a model, we may need to translate this into natural language, due to domain experts not being familiar with process modeling languages (third discovery challenge). Validation typically leads to the need of interviewing the person again to clarify certain parts of the process. A second iteration of the cycle in Figure 5.4 is often enough to get the approval of the interviewee. However, especially for complex processes, more than two iterations may be required.

In summary, interview-based discovery offers a rich and detailed picture of the process and its participants. Interviewing multiple process participants (also for the same role) has the potential to reveal inconsistent perceptions that different domain experts may have on how a particular process operates. It also helps the process analyst to understand the process in detail. However, it is a labor-intensive discovery method which requires ample time of different individuals.

Exercise 5.4 After collecting relevant information on the student admission process (see Exercise 5.3 on page 167), you interviewed some representatives for the two roles involved in this process: Mary Adams and Louise Smith as student admission officers, and Peter Capello as a member of the academic committee (Mark Johnson, the process owner, confirmed that the enrollment office is not involved in this process). The relevant parts of the interview transcripts are provided below.

Student admission officer (Mary Adams):

"My process starts when I receive an application for admission. First, I check the completeness of this document. If the application is incomplete, I need to send a request for clarification back to the applicant. Otherwise, I forward it to the academic committee. I then receive a response from the academic committee which can be either of the below:

- A notification of acceptance from the academic committee. In this case, I prepare a letter of offer and send it to the applicant via post to collect his or her signature. Most of the times, I receive a signed offer back from the applicant, but sometimes I don't.
- A notification of rejection. In this case, I send a rejection letter to the applicant via ordinary post.

The problem is that the academic committee is often too slow to reply. I wonder if these academics are just too overloaded with work to care about student admissions..."

Student admission officer (Louise Smith):

"When I get a fresh application, it's important that this contains all the required information, including name, address, phone number, and email address of the applicant. Unfortunately, the Web portal has many bugs and sometimes lets through incomplete applications, which are a nightmare to rectify! This means going back and forth with the student at least a couple of times. Anyway, once the application is complete, I pass it to a member of the academic committee using our internal student admission system—the same that collects applications via the Web portal. Most of the times, the member of the academic committee replies with a notification of acceptance, in which case I need to prepare a letter of offer and send it to the applicant via post. Our policies are such that applicants must reply within four weeks. In fact, we are flooded by applications, so if they do not hurry to reply, we will offer the place to someone else. Sometimes I receive a notification of rejection. Well, in this case I formulate a rejection letter and send it to the applicant via post".

Member of academic committee (Peter Capello):

"When I receive an application from the admission officer, I assess its quality. I extract the grade of the applicant from his or her previous degree and convert it to a standard score based on a conversion table. The score must be at least 70%; otherwise the student is out. Next, I perform a plagiarism check of the essay contained in the application using our plagiarism detection software. Most of the times, the essay is plagiarism-free. If so, I proceed to read it and assign it a score. Finally, I read the two reference letters attached to the application. There's a lot you can learn from a reference letter. Often there are subtle messages that the referee wants you to get, like "This is a great student, but I've had better ones". In any case, based on the score, quality of the essay, and reference letters, if I deem that the applicant is qualified, I send an acceptance notification to the admission officer, otherwise I send a rejection notification. In either case, I archive the results of my assessment in my database. Ah, I communicate with the student admission office using our internal student admission system. A piece of junk, sometimes messages get lost and I have to send them again, if I'm lucky to find it out!"

Next, you took an active role in observing how this process works by acting as the applicant. Using a fake identity (in agreement with the process owner), you triggered this process several times by submitting various applications via the Web portal. After this, you came up with the following observations.

Applicant:

> To apply for admission, the applicant needs to prepare an admission application and submit it to the university via a Web portal. The application must include academic transcripts, an essay, and two reference letters. The applicant will then receive a response from an admission officer via ordinary mail, which can be:
>
> - A letter of offer. In this case, the applicant needs to sign the letter of offer and return it to the admission officer via post within four weeks.
> - A rejection letter. In this case, the applicant does not do anything further and the process is finished.
> - A request for clarification from the admission officer. This is an email notification. In this case, the applicant provides the required documentation to the admission officer by submitting an updated application through the same Web portal used for the initial submission, and then gets a response that is the letter of offer, the rejection letter, or again a request for clarification.

Using the information above, create a draft BPMN model of the as-is student admission process. This draft will then be validated with the people that have been interviewed, before sign-off by the process owner. Make appropriate assumptions.

5.2.3 Workshop-Based Discovery

Workshop-based discovery also offers the opportunity to get a rich understanding of the business process, with the advantage of resolving inconsistent views between domain experts more quickly than interviews. In fact, in contrast to interviews, a workshop involves multiple process participants at the same time. Moreover, it may include two further roles in place of or in addition to the business analyst. A *facilitator* may be invited to coordinate the verbal contributions of the participants, while a *process modeler* may be invited to create the process model as the workshop unfolds. If these two figures are available, the business analyst monitors the workshop and acts as a *scribe* taking note of all relevant concerns that may require further investigation. For example, if a passage of the process may not be clear, but the discussion moves elsewhere, the scribe would record this point to come back to it later, in order not to stop the flow of thoughts. In small contexts, facilitator and modeler may coincide with the process analyst, but in contexts where the business process in question is complex and where a large number of participants are attending, it is advisable to tap into these extra roles, budget allowing.

In terms of effort, an end-to-end detailed process model can hardly be completed within a single workshop session. Typically, three to five sessions of no more than

3 h each are required to complete the modeling effort, including consolidating the model between sessions to ensure a high level of quality.

The involvement of multiple domain experts requires diligent scheduling and preparation. The sessions should be scheduled well in advance to ensure the simultaneous availability of domain experts with different involvement in the business process. This includes at least one representative of each role participating in the process (e.g., a customer relationship manager, a warehouse worker, and a financial officer for the order-to-cash process of our online bookstore example). It is useful to also involve technical staff managing the systems supporting the process, even if these people are not directly involved in the process (e.g., the system administrator of the ERP system used to automatically check stock availability). It is further advisable that the project sponsor (typically the process owner) also participates, at least in the first session, to stress the importance of the project. In any case, there should not be more than ten to twelve domain experts per session, otherwise there will not be enough time for each to take parole. If the process is available in multiple variants (e.g., distributed geographically or per product), it is better to discover each variant in a separate session to avoid confusion between variants. This is also the case if there is a need to create a consolidated as-is process model for all variants, as this consolidated model may be achieved off-line after the various sessions.

At the beginning of the first workshop session the analyst should reset expectations and illustrate the format of the workshop. Participants may have a different understanding of the goals of the workshop, so it is important to clarify objectives (what process should be discovered), importance (how this project contributes to the company's strategy), and scope (how deep the process modeling should go). In the first workshop session it can also be beneficial to take a lightweight yet participative approach to process modeling. One technique to engage workshop participants is to ask them to collectively build a rough model of the process (a sketch) using sticky notes on a wall. The facilitator starts with a pad of sticky notes. Each sticky note is meant to represent a task or event. The group begins with discussing how the process typically starts, i.e., what its possible triggers are and what tasks are performed next. The facilitator then writes the name of the start event on a sticky note and posts it on the wall. Then they ask what can happen next. The participants start mentioning one or more possible tasks. The facilitator writes these down on new sticky notes and posts these on the wall, organizing them for example from left to right or top to bottom to capture the temporal order of tasks. In this exercise, no lines are drawn between the tasks and no gateways are discovered. The purpose is to build a sequence of process tasks. Sometimes, participants disagree on whether something is one or two tasks. If the disagreement cannot be resolved, the two tasks can be written down as two sticky notes bundled together, hence forming a composite activity, e.g., in certain processes tasks "Prepare invoice" and "Post invoice" may be done by the same resource, hence they form a sub-process "Handle invoice". In general, it is important to avoid too much deliberation in order to keep the workshop moving. The facilitator also needs to pay attention to the fact that the tasks being posted are at the same level of granularity. When people start mentioning micro-steps, e.g., "Put the document on a fax machine", the facilitator should lift the level of abstraction back to a conceptual process model level. In the end, this exercise leads to a sketch process model that the process analyst can take as input to construct an initial BPMN model after the workshop session. This can be done during the session if a process modeler is available.

At the beginning of the second session, the analyst may provide the participants with a quick introduction to the core set of BPMN elements (start and end events, activities, XOR and AND gateways) in order to show the model that has been prepared as a result of the first workshop session. This model, which can be shown on a whiteboard or directly in a modeling tool through a beamer, can be used to frame the discussion with the aim of validating the current understanding of the business process. It is important, however, not to get lost in the details of the modeling notation to avoid steering attention away from the actual discovery effort.

Workshop-based process discovery requires an organized facilitation and an atmosphere of openness. The facilitator must ensure that parole is balanced between the different participants. This means on the one hand restricting the speech time of talkative participants and, on the other hand, encouraging more introverted participants to express their perspective. Moreover, an atmosphere of openness is indispensable to everybody's participation.

Example 5.2 Consider the following two companies.

> Company A is young, founded three years ago, and has grown rapidly to a current toll of one hundred employees. Company B is owned by the state and operates in a domain with extensive health and security regulations. How might these different characteristics influence workshop-based discovery?

An atmosphere of openness is influenced by the culture of the company. In organizations with a strongly emphasized hierarchy, ideas and critique may be held back, so it may be difficult for domain experts to express their view openly if their boss is also present. In contrast, if creativity and independent thinking are appreciated, participants are more likely to feel at ease with uttering their ideas and issues, even in the presence of their boss. In our example, it might be the case that the young dynamic company has a more open culture than the company with extensive regulations. This must be taken into account when organizing a workshop.   □

It is the responsibility of the analyst to carefully choose the participants depending on the organizational culture. Further, it is the responsibility of the facilitator to always try to stimulate constructive interactions among participants, while remaining neutral when diverging opinions arise. Meantime, while criticism should be allowed, the facilitator should keep negative comments from participants at a minimum to avoid creating unnecessary attrition between them. The facilitator should also challenge viewpoints until a consolidated opinion on the process is formed.

Exercise 5.5 Consider the complaints that have emerged from the interviews reported in Exercise 5.4 (page 170). As a facilitator, what questions would you ask the various participants to investigate these further in a workshop?

5.2.4 Strengths and Weaknesses

The different methods of process discovery have each strengths and weaknesses. These can be discussed in terms of objectivity, richness, time consumption, and immediacy of feedback (see Table 5.1).

- *Objectivity*: Evidence-based discovery methods typically provide the best level of objectivity. Existing documents, existing logs, and observation provide an unbiased account of how a process works. Interview-based and workshop-based discovery both have to rely on the descriptions and interpretations of domain experts who are involved with the process. This bears the risk that those persons may have perceptions and ideas of how the process operates, which may be partially incorrect. Even worse, domain experts may opportunistically hide relevant information about the process from the analyst. This may be the case if the process discovery project happens in a political environment where groups of process stakeholders fear loss of power, loss of influence, or loss of position.
- *Richness*: While interview-based and workshop-based discovery methods show some weaknesses in terms of objectivity, they can provide rich insights into the process. Domain experts involved in interviews and workshops are a good source to clarify reasons why a process is set up as it is. Evidence-based methods might show issues that need to be discussed and raise questions, but they often do not provide an answer. Talking to domain experts also offers a view into the history of the process and the surrounding organization. This is important for understanding which stakeholders have which agenda. Evidence-based discovery methods sometimes provide insights into strategic considerations about a process when they are documented in white papers, but they hardly allow conclusions about the personal agendas of the different stakeholders.
- *Time consumption*: Discovery methods differ in the amount of time they require. While documentation around a particular process can easily be made available to a process analyst, it is much more time-consuming to conduct interviews and workshops. While interview-based discovery requires several feedback iterations, it is difficult to schedule a workshop session with various domain experts at the same time, especially on short notice. Automated process discovery often involves a significant amount of time for extracting, reformatting, and filtering event logs. Passive observation also requires coordination and approval

Table 5.1 Relative strengths and weaknesses of process discovery methods

Aspect	Evidence-based	Interviews	Workshops
Objectivity	High	Medium-high	Medium-high
Richness	Medium	High	High
Time consumption	Low-medium	Medium	Medium
Immediacy of feedback	Low	High	High

time. Thus, it is a good idea to start with document analysis, since documentation can often be made accessible on short notice.

- *Immediacy of feedback*: Those methods that directly build on the conversation and interaction with domain experts are best for getting immediate feedback. Workshop-based discovery is best in this regard since inconsistent perceptions about the operation of a process can directly be resolved by the involved parties. Interviews offer the opportunity to ask questions whenever process-related aspects are unclear. However, not all issues can be resolved directly with a single domain expert. Evidence-based discovery methods raise various questions about how a process works. These questions can often only be answered by talking to domain experts.

The above strengths and weaknesses are summarized in Table 5.2. Since each discovery method has strengths and weaknesses, we recommend employing a mixture of them in a discovery project, if budget allows. The process analyst typically starts with documentation that is readily available. It is essential to organize the project in such a way that the information can be gathered from the relevant domain experts in an efficient and effective way. Interviews and workshops have to be scheduled during the usual work time of domain experts. Thus, experts

Table 5.2 Summary of strengths and weaknesses per discovery method

Method	Strengths	Weaknesses
Document analysis	• Structured information • Independent from stakeholders availability	• Outdated material • Wrong level of abstraction
Observation	• Context-rich insights	• Potentially intrusive • Stakeholders likely to behave differently • Only few cases and not all processes can be observed
Automated discovery	• Extensive set of cases • Objective data	• Potential issue with data quality and level of abstraction • Data may not be available or be available only in part • Data extraction and preparation is time-consuming
Interviews	• Context-rich insights	• Requires sparse time of stakeholders • Time-consuming: several iterations required before sign-off
Workshops	• Context-rich insights • Direct resolution of conflicting views	• Requires simultaneous availability of multiple stakeholders • Time-consuming: multiple sessions typically required

have to be motivated to participate and involved in such a way that it is the least time-consuming for them. Once issues arise about specific details of a process, it might be required to turn back to evidence-based discovery methods.

Question In what situations is it simply not possible to use one or more of the described discovery methods?

There are various circumstances that may restrict the application of different discovery methods. Direct observation may not be possible if the process partially runs in a remote or dangerous environment. For instance, the discovery of an oil-extraction process at an offshore oil platform might belong to this category. There might also be cases where documentation does not exist, for example when a startup company which has gone through a period of rapid growth wants to structure its purchasing process. Lack of input may also be a problem for automated process discovery based on event log data. If the process under consideration is not yet supported by an IT system, or it is only supported in part, there is no data available for the automated discovery of the end-to-end process. In general, interviews are always possible. It might still be a problem though to gain commitment of domain experts to participate in interviews, especially because more than one interview is typically required. Moreover, this may be the case when the process discovery project is subject to company-internal politics and hidden agendas. Workshop-based discovery can be critical in strictly-hierarchical companies with a non-open culture.

Exercise 5.6 The order-to-cash process of your favorite online bookstore has ten major activities conducted by ten people with five different roles. How much time do you approximately need for creating a process model that is validated by the various stakeholders and approved by the process owner? Consider two scenarios: one in which you run interviews, the other in which you run workshops. You may also use other discovery methods in these two scenarios, in addition to either interviews or workshops. Can you estimate the difference in time effort between the two scenarios? Make appropriate assumptions.

5.3   Process Modeling Method

Modeling a business process during process discovery is a complex task. Thus, it is good to follow a predefined procedure in order to approach this task in a systematic way. One way to do so is to work in five steps as follows:

1. Identify the process boundaries
2. Identify activities and events
3. Identify resources and their handoffs
4. Identify the control flow
5. Identify additional elements.

5.3.1 Step 1: Identify the Process Boundaries

The identification of the process boundaries is essential for understanding the scope of the process. As such, part of this work might have already been done with the definition of a process architecture during the process identification phase. The process boundaries vary depending on the perspective of the party we take. For example, let us consider again the order-to-cash process that we modeled in Chapter 3. Three parties are involved in this process: seller, customer, and supplier (for simplicity, we only consider one supplier rather than two). Let us assume we are a process analyst working for the seller company. Thus, in Step 1 we need to identify the boundaries of this process from the perspective of the seller, which is our party of interest. Technically, this means we need to identify the events that trigger our process and those that signal its completion. One way to do so is to identify the business objects that are required as input and provided as output of the process. Another option, as far as the end events are concerned, is to identify the possible outcomes of the process. For example, our order-to-cash process is triggered by the receipt of a purchase order from the customer (so the input object to the process is a purchase order) and completes with the fulfillment of the order (the final outputs are an invoice and a product, which are required to fulfill the order). Accordingly, we can identify one start message event (purchase order received) and one end event (order fulfilled). These two events mark the boundaries of our process from the perspective of the seller. If the process had negative outcomes, we would model these via terminate end events.

Exercise 5.7 Identify the process boundaries for the procure-to-pay process described in Exercise 1.7 (page 31).

5.3.2 Step 2: Identify Activities and Events

The goal of the second step is to identify the main process activities and intermediate events. The advantage of starting with activities in workshops or interviews is that domain experts will be able to articulate what they are doing even if they are not fully aware of the overarching business process. In this step, we also need to identify the events that occur during the process, which we will model with intermediate events in BPMN. Figure 5.5 lists the twelve activities and two events in our order-to-cash example (there are no intermediate events in this example). The initial set of activities and events obtained in this step may undergo revisions, e.g., more activities may be added as we add more details to our model. If the process is too complex, we suggest you only focus on the main activities and intermediate events at this stage, and add the others at a later stage when a deeper understanding of these elements and their relations has been gained.

Fig. 5.5 The activities and events of the order-to-cash process

Exercise 5.8 Identify the main activities and events for the procure-to-pay process of Exercise 1.7 (page 31).

5.3.3 Step 3: Identify Resources and Their Handoffs

Once we have identified the set of main activities and intermediate events, we can turn to the question of *what resource* is responsible for which activity. This information provides the basis for the definition of pools and lanes, as well as for the assignment of activities and events to these elements. At this stage, the order of the activities is not defined yet. Therefore, it is good to first identify those points in the process where work is handed over from one resource to another, e.g., from one department to another. These handoff points are important since a participant being assigned a new task to perform usually has to make assumptions about what has been completed before. Making these assumptions explicit is an essential step in process discovery. Figure 5.6 shows the set of activities and events of the order-to-cash process now being assigned to the lanes of the seller pool, with sequence flows indicating handoffs. The handoff points also help to identify parts of the process that can be studied in isolation from the rest. These parts can be refined into sub-processes by the help of the involved stakeholders. For example, in the order-to-cash

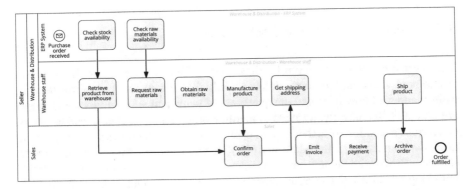

Fig. 5.6 The activities and events of the order-to-cash process assigned to lanes

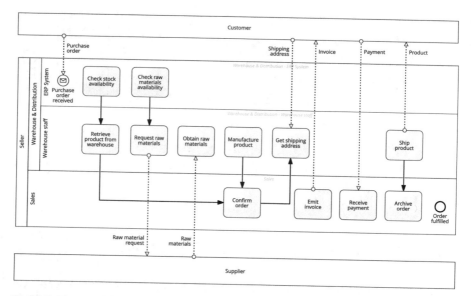

Fig. 5.7 The handoff of work between the seller, the customer, and the supplier

process the acquisition of raw materials (see Figure 4.15 on page 131) could be handled in isolation from the rest of the process, since this part involves the suppliers and personnel from the warehouse & distribution department.

If the process involves external parties such as customers, business partners, or suppliers, we use pools to model these external parties and message flows to capture the handoff between them. For our order-to-cash example we obtain the model in Figure 5.7.

Exercise 5.9 Using the process description in Exercise 1.7 (page 31), first identify the involved resources; next, assign the activities and events you obtained in Exercise 5.8 to these resources; and finally identify the handoffs.

5.3.4 Step 4: Identify the Control Flow

The internal handoffs within our business party of interest, i.e., those that we have represented via sequence flows, define an initial structure for the control flow. In essence, control flow relates to the questions of *when* and *why* activities and events are executed. Technically, we need to identify order dependencies, decision points, concurrent execution of activities and events, and potential rework and repetition. Decision points require the addition of (X)OR-splits and relevant conditions on the sequence flows originating from these splits. Rework and repetition can be modeled with loop structures. Concurrent activities that can be executed independently from each other are linked to AND gateways. Event-based splits are used to react to

Fig. 5.8 The control flow of the order-to-cash process

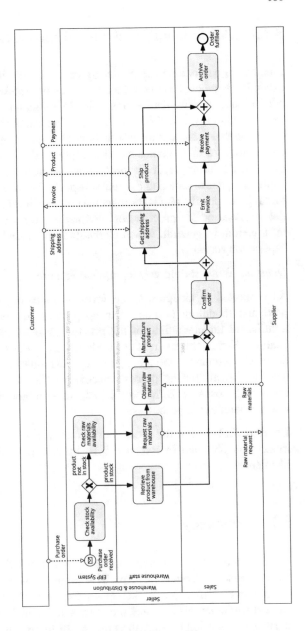

decisions taken outside the process. Figure 5.8 shows how order constraints are captured by control-flow arcs in the seller pool of the order-to-cash process. Here we can see that the handoffs that we identified in the previous step have now been refined in more elaborate dependencies.

Exercise 5.10 Using the process description in Exercise 1.7 (page 31), refine the model you obtained in Exercise 5.9 by defining the full control flow.

5.3.5 Step 5: Identify Additional Elements

Finally, we can extend the model by capturing the involved business objects and exception handlers based on the purpose of our model. For the objects, this means adding data objects, data stores, and their relations to activities and events via data associations. For the exception handlers, this means using boundary events, exception flows, and compensation handlers. As we mentioned in Chapters 3 and 4, the addition of data elements and exceptions depends on the particular modeling purpose. For example, if the process is meant to be automated, it is desirable to explicitly capture data and exception aspects. We may also add further annotations to support specific application scenarios. For instance, if the model is used for risk analysis or for process cost estimation, we may need to add risk and cost information. In general, which elements to be added depends upon the particular application scenario.

Question When should we stop modeling a process?

As discussed in Chapter 3, the level of modeling detail is determined by the particular modeling purpose. During process discovery, the purpose is to gain a sufficient understanding of the process as required to perform the subsequent analysis. Hence, there is no need to document the process in a level of excruciating detail. Unfortunately, though, many organizations fall into the trap of creating very detailed models during process discovery. This may have a negative impact on the overall cost of a BPM project, and most importantly, it will delay the actual improvement of the processes.

Exercise 5.11 Using the process description in Exercise 1.7 (page 31), refine the model you obtained in Exercise 5.10 by adding business objects and exception handlers.

5.3.6 Summary

In this section, we illustrated a method for constructing a business process model via a number of incremental steps. This method lends itself well to workshops, as it can be run over multiple workshop sessions. For example, we can do Steps 1–2 in the first workshop session, and then Steps 3, 4, and 5 in a subsequent session each, starting each session by validating the results of the previous step with the workshop participants.

   If you are an expert analyst combining a strong knowledge of BPMN with excellent facilitation abilities, you may run this method in an integrated manner. In this alternative, you would model the control flow on-the-fly as you add resources, i.e., you would do Steps 3 and 4 simultaneously.

5.4 Process Model Quality Assurance

As discussed, gathering and organizing process-related information in a process model is typically a sequential activity (e.g., we conduct different workshop sessions or interviews), which involves at least one process analyst and multiple domain experts. Therefore, there is a need to assure that the model we produce is of high quality. As shown in Figure 5.9, a process model is subjected to three quality aspects: syntactic, semantic, and pragmatic quality. Verification is the activity of assuring syntactic quality, validation that of assuring semantic quality, and certification that of assuring pragmatic quality. In addition, modeling guidelines and conventions can be used to achieve a high quality right from the start.

5.4.1 Syntactic Quality and Verification

Syntactic quality relates to the conformance of a process model to the syntactic rules of the modeling language used. We distinguish two types of syntactic rules: structural and behavioral rules. *Structural rules* relate to the way the various model elements are connected with each other while *behavioral rules* relate to the way a process model can be instantiated. Syntactic rules are important because they are meant to increase model understandability and to avoid ambiguity.

Below we list the main structural rules that apply to a BPMN model:

1. **Element level:**

   - Activities: activities must have at least one incoming and one outgoing sequence flow.
   - Events:

     – start events must not have incoming sequence flows;

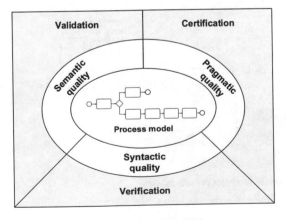

Fig. 5.9 Process model quality aspects and assurance activities

- end events must not have outgoing sequence flows;
- intermediate events must have at least one incoming and one outgoing sequence flow;
- only intermediate catching boundary events can be attached to an activity's border.

- Gateways:

  - split gateways must have exactly one incoming and at least two outgoing sequence flows;
  - join gateways must have at least two incoming and exactly one outgoing sequence flows;
  - the outgoing arcs of an (X)OR-split gateway must bear conditions.

- Flows:

  - a sequence flow must connect two flow nodes (activities, events, and gateways) of the same pool, i.e., sequence flows cannot cross the boundaries of pools;
  - a message flow must connect (an activity or a throwing message event in) one pool with (an activity or a catching message event in) a different pool;
  - a directed data association must connect a data object with an activity or message event, or a data store with an activity, or vice versa;
  - an indirected data association must connect a data object with a sequence flow, or a text annotation with any element.

2. **Model level:** all flow nodes must be on a path from a start to an end event.

The element-level rules restrict the way each model element is used, while the model-level rule ensures that the model is not disconnected. A model is *structurally correct* if it satisfies all the above structural rules. Such rules can be checked by inspecting the graph-based structure of the process model. For example, it is easy to see that the model in Figure 5.10 is structurally incorrect.

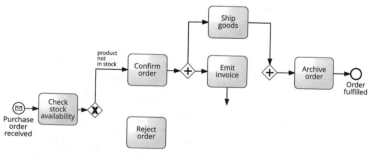

Fig. 5.10 A structurally incorrect process model

Behavioral rules are required to avoid behavioral anomalies such as deadlocks and livelocks during the execution of a process model. We have already introduced some of these behavioral anomalies in Chapter 3 (see e.g., the discussion on Figure 3.11 on page 88). Let us now take a systematic look at them. A *deadlock* occurs when a running process instance is not able to progress any further once a given state is reached, i.e., a token gets stuck at that state. A *livelock* is another type of behavioral anomaly which occurs when a process instance keeps cycling in a loop. In other words, a token is trapped within a loop structure: it is free to move but only within the loop. For example, this may arise if the condition of a loop always evaluates to true. Both deadlocks and livelocks may prevent tokens from reaching an end event, so the process instance may not be able to complete altogether. Another behavioral anomaly is the *lack of synchronization*. This occurs when two or more tokens are in the same sequence flow because they are not synchronized at some join gateway. Finally, a *dead activity* is an activity that can never be executed in any instance of the process model.

It is easy to see that these behavioral anomalies can arise when mixing a split with a join of a different type in the same block structure, as shown in Figure 5.11. A *block structure* is a single-entry single-exit process model fragment, such that the entry and exit points are two gateways (one split and one join) and each path from one gateway leads to the other gateway. If the split and join match in type no behavioral anomaly can arise, while if the two gateways are different, as in the models of Figure 5.11, this will lead to different behavioral anomalies. Such anomalies, though, can also arise outside of block structures, in which case they are harder to spot. For example, Figure 5.12a shows a model with a deadlock that occurs at the AND-join if activity G is executed. This is because there is an injection of a branch into what would otherwise be a perfect AND-block. A token may come back from this branch and reach the AND-join after E is performed. The AND-join, however, will deadlock because it will never receive a token from C after F has been executed.

Exercise 5.12 Have a look at Figure 5.11. What is precisely going wrong in each block structure?

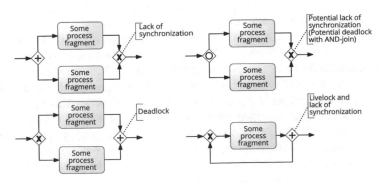

Fig. 5.11 Common behavioral anomalies in block structures

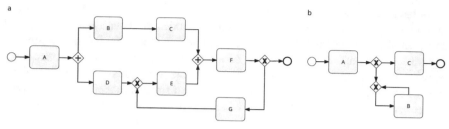

Fig. 5.12 A process model with a deadlock (**a**) and one with a livelock (**b**)

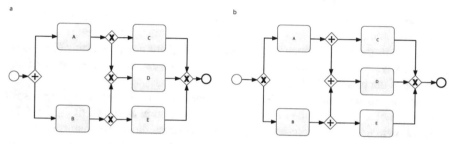

Fig. 5.13 A process model with lack of synchronization (**a**) and one with a dead activity (**b**)

We say that a process model is *behaviorally correct*, or *sound*, if and only if it satisfies the following behavioral rules:

1. **Option to complete:** any running process instance must eventually complete,
2. **Proper completion:** at the moment of completion, each token of the process instance must be in a different end event,
3. **No dead activities:** any activity can be executed in at least one process instance.

Option to complete implies that there are no deadlocks nor livelocks that prevent the instance from completing, while proper completion implies that there is no lack of synchronization. For example, the model in Figure 5.12a violates the option to complete due to a deadlock if the path via G is chosen. Another example of no option to complete is provided by the model in Figure 5.12b, though this time it is because of a livelock. In addition, this model is structurally incorrect because B is not on a path from a start to an end event. An example of improper completion is given by the model in Figure 5.13a. This model has a lack of synchronization (the last sequence flow will always have two tokens), and in some instances activity D may even be executed twice. Finally, the model in Figure 5.13b violates the no dead activities property, as D can never be executed. Moreover, this model suffers from improper completion, since when the end event is reached a token remains trapped before the AND-join. However, this is not due to lack of synchronization (there can never be two tokens on the same sequence flow), but rather to a deadlock at the AND-join. Thus, while proper completion excludes lack of synchronization, the latter is not the only cause for improper completion.

The above definition of *soundness* only takes into account the control flow of a process model. It assumes all input data objects and incoming messages are available when an activity is to be executed, and all output data objects and outgoing messages are produced upon an activity's completion. Properties such as soundness can be checked after a process model is created. Alternatively, a process modeling tool can enforce that a model is correct by design. This can be achieved by allowing only edit operations that preserve structural and behavioral correctness. One easy way to achieve that is to construct models where gateways appear only in block structures and are of matching type (so-called *structured* process models) as the model in Figure 3.12 (see page 90). However, this type of model has limited expressiveness compared to unstructured models, as discussed in Section 4.1 in the context of cycles.

Those parts of a model that cause unsoundness should be reworked. Typically, these parts trigger questions about specific behavior of the process that need to be clarified with domain experts. *Verification* is the activity of checking that a process model is syntactically correct, i.e., that it is both structurally and behaviorally correct. Verification addresses formal properties of a model that can be checked without knowing the corresponding real-world process.

Exercise 5.13 Which behavioral rules are violated in the model of Figure 5.14? How can this model be made sound?

5.4.2 Semantic Quality and Validation

Semantic quality deals with the adherence of a process model to its real-world process. *Validation* is the activity of checking the semantic quality of a model by comparing it with its real-world business process. The particular challenge of validation is that there is no set of formal rules that can be used to easily check semantic quality; rather the focus is on the overall meaning of the model, and

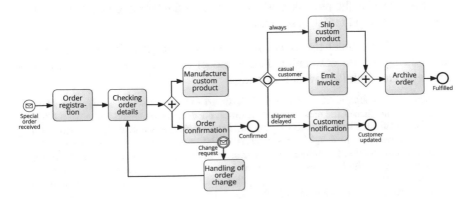

Fig. 5.14 A process model for fulfilling special orders

therefore, this can only be done by talking to the process participants and by consulting the available documentation.

There are two essential aspects of semantic quality: validity and completeness. *Validity* means that all statements that one can make from the model are correct and relevant to the real-world process. Validity can be assessed by explaining to domain experts how the processing is captured in the model. The domain expert is expected to point out any difference between what the model states and what is possible in reality. *Completeness* means that the model contains all relevant statements about the corresponding business process. Completeness is more difficult to assess. Here, the process analyst has to ask about various alternative processing options at different stages of the process to ensure nothing is missing. For example, the model in Figure 5.8 (see page 181) is incomplete because it does not capture exceptional paths such as that to handle an order cancelation from the customer. It is the job of the process analyst to judge the relevance of these additional elements. This judgement has to be done against the background of the modeling objective, which the process analyst should be familiar with. Let us consider an example to understand the difference between validity and completeness. If a process model for loan assessments states that any financial officer may carry out the task of checking the credit history of a particular applicant while in practice this requires a specific authorization, the model has a semantic problem due to an invalid statement. If the task of checking the credit history is omitted then the model has a semantic problem due to incompleteness.

Exercise 5.14 What can we say about the semantic quality of the model in Figure 3.9 (page 87)? Refer to the process description in Example 3.5 on page 86.

Validation can be supported by methods like interviews or workshops. Alternatively, there are tools that provide truthfulness by design. This is, for instance, achieved by automatically discovering a process model from an event log, as we will see in Chapter 11. In practice, process models often require the *approval* from the process owner. This approval is a special validation step, since it is an endorsement of the validity and completeness of the model. Beyond that, the approval of the process owner establishes the normative character of the process model at hand. As a consequence, the process model can then be published, used as an input for process analysis and redesign, or archived.

Exercise 5.15 Consider the model in Figure 5.14 (page 187) with reference to the following process description. Is this model valid and complete? If not, what statements are invalid and what is missing?

When a special order is received, it is first registered and then its details are checked. Next, the order is confirmed and meantime the custom product is manufactured. Once the product has been made, the shipment can be planned. Afterwards, the customer type and shipment status are checked. In fact, if a customer is casual an ad hoc invoice must be emitted, which is not required for ordinary customers. In the latter case, the customer account is simply charged with the costs related to the order fulfillment. Moreover, if the shipment has been delayed, the customer must be updated on the expected delay. Concomitantly to these activities, the custom product is shipped. After the latter activity and after the invoice has been emitted, the process completes with the archival of the order. Any time during the confirmation of the order and the manufacturing of the respective product, an order change request may be received, in which case any activity must be interrupted to handle the change request. This includes the registration of the order variation and a notification to the customer, after which the process resumes from the order checking.

5.4.3 Pragmatic Quality and Certification

Pragmatic quality relates to the usability of a process model. The particular challenge of pragmatic quality assessment is to anticipate the actual usage of a process model. This aspect focuses on how people interact with a model. For instance, a process model of good pragmatic quality can be checked by testing how well a user understands the model.

Certification is the activity of checking the pragmatic quality of a process model by investigating its use. There are several aspects of usability including understandability, maintainability, and learning. *Understandability* relates to how easy it is to read and comprehend a process model. *Maintainability* points to the ease of applying changes to the model. *Learning* relates to how good a process model reveals how its corresponding business process works in reality. There are several characteristics of a model that influence usability including its size, its structural complexity, and its graphical layout.

Certification can be achieved via interviews or experiments with model users, i.e., with those that are meant to use the model in their job, e.g., a process owner using a model for communication purposes or a process analyst using it as input to process analysis and redesign. Alternatively, there are rules that strive to provide usability by design. One of these is *block-structuredness*: a structured process model, besides being always sound, has been shown to often be easier to understand than its unstructured counterpart. As an example, Figure 5.15a shows an unstructured process model while Figure 5.15b shows the structured version of this model, where one activity has been duplicated to avoid crossing arcs, and splits and joins within the same block match in type. This model is semantically equivalent to, yet simpler to understand than that of Figure 5.15a.

There are two essential checks for understandability, and learning. The first one relates to the consistency between visual structure and logical structure. Figure 5.16a and b show the same fragment of the order-to-cash process model. The second model is a rework of the first one in terms of layout, where all elements are laid out following a top-left to bottom-right orientation, and where there are no crossing arcs. Here the elements' position has been changed with the aim to improve the consistency between visual structure and logical structure. Block-structuring a process model, where possible, is also another mechanism to improve this consistency.

The second check is concerned with meaningful labels. Activities, events, and other elements must use labels that follow specific naming conventions. For example, the labels in the model of Figure 5.17 follow inconsistent labeling

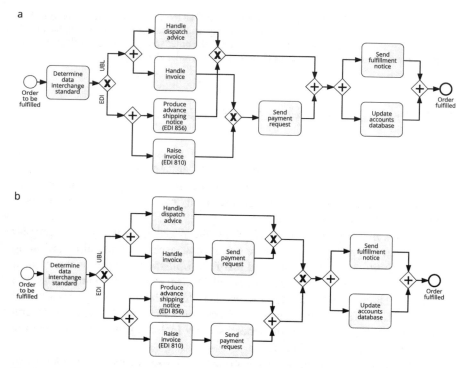

Fig. 5.15 An unstructured process model (**a**) and its structured counterpart (**b**).

Acknowledgement This example is taken from [40]

styles and lack the use of a common glossary, resulting in ambiguous meaning which affects the model understandability. Activity "Get approval for expenses" follows the *verb-object* style (imperative verb + business object), which has been shown to be the most effective style for labeling activities. In contrast, activities "Cost planning" and "Recalculation of costs" capture the actions of planning and recalculating as nouns at different positions in the label, following the *action-noun* style. As a result of mixing different labeling styles, the meaning of activity "Plan data transfer" is ambiguous: it could mean either to plan a data transfer or to transfer a record of plan data. In addition, due to the lack of a common glossary, two activities use the term "costs" while another the term "expenses", though they probably refer to the same thing. Moving to the labels of events and gateways, we see that the label of the end event "Approved" lacks a reference to a business object (it should be "Expenses approved", following an object-verb style: business object + past participle verb). The XOR-split's label "Acceptable?" hides the existence of a decision activity "Check plan acceptability". In fact, as discussed in Section 3.2 (see page 79), it is preferable to avoid labeling (X)OR-split gateways and to use more explicative conditions than "yes" or "no" in the outgoing arcs of the split, e.g., "plan acceptable" and "plan unacceptable".

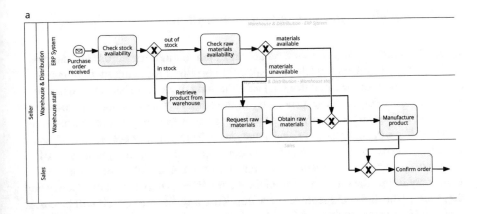

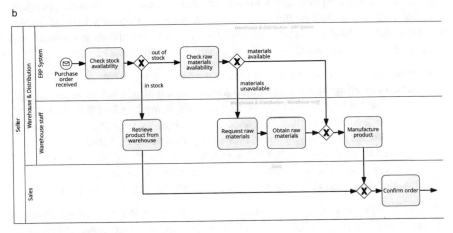

Fig. 5.16 Extract of the order-to-cash process model: with bad layout (**a**), with good layout (**b**)

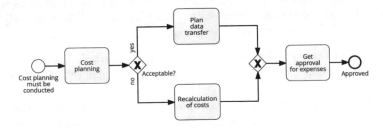

Fig. 5.17 A process model for cost planning.

Acknowledgement This example is taken from [87]

Exercise 5.16 Is the process model in Figure 5.14 (page 187) of good pragmatic quality? If not, how can it be improved?

5.4.4   *Modeling Guidelines and Conventions*

Modeling guidelines and *conventions* are an important tool for improving the pragmatic quality of process models. The specific objectives for using modeling guidelines and conventions are manifold: (i) safeguarding model consistency and improving standardization and reuse, especially in the context of large modeling initiatives
involving various process analysts; (ii) reducing the dependency on process analysts,
who may leave the company at some stage; and (iii) facilitating access to models by
non-modeling experts. For example, consider an insurance company that has a BPM
team within each line of business (home, motor, commercial). The various BPM
teams may follow the same set of modeling guidelines to maximize consistency and
reuse across the different insurance services. This way, for example, it will be easier
to standardize common parts across all the variants of their claim handling process.

The difference between guidelines and conventions is essentially that the former
are suggestions while the latter are mandatory rules. Modeling guidelines and
conventions are restrictions to the following aspects of a process model:

1. **Vocabulary:** avoiding certain elements, e.g., never using event sub-processes.
2. **Structure:** limiting the structure of the model, e.g., setting a threshold on the size
   or the number of hierarchical layers, or modeling using block-structures only.
3. **Semantics:** avoiding particular element meanings (rarely used), e.g., using
   boundary events to model business faults only, excluding technology faults.
4. **Appearance:** restricting the model appearance in terms of labels, layout, and
   notation, e.g., using the verb-noun style to label activities, using terms only taken
   from a glossary, or modeling with a top-left to bottom-right orientation.

Below we propose a set of modeling guidelines called the *Seven Process
Modeling Guidelines (7PMG)*. This set was developed as an amalgamation of
insights from available research. Specifically, the analysis of large collections of
process models by various researchers identified many syntactical errors as well as
complex structures that reduce pragmatic quality. These guidelines are helpful to
guide users towards mitigating such problems.

G1:   *Use as few model elements as possible.* Studies have shown that models of
         large size tend to be more difficult to understand and have a higher syntactic
         error rate.
G2:   *Minimize the routing paths per element.* For each element in a process model,
         it is possible to determine the number of incoming and outgoing arcs. This
         summed figure gives an idea of the routing paths through the element. A
         high number makes it harder to understand the model. Also, the number of
         syntactic errors in a model seems strongly correlated to the use of model
         elements with a high number of routing paths.
G3:   *Use one start event for each trigger and one end event for each outcome.*
         Empirical studies have established that the number of start and end events is
         positively connected with an increase in error probability. Models satisfying
         this requirement are easier to understand.

G4:   *Model as structured as possible.* Unstructured models are not only more likely to include behavioral anomalies, but they also tend to be harder to understand. Nonetheless, as shown in Section 4.1, it is sometimes not possible or not desirable to turn an unstructured model fragment (e.g., an unstructured cycle) into a structured one. This is why this guideline states "as structured as possible".

G5:   *Avoid OR gateways where possible.* Models that have only AND and XOR gateways are less error-prone. This empirical finding is apparently related to the fact that the combinations of choices represented by an OR-split are more difficult to grasp than behavior captured by other gateways. Moreover, the semantics of the OR-join is complex, as it needs to check that each of its incoming branches is active (see Section 3.2.3 on page 86), and as such hampers understandability.

G6:   *Use verb-object activity labels.* A wide exploration of labeling styles used in process models from practice disclosed the existence of a number of popular styles. From these, model users consider the verb-object style, like "Inform complainant", as significantly less ambiguous and more useful than action-noun labels (e.g., "Complaint analysis") or labels that follow neither of these styles (e.g., "Incident agenda").

G7:   *Decompose a model with more than 30 elements.* This guideline relates to G1 that is motivated by a positive correlation between size and syntactic errors. For models with more than 30 elements the error probability tends to climb sharply. Thus, large models should be split up into smaller ones. For example, large fragments with a single entry and a single exit can be replaced by a collapsed sub-process activity.

Exercise 5.17   Consider the process model of Figure 5.18, which captures a business process for handling complaints, as described below. Identify improvements for this model by assessing which of the 7PMG guidelines are not followed. Next, remodel the process based on your observations.

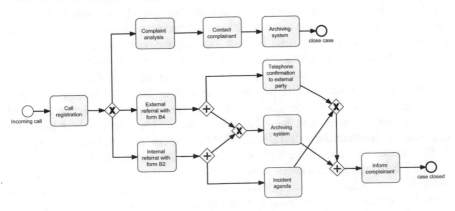

Fig. 5.18 A process model for handling complaints, as found in practice

A complaint is triggered by a phone call by a complaining customer. It is decided whether the complaint can be handled or whether it has to be referred to an internal or external party. An external referral leads to a telephone confirmation to the external party. An internal referral is added to the incident agenda. If no referral is needed, a complaint analysis is conducted and the complainant is contacted. In either case, the complaint is archived and the case is closed.

Process modeling tools such as Apromore, ARIS or Signavio Process Manager come with a predefined list of modeling guidelines that can be automatically checked against a model, and allow the possibility of defining custom guidelines. For example, one can check that each activity follows a verb-object labeling style or that the model is laid out from top-left to bottom-right. While support for the automated checking of modeling guidelines is common, much less common is the support for the automated checking of the BPMN syntactic rules, where the focus is mostly on structural rules.

5.5 Recap

This chapter described how to conduct the different tasks of process discovery: (i) defining the setting, (ii) gathering the required information, (iii) modeling the process, and (iv) assuring model quality. The chapter stressed the complementary skills of process analysts and domain experts. While process analysts are skilled in analyzing and modeling processes, they often lack detailed domain knowledge. In contrast, domain experts have typically limited modeling skills, but a detailed understanding of the part of the process they are involved with. This implies several challenges of process discovery that analysts have to face.

Next, the chapter illustrated different discovery methods. Evidence-based methods typically provide the most objective insight into the execution of the process. However, the immediacy of feedback is low and the richness of the insights can be mediocre. Interviews can be biased towards the perspective of the interviewee, but reveal rich details of the process. Interviews offer a chance to gain direct feedback on process-related matters. Workshops can help to resolve inconsistent views of different domain experts. On the downside, it is difficult to have all required domain experts available at the same time. Budget allowing, we recommend using a mixture of discovery methods based on the specifics of the discovery project.

We then presented a five-step process modeling method. First, we suggest identifying the boundaries of the process in terms of its start and end events. Second, we determine the main activities and events, the different resources involved (internal and external), and their handoff of work. Once this aspect has been clarified, we can determine the full control flow, and complete the model by adding additional elements such as business objects and exception handlers.

In the last section we discussed three measures of quality assurance: syntactic, semantic, and pragmatic quality, and discussed the respective quality assurance activities: verification, validation, and certification. We concluded the chapter by illustrating a set of modeling guidelines that can help improve pragmatic quality.

5.6 Solutions to Exercises

Solution 5.1 Domain knowledge can be very helpful for analyzing processes. It helps to ask the right questions and to build analogies from prior experience. On the other hand, the skills of an experienced process analyst should not be underestimated. These skills are domain-independent and relate to how a process discovery project can be organized. Experienced process analysts are skilled in scoping and driving a project into the right direction. They possess problem-solving skills for handling various critical situations of a process discovery project. There is clearly a trade-off between the two sets of skills. It should be assured that a certain level of process modeling analysis experience is available. If that is not the case for the applying domain expert, the process analyst would be preferred.

Solution 5.2 To obtain a complete and systematic view of our process, we must overcome two of the three challenges related to domain experts, namely: (i) fragmented process knowledge and (ii) thinking on a case level. To overcome the first challenge, we first need to understand how each of the three domain experts (customer relationship manager, warehouse worker, and financial officer) participates in the process. To this end, we can ask them what tasks they are responsible for, and, for each of these, what inputs are required and what outputs are produced. This will help us understand which handoffs of work exist between them (assuming there is no other resource involved in the process), so as to infer an initial order between their tasks. For example, from this first battery of questions we may realize that the warehouse worker picks books from the warehouse for shipment only upon the receipt of a confirmed order, which is emitted by the customer relationship manager. This suggests a handoff of work between customer relationship manager and warehouse worker.

If inconsistent descriptions of the process emerge out of these initial discussions, we have to ask additional questions to uncover hidden assumptions and conditions underlying these descriptions. For example, the warehouse worker may expect to receive a single confirmed order for all books in a given purchase order, assuming that any shipment should be put on hold until all the ordered books are available. However, the customer may have opted for their books to be shipped in different packages as soon as they become available. In this case, the customer relationship manager may confirm a set of sub-orders (one per package), rather than a single order. To clarify these diverging assumptions between the customer relationship manager and the warehouse worker, we may ask the customer relationship manager about the different shipment options that are available to customers, and assess what implications there should be for the warehouse worker, as opposed to what the latter actually does. This investigation into inconsistent views by the involved stakeholders can already help us identify opportunities for improving the process.

To overcome the second challenge (resources thinking on a case level), we may inquire about exceptions due to *business faults* such as what happens if an order is canceled by the customer, or if an ordered product is unavailable or discontinued. We may also inquire about the existence of *timeouts*, for example by asking if there is a prescribed timeframe to fulfill an order, and if so, what happens if this deadline is not met. These are examples of questions that help us reason on a process level, because they focus on different conditions and different outcomes, rather than on the case level, i.e., with reference to a specific order. By doing so, we can identify the routing constructs that are required to link all the tasks together and infer the complete control flow. For example, an order is confirmed by the customer relationship manager only if the ordered books are available. If they are not available, the customer is informed accordingly and the order is declined. These two (intermediate) outcomes are mutually exclusive, suggesting the presence of an XOR-split after the stock availability check.

Solution 5.3 The methods in the classes of the UML class diagram may suggest possible process activities, while the organizational policies may provide the conditions underpinning certain decision activities in the process. Looking at the class diagram, some classes map to organizational roles that participate in our process, such as Applicant, Admission officer, and Academic committee member; other classes map to documents, such as Assessment and Application. However, considering that this class diagram models the functionality of an entire system and that this system likely supports other processes within the university, some of these classes are irrelevant for our specific process. For example, Visitor and Visit probably refer to a process similar to the student admission process, i.e., that for admitting academic visitors to the university.

Taking a closer look at the methods for AdmissionOfficer, we can derive three candidate activities for our process: "Provide information", "Check application", and "Request clarification". Which of these are actually activities of our process will have to be assessed by talking directly to an admission officer. Likewise, looking at AcademicCommitteeMember, other candidate activities are "Assess application", "Accept application", "Reject application", and "Archive assessment". Similar conclusions can be derived from the Applicant class. Observe, however, that not all activities performed by a given participant are reflected in a UML class diagram. This is because some of these activities may be manual or simply not supported by the system in question. Again, this is something that will have to be discussed with domain experts.

Moving to the list of organizational policies, we can infer the conditions underpinning the final decision on an admission application (e.g., based on consistency of prior education and quality of essay). These conditions are probably checked by a member of the academic committee via activity "Assess application", while via activity "Check application" an admission officer probably checks that all required documents (academic transcripts, essay, reference letters, etc.) are present in the application. If something is missing or unclear they may request more information or documents by performing activity "Request clarification". In addition, the last policy suggests the presence of a deadline of four weeks for the applicant to accept a letter of offer. We can model this timeout with an event-based XOR-split followed by a timer event (4 weeks) in one branch and an intermediate catching message event on the other, to receive the signed letter of offer. However, from the available documentation it is not possible to infer which resource will perform this check. It may likely be a student admission officer, if this role handles all communications with the applicant.

Finally, we use the organization chart to determine the persons to interview and their supervisors to ask for permission. Candidates for interview are all officers within the student admission office (with Mark Johnson being their supervisor) and all members of the academic committee (with Liza Stewart being their supervisor). It is not clear at this stage if the enrollment office is involved at all in our process. Probably this office is only relevant to the enrollment process, which follows the admission process and allows students to enroll in particular subjects. Mark can help us figure this out.

Solution 5.4

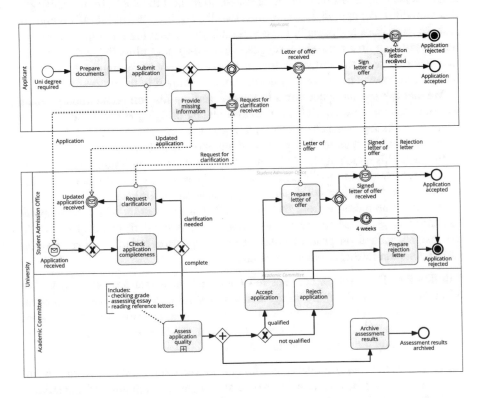

Solution 5.5 Three complaints emerge from the interviews. Louise Smith complains that the Web portal has bugs and as such it lets through incomplete applications. She points out that rectifying these applications is time-consuming. Peter Capello also complains about technology. He points out to communication issues with the student admission office due to the student admission system losing messages that he needs to resend. He adds that he can only resend messages if he finds out that these went missing, alluding to the fact that sometimes he does not

realize that messages got lost. Also in this case, this problem leads to rework and so to process slowdowns. Finally, Mary Adams laments that the academic committee is too slow to reply.

As discussed, process discovery can provide opportunities to isolate process issues, the impact of which can then be assessed during process analysis. However, before capturing these issues into the model and flagging them for process analysis, it is important to investigate these issues. The purpose is to understand whether they are really issues, in which case they should be captured in the model, or rather sporadic exceptions, which we may neglect to avoid cluttering the model. This can be done during a workshop, where such complaints are discussed directly with all relevant stakeholders. For example, for each complaint we can ask the person who raised it how frequently the particular issue occurs. In our example, we can ask Louise how many times on average she needs to request the applicant to rectify and resubmit his or her application, and when was the last time she did so. If we find out that the issue does not actually happen frequently, or that the last time it occurred was a very long time ago, which suggests that it may have already been fixed (e.g., in a new release of the software), then the issue may not be so important, or it has become irrelevant, and so we may decide not to capture it in the process model.

We can ask the same questions to Peter regarding his communication problem with the student admission office. Interestingly, by bringing everyone at the same table, a workshop can help us to understand the root causes of certain issues. This could be the case for Mary's complaint about the slowness of the academic committee. This issue may likely be caused by the student admission system, which as Peter reported, seems to frequently fail to send messages to the student admission office. So per se this does not depend on the academic committee.

A take-home message from this exercise is that the results of a workshop are not narrowly restricted to the process model that is created, but they extend to the insights gained on process issues, and also provide a forum where process participants can further explore these issues.

Solution 5.6 This process contains ten major activities that are assigned to five different roles, and there are altogether ten domain experts besides the process owner. We can assume that there will be a kickoff meeting with the process owner and some important domain experts on day one. Furthermore, 1 day might be required to study the available documentation.

Scenario 1: Interviews. An interview with one domain expert can take from 2 to 3 h, such that we would be able to meet two persons a day, and document the interview results later in the same day. Let us assume that we meet some persons only once while we seek feedback from important domain experts in two additional interviews. Then, there would be a final approval from the process owner. This adds up to 1 day for the kickoff, one for document study, 5 days for the first iteration interviews, and further 5 days if we assume that we meet five of the ten experts three times. Then, we need maximum 1 day to prepare for the meeting to gain final approval from the process owner, which would be on the following day. If there are no delays and scheduling problems, using document analysis and interviews yields a total of 2 + 5 + 5 + 2 = 14 work days as a minimum.

Scenario 2: Workshop. Given the relatively low complexity of this process (ten main activities overall, five different roles and ten participants), three workshop sessions of 3 h each should be enough to create a complete process model and validate it. Clearly, this is only feasible assuming that we can simultaneously access at least one representative for each of the ten roles. This will lead to a minimum of five and a maximum of ten people participating in each workshop session, which is feasible (recall that no more than ten to twelve people should attend a workshop to avoid it to become unmanageable). We can use the first session to create a sketch of the model including relevant resources, the second to validate this sketch and identify the main routing constructs, and the final session to refine the control flow and validate the final model. Between each session we can spend 2–3 h to consolidate the results of each session and prepare for the next session. Then, similarly to the first scenario, we need maximum 1 day to prepare for the meeting to gain final approval from the process owner, which would be on the following day. If there are no delays and scheduling problems, using document analysis and workshops yields a total of 2 + 3 + 2 = 7 work days as a minimum.

In conclusion, we would take about half the time if conducting workshops instead of interviews.

Solution 5.7 We take the perspective of the company and consider the employee as the customer. Accordingly, we identify one start event, namely "Request for purchase received", and three end events, namely "Goods received & paid" (positive outcome), "Purchase request rejected", and "Goods returned" (negative outcomes).

Solution 5.8 We identify 16 main activities and four intermediate events. As for the activities, given that the approval for the necessity of purchase and for the conformance to the company's policies are done by the same supervisor, we can capture these two approvals with a collapsed sub-process. As for the events, we use three intermediate throwing message events to communicate the results of the checks done by the supervisors and by the purchasing department back to the employee, and one intermediate catching message event to model the receipt of the goods.

Solution 5.9 We identify one pool for the employee, one for the vendor, and one for our company. The latter includes the following lanes: supervisor, purchasing department, enterprise system, accounts payable office, and goods receipt department. In the lane for the supervisor we add a text annotation to specify that a four-eye principle applies to the two approval activities ("Approve finance" and "Approve necessity of purchase & policy conformance"). Activity "Archive paper-based note" is performed by both the purchasing department and by the accounts payable office.

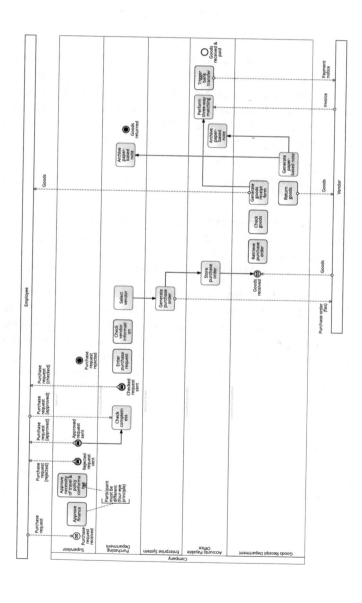

Solution 5.10

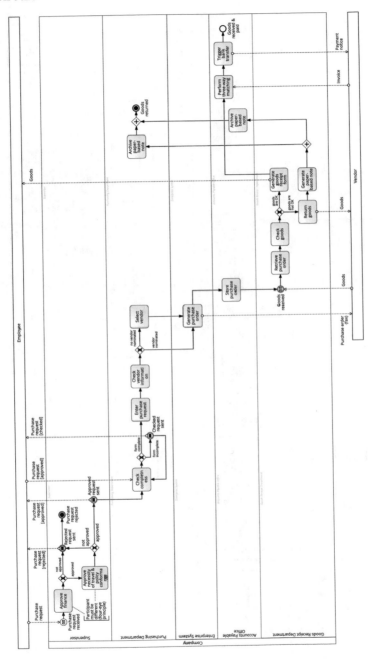

Solution 5.11

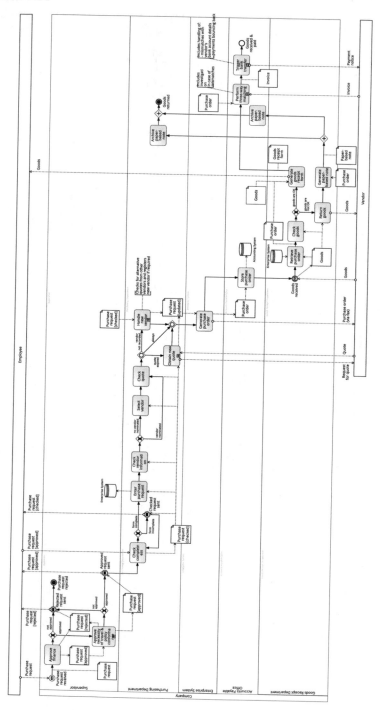

Solution 5.12   We can observe the following behavioral anomalies:

- On the top-left structure we have a *lack of synchronization*, because an AND-split is followed by an XOR-join. The two tokens created from the AND-split are not synchronized by the XOR-join, leading to two tokens being placed on the arc emanating from the XOR-join.
- On the bottom-left structure we have a *deadlock*. The AND-join requires a token on each of its incoming arcs. However, XOR-split will create a token only on one of its outgoing arcs leading to the process getting stuck at the AND-join, waiting for a second token to arrive.
- On the top-right structure, if the OR-split is followed by an XOR-join we may get a *lack of synchronization*. This occurs if multiple tokens are generated by the OR-split (one per branch). Similarly, there is a potential *deadlock* if the OR-split is followed by an AND-join. The deadlock occurs if the OR-split sends only one token out.
- On the bottom-right structure, there is an XOR-join used as the entry to the loop, while the loop exit is modeled with an AND-split. This has the consequence that one token will remain trapped in the loop at each iteration of the loop, causing a *livelock*. Meantime, each time the AND-split is reached, a second token is created and put on the split's outgoing arc, leading to a *lack of synchronization* (more than one token will be on this latter arc).

Solution 5.13   This model is unsound because two soundness properties are violated. First, if the exception flow emanating from the boundary event is taken, two tokens will be put on the top branch of the AND-split. This lack of synchronization leads to improper completion, as two tokens will reach the same end event. Second, the model will deadlock at the AND-join if the middle branch out of the OR-split is not taken. This violates the option to complete property.

The model can be made sound by replacing the AND-join with an OR-join and by enclosing the two parallel activities "Manufacture custom product" and "Order confirmation" into an expanded sub-process, to which the boundary event "Change request" is attached. This way, if a request for change is received both the order confirmation and the product manufacturing will be interrupted, preventing any token from proceeding forward if a token is coming back through the exception flow.

Solution 5.14   Products should be stored in either Amsterdam or Hamburg. However, the model also allows products not to be stored in any of the two warehouses, if the top branch out of each of two XOR-splits is taken. This leads to an invalid statement, so the model is semantically incorrect.

Solution 5.15   The model is semantically incorrect for the following reasons. First, there are no activities to plan the shipment and to check the customer type and shipment status. This means that any process instance of this model that leads to the fulfillment of an order is invalid.

Second, after the handling of a change request, the process should resume from the order checking, but the model suggests that the order registration is also to be repeated. Moreover, the receipt of a change request only interrupts the order confirmation, but it should also interrupt the manufacturing of the product. Therefore, all instances that lead to a change request are invalid.

Finally, the model is incomplete as it does not cover the case of ordinary customers, whose account is to be charged before the order can be archived.

Solution 5.16 This model employs different labeling styles. For example, activities "Order registration" and "Checking order details" follow the action-noun style, while "Ship customer product" and "Emit invoice" follow the verb-object style. Moreover, the label of events "Confirmed" and "Fulfilled" lacks a reference to a business object (the order). The same applies to the boundary message event "Change request", which in addition lacks the past-participle verb "received". To improve the pragmatic quality of this model we need to homogenize the various labeling styles, e.g., using a verb-object style for activities and an object-verb style for events. The layout of this model is consistent with a left-to-right orientation, so there is no need to re-layout the model. Taking the results from Solution 5.15 as input, the resulting model is shown in Figure 5.19.

Solution 5.17 The process model reveals various problems. Several elements with the same name are shown twice (end event and archiving activity), therefore G1 is violated. Also the control structure is very complicated and the model is not structured, violating G4. Finally, several activities do not follow the naming conventions of G6. The model can be reworked to the one in Figure 5.20 which is much simpler, yet semantically equivalent.

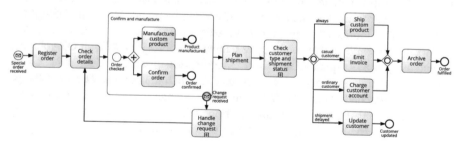

Fig. 5.19 The process model for fulfilling special orders, syntactically and semantically correct, and of high pragmatic quality

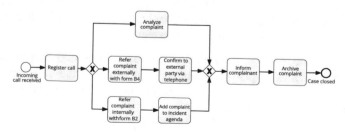

Fig. 5.20 The reworked complaint handling process model

5.7 Further Exercises

Exercise 5.18 As the person responsible for the human resources department of a consultancy company, how would you develop the skills of your junior process analysts?

Exercise 5.19 As a process analyst, how would you prepare for an interview with a domain expert for the loan assessment process in Solution 3.8 (page 111)? Consider three different domain experts: the process owner, the loan officer, and the financial officer.

Exercise 5.20 As a process analyst working for a car insurer, you are engaged in a project that aims at improving the company's insurance claim registration process. The first step is to model the as-is process. You have interviewed a few representatives for three key roles participating in this process: a customer service representative from the customer service department, a claims handler from the claims handling department, and a claims manager. The relevant parts of the interview transcripts for each role are provided below.

Customer service representative:

"When I receive a claim from a customer, I first check it for completeness. If it is not complete, I ask the customer to complete the missing information and resubmit the claim. When receiving a complete claim, I register it and send it to the claims handling department. I then wait for a notification from the claims manager that a decision has been taken. After receiving this notification, I send a customer satisfaction survey to the customer. If the customer sends back a completed survey, I first add it to our customer satisfaction database. I then have a closer look at it to evaluate if the overall satisfaction indicated by that customer is at least 5 on a scale from 1 to 10. If it is, my job is done. If it is not, all that is left for me to do is to notify the claims manager. If, after sending out the survey to the customer I do not get a response within two months, I make a *no reply* entry in the customer satisfaction database".

Claims handler:

"When I receive a claim from the customer service department, I first check whether the claimant has a valid insurance policy. If not, I inform the claimant that the claim is rejected due to an invalid policy. Otherwise, I evaluate the severity of the claim. Based on the outcome of this evaluation, I send relevant forms to the claimant. I also check whether the form is complete. Only if the form is complete, I register the claim in the claims management system. Otherwise, I ask the claimant to update and complete the form. Upon receiving the updated form, I check it again for completeness. After the claim is registered, I start evaluating it as either simple (for minor car accidents) or complex (for major car accidents). When a claim is complex, I need to additionally retrieve the corresponding car accident report from a police reports database. Based on the claim, and on the police report if required, I calculate an initial claim estimate and create an action plan. Finally, I send both the initial claim estimate and the action plan to the claims manager".

Claims manager:

"After receiving an initial claim estimate and action plan from the claims handling department, I make a final decision. Depending on the outcome of the decision (accept or reject), I notify the customer about my decision. I then update the claim file to record this decision and notify the customer service that a decision has been taken. After that, there are two possibilities:

- I receive a notification from the customer service that the results of a customer satisfaction survey indicate that the overall satisfaction of the customer is very low (i.e., less than 5). In this case, I retrieve the corresponding survey and claim from our databases. I analyze them thoroughly to identify whether our internal operations could have been done differently, or could be improved in the future to better satisfy our customers. Finally, I send a letter to the claimant to apologise and promise to provide better services in the future.
- I do not hear back from the customer service within two months. In this case, no further action is required from me."

Next, you took an active role in observing how this process works by acting as the claimant. Using a fake identity (in agreement with the process owner), you triggered this process several times and came up with the following observations.

Claimant:

The claimant completes a claims form and submit it to the customer service of the car insurer. Then the claimant has to wait for a response, which can be either of the following:

- Notification from customer service of the approval of my claim; in this case the claimant does not have to do anything further.
- Request from customer service to provide missing information on the forms, in which case the claimant updates the form and resends it to claims handling.
- Rejection from claims handling; in this case the claimant does not proceed any further with his or her claim.

After submitting a completed form to the claims handling department, the claimant waits for the claims manager to send him or her the final decision about the claim. After that, the claimant receives a customer satisfaction survey from the customer service. The claimant may choose to simply ignore this form. He or she may also choose to fill it out (typically the claimant does so when he or she is not satisfied with the service) and sends it back to the customer service. In this case, the claimant may receive a letter of apology from the claims manager within two months; otherwise the claimant is done.

Using the information above, create a draft BPMN model of the as-is claim registration process. This draft will then be validated with the people that have been interviewed before sign-off by the process owner. Make appropriate assumptions.

Acknowledgement This exercise is adapted from a similar exercise developed by Wasana Bandara, Queensland University of Technology.

Exercise 5.21 As a process analyst working for a financial institution, you are engaged in a project that aims at improving the company's credit application process. The first step is to model the as-is process. You have interviewed a few representatives for three key roles participating in this process: customer service, corporate risk assessor and risk management. The relevant parts of the interview transcripts for each role are provided below.

Customer service:

"After I receive a credit application from the customer, I check if the application is complete. If the application is incomplete, I send a request for clarification to the customer. Once I receive this clarification, I check the application again for completeness. When I assess the application as complete, I pass it on to a corporate risk assessor. I then prepare some further marketing material (e.g., a selection of investment options) for the customer. After that, I will eventually receive one of the following:

a A notification of approval from the corporate risk assessor,
b A notification of rejection from the corporate risk assessor, or
c A request for clarification from the risk manager.

In case of (a), I send a credit approval together with the marketing material to the customer, after which the process is finished for me. In case of (b), I send a credit rejection, after which the process is finished for me. In case of (c), I send a request for clarification to the customer. After receiving the clarification, I pass it on to the risk manager. I will then receive again one of the three documents listed above".

Corporate risk assessor:

"When I receive a credit application from the customer service, I first check it. Afterwards, I send it to the risk manager, from whom I then receive either a notification of approval or a notification of rejection. In both cases, I forward the notification to the customer service, after which the process is finished for me".

Risk manager:

"After receiving a credit application from the corporate risk assessor, I check it for completeness. If it is not complete, I send a request for clarification to the customer service. After the customer service responds with a clarification, I check the credit application again. Once an application successfully passes the completeness check, I assess its content. There are three possible outcomes of this assessment:

- The credit application satisfies our criteria for approval. In this case, I send a notification of approval to the corporate risk assessor. Then I formally authorize the credit in our IT systems, after which the process is finished for me.
- The credit application does not satisfy our criteria for approval. In this case, I send a notification of rejection to the corporate risk assessor, after which the process is finished for me.
- Some information in the application is unclear. In this case, I send a request for clarification to the customer service. After receiving the clarification, I assess the content of the credit application once again. This leads to one of the three outcomes listed here".

Next, you took an active role in observing how this process works by acting as the customer. Using a fake identity (in agreement with the process owner), you triggered this process several times and came up with the following observations.

Customer:

To apply for credit, the customer needs to fill out a credit application and send it to the financial institution. They will eventually get a response, which can be either:

- A credit approval with additional marketing material or a credit rejection. In these two cases, the process is finished for the customer.
- A request for clarification. In this case, the customer can proceed by preparing a clarification and sending it to the financial institution. After that, he or she will get a response that may be a credit approval with additional marketing material, a credit rejection, or again a request for clarification.

Using the information above, create a draft BPMN model of the as-is credit application process. This draft will then be validated with the people that have been interviewed before sign-off by the process owner. Make appropriate assumptions.

Acknowledgement This exercise is adapted from a similar exercise developed by Wasana Bandara, Queensland University of Technology.

Exercise 5.22 How can the model in Figure 5.12a (page 186) be fixed without affecting the cycle, i.e., such that activities F, G, and E all remain in the cycle?

Exercise 5.23 Consider the process model in Figure 5.21. Does this model suffer from soundness problems? If so, what behavioural rules does it violate? If the model is unsound, how can it be fixed without removing any activity?

Exercise 5.24 Consider the process model for loan risk assessment of Figure 5.22. Does it suffer from soundness problems? If so, what behavioural rules does it violate? If the model is unsound, how can it be fixed without removing any activity?

Exercise 5.25 Consider the model in Figure 5.23 with reference to the process for damage compensation described in Exercise 3.16 (page 113). Is this model valid and complete? If not, which statements are invalid and what is missing?

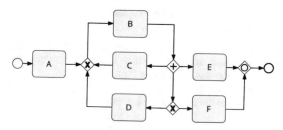

Fig. 5.21 A process model

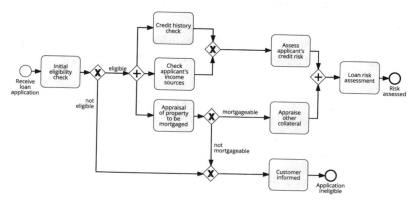

Fig. 5.22 A process model for loan risk assessment

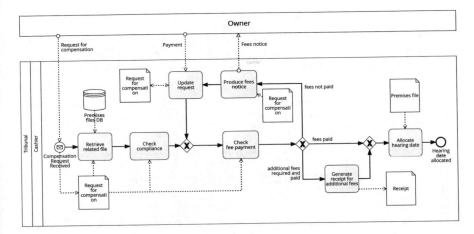

Fig. 5.23 A process model for damage compensation

Exercise 5.26 Consider the model in Figure 5.24 with reference to the process for handling motor claims described in Exercise 3.20 (page 113). Is this model valid and complete? If not, which statements are invalid and what is missing?

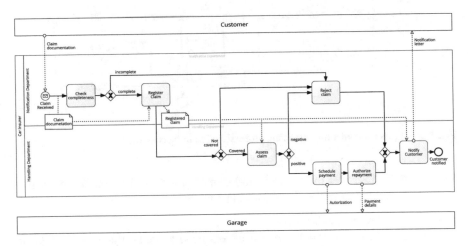

Fig. 5.24 A process model for handling motor claims

Exercise 5.27 Consider the model in Figure 5.25 with reference to the process for handling claims described in Exercise 3.21. Is this model valid and complete? If not, what statements are invalid and what is missing?

Exercise 5.28 Propose improved labels where appropriate for the model of Figure 5.22.

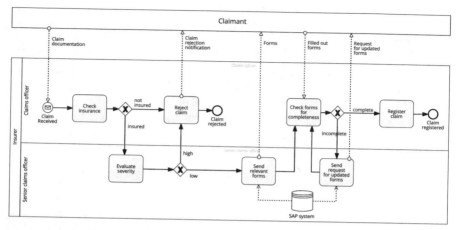

Fig. 5.25 A process model for handling claims

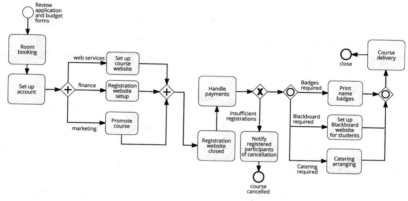

Fig. 5.26 A process model for organizing professional training courses

Exercise 5.29 Consider the process model of Figure 5.26. This model refers to a process for organizing professional training courses.

1. Is the model semantically correct?
2. What modeling conventions should be enforced to make this model easier to understand and maintain?
3. Rewrite this model by taking into account the observations on semantic and pragmatic quality made from the above two points.

Hint. For (1) you do not have any reference process description, so just use common sense.

Exercise 5.30 Consider the sales campaign process model of Figure 5.27. Describe which 7PMG guidelines can be used to improve this model.

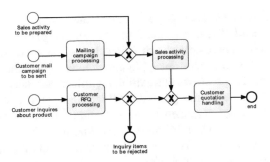

Fig. 5.27   A sales campaign process model

5.8   Further Readings

Detailed practical advice on all tasks of process discovery, and specifically information gathering and workshop organization, is provided in the book by Sharp
& McDermott [161] and in that by Jeston & Nelis [71]. Other practical advice
on workshop organization is offered by Verner [185] and by Stirna et al. [169].
Interview techniques are widely discussed as a social science research method for
instance in the book by Berg & Lune [20] or in the book by Seidman [160]. General
concerns regarding information gathering are discussed in the area of requirements
engineering, for instance in the books by van Lamsweerde [181], Pohl [127], and
Dick et al. [36].

Frederiks & van der Weide [48] discuss the skills required from process analysts,
particularly when engaging in process discovery efforts. In a similar vein, Schenk et
al. [157] and Petre [126] discuss the capabilities that expert process analysts (as
opposed to novice ones) generally display when engaging in process discovery,
while different facets of the facilitator role are explored by Rosemann et al. [147].
The five-factor personality structure model introduced on page 163 is proposed by
Digman [37] and applied to system analyst and development by Clark et al. [26].

In this chapter, we emphasized manual process discovery methods, wherein
process models are manually constructed based on information collected from
various process stakeholders by means of interviews, workshops, or observation. As
mentioned in Section 5.2.1, there is also a whole range of complementary techniques
for automated discovery of process models from event logs. These techniques are
presented in Chapter 11.

The modeling method introduced in Section 5.3 revolves around the discovery of
activities and control-flow relations between activities. This family of approaches
is usually called *activity-based modeling* [129]. An alternative approach to process
modeling is known as *artifact-centric modeling* [27]. Here the emphasis is not on
identifying activities, but *artifacts* (physical or electronic business objects) that are
manipulated within a given process, such as a purchase order or an invoice in an
order-to-cash process. Once these artifacts have been identified, they are analyzed
in terms of the data that they hold and the states they go through during the process.

For example, a purchase order may go through states such as *received, confirmed, shipped,* and *invoiced.* These states and the transitions between them are called the *artifact lifecycle.* Discovering such lifecycles is the focus of artifact-centric process modeling. Several industrial applications have shown that this approach is particularly suitable for processes that exhibit significant amounts of variation, e.g., variation between business units, geographical regions, or types of customers.

The quality of conceptual models in general, and of process models specifically, has received extensive attention in the research literature. The *Sequal* framework introduced by Lindland et al. adapts semiotic theory, namely the three perspectives of syntax, semantics, and pragmatics, to the evaluation of conceptual model quality [91]. An extended and revised version of this framework is presented in the book by Krogstie [83].

Verification and validation of process models have also received extensive attention in the literature. Mendling [109] for example provides numerous pointers to related research. The verification of Workflow nets, another process modeling language, is specifically investigated by Van der Aalst [2] who connects soundness analysis of process models with formal properties of Petri nets.

In this chapter we listed the main structural rules of BPMN. The complete list of rules can be found in Silver's Method & Style website.[2]

The 7PMG discussed in this chapter originate from [110]. These guidelines build on empirical work on the relation between process model metrics on the one hand and error probability and understandability on the other hand [108, 111, 112, 123, 133, 136, 143, 144], and have been widely used in practice. The 7PMG are one of the available sets of modeling guidelines. For example, another set of guidelines are those by Becker et al. [18]. Moreover, research in the area of process model quality is still developing. So, as insights develop further, it is likely and favorable that these guidelines will be updated and expanded.

As a complement to process modeling guidelines and conventions, it is useful to also keep in mind potential pitfalls to be avoided in process modeling projects. For example, Rosemann [145, 146] draws a list of 22 pitfalls of process modeling, including a potential lack of strategic connection and getting lost in modeling details, to name but a few. His bottom line is that modeling success does not directly equate with business process success.

---

[2]https://methodandstyle.com/the-rules-of-bpmn.

Chapter 6
Qualitative Process Analysis

> *Quality is free, but only to those who are willing to pay heavily for it.*
> Tom DeMarco (1940–)

Analyzing business processes is both an art and a science. In this respect, qualitative analysis is the artistic side of process analysis. Like fine arts, such as painting, there is not a single way of producing a good process analysis, but rather a range of principles and techniques that tell us which practices typically lead to a "good" process analysis.

In this chapter, we introduce a selected set of principles and techniques for qualitative process analysis. First, we present two techniques aimed at identifying unnecessary steps of the process (value-added analysis) and sources of waste (waste analysis). Next, we present techniques to identify and document issues in a process from multiple perspectives and to analyze the root causes of these issues.

6.1 Value-Added Analysis

Value-added analysis is a technique to identify unnecessary steps in a process in view of eliminating them. In this context, a *step* may be a task in the process or part of a task. It is often the case that one task involves several steps. For example, a task "Check invoice" may involve the following steps:

1. Retrieve the PO that corresponds to the invoice.
2. Check that the amounts in the invoice and those in the PO coincide.
3. Check that the products or services referenced in the PO have been delivered.
4. Check that the supplier's name and banking details in the invoice coincide with those recorded in the supplier management system.

In some cases, steps within a task are documented in the form of checklists. The checklists tell the process participants what things need to be in place before a task is considered to be complete. If detailed checklists are available, the process analyst

© Springer-Verlag GmbH Germany, part of Springer Nature 2018
M. Dumas et al., *Fundamentals of Business Process Management*,
https://doi.org/10.1007/978-3-662-56509-4_6

can use them to decompose tasks into steps. Unfortunately, such checklists are not always available. In many cases, process participants have an implicit understanding of the steps in a task because they perform the task day in and day out. But this implicit understanding is not documented anywhere. In the absence of such documentation, the process analyst needs to decompose each task into steps by means of observation and interviewing.

Having decomposed the process into steps, a second prerequisite for value-added analysis is to identify who is the customer of the process and what are the positive outcomes that the customer seeks from the process. These outcomes are said to add value to the customer, in the sense that fulfilling these outcomes is in the interest or for the benefit of the customers.

Having decomposed the process into steps and having identified the positive outcomes of a process, we can then analyze each step in terms of the value it adds. Steps that directly contribute to positive outcomes are called *Value Adding* (VA) steps. For example, consider a process for repairing a washing machine or other appliance. The steps where the technician diagnoses the problem with the machine are value adding, as they directly contribute to the outcome the customer wishes to see, which is that the machine is repaired. Also, the steps related to repairing the machine are value adding.

Some steps do not directly add value to the customer but they are necessary for the business. Consider again the example of a process for repairing a washing machine. Imagine that this process includes a step "Record defect" in which the technician enters data into an information system about the washing machine and an explanation of the defect found in it. This step per se is not value adding for the customer. The customer wishes the machine to be fixed and does not get value by the fact that the defect in their machine was recorded in an information system. However, recording defects and their resolution helps the company to build up a knowledge base of typical defects and their resolution, which is valuable when new technicians are recruited. Also, such data allows the company to detect frequent defects and to report such defects to the manufacturer or distributor of the washing machine. Steps such as "Record defect" are termed *Business Value Adding* (BVA) steps. BVA steps are those that the customer is neither willing to pay for, nor gains satisfaction from (so they are not value adding), but they are necessary or useful to the company where the process is performed.

Steps that are neither VA nor BVA are called *Non-Value Adding* (NVA).

In summary, value-added analysis consists in breaking down each task in a process into steps, such as a preparation step, an execution step, and a handoff step. We then classify each step into one of three categories, namely:

- Value Adding (VA): This is a step that produces value or satisfaction to the customer. When determining whether or not a step is VA, it may help to ask the following questions: Would the customer be willing to pay for this step? Does the customer value this step enough to keep conducting business with us? And conversely, if we remove this step, would the customer perceive that the outcome of the process is less valuable?

- **Business Value Adding (BVA):** The step is necessary or useful for the business to run smoothly, to collect revenue, or it is required due to the regulatory environment of the business. When determining whether or not a step is BVA, it may help to ask the following questions: Is this step required in order to collect revenue, to improve or grow the business? Would the business (potentially) suffer in the long term if this step were removed? Does it reduce risk of business losses? Is this step required in order to comply with regulatory requirements?
- **Non-Value Adding (NVA):** The step does not fall into any of the other two categories.

Example 6.1 We consider the equipment rental process described in Example 1.1 (page 3). The customer of this process is the site engineer who submits an equipment rental request. From the perspective of the site engineer, the positive outcome of the process is that the required piece of equipment is available in the construction site when needed. Let us analyze the fragment of this process described in Figure 1.6, which we reproduce as Figure 6.1 for convenience. To identify the relevant steps, we walk through this model task by task, and we classify each step into VA, BVA, and NVA.

- The first task in the process model is the one where the engineer lodges the request. From the description in Example 1.1, we observe there are three steps in this task:

  1. Site engineer fills in the request.
  2. Site engineer sends the request to the clerk via email (handoff step).
  3. Clerk opens and reads the request (handoff step).

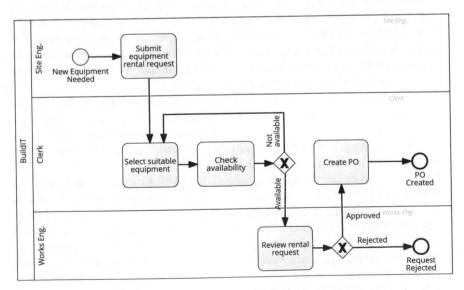

Fig. 6.1 Process model for the initial fragment of the equipment rental process

Arguably, filling the request is VA insofar as the site engineer cannot expect the equipment to be rented if they do not ask for it. In one way or another, the site engineer has to request the equipment in order to obtain it. On the other hand, the site engineer does not get value out of sending the request to the clerk by email nor does get value out of the clerk having to open and read the request. More generally, steps associated to handoffs between process participants, such as sending and receiving internal messages, are NVA.

- The second task is the one where the clerk selects a suitable equipment from the supplier's catalog. We can treat this task as a single step. This step is VA insofar as it contributes to identifying a suitable equipment to fulfill the needs of the site engineer.
- In the third task, the clerk calls the supplier to check the availability of the selected equipment. This "call supplier" step is value adding insofar as it contributes to identifying a suitable and available equipment. If the equipment is available, the clerk recommends that this equipment be rented. To this end, the clerk adds the details of the recommended equipment and supplier to the rental request form and forwards the form to the works engineer for approval. Thus we have two more steps: (i) adding the details to the rental request and (ii) forwarding the rental request to the works engineer. The first of these steps is BVA since it helps the company to keep track of the equipment they rent and the suppliers they rent from. Maintaining this information is valuable when it comes to negotiating or re-negotiating bulk agreements with suppliers. On the other hand, the handoff between the clerk and the works engineer (i.e. the "forwarding" step) is not value adding.
- Next, the works engineer examines the rental request in view of approving it or rejecting it. We can treat this examination as one step. This step is a *control step*, that is, a step where a process participant or a software application checks that something has been done correctly. In this case, this control step helps the company to ensure that equipment is only rented when it is needed and that the expenditure for equipment rental in a given construction project stays within the project's budget. Control steps are generally BVA.
- If the works engineer has an issue with the rental request, the works engineer communicates it to the clerk or the site engineer. This communication is another step and it is BVA since it contributes to identifying and avoiding misunderstandings within the company. If approved, the request is sent back to the clerk; this is a handoff step and it is thus NVA.
- Finally, assuming the request is approved, the clerk creates and sends the PO. Here we can identify two more steps: creating the PO and sending the PO to the corresponding supplier. Creating the PO is BVA. It is necessary in order to ensure that the rental request cost is correctly accounted for and eventually paid for. Sending the PO is value adding: It is this act that makes the supplier know when the equipment has to be delivered on a given date. If the supplier did not get this information, the equipment would not be delivered. Note however that what is value adding is the fact that the supplier is explicitly requested by the

Table 6.1 Classification of steps in the equipment rental process

Step	Performer	Classification
Fill request	Site engineer	VA
Send request to clerk	Site engineer	NVA
Open and read request	Clerk	NVA
Select suitable equipment	Clerk	VA
Check equipment availability	Clerk	VA
Record recommended equipment & supplier	Clerk	BVA
Forward request to works engineer	Clerk	NVA
Open and examine request	Works engineer	BVA
Communicate issues	Works engineer	BVA
Forward request back to clerk	Works engineer	NVA
Create PO	Clerk	BVA
Send PO to supplier	Clerk	VA

construction company to deliver the equipment on a given date. The fact that this request is made by sending a PO is secondary in terms of adding value to the site engineer.

The identified steps and their classification are summarized in Table 6.1.

□

One may wonder whether creating the PO is a VA step or a BVA step. Arguably, in order for the equipment to be available, the supplier needs to have an assurance that the equipment rental fee will be paid. So one could say that the creation of the PO contributes to the rental of the equipment since the PO serves to assure the supplier that the payment for the rental equipment will be made. However, as mentioned above, what adds value to the site engineer is the fact that the supplier is notified that the equipment should be delivered at the required date. Whether this notification is done by means of a PO or by means of a simple electronic message sent to the supplier is irrelevant, so long as the equipment is delivered. Thus, producing a formal document (a formal PO) is arguably not value adding. It is rather a mechanism to ensure that the construction company's financial processes run smoothly and to avoid disputes with suppliers, e.g., avoiding the situation where a supplier delivers a piece of equipment that is not needed and then asks for payment of the rental fee. More generally, we will take the convention that documentation and control steps imposed by accounting or legal requirements are BVA.

Exercise 6.1 Consider the process for university admission described in Exercise 1.1 (page 5) and modeled in Figure 5.4 (page 197). What steps can you extract from this process? Classify these steps into VA, BVA, and NVA.

Having identified and classified the steps of the process as discussed above, one can then proceed to determining how to minimize or eliminate NVA steps. Some NVA steps can be eliminated by means of automation. This is the case of handoffs for example, which can be eliminated by putting in place an information system that allows all stakeholders to know what they need to do in order to move forward the rental requests. When the site engineer submits a rental request via this information system, the request would automatically appear in the to-do list of the clerk. Similarly, when the clerk records the recommended supplier and equipment, the works engineer would be notified and directed to the request. This form of automation makes these NVA steps transparent to the performers of the steps. The topic of process automation will be discussed in further detail in Chapter 10.

A more radical approach to eliminate NVA steps in this example is to eliminate the clerk altogether from the process. This means moving some of the work to the site engineer so that there are less handoffs in the process. Of course, the consequences of this change in terms of added workload to the site engineer need to be carefully considered. Yet another approach to eliminate NVA (and BVA) steps would be to eliminate the need for approval of rental requests in cases where the estimated cost is below a certain threshold. Again, this option should be weighted against the possible consequences of having less control steps in place. In particular, if the site engineers were given full discretion to rent equipment at their own will, there would need to be a mechanism in place to make them accountable in case they rent unnecessary equipment or they rent equipment for excessively and unnecessarily long periods.

While elimination of NVA steps is generally considered a desirable goal, elimination of BVA steps should be considered as a trade-off given that BVA steps play a role in the business. Prior to eliminating BVA steps, one should first map BVA steps to business goals and business requirements, such as regulations that the company must comply to and risks that the company seeks to minimize. Given a mapping between BVA steps on the one hand and business goals and requirements on the other, the question then becomes the following: What is the minimum amount of work required in order to perform the process to the satisfaction of the customer, while fulfilling the goals and requirements associated to the BVA steps in the process? The answer to this question is a starting point for process redesign (see Chapter 8).

6.2   Waste Analysis

Waste analysis can be seen as the reverse of value added analysis. In value added analysis we look at the process from a positive angle. We try to identify value adding steps, and then we classify the remaining steps into business-value adding and non-value adding. Waste analysis takes the negative angle. It tries to find waste everywhere in the process. Some of these wastes can be traced down to specific steps in the process, but others, as we will see, are hidden in between steps or sometimes throughout the process.

Waste analysis is one of the key techniques of the *Toyota Production System* (TPS) developed by Taiichi Ohno and colleagues in the 1970s. This technique has been integrated in various management paradigms such as Lean management [115]. Ohno used to describe the TPS as follows: What we are doing, all the time, is to look at a timeline from the moment a customer puts an order to the point that the cash for that order is collected. And looking at the timeline, we are trying to reduce the *muda*. Muda is a Japanese term for waste. Ohno and his colleagues came up with a classification of waste into seven types, which we group into three higher-level categories to make them easier to remember:

- *Move*: Wastes that are related to movement. This category includes two types of waste: *transportation* and *motion*.
- *Hold*: Wastes arising from holding something. Again, this category includes two types of waste: *inventory* and *waiting*.
- *Overdo*: Wastes arising from doing more than is necessary in order to deliver value to the customer or the business. This category encompasses three types of waste: *defects*, *overprocessing*, and *overproduction*.

6.2.1   Move

The first and perhaps most pervasive source of waste is *transportation*. In a manufacturing process, transportation means moving materials from one location to another one, such as from a warehouse to a production facility. In a business process, physical transportation occurs, for example, when documents are sent from one process participant to another—often signaling a handoff of work between participants—or when physical documents are exchanged with an external party. In modern business processes, physical document exchanges have been largely replaced with electronic exchanges. For example, purchase orders, shipment notifications, delivery receipts and invoices are often exchanged via *Electronic Data Interchange* (EDI) channels. Meanwhile, internal handoffs between process participants are generally automated by means of Process-Aware Information Systems, as we will discuss in Chapter 9. But despite the replacement of physical document flows with electronic ones, which we have witnessed in the past decades, transportation remains nonetheless a source of waste. Indeed, every time that a handoff occurs between participants, this handoff entails some delay, as the participant who needs to take the relay is likely to be busy with other work when the handoff occurs.

A process model with lanes and pools can help us to identify transportation waste. Typically, there is transportation waste wherever a sequence flow goes from one lane to another in a pool. Such a sequence flow represents a handoff. In a similar vein, if the process model has multiple pools, every message flow is a potential transportation waste.

Example 6.2 Let us consider the equipment rental process model introduced in Example 1.1 (page 3). The fragment of the process from the creation of the rental request up to its approval is shown in Figure 6.2. The figure highlights four transportation wastes. The first three come from handoffs between process

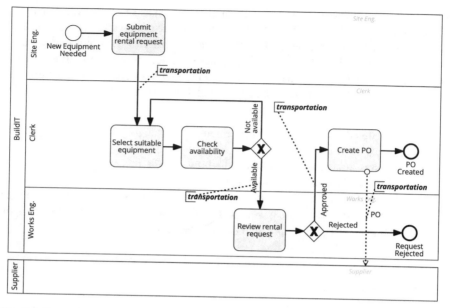

Fig. 6.2 Fragment of the equipment rental process from creation of rental request up to creation of the PO

participants: (i) from the site engineer to the clerk; (ii) from the clerk to the works engineer; and (iii) from the works engineer back to clerk. The fourth transportation waste occurs when the clerk sends the purchase order to the supplier.

Later in the process, we can note two other transportation events: the delivery of the equipment to the construction site and its subsequent removal at the end of the renting period. One might argue that these two transportation events are value adding, since the delivery of the equipment is precisely what the site engineer seeks. Still, the rental company would strive to minimize this transportation, for example, by optimizing the placement of equipment so that it is close to the construction sites where it is likely to be used.

A final transportation waste occurs when the supplier submits the invoice.   □

This example shows that not all transportation waste in a process can be eliminated. In particular, the transportation of equipment cannot be fully eliminated. But we can strive to reduce it or we can strive to reduce its cost. For example, to reduce the cost of physical transportation of goods, we can batch together several deliveries. Similarly, transportation of physical documents can in some cases be replaced by electronic exchanges. In other situations, it may be possible to reduce the number of handoffs, so as to reduce the waiting times and context switches that these exchanges create.

The second type of waste related to movement is *motion*. Motion refers to process participants moving from one place to another during the execution of a process. Motion is common in a manufacturing process where workers move pieces from one place to another in the production line. In the field of business processes, motion wastes are less common than in manufacturing process, but they are nonetheless present.

Consider, for example, a vehicle inspection process where customers have their vehicles inspected in order to assess their roadworthiness and their compliance with respect to gas emission requirements. In this process, vehicles have to go through different inspection bases in order to undergo different tests. Oftentimes, process participants have to move equipment or tools from one inspection base to another to perform certain tests. This is a motion waste.

Another form of motion waste—which can be found in digitized processes—arises when a process participant has to switch from one application to another during the performance of a task. For example, when doing a vehicle inspection booking for a new customer, the receptionist may need to record the customer details in one application, and then schedule the inspection in another application. The movement between these two applications is motion waste. A set of techniques and tools known under the name of Robotic Process Automation (RPA) [15] aim at reducing this type of motion waste. RPA will be further discussed in Chapter 9.

6.2.2   Hold

We can also generate waste by having materials, work items, or resources on hold. The first type of hold waste is called *inventory*. In manufacturing processes, inventory waste arises whenever we hold more inventory than what is strictly necessary at a given point in time in order to maintain the production lines working. In the field of business processes, inventory waste usually does not take the form of physical inventory. Instead, inventory waste shows up in the form of *Work-In-Process* (WIP). WIP is the number of cases that have started and have not yet completed.

For example, in the vehicle inspection process mentioned above, it may happen that a vehicle does not pass the inspection the first time due to a minor issue (e.g., worn tyres). In this case, the customers is asked to correct the issue at their preferred garage and to come back for a second inspection. At any point in time, it may be that dozens of vehicles are in a state between their first inspection and their second inspection. Those vehicles contribute to high levels of WIP and hence they constitute inventory waste. One may ask why do we consider these pending inspections a form of waste? The reason is that these pending inspections are *unrealized value*. The customers only get value out of this process once their vehicle has passed the inspection. Ideally, we would like cases to arrive and leave as fast as possible, so as to generate as much value as possible.

Another type of waste falling under the hold category is *waiting*. In manufacturing processes, waiting waste occurs, for example, when unfinished products come out from one production line and they need to wait for the workers in the next production line to become available in order to proceed. In the case of a business process, waiting waste occurs when a task waits for a process participant to become available. Waiting waste can also occur in the opposite direction: Instead of the task waiting for a resource, we might have a resource waiting for a task. This sub-type of waiting waste is called *idleness*.

Let us consider again the vehicle inspection process. At some point in time, it might be that there is a technician at an inspection base waiting for the next car, because the next car is still being inspected at the previous base. This is an example of idleness.

On the other hand, consider the case of a travel request that has undergone one approval, but needs to undergo a second one. This second approval is a task. If the participant responsible for the second approval is not available when the first approval is completed, the request is put on hold. The time that the request spends on hold is waiting waste.

Transportation waste often implies waiting waste. For example, the three flows going across lanes in Figure 6.2 induce waiting waste because process participants who receive the rental request will often not be available when the request is handed off to them.

6.2.3   Overdo

The third category of waste are those related to overdoing. The first type of overdo waste is called *defect* waste. Defect waste refers to all work performed in order to correct, repair, or compensate for a defect in a process. Defect waste encompasses *rework*, meaning situations where we have to perform again a task that we have previously executed in the same case, because of a defect the first time the task was performed. In a travel requisition process, an example of a defect waste is when a travel requisition request is sent back by the approver to the requestor for revision because some data was missing.

Another type of waste in this category is called *overprocessing*. Overprocessing refers to work that is performed unnecessarily given the outcome of a process instance. It includes unnecessary perfectionism, but it also includes tasks that are performed and later found not to be necessary.

Coming back to the vehicle inspection process, let us assume that the technicians take a lot of time to measure the vehicle emissions with a higher degree of accuracy. This perfectionism is waste. If in addition we find out later that the said vehicles for which the emissions were measured so accurately, end up not fulfilling the emissions levels by a big margin, then all this accuracy was unnecessary.

Consider now the example of the travel approval and assume that about 10% of the requests are rejected trivially after several tasks have been completed, because there is not enough budget for the travel. These unnecessary task executions could be avoided by doing a budget check earlier in the process, so as to avoid wasting the time of the approvers. This example illustrates that simple verification steps at the start of a process can help to minimize overprocessing. This approach to minimize overprocessing will be further discussed in Chapter 8.

The final type of waste, namely *overproduction*, is closely related to overprocessing. While overprocessing occurs when a task is executed and later found to be unnecessary, overproduction occurs when we execute an entire process instance that does not add value upon completion.

Consider a quote-to-cash process in which the quote-to-order sub-process produces many quotes that are later rejected by the customer. In other words, the customer obtains a quote but does not submit a subsequent purchase order. The rejected quotes are overproduction waste. We should strive to minimize this waste by not attracting requests for quote that will not lead to an order, or by trying to convert every possible request for quote we get into an order, because the fulfilled order is what adds value to the organization.

Another typical example of overproduction occurs when a process instance is canceled by its initiator (the customer). For example, consider a travel approval process in which some travel requests are created just in case the trip is needed (without certainty). If it turns out that the travel is not needed, the travel request is canceled. These canceled instances create non-value adding work for the process participants. Ideally, we would like to minimize this waste and only have to handle the necessary requests.

Similarly, travel requests that are rejected for reasons that could have been foreseen prior to the process instance being created constitute overproduction waste. For example, a travel request that is rejected due to lack of budget, in a way that could have been detected upfront, is an overproduction waste.

This latter example illustrates that the boundary between overproduction and overprocessing is sometimes subtle. The key difference is that overprocessing occurs when it is necessary to start the process instance in order to discover that the instance cannot be fulfilled, whereas overproduction occurs in two cases:

- When the instance ends up in a positive outcome, but it turns out that the instance was not needed.
- When the instance ends up in a negative outcome that could have been foreseen prior to the instance being created.

Example 6.3 Consider the fragment of the equipment rental process captured in Figure 6.2 (page 220). After performing the task "Check availability", it may happen that the selected equipment is not available. In this case, the clerk needs to go back and select an alternative equipment. In other words, there is a rework loop. This rework is a defect waste.

Once the clerk has found a suitable and available equipment item, the works engineer might reject the request because the job for which the equipment is required can be done using an equipment item available at a nearby construction site. In other words, the creation of the rental request could have been avoided if the site engineer was able to check which other equipment items are available at nearby sites. The latter is an example of overproduction waste. □

Exercise 6.2 Identify wastes in the university admission process of Exercise 1.1 (page 5) and classify them according to the seven types of waste. Consider the following additional information.

Each year, the university receives in total 3,000 online applications. There are 10 study programs. Each study program has 30 study places. The top-5 applicants in each study program are offered scholarships in addition to a study place. Applicants initially ranked in positions 6 to 30 in their study program are offered a study place but without a scholarship. After the committee has examined the applications, each application is either: (i) accepted with a scholarship, (ii) accepted without scholarship, (iii) admissible but not accepted unless a study place is freed up by a higher-ranked applicant, or (iv) rejected due to low scores or plagiarism.

Successful applicants must accept or decline the offer at most two weeks after notification. If an applicant declines the offer, his or her study place is allocated to the next admissible non-admitted applicant in the ranking of his or her study program. If an applicant with an allocated scholarship rejects his or her study place, the scholarship is allocated to the next applicant in the corresponding ranking who does not yet have an allocated scholarship. Applications are rejected or discarded for the following reasons:

- 20% of applications are rejected initially due to deficiencies in the online application form (e.g., missing documents). In half of the cases, the applicant manages to fix the identified issues and the application passes the administrative check after the second try.
- 10% of applications are rejected because the hard copy is not received on time.
- 3% rejected due to a negative advice from the academic recognition agency.
- 2% rejected due to invalid English language test.
- 5% rejected due to plagiarized motivation letter.
- 5% rejected due to poorly written motivation letters.
- 15% rejected due to low GPA.
- 20% of applicants are offered a place but decline it. In 60% of these cases, the applicant declines because he or she expected to get a scholarship, but his or her score was insufficient. In another 30% of cases, applicants decline because they had already accepted an offer elsewhere. The rest of cases where applicants decline an offer are due to personal reasons.
- 20% of applicants are declared admissible but do not receive an offer due to lack of study places.

The admissions office handles circa 10,000 emails from applicants concerning the application process, including questions about the application form, the required documents, the eligibility conditions, the application status, etc.

6.3 Stakeholder Analysis and Issue Documentation

When analyzing a business process, it is worth keeping in mind that "even a good process can be made better" [61]. Experience shows that any non-trivial business process, no matter how much improvement it has undergone, suffers from a number of issues. There are always errors, misunderstandings, incidents, unnecessary steps and other waste when a business process is performed on a day-to-day basis.

Part of the job of a process analyst is to identify and to document the *issues* that affect the performance of a process. To this end, an analyst will typically gather data from multiple sources and will interview several stakeholders, chiefly the process participants but also the process owner and managers of organizational units involved in the process. Each stakeholder has a different view on the process and will naturally have a tendency to raise issues from his or her own perspective. The same issue may be perceived differently by two stakeholders. For example, an executive manager or a process owner will typically see issues in terms of performance objectives not being met or in terms of constraints imposed for example by external pressures (e.g., regulatory or compliance issues). Meanwhile, process participants might complain about insufficient resources, hectic timelines as well as errors or exceptions perceived to be caused by other process participants or by customers.

Below, we introduce three complementary techniques to collect, document and analyze issues in a process:

1. Stakeholder analysis, which allows us to collect issues from complementary perspectives.
2. Issue register, which allows us to document issues in a structured manner.
3. Pareto analysis and PICK charts, which allow us to select a subset of issues for further analysis and redesign.

6.3.1   Stakeholder Analysis

Stakeholder analysis is a widely used technique in the field of project management. This analysis is generally undertaken at the start of a project in order to understand who has an interest in the project and could therefore contribute to, affect, or be affected by the project's execution, and how.

In the field of BPM, stakeholder analysis is commonly used to gather information about issues that affect the performance of the process from different perspectives. In this context, there are typically five categories of stakeholders:

- The customer(s) of the process.
- The process participants.
- The external parties (e.g., suppliers, sub-contractors) involved in the process.
- The process owner and the operational managers who supervise the process participants.
- The sponsor of the process improvement effort and other executive managers who have a stake in the performance of the process.

Each of these categories of stakeholders bring their own viewpoint and are likely to perceive different issues in the process. The customers are likely to be concerned with issues such as slow cycle time, defects, lack of transparency, or lack of traceability (i.e., inability to observe the current status of the process).

Process participants might be rather concerned about high resource utilization, as this means that they have to work under stress. They might also be concerned about defects, though not necessarily the same defects as the customer since the process participants see the process from the inside. Specifically, process participants are likely to see defects arising from handoffs in the process, whereas customers do not necessarily see these defects if they are internally fixed. More generally, process participants are usually able to provide insights regarding wastes in the process, not only defects, but also transportation, movement and waiting waste (arising from handoffs), as well as overprocessing.

External parties can have a variety of concerns, depending on their role in the process. Suppliers and sub-contractors (which are a common type of external party) are generally concerned about having a steady or growing stream of work from the process, being able to plan their work ahead, and being able to meet contractual requirements. In other words, they are concerned about predictability, and they might see opportunities to improve the interactions between their own process and the processes with which they are integrated.

The process owner and the operational managers are likely to be concerned with the performance measures of the process, be it high cycle times or high processing times. Indeed, processing times are directly related to labor costs and hence they affect the efficiency of the process. A process owner might also be concerned about common defects in the process, as well as overproduction. The process owner and other managers are generally also concerned about compliance with internal policy and external regulations.

The sponsor and other high-level managers are generally concerned with the strategic alignment of the process and the contribution of the process to the key performance measures of the organization. They might also be concerned about the ability of the process to adapt to evolving customer expectations, external competition, and changing market conditions. Sponsors and high-level managers might also raise opportunities (as opposed to issues), for example opportunities to attract additional customers, to expand into a new market segment, or to cross-sell or up-sell products or services to existing customers.

When a process improvement effort starts, the sponsor and the process owner will generally put forward a set of objectives and targets to be achieved by the improvement effort. They may also put forward one or more hypotheses regarding the main bottlenecks and issues in the process. The analyst takes this initial set of objectives, targets, and perceived issues as a starting point. The analyst then identifies and conducts interviews with stakeholders in each of the above categories in order to collect additional perceived issues. By cross-checking the perceived issues raised during these interviews, and by validating them via additional data collection, the analyst identifies a set of validated issues from the perspective of each category of stakeholder. These validated issues are the input to construct an issue register as discussed below.

Example 6.4 Consider the equipment rental process discussed in previous examples. The owner of this process is BuildIT's purchasing manager. The purchasing manager is concerned by the growing volume of equipment rental expenses. In the past year, these expenses have grown by 12% whereas the overall volume of construction activity (measured by revenue) has grown by only 8%. The purchasing manager launches an improvement effort to bring down the rental expenses by 5%. This objective is in line with overall target set by the CFO of 5% of company-wide cost reductions.

An analyst is asked to review the rental process. The analyst identifies the following stakeholders:

- Customer: the site engineers.
- Process participants: the clerks, the works engineers and the accounts payable team at the financial department (who handle the invoice).
- Process owner and operational managers: purchasing manager, construction project managers, accounts payable team lead.
- Upper management: the CFO, acting as the business sponsor as part of the broader mandate for cost reduction.
- External party: the equipment rental suppliers.

After interviewing the process owner, the analyst notes two perceived issues in the process:

- Equipment is often hired for longer than needed, leading to inventory waste.
- Penalties are often being paid to the suppliers due to: (i) equipment being returned upon receipt because it was not suitable for the job; and (ii) late invoice payments. In both cases, these penalties arise from wastes of type defect.

The above observations illustrate that oftentimes, issues raised during the stakeholder analysis (particularly issues raised by the process owner and the process participants) are associated with wastes. Hence, the output of waste analysis can be helpful when engaging in a stakeholder analysis.

The analyst decides to start by gathering data from the site engineer, the clerk and the works engineer, given their central role in the process. He proceeds with interviews in order to derive deeper qualitative insights. The interviews are partly driven by the waste analysis—in particular transportation, waiting, and defects, as well as the inventory waste raised by the process owner.

After interviewing three site engineers, the analyst retains that the main concern of the site engineers is the delay between the moment they create an equipment rental and the moment the corresponding equipment arrives. The analyst determines that this delay is of 3.5 working days on average (sometimes three, sometimes 4 days, rarely less or more). The site engineer also confirmed that sometimes they have to reject equipment when they receive it because the equipment is not suitable for the job—even though they claim that in their requests, they clearly indicate what type of equipment is needed and for what purpose.

On the other hand, the clerks' main concerns are:

- Lack of clarity in the requirements they receive from the site engineers, which somehow contradicts the viewpoint of the latter.
- Inaccurate and incomplete equipment descriptions in the catalogs of the site engineer vendors.
- Slow turnaround times when asking the works engineers to approve the rental requests.

The works engineers echo the concerns of the purchasing managers that site engineers are sometimes retaining the rented equipment for longer than strictly needed (inventory waste). They are aware that sometimes the delivered equipment does not match the requirements of the site engineers and is hence returned, but they do not perceive that this is a major issue.

The accounts payable team claims that they are aware of the fact that penalties are being paid for late invoice payments. However, they claim that it is not their fault. In 98% of cases, invoices are being paid at most three working days after their internal approval. The accounts payable department claims that it is not possible to do faster, and that in any case, the penalties of late invoices would still occur even if they could reduce the payment time from 3 days to 2 days.

The analyst also interviewed two suppliers, who echoed the fact that sometimes the delivered equipment was rejected by the site engineer, and that invoices took too long to be paid. The suppliers additionally perceived that there is a lack of integration between their systems and the ones used internally at BuildIT. A supplier commented that this lack of integration could be one of the reasons why mistakes were being made along the way.

The analyst retains that the issues raised by the process owner are being echoed in several ways by other stakeholders. The analyst also takes note of the slow cycles times reported by the site engineer, and the misunderstandings and data quality issues raised by the clerk.

□

Exercise 6.3 Let us consider again the university admission process for international students described in Exercise 1.1 (page 5). The owner of this process is the Head of the Admissions Office, who reports to the university's Deputy Vice-Chancellor for Student Affairs. The Head of Admissions Office is simultaneously concerned about the cost of running the admissions process, but equally as much by the fact that the university is losing talented admission candidates to competing universities.

Regarding the costs, the process owner reports that each instance of the admission process generates € 100 in labor cost, including the time spent by the admissions office as well as the time spent by the academic committees responsible for assessing and ranking the applications. The admissions office additionally pays a fee of € 30 to an external agency to verify the validity and equivalence of each submitted diploma, plus € 20 per submitted application to the provider of the online application system that students use to submit and track their applications. The university's marketing office additionally spends € 100 in marketing per application. The university charges to the applicant a non-reimbursable application fee of € 100 per application. As discussed in Exercise 6.2 (page 224), out of 3,000 applications only 300 applicants end up joining a study program. The remaining students drop out during the process for the reasons enumerated in Exercise 6.2.

Regarding the loss of candidates during the admission process, the process owner is particularly concerned about the relatively high number of applicants who receive an admission offer but do not accept it. Specifically, 30% of applicants who receive an offer reject it as mentioned in Exercise 6.2 (page 224) and 30% of those who reject the offer do so in favor of a competing university.

You are tasked with doing an analysis of the above process in order to come up with a list of issues. Given the description of the process in Exercise 1.1 (page 5) and the information given above, prepare a plan including:

- The list of stakeholders you would interview (justify your choice).
- For each stakeholder, discuss what types of issues you would expect him or her to raise (hypothesized issues) and what questions you could ask to each stakeholder in order to determine if these hypothesized issues indeed exist, and if so, what is their impact.

6.3.2 Issue Register

Stakeholder analysis allows us to identify issues in a business process from multiple perspectives. The next natural step is to organize and document these issues and to assess their impact both quantitatively, for example in terms of time or financial loss, as well as qualitatively in terms of perceived nuisance to the customer or perceived risks that the issue entails. This is the role of the *issue register*. Concretely, an issue register is a listing that provides a detailed analysis of each issue and its impact in the form of a table with a pre-defined set of fields. The following fields are typically described for each issue:

- *Name of the issue*. This name should be kept short, typically 2–5 words, and should be understandable by all stakeholders in the process.
- *Description*. A short description of the issue (e.g., 1–3 sentences) focused on the issue itself as opposed to its consequences or impact, which are described separately.
- *Priority*. A number (1, 2, 3, ...) stating how important this issue is relative to other issues. Note that multiple issues can have the same priority number.
- *Data and assumptions*. Any data used or assumptions made in the estimation of the impact of the issue, such as for example number of times a given negative outcome occurs, or estimated loss per occurrence of a negative outcome. In the early phases of the development of the issue register, the numbers in this column will be mainly assumptions or ballpark estimates. Over time, these assumptions and rough estimates will be replaced with more reliable numbers derived from actual data about the execution of the process.
- *Qualitative impact*. A description of the impact of the issue in qualitative terms, such as impact of the issue on customer satisfaction, employee satisfaction, long-term supplier relationships, company's reputation, or other intangible impact that is difficult to quantify.
- *Quantitative impact*. An estimate of the impact of the issue in quantitative terms, such as time loss, revenue loss, or avoidable costs. This field in the issue register provides a link between qualitative and quantitative analysis techniques.

Quantitative analysis techniques, such as those to be presented in the next chapter, allow us to obtain refined estimates of the quantitative impact of an issue.

Other fields may be added to an issue register. For example, in view of process redesign, it may be useful to include an attribute *possible resolution* that describes possible mechanisms for addressing the issue.

Example 6.5 We consider again the equipment rental process described in Example 1.1 (page 3) and the stakeholder analysis summarized in Example 6.4. As a result of the stakeholder analysis, the analyst concluded that the issues raised by the process owner were echoed by the customer (site engineer) and the other process participants. The analyst also found three other perceived issues: one raised by the site engineer (delays in the rental process) and two by the clerk (unclear site engineer requirements and inaccurate or incomplete catalog data). The analyst decided not to include these perceived issues in the initial issue register, because they appeared to be possible causes of the issues raised by the process owner, rather than top-level issues on their own. Accordingly, the analyst proceeded to analyze the issues raised by the process owner by gathering additional data about their frequency and the impact of each occurrence of those issues.

Based on the collected data, the analyst prepared the issue register in Table 6.2.[1]

□

Question Issue or factor?

An issue register may contain a mixture of issues that have a direct impact business performance as well as other issues that are causal or contributing factors of issues that then impact on business performance. In other words, the issue register contains both *issues* and *factors*. For example, when preparing the issue register of the equipment rental process, one could be tempted to include entries such as the following ones:

- Clerk misunderstood the site engineer's requirements for an equipment.
- Clerk did not select the correct equipment from the supplier's catalog due to inattention.
- Clerk indicated an incorrect delivery date in the PO.
- Supplier did not deliver the equipment that had been ordered.
- Delivered equipment is faulty or is not ready-for-use.
- Supplier delivered the equipment to the wrong construction site or at the wrong time.
- The equipment arrived five working days after the site engineer had requested it, but the site engineer needed the equipment earlier.

All of the above issues are possible causal or contributing factors of a top-level issue, namely "Equipment is rejected by the site engineer". The fact that the site

---

[1]In this issue register we do not use one column per field, but rather one row per field. This is a pragmatic choice to better fit the issue register within the width of the page.

Table 6.2 Issue register of equipment rental process

Issue 1: Equipment kept longer than needed

Priority: 1

Description: Site engineers keep the equipment longer than needed

Data and assumptions: BuildIT rents 3,000 pieces of equipment per year. In 10% of cases, site engineers keep the equipment 2 days longer than needed. On average, rented equipment costs € 100 per day

Qualitative impact: Not applicable

Quantitative impact: $0.1 \times 3,000 \times 2 \times 100 = $ € 60,000 in additional rental expenses per year

---

Issue 2: Rejected equipment

Priority: 2

Description: Site engineers sometimes reject the delivered equipment due to non-conformance to their specifications

Data and assumptions: BuildIT rents 3,000 pieces of equipment per year. Each time an equipment is rejected due to a mistake on BuildIT's side, BuildIT is billed the cost of 1 day of rental, that is € 100. 5% of them are rejected due to an internal mistake within BuildIT (as opposed to a supplier mistake)

Qualitative impact: These events disrupt the construction schedules and create frustration and internal conflicts

Quantitative impact: $3,000 \times 0.05 \times 100 = $ € 15,000 per year

---

Issue 3: Late payment fees

Priority: 3

Description: BuildIT pays late payment fees because invoices are not paid by the due date

Data and assumptions: BuildIT rents 3,000 pieces of equipment per year. Each equipment is rented on average for 4 days at a rate of € 100 per day. Each rental leads to one invoice. About 10% of invoices are paid late. On average, the penalty for late payment is 2% of the amount of the invoice

Qualitative impact: Suppliers are annoyed and later unwilling to negotiate more favorable terms for equipment rental

Quantitative impact: $0.1 \times 3,000 \times 4 \times 100 \times 0.02 = $ € 2,400 per year

---

engineer rejects the equipment creates a direct impact for BuildIT, for example in terms of delays in the construction schedule. Meanwhile, the issues listed above have an indirect business impact, in the sense that they lead to the equipment being rejected and the needed equipment not being available on time, which in turn leads to delays in the construction schedule.

When an issue register contains a combination of issues and factors, it may be useful to add two fields to the register, namely "caused by" and "is cause of", that indicate for a given issue, which other issues in the register are related to it via a cause-effect relation. This way it becomes easier to identify which issues are related between them so that related issues can be analyzed together. Also, when an issue X is a factor of an issue Y, instead of analyzing the impact of both X and Y, we can analyze the impact of Y and in the qualitative and quantitative impact fields of X we can simply refer to the impact of Y. For example, in the impact field of issue "Clerk misunderstood the site engineer's requirements" we can simply refer to the impact of "Equipment is rejected by the site engineer".

Alternatively, we can adopt the convention of including in the issue register only top-level issues, meaning issues that have a direct business impact, and separately, we can use why-why diagrams and cause-effect diagrams to document the factors underpinning these top-level issues. This convention is followed in the rest of this chapter, meaning that the issue registers shown below only contain top-level issues rather than factors. The analysis and documentation of the causes of each issue is undertaken outside the issue register by means of root cause analysis techniques, which we will discuss later in this chapter. Hence, for each issue we put in an issue register, there is at least one stakeholder who is directly impacted by the issue, and hence we can do an impact analysis of each issue.

In the above example, the number of issues is small. In a large organization, a stakeholder analysis of a core process can lead to dozens of issues. Moreover, when we engage in a BPM program covering many processes, the number of issues across all processes can be in order of hundreds. In these cases, it pays off to use an *Issue Tracking system* to maintain the issue register. An issue tracking system is a collaboration tool that allows its users (among other things) to create, document, edit, and comment on issues, and to generate filtered and sorted lists of issues according to a range of criteria.

Exercise 6.4 We consider again the university admission process. As discussed in Exercise 6.3 (page 228), the process owner is concerned by the costs of the process and by the fact that good candidates are being lost to competing universities during the admission process. Concretely, we saw in Exercise 6.2 (page 224) that 30% of students who receive an offer reject it, and that out of those, 30% of them reject the offer because they received an offer from a competing university. The interviews as well as data from applicant surveys reveal that one of the issues faced by the university is that students have to wait too long to know the outcome of their application. It often happens that by the time a student is admitted, the student has decided to go to another university instead. Write an issue register to document this issue (only this issue). Take into account the data in Exercises 6.2 and 6.3.

6.3.3 Pareto Analysis and PICK Charts

The impact assessment conducted while building the issue register can serve as input for *Pareto analysis*. The aim of Pareto analysis is to identify which issues or which causal factors of an issue should be given priority. Pareto analysis rests on the principle that a small number of factors are responsible for the largest share of a given effect. In other words:

- A small subset of issues in the issue register are likely responsible for the largest share of impact.
- For a given issue, a small subset of factors behind this issue are likely responsible for the largest share of occurrences of this issue.

Sometimes this principle is also called the 80-20 principle, meaning that 20% of issues are responsible for 80% of the effect. One should keep in mind however that the specific proportions are only indicative. It may be for example that 30% of issues are responsible for 70% of the effect.

A typical approach to conduct Pareto analysis is as follows:

1. Define the effect to be analyzed and the measure via which this effect will be quantified. The measure might be for example:

   - Financial loss for the customer or for the business.
   - Time loss by the customer or by the process participants.
   - Number of occurrences of a negative outcome, such as number of unsatisfied customers due to errors made when handling their case.

2. Identify all relevant issues that contribute to the effect to be analyzed.
3. Quantify each issue according to the chosen measure. This step can be done on the basis of the issue register, in particular, the quantitative impact column of the register.
4. Sort the issues according to the chosen measure (from highest to lowest impact) and draw a so-called *Pareto chart*. A Pareto chart consists of two components:

   a. A bar chart where each bar corresponds to an issue and the height of the bar is proportional to the impact of the issue or factor.
   b. A curve that plots the cumulative percentage impact of the issues. For example, if the issue with the highest impact is responsible for 40% of the impact, this curve will have a point with a y-coordinate of 0.4 and an x-coordinate positioned so as to coincide with the first bar in the bar chart.

Example 6.6 Consider again the equipment rental process described in Example 1.1 (page 3) and the issue register in Example 6.5. All three issues in this register have in common that they are responsible for unnecessary rental expenditure, which is a form of financial loss. From the data in the impact column of the register, we can plot the Pareto chart in Figure 6.3.

This Pareto chart shows that issue "Slow rental approval" is responsible already for 78% of unnecessary rental expenditure. Given that in this example there are only three issues, one could have come to this conclusion without conducting Pareto analysis. In practice though, an issue register may contain dozens or hundreds of issues, making Pareto analysis a useful tool to summarize the data in the issue register and to focus the analysis and redesign efforts on the set of issues that would lead to the most visible impact.   □

Exercise 6.5 Let us consider again the equipment rental process. This time we take the perspective of the site engineer, whose goal is to have the required equipment available on site when needed. From this perspective, the main issue is that in about 10% of cases, the requested equipment is not available on site the day when it is required. When this happens, the site engineer contacts the suppliers directly to resolve the issue, but still, resolving the issue may take several days. It is estimated that each such delay costs € 400 per day to BuildIT. By inspecting a random sample

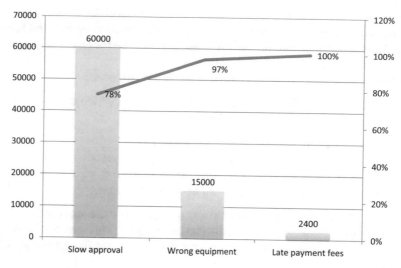

Fig. 6.3 Pareto chart for excessive equipment rental expenditure

of delayed equipment deliveries during a one-year period and investigating the cause of each occurrence, an analyst found that:

1. In total, five occurrences were due to the site engineer not having ordered the equipment with sufficient advance notice: The site engineers ordered the equipment the day before it was needed, when at least 2 days are needed. These cases cause delays of 1 day on average.
2. Nine occurrences were due to the fact that none of BuildIT's suppliers had the required type of equipment available on the requested day. These cases cause delays of 1 to 4 days (3 days on average).
3. 13 occurrences were due to the approval process taking too long (more than a day) due to mistakes or misunderstandings. For these cases, the delay was 1 day on average.
4. 27 occurrences were due to the equipment having been delivered on time, but the equipment was not suitable and the site engineer rejected it. These cases cause delays of 2 days on average.
5. Four occurrences were due to mistakes or delays attributable entirely to the supplier. These cases lead to delays of one day. However, in these cases, the supplier compensated BuildIT by providing the equipment 2 days for free (the remaining days are still charged). Recall that the average cost of an equipment rental per day is € 100.
6. For two occurrences, the analyst did not manage to determine the cause of the delay (the process participants could not recall the details). The delays in these cases where 2 days per occurrence.

The sample of analyzed occurrences represents around 20% of all occurrences of the issue during a one-year period.

Fig. 6.4 PICK chart
visualizing the payoff and
difficulty of addressing each
issue

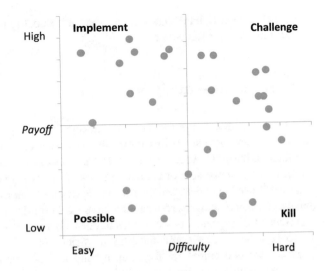

Draw a Pareto chart corresponding to the above data.

It is worth highlighting that Pareto analysis focuses on a single dimension. In the example above, the dimension under analysis is the impact in monetary terms. In other words, we focus on the estimated payoff of addressing an issue. In addition to payoff, there is another dimension that should be taken into account when deciding which issues should be given higher priority, namely the level of difficulty of addressing an issue. This level of difficulty can be quantified by the investment required to change the process, such that the issue in question is addressed.

A type of chart that can be used as a complement to Pareto charts in order to take into account the difficulty dimension is the *PICK chart*. PICK is an acronym standing for Possible, Implement, Challenge, and Kil. These are the names of the four quadrants of a PICK chart (see Figure 6.4). In a PICK chart, each issue appears as a point. The horizontal coordinate of a point captures the difficulty of addressing the issue (or more specifically the difficulty of implementing a given improvement idea that addresses the issue). Meanwhile, the vertical coordinate of an issue captures its potential payoff. The horizontal axis (difficulty) is split into two sections (easy and hard) while the vertical axis (payoff) is split into low and high. These splits lead to four quadrants that allow analysts to classify issues according to the trade-off between payoff and difficulty:

- *Possible* (low payoff, easy to do): issues that can be addressed if there are sufficient resources to do so.
- *Implement* (high payoff, easy to do): issues that should definitely be implemented as a matter of priority.
- *Challenge* (high payoff, hard to do): issues that should be addressed but require significant amount of effort. In general one would pick one of these challenges and focus on it rather than addressing all or multiple challenges at once.

- *Kill* (low payoff, hard to do): issues that are probably not worth addressing or at least not to their full extent.

6.4 Root Cause Analysis

Root cause analysis is a family of techniques that helps analysts to identify and understand the root cause of issues or undesirable events. Root cause analysis is not confined to business process analysis. In fact, root cause analysis is commonly used in the context of accident or incident analysis as well as in manufacturing processes where it is used to understand the root cause of defects in a product. In the context of business process analysis, root cause analysis is helpful to identify and to understand the issues that prevent a process from having a better performance.

Root cause analysis encompasses a variety of techniques. In general, these methods include guidelines for interviewing and conducting workshops with relevant stakeholders, as well as techniques to organize and to document the ideas generated during these interviews or workshops. Below, we will discuss two of these techniques, namely *cause-and-effect diagrams* and *why-why diagrams*.

6.4.1 Cause-Effect Diagrams

Cause-effect diagrams depict the relationship between a given *negative effect* and its potential causes. In the context of process analysis, a negative effect is usually either a recurrent issue or an undesirable level of process performance. Potential causes can be divided into causal and contributing factors (hereby called *factors*) as explained in the box below.

CAUSAL VERSUS CONTRIBUTING FACTORS

Two broad types of causes are generally distinguished in the area of root cause analysis, namely *causal factors* and *contributing factors*. Causal factors are those factors that, if corrected, eliminated or avoided would prevent the issue from occurring in future. For example, in the context of an insurance claims handling process, errors in the estimation of damages lead to incorrect claim assessments. If the damage estimation errors were eliminated, a number of occurrences of the issue "Incorrect claim assessment" would definitely be prevented. Contributing factors are those that set the stage for, or that increase the chances of a given issue occurring. For example, consider the case where the user interface for lodging the insurance claims requires the claimant to enter a few dates (e.g., the date when the claim incident occurred), but the

---

(continued)

interface does not provide a calendar widget so that the user can easily select the date. This deficiency in the user interface may increase the chances that the user enters the wrong date. In other words, this deficiency contributes to the issue "Incorrect claim data entry".

While the distinction between causal and contributing factor is generally useful when investigating specific incidents (for example investigating the causes of a given road accident), the distinction is often not relevant or not sufficiently sharp in the context of business process analysis. Accordingly, in this chapter we will use the term *factor* to refer to causal and contributing factors collectively.

In a cause-effect diagram, factors are grouped into categories and possibly also sub-categories. These categories help to guide the search for potential causes. Concretely, when organizing a brainstorming session for root cause analysis, one way to structure the session is to first go around the table asking all participants to give their opinion on the potential causal or contributing factors of the issue at hand. These potential factors are listed in no particular order. Next, the potential factors are classified according to certain categories and the discussion continues in a more structured way using these categories as a framework. The outcome of this discussion is a list of potential (or hypothesized) factors. Each of these hypothesized factors should be validated subsequently by collecting data from the relevant information systems or by observing executions of the process during a period of time in order to determine if occurrences of the negative effect can indeed be traced back to occurrences of the potential factor.

A well-known categorization for cause-effect analysis are the so-called 6 M's, which are described below together with possible sub-categorizations.

1. **Machine** (technology)—factors pertaining to the technology used, like for example software failures, hardware failures, network failures, or system crashes that may occur in the information systems that support a business process. A useful sub-categorization of Machine factors is the following:

   a. Lack of functionality in application systems.
   b. Redundant storage of data across systems, leading for example to double data entry (same data entered twice in different systems) and data inconsistencies across systems.
   c. Low performance of IT of network systems, leading for example to low response times for customers and process participants.
   d. Poor user interface design, leading for example to erroneous customer or process participants not realizing that some data is missing or that some data is provided but not easily visible.
   e. Lack of integration between multiple systems within the enterprise or with external systems such as a supplier's information system or a customer's information system.

2. **Method** (process)—factors stemming from the way the process is defined or understood or in the way it is performed. An example of this is when a given process participant A thinks that another participant B will send an email to a customer, but participant B does not send it because it is not aware it has to send it. Possible sub-categories of Method factors include:

   a. Unclear, unsuitable, or inconsistent assignment of decision-making and processing responsibilities to process participants.
   b. Lack of empowerment of process participants, leading to process participants not being able to make necessary decisions without consulting several levels above in their organizational hierarchy. Conversely, excessive empowerment may lead to process participants having too much discretion and causing losses to the business through their actions.
   c. Lack of timely communication between process participants or between process participants and the customer.

3. **Material**—factors stemming from the raw materials, consumables, or data required as input by the tasks in the process, like for example incorrect data leading to a wrong decision being made during the execution of process. The distinction between raw materials, consumables, and data provides a possible sub-categorization of these factors.

4. **Man**—factors related to a wrong assessment or an incorrectly performed step, like for example a claims handler accepting a claim even though the data in the claim and the rules used for assessing the claim require that the claim be rejected. Possible sub-categories of Man factors include:

   a. Lack of training and clear instructions for process participants.
   b. Lack of incentive system to motivate process participants sufficiently.
   c. Expecting too much from process participants (e.g., overly hectic schedules).
   d. Inadequate recruitment of process participants.

5. **Measurement**—factors related to measurements or calculations made during the process. In the context of an insurance claim, an example of such a factor is one where the amount to be paid to the customer is miscalculated due to an inaccurate estimation of the damages being claimed.

6. **Milieu**—factors stemming from the environment in which the process is executed, like for example factors originating from the customer, suppliers, or other external actors. Here, the originating actor is a possible sub-categorization. Generally, Milieu factors are outside the control of the process participants, the process owner, and other company managers. For example, consider a process for handling insurance claims for car accidents. This process depends partly on data extracted from police reports (e.g., police reports produced when a major accident occurs). It may happen in this context that some errors during the claims handling process originate from inaccuracies or missing details in the police reports. These factors are to some extent outside the control of the insurance company. This example illustrates that milieu factors may need to be treated differently from other (internal) factors.

These categories are meant as a guideline for brainstorming during root cause analysis rather than gospel that should be followed to the letter. Other ways of categorizing factors may be equally useful. For example, one alternative categorization is known as the 4 P's (Policies, Procedures, People and Plant). Also, it is sometimes useful to classify factors according to the tasks in the process from where they originate (i.e., one category per major task in the process).

The above categories are useful not only as a guide for brainstorming during root cause analysis, but also as a basis for documenting the potential root causes in the form of a cause-effect diagram. Concretely, given a categorization of potential causes, such as the 6 M's above, a cause-effect diagram consists of a main horizontal line (the *trunk*) from which a number of branches stem (see Figure 6.5). At one end of the trunk is a box containing the negative effect that is being analyzed (in our case the *issue* being analyzed). The trunk has a number of main branches corresponding to the categories of factors (e.g., the 6 M's). The root causes are written in the sub-branches. Sometimes, it is relevant to distinguish between *primary factors*, meaning factors that have a direct impact on the issue at hand, from *secondary factors*, which are factors that have an impact on the primary factors. For example, in the context of an insurance claims handling process, an inaccurate estimation of the damages leads to a miscalculation of the amount to be paid for a given claim. This inaccurate estimation of the damages may itself stem from a lack of incentive from the repairer to accurately calculate the cost of repairs. Thus, "Inaccurate damage estimation" can be seen as a primary factor for "Liability miscalculation", while "Lack of incentive to calculate repair costs accurately" is a secondary factor behind the "Inaccurate damage estimation". The distinction between primary and secondary factors is a

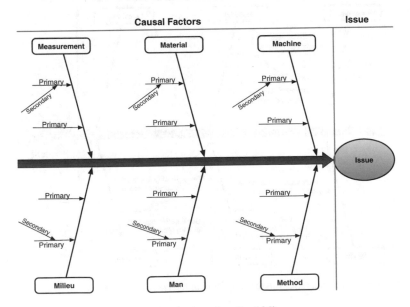

Fig. 6.5 Template of a cause-effect diagram based on the 6 M's

first step towards identifying chains of factors behind an issue. We will see later in this chapter that why-why diagrams allow us to dig deeper into such chains of factors.

Because of their visual appearance, cause-effect diagrams are also known as *Fishbone diagrams*. Another common name for such diagrams is *Ishikawa diagrams* in allusion to one of its proponents—Kaoru Ishikawa—one of the pioneers of the field of quality management.

Example 6.7 We consider again the equipment rental process described in Example 1.1 (page 3) and the issue register in Table 6.2 (page 231). One of the issues identified in the issue register is that sometimes, the delivered equipment is rejected by the site engineer. We can see three primary causes from the issue, which are summarized in the cause-effect diagram in Figure 6.6. The diagram also shows secondary causes underpinning each of the primary causes. Note that the factor "clerk selected equipment with incorrect specs" has been classified under the Material category because this factor stems from incorrect input data. A defect in input data used by a process falls under the Material category.   □

Exercise 6.6 As discussed in Exercise 6.4 (page 232), one of the main issues of the university admission process is that students have to wait too long to know the outcome of their application. It often happens that by the time a student is admitted, the student has decided to go to another university instead. Analyze the possible causes of this issue using a cause-effect diagram.

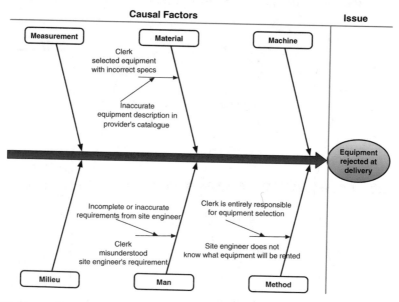

Fig. 6.6 Cause-effect diagram for issue "Equipment rejected at delivery"

6.4.2   Why-Why Diagrams

Why-why diagrams (also known as *tree diagrams*) constitute another technique to analyze the cause of negative effects, such as issues in a business process. The emphasis of root cause analysis is to capture the series of cause-to-effect relations that lead to a given effect. The basic idea is to recursively ask the question: Why has something happened? This question is asked multiple times until a factor that stakeholders perceive to be a *root cause* is found. A common belief in the field of quality management—known as the 5 Why's principle—has it that answering the "why" question five times recursively allows one to pin down the root causes of a given negative effect. Of course, this should not be treated as gospel, but as a guideline of how far one should go during root cause analysis.

   Why-why diagrams are a technique for structuring brainstorming sessions (e.g., workshops) for root cause analysis. Such a session would start with an issue. The first step is to give a name to the issue that stakeholders agree on. Sometimes it is found that there is not one issue, but multiple issues, in which case they should be analyzed separately. Once the issue has been identified and a name has been agreed upon, this becomes the root of the tree. Then at each level the following questions are asked: "Why does this happen?" and "What are the main sub-issues that may lead to this issue?". Possible factors are then identified. Each of these factors is then analyzed using the same questions. When getting down in the tree (e.g., to levels 3 or 4) it is recommended to start focusing on factors that can be resolved, meaning that something can be done to change them. The leaves of the tree should correspond to factors that are fundamental in nature, meaning that they cannot be explained in terms of other factors. Ideally, these factors, called root causes, should be such that they can be eliminated or mitigated, but this is not necessarily the case. For example, in the context of an insurance claims handling process, a certain type of error in a police report may be due to lack of time and hectic schedules on the side of police agents involved in filling these reports. There is relatively little the insurance agency can do in this case to eliminate the error, other than raising the issue with the relevant authorities. Yet, the impact of this factor could be mitigated by putting in place checks to detect such errors as early as possible in the process.

   A simple template for why-why diagrams is given in Figure 6.7. An alternative way of presenting the information in such diagrams is by means of nested bullet-point lists. In the rest of this chapter we will opt for this latter representation.

Example 6.8 We consider again the equipment rental process described in Example 1.1 (page 3) and the issue register in Table 6.2 (page 231).

   Regarding the first issue, the analyst identified a dozen examples where equipment had been kept for more than 10 working days and reportedly not used during the whole rental period. The analyst found that in the majority of these cases, the equipment had been initially rented for a period of less than 10 days, but it was kept for longer by means of a deadline extension. By analyzing the data further, the analyst found that deadline extensions were quite common. It turned out that site engineers found it easy to get a deadline extension. They also knew that getting

Fig. 6.7 Template of a
why-why diagram

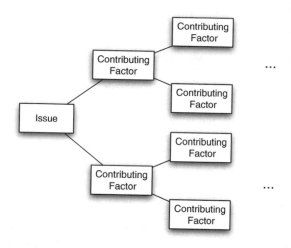

equipment rental requests approved took a couple of days or more, and the larger the cost and the longer the duration of the rental, the slower it was to get it approved. As a workaround, site engineers were renting equipment several days before the date when they actually needed it. Also, they were specifying short periods in their equipment rental requests in order to get them approved quicker. When the deadline for returning an equipment approached, they just called the supplier to keep the equipment for a longer period.

The analyst then had a closer look at the second issue (equipment being rejected). The initial interviews with the clerks had already provided some hints as to the causes of this issue. The clerks often misunderstood the site engineer's requirements for an equipment. They also found that the data in the suppliers' catalogs was inaccurate and incomplete. Further interviews with the site engineers also revealed that the site engineers often did not know what equipment had been ordered as a result of their rental request. Had they known it, they could have rectified the mistakes before the equipment reached the construction site.

Finally, the analyst took a closer look at the issue of penalties for late payment of invoices. Again, by taking some concrete examples and talking about them with the clerks, the analyst found that the issue partially came from the fact that clerks were having a hard time getting the site engineers to confirm that the data in the invoices are correct. Site engineers did not feel that verifying the invoices was a priority for them. The clerks also pointed out that there were often inconsistencies between the PO and the invoice. One of the causes for these inconsistencies was that, to avoid the hassle of taking back the equipment and exchanging it for another one, some of the suppliers had developed a workaround: Every time the supplier received a PO, the supplier contacted directly the site engineer to negotiate exactly which equipment should be delivered. As a result of this negotiation, very often the equipment that was actually delivered differed from the one specified in the PO.

Based on the above observations and others made during the interviews, the analyst wrote the following why-why diagrams (represented as nested bullet-point lists).

Issue 1 Site engineers sometimes reject delivered equipment, why?

- wrong equipment is delivered, why?
  - miscommunication between site engineer and clerk, why?
    - o site engineer provides an incomplete or inaccurate description of what they want.
    - o site engineer does not always see the supplier catalogs when making a request and does not communicate with the supplier, why?
      - · site engineer generally does not have Internet connectivity.
    - o site engineer does not check the choice of equipment made by the clerk.
  - equipment descriptions in supplier's catalog not accurate.

Issue 2 Site engineers keep equipment longer than needed via deadline extensions, why?

- site engineer fears that equipment will not be available later when needed, why?
  - time between request and delivery too long, why?
    - o excessive time spent in finding a suitable equipment and approving the request, why?
      - · time spent by clerk contacting possibly multiple suppliers sequentially;
      - · time spent waiting for works engineer to check the requests;

Issue 3 BuildIT often has to pay late payment fees to suppliers, why?

- Time between invoice received by clerk and confirmation is too long, why?
  - clerk needs confirmation from site engineer, why?
    - o clerk cannot assert when the equipment was delivered and picked up, why?
      - · delivery and pick-up of equipment are not recorded in a shared information system;
      - · site engineer can extend the equipment rental period without informing the clerk;
    - o site engineer takes too long to confirm the invoice, why?
      - · confirming invoices is not a priority for site engineer;

□

Exercise 6.7 Consider again the process for university admission described in Exercise 1.1 (page 5) and the issue described in Exercise 6.6 above. Analyze this issue using a why-why diagram.

6.5 Recap

In this chapter, we presented a selection of techniques for qualitative analysis of business processes. The first technique, namely value-added analysis, allows us to identify steps in the process that do not provide value to the customer or to the business. We then presented a complementary technique, which allows us to identify different types of waste. These two techniques allow us to identify potential inefficiencies in the process.

Next, we presented a technique to collect issues from multiple perspectives, namely stakeholder analysis, as well as a template to document these issues in an issue register. The purpose of an issue register is to document issues in a semi-structured way and to analyze their impact on the business both from a qualitative and a quantitative angle. In particular, the issue register provides a starting point to build Pareto charts and PICK charts—two visualization techniques that provide a bird's-eye view of a set of issues. These charts help analysts to focus their attention on issues that offer the highest payoff (in the case of Pareto charts) or the best trade-off between payoff and difficulty (in the case of PICK charts).

Finally, we presented two techniques to uncover the causes behind a given issue, namely cause-effect analysis and why-why analysis. Whereas cause-effect analysis focuses on classifying the factors underpinning the occurrences of an issue, why-why analysis focuses on identifying the recursive cause-effect relations between these factors.

6.6 Solutions to Exercises

Solution 6.1

- VA: receive online application, evaluate academic admissibility, send notification to student
- BVA: check completeness, academic recognition agency check, English test check
- NVA: receive physical documents from students, forward documents to committee, notify students service of outcomes of academic admissibility.

Note. In this solution we treat the entire agency check as BVA. Part of this agency check consists in the admissions office sending the documents to the agency and the agency sending back the documents and their assessment to the admissions office. These two sub-steps could be treated as NVA. However, if we assume that the agency requires the documents to be sent by post to them, these sub-steps cannot be easily separated from the agency check itself. In other words, it would not be possible to eliminate these handoff steps without eliminating the entire agency check. Thus the entire agency check should arguably be treated as a single step.

Solution 6.2

Transportation.   Right from the start of the process, we can spot transportation waste in the form of physical documents sent by the student to the admissions office, emails from the admission office to the student, and further documents sent by the applicant if the initial application is incomplete. The latter events can also be seen as defect waste. We also note that there is a handoff from the admissions office to the committee and back. These handoffs are transportation wastes too. Other transportation wastes come from the interactions between the admissions office and the external academic recognition agency.

Waiting.   When the admissions office finds that an application is incomplete, an email is sent to the student asking for the missing information or documents. The fact that the application is put on hold until additional input is received from the candidate is waiting waste. Later in the process, the committee batches the applications and examines them every three months. This batching generates waiting waste. There may also be idleness waste during the period when the admissions office is waiting for the decisions of the academic committee, but without further information, it is not possible to assert that this idleness indeed occurs in practice (it may be that the office handles other work in the meantime).

Inventory.   Given the committee meets every three months, we can hypothesize that at a given point in time, there are several hundred applications in a pending state. This constitutes inventory waste.

Defect.   When an incomplete application is sent back to the applicant, the application needs to be checked again after the student resubmits a revised application. This second verification of completeness is rework, hence defect waste.

Overprocessing.   Officers in the admissions office spend time verifying the authenticity of around 3,000 diplomas and language test results submitted by the applicants. In the end, however, only 5% of cases reveal any issues. Later on in the process, three quarters of the applications are passed on to the admission committees. The university ends up making a study place offer to only 20% of the applications that they receive. The fact that the document authenticity was verified for all the applications rejected by the committee is an example of overprocessing.

Overproduction.   We can see two sources of overproduction waste: cases where an applicant rejects the admission offer he or she receives (20% of cases) and cases where the applicant is declared admissible but does not receive a study offer due to lack of places (20%).

Solution 6.3 The customer of the admissions process is the applicant. We distinguish between applicants who do not get an admission offer and those who get one.

Among those who get an admission offer, we distinguish between those who accept the admission offer and those who reject it. Additionally, we could distinguish those students who get an admission offer with scholarship from those who do not. Based on this classification, we may wish to interview at least one applicant whose application was rejected; one whose application who was accepted without scholarship and did not accept the offer; one whose application was accepted with scholarship and did not accept the offer; and one whose application was accepted without scholarship and accepted the offer. We could also interview one who was admitted with scholarship and accepted the offer but it is unclear if this would bring additional insights given the objectives of the process owner.

The main process participants are the admission officers and the admission committees (we assume there is one committee per curriculum). We should interview at least one representative from each of these two groups, and in the case of the admission committees, we should consider interviewing representatives of at least two committees.

There is one external party in the process (the academic recognition agency). However, given that their role in the process is punctual and given the objectives of the process owner, it does not seem that getting input from the academic recognition agency is necessary.

Given the description of the process, we hypothesize that the students are concerned by the complexity and slowness of the process, and hence we should be prepared to ask questions about the amount of effort that the process requires from them, and their perception about the response times in the process. They might also raise issues (defects) during the process, like for example wrong answers to their questions, and hence questions could be prepared to explore this possibility.

The admission officers have a large amount of applications to handle, so they might be concerned about excessive workload. But they could also be concerned about the amount of inquiries they get from students. There is a back-and-forth handoff with the admission committee in the process, and hence defects and waiting times associated to these handoffs. More generally, we could take each of the wastes identified in Solution 6.2 and prepare questions to shed light into the magnitude and impact of each waste.

The admission committee has to examine the applications from multiple perspectives and has to deal with discrepancies between different grading systems, as students come from different countries. They also have to assess the motivation letters and reference letters, which are free-form. One can expect them to raise issues about the complexity of tasks they perform. Questions could also be prepared to shed further light into the wastes identified in Solution 6.2, particularly with regard to handoffs.

Solution 6.4 In the following issue register, we only analyze the issue described in this chapter, namely that the admission process takes too long. In practice, the issue register would include multiple issues.

Issue 1: Students reject offer due to long waiting times

Priority: 1

Description: The time between online submission of an application to notification of acceptance takes too long, resulting in some students rejecting their admission offer.

Data and assumptions: Out of 3,000 applicants, 20% (i.e., 600) get an admission offer and reject it. Out of them 30% (i.e. 180) reject the offer because they accepted the admission offer elsewhere. In addition to these data, we assume that half of those who accept an admission offer elsewhere (i.e., 90 students) would have accepted our admission offer if we had made our offer earlier. According to the data in Exercise 6.3 (page 228), the assessment of each application costs € 100 per student to the university in time spent by the admissions office, plus € 50 of academic recognition agency fee and online application service fee. The university spends € 100 in marketing for each application it attracts, but this is covered by the € 100 application fee.

Qualitative impact: Students who would contribute to the institution positively are lost. Delays in the admission process affect the image of the university vis-à-vis future students, and generate additional effort to handle enquiries from students while they wait for the admission decisions.

Quantitative impact: $90 \times € 150 = € 13,500$ per admission round

In the above issue analysis, the effort required to deal with enquiries during the pre-admission period is listed in the qualitative impact field. If it were possible (with a reasonable amount of effort) to estimate how many such enquiries arrive and how much time they consume, it would be possible to turn this qualitative impact into a quantitative one.

Solution 6.5 First, we analyze the cost incurred by each type of occurrence (i.e., each causal factor) in the sample:

1. Last-minute request: 1 day delay (because normally 2 days advance notice are needed), thus € 400 cost $\times 5 = € 2,000$.
2. Equipment out-of-stock: 3 days delay $= € 1,200 \times 9 = € 10,800$.
3. Approval delay: 1 day delay $= € 400 \times 13 = € 5,200$.
4. Rejected equipment: 2 days delay $= € 800 \times 27 = € 21,600$. Note that in Example 6.5 we mentioned that when an equipment is rejected, a fee of € 100 (on average) has to be paid to the supplier for taking back the equipment. However, we do not include this fee here because we are interested in analyzing the costs stemming from equipment not being available on the required day, as opposed to other costs incurred by rejecting equipment.
5. Supplier mistake: 1 day delay $= € 400$ minus € 200 in rental cost saving $= € 200 \times 4 = € 800$.
6. Undetermined: 2 days delay $= € 800 \times 2 = € 1,600$.

Since the sample represents 20% of occurrences of the issue over a year, we multiply the above numbers by 5 in order to estimate the total yearly loss attributable to each causal factor. The resulting Pareto chart is given in Figure 6.8.

Solution 6.6 The cause-effect diagram corresponding to this exercise should include at least the name of the issue (e.g., "Student waiting time too long") and the following factors:

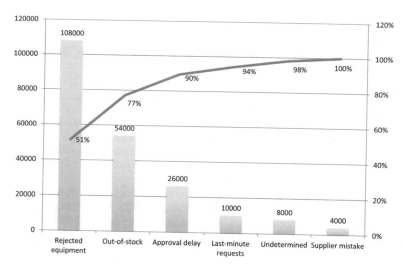

Fig. 6.8 Pareto chart of causal factors of issue "Equipment not available when needed"

- Process stalls due to agency check. This is a Method issue, since the issue stems from the fact that the process essentially stalls until a response is received from the agency. One could argue that to some extent this is a Milieu issue. But while the slowness of the agency check is a Milieu issue, the fact that the process stalls until a response is received from the agency is a Method issue.
- Agency check takes too long. This is a Milieu issue since the agency is a separate entity that imposes its own limitations.
- Academic committee assessment takes too long. This is a Method issue since the process imposes that the academic committee only assesses applications at certain times (when it meets), rather than when applications are ready to be evaluated.
- Physical documents take too long to be received. This is a Milieu issue for two reasons. First, the physical documents are needed for the purpose of the agency check and the delays in the arrival of physical documents are caused by the applicants themselves and postal service delays.
- Admission office delays the notification after academic assessment. This seems to be a Method issue, but the description of the process does not give us sufficient information to state this conclusively. Here, a process analyst would need to gather more information in order to understand this issue in further detail.

Solution 6.7

- Admission process takes too long, why?

  – Process stalls until physical documents arrive, why?

    · Agency check requires physical documents;
    · Other tasks are performed only after agency check, why?

- · Traditionally this is how the process is set up but there is no strong reason for it;

- Agency check takes too long, why?

  - · Exchanges with the agency are via post, why?

    - · Agency requires original (or certified) documents due to regulatory requirements.

- Academic committee takes too long, why?

  - Documents are exchanged by internal mail between admissions office and committee.
  - Academic committee only meets at specified times.

- Admission office delays the notification after academic assessment, why?

  - Not enough information available to analyze this issue (probably due to batching—admissions office sends notifications in batches).

The above analysis already suggests one obvious improvement idea: perform the academic committee assessment in parallel to the agency check. Another improvement opportunity is to replace internal mail communication between admissions office and academic committee with electronic communication (e.g., documents made available to committee members via a Web application).

6.7 Further Exercises

Exercise 6.8 Consider the pharmacy prescription fulfillment process described in Exercise 1.6 (page 30). Identify the steps in this process and classify them into VA, BVA, and NVA.

Exercise 6.9 Consider the procure-to-pay process described in Exercise 1.7 (page 31). Identify the steps in this process and classify them into VA, BVA, and NVA.

Exercise 6.10 Consider the pharmacy prescription fulfillment process described in Exercise 1.6 (page 30). Which types of waste can you identify in this process?

Exercise 6.11 Consider the booking-to-cash process at a photography company (Fotof) described in Exercise 4.31 (page 155). Which types of waste can you identify in this process?

Exercise 6.12 Consider the following summary of issues reported in a travel agency.

A travel agency has recently lost several medium-sized and large corporate customers due to complaints about poor customer service. The management team of the travel agency decided to appoint a team of analysts to address this problem. The team gathered data by conducting interviews and surveys with current and past corporate customers and also by gathering customer feedback data that the travel agency has recorded over time. About 2% of customers complained about errors that had been made in their bookings. In one occasion, a customer had requested a change to a flight booking. The travel agent wrote an email to the customer suggesting that the change had been made and attached a modified travel itinerary. However, it later turned out that the modified booking had not been confirmed in the flight reservation system. As a result, the customer was not allowed to board the flight and this led to a series of severe inconveniences for the customer. Similar problems had occurred when booking a flight initially: the customer had asked for certain dates, but the flight tickets had been issued for different dates. Additionally, customers complained of the long times it took to get responses to their requests for quotes and itineraries. In most cases, employees of the travel agency replied to requests for quotes within 2–4 working hours, but in the case of some complicated itinerary requests (about 10% of the requests), it took them up to 2 days. Finally, about 5% of customers also complained that the travel agents did not find the best flight connections and prices for them. Several customers reported that they had found better itineraries and prices on the Web by searching by themselves.

1. Document the issues in the form of an issue register. To this end, you may assume that the travel agency receives around 100 itinerary requests per day and that the agency makes 50 bookings per day. Each booking brings a gross profit of € 100 to the agency.
2. Analyze the issues described above using root cause analysis techniques.

Exercise 6.13 Consider the booking-to-cash process at a photography company (Fotof) described in Exercise 4.31 (page 155) as well as the following data:

- Fotof has 25 photo studios and its latest annual turnover from photography services is 17.6 million, out of which 25% from sales to corporate customers and the rest from private customers.
- The company makes an additional 5 million revenue in sales of photography equipment and accessories at its studios.
- There are on average 3.5 photographers and 2 technicians per studio.
- On average, an in-studio session lasts 45 min, while an on-location session lasts 3.5 h (including transportation time).
- 20% of private customer shootings and 100% of corporate customer shootings are on-location. The remaining ones are on-studio.

An analyst conducted a stakeholder analysis focusing on three types of a stakeholders: the customer, the process participants, and the management (process owner and business sponsor). The main findings of this analysis are summarized below.

Customer According to the latest customer survey, customer satisfaction stands at 80% (declining from 85% in the previous year) and net promoter score at 70% (declining from 80% in the previous year). Common customer complaints exist in regards to: (i) turnaround times between the photo shooting session and the availability of pictures for review, as well as the turnaround times for delivery of digital copies and printouts; (ii) turnaround times for resolving customer complaints particularly with regard to perceived defects in the delivered digital and printed copies; (iii) mishandled or forgotten orders or special requests. Customers often make changes to their orders or additional special requests via phone or email and these changes/requests are sometimes not recorded (or recorded incorrectly) in the order management system. Changes to orders are currently handled manually.

Process Participants Staff satisfaction is also low. Over 60% of customer service staff consider that their job is stressful. The staff turnover rate overall is at an all-times high: 10% of staff left the company in the previous year and had to be replaced up from 6% the year before. The average Cost-To-Company (CTC) of a photographer at a Fotof studio is 41K per year (35K for technicians and 37K for customer service staff). The CTC at Fotof is generally in line with industry averages. The company additionally employs 20 staff at the company headquarters at an average CTC of 46K. Interviews with staff have highlighted the following issues in the process:

- Customer service staff perceive that appointment management is too time-consuming. Customers sometimes call or email multiple times to find a suitable appointment time. Customers also call frequently to change their appointments for shooting sessions or to cancel their session. About 1% of corporate orders result in a cancelation prior to the shooting, while 5% of private orders are canceled prior to the shooting.
- The late-show and no-show rates for appointments are high: 10% late-shows for in-studio sessions, 2% for on-location sessions, 3% of no-shows for on-studio sessions, and 1% for on-location.
- There are numerous customer enquiries via phone and email (on average three per order, in addition to booking-related calls or emails), be it to enquire about the status of orders or deliveries, to make changes to the order, to discuss special requests, pricing questions, as well as to report complaints with received pictures.

Management Fotof's three-years strategy is focused on revenue growth. The company seeks to achieve a revenue increase of 50% by end of 2018 organically, meaning via growth of the existing business, without company acquisitions and without opening additional retail outlets. To achieve this goal, Fotof's management is receptive to ideas to improve customer service and to expand the range of added-value services. Fotof's management perceives that additional revenue could come in great part from wedding photos, parties and ceremonies. At present only the customer who initiates the booking can place orders. But in the case of personal events and if the customer consents, there is an opportunity to sell to other event participants. Fotof's management also perceives that faster cycle times could also help to enhance sales.

Write an issue register based on the above information.

Exercise 6.14 Write an issue register for the pharmacy prescription fulfillment process described in Exercise 1.6 (page 30). Analyze at least the following issues:

- Sometimes, a prescription cannot be filled because one or more drugs in the prescription are not in stock. Customers only learn this when they come to pick up their prescription.

- Oftentimes, when customers arrive to pick up the drugs, they find out that they have to pay more than what they expected because their insurance policy does not cover the drugs in the prescription, or because the insurance company covers only a small percentage of the cost of the drugs.
- In a very small number of cases, the prescription cannot be filled because there is a potentially dangerous interaction between one of the drugs in the prescription and other drugs that the customer has been given in the past. Customers only find out about this issue when they arrive to pick up the prescription.
- Some prescriptions can be filled multiple times. This is called a "refill". Each prescription explicitly states whether a refill is allowed and if so how many refills are allowed. Sometimes, a prescription cannot be filled because the number of allowed refills has been reached. The pharmacist then tries to call the doctor who issued the prescription to check if the doctor would allow an additional refill. Sometimes, however, the doctor is unreachable or the doctor does not authorize the refill. The prescription is then left unfilled and customers will only find out when they arrive to pick-up the prescription.
- Oftentimes, especially during peak time, customers have to wait for more than 10 min to pick up their prescription due to queues. Customers find this annoying because they find that having to come twice to the pharmacy (once for drop-off and once for pick-up) should allow the pharmacy ample time to avoid such queues at pick-up.
- Sometimes, the customer arrives at the scheduled time, but the prescription is not yet filled due to delays in the prescription fulfillment process.

When making assumptions to analyze these issues, you may choose to equate "oftentimes" with "20% of prescriptions", "sometimes" with "5% of prescriptions" and "very small number of cases" with "1% of prescriptions". You may also assume that the entire chain of pharmacies consists of 200 pharmacies that serve 4 million prescriptions a year and that the annual revenue of the pharmacy chain attributable to prescriptions is € 200 million. You may also assume that every time a customer is dissatisfied when picking up a prescription, the probability that this customer will not come back after this experience is 20%. You may also assume that on average a customer requires 5 prescriptions per year.

Based on the issue register, apply Pareto Analysis to determine a subset of issues that should be addressed to reduce the customer churn due to dissatisfaction by at least 70%. Customer churn is the number of customers who stop consuming services offered by a company at a given point in time. In this context, this means the number of customers who stop coming to the pharmacy due to a bad customer experience.

Exercise 6.15 Write an issue register for the procure-to-pay process described in Exercise 1.7 (page 31).

Exercise 6.16 Consider the pharmacy prescription fulfillment process described in Exercise 1.6 (page 30) and the following issue:

- Sometimes, the customer arrives at the scheduled time, but the prescription is not yet filled due to delays in the prescription fulfillment process.

Analyze the possible causes of this issue using a cause-effect diagram or why-why diagram.

6.8 Further Readings

Value-added analysis, cause-effect analysis, why-why analysis, Pareto analysis and PICK charts are all part of a wide array of techniques included in the Six Sigma method (see the box on "Related Disciplines" in Section 1.2 on page 3). Conger [28] shows how these and other Six Sigma techniques are applicable to business process analysis. Meanwhile, waste analysis is one of the core techniques of Lean Six Sigma, which combines Six Sigma with elements from the lean manufacturing, which itself stems from the Toyota Production System.

A comprehensive listing of Six Sigma techniques is maintained in the iSixSigma portal.[2] A given business process improvement project will generally only make use of a subset of these techniques. In this respect, Johannsen et al. [72] provide guidelines for selecting analysis techniques for a given BPM project.

Straker's Quality Encyclopedia[3] provides a comprehensive compendium of concepts used in Six Sigma and other quality management disciplines. In particular, it provides definitions and illustrations of the 6 M's and the 4 P's used in cause-effect diagrams and other concepts related to root cause analysis. A related resource—also by Straker—is the Quality Toolbook, which summarizes a number of quality management techniques. Originally the Quality Toolbook was published as a hardcopy book [170], but it is nowadays also available freely.[4]

Why-why diagrams allow us to document sequences of cause-effect relations that link factors to a given issue. A related technique to capture cause-effect paths is the *causal factor chart* [142]. Causal factor charts are similar to why-why diagrams. A key difference is that in addition to capturing factors, causal factor charts also capture conditions surrounding the factors. For example, in addition to stating that "the clerk made a data entry mistake when creating the PO", a casual factor chart might also include a condition corresponding to the question "in which part of the PO the clerk made a mistake?" These additional conditions allow analysts to more clearly define each factor.

The issue register has been proposed as a process analysis tool by Schwegmann & Laske [159][5] who use the longer term "list of weaknesses and potential improvements" to refer to an issue register. Schwegmann & Laske suggest that the issue register should be built up in parallel with the as-is model. The rationale

---

[2]http://www.isixsigma.com/tools-templates/.

[3]http://www.syque.com/improvement/a_encyclopedia.htm.

[4]http://www.syque.com/quality_tools/toolbook/toolbook.htm.

[5]The sub-categorization of the 6 M's given in Section 6.4.1 also comes from Schwegmann & Laske [159].

is that during the workshops organized for the purpose of process discovery (see Chapter 5), workshop participants will often feel compelled to voice out issues related to different parts of the process. Therefore, process discovery is an occasion to start listing issues.

Another framework commonly used for qualitative process analysis is Theory of Constraints (TOC) [56]. TOC is especially useful when the goal is to trace weaknesses in the process to bottlenecks. The application of TOC to business process analysis and redesign is discussed by Laguna & Marklund [85, Chapter 5] and by Rhee et al. [140].

Chapter 7
Quantitative Process Analysis

> *It is better to be approximately right than precisely wrong.*
> Warren Buffett (1930–)

Qualitative analysis is a valuable tool to gain systematic insights into a process. However, the results obtained from qualitative analysis are sometimes not detailed enough to provide a solid basis for decision making. Think of the process owner of BuildIT's equipment rental process who wants to convince the *Chief Operations Officer* (COO) that every site engineer should be given a tablet computer with wireless access in order to query the suppliers' catalogs and to create or modify rental requests from any construction site. The process owner will be asked to substantiate the benefits of this investment in quantitative terms by providing estimates of how the performance of the process will be measurably improved. To make such estimates, we need to go beyond qualitative analysis.

This chapter introduces techniques for analyzing business processes quantitatively in terms of process performance measures such as cycle time, waiting time, cost, and other measures we already discussed in Section 2.3.2. Specifically, the chapter focuses on three techniques: flow analysis, queueing analysis and simulation.

7.1 Flow Analysis

Flow analysis is a family of techniques to estimate the overall performance of a process given some knowledge about the performance of its tasks. For example, using flow analysis we can calculate the average cycle time of an entire process if we know the average cycle time of each task and the probability of taking each flow stemming from a decision gateway. A decision gateway is either an XOR-split or an OR-split. Similarly, we can use flow analysis to calculate the average cost of a process instance knowing the cost-per-execution of each task or to calculate the error rate of a process given the error rate of each task.

© Springer-Verlag GmbH Germany, part of Springer Nature 2018
M. Dumas et al., *Fundamentals of Business Process Management*,
https://doi.org/10.1007/978-3-662-56509-4_7

In order to understand the scope and applicability of flow analysis, we start by showing how flow analysis can be used to calculate the average cycle time of a process. As a shorthand, we will use the term *cycle time* to refer to *average cycle time* in the rest of this chapter.

7.1.1   Calculating Cycle Time Using Flow Analysis

We recall that the cycle time of a process is the average time it takes between the moment the process starts and the moment it completes. By extension, we say that the cycle time of a task is the average time it takes between the moment the task starts and the moment it completes.

To understand how flow analysis works it is useful to start with an example of a purely sequential process as in Figure 7.1. The cycle time of each task is indicated between brackets. Since the two tasks in this process are performed one after the other, we can conclude that the cycle time of this process is $20 + 10 = 30$ h.

More generally, we can state that the cycle time of a sequential fragment of a process is the sum of the cycle times of the tasks in the fragment. We use T as the set of tasks with an index i and define:

$$CT = \sum_{i=1}^{n} T_i \qquad (7.1)$$

When a process model or a fragment of a model contains gateways, the cycle time is on average no longer the sum of the task cycle times. Let us consider the example shown in Figure 7.2. Here, it is clear that the cycle time of the process is

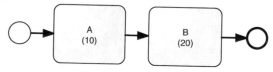

Fig. 7.1 Fully sequential process model (durations of tasks in hours are shown between brackets)

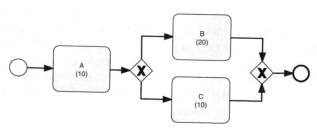

Fig. 7.2 Process model with XOR-block

not 40 (the sum of the task cycle times). Indeed, in a given instance of this process, either task B or task C is performed. If B is performed, the cycle time is 30 h, while if C is performed, the cycle time is 20 h. So we can conclude that the cycle time must be lower than 30 h.

Whether the cycle time of this process is closer to 20 h or closer to 30 h depends on how frequently each branch of the XOR-split is taken. For instance, if in 50% of instances the upper branch is taken and the remaining 50% of instances the lower branch is taken, the overall cycle time of the process is 25 h. On the other hand, if the upper branch is taken 90% of the times and the lower branch is taken 10% of the times, the cycle time should be intuitively closer to 30 h. Generally speaking, the cycle time of the fragment of the process between the XOR-split and the XOR-join is the weighted average of the cycle times of the branches in-between. Thus, if the upper branch has a frequency of 90% and the lower branch a frequency of 10%, the cycle time of the fragment between the XOR-split and the XOR-join is: $0.9 \times 20 + 0.1 \times 10 = 19$ h. We then need to add the cycle time of task A in order to obtain the total cycle time, that is, $10 + 19 = 29$ h. In the rest of this chapter, we will use the term *branching probability* to denote the frequency with which a given branch of a decision gateway is taken.

In more general terms, the cycle time of a fragment of a process model with the structure shown in Figure 7.3 is:

$$CT = \sum_{i=1}^{n} p_i \times T_i \qquad (7.2)$$

In Figure 7.3, p_1, p_2, etc. are the branching probabilities. Each cloud represents a fragment that has a single entry flow and a single exit flow. The cycle times of these nested fragments are T_1, T_2, etc. This type of fragment is called a *XOR-block*.

Let us now consider the case where parallel gateways are involved as illustrated in Figure 7.4. Again, we can observe that the cycle time of this process cannot be 40 (the sum of the task cycle times). Instead, since tasks B and C are executed in parallel, their combined cycle time is determined by the slowest of the two tasks, that is, by B. Thus, the cycle time of the process shown in Figure 7.4 is $10 + 20 = 30$ h.

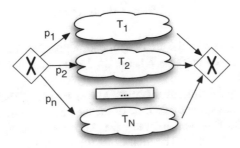

Fig. 7.3 XOR-block pattern

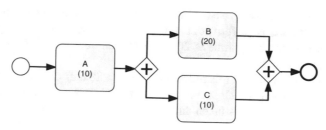

Fig. 7.4 Process model with AND-block

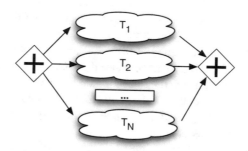

Fig. 7.5 AND-block pattern

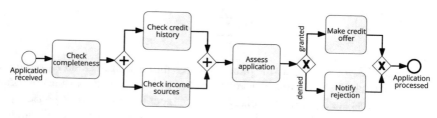

Fig. 7.6 Credit application process

More generally, the cycle time of an *AND-block* such as the one shown in Figure 7.5 is:

$$CT = Max(T_1, T_2, \ldots, T_n) \tag{7.3}$$

Example 7.1 Let us consider the credit application process model in Figure 7.6 and the task cycle times given in Table 7.1. Let us also assume that in 60% of the cases the credit is granted.

To calculate the cycle time of this process, we first note that the cycle time of the AND-block is 3 days (the cycle time of the slowest branch). Next, we calculate the cycle time of the fragment between the XOR-block using Eq. (7.2), that is, $0.6 \times 1 + 0.4 \times 2 = 1.4$ days. The total cycle time is then: $1 + 3 + 3 + 1.4 = 8.4$ days.

□

Table 7.1 Cycle times for credit application process

Task	Cycle time
Check completeness	1 day
Check credit history	1 day
Check income sources	3 days
Assess application	3 days
Make credit offer	1 day
Notify rejection	2 days

Exercise 7.1 Consider the process model given in Figure 3.8 (page 86). Calculate the cycle time under the following assumptions:

- Each task in the process takes 1 h on average.
- In 40% of the cases the order contains only Amsterdam products.
- In 40% of the cases the order contains only Hamburg products.
- In 20% of the cases the order contains products from both warehouses.

Compare the process model in Figure 3.8 (page 86) with the one in Figure 3.10 (page 88). Does this comparison give you an idea of how to calculate cycle times for process models with OR gateways?

Another recurrent pattern is the one where a fragment of a process is repeated any number of times. This pattern is illustrated in Figure 7.7. In this figure, the decimal numbers attached to the flows denote the probability that the flow will be taken whenever the XOR-split gateway is reached. Looking at the figure, we can say for sure that task B will be executed once. Next, we can say that task B may be repeated once (i.e., executed a second time) with a probability of 20% (i.e., 0.2), which is the probability of going back from the XOR-split gateway to the XOR-join gateway. If we continue this reasoning, we can conclude that the probability that task B is repeated twice (in addition to the first execution) is $0.2 \times 0.2 = 0.04$. More generally, the probability that task B is repeated N times (in addition to the first execution) is 0.2^N.

If we sum up the cycle time of the first execution of B, plus the cycle times of the cases where B is repeated once, twice, three times, etc., we get the following summation: $\sum_{n=0}^{\infty} 0.2^n$. This is the expected number of executions of task B. If we replace 0.2 with a variable r, this summation is a well-known series, known as the *geometric series*, and it can be shown that this series is equivalent to $1/(1 - r)$.

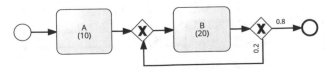

Fig. 7.7 Example of a rework block

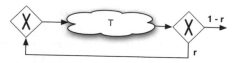

Fig. 7.8 Rework pattern

Hence, the average number of times that B is expected to be executed is $1/(1 - 0.2) = 1.25$. Now, if we multiply this expected number of instances of B times the cycle time of task B, we get $1.25 \times 20 = 25$. Thus the total cycle time of the process in Figure 7.7 is $10 + 25 = 35$.

More generally, the cycle time of a fragment with the structure shown in Figure 7.8 is:

$$CT = \frac{T}{1 - r}. \tag{7.4}$$

In this formula, the parameter r is called the *rework probability*, that is, the probability that the fragment inside the cycle will need to be reworked. This type of block is called a *rework block* or *repetition block*.

In some scenarios, a task is reworked at most once. This situation would be modeled as shown in Figure 7.9. Using what we have seen, we can already calculate the cycle time of this example. First, we observe that the cycle time of the fragment between the XOR-split and the XOR-join is $0.2 \times 20 + 0.8 \times 0 = 4$. Here, the zero comes from the fact that one of the branches between the XOR-split and the XOR-join is empty and, therefore, does not contribute to the cycle time. To this, we have to add the cycle time of the preceding tasks, giving us a total cycle time of 34.

In summary, we have seen that the cycle time of a process can be calculated using the following four equations:

- The cycle time CT of a sequence of fragments with cycle times $CT_1, \ldots CT_n$ is the sum of the cycle times of these fragments: $CT = \Sigma_{i=1}^{n} CT_i$.
- The cycle time CT of an XOR-block is the weighted average of the cycle times of its branches (CT_i), using the branching probabilities p_i as the weights: $CT = \Sigma_{i=1}^{n} p_i \times CT_i$.

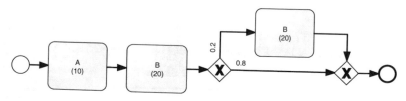

Fig. 7.9 Situation where a fragment (task) that is reworked at most once

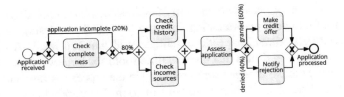

Fig. 7.10 Credit application process with rework

- The cycle time CT of an AND-Block is the cycle time of its slowest branch or, in other words, the maximum of the cycle times of the branches: $CT = Max(CT_1, \ldots CT_n)$.
- The cycle time CT of a rework block with a rework probability r is the cycle time of each iteration of the loop (let us call it CT_b) divided by $(1 - r)$: $CT = CT_b/(1 - r)$.

Example 7.2 Let us consider the credit application process model in Figure 7.10 and the cycle times previously given in Table 7.1. Let us assume that after each execution of "Check completeness", in 20% of the cases the application is incomplete. And let us also assume that in 60% of the cases the credit is granted.

The cycle time of the rework block is $1/(1 - 0.2) = 1.25$ days. The cycle time of the AND-block is 3 days and that of the XOR-block is 1.4 days as discussed in Example 7.1. Thus the total cycle time is $1.25 + 3 + 3 + 1.4 = 8.65$ days. □

7.1.2 Cycle Time Efficiency

The cycle time of a task or of a process can be divided into *waiting time* and *processing time*. Waiting time is the portion of the cycle time where no work is being done to advance the process. Processing time, on the other hand, refers to the time that participants spend doing actual work. In many, if not most processes, a considerable proportion of the overall cycle time is waiting time. Waiting time typically arises when there is a handoff between two participants. In this case, there is usually a waiting time between the moment the first participant finishes its task, and the moment when the next participant starts the next task. This waiting time may become relatively long if the process participants perform their work in batches. For example, in a purchase requisition process, the supervisor responsible for purchase approvals might choose to *batch* all purchase requisitions that arrive during a given day and approve them all at once at the end of the working day. Also, sometimes time is spent waiting for an external party to provide input for a task. For example, in the context of fulfilling a medical prescription, a pharmacist may require a clarification from the doctor. To do so, the pharmacist would try to call the doctor. But the doctor might be unavailable such that the pharmacist needs to put the prescription aside and wait until the doctor returns the call.

When analyzing a process with the aim of addressing issues related to cycle time, it may be useful to start by evaluating the ratio of overall processing time relative to the overall cycle time. This ratio is called *cycle time efficiency*. A cycle time efficiency close to 1 indicates that there is little room for improving the cycle time unless relatively radical changes are introduced in the process. A ratio close to zero indicates that there is a significant amount of room for improving cycle time by reducing the waiting time.

Concretely, the cycle time efficiency of a process is calculated as follows. First, we need to determine the cycle time and the processing time of each task. Given this information, we then calculate the cycle time CT of the process using the four equations we saw above. Next, we calculate the so-called the *Theoretical Cycle Time* (TCT) of the process. The TCT is the average amount of time that a case would take if there was no waiting time at all. The TCT is calculated using the same four equations we introduced above, but instead of using the cycle time of each task, we must use instead the processing time of each task. Once we have calculated the TCT, we calculate the Cycle Time Efficiency (CTE) as follows:

$$CTE = \frac{TCT}{CT} \tag{7.5}$$

Example 7.3 Let us consider the credit application process model in Figure 7.10 and the processing times given in Table 7.2. The task cycle times (including both waiting and processing time) are those previously given in Table 7.1. We assume again that in 20% of the cases the application is incomplete and in 60% of the cases the credit is granted. Let us additionally assume that 1 day is equal to 8 working hours.

We have seen in Example 7.2 that the total cycle time of this process is 8.65 days, which translates to 69.2 working hours. We now calculate the theoretical cycle time using the processing times given in Table 7.2. This gives us: $2/(1 - 0.2) + 3 + 2 + 0.6 \times 2 + 0.4 \times 0.5 = 8.9$ working hours. The cycle time efficiency is thus $8.9/69.2 = 12.9\%$. □

Exercise 7.2 Calculate the overall cycle time, theoretical cycle time, and cycle time efficiency of the ministerial enquiry process introduced in Example 3.7 (page 90). Assume that the rework probability is 0.2 and the waiting times and processing times are those given in Table 7.3.

Table 7.2 Processing times for credit application process

Task	Processing time
Check completeness	2 h
Check credit history	30 min
Check income sources	3 h
Assess application	2 h
Make credit offer	2 h
Notify rejection	30 min

Table 7.3 Task cycle times and processing times for ministerial enquiry process

Task	Cycle time	Processing time
Register ministerial enquiry	2 days	30 min
Investigate ministerial enquiry	8 days	12 h
Prepare ministerial response	4 days	4 h
Review ministerial response	4 days	2 h

Table 7.4 Analysis of cycle times in white-collar processes [21]

Industry	Process	CT	TCT	CTE
Life Insurance	New policy application	72 h	7 min	0.16%
Consumer Packaging	New graphic design	18 days	2 h	0.14%
Commercial Bank	Consumer Loan	24 h	34 min	2.36%
Hospital	Patient Billing	10 days	3 h	3.75%
Automobile Manufacture	Financial Closing	11 days	5 h	5.60%

An important question is in what range we would typically observe cycle time efficiency in practice. Actual measurements are reported in a study by Blackburn from 1992 on white-collar processes, see Table 7.4 and [21]. These measurements appear to be around 5% or lower, which indicates that there are substantial waiting times in many business processes. This is a valuable observation. It implies that cycle times and cycle time efficiency can often be improved by reducing these waiting times. Process-Aware Information Systems and specifically Business Process Management Systems provide several features that are helpful in this regard, as we will see in Chapter 9.

Exercise 7.3 The measurements reported in Table 7.4 stem from 1992. How do you expect that these measurements have changed since then? What role do information systems play in this context?

7.1.3 Critical Path Method

A low cycle time efficiency raises the question of which parts of the process should be improved. In order to answer that question, we need to more precisely understand which tasks contribute to the theoretical cycle time. The *Critical Path Method* (CPM) is a well-known method for addressing this question in the context of project planning. This method can be applied to process models that do not contain decision gateways. This means that if the process model contains XOR or OR gateways, we need to simplify it by removing all such gateways, before we can apply the CPM method. We can do this by either replacing every XOR, OR, and loop block with a single task, or by considering only specific paths of our process and focusing on those ones. For example, we can eliminate the branches of an XOR-split that lead to an early completion of the case as well as those gateways associated with rework loops (like the rework loop in Figure 7.10). Indeed, if we optimize the theoretical

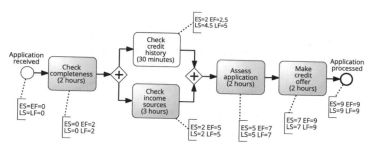

Fig. 7.11 Credit application process without XOR gateways

cycle time of the process without its rework loops, this would contribute to also optimizing the process with the rework loop.

Let us consider again the credit application process without repetition and with a positive credit assessment as shown in Figure 7.11. The theoretical cycle time is determined by the processing time of tasks "Check completeness", "Check income sources", "Assess Application", and "Make credit offer", which all take 2, 3, 2 and 2 h, respectively. These tasks are part of the *critical path* of this process (highlighted in grey). The critical path of a process is the sequence of tasks that determines the theoretical cycle time of the process. When optimizing a process with respect to theoretical cycle time, one should focus the attention on the processing times of the tasks that belong to the critical path.

CPM identifies the critical path based on the notions of *early start (ES)*, *early finish (EF)*, *late start (LS)*, and *late finish (LF)* of each task of the process. Early start and early finish are determined in a forward pass over the process. We start with time zero at the start event. Each task is assigned as early start the early finish time of its predecessor. Its early finish is its early start time plus its processing time. If this predecessor is the entry (split) gateway of an AND-block, it is assigned the early finish time of the preceding fragment. If it is the exit (join) gateway of an AND-block, it is assigned the maximum of the early finish from all its parallel branches. Using this procedure, we can determine at what time each task has to start and finish such that the cycle time is equal to the theoretical cycle time.

Not all tasks are equally critical for finishing the process within the theoretical cycle time. Consider the two verification (check) tasks of the credit application process. They are part of an AND-block. If the more time-consuming task "Check income sources" (3 h) gets delayed, this will delay the process altogether. If "Check credit history" (taking 30 min) is delayed, this will only delay the process if it takes longer than the processing time of the more time-consuming task "Check income sources". For this reason, we also have to determine the late start and late finish of all tasks in a backward pass over the process. Now, we start from the end event with the time set to the theoretical cycle time. For each task, its late finish is assigned the late start of its successor. Its late start is the late finish minus its processing time. We continue our pass from right to left of the process, now taking the earlier time at the entry split an AND-block.

Example 7.4 Let us now apply these calculation steps for the credit application process shown in Figure 7.11 and the processing times given in Table 7.2. We start with calculating the early start and early finish times (ES and EF).

- The start event "Application received" gets zero assigned ($ES = EF = 0$).
- Early start of "Check completeness" is the same as the early finish of its predecessor. This means $ES = 0$. We calculate $EF = ES + processingtime = 2$.
- Each task after the AND-split gets the same ES as the preceding task. Its EF is this ES plus the respective processing time. This means, for "Check credit history" we get $ES = 2$ and $EF = 2.5$ and for "Check income sources" we have $ES = 2$ and $EF = 5$.
- At the AND-split, we have to determine the maximum EF of its preceding tasks. This is $Max(2.5, 5) = 5$.
- The subsequent task "Assess application" gets this maximum as its $ES = 5$. Considering the processing time, its $EF = 7$.
- For "Make credit offer" we get $ES = 7$ and $EF = 9$.
- Therefore, $ES = EF = 9$ holds for the end event "Application processed" and for the overall process.

With this value of $EF = 9$, we start our pass backwards to calculate late start and late finish (LS and LF).

- For the task "Make credit offer", we assign the late finish time from the end event ($LF = 9$) and subtract the processing time to get $LS = 7$.
- In the same way, we first obtain $LF = 7$ and then $LS = 5$ for "Assess application".
- For the tasks preceding the AND-join, we obtain their late finish from the late start of the task after it. Therefore, both "Check credit history" and "Check income sources" have $LF = 5$. We subtract their respective processing times to get $LS = 4.5$ and $LS = 2$.
- At the AND-split, we determine the minimum LS of its successor tasks. This is $Min(4.5, 2) = 2$.
- The preceding task "Check completeness" gets this minimum as $LF = 2$. Considering its processing time, we get $LS = 0$.
- Therefore, we also have $LS = LF = 0$ for the start event.

□

In this example, we observe that the early start and finish times are the same for most tasks. The *critical path* is the set of tasks for which these two values are equal. Those tasks with a late start greater than the early start ($LS > ES$) or late finish greater than early finish ($LF > EF$) have *slack*. This means that even when they start or complete later, it might still be possible to finish the process without delay. This is the case of "Check credit history" in our example. Slack tasks are typically the less time-consuming tasks in AND-blocks.

Exercise 7.4 Consider the process model shown in Figure 7.4 with the processing times indicated in the brackets of the tasks. What is its critical path? How much slack is there on the task that is not on the critical path?

7.1.4 Little's Law

Cycle time is directly related to two measures that play an important role when analyzing a process, namely arrival rate and Work-In-Process (WIP).

The *arrival rate* of a process is the average number of new instances of the process that are created per time unit. For example, in a credit application process, the arrival rate is the number of credit applications received per day (or any other time unit we choose). Similarly, in an order-to-cash process, the arrival rate is the average number of new orders that arrive per day. Traditionally, the symbol λ (lambda) is used to refer to the arrival rate.[1]

The *Work-In-Process* (WIP) is the average number of instances of a process that are active at a given point in time, meaning the average number of instances that have not yet completed. For example, in a credit application process, the WIP is the average number of credit applications that have been submitted and not yet granted or rejected. Similarly, in an order-to-cash process, the WIP is the average number of orders that have been received, but not yet delivered and paid for.

Cycle time (CT), arrival rate (λ), and WIP are related by a fundamental law known as Little's law, which states that:

$$WIP = \lambda \times CT \qquad (7.6)$$

In essence, what this law tells us is that:

- WIP increases if the cycle time increases or if the arrival rate increases. In other words, if the process slows down—meaning that its cycle time increases—there will be more instances of the process active at the same time. Also, the faster new instances are created, the higher will be the number of instances in an active state.
- If the arrival rate increases and we want to keep the WIP at current levels, the cycle time must decrease.

Little's law holds for any stable process. By stable, we mean that the number of active instances is not increasing infinitely. In other words, in a stable process, the amount of work waiting to be performed is not growing beyond control.

---

[1] A related concept is that of *throughout*, which is the average number of instances completed per time unit. In a stable system and over long periods of time, the throughput should be equal to the arrival rate (otherwise it means that we are not able to handle all the workload).

Although simple, Little's law can be an interesting tool for what-if analysis. We can also use Little's law as an alternative way of calculating the total cycle time of a process if we know the arrival rate and WIP. This is useful because determining the arrival rate and WIP is sometimes easier than determining the cycle time. For example, in the case of the credit application process, the arrival rate can be easily calculated if we know the total number of applications processed over a period of time. For example, if we assume there are 250 business days per year and we know the total number of credit applications over the last year is 2,500, we can infer that the average number of applications per business day is 10. WIP on the other hand can be calculated by means of sampling. We can ask how many applications are active at a given point in time, then ask this question again one week later and again two weeks later. Let us assume that on average we observe that 200 applications are active at the same time. The cycle time is then $WIP/\lambda = 200/10 = 20$ business days.

Exercise 7.5 A restaurant receives on average 1,200 customers per day (between 10 a.m. and 10 p.m.). During peak times (12 p.m. to 3 p.m. and 6 p.m. to 9 p.m.), the restaurant receives around 900 customers in total and, on average, 90 customers can be found in the restaurant at a given point in time. At non-peak times, the restaurant receives 300 customers in total and, on average, 30 customers can be found in the restaurant at a given point in time.

- What is the average time that a customer spends in the restaurant during peak times?
- What is the average time that a customer spends in the restaurant during non-peak times?
- The restaurant's premises have a maximum capacity of 110 customers. This maximum capacity is sometimes reached during peak times. The restaurant manager expects that the number of customers during peak times will increase slightly in the coming months. What can the restaurant do to address this issue without investing in extending its building?

7.1.5 Capacity and Bottlenecks

The calculations of Little's law rely on the assumption that the process is stable. In order to assess whether or not this assumption is applicable, we have to know the *theoretical capacity* of the process and the *resource utilization* of the resources involved in the process.[2]

The *theoretical capacity* of a process is the maximum amount of instances that can be completed per time unit given a set of resources. The theoretical capacity is reached when a subset of the resources are working at full capacity (no idle time)

---

[2]The term *occupation rate* is sometimes used a synonym for resource utilization.

and the other resources cannot help them due to the existing division of labor in the process. When this limit is reached, the resources who are at full capacity cannot handle more work per time unit.

To better understand the notion of theoretical capacity, we need to introduce the notion of *resource pool*. A resource pool R is a set of interchangeable resources who are responsible for executing a set of tasks in a process. For example, let us assume that in the loan application process, tasks "Check completeness", "Check credit history", and "Check income sources" are performed by *clerks*, whereas "Assess application", "Make credit offer", and "Notify rejection" are performed by *credit officers*. Therefore, this process has two resource pools (clerks and credit officers). Most likely, there are multiple clerks and multiple credit officers. This means that each resource pool has a given size.

Each instance of the process demands a given amount of time (on average) from each resource pool. The amount of time that a resource pool p needs to spend on one instance of the process is called the pool's *unit load* (ul). Each task assigned to a resource pool adds up to its unit load. And the more times a task is executed per instance, the more this task adds up to the load of its resource pool. For example, if two tasks a_1 and a_2 have the same processing time, but a_1 is executed on average 0.5 times per instance, while a_2 is executed on average twice per instance, then a_2 contributes four times more to the unit load than a_1. Hence, to calculate the unit load, we add up the processing times of each task a assigned to resource pool p, taking into account how many times each task is executed per instance of the process.

Below we present a two-step method to calculate ul (for a given pool p) using equations similar to the ones we used to calculate cycle time and theoretical cycle time. In the first step, we assign a unit load to each task with respect to pool p as follows:

- For each task assigned to resource pool p, its unit load is equal to its processing time.
- For each task not assigned to resource pool p, its unit load is zero.

In the second step, we use the following equations to calculate ul for a pool:

- The unit load ul of a sequence of fragments with unit loads $ul_1, \ldots ul_n$ is the sum of the unit loads of the fragments: $ul = \Sigma_{i=1}^{n} ul_i$.
- The unit load ul of an XOR-block is the weighted average of the unit loads of its branches (ul_i), using the branching probabilities p_i as the weights: $ul = \Sigma_{i=1}^{n} p_i \times ul_i$.
- The unit load ul of an AND-Block is the sum of the unit loads of its branches: $ul = \Sigma_{i=1}^{n} ul_i$. This is the same equation for sequences of fragments. The reason is that if a resource pool is involved in multiple branches of an AND-Block, each of these branches adds up to the load of this resource pool (i.e., each branch requires some effort and these efforts have to be added up).
- The unit load ul of a rework block with a rework probability r is the unit load of each iteration of the loop (let us call it ul_b) divided by $1 - r$: $ul = ul_b/(1 - r)$.

Example 7.5 Let us consider the credit application process model in Figure 7.10 and the processing times given in Table 7.2. Tasks "Check completeness", "Check credit history", and "Check income sources" are performed by *clerks*, whereas "Assess application", "Make credit offer", and "Notify rejection" are performed by *credit officers*.

Using the above equations, the unit loads of the three tasks assigned to the clerk are 2 h ("Check completeness"), 3 h ("Check credit history"), and 0.5 h ("Check income sources"). The remaining tasks after the AND-join gateway do not contribute to the unit load of the clerk pool. Hence, the unit load pool is $2/(1 - 0.2) + 3 + 0.5 = 6$ working hours. This means that each loan application takes 6 h of time from the clerk pool.

Meanwhile, the unit loads of the tasks assigned to the credit officer are 2 h for both "Assess application" and for "Make credit offer", but 0.5 h for "Notify rejection". The first three tasks do not contribute to the unit load of credit officers. Taking into account the branching probabilities of the XOR-split, the unit load of the credit office pool is $2 + 0.6 \times 2 + 0.4 \times 0.5 = 5.2$ working hours. Again, this means that each loan application takes on average 5.2 h from the credit officers pool. □

We have seen how to calculate the unit load ul of a resource pool p, which means the amount of time that a resource pool p spends per instance of the process. To calculate the theoretical capacity, we now need to determine how much time each resource pool can deliver per time unit. This is called the *unit capacity* of the pool. To do this, it is convenient to lift the temporal granularity by one level. Since we have been working in terms of hours above, we will now move to the next higher granularity, which is the working day. Let us assume that a working day is 8 h. This means that one resource in a pool can deliver 8 h of work per day. This is called the unit capacity of a resource. By extension, the unit capacity of a resource pool uc is the size of the pool times the capacity of one resource.

Given the above, the theoretical capacity $\mu_p{}^3$ of pool p is:

$$\mu_p = \frac{uc}{ul} \tag{7.7}$$

Example 7.6 Continuing the previous example, let us assume that the size of the clerk resource pool is 3, while the same holds for the credit officer pool. Let us also assume that 1 day is equal to 8 working hours. The unit capacity of a clerk (and same for a credit officer) is 8 h/day. The unit capacity of the clerk pool is 24 h/day (same for the credit officer pool). This means that the clerks can dedicate up to 24 h of effort per business day. Since each instance takes 6 h from them, they can collectively handle $24/6 = 4$ applications per day (i.e., $\mu = 4$ instances/day for the clerk pool). Similarly, three credit officers can dedicate up to 24 h/day. And since each instance requires 5.2 h from them, their theoretical capacity is $24/5.2 = 4.62$ loan applications per day (i.e., $\mu = 4.62$ for the credit officer pool). □

---

[3]Letter μ is pronounced mu.

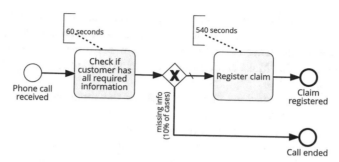

Fig. 7.12 Process model of a call center

We see that the clerks can handle less loan applications per day than the credit officers (4 versus 4.62). So, if we start receiving a lot of loan applications, the clerks will be the first ones to reach their theoretical capacity. We say that the clerk pool is the *bottleneck* of the process. More generally, the bottleneck is the resource pool with the minimum theoretical capacity among all pools in a process.

The *theoretical capacity of a process* is the theoretical capacity of its bottleneck pool. In our example, this is four instances per day. In the long term, there is no way we can deliver more instances per day unless something is changed, like for example if we add more resources to the resource pool or reduce the processing time of the tasks in which they are involved.

Another useful and related concept is that of *resource utilization*. The resource utilization ρ_p[4] of a pool p is the arrival rate λ of instances of the process (which we saw in Little's law) divided by the theoretical capacity μ_p of the pool, i.e.

$$\rho_p = \lambda / \mu_p \tag{7.8}$$

When there is no ambiguity, we will omit the subscript of ρ_p, meaning that we will simply write ρ if it is clear which pool we are referring to.

Example 7.7 Continuing from the previous example, and assuming that 3 loan applications arrive per day (i.e., $\lambda = 3$), the resource utilization of the clerk pool is $3/4 = 0.75$ and that of the credit officer pool is $3/4.62 \sim 0.65$. This means the pools are running at 75% and 65% of their theoretical capacity, respectively. □

Exercise 7.6 An insurance company receives 220 calls per day from customers who want to lodge an insurance claim. All calls are handled by 7 call center agents who work from 8 a.m. to 5 p.m. every day. The way calls are handled is captured in Figure 7.12. The process model in this figure also shows the processing times and branching probabilities.

---

[4]Letter ρ is pronounced rho.

Based on this information, answer the following questions:

- What is the unit load of the "Call center agent" pool?
- What is the unit capacity of the "Call center agent" pool? Specifically, how many seconds per hour can the agents collectively dedicate to the process?
- What is the theoretical capacity of the "Call center agent" pool?
- What is the resource utilization of the "Call center agent" pool?

7.1.6 Flow Analysis for Cost

As mentioned earlier, flow analysis can also be used to calculate other performance measures besides cycle time. For example, assuming we know the average cost of each task, we can calculate the cost of a process more or less in the same way as we calculate cycle time. In particular, the cost of a sequence of tasks is the sum of the costs of these tasks. Similarly, the cost of an XOR-block is the weighted average of the cost of the branches of the XOR-block and the cost of a rework pattern, such as the one shown in Figure 7.8, is the cost of the body of the loop divided by $1 - r$. The only difference between calculating cycle time and calculating cost relates to the treatment of AND-blocks. The cost of an AND-block, such as the one shown in Figure 7.5, is not the maximum of the cost of the branches of the AND-block. Instead, the cost of such a block is the sum of the costs of the branches. This is because after the AND-split is traversed, every branch in the AND-join is executed. Therefore the costs of these branches add up to one another.

Example 7.8 Let us consider again the credit application process model in Figure 7.10 and the processing times given in Table 7.2. As previously, we assume that in 20% of cases the application is incomplete and in 60% of cases the credit is granted. We further assume that the tasks "Check completeness", "Check credit history" and "Check income sources" are performed by a clerk, while "Assess application", "Make credit offer" and "Notify rejection" are performed by a credit officer. The hourly cost of a clerk is € 25 while the hourly cost of a credit officer is € 50. Performing a credit history requires that the bank submit a query to an external system. The bank is charged € 1 per query by the provider of this external system.

From this scenario, we can see that the cost of each task can be split into two components: the *labor cost* and *other costs*. The labor cost is the cost of the human resource that performs the task. This can be calculated as the product of the hourly cost of the resource and the processing time (in hours) of the task. Other costs correspond to costs that are incurred by an execution of a task, but are not related to the time spent by human resources on the task. In this example, the cost per query to the external system would be classified as "other costs" for the task "Check credit history". The remaining tasks do not have an "other costs" component. For the example at hand, the breakdown of resource cost, other cost and total cost per task is

Table 7.5 Cost calculation table for credit application process

Task	Resource cost	Other cost	Total cost
Check completeness	2× € 25 = € 50	€ 0	€ 50
Check credit history	0.5× € 25 = € 12.5	€ 1	€ 13.5
Check income sources	3× € 25 = € 75	€ 0	€ 75
Assess application	2× € 50 = € 100	€ 0	€ 100
Make credit offer	2× € 50 = € 100	€ 0	€ 100
Notify rejection	0.5× € 50 = € 25	€ 0	€ 25

given in Table 7.5. Given this input, we can calculate the total cost-per-execution of the process as follows: $50/(1-0.2)+13.5+75+100+0.6 \times 100+0.4 \times 25 = 321$.

□

Exercise 7.7 Calculate the cost-per-execution of the ministerial enquiry process introduced in Exercise 3.7 (page 90). Assume that the rework probability is 0.2 and the times as given in Table 7.3. The task "Register ministerial enquiry" is performed by a clerk, task "Investigate ministerial enquiry" is performed by an adviser, "Prepare ministerial response" is performed by a senior adviser, and "Review ministerial response" is performed by a minister counselor. The hourly resource cost of a clerk, adviser, senior adviser and minister counselor are € 25, € 50, € 75, and € 100, respectively. There are no other costs attached to these tasks besides the resource costs.

7.1.7 Limitations of Flow Analysis

Before closing the discussion on flow analysis, it is important to highlight some of its pitfalls and limitations. First of all, we should note that the equations presented in Section 7.1.1 do not allow us to calculate the cycle time of any given process model. In fact, these equations only work in the case of *block-structured* process models. In particular, we cannot use these equations to calculate the cycle time of an unstructured process model such as the one shown in Exercise 3.12 (page 112). Indeed, this example does not fit into any of the patterns we have seen above. Also, if the model contains other modeling constructs besides AND and XOR gateways, the method for calculating cycle time becomes more complicated.

Fortunately, this is not a fundamental limitation of flow analysis, but only a limitation of the equations discussed in Section 7.1.1. There are more sophisticated flow analysis techniques that can be used for any process model. The maths can get a bit more complex. But this is generally not a problem given that several modern process modeling tools include functionality for calculating cycle time, cost and other performance measures of a process model using flow analysis.

A more fundamental roadblock faced by analysts when applying flow analysis is the fact that they first need to estimate the average cycle time of each task in the process model. In fact, this is a typical obstacle when applying any quantitative process analysis technique. There are at least two approaches to address this obstacle. The first one is based on interviews or observation. In this approach, analysts interview the stakeholders involved in each task or they observe how the stakeholders work during a given day or period of time. This allows analysts to at least make an informed guess regarding the average time a case spends in each task, in terms of both waiting time and processing time. In practice, the collection of data using interviews and observation should best be integrated with the process discovery as described in Section 5.2. A second approach is to collect logs from the information systems used in the process. For example, if a task "Approve purchase requisition" is performed via a Web portal, the portal's administrators may be able to extract execution logs to estimate the average time that a requisition spends in the "waiting for approval" state and the average time between the moment the supervisor opens a requisition for approval and the moment they approve it.

A more fundamental limitation of flow analysis is that it does not take into account the fact that a process behaves differently depending on the load. Intuitively, the cycle time of a process for handling insurance claims would be much slower if the insurance company is handling thousands of claims at once, due for example to a recent natural disaster such as a storm, versus the case where the load is low and the insurance company is only handling a hundred claims at once. When the load goes up and the number of resources (e.g., claim handlers) remains relatively constant, it is clear that the waiting times are going to be longer. This is due to a phenomenon known as *resource contention*. Resource contention occurs when there is more work to be done than resources available to perform the work, like for example more claims than insurance claim handlers. In such scenarios, some tasks will be in waiting mode until one of the necessary resources is freed up. Flow analysis does not directly inform us about the effects of increased resource contention. Instead, the estimates obtained from flow analysis are only applicable if the level of resource contention remains relatively stable over the long run.

7.2 Queues

Queueing theory is a collection of mathematical techniques to analyze systems that have resource contention. Resource contention inevitably leads to queues as we all probably have experienced in supermarket check-out counters, at a bank branch, post office, or government agency. Queueing theory gives us techniques to analyze important parameters of a queue such as the expected length of the queue or the expected waiting time of an individual case in a queue.

7.2.1   Basics of Queueing Theory

In basic queueing theory, a *queueing system* consists of one or multiple *queues* and a *service* that is provided by one or multiple *servers*. The elements inside a queue are called *jobs* or *customers*, depending on the specific context. In the following, we stick to the generic term *process instance*. For example, in the case of a supermarket, the service is that of checking out. This service is provided by multiple cashiers (the servers). Meanwhile, in the case of a bank office, the service is to perform a banking transaction, the servers are tellers, and there is generally a single queue that leads to multiple servers (the tellers). These two examples illustrate an important distinction between multi-line (i.e., multi-queue) queueing systems (like the supermarket) and single-line queueing systems (like the bank office).

Queueing theory provides a very broad set of techniques. Instead of trying to present everything that queueing theory has to offer, we will present two queueing theory models that are relatively simple, yet useful when analyzing business processes or tasks within a process.

In the two models we will be presenting there is a single queue (single-line queueing system). Instances arrive at a given average arrival rate λ. This is the same concept of arrival rate that we discussed above when presenting Little's law. For example, we can say that customers arrive to the bank office at a mean rate of 20 per hour. This implies that, on average, one customer arrives every 3 min ($\frac{1}{20}$ h). This latter number is called the mean *inter-arrival time*. We observe that if λ is the arrival rate per time unit, then $1/\lambda$ is the mean inter-arrival time.

It would be illusory to think that the time between the arrival of two customers at the bank office is always 3 min. This is just the mean value. In practice, customers arrive independently from one another, so the time between the arrival of one customer and the arrival of the next customer is completely random. Moreover, let us say the time between the arrival of the first customer and the arrival of the second customer is 1 min. This observation does not tell us anything about the time between the arrival of the second customer and the arrival of the third customer. It might be that the third customer arrives 1 min after the second, 5 min, or 10 min. We will not know until the third customer arrives.

Such an arrival process is called a *Poisson process*. In this case, the distribution of arrivals follows a so-called *exponential distribution* (specifically a *negative exponential distribution*) with a mean of $1/\lambda$. In a nutshell, this means that the probability that the inter-arrival time is exactly equal to t (where t is a positive number) decreases in an exponential manner when t increases. For instance, the probability of an inter-arrival time of 10 min is considerably smaller than the probability of the inter-arrival time being 1 min. Hence, shorter inter-arrival times are much more probable than longer ones, but there is always a probability (perhaps a very small one) that the inter-arrival time will be large.

In practice, the Poisson process and the exponential distribution describe a large class of arrival processes. So, we will be using them to capture the arrival of jobs or customers into a business process or a task in a business process. The Poisson process can also be observed when we examine how often cars enter a given segment of a highway or how often calls go through a telephone exchange.

Having said this, one must always cross-check that cases arrive at a given process or task in an exponentially distributed manner. This cross-check can be done by recording the inter-arrival times for a given period of time and then feeding these numbers into a statistical tool such as R, Mathworks's Statistical Toolbox, and EasyFit. These tools use the input of a set of observed inter-arrival times to check if it follows a negative exponential distribution.

Exponential distributions are not only useful when modeling the inter-arrival time. They are also in some cases useful when describing the processing time of a task. In queueing theory, the term *service time* is often used instead of processing time. In the case of tasks that require a diagnosis, a non-trivial verification, or some non-trivial decision making, it is often the case that the processing time is exponentially distributed. Take, for example, the amount of time it takes for a mechanic to make a repair on a car. Most repairs are fairly standard and the mechanics might take 1 h to do them. However, some repairs are complex and in such cases it can take the mechanic several hours to complete. A similar remark can be made of a doctor receiving patients in an emergency room. A large number of emergencies are quite standard and can be dispatched in less than an hour, but some emergencies are extremely complicated and can take hours to deal with. So, it is likely that such tasks will follow an exponential distribution. As mentioned above, when making such a hypothesis, it is important to verify it by taking a random sample of processing times and feeding them to a statistical tool.

In the queueing theory field, a single-queue system is called an *M/M/1 queue*[5] if the inter-arrival times of customers follow an exponential distribution, the processing times follow an exponential distribution, there is one single server and instances are served on a First-In-First-Out (FIFO) basis. In the case of M/M/1 queue, we also assume that when an instance arrives it enters the queue and it stays there until it is taken on by the server.

If the above conditions are satisfied, but there are multiple servers instead of a single server, the queueing system is said to be *M/M/c*, where c is the number of servers. For example, a system is M/M/5 if the inter-arrival times of customers follow an exponential distribution, the processing times follow an exponential distribution, and there are 5 servers at the end of the queue. The "M" in this denomination stands for "Markovian", which is the name given to the assumptions that inter-arrival times and processing times follow an exponential distribution. Other queueing models exist that make different assumptions. Each such model is different, so the results we will obtain for an M/M/1 or M/M/c queue are quite different from those we would obtain from other distributions.

---

[5]This notation is commonly known as Kendall's notation.

7.2.2 M/M/1 and M/M/c Models

The previous discussion, an M/M/1 queue or M/M/c queue can be defined by means of the following parameters:

- λ is the mean arrival rate per time unit. The mean inter-arrival time is then $1/\lambda$. For example, $\lambda = 5$ means that there are 5 arrivals per hour and this entails that the mean inter-arrival time between two consecutive instances is $1/5$ h, that is 12 min.
- μ is the theoretical capacity per server (i.e., theoretical capacity per resource) or in other words, the number of instances that a server can execute per time unit. For example, $\mu = 6$ means that 6 instances are served per hour, which means that one instance is served in 10 min (on average).[6]
- In the case of M/M/c, the number of servers is c.

Given parameters λ and μ, we defined in Section 7.1.5 the *resource utilization* $\rho = \lambda/\mu$. In the above example, the resource utilization is 5/6 = 83.34%. It should be noted that this is a relatively high resource utilization. A system with a resource utilization of more than 100% is unstable, which means that the queue will become longer and longer forever because the server cannot cope with all the demand. In fact, even a system with a resource utilization close to 100% is unstable because of the randomness with which new instances arrive and the variability in the processing times per instance. To understand why this is the case, just imagine a doctor receiving patients at a rate of 6 per hour for 8 h, knowing that every patient takes 10 min on average to be treated (sometimes less but sometimes more). Without any slack, the doctor will end up with a tremendous backlog at the end of the day.

In the case of an M/M/c system, the resource utilization is $\frac{\lambda}{c\mu}$ since the system consists of a pool of resources that can collectively handle instances at a rate of $c\mu$. For example, if the system has 2 servers and each server can handle 2 instances per hour, the system can handle 4 instances per hour. If instances arrive at a mean rate of 3 per hour, the resource utilization of the system is $3/4 = 75\%$.

Given an M/M/1 or M/M/c system, queueing theory allows us to calculate the following parameters:

- L_q is the average number of instances in the queue.
- W_q is the average time one instance spends in the queue.
- W is the average time one instance spends in the entire system. This includes both the time the instance spends in the queue but also the time it spends being serviced.
- L is the average number of instances in the system (i.e., the Work-In-Process referenced in Little's law).

---

[6]In Section 7.1.5, we used symbol μ to refer to the theoretical capacity of a resource pool, while here we are using symbol μ to refer to the theoretical capacity of each individual resource (or server) in a pool. This is because the size of the pool is handled separately using parameter c.

Fig. 7.13 Structure of an
M/M/1 or M/M/c system,
input parameters and
computable parameters

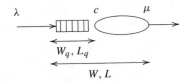

To summarize, the general structure of a single-queue system, which consists of one queue and one or many servers, is depicted in Figure 7.13. The parameters of the queue (λ, c and μ) are shown at the top. The parameters that can be computed from these three input parameters are shown under the queue and the server. The average time an instance waits in the queue is W_q, while the average length of the queue is L_q. Eventually, an instance goes into the server and in there it spends on average $1/\mu$ time units.[7] The average time between the moment an instance enters the system and the moment it exits is W, while the average number of instances inside the system (in the queue or in a server) is L.

Queueing theory gives us the following equations for calculating the above parameters for M/M/1 models:

$$L_q = \rho^2/(1-\rho) \tag{7.9}$$

$$W_q = \frac{L_q}{\lambda} \tag{7.10}$$

$$W = W_q + \frac{1}{\mu} \tag{7.11}$$

$$L = \lambda W \tag{7.12}$$

Formulas (7.10), (7.11) and (7.12) can be applied to M/M/c models as well. The only parameter that needs to be calculated differently in the case of M/M/c models is L_q. For M/M/c models, L_q is given by the following formula:

$$L_q = \frac{(\lambda/\mu)^c \rho}{c!(1-\rho)^2 \left(\frac{(\lambda/\mu)^c}{c!(1-\rho)} + \sum_{n=0}^{c-1} \frac{(\lambda/\mu)^n}{n!} \right)} \tag{7.13}$$

This formula is particularly complicated because of the summations and factorials. Fortunately, there are tools that can do this for us. For example, the Queueing Toolpack[8] supports calculations for M/M/c systems (called *M/M/s* in the Queueing Toolpack) as well as M/M/c/k systems, where k is the maximum number of instances allowed in the queue. Instances that arrive when the length of the queue

---

[7] This is equivalent to what we called the unit load in Section 7.1.5.
[8] http://queueingtoolpak.org.

is k are rejected (and may come back later). Other tools for analyzing queueing systems include QSim[9] and PDQ.[10]

Example 7.9 A company designs customized electronic hardware for a range of customers in the high-tech electronics industry. The company receives orders for designing a new circuit every 20 working days on average. It takes a team of engineers on average 10 working days to design a hardware device.

This problem can be mapped to an M/M/1 model, assuming that the arrival of designs follows a Poisson process, that the distribution of times for designing a circuit follows an exponential distribution, and that new design requests are handled in a FIFO manner. Note that even though the team includes several people, they act as a monolithic entity and therefore should be treated as a single server. Let us take the working day as a time unit. On average, 0.05 orders are received per day ($\lambda = 0.05$), and 0.1 orders are fulfilled per day ($\mu = 0.1$). Thus, the resource utilization of this system $\rho = 0.05/0.1 = 0.5$. Using the formulas for M/M/1 models, we can deduce that the average length of the queue L_q is $0.5^2/(1 - 0.5) = 0.5$ orders. From there we can conclude that the average time an order spends in the queue is $W_q = 0.5/0.05 = 10$ days. Thus, it takes on average $W = 10 + 1/0.1 = 20$ working days for an order to be fulfilled. □

Exercise 7.8 Consider now the case where the engineering team in the previous example requires 16 working days to design a hardware device. What is then the average amount of time an order takes to be fulfilled?

Exercise 7.9 An insurance company receives 220 calls per day from customers who lodge insurance claims. The call center is open from 8 a.m. to 5 p.m. The arrival of calls follows a Poisson process. Looking at the intensity of arrival of calls, we can distinguish three periods during the day: the period 8 a.m. to 11 a.m., the period 11 a.m. to 2 p.m. and the period 2 p.m. to 5 p.m. During the first period, around 60 calls are received. During the 11 a.m. to 2 p.m. period, 120 calls are received, and during the 2 p.m. to 5 p.m. period, 40 calls are received. A customer survey has shown that customers tend to call between 11 a.m. and 2 p.m. because during this time they have a break at work.

Statistical analysis shows that the durations of calls follow an exponential distribution. According to the company's customer service charter, customers should not wait more than 1 min on average for their call to be answered.

- Assume that the call center can handle 70 calls per hour using 7 call center agents. Is this enough to meet the 1-min constraint set in the customer service charter? Please explain your answer by showing how you calculate the average length of the queue and the average waiting time.
- What happens if the call center's capacity is increased so that it can handle 80 calls per hour (using 8 call center agents)?

---

[9]http://www.stat.auckland.ac.nz/~stats255/qsim/qsim.html.
[10]http://www.perfdynamics.com/Tools/PDQ.html.

- The call center manager has a mandate to cut costs by at least 20%. Give at least two ideas to achieve this cut without reducing the salaries of the call center agents and while keeping an average waiting time below or close to 1 min.

7.2.3 Limitations of Basic Queueing Theory

The basic queueing analysis techniques presented above allow us to estimate waiting times and queue lengths based on the assumptions that inter-arrival times and processing times follow an exponential distribution. When these parameters follow different distributions, one needs to use different queueing models. Fortunately, queueing theory tools nowadays support a broad range of queueing models and of course they can do the calculations for us. The discussion above must be seen as an overview of single-queue models, with the aim of providing a starting point from where you can learn more about this family of techniques.

A more fundamental limitation of the techniques introduced in this section is that they only deal with one task at a time. When we have to analyze an entire process that involves several tasks, events, and resources, these basic techniques are not sufficient. There are many other queueing analysis techniques that could be used for this purpose, like for example queueing networks. Essentially, queueing networks are systems consisting of multiple inter-connected queues. However, the maths behind queueing networks can become quite complex, especially when the process includes concurrent tasks. A more popular approach for quantitative analysis of process models under varying levels of resource contention is process simulation, as discussed below.

7.3 Simulation

Process simulation is arguably the most popular and widely supported technique for quantitative analysis of process models. The essential idea underpinning process simulation is to use the process simulator for generating a large number of hypothetical instances of a process, executing these instances step-by-step, and recording each step in this execution. The output of a simulator then includes the logs of the simulation as well as statistics of cycle times, average waiting times, and average resource utilization.

7.3.1 Anatomy of a Process Simulation

During a process simulation, the tasks in the process are not actually executed. Instead, the simulation of a task proceeds as follows. When a task is ready to be executed, a so-called *work item* is created and the simulator first tries to find a resource to which it can assign this work item. If no resource able to perform the work item is available, the simulator puts the work item in waiting mode until a suitable resource becomes available. Once a resource is assigned to a work item, the simulator determines the duration of the work item by drawing a random number according to the probability distribution of the task processing time. This probability distribution and the corresponding parameters need to be defined in the simulation model.

Once the simulator has determined the duration of a work item, it puts the work item in sleeping mode for that duration. This sleeping mode simulates the fact that the task is being executed. Once the time interval has passed (according to the simulation clock), the work item is declared to be completed and the resource that was assigned to it becomes available.

In reality, the simulator does not effectively wait for tasks to come back from their sleeping mode. For example, if the simulator determines that the duration of a work item is 2 days and 2 h, it will not wait for this amount of time to pass by. You can imagine how long a simulation would take if that was the case. Instead, simulators use smart algorithms to complete the simulation as fast as possible. Modern business process simulators can effectively simulate thousands of process instances and tens of thousands of work items in a matter of seconds.

For each work item created during a simulation, the simulator records the identifier of the resource that was assigned to this instance as well as three timestamps:

- The time when the task was ready to be executed.
- The time when the task was started, meaning that it was assigned to a resource.
- The time when the task completed.

Using the collected data, the simulator can compute the average waiting time for each task. These measures are quite important when we try to identify bottlenecks in the process. Indeed, if a task has a high average waiting time, it means that there is a bottleneck at the level of this task. The analyst can then consider several options for addressing this bottleneck.

Additionally, since the simulator records which resources perform which work items and it knows how long each work item takes, the simulator can find out the total amount of time during which a given resource is busy handling work items. By dividing the amount of time that a resource was busy during a simulation by the total duration of the simulation, we obtain the *resource utilization*, that is, the percentage of time that the resource is busy on average.

7.3.2   Input for Process Simulation

From the above description of how a simulation works, we can see that the following information needs to be specified for each task in the process model in order to simulate it:

- The probability distribution for the processing time of each task.
- Other performance attributes for the task such as cost and added-value produced by the task.
- The *resource pool* that is responsible for performing the task. In the loan application process, there are three resource pools: the claim handlers, the clerks and the managers. For each resource pool, we need to specify its size (e.g., the number of claim handlers or the number of clerks) and optionally their cost per time unit (e.g., the hourly cost of a claims handler). If we specify the cost per time unit for every resource pool, the simulation will calculate the mean labor cost per case in addition to calculating cycle times and waiting times.

Common probability distributions for task durations in the context of process simulation include:

- *Fixed.* This is the case where the processing time of the task is the same for all executions of this task. It is rare to find such tasks because most tasks, especially those involving human resources, would exhibit some variability in their processing time. Examples of tasks with fixed processing time can be found among automated tasks such as for example a task that generates a report from a database. Such a task would take a relatively constant amount of time, say for example 5 s.
- *Exponential distribution.* As discussed in Section 7.2, the exponential distribution may be applicable when the processing time of the task is most often around a given mean value, but sometimes it is considerably longer. For example, consider a task "Assess insurance claims" in an insurance claims handling process. For normal cases, the claim is assessed in an hour, or perhaps less. However, some insurance claims require special treatment, for example because the assessor considers that there is a risk that the claim is fraudulent. In this case, the assessor might spend several hours or even an entire day assessing a single claim. A similar observation can be made of diagnostics tasks, such as diagnosing a problem in an IT infrastructure or diagnosing a problem during a car repair process.
- *Normal distribution.* This distribution is used when the processing time of the task is around a given average and the deviation around this value is symmetric, which means that the actual processing time can be above or below the mean with the same probability. Simple checks, such as for example checking whether or not a paper form has been fully completed might follow this distribution. Indeed, it generally takes about 3 min to make such a check. In such cases, this time can be lower because for example the form is clearly incomplete or clearly complete. In other cases, it can take a bit longer, because a couple of fields have been left empty and it is unclear if these fields are relevant or not for the specific customer who submitted the form. Some simulators also support the *half-normal distribution*, which is similar to the normal distribution but it only allows for positive values. Negative values do not make sense when applied to processing times or costs.

When assigning an exponential distribution to a task duration the analyst has to specify the mean value. Meanwhile, when assigning a normal distribution, the analyst has to specify two parameters: mean value and standard deviation. These values are determined based on an informed guess (based on interviews with the relevant stakeholders), but preferably by means of sampling (the analyst collects data for a sample of task executions) or by analyzing execution logs of relevant information systems. Some simulation tools allow the analyst to import logs into the simulation tool and assist the analyst in selecting the right probability distribution for task durations based on these logs. This functionality is called *simulation input analysis*.

In addition to the above per-task simulation data, a branching probability needs to be specified for every flow coming out of a decision gateway. These probabilities may be determined by interviewing relevant stakeholders, observing the process during a period of time, or collecting logs from relevant information systems.

Finally, in order to run a simulation, the analyst additionally needs to specify at least the following:

- The mean inter-arrival time and its associated probability distribution. As explained above, a very frequent distribution of inter-arrival times is the exponential distribution and this is usually the default distribution supported by business process simulators. It may happen however that the inter-arrival times follow a different distribution such as for example a *normal distribution*. By feeding a sample of inter-arrival times during a certain period of time to a statistical tool, we can find out which distribution best matches the data. Some simulators provide a module for selecting a distribution for the inter-arrival times and for computing the mean inter-arrival time from a data sample.
- The starting date and time of the simulation (e.g., "11 Nov. 2017 at 8:00").
- One of the following:

  - The end date and time of the simulation. If this option is selected, the simulation will stop producing more process instances once the simulation clock reaches the end time.
  - The real-time duration of the simulation (e.g., 7 days, 14 days). In this way, the end time of the simulation can be derived by adding this duration to the starting time.
  - The required number of process instances to be simulated (e.g., 1,000). If this option is selected, the simulator generates process instances according to the arrival rate until it reaches the required number of process instances. At this point, the simulation stops. Some simulators will not stop immediately, but will allow the active process instances to complete before stopping the simulation.

Example 7.10 We consider the process for loan application approval modeled in Figure 4.2 (page 118). We simulate this model using the BIMP simulator.[11] This

---

[11] http://bimp.cs.ut.ee.

simulator takes as input a BPMN process model. We provide the following inputs for the simulation.

- Three loan applications arrive per hour on average, meaning an inter-arrival time of 20 min. Loan applications arrive only from 9 a.m. to 5 p.m. during weekdays.
- The tasks "Check credit history" and "Check income sources" are performed by clerks.
- The tasks "Notify rejection", "Make credit offer", and "Assess application" are performed by credit officers.
- The task "Receive customer feedback" is in fact an event. It takes zero time and it only involves the credit information system (no human resources involved). To capture this, the task is assigned to a special "System" role.
- There are two clerks and two credit officers. The hourly cost of a clerk is € 25 while that of a credit officer is € 50.
- Clerks and credit officers work from 9 a.m. to 5 p.m. during weekdays.
- The cycle time of the task "Assess application" follows an exponential distribution with a mean of 20 min.
- Cycle times of all other tasks follow a normal distribution. The tasks "Check credit history", "Notify rejection", and "Make credit offer" have a mean cycle time of 10 min with a 20% standard deviation, while "Check income sources" has a cycle time of 20 min with a 20% standard deviation as well.
- The probability that an application is accepted is 80%.
- The probability that a customer, whose application was rejected, asks that the application be re-assessed is 20%.

We run a simulation with 2,400 instances, which means 100 working days given that 24 loan applications arrive per day. The simulation gives an average cycle time of around 7.5 h if we count the time outside working hours (*cycle time including off-timetable hours* in BIMP). If we count only working hours, the cycle time is 2 h. The latter is called the *cycle time excluding off-timetable hours* in BIMP. These cycle time measurements may vary by about ± 10% when we run the simulation multiple times. These variations are expected due to the stochastic nature of the simulation. For this reason, we recommend running the simulation multiple times and to take averages of the simulation results.

Figure 7.14 shows the histograms for process cycle times (both including and excluding off-timetable hours), waiting times (excluding off-timetable costs), and costs. It can be seen that the waiting times are relatively low. This is because the resource utilization of clerks and credit officers is around 76–80%. □

Exercise 7.10 The insurance company called Cetera is facing the following problem: Whenever there is a major event (e.g., a storm), their claim-to-resolution process is unable to cope with the ensuing spike in demand. During normal times, the insurance company receives about 9,000 calls per week, but during a storm scenario the number of calls per week doubles.

The claim-to-resolution process model of Cetera is presented in Figure 7.15. The process starts when a call related to lodging a claim is received. The call is routed

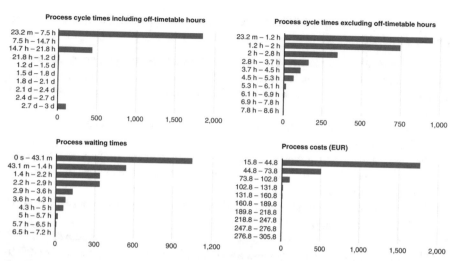

Fig. 7.14 Histograms produced by simulating the credit application process with BIMP

to one of two call centers depending on the location of the caller. Each call center receives approximately the same amount of calls (50–50) and has the same number of operators (40 per call center). The process for handling calls is identical across both call centers. When a call is received at a call center, the call is picked up by a call center operator. The call center operator starts by asking a standard set of questions to the customer to determine if the customer has the minimum information required to lodge a claim (e.g., insurance policy number). If the customer has enough information, the operator then goes through a questionnaire with the customer, enters all relevant details, checks the completeness of the claim, and registers the claim.

Once a claim has been registered, it is routed to the claims handling office, where all remaining steps are performed. There is one single claims handling office, so regardless of the call center agent where the claim is registered, the claim is routed to the same office. In this office, the claim goes through a two-stage evaluation process. First of all, the liability of the customer is determined. Secondly, the claim is assessed in order to determine if the insurance company has to cover this liability and to what extent. If the claim is accepted, payment is initiated and the customer is advised of the amount to be paid. The tasks of the claims handling department are performed by *claims handlers*. There are 150 claims handlers in total.

The mean cycle time of each task (in seconds) is indicated in Figure 7.15. For every task, the cycle time follows an exponential distribution. The hourly cost of a call center agent is € 30, while the hourly cost of a claims handler is € 50.

Describe the input that should be given to a simulator in order to simulate this process in the normal scenario and in the storm scenario. Using a simulation tool, encode the normal and the storm scenarios, and run a simulation in order to compare these two scenarios.

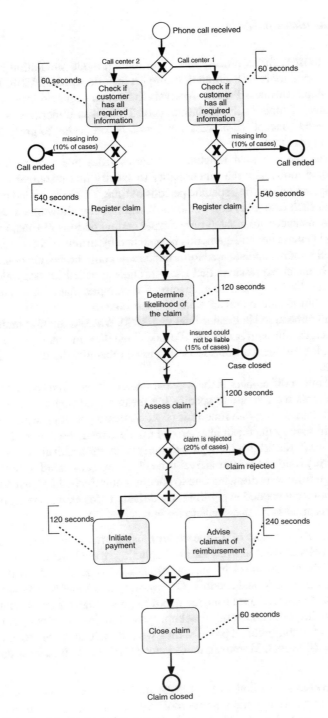

Fig. 7.15 Cetera's claim-to-resolution process

7.3.3   Simulation Tools

Nowadays, most business process modeling tools provide simulation capabilities. Examples of such tools with simulation support include Appian, ARIS, IBM BPM, Logizian, Oracle Business Process Analysis Suite, and Signavio Process Manager. The landscape of tools evolves continuously. Thus, it is important to understand the fundamental concepts of process simulation before trying to grasp the specific features of a given tool.

In general, the provided functionality varies from one tool to another. For example, some tools offer the functionality to specify that resources do not work continuously, but only during specific periods of time. This is specified by attaching a calendar to each resource pool. Some tools additionally allow one to specify that new process instances are created only during certain periods of time, for example only during business hours. Again, this is specified by means of a calendar.

Some of the more sophisticated tools capture not only branching conditions, but also actual boolean expressions that use attributes attached to data objects in the process model. In this way, we can specify, for example, that a branch coming out of an XOR-split should be taken when the attribute *loanAmount* of a data object called "loan application" is greater than € 10,000, whereas another branch should be taken when this amount is up to € 10,000. When the simulator generates objects of type loan, it gives them a value according to a probability distribution attached to this attribute.

There are minor differences in the way parameters are specified across simulation tools. Some tools require one to specify the mean arrival rate, that is the number of cases that start during one time unit (e.g., 50 cases per day), while other tools require one to specify the mean inter-arrival time between cases (e.g., 2 min until a new case arrives). Recall that the distinction between mean arrival rate (written λ in queueing theory) and mean inter-arrival time ($1/\lambda$) was discussed in Section 7.2.1. Other tools go further by allowing one to specify not only the inter-arrival time, but how many cases are created every time. By default, cases arrive one by one, but in some business processes, cases may arrive in batches.

Example 7.11 An example of a process with batch arrivals is an archival process at the Macau Historical Archives. At the beginning of each year, transfer lists are sent to the Historical Archives by various organizations. Each transfer list contains approximately 225 historical records. On average, two transfer lists are received each year. Each record in a transfer list needs to go through a process that includes appraisal, classification, annotation, backup, and re-binding. If we consider that each record is a case of this archival process, then we can say that cases arrive in batches of $225 \times 2 = 450$ cases. Moreover, these batches arrive at a fixed inter-arrival time of one year.

□

Finally, process simulation tools typically differ in terms of how resource pools and resource costs are specified. Some tools restrict the specification to a resource pool and its number of resources. A single cost per time unit is then attached to the entire resource pool. Other tools support a more fine-grained specification of the resources of a pool one by one with specific cost rates for each created resource (e.g., create 10 clerks one by one, each with its name and hourly cost).

The above discussion illustrates some of the nuances found across simulation tools. In order to avoid diving straight away into the numerous details of a tool, it may be useful for beginners to take their first steps using the BIMP simulator referred to in Example 7.10. BIMP is a rather simple BPMN process model simulator that provides the core functionality found in commercial business process simulation tools.

7.3.4 A Word of Caution

One should keep in mind that the quantitative analysis techniques we have seen in this chapter, and simulation in particular, are based on models and on simplifying assumptions. The reliability of the output produced by these techniques largely depends on the accuracy of the numbers that are given as input. Additionally, simulation assumes that process participants work mechanically. However, process participants are not robots. They are subject to unforeseen interruptions, they display varying performance depending on various factors, and they may adapt differently to new ways of working.

It is good practice whenever possible to derive the input parameters of a simulation from actual observations, meaning from historical process execution data. This is possible when simulating an as-is process that is being executed in the company, but not necessarily when simulating a to-be process. In a similar spirit, it is recommended to cross-check simulation outputs against expert advice. This can be achieved by presenting the simulation results to process stakeholders (including process participants). The process stakeholders are usually able to provide feedback on the credibility of the resource utilization levels calculated via simulation and the bottlenecks put into evidence by the simulation. For instance, if the simulation points to a bottleneck in a given task, while the stakeholders and participants perceive this task to be uncritical, there is an indication that incorrect assumptions have been made. Feedback from stakeholders and participants helps to reconfigure the parameters such that the results are closer to matching the actual behavior. In other words, process simulation is an iterative analysis technique.

Finally, it is advisable to perform sensitivity analysis of the simulation. Concretely, this means observing how the output of the simulation changes when adding one resource to or removing one resource from a resource pool, or when changing the processing times by $\pm 10\%$, for example. If such small changes in the simulation input parameters significantly affect the conclusions drawn from the simulation outputs, one must be careful when interpreting the simulation results.

7.4 Recap

In this chapter we saw three quantitative process analysis techniques, namely flow analysis, queueing theory, and simulation. These techniques allow us to derive process performance measures, such as cycle time or cost, and to understand how different tasks and resource pools contribute to the overall performance of a process.

Flow analysis allows us to calculate performance measures from a process model and performance data pertaining to each task in the model. We also analyzed the critical path of a process using the Critical Path Method. Finally, we studied the capacity of a process and defined the notion of resource utilization. The waiting times of a process are highly dependent on resource utilization—the busier the resources are, the longer the waiting times.

Basic queueing theory models, such as the M/M/1 model, allow us to calculate waiting times for individual tasks given data about the number of resources and their processing times. Other queueing theory models such as queueing networks can be used to perform fine-grained analysis at the level of entire processes. However, in practice it is convenient to use process simulation for fine-grained analysis. Process simulation allows us to derive process performance measures (e.g., cycle time or cost) given data about the tasks (e.g., processing times) and data about the resources involved in the process. Process simulation is a versatile technique supported by a range of process modeling and analysis tools.

7.5 Solutions to Exercises

Solution 7.1 First we observe that the cycle time of the AND-block is 1. Next, we calculate the cycle time of the XOR-block as follows: $0.4 \times 1 + 0.4 \times 1 + 0.2 \times 1$ h. The total cycle time is thus: $1 + 1 + 1 = 3$ h.

Solution 7.2 The cycle time of the process is $2 + 8 + \frac{4+4}{1-0.2} = 20$ days. Assuming 8 working hours per day, this translates to 160 working hours. The theoretical cycle time is $0.5 + 12 + \frac{4+2}{1-0.2} = 20$ h. Hence, cycle time efficiency is 12.5%.

Solution 7.3 It can be expected that the average cycle times of the reported process have generally improved. Since 1992, several technological advancements have drastically improved white-collar work productivity. These relate to a better coordination and routing of tasks using information technology including office applications, enterprise systems, and Internet technology. In Chapter 9, we will discuss how Business Process Management Systems and different types of Process-Aware Information Systems have contributed to better coordination and task automation. These advancements have likely reduced waiting times in many business processes. Therefore, also cycle time efficiency should have improved since 1992.

Solution 7.4 The process model shown in Figure 7.4 has three tasks with the following ES, EF, LS, and LF:

- Start event: $ES = EF = LS = LF = 0$.
- Task A: $ES = LS = 0$ and $EF = LF = 10$.
- Task B: $ES = LS = 10$ and $EF = LF = 30$.
- Task C: $ES = 10$ and $EF = 20$. Here is slack, because $LS = 20$ and $LF = 30$.
- End event: $ES = EF = LS = LF = 30$.

Task B has slack of 10. The critical path includes all tasks except B.

Solution 7.5 Little's law tells us that $CT = WIP/\lambda$. At peak time, there are 900 customers distributed across 6 h, so the mean arrival rate $\lambda = 150$ customers per hour. On the other hand, $WIP = 90$ during peak time. Thus, $CT = 90/150 = 0.6$ h (i.e., 36 min). During non-peak time, $\lambda = 300/6 = 50$ customer per hour while $WIP = 30$, thus $CT = 30/50 = 0.6$ h (again 36 min). If the number of customers per hour during peak times is expected to go up, but the WIP has to remain constant, we need to reduce the cycle time per customer. This may be achieved by shortening the serving time, the interval between the moment a customer enters the restaurant and the moment he or she places an order, or the time it takes for the customer to pay. In other words, the process for order taking and payment may need to be redesigned.

Solution 7.6

- A call center agent spends $60 + 0.9*540 = 546$ s per instance.
- One call center agent can deliver 3,600 s per hour, hence 7 agents can deliver 25,200 s per hour.
- $\mu = 25,200/546 = 46.15$ calls per hour.
- For convenience, we use the hour as the time unit. Hence, $\lambda = 24.44$ and $\mu = 46.15$, and therefore $\rho = 24.44/46.15 = 0.53$

Solution 7.7 Given that there are no other costs, we calculate the cost of the process by aggregating the resource costs as follows: $0.5 \times €25 + 12 \times €50 + (4 \times €75 + 2 \times €100)/(1 - 0.2) = €1,237.50$.

Solution 7.8 On average, 0.05 orders are received per day ($\lambda = 0.05$), and 0.0625 orders are fulfilled per day ($\mu = 0.0625$). Thus, the resource utilization of this system $\rho = 0.05/0.0625 = 0.8$. Using the formulas for M/M/1 models, we can deduce that the average length of the queue L_q is: $0.8^2/(1 - 0.8) = 3.2$ orders. From this, we can conclude that the average time an order spends on the queue is $W_q = 3.2/0.05 = 64$ days. Thus, it takes on average $W = 64 + 16 = 80$ working days for an order to be fulfilled.

Solution 7.9 Strictly speaking, we should analyze this problem using an M/M/c queueing model. However, the formulas for M/M/c are quite complex to show the calculations in detail. For this reason, we will assume in this solution that the entire call center behaves as a single monolithic team, so that we can use an M/M/1 queueing model to analyse the problem. Because of this assumption, the results will not be exact.

If we only had 7 call center agents, then the resource utilization $\rho = 40/70 = 0.57$, $L_q = \rho^2/(1-\rho) = 0.57^2/(1-0.57) = 0.76$, and $W_q = L_q/\lambda = 0.76/40 = 0.0189$ h $= 1.13$ min. So we cannot meet the customer service charter.

If we can handle 80 calls per hour (8 call center agents), then the resource utilization $\rho = 40/80 = 0.5$, $L_q = \rho^2/(1-\rho) = 0.5^2/(1-0.5) = 0.5$, and $W_q = L_q/\lambda = 0.5/40 = 0.0125$ h $= 45$ s, so we meet the customer service charter.

Ways to reduce costs while staying as close as possible to the customer service charter are:

- We could reduce the number of call center agents to 7 and still have an average waiting time of 1.13 min. That reduces costs by 12.5% (one call center agent less).
- We could introduce a self-service system, whereby people lodge their application online (at least for simple claims).
- We could extend the call center working times (e.g., work until 6 p.m. or 7 p.m. instead of 5 p.m.), so that people can call after work. In this way, we might ease the call center load during its peak time.
- Reduce the time of each call by providing better training to call center agents.

Solution 7.10 For this problem, we will reason exclusively in terms of working hours as a unit of time, as opposed to calendar hours. We assume that a week consists of 40 working hours. Calls arrive only during these 40 working hours and call center operators and claims handlers work only during these 40 h. By taking working hours as a time unit, we avoid the need to attach calendars resources.

In the normal scenario (no storm), the arrival rate is 9,000 cases per week, that is one case every 16 s (this is the inter-arrival time). In the storm scenario the inter-arrival time is 8 s. In both cases, we use an exponential distribution for the inter-arrival time. We run simulations corresponding to 1 week of work, which means 9,000 cases for the normal scenario and 18,000 cases for the storm scenario.

In order to distinguish between the two call centers, we define two separate resource pools called "Call Center Operator 1" and "Call Center Operator 2" each one with 40 resources at an hourly cost of 30, plus a resource pool "Claims Handler" with 150 resources. We assign tasks to resource pools as indicated in the scenario and we use the cycle times indicated in the process model as input for the simulation. Running the simulation using the BIMP simulator gives us the following outputs. In the normal scenario, we obtain a resource utilization of around 48% for claims handlers and 34–36% for call center operators. The average cycle time (excluding off-timetable hours) is around 0.5 working hours and the maximum observed cycle time is around 3.3 working hours. In other words, the resources are under-utilized and, thus, the cycle time is low.

In the storm season, resource utilization of claims handlers is above 95% and around 78% for the call center agents. The average cycle time is 2 h while the maximum is around 7.5 h (excluding off-timetable time). The high resource utilization indicates that the claims handling office is overloaded during storm season. On the other hand, the call center has sufficient capacity. The average waiting time in the call center is in the order of seconds.

A BPMN model of this process together with the simulation parameters (in the format required by BIMP) can be found in the book's companion website.[12]

7.6 Further Exercises

Exercise 7.11 Calculate the cycle time, cycle time efficiency, and cost of the university admission process described in Exercise 1.1 (page 5), assuming that:

- The process starts when an online application is submitted.
- It takes on average 2 weeks (after the online application is submitted) for the documents to arrive to the students service by post.
- The check for completeness of documents takes about 10 min. In 20% of the cases, the completeness check reveals that some documents are missing. In this case, an email is sent to the student automatically by the university admission management system based on the input provided by the international students officer during the completeness check.
- A student services officer spends on average 10 min to put the degrees and transcripts in an envelope and to send them to the academic recognition agency. The time it takes to send the degrees and transcripts to the academic recognition agency and to receive back a response is 2 weeks on average.
- About 10% of applications are rejected after the academic recognition assessment.
- The university pays a fee of € 5 each time it requests the academic recognition agency to accept an application.
- Checking the English language test results takes 1 day on average, but the officer who performs the check only spends 10 min on average per check. This language test check is free.
- About 10% of applications are rejected after the English language test.
- It takes on average 2 weeks between the time students service sends the copy of an application to the committee members and the moment the committee makes a decision (accept or reject). On average, the committee spends 1 h examining each application.
- It takes on average 2 days (after the decision is made by the academic committee) for the students service to record the academic committee's decision in the university admission management system. Recording a decision takes on average 2 min. Once a decision is recorded, a notification is automatically sent to the student.
- The hourly cost of the officers at the international students office is € 50.
- The hourly cost of the academic committee (as a whole) is € 200.

---

[12]http://fundamentals-of-bpm.org/supplementary-material/.

Exercise 7.12 Let us consider the following process performed by an IT helpdesk that handles requests from clients. The clients are employees of a company. There are about 500 employees in total. A request may be an IT-related problem of a client or an access request (e.g., requesting rights to access a system). Requests need to be handled according to their type and their priority. There are three priority levels: "critical", "urgent", or "normal". The current process works as follows.

> A client calls the help desk or sends an email in order to make a request. The help desk is staffed with 5 Level-1 support staff who, typically, are junior people with less than 12 months experience, but are capable of resolving known problems and simple requests. The hourly cost of a Level-1 staff member is € 40.
>
> When the Level-1 employee does not know the resolution to a request, the request is forwarded to a more experienced Level-2 support staff. There are 3 Level-2 staff members and their hourly cost is € 60. When a Level-2 employee receives a new request, he or she evaluates it in order to assign a priority level. The ticketing system that tracks the process will later assign the request to the same or to another Level-2 staff depending on the assigned priority level and the backlog of requests.
>
> Once the request is assigned to a Level-2 staff member, the request is researched by the Level-2 employee and a resolution is developed and sent back to the Level-1 employee. Eventually, the Level-1 employee forwards the resolution to the client who tests the resolution. The client notifies the outcome of the test to the Level-1 employee via email. If the client states that the request is fixed, it is marked as complete and the process ends. If the request is not fixed, it is resent to Level-2 support for further action and goes through the process again.
>
> Requests are registered in a ticketing system. The ticketing system allows help desk employees to record the details of the request, the priority level and the name of the client who generated the request. When a request is registered, it is marked as "open". When it is moved to Level-2, it is marked as "forwarded to Level-2". When the resolution is sent back to Level-1, the request is marked as "returned to Level-1". Finally, when a request is resolved, it is marked as "closed". Every request has a unique identifier. When a request is registered, the ticketing system sends an email to the client. The email includes a so-called request reference number that the client needs to quote when asking questions about the request.

Calculate the cycle time efficiency and the cost-per-execution of the as-is process assuming that:

- Submitting and registering a new request takes 5 min on average.
- Requests spend on average 1 h waiting for a Level-1 staff member to check them. This applies both to new requests and to resubmitted requests.
- Checking if a new request is known takes on average 10 min. In 20% of the cases, the request is known. In this case, it takes between 2 and 10 min (average 5 min) for the Level-1 staff member to communicate the resolution to the client. Once this is done, the request is marked as "closed". On the other hand, if the request is not known, the request is automatically forwarded to Level-2.
- New requests spend on average 2 h waiting for a Level-2 staff member to evaluate them. Level-2 staff take on average 20 min to evaluate a new request.
- Level-2 staff take 5 min to prioritize a request.
- The time between the moment a request has been prioritized and the moment the request is picked up by a Level-2 staff member is 20 h.
- The time required to research and resolve a request is on average 2 h.

- The time to write the resolution to a request is on average 20 min.
- Once a Level-2 staff member has written the resolution of a request, it takes on average 20 h before a the request is fetched from the ticketing system by a Level-1 staff member.
- It takes on average 20 min for a Level-1 staff member to send to the client a problem resolution previously written by a Level-2 staff member.
- It takes on average 20 h between the moment a resolution is sent by the Level-1 staff member and the moment the resolution is tested by the client.
- It takes the client around 10 min to email the test results to the Level-1 staff.
- In 20% of the cases, the request is not resolved and it needs to be forwarded to Level-2 again. In this latter case, it takes about 2 min for the Level-1 staff to forward the request to the Level-2 staff. Unresolved requests that are forwarded in this way are automatically marked as prioritized, since they have already been prioritized in the previous iteration.
- There are no other costs besides the resource costs.

Hint   To calculate theoretical cycle time and cost, only take into consideration time spent doing actual work, excluding waiting times and handoffs.

Acknowledgement   This exercise is inspired by an example found in [28].

Exercise 7.13   We consider a simplified process for handling a Request for Quote (RFQ) for custom-made metal products at a company called MetalWorks. The process model including processing times and branching probabilities is shown in Figure 7.16. There are two production sales engineers dedicated to this process and one production manager. The production sales engineers work can dedicate up to 32 h per week to this process (each) while the production manager can only dedicate up to 18 h per week to this process. Calculate the theoretical capacity of each of these two resource pools. Which of the pools is the bottleneck pool?

Exercise 7.14   Consider the scenario described in Exercise 7.8 (page 278). The company in question is being pressed by several of its customers to fulfill their orders faster. The company's management estimates that the company stands to lose

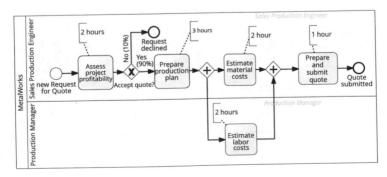

Fig. 7.16   Request for handling a request for quote at MetalWorks

€ 250,000 in revenue, if they do not reduce their order fulfillment time below 40 working days. Adding one engineer to the existing team would reduce the time to design a hardware down to 14 working days (from 16 days). An additional engineer would cost the company € 50,000. On the other hand, hiring a second engineering team would cost € 250,000. Analyze these two scenarios and formulate a recommendation to the company.

Exercise 7.15 We consider a Level-2 IT service desk with 2 staff members. Each staff member can handle one service request in 4 working hours on average. Service times are exponentially distributed. Requests arrive at a mean rate of one request every 3 h according to a Poisson process. What is the average time between the moment a service request arrives to this desk and the moment it is fulfilled?

Exercise 7.16 Consider the Level-2 IT service desk described in Exercise 7.15. Let us assume that the number of requests is one per hour. How many level-2 staff members are required in order to ensure that the mean waiting time of a request is less than two working hours?

Exercise 7.17 Consider again the IT helpdesk process described in Exercise 7.12 (page 291). Model and simulate it assuming that cases arrive at a rate of 50 per day according to an exponential distribution. Assume that all the task cycle times follow an exponential distribution with the average given in Exercise 7.12.

Note When modeling the process, do not model the waiting times between tasks, only the tasks themselves.

Exercise 7.18 Consider the process model in Figure 7.17. This model captures a simplified process for handling mortgage applications. There are two checks involved. CT1 deals with a check of the financial coverage of the mortgage application. The second check CT2 concerns the verification of the property that is to be mortgaged. If the result of both checks is positive, the application is accepted (task AC). On average, after the execution of task CT1, 20% of all applications

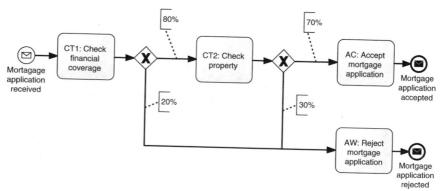

Fig. 7.17 Mortgage process model

are rejected. Meanwhile, task CT2 leads to 30% of further rejections. If either of the checks has an unsatisfactory result, the application is rejected (task AW). The arrival process is Poisson with an average arrival of 5 cases per hour during business hours. For each task, exactly one dedicated resource is available. The processing time of every task follows an exponential distribution. The mean processing times for tasks CT1, CT2, AC, and AW are respectively 5, 4, 3, and 3 min. The wage of each resource is € 20 per hour. Business hours are from Monday to Friday from 9 a.m. to 5 p.m. Resources are only available during these hours.

a. Determine the resource utilization of each resource.
b. Determine the average cycle time of the process.
c. Determine the cycle time efficiency of the process.
d. Determine the average number of mortgage applications that are being handled at any given point in time.

Hint For this exercise, it might be convenient to use a combination of process simulation, Little's law, and flow analysis.

7.7 Further Readings

In Section 7.1, we showed how flow analysis techniques can be used to calculate cycle time and cost. Laguna & Marklund [85] discuss flow analysis in detail. Another possible application of flow analysis is to estimate the error rate of the process, meaning the number of cases that will end up in a negative outcome. This latter application of flow analysis is discussed for example by Yang et al. [196]. Yang et al. also present a technique for flow analysis that is applicable not only to block-structured process models but also to a much broader class of process models.

As mentioned in Section 7.2, the formula for determining the average queue length in the context of the M/M/c model is particularly complicated. Laguna & Marklund [85, Chapter 6] analyze the M/M/c model (including the formula for average queue length) and its application to process analysis. They also analyze the M/M/c/K model, where an upper-bound to the length of the queue is imposed (this is parameter K in the model). The M/M/c/K model is suitable for example when there is a maximum length of queue beyond which customers are rejected from the queue. Adan & Resing [3] give detailed introductions to M/M/1, M/M/c, M/M/c/K and other queueing theory models.

As stated in Section 7.3, business process simulation is a versatile approach for quantitative process analysis. Numerous case studies illustrating the use of process simulation in various domains can be found in the literature. For example, Greasley [58] illustrates the use of business process simulation for redesigning a process for road traffic accident reporting. In a similar vein, Van der Aalst et al. [178] discuss the use of business process simulation to evaluate different strategies to avoid or to mitigate deadline violations in the context of an insurance claims handling process in an insurance company. Exercise 7.10 is based on this latter paper.

Current tools for business process simulation have various limitations. Several of these limitations are discussed at length by Van der Aalst et al. [177]. Research by Martin et al. discusses how data about previous executions of the process can be used to build more accurate simulation models [104, 105]. Van der Aalst et al. [177] propose to use more sophisticated tools for process simulation, namely Discrete-Event Simulation (DES) tools. They specifically put forward *CPN Tools* as a possible DES that can be used for business process simulation. CPN Tools is based on *Colored Petri Nets*—a language that extends Petri nets. Other DES tools that can be used for business process simulation include ExtendSim [85] and Arena [75]. For example, Arena is used in the aforementioned case study of a road traffic reporting process [58]. DES tools are clearly more powerful than specialized business process simulation tools. However, the choice of a DES tool means that one cannot directly use a BPMN model for simulation. Instead the model has to be re-encoded in another notation. Moreover, the use of DES tools requires more technical background from the analyst. These trade-offs should be considered when choosing between DES tools and specialized business process simulation tools based for example on BPMN.

We saw throughout the chapter that quantitative analysis techniques allow us to identify critical paths and bottlenecks. These are essentially paths in the process that require special attention if the goal is to reduce cycle time. Anupindi et al. [9] offer detailed advice on how to deal with critical paths and bottlenecks in business processes as well as how to reduce waste and repetition. The following chapter will discuss some of these insights.

Chapter 8
Process Redesign

Check for updates

We know what we are, but not what we may be.
William Shakespeare (1564–1616)

The thorough analysis of a business process may lead to the identification of a range of issues. For example, bottlenecks slow down the process or the cost of process execution is too high. These issues spark various directions for redesign. The problem is, however, that redesign is often approached as an ad hoc activity. The downside to this is that interesting redesign opportunities may be overlooked. For this reason, it is important to become aware of *redesign methods*, which can be used to systematically generate redesign options.

This chapter deals with the methods that help to rethink and re-organize business processes to make them perform better. We first clarify the motivation for redesign and delve deeper into what improving process performance actually means. Then, we present the spectrum of redesign methods and discuss representative sample methods in some detail. More specifically, we distinguish between transactional and transformational methods.

8.1 The Essence of Process Redesign

In this section, we describe the motivation behind redesign and discuss what lies within the scope of this concept. We will also introduce the Devil's Quadrangle [22], which provides a perspective on the different performance dimensions that are involved in a redesign effort.

© Springer-Verlag GmbH Germany, part of Springer Nature 2018
M. Dumas et al., *Fundamentals of Business Process Management*,
https://doi.org/10.1007/978-3-662-56509-4_8

8.1.1 *Product Versus Process Innovation*

Before explaining what redesign is about, let us again consider why it is beneficial to focus on business processes at all. In any firm, innovation can take place along the line of its *products* or its *processes*. *Product innovation* is concerned with the development of new products or the addition of new features to existing ones. For example, think of Apple's introduction of the first iPhone in 2007. In the years following, new generations of this smartphone were developed, each of which included better features than its predecessor. The opportunities to attract new clients and retain existing ones through product innovation, however, are not endless. That is why a second mode of innovation, *process innovation*, has become popular with many firms. In this mode, the focus is on redesigning business processes such that customers are drawn to them to acquire the products or services that they generate. A good example of an organization that heavily relies on process innovation is Amazon. This company continually finds ways to improve its processes. For example, in 2009, it patented the 1-Click ordering technique to simplify the ordering process for its clients. More recently, Amazon introduced robots to improve warehouse operations and drones to speed up its delivery process.

Research has indicated that it is natural for many firms that their initial emphasis on product innovation is at some point followed up by a focus on process innovation [174]. These two successive waves are shown in Figure 8.1. From the curves in the figure, it becomes clear why the innovation of a business process is also referred to as "the second wave of innovation".

Question Can you think of firms or organizations for which product innovation is not an option at all?

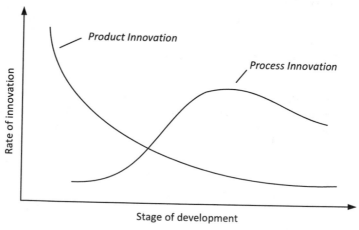

Fig. 8.1 The waves of product and process innovation

An innovation view is one angle to appreciate why organizations wish to improve their business processes. We see this as an *positive* motive, since it takes the noble urge to innovate as a starting point. There is also a less positive, more reactive motivation, which relates to the phenomenon of *organizational entropy*: All business processes evolve over time. As a result, they grow more complex and their performance gradually deteriorates. Consider the following examples:

- A clerk in a warehouse forgets to carry out a quality check for a specific order. The client, who receives the flawed product, becomes upset. To prevent such a situation from happening again, the firm's management decides to add an extra check to the process: A second clerk will verify whether the quality check is properly performed by the first. This is a good fix, but after some time the initial quality check becomes automated through the introduction of a new production system. The check-on-the-check has become superfluous, but is still part of the process. In this way, it keeps on consuming unnecessary resources and time.
- The marketing department of an organization introduces a special campaign. Each time a customer engages with this organization, their account manager asks for extra information beyond what is normally asked. By doing so, the marketing team can make a perfectly customized offer to each customer. Yet, the information comes on top of the information that the customer needs to provide anyway. After some time, the marketing campaign came to an end, but the account managers will still ask for the extra information whenever they interact with the particular kind of customer. It has become an unnecessary and time-consuming step.
- An internal auditing department demands that the monetary value of financial activities should be reported whenever these are carried out. This causes an extra calculation and an extra reporting step in each of the business processes that are affected. Over time, the management of the auditing department changes its priorities and starts looking into other, non-financial information. The reports, nonetheless, keep coming in.

All of the issues mentioned in the three examples can be overcome, of course. The point is that people who are concerned with carrying out day-to-day operations are usually neither inclined nor equipped to start rethinking existing business processes within their organization. Specifically, it is very common that people have a limited insight into why a business process is organized in the way it is: People know how to perform their own work and, perhaps, some of the activities up- and downstream from what they do. But that is about where it ends. Even managers, who are expected to exert a "helicopter view", are normally more concerned with day-to-day execution than structural improvement. People, it seems, are creatures of habit. A business process perspective helps to overcome the inhibition to improve. So, to fight the troubles that go hand in hand with the organical deterioration of a process, redesign is a good weapon.

Exercise 8.1 Can you identify business processes from your own experience that were efficient at some stage, but which have become unnecessarily complex?

While both (1) the positive impetus of organizations to innovate and (2) the phenomenon of organizational entropy show the importance of improving *existing* processes, the principles behind redesign approaches are also helpful to develop *entirely new* business processes. New business processes appear continuously. For example, think of how new legislation may require the development of new business processes. In response to the financial crisis earlier this century, many national governments invoked guardian institutes to watch over banks. The business processes that governed their interaction with the national banks often had to be developed from scratch. Other examples of new business processes can also be clearly seen in healthcare settings, where new medical knowledge triggers entirely new treatment processes. What is important to remember is this: Each business process in existence had to be developed at some stage. Redesign methods can be helpful for new processes, too.

Exercise 8.2 Can you come up with other examples that call for the development of entirely new business processes?

Note that even when new business processes must be developed, we will still refer to such occasions as process *redesign*. Technically, of course, this is a misnomer—it would be more precise to refer to this as process *design*. We will specifically return to the issue of developing processes from scratch when we will be discussing the various types of redesign approaches.

8.1.2 Redesign Concepts

Let us now take a closer look at what process redesign is. If you adopt a very broad interpretation of the term, *any* change to an existing process, be it minor or major, qualifies. Since business processes are complex artifacts with many facets, they concern, among other things, the steps in a process, the workforce that is committed to carrying out the process, the information that is being exchanged, and the information systems employed. So, when we talk about process redesign in the context of this book, we will not refer to minor updates of a business processes, neither to changes of parts that are peripheral to a process, nor to changes that are unrelated to the business process concept whatsoever.

For example, let us suppose that a bank prints the conditions under which a mortgage is granted on ordinary paper. It is also accustomed to sending the paperwork to applicants when the conditions are completely settled and approved. In this setting, we would not consider a change of the company logo on the paperwork as an act of process redesign. If, on the other hand, the client would be provided at any time with an insight into a digital file that shows the conditions as they are developed during the execution of the process, we would be much more confident in calling this process redesign. This would be particularly so if the idea behind it is to improve a customer's satisfaction with the service provided.

Another point that may need clarification is how the terms "redesign" and "innovation" relate to one another. The latter term is used by a number of scholars as special type of process redesign, namely the kind that leads to a groundbreaking shift from how things were done before. We do not follow this distinction exactly and use the terms interchangeably. We do acknowledge that there is a fundamental difference between incremental versus radical methods for process redesign, as we will see later on (see Section 8.1.5).

At this point, we will present a list of elements that helps to think and reason about the most important manifestations of process redesign. These are the following:

1. the internal or external *customers* of the business process,
2. the *business process operation* view, which relates to how a business process is implemented, specifically the number of activities that are identified in the process and the nature of each, and
3. the *business process behavior* view, which relates to the way a business process is executed, specifically the order in which activities are executed and how these are scheduled and assigned for execution,
4. the *organization* and the participants in the business process, captured at two levels: the organization structure (elements: roles, users, groups, departments, etc.), and the organization population (individuals: agents which can have activities assigned for execution and the relationships between them),
5. the *information* that the business process uses or creates,
6. the *technology* the business process uses, and
7. the *external environment* the process is situated in.

With these elements in mind, process redesign can be said to be a substantial and intentional change of a business process. It is primarily concerned with changing the business process itself, covering both its *operational* and *behaviorial* view. Process redesign extends to changes that are on the interplay between the process on the one hand and on the other the *organization* or even the *external environment* that the process operates in, the *information* and *technology* it employs, as well as the products it delivers to its *customers*.

Note that this is still a comprehensive way of looking at process redesign, but it does exclude some activities. For example, out of scope are: the way to train people to optimally perform certain activities, the decision which products to phase out, and the acquisition of a competitor.

Exercise 8.3 Consider the following list and indicate which of these you would consider as process redesign initiatives. Motivate your answer and, if applicable, provide the links to the elements discussed.

1. An airline has seen its profits falling over the past year. It decides to start a marketing campaign among its corporate clients in the hope that it can extend its profitable freight business.
2. A governmental agency notices that it is structurally late to respond to citizens' queries. It decides to assign a manager to oversee this particular process and mandates her to take appropriate counter actions.

3. A video rental company sees that its customer base is evaporating. It decides to switch to the business of promoting and selling electronic services through which clients can see movies online and on-demand.
4. A bank notices internal conflicts between two different departments over the way mortgage applications are dealt with. It decides to analyze the role of the various departments in the way applications are received and handled to come up with a new role structure.
5. A clinic wants to introduce the one-stop-shop concept to improve over the situation that its patients need to make separate appointments for the various diagnostic tests that are part of a procedure for skin cancer screening.

Not each business domain is equally suitable for the application of business process redesign. To appreciate this, consider the differences between industries that deliver physical objects on the one hand and informational products on the other. To deliver a *physical product*, the emphasis is on transforming raw materials into tangible products, which often relies on the use of robots and advanced machinery. For an *informational product*, the emphasis is on the collection, processing, and aggregation of information. Compare, for example, a car manufacturing company with an insurance company as two characteristic examples of the respective domains. In general, it is fair to say that for organizations that primarily deliver informational products the following properties hold:

- Making a copy is easy and cheap. In contrast to making a copy of a product like a car, it is relatively easy to copy a piece of information, especially if the information is in electronic form.
- There are no real limitations with respect to the in-process inventory. Informational products do not require much space and are easy to access, especially if they are stored in a database.
- There are less requirements with respect to the order in which activities are executed: Human resources are flexible in comparison with machines; there are few technical constraints with respect to the layout of the service process.
- Quality is difficult to measure. Criteria to assess the quality of a service, an informational product, are usually less explicit than those in a manufacturing environment.
- Quality of end products may vary. A manufacturer of goods usually has a minimal number of components that any product should incorporate. However, in the services domain it might be attractive to skip certain checks in producing the informational product to reduce the workload.
- Transportation of electronic data is timeless. In a computer network, information travels almost at the speed of light; in a manufacturing environment, the transportation of parts is an essential share of the total cycle time, for example think of parts and sub-assemblies that have to be moved from one plant to the other.

From these differences, it can be concluded that there are more degrees of freedom in redesigning business processes that create informational products than physical products. To optimize a manufacturing process, one has to look for redesign opportunities while juggling many physical constraints. For example, concrete parts that have to be assembled must be transported to the same geographical location; by contrast, pieces of information can be put together while their digital representation is stored in different locations. Similarly, where logistics has evolved as a field to deal with the inventory of parts and half-products, the storage of (digital) information is usually a matter of the right amount of hardware. Business process redesign, therefore, is easier to apply in the informational domain. In physical environments, this is more difficult, which results in a greater emphasis on the optimization of planning and the management of inventories.

Exercise 8.4 Consider the following business processes and decide whether they are suitable for being redesigned. Use the properties that distinguish the manufacturing and services domain as a mental checklist to support your choice.

1. Dealing with a customer complaint.
2. Carrying out cardiovascular surgery.
3. The production of a wafer stepping machine.
4. Transporting a package.
5. Providing financial advice on composing a portfolio.
6. Designing a train station.

While the opportunities for process redesign differ across domains, it important to signal this trend: Manufacturing and high-tech organizations that used to focus on the production of physical products are increasingly making money with providing informational services along with their physical products. Therefore, for organizations in this domain process redesign is gaining in importance.

8.1.3 The Devil's Quadrangle

So far, we have not been very specific about the goals behind redesign other than that we said that the purpose is to make business process perform better. Since there are, in fact, various directions for improvement, it is time that we should.

Question What do we want to achieve exactly when a process is redesigned?

A framework that is helpful in answering this question is the *Devil's Quadrangle*, which is depicted in Figure 8.2. This framework is based on the four performance dimensions discussed in Chapter 2, namely time, cost, quality, and flexibility. In an ideal world, a business process redesign *decreases* the time required to handle a case, it *lowers* the required cost of executing the process, it *improves* the quality of the service delivered, and it *increases* the resilience of the business process to deal with variation.

The vexing aspect of the Devil's Quadrangle is this: It suggests that improving a process along one dimension may very well weaken its performance along another.

Fig. 8.2 The Devil's
Quadrangle

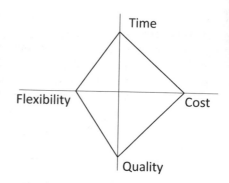

If you were to move one vertex of the quadrangle it may set another one in motion in an undesirable direction. For example, suppose that a process is extended with a reconciliation activity such that the quality of the delivered service is *improved*. This extension may actually *slow down* the delivery time of the service in question, which would be an undesirable side effect. The ominous name of the framework refers to the difficult trade-offs that sometimes have to be made. Awareness of these trade-offs is utterly important to arrive at an effective redesign for a process.

Exercise 8.5 Consider the following redesign acts. Which performance measures are affected by these, either positively or negatively?

1. A new computer application is developed that speeds up the calculation of the maximum loan amount that a given client can be offered.
2. Whenever a quote is needed from a financial provider, a clerk must use a direct messaging system instead of email.
3. By the end of the year, temporary workers are hired and assigned to picking items for fulfilling Christmas orders.
4. A robot carries out part of a surgical procedure, in this way replacing an activity that was previously completely carried out by a surgeon.

While the performance dimensions of the Devil's Quadrangle are helpful to think of the desired effects of business process redesign in general and for a specific business process in particular, they are also useful to think about common approaches to improve business processes. We will devote more attention to this topic when dealing with a specific redesign approach later on, i.e., Heuristic Process Redesign (see Section 8.2.3).

8.1.4 Approaches to Redesign

There is a great variety of books and articles on process redesign. These deal with different methods, present case studies, and suggest management lessons. Since the supply may be a bit overwhelming, the following classification can help us to see the forest for the trees. There are three levels of abstractions to reason about process redesign: methods, techniques, and tools.

Methods sit at the highest level of abstraction in the redesign landscape; they refer to a collection of problem-solving approaches governed by a set of principles and a common philosophy for solving targeted problems. Specific process redesign methods have been proposed by management gurus, consulting firms, and academic scholars, each with its own emphasis. Methods typically stretch out from the early analysis phase of a redesign project until the implementation of the proposed changes.

At the next, lower level of abstraction, a *technique* is defined as a set of precisely described procedures for achieving a standard task. Some techniques that are often encountered to analyze a business process are, for example, fishbone diagramming, Pareto analysis, and cognitive mapping (see Chapter 6). To support the act of rethinking a process, creativity techniques like brainstorming, SCAMPER, Six Thinking Hats, and Delphi are available. In turn, to model and evaluate business processes, other techniques are in use, such as flowcharting, IDEF3, speech act modeling, activity-based costing, time motion studies, Petri nets, role-playing, and simulation, among many others.

At the lowest, most concrete level, a *tool* is defined as a computer software package to support the execution of one or more techniques. The majority of what some would call *process redesign tools* are in fact merely process modeling tools: They support the use of a notation to capture a business process in a diagram, sometimes in a collaborative fashion. A large number of tools are also available for the evaluation of business process models, in particular supporting the technique of simulation (see Chapter 7). Few tools exist to structurally capture knowledge about the redesign directions or to support creativity techniques.

Our foremost concern in this chapter is with *redesign methods*. A general observation that can be made about these is that they tend to be very specific about the preliminary steps in a process redesign project, e.g., the assembly of the project team, and similarly specific towards the end, e.g., how to evaluate the benefits of a newly implemented business process. They less frequently cover details on *how* to turn an existing process into a better performing one. We will refer to this middle part as the *technical challenge* of process redesign. It is, curiously enough, the most underdeveloped part of many redesign methods, but arguably the most important. After all, the start and end of a redesign project are more often than not simply a matter of good project management. Alec Sharp and Patrick McDermott made a witty observation on this phenomenon:

> How to get from the as-is to the to-be [in a process redesign project] isn't explained, so we conclude that during the break, the famous *ATAMO procedure* is invoked ("And Then, A Miracle Occurs").

Our aim with the remaining part of this chapter is to focus on methods that provide concrete guidance for the technical challenge of process redesign. Before we embark on the explanation of a number of these, we need to take a look at the factors that distinguish them from each other.

8.1.5   The Redesign Orbit

We can distinguish a whole spectrum of business process redesign methods. We visualized this spectrum as the *Redesign Orbit* in Figure 8.3. The vertical axis distinguishes the *transactional methods* that are positioned on the left-hand side of the figure, such as Six Sigma, from the *transformational methods* on the right-hand side, such as NESTT. Similarly, the horizontal axis in the Redesign Orbit shows the distinction between the *creative methods* like 7FE at the top side of the figure and the *analytical methods* like Business Process Reengineering, which are below the vertical axis. The inner circle of the Redesign Orbit contains the methods that can be characterized as *inward-looking*, while the methods outside this circle are *outward-looking* in nature. An example of the former is, again, 7FE, while an example of the latter would be Lean. The three respective axes in this Redesign Orbit concern the *ambition* behind the method, the *nature* of the techniques it embodies, and the *perspective* it assumes on the business process. We will now explain these in more detail.

The *ambition* behind a redesign method refers to the magnitude of the change that it seeks to bring about. We distinguish between transactional and transformational methods. A *transactional method* supports the identification of problems or bottlenecks in a process and then helps to resolve these in an incremental way. As such, a transactional method does not challenge the foundations of the existing process, but seeks to improve the overall process gradually. A *transformational method* aims to achieve a breakthrough: change on a grand scale. This type of method disputes the fundamental assumptions and principles behind an existing process and aims to radically break away from these. The distinction between transactional and

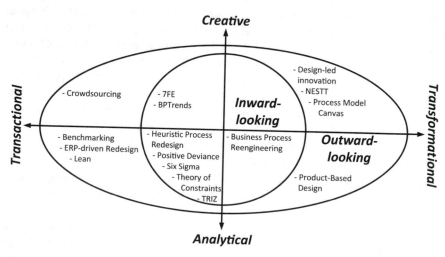

Fig. 8.3   The Redesign Orbit: A spectrum of business process redesign methods

transformational redesign methods can also be framed as the difference between *evolutionary* and *revolutionary* approaches to process redesign.

Redesign methods also differ with respect to their *nature*, with analytical and creative methods as antipoles. An *analytical redesign method* is characterized by a mathematical basis and the use of quantitative techniques. This type of method is also likely to employ tools to support its various stages, in particular to analyze process deficiencies or to generate process alternatives. By contrast, a *creative redesign method* embraces human creativity and ingenuity. It often builds on the advantages that are gained through the phenomenon of *group dynamics*: People stimulate each other to come up with new ideas on how to organize a business process, typically within the setting of a workshop.

A final differentiating factor is the *perspective* that is being taken by the redesign method. An *inward-looking redesign method* assumes the viewpoint of the organization that hosts the business process. With such a method, the concerns and interests of that organization itself take center stage. The information that is gathered about the process also often comes from within the organization itself. Its obvious counterpart is an *outward-looking redesign method*. Such a method takes an outsider's perspective on the process, very often that of the customer or even a third party. In addition, an outward-looking method is typically driven by opportunities and developments that are taking place outside the organization that is redesigning.

It is important to note that the choices along the axes we discussed here are orthogonal. A method, for example, could be transactional, creative, as well as inward-looking; see 7FE in Figure 8.3. Another thing to note is that some of the methods have evolved from others. For example, Heuristic Process Redesign is a method that has been derived from core ideas behind Business Process Reengineering and Lean.

Exercise 8.6 It could be argued that Total Quality Management is a redesign method in its own right (see the "Related Disciplines" box in Chapter 1 on page 7). How would you position this method in the Redesign Orbit with respect to its ambition?

The remainder of this chapter will focus on describing the various redesign methods as included in the Redesign Orbit. We will first discuss the transactional methods and then follow up with the transformational methods.

8.2 Transactional Methods

We will briefly characterize the various transactional methods that exist. Specifically, we will deal with the ones mentioned in Figure 8.3. After this walkthrough, we will discuss two methods in considerable more detail: 7FE and Heuristic Process Redesign.

8.2.1 Overview of Transactional Methods

The transactional part of the Redesign Orbit can be further broken down using the *nature* axis, which distinguishes between creative and analytical methods. Probably the most well-known example of an *analytical* method in this setting is *Six Sigma*, which we encountered before (see the "Related Disciplines" box in Chapter 1 and "Further Readings" in Chapter 6). The core idea behind Six Sigma is that a number of process performance measures is closely monitored for deviations of a norm or target value. Such measures typically relate to resource consumption, cost, cycle time, or customer satisfaction. The goal is to bring back any deviations to a very small fraction in proportion to the desired outcomes.[1] Six Sigma consists of a large collection of techniques to specify measures, quantitatively analyze deviations, and determine the causes for detected deviations. It emphasizes the use of statistical tools to determine the size of deviations. In this way, Six Sigma is rather more focused on the identification and justification of process improvement opportunities than on the generation of concrete redesign measures itself.

Another well-known analytical method is associated with the *Theory of Constraints* (TOC). The TOC holds that any production system is limited in reaching its goals by at least one constraint. For instance, in Section 7.1.5, we identified the cook as the bottleneck in the restaurant. The idea is, therefore, to focus on lifting that constraint to improve the productivity of the overall system. If successful, performance will improve yet another constraint will manifest itself. So, the steps of identifying and lifting a constraint need to be repeated. As such, the TOC puts much emphasis on process improvement as an ongoing process. Examples of constraints that may be relevant in a particular business process context are: the equipment or infrastructure that is available, the skills of the people involved in the process, and the policies that govern the execution of the process. The TOC embraces a set of tools that help project team members to converge on their assessment of performance problems and solutions for these, with much emphasis on the logical connections between the outcomes of these different tools as a basis for validation and decision-making.

Relatively unknown outside East Europe is *TRIZ*, which emerged as a generic theory of problem solving. Its creator, Genrich Altshuller, studied more than 40,000 patents to find out how product innovations take place. His main insight was that innovations follow up on each other through an evolution of *patterns*. For example, one such pattern is that if the possibilities are exhausted to further significantly improve a technical system, then the next step is that it will be included in a super-system, as a part of it. Various researchers have picked up the TRIZ patterns to try and translate them to the improvement of socio-technical systems, services, and, in particular, business processes. REPRO is a good example of a contemporary redesign method that encapsulates various TRIZ principles for the specific purpose

---

[1]The "sigma" (σ) refers to the common symbol used in statistics for a standard deviation, which quantifies the amount of variation.

of generating evolutionary improvements of existing processes [183]. One of its patterns is to let employees generate feedback at any given point in a process, while another pattern concerns the introduction of short-cuts through a process. Methods that are based on TRIZ all share the analytical component of using a set of explicit principles to generate redesign options.

A rather different approach to process redesign aims at the identification and utilization of deviant behavior within organizational contexts. The assumption is that individuals or groups sometimes intentionally behave differently than what is considered the norm, yet with remarkable positive effects. Such *Positive Deviance* can be used as a blueprint for spreading that behavior, hopefully with similarly positive effects. It was established, for example, that in the setting of bakery trading departments in a large retail organization some of these strategically minimized the offer at the end of the day in order to minimize waste, while this was against company policy [114]. A Positive Deviance approach may build on either qualitative (interviews and observations) or quantitative techniques (statistics). What is crucial is that a reliable link is established between the intent, the actual behavior, and the desired outcome. So, similarly to Six Sigma, it is important to precisely define relevant measures and establish the links between these.

Six Sigma, TOC, TRIZ, and Positive Deviance methods all have in common that they strongly focus on the existing process in an organization as a starting point. This is a clear indication of an *inward-looking* perspective. This also holds for Heuristic Process Redesign, which we will be discussing in more detail in Section 8.2.3. Of course, to some extent all the methods mentioned take into account some influences from the external environment. Yet, other methods are *fundamentally* outward-looking. We will now discuss Benchmarking, ERP-driven Redesign, and Lean, which all assume a fundamental outward-looking perspective.

Benchmarking in the context of BPM is a collective term for a range of approaches. All of these aim to compare competing designs for a particular process and to enable a choice between these according to the criteria that are most relevant for a firm. In principle, organizations can carry out a benchmarking study themselves. A case in point is the Dutch CoSeLoG project, which pitted together five Dutch municipalities that wished to compare their business processes with respect to their design and performance.[2] It is more common that the comparison is done by a consultancy company, IT solution provider or standardization consortium, which then develops *standardized* versions of business processes for a particular industry. These standardized processes are then presented as *blueprints*, *best practices*, *industry prints*, or *reference models*. Examples are the Information Technology Infrastructure Library (ITIL) for IT service management and the Supply-Chain Operations Reference model (SCOR) for supply chain management (previously mentioned in Chapter 2). The attraction of such standardized processes for individual firms is that they may decrease the efforts to develop new processes or to change existing ones, while there is also the suggestion that the pre-packaged

---

[2]http://www.win.tue.nl/coselog/wiki.

process designs are in some sense superior to what individual firms can come up with. Since these designs represent to some extent how an industry is taking care of certain crucial processes, they are rather conventional in their set-up. This also explains why a benchmarking approach should be considered as *transactional* in nature.

A specific variation of the benchmarking approach is one where a process redesign effort is *driven by an enterprise IT system*. Such a system supposes that important business processes take on a particular form. This is, in more specific terms, the case when an organization starts the implementation of an ERP system, such as SAP, Oracle ERP, or Microsoft Dynamics ERP. An ERP system is a standardized software system, based on an integrated database, which consists of several modules that support specific business functions, such as purchasing, finance, and human resource management. The key insight for process redesign is that the logic underpinning the modules of an ERP system already suppose to quite an extent how the business processes they aim to support are organized. This logic is often grounded in the vendor's conception of how business processes in certain industries are typically organized. This implies that organizations adopting an ERP system in fact also accept the vendor's view of how certain business processes should be organized. This is the link to the benchmarking approach we just discussed. As to the flexibility that firms have to adapt ERP systems to their specific preferences, notable progress is being made through making such systems more "process-aware" (see Chapter 10 for a discussion on this concept). It still seems fair to say that the majority of efforts that an organization needs to make to implement an ERP system relate to the alignment of that system's functionalities and the characteristics of the organization itself.

The last analytical redesign method that is left to be discussed on the transactional side of the Redesign Orbit is *Lean*. We already briefly touched on this philosophy in our "Related Disciplines" box in Chapter 1 on page 7. Lean is concerned with improving business activities (1) on the overall enterprise level as well as (2) on the more operational business process level. The main tool for the former is value-stream mapping, which aims at capturing an entire value chain. This is highly similar to the end-to-end process concept that we saw before in Chapter 2. A core Lean guideline is that such a value stream must show how value is generated from the perspective of a customer. Mapping value streams serves the purpose of identifying dependencies between processes and, if possible, shaping them into so-called Just-In-Time dependencies. It diminishes inventories when raw materials or sub-assemblies are handed over from one process to the other in such a fashion. On the operational business process level, Lean's main emphasis is on the elimination of waste (see Section 6.2). In a Lean initiative, individual process activities are assessed on whether they add value or do not, once again considering the perspective of the customer. In fact, the customers' interests are so central in the Lean philosophy that "the voice of the customer" (VOC) has become a standing term. This also explains that we consider the overall method as outward-looking. It should also be noted that Lean principles to improve processes are often used in succession to the process assessment activities of Six Sigma, even to the extent that this has evolved into the overarching *Lean Six Sigma* method.

We now turn our attention to the *creative* counterparts of the transactional methods that we discussed so far. We have seen that methods like Six Sigma, TRIZ, and benchmarking employ all kinds of tools, involve statistics, and are strongly rationalized in that they aggregate information collected within an entire industry. Compared to this analytical angle, the more conventional approach to process redesign for many organizations is to unleash the creativity of people. This in particular relates to the people who are already working within the setting of internal business processes or otherwise hold deep knowledge of such processes. In Figure 8.3, we included two methods that are representative for a wide variety of such methods: *7FE* and *BPTrends*. These involve similar steps and a similar logic to redesign processes. Essentially, they aim to bring together people with knowledge of an existing business process during a series of workshops. Typically, such people represent the various business functions and roles that are relevant in a particular business context. Under the guidance of a professional facilitator, workshop participants identify process weaknesses, question the assumptions underlying the process, and then generate ideas to change aspects of that process for the better. To stimulate people to come up with ideas, creativity techniques such as brainstorming, SCAMPER, and group ideation are applied. Workshop participants may scribble down ideas on Post-it notes, which can then be visualized to all participants on whiteboards, shuffled around to identify synergies or similarities with other ideas, or put aside if they do not find sufficient support. All major consultancy companies have developed their own proprietary versions of this type of redesign method, which they offer to their clients, along with the facilitators that are versed in applying these. To get a more profound understanding of this type of method, we will be looking at the different steps of 7FE in more detail in Section 8.2.2.

Both 7FE and BPTrends are distinctly inward-looking with their emphasis on engaging professionals that already play a role within a targeted business process. Interestingly, through the advent of *crowdsourcing* and *open innovation*, it has become feasible for firms to more easily than before tap into the skills and knowledge of people outside their organizational borders. This may affect how process redesign is taking place, even to the extent that this at some point may lead to an *outward-looking* variant of a transactional, creative redesign method. While no full-fledged methods in this sphere yet exist, it can be imagined how crowds of customers or suppliers may help to identify process weaknesses and generate improvement ideas. Experiments in healthcare settings, for example, have already identified the potential of soliciting the ideas of patients to improve the non-clinical parts of treatments. Also, airlines actively scan social media to identify structural performance issues. Of course, it is likely that the mobilization of external knowledge and viewpoints will need to be combined with internal efforts to change any process for the better. That such people-centered methods will shift the attention from the internal perspective to that of outsiders still makes them distinctly *outward-looking*.

Exercise 8.7 Are you familiar with a transactional redesign method that is not included in the Orbit? If so, what other method does it resemble most?

This ends our discussion of the characteristics of the transactional redesign methods within the Redesign Orbit. As announced, we will now be looking at two transactional redesign methods in more detail.

8.2.2 7FE

Jeston and Nelis' *7FE* is essentially a framework for BPM projects or even BPM programs, which involve multiple BPM projects. The 7FE framework[3] consists of a number of phases to bring a BPM project to a successful end. This ranges all the way from the formulation of the organization strategy at the start, through phases that involve the composition of the project team and an analysis of the current situation, towards the redesign of a process and its final implementation. In this sense, 7FE is considerably more extensive than what we refer to in this chapter as a redesign method. Nonetheless, the specific *Innovate* phase of 7FE covers what we referred to as the *technical challenge* of process redesign. 7FE explicitly underpins this phase by the view that workshops are the best way to develop new process options and alternatives, which puts it in the *creative* sphere of the Redesign Orbit. It is this part of the framework that we will focus on now.

There are roughly three stages that can be distinguished in the 7FE process redesign method:

1. *Prepare*: In this stage, all necessary inputs for the workshops are collected. Specifically, it needs to be clarified (a) how the redesign project and the new process link with the organizational strategy, (b) what the goals are for the process as well as the associated performance measures, (c) what constraints are placed on the redesign options, and (d) what the desired timeframe is for the redesigned process to get implemented. With respect to creating an understanding of the position of the business process in its organizational context it makes sense to consult the process architecture (see Chapter 2). From the perspective of managing stakeholder expectations, it is also wise to gather information from external stakeholders on how they would preferably like to interact with the process in future. Finally, it may also make sense to make an inventory of state-of-the-art technologies that may be relevant for automating (parts of) the business process in question.
2. *Generate*: During the actual workshops, the emphasis is on the generation of ideas for a redesign of the business process in focus. 7FE insists on the incorporation of an external, independent facilitator to lead these workshops. In this way, it is expected that a neutral, "baggage-free" view on the process is maintained. The other participants should be recruited from those who have an intimate knowledge of the process. If the time frame for the redesign extends

---

[3]The name is derived from four foundational concepts for this framework that start with an F and three that start with an E: seven in total.

across 24 months, it is also important to include senior executives that can make decisions about strategic issues. The character of this stage is to first generate a range of ideas, after which convergence and consensus is pursued. Preferably, this leads to one or more scenarios for an improved process.

3. *Validate*: Once the scenarios have been determined, it becomes important to test these on their effectiveness and feasibility. In 7FE, the preferred technique to assess these elements is the use of simulation (see Chapter 7). The most attractive of the generated scenarios should then be further assessed to determine whether they meet all stakeholder needs. Once again, this is an activity that can be carried out in a workshop setting. At this stage, it becomes relevant to include participants with expertise in compliance, IT, operational risks, and auditing, such that it can be determined whether the redesign accommodates concerns from these areas as well. A final technique to assess the quality of a redesign scenario, especially one that relies on automation, is to develop a prototype of the process. An alternative is to carry out virtual walkthroughs of the intended, new process. The redesign effort ends with documenting the process, the motivation behind it, and the results of the various evaluation actions.

We will now focus the presentation of 7FE on the various techniques that are proposed to stimulate workshop participants in the creation of redesign options, which is situated in the *Generate* stage that we just described. They relate to facilitation, the customer perspective, and triggers.

The *facilitator* has a special role in the execution of the workshop and is to a large extent responsible for creating the right climate for the generation of ideas. The first objective for the facilitator is to prevent any judgment from workshop participants during the initial part of the *Generate* stage. Only in a further phase it becomes important to start filtering out ideas that are infeasible or impractical. Jeston and Nelis specifically recommend the facilitator to:

- Ask lots of "what if" and "why this" questions,
- Not accept what he is or she is told (the first time),
- Look for the second 'right' answer,
- Regularly change the question and come it at from a different direction,
- Challenge the rules of the process,
- Rely on intuition.

Exercise 8.8 The specific recommendations that are mentioned here strongly resemble those of a group creativity technique called *brainstorming*. While this approach is quite popular in industry for problem-solving, it has its drawbacks too. Can you think of any?

From the list, it becomes clear that a facilitator needs to rely on vast experience to successfully apply these principles.

7FE suggests that a good way for getting workshop participants in the mood to generate ideas is to have them model the process to be redesigned from a *customer's perspective*. In other words, they should identify when customers interact with the process, how the interaction takes place, what the information is that is being exchanged, etc. This may be quite a different perspective from what the workshop participants are accustomed to when thinking about a process. After all, a customer is often not interested in what exactly goes on within an organization, while process participants do carry out different steps that do not involve direct contact with the client. Looking at the process through a customer's eyes may enable workshop participants to identify flaws or inefficiencies within the business process that they would otherwise overlook. Additional to this exercise, it may also be useful to compare what a costumer would experience when interacting with a competitor of the organization that the workshop participants work for.

The recommendation to take a customer's perspective on a business process is highly related to the identification of the *customer journey*. This has become one of the most widely used tools in service design, where it also includes the feelings, motivations, and issues that customers may have about the so-called *touch points* with an organization. It is clear that these latter types of information may not always be directly available in the setting of a 7FE workshop, although this may be information that could be collected up front, e.g., through customer surveys.

Another similarity that comes to mind in this context is that of the *mystery shopper*. This is a technique used in market research where a specifically hired professional performs tasks such as purchasing a product, asking questions, registering complaints, or behaving in a certain way to collect insights in how an establishment performs. That a walkthrough of a process is useful for the purpose of understanding its inefficiencies will also become apparent in Exercise 8.15 (page 333).

Another way to stimulate the stream of ideas is to guide participants to *problematic elements* of a business process as well as *generic solutions* that may be applicable for the business process under consideration. In 7FE, both problems and solutions can be used as *triggers* for generating a better process design.

An example of a typical *problem* that could be used as a trigger is the concept of *handoffs*. These concern the points where transfers of cases take place from one organizational unit or role to the other. At handoffs, the tension is the strongest between the traditional, functional orientation of an organization and a horizontal, process-oriented view on it. After all, the goals of the independent departments themselves may not be conducive to properly coordinating the work between those departments. For instance, in many organizations people from the sales department close a deal, which needs to be registered and fulfilled by people from other departments. It then makes sense to investigate how much time it takes before information on the closed deal is picked up by the other process participants. If this consumes too much time, this can be a specific issue that may trigger improvements to the overall process. For this example specifically, workshop participants could then propose that the transfer of information from a sales rep to an administrative clerk be improved by integrating the IT systems of the separate departments.

An example of a trigger in the form of a *generic solution* is to let workshop participants consider the use of a particular technology, such as RFID (Radio Frequency Identification) technology. RFID allows for an economically more reasonable way of tracking the whereabouts of important physical elements in a business process than many older approaches. RFID may be useful if inefficiencies of the process seem related to items getting lost and considerable effort is needed to locate them again. Also, this type of technology may help to provide customers or suppliers with more accurate information on the progress of the work that is relevant to them. In 7FE, a range of other examples of generic solutions are mentioned. They are, in fact, to a large extent similar to some of the redesign heuristics that form the core of the redesign method we will be looking at next: Heuristic Process Redesign.

8.2.3 Heuristic Process Redesign

In contrast to 7FE, the use of workshops is not an important ingredient for the *Heuristic Process Redesign* method. Rather, the emphasis is on the systematic consideration of a wide range of redesign principles, which makes it an *analytical* instead of a *creative* approach. These *redesign heuristics* are similar in nature to some of the triggers we have seen in 7FE. However, their number is much larger than the principles that can be found within 7FE and comparable redesign methods. This wide range of heuristics is, in fact, where the strength of Heuristic Process Redesign lies.

For the explanation of Heuristic Process Redesign, we will again focus on the *technical challenge* of generating a new process design. We will also provide pointers to other parts of the book here. First, we will outline the stages and then turn to its most important ingredient in more detail, i.e., the redesign heuristics that are important to the *Design* stage.

1. *Initiate*: In the first stage, the redesign project is set up. There are various organizational measures that have to be taken, e.g., setting up the project team, but from a technical perspective the most important goals are: (a) to create an understanding of the existing situation and (b) to set the performance goals for the redesign project. For (a), the modeling techniques that have been discussed in Chapters 3 and 4 are useful, as well as the analysis techniques explained in Chapters 6 and 7 to gain an understanding of performance issues, bottlenecks, and improvement opportunities. To arrive at a clearer picture for (b), the Devil's Quadrangle that has been discussed in this chapter is a great asset.

2. *Design*: Given the outcomes of the initiate stage, the design stage makes use of a fixed list of redesign heuristics to determine potential improvement actions on the existing process. For each of the performance goals, there needs to be a reflection by the project team on relevant heuristics that may be applied. A redesign heuristic is desirable to apply if it helps to attain the desired performance improvement of the process under consideration. After it has been determined which redesign heuristics may be helpful, it makes sense to see whether clusters of these can be formed. For some of the heuristics it may make sense to be applied together, for others this is not the case. For example, if you decide to automate a certain activity, it makes no sense to empower the resource that initially carried out that activity. On basis of relevant clusters, a set of scenarios can be generated,

each of which describes which redesign heuristics are applied in this scenario and, importantly, how this is done. For example, if the heuristic to automate an activity is applied it needs to be specified which activities are subjected to it. The scenarios, therefore, should be seen as *alternatives* for the process redesign.

3. *Evaluate*: This is the stage where the different redesign scenarios as developed in the previous stage need to be evaluated. This evaluation can be done in a qualitative way, e.g., employing the techniques from Chapter 6, or in a quantitative way, see Chapter 7. In many practical settings, a combination of the two is used where a panel of experts assesses the attractiveness of the various scenarios and where simulation studies are used to underpin the choice for one particular scenario to be developed further, potentially all the way to implementing it. An outcome of the evaluation stage may also be that none of the scenarios are attractive to pursue or are seen as powerful enough to establish the desirable performance improvement. Depending on the exact outcome, the decision may be to adjust the performance goals, to step back to the design stage, or to drop the redesign project altogether.

The description of the stages are here described as separate ones, but in practice they will be executed in highly iterative and overlapping ways.

We will now focus the discussion of the Heuristic Process Redesign method on how to employ heuristics during the *design* stage.

Redesign Heuristics

The main component of the design stage is the methodological evaluation of a set of *redesign heuristics*. Redesign heuristics can be seen as rules of thumb for deriving a different process from an existing one. The full set we consider in this book consists of 29 redesign heuristics, which can be found in Appendix A. All heuristics are based on historic redesign projects, where they were applied successfully to generate redesign scenarios. The reader who is interested in the derivation of this set is referred to [135].

During the design stage, for each of the set performance goals, an evaluation of the set of redesign heuristics should take place. This evaluation must focus on those heuristics that are known to bring about improvements along the particular dimension of the performance goal in question. For example, if the performance goal is to reduce the average cycle time of a particular business process by 15%, then that performance dimension would be *time*. For each of the redesign heuristics, it is known to which performance dimensions of the Devil's Quadrangle it generally makes a positive contribution, based on what was accomplished with that redesign heuristic established on previous occasions. While that may be no guarantee for a successful application in a new context, it is nonetheless a good starting point.

To explain how this may work, consider the selection of redesign heuristics in Figure 8.4.

Time	Cost	Quality	Flexibility
Parallellism Case-based work	Activity elimination Empower	Empower Triage	Flexible assignment Centralization

Fig. 8.4 A selection of redesign heuristics

For each of the four performance dimensions of the Devil's Quadrangle, two sample redesign heuristics are listed in Figure 8.4. These are the following:

Parallelism: "Put activities in parallel". Activities in a business process are often ordered in a strictly sequential way even though there is no good reason for doing so. Some activities may well be carried out in an arbitrary order or even simultaneously. By allowing a less restrictive choice on the order in which activities are executed, a business process can be carried out faster.

Case-based work: "Remove batch-processing and periodic activities". Notable sources of delays in business processes exist where individual cases (a) get piled up in a batch that is only processed once all its items are available or (b) are slowed down by periodic triggers, e.g., a computer system is only available at one specific slot during the day. Getting rid of such constraints is in general a good way to significantly speed up a process.

Activity elimination: "Eliminate unnecessary activities". Over time, processes get clogged up with activities that were useful at some point but have lost their purpose or rationale. Control activities, i.e., activities that are incorporated in a process to fix problems, are prime examples of non-value adding activities. Getting rid of unnecessary activities is an effective way to reduce the cost of handling a case.

Empower: "Give workers decision-making authority". In traditional settings, people have to authorize the outcomes of activities that have been performed by others. If workers are empowered to take decisions autonomously, this may render much of the work of middle managers superfluous, in this way reducing cost significantly.

Triage: "Split an activity into alternative versions". By creating alternative versions of an activity, it is possible to better deal with the variety of cases that need to be processed. An alternative activity essentially pursues the high-level goal of the original activity but is either geared specifically to a sub-category of cases that are being encountered (e.g., orders of special customers vs. all customers) or exploits the characteristics of the resource class that is assigned to it (e.g., senior clerks vs. all clerks). By aligning work more specifically to the properties of particular cases, the quality of work delivered improves.

Case assignment: "Let participants perform as many steps as possible". If someone carries out an activity, then that person becomes acquainted at some level with the case for which the work is done. That knowledge accumulates with each activity that is done for the same case. By making one participant the preferred resource for any work that needs to be carried out for a particular case, this knowledge can be leveraged to deliver a high standard of work.

Flexible assignment: "Keep generic participants free for as long as possible". Suppose that an activity can be executed by either of two available participants, then it should be assigned to the most specialized person. In this way, the likelihood to commit the free, more generally qualified participant to another work package is maximal. The advantage of this heuristic is that an organization stays flexible with respect to assigning work.

Centralization: "Let geographically dispersed resources act as if they are centralized". This heuristic is explicitly aimed at exploiting the benefits of a Business Process Management System (BPMS) (see Chapter 10). After all, if a BPMS takes care of assigning work to process participants it becomes less relevant where these resources are located geographically. In this way, resources can be committed more flexibly.

Let us now look at how this may work. Imagine the hypothetical car rental agency *Frequenz*, which wishes to improve the business process that takes care of collecting rental cars on their return. Their interest is to improve that process from both a time and quality perspective. The existing business process involves four major steps, which are carried out in the following order for all returned cars: (a) an interview with the tenant on specific circumstances during the rental period; (b) an inspection of the exterior of the returned car; (c) an inspection of the interior of the returned car; (d) the completion of the customer invoice on the basis of the outcomes of the previous activities.

To improve the timeliness of the business process, *Frequenz* would need to consider the parallelism and case-based work heuristics first. Indeed, the agency may want to consider carrying out activities (a), (b), and (c) simultaneously (parallelism). No constraints can be lifted through the application of the case-based work heuristic, though; this heuristic is not applicable in this situation.

From a quality perspective, the triage and case assignment heuristics are the first relevant heuristics to look at. On reflection, it may indeed make sense to develop specific versions of activities (b) and (c) for *off-road* vehicles, because they generally suffer more during rental contracts; in this way, a more thorough inspection of returned off-road vehicles can take place, improving the quality of activities (b) and (c). It may also be beneficial to have one participant carry out all steps (case assignment), such that for example all information gathered during (a) can be used to improve the thoroughness of activities (b) and (c), as well as the completeness of (d). *Frequenz*, however, realizes how this may interfere with their earlier decision to carry out these steps simultaneously to gain time. On reflection, the agency prefers to not implement this heuristic in favor of the parallelism heuristic.

Note how in this example both a reflection on the heuristics individually and the clustering of feasible heuristics has taken place. These are essential elements of the *design* stage of the Heuristic Process Redesign method. In the above case, only one scenario is generated. What also becomes clear from the example is that it may be necessary to gather specific insights into the process itself, the circumstances under which it operates, and its historic performance.

Exercise 8.9   In recognition of the Devil's Quadrangle, each heuristic can also have negative side-effects when applied. Can you imagine what negative impact the *Frequenz* redesign scenario may have on the performance of the rental car collection process in terms of Cost and Flexibility?

This ends our description of Heuristic Process Redesign specifically and our discussion of transactional process redesign methods on a more general level. The next section will look into transformational methods for process redesign.

8.3   Transformational Methods

In the same way as we did for the transactional redesign methods, we will provide an overview of existing transformational methods. We will deal with all the examples that are mentioned in Figure 8.3. After this walkthrough, we will discuss three methods in more detail, focusing again on the *technical challenge* of redesign. The methods we will discuss are: NESTT, Business Process Reengineering, and Product-Based Design.

8.3.1   Overview of Transformational Methods

What can be immediately noticed in Figure 8.3 is that fewer methods populate the transformational, right-hand side of the Redesign Orbit than the transactional, left-hand side of this figure. This characterizes the state of the art quite well, which may be a bit surprising given how process redesign started out. What is generally considered as the first call for the redesign of business processes and the first attempt to identify enduring patterns for this endeavor is known as *Business Process Reengineering*, as pioneered by the late Michael Hammer [59]. One of the core concepts in this method, as we will discuss in more detail in Section 8.3.2, is that it assumes a *clean slate* for the design of a process. As Hammer put it:

> For many, reengineering is the only hope for breaking away from the antiquated processes that threaten to drag them down.

Such a sentiment clearly embraces a breakthrough type of change, a transformation in fact. In other words, process redesign started out as purely transformational through the advent of Business Process Reengineering, but over time transactional redesign methods have become more prevalent and more popular than the revolutionary approach Hammer evangelized.

Exercise 8.10 Can you think of a reason why transactional methods for redesign have become more popular than transformational methods?

Despite the noted imbalance between the two halves of the Redesign Orbit, transformational methods are indeed being applied by organizations and new methods do appear regularly on the horizon. Interestingly, a number of these methods have actually become popular *without* a particular focus on business processes at first. After an initial focus on entire organizations or products, process-specific applications of such methods were developed. A good example is *Design-led Innovation* (or *Design-driven Innovation*). This foundational method aims to provide organizations with an understanding of the deep emotional ties that consumers develop with their products. Its basic tenet is that people are not only served by the form and function of a product, but also through the *experience* its usage invokes. Based on this understanding, organizations may pursue innovations that customers do not expect, but which they eventually grow passionate about. The method was developed by Roberto Verganti [184], who over a period of 10 years studied successful design companies, such as Apple, Nintendo, and Alessi. The method goes through stages of listening (gaining knowledge on what people desire), interpreting (combining user knowledge with a firm's capabilities), and addressing (preparing customers and supporting socio-cultural change). Crucial aspects of the method are: (1) the aim for radical innovation, which explains the *transformational* characterization of the method, (2) the exploitation of the network of outsiders to gain that crucial understanding in the listening stage, which makes the method specifically *outward-looking*, and (3) its reliance on the ingenuity of designers, scientists, and artists, which gives it its *creative* flavor. Particularly those business processes where customer interaction is a crucial element are good candidates to be overhauled through Design-led Innovation: new ways of how an organization interacts with its clients may contribute to a more meaningful experience.

Exercise 8.11 Can you come up with examples of business processes where customer interaction is crucial?

Another example of an inspiring model for a method to redesign business processes in a transformative way is the *Business Model Canvas*, as developed by Alexander Osterwalder and Yves Pigneur [122]. The Business Model Canvas is a visual chart that shows how an organization's value proposition relates to its infrastructure, customers, and financial structure. It is particularly valuable to develop and assess new value propositions because it supports the strategic evaluation of important organizational assets. Inspired by this way of thinking, the so-called Process Model Canvas has been developed that allows firms to reason about the value proposition behind their business processes in a similarly visual way. The *Process Model Canvas*[4] is shown in Figure 8.5.

As can be seen, the canvas shows blank spaces under the various headings, which are to be discussed and filled in during a workshop session. The key way

---

[4] See www.processmodelcanvas.org.

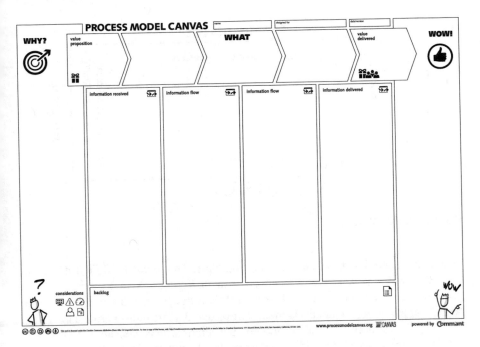

Fig. 8.5 The Process Model Canvas

of using the canvas is to start reasoning from the *wow!* factor behind a business process (see the right-hand side of the figure), i.e., what people in such a workshop think would truly impress customers. This vision is then used to determine *what* is necessary to establish this effect in terms of the major steps in the business process and the information that is required to support those steps. The final connection that needs to be made is that from the business process to the strategic focus of the firm, the *why?* on the left-hand side. In this way, the method reasons from the expectations of the customer (*outward-looking*) to create a breakthrough process design (*transformative*) through a workshop-based use of a visual aid (*creative*).

Exercise 8.12 What do you find to be the key similarity between designing processes according to the principles of Design-led innovation and the Process Model Canvas?

The final redesign method that is part of the same intersection as Design-led Innovation and the Process Model Canvas is *NESTT*, a recent addition to the spectrum. The method has been developed at Queensland University of Technology. The NESTT acronym captures the four main stages of the method: Navigate, Expand, Strengthen, and Tune/Take-off. Its defining feature is how participants in a workshop setting use the spatial affordances of a dedicated room (see Figure 8.6).

Between 8 to 10 people use the four walls and the floor of the room to visualize and address different viewpoints on a business process. They start at formulating a vision on the new process, which may be inspired by, for example, vendors

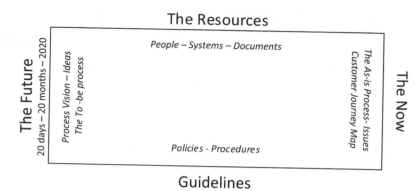

Fig. 8.6 The NESTT room

of new technologies or benchmark organizations. This gives NESTT a dominant *outward-looking* perspective. As can be seen in Figure 8.6, that future vision is given shape over three different time horizons: 20 days from the initiation of the NESTT application, 20 months from that time, and 3 years (considering a start time in 2017). By committing to this vision, the participants determine how to overcome problems and seize opportunities to realize that vision, while using insights from the existing process (the Now), available and required resources, as well as relevant procedures. The creative element is strong in this method, since it exploits a range of techniques to help people design a new process together. Although it is important that there is an outcome in the short term, NESTT is indeed a transformative method because of the long-term perspective it also fosters.

Exercise 8.13 What do you find the key similarity between designing processes according to the Process Model Canvas on the one hand and the principles of NESTT on the other? What is different?

This discussion ends the overview of transformational redesign methods. As can be seen in the Redesign Orbit, the intersection of inward-looking and transformational methods is actually empty. This signals a wide-held belief that true transformations hardly emanate from reasoning from an internal perspective only. This does not mean that the internal perspective is completely ignored, of course (consider NESTT, for example). What is striking is that all transformational methods we discussed so far are *creative* in nature. This is, however, not a universal feature. There are two transformational methods in the Redesign Orbit that are not discussed so far: Business Process Reengineering and Product-Based Design. We will be looking at these methods, which are both analytical in nature, in the coming sections.

8.3.2 Business Process Reengineering

Business Process Reengineering as a concept was coined by Michael Hammer at the start of the 1990s. This point in time is considered by many as the true start of process redesign methods and even that of Business Process Management as a discipline. Hammer had been studying a number of businesses that were under huge pressure but managed to survive and even thrive. The most famous case study is that of the Ford Motor Company, which we presented on page 11 in Chapter 1.

There are three main insights that Hammer distilled from his observations. First of all, no successful organization relies on piecemeal improvement of what was already carried out. Rather, strong ambition leads to huge rewards. Secondly, while information technology is a crucial asset in redesigning business processes, it is necessary to go beyond pure automation of what is already being done. Hammer summarized these two insights:

> We have the tools to do what we need to do. Information technology offers many options for reorganizing work. But our imaginations must guide our decisions about technology— not the other way around. We must have the boldness to imagine taking 78 days out of an 80-day turnaround time, cutting 75% of overhead, and eliminating 80% of errors. These are not unrealistic goals. If managers have the vision, reengineering will provide a way.

The third of Hammer's insights is that organizations need to break away from a set of ingrained patterns of organizing work that prevent business processes from being carried out in an integrated, cross-functional way. Instead, a set of new principles need to be adopted. The reliance on such a set of clearly defined principles, in contrast to what a group of people comes up with, is what makes Business Process Reengineering a decidedly *analytical* method. At the same time, it is mostly *inward-looking* as it still operates within the scope and context of the existing process it aims to overhaul.

Unlike the transactional methods we discussed in detail in Sections 8.2.2 and 8.2.3, the principles of Business Process Reengineering are not embedded in an explicit, staged view on how to carry out process redesign. This can be explained by the pioneering nature of the method. At the time of its inception, it was more important to convince people of the viability of redesign itself than to exactly prescribe it. The principles are, nonetheless, clearly linked to the *technical challenge* of creating a new process design. We will now take a look at a number of these principles.

The first ingrained yet antiquated pattern that Hammer identified is that many organizations collect the same information repeatedly, even to the extent that different departments and units use their own requirements and forms for obtaining the same information. Even though this may have made sense in times when it was difficult to share and distribute data within a single organization, nowadays database technology, networking facilities, and cloud solutions make this information gathering behavior obsolete.

The positive counter principle is to make sure that information is captured fresh, at the moment it is produced, and at the source by the stakeholder who is producing it. This information needs to be made available to others who are in need of and authorized for its reuse, principally through a shared data store. This will render superfluous sending documents or emails around with the data produced in the process. Equally important, it will prevent clients from getting annoyed being asked for the same information time and again. Anybody who has been through some type of mildly complex procedure in a hospital may recognize this phenomenon.

The second problem that Hammer identified is that workers who are producing a particular piece of valuable information cannot follow up on that information, either because they are not allowed to do so or lack the facilities. This arrangement particularly reflects the belief that people at lower organizational levels are incapable of acting on information they generate. As a result, many organizations end up with units that do nothing else than collecting and processing information that other departments created. Needless to say, this creates inefficiencies and introduces delays.

To counter this problem, the second principle behind Business Process Reengineering is that information processing work, i.e., work that involves capturing or processing information, is to be integrated with the real work where this information is produced. Clearly, this may require a different level of trust and may also involve training people to take on more types of work. What it may bring is that work flows much more smoothly.

The third, undesirable situation as found within many organizations is that hyperspecialized departments have emerged. These handle everything that looks like "their work". In this way, one department ends up being the customer of a sister department for something they desire themselves, could in principle take care of themselves, but are not longer allowed to do so. Think, for example, of a group who wishes to purchase office items but can only do so through dealing with its specialized purchasing department, which is also taking care of purchasing the expensive raw materials that the company uses for its main products. While a centralized approach pursues the benefits of specialization and economies of scale, many internal processes are slow and bureaucratic. The main reason behind this is that the unit that takes care of a process is not the prime beneficiary of its outcomes and may find it has more important things to do.

In a setting where process participants and even clients can be supported by data and technology to accomplish their objectives, it makes sense to allow, at least in a number of situations, that workers who need something should take care of it. Those who have an interest in the output of a process should not only participate in it but potentially drive it all the way. Another way of looking at it is that according to this principle work can be pushed to the actor that has the best incentive to do it, which may positively influence the timeliness and quality of what is accomplished.

The last ingrained pattern of many organizations that they get rid of is the sharp distinction between those who do the work from those who monitor the work and make decisions about it. As Hammer puts it:

The tacit assumption is that the people actually doing the work have neither the time nor the inclination to monitor and control it and that they lack the knowledge and scope to make decisions about it. The entire hierarchical management structure is built on this assumption.

As a result of this pattern, a surplus of accountants, auditors, and supervisors are in place in organizations to check, record, and monitor work. Needless to say that these people induce delays and incur considerable cost.

The principle that is to replace this anti-pattern is to put every decision point in a process preferably at the place where work is performed. Specifically, this relates to work that produces the information that is required to make the decision. In addition, it is a call to seamlessly integrate all control activities into activities that form the core tasks of a process. The counterpart of this is, of course, that process participants have to be provided with the information they need to make the decisions themselves. The importance of this principle is that back-and-forth handoffs between process workers and process managers can be replaced by well-designed controls in the hands of empowered process workers.

Exercise 8.14 Consider the Ford case study described in Section 1.3.2 (page 11) again. Which of the above principles have been applied?

The initial set of principles were just the start of the Business Process Reengi-neering wave of the early 1990s. Hammer himself added new ones and gradually developed additional insights into the success behind redesign programs. The last and rather recent contribution in this line is an instrument for organizations to assess their level of maturity in managing processes. In its turn, Business Process Reengineering influenced the development of many other methods. This can be seen back, for example, in the heuristics that form the core of Heuristic Process Redesign (see Section 8.2.3).

We will now take a look at the last remaining transformational redesign method: Product-Based Design.

8.3.3 Product-Based Design

The *Product-Based Design* method was developed at Eindhoven University of Technology at the start of the century [134]. It is *analytical* in nature since it relies on a formal, almost purely algorithmic way of developing a new business process. The objective is to completely overhaul a process, which puts it in the *transformative* sphere. To explain why it is *outward-looking*, one needs to consider the artifact that takes center stage in this method: It is the *product* that a business process aims to deliver. The characteristics of that particular product (or the service) are used to, in fact, *reason back* to determine what the process should look like. Think of it as follows: If you like to produce a red, electric car with four wheels, you are certain that the production process at some stage must involve the production or purchasing of a chassis, that there is a step needed to assemble four wheels to that chassis, that you will need to insert a battery at some point, and that you will need to paint the vehicle (if you cannot get your hands on red parts, that is). Perhaps you are not sure in what order these things need to take place exactly, but you can at least identify some logical dependencies. For example, you would be better off painting the vehicle *after* you acquired the chassis.

The idea behind Product-Based Design is that by *ignoring* the existing process and purely considering the features of the product, it becomes feasible to develop the leanest, most performative process possible. While Product-Based Design is more ambitious in nature than transactional redesign methods, it is also more limited in its application scope. It has been specifically developed to design processes that produce *informational* products, e.g., decisions, proposals, documents, permits, etc. It is this informational product that is analyzed and laid down in a *product data model*. There is a striking resemblance between this model and the *bill-of-material* (BOM) as used in the manufacturing domain. The product data model is the main vehicle that a process designer uses to determine the best process structure to create and deliver that product. Given that there are, in general, multiple ways to produce an informational product, Product-Based Design discloses insights into all of these possibilities.

The most important stages of Product-Based Design are the following:

1. Scoping: In this initial phase the business process is selected that will be subjected to the redesign. The performance targets for this process are identified, as well as the limitations to be taken into consideration for the final design.
2. Analysis: A study of the product specification leads to its decomposition into information elements and their logical dependencies in the form of a *product data model*. The existing business process—if any—is diagnosed to retrieve data that is both significant for designing the new business process and for the sake of evaluation.
3. Design: Based on the redesign performance objectives, the product data model, and estimated performance figures, one or more process designs are derived that best match with the design goals.
4. Evaluation: The process designs are verified, validated with end users, and their estimated performance is analyzed in more detail. The most promising designs can be presented to the commissioning management to assess the degree in which objectives can be realized and to select the most favorable design to be implemented.

These phases are presented in a sequential order, but in practice it is often desirable that iterations will take place. For example, the evaluation phase is explicitly aimed at identifying design errors, which may result in rework on the design. The remainder of this section will focus on two important elements of the method: The product data model and the derivation of a process design from it.

The Product Data Model

In the analysis phase, sources are gathered that may shed light on what producing a particular product exactly entails. The purpose is to identify:

1. information elements: the pieces of information that are needed at some stage in creating an informational product,
2. dependencies between information elements: insights into which pieces of information are needed to derive other pieces, and
3. production logic: the way information elements can be combined to arrive at new information.

For example, to design a process that evaluates loan applications, we can identify a number of *information elements* that will play a role in this process: the purpose of the loan, the requested amount, and the financial status of the applicant. The decision to grant a loan will *depend* on these three elements. The involved logic may be that loans for certain purposes are automatically declined, for example when they relate to ecologically damaging projects, but otherwise granted if the financial position of the client at least meets a range of criteria.

For a proper representation of this information, a tree-like structure is used, which is referred to as a *product data model*. This structure is different from the traditional BOM found in manufacturing. This is due to several differences between informational products and physical products. These differences lead to two important characteristics of a product data model. First, the same piece of information may be used to derive various other information elements. For example, the age of an applicant for a life insurance may be used to estimate both (a) the involved health risks for that patient and (b) the risks of work-related accidents. Secondly, there may be multiple ways to derive the same piece of information. For example, health risks may be estimated using either a patient questionnaire or a full medical examination of that patient.

A graphical example of a product data model is shown in Figure 8.7. All nodes in this figure correspond to information elements that may be used in a hiring process of helicopter pilots by the Dutch Air force. Arcs are used to express the dependencies between the various pieces of information, i.e., the information elements.

The meaning of the information elements is as follows:

- A: the candidate's suitability to become a helicopter pilot,
- B: the candidate's psychological fitness,
- C: the candidate's physical fitness,
- D: latest outcome of tests on candidate in the previous two years,
- E: quality of the candidate's reflexes,
- F: quality of the candidate's eye-sight.

In general, each incoming arc of a node in a product data model signifies an *alternative way* of determining a value for the corresponding information element for a specific case. If outgoing arcs of multiple nodes are *joined*, this means that

Fig. 8.7 A sample product
data model

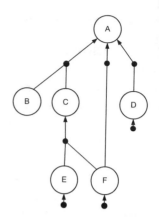

values of all of the corresponding information elements are required to determine
a value for the information element the arrow leads to. There are also information
elements which have incoming arrows that do not originate from other information
elements. These relate to those elements that do not rely on the values of other
information elements, e.g., element B. We will refer to such information elements
as *leaf elements*.

One of the things that is expressed in Figure 8.7 is that there are three ways to
determine a value for information element A. The suitability of a candidate (a) can
be determined on the basis of:

1. the combined results of the candidate's psychological test (B) and physical test
   (C),
2. the result of a previous suitability test (D), or
3. the candidate's eye-sight quality (F).

The way in which a new piece of information can be determined on the basis of
one or more pieces of other information is called a *production rule*. A production
rule specifies how the value of an output information element may be determined
on the basis of the values of its inputs. The description of a production rule may be
given in pseudo code or another rather precise specification language. For example,
using the Helicopter Pilot product data model again, the production rule that relates
to the use of a value for F to determine a value for A may be: "If a candidate's
vision of either or both eyes as expressed in diopters is above $+0.5$ or below
-0.5, then such a candidate is considered as *unsuitable* to become a helicopter
pilot". A complete product data model describes all the involved production rules.
Such a complete description is referred to as the *production logic*. In reality,
different production rules may be applicable under different circumstances. We just
considered the example that a candidate's eye-sight is so bad (F) that the candidate
is not considered suitable (A). However, in the more common case, the quality of
eye-sight is only one of the many aspects that are incorporated in a physical test
(B), which should be combined with the outcome of the psychological test (C) to
determine the suitability result (A).

Deriving a Process

From a product data model and the production logic, it becomes clear what the relevant information is, what the dependencies are, and what logic is involved. This is the basis to derive alternative designs for a process. The essential principle is that each *walk* through a product data model, i.e., starting from one or more of the leaf elements, through the derivation of information elements in the middle layer of a product data model, all the way up to the top element, is a valid way of executing a business process to create the desired product. Against this background, a process design is nothing more than determining what the preferred way of traversing a product data model is from bottom to top.

What is crucial to note is that for many products that are decomposed in the form of product data models, it becomes clear that there are different paths to establish the same end result. Each of these paths has its own performance characteristics, which renders it more or less attractive than its alternatives. For example, in the case of the hiring example, the target may be to minimize cost. In that case, it may be wise to first check what the quality of a candidate's eyes are: if this does not lead to an immediate rejection, then the other tests are carried out. If overall speed of the process is more important than cost, it may be preferred that the hiring staff immediately start checking the quality of eye-sight *and* the reflexes of a candidate.

Obviously, the expected performance, speed, and cost of determining pieces of information are crucial aspects in determining what the best process design is. Accordingly, Product-Based Design involves various steps to collect and validate this important information. The most algorithmic indication of the overall method is that tools are available to generate various process designs on the basis of a complete product data model. The newest version of the method does not even prescribe a single best way of traversing the product data model anymore, but allows process participants to decide on this by a case to case basis [182]. Flexible case management technology with knowledge of the product data model supports a process participant in deciding how to best carry out the process for each individual case.

8.4 Recap

In this chapter, we discussed the motivation for process redesign. We offered two views on the importance of process redesign: one from a positive angle, which shows how process innovation is often a good follow-up strategy for organizations after they spent time innovating their products; the other view considers redesign as a necessary medicine against organizational entropy. We also stressed that process redesign methods may be useful for the design of entirely new processes.

We delineated process redesign closer by focusing on a number of relevant elements: customers, business process operation, business process behavior, organization structure, organization population, information, technology, and the external environment. Using these elements, we explained how process redesign is different from other organizational measures or programs. The Devil's Quadrangle helped us to clarify that many redesign options have to be discussed from the perspective of a trade-off between time, cost, quality, and flexibility.

We also sketched the spectrum of redesign methods in the form of the Redesign Orbit. We identified three axes to distinguish such methods from each other: nature, ambition, and perspective. The remainder of the chapter was devoted to a discussion of transactional redesign methods on the one hand and transformational methods on the other. For each side, two methods were discussed in detail, in particular with respect to the technical challenge of redesign: 7PE, Heuristic Process Redesign, Business Process Reengineering, and Product-Based Design.

8.5   Solutions to Exercises

Solution 8.1 This is a hands-on exercise. A potential approach to this question might be to think of companies that offered services which are now provided by other companies via the Internet.

Solution 8.2 This is a hands-on exercise. Aside from new regulations or healthcare innovations, new processes may spring from the business models of start-ups, the integration of a new service along with an existing product (e.g., maintenance contract), a new source of data collection (e.g., fitness information from a smartwatch that is turned into health advice), etc.

Solution 8.3

1. "An airline has seen its profits falling over the past year. It decides to launch a marketing campaign among its corporate clients in the hope that it can extend its profitable freight business": Not a redesign initiative, no link to process.
2. "A governmental agency notices that it is structurally late to respond to citizens' queries. It decides to assign a manager to oversee this particular process and to take appropriate counter actions": Redesign, refers to *participants* and the *business process* itself.
3. "A video rental company sees that its customer base is evaporating. It decides to switch to the business of promoting and selling electronic services through which clients can see movies online and on-demand": Not so much a process redesign initiative; although there is certainly a link to process and products, this is much more a strategic initiative.
4. "A bank notices internal conflicts between two different departments over the way mortgage applications are dealt with. It decides to analyze the role of the various departments in the way applications are received and handled to come up with a new role structure": A redesign initiative, touches *process* and *participants*.

5. "A clinic wants to introduce the one-stop-shop concept to improve over the situation that its patients need to make separate appointments for the various diagnostic tests that are part of a procedure for skin cancer screening": A redesign initiative, touches *process* and *customers*.

Solution 8.4

1. Dealing with a customer complaint: Suitable.
2. Carrying out cardiovascular surgery: Mildly suitable, there are physical constraints involved here.
3. The production of a wafer stepping machine: Not very suitable, highly physical process.
4. Transporting a package: Mildly suitable, there are physical constraints involved here.
5. Providing financial advice on composing a portfolio: Suitable.
6. Designing a train station: Suitable.

Solution 8.5

1. "A new computer application is developed that speeds up the calculation of the maximum loan amount that a given client can be offered": Time is positively affected, development of the application may be costly.
2. "Whenever a clerk wants to have a quote from a financial provider, the clerk must use a direct messaging system instead of email": Quality and time may be positively influenced since the feedback is obtained directly and may be more to the point. Quality may also be negatively affected, depending on the kind of feedback this interaction generates.
3. "By the end of the year, additional, temporary workers are hired and assigned to picking items for fulfilling Christmas orders": This provides more flexibility which may also be exploited to improve timeliness. It's clearly a costly affair and temporary workers may deliver lower quality since they are less familiar with the operations.

Solution 8.6 TQM is seen by many as a predecessor to BPM and its focus on process redesign. What is clear is that TQM is not about making breakthrough innovations, but aims at continuous and gradual improvement. In this sense, it should be considered as *transactional*.

Solution 8.7 This is a hands-on exercise. The interested reader who is looking for inspiration to test his or her knowledge may want to take a look at the Wikipedia entry for business process reengineering[5] for a list of industrial redesign methods.

Solution 8.8 A variety of critical views on brainstorming exist, which can easily be found by an Internet search. A concise overview of explanations why brainstorming

---

[5]https://en.wikipedia.org/wiki/Business_process_reengineering.

may be not be so effective to solve problems or stimulate creativity can be found in [24], which mentions *social loafing*, *social anxiety*, *regression to the mean*, and *production blocking*.

Solution 8.9

- Cost: To carry out the various activities truly simultaneously, different participants must be available to carry out those activities. Depending on the situation, this may incur cost.
- Flexibility: By creating alternatives of a single activity, the process becomes more complex. If these alternative tasks all need to be changed for the same reason, for example due to new legislation or technology, the process has becomes less flexible.

Solution 8.10 In general, transformational methods tend to be more risky as they break away from existing, known procedures. This has a negative effect on the success rate of programs that rely on transformational methods. Over time, organizations have tended to favor redesign projects with an almost guaranteed level of establishing at least some level of improvement; hence, the popularity of transactional redesign methods.

Solution 8.11 You may think of services where the interaction with an advisor is actually what would make the process attractive for a customer. For example, private banking is an area of financial services where so-called "high net worth individuals" are provided with personalized advice on how to manage their assets. Similarly, specialized travel agencies that develop customized travel plans would rely on excellent customer interaction.

Solution 8.12 Clearly, different similarities exist. Both methods heavily rely on the creative input of people. Even more strikingly, both methods pursue deeply impressing a customer as the design starting point.

Solution 8.13 Again, various similarities can be picked out. The use of a physical aid (canvas, walls, room) to support the redesign process is a strong similarity. A decidedly different aspect is the explicit identification of different timelines within the NESTT approach versus the single timeline in the application of the Process Model Canvas.

Solution 8.14 The decision to let warehouse personnel immediately check whether a delivery actually matched what was originally purchased is an example of *subsuming information-processing work into real work*. To not collect the same information from the vendor through both an invoice and a notice can be seen as an instantiation of *capturing information once*.

8.6   Further Exercises

Exercise 8.15 The following text is the literal description of a redesign case at IBM Credit Corporation, taken from the book "Reengineering the Corporation" by Hammer and Champy [62]. It is split up into several parts. Please read these and answer the questions.

> Our first case concerns IBM Credit Corporation, a wholly owned subsidiary of IBM, which, if it were independent, would rank among the Fortune 100 service companies. IBM Credit is in the business of financing the computers, software, and services that the IBM Corporation sells. It is a business of which IBM is fond, since financing customers' purchases is an extremely profitable business. In its early years, IBM Credit's operation was positively Dickensian. When IBM field salespersons called in with a request for financing, they reached one of fourteen people sitting around a conference room table in Old Greenwich, Connecticut. The person taking the call logged the request for a deal on a piece of paper. That was step one. In step two, someone carted that piece of paper upstairs to the credit department, where a specialist entered the information into a computer system and checked the potential borrower's creditworthiness. The specialist wrote the results of the credit check on the piece of paper and dispatched it to the next link in the chain, which was the business practices department. The business practices department, step three, was in charge of modifying the standard loan covenant in response to customer request. Business practices had its own computer system. When done, a person in that department would attach the special terms to the request form. Next, the request went to a pricer, step four, who keyed the data into a personal computer spreadsheet to determine the appropriate interest rate to charge the customer. The pricer wrote the rate on a piece of paper, which, with the other papers, was delivered to a clerical group, step five. There, an administrator turned all this information into a quote letter that could be delivered to the field sales representative by Federal Express.

(a) Model the described business process. Use pools and lanes where needed.

> The entire process consumed 6 days on average, although it sometimes took as long as 2 weeks. From the sales reps' point of view, this turnaround was too long, since it gave the customer 6 days to find another source of financing, to be seduced by another computer vendor, or simply to call the whole deal off. So the rep would call and call and call to ask, "Where is my deal, and when are you going to get it out?" Naturally, no one had a clue, since the request was lost somewhere in the chain.

(b) Which dimension of the Devil's Quadrangle would be dominant for a redesign? Give an exact definition of the performance criterion.

> In their efforts to improve this process, IBM Credit tried several fixes. They decided, for instance, to install a control desk, so they could answer the rep's questions about the status of the deal. That is, instead of each department forwarding the credit request to the next step in the chain, it would return it to the control desk where the calls were originally taken. There, an administrator logged the completion of each step before sending the paper out again. This fix did indeed solve one problem: The control desk knew the location of each request in the labyrinth and could give the rep the information they wanted. Unfortunately, this information was purchased at the cost of adding more time to the turnaround.

(c) Model the adapted process. Use pools and lanes where needed. (d) Can you explain in terms of the performance dimensions of the Devil's Quadrangle what has happened?

Eventually, two senior managers at IBM Credit had a brainstorm. They took a financing request and walked it themselves through all five steps, asking personnel in each office to put aside whatever they were doing and to process this request as they normally would, only without the delay of having it sit in a pile on someone's desk. They learned from their experiments that performing the actual work took in total only 90 min—one and a half hours. The remainder—now more than 7 days on average—was consumed by handing the form off from one department to the next. Management had begun to look at the heart of the issue, which was the overall credit issuance process. Indeed, if by the wave of some magic wand the company were able to double the personal productivity of each individual in the organization, total turnaround time would have been reduced by only 45 min. The problem did not lie in the activities and the people performing them, but in the structure of the process itself. In other words, it was the process that had to change, not the individual steps.

In the end, IBM Credit replaced its specialists-the credit checkers, pricers, and so on-with generalists. Now, instead of sending an application from office to office, one person called a deal structurer processes the entire application from beginning to end: No handoffs.

How could one generalist replace four specialists? The old process design was, in fact, founded on a deeply held (but deeply hidden) assumption: that every bid request was unique and difficult to process, thereby requiring the intervention of four highly trained specialists. In fact, this assumption was false; most requests were simple and straightforward. The old process had been over-designed to handle the most difficult applications that management could imagine. When IBM Credit's senior managers closely examined the work the specialists did, they found that most of it was little more than clerical: finding a credit rating in a database, plugging numbers into a standard model, pulling boilerplate clauses from a file. These activities fall well within the capability of a single individual when this is supported by an easy-to-use computer system that provides access to all the data and tools the specialists would use.

IBM Credit also developed a new, sophisticated computer system to support the deal structurer. In most situations, the system provides the deal structurer with the guidance needed to proceed. In really tough situations, the deal structurer can get help from a small pool of real specialists-experts in credit checking, pricing, and so forth. Even here, handoffs have disappeared because the deal structurer and the specialists he or she calls in work together as a team.

The performance improvement achieved by the redesign is extraordinary. IBM Credit slashed its seven-day turnaround to 4 h. It did so without an increase in head count-in fact, it has achieved a small head-count reduction. At the same time, the number of deals that it handles has increased a hundredfold. Not 100 percent, but one hundred times.

(e) Consider the list of heuristics dealt with in this chapter. Which of these can you recognize in the new process redesign?

Exercise 8.16 Indicate in what respect the application of the *Outsourcing* heuristic and the composition of larger activities as a specific case of the *Activity composition* heuristic can lead to similar or different results. Use the performance dimensions of the Devil's Quadrangle and provide specific interpretations.

Exercise 8.17 Consider the equipment rental process described in Example 1.1 (page 3) and the corresponding issues documented in Example 6.5 (page 230).

a Apply the redesign heuristics from Appendix A in order to address the issues documented in Example 6.5.

b Capture the resulting to-be model in BPMN.

c Explain the impact of the changes you propose in terms of the performance dimensions of the Devil's Quadrangle.

Exercise 8.18 Consider the university admission process described in Exercise 1.1 (page 5) and the corresponding issues documented in Exercise 6.4 (page 232).

a Apply the redesign heuristics from Appendix A in order to address the issues documented in Exercise 6.4.
b Capture the resulting to-be model in BPMN.
c Explain the impact of the changes you propose in terms of the performance dimensions of the Devil's Quadrangle.

Exercise 8.19 Consider the process for prescription fulfillment described in Exercise 1.6 (page 30) and the corresponding issues documented in Exercise 6.14 (page 251).

a Apply the redesign heuristics from Appendix A in order to address the issues documented in Example 6.14.
b Capture the resulting to-be model in BPMN.
c Explain the impact of the changes you propose in terms of the performance dimensions of the Devil's Quadrangle.

Exercise 8.20 Consider the procure-to-pay process described in Exercise 1.7 (page 31) and the corresponding issues documented in Exercise 6.15 (page 252).

a Apply the redesign heuristics from Appendix A in order to address the issues documented in Example 6.15.
b Capture the resulting to-be model in BPMN.
c Explain the impact of the changes you propose in terms of the performance dimensions of the Devil's Quadrangle.

Exercise 8.21 Consider the following business process that is carried out at a healthcare institute. Figure 8.8. It shows the Intake process for elderly patients with mental problems, which is styled after the way this is carried out in the Eindhoven region.

The Intake process starts with a notice by telephone at the secretarial office of the healthcare institute. This notice is delivered by the family doctor of the person who is in need of mental treatment. The secretarial worker inquires after the name and residence of the patient. On basis of this information, the doctor is put through to the nursing officer responsible for the part of the region that the patient lives in.

The nursing officer makes a full inquiry into the mental, health, and social status of the patient in question. This information is recorded on a registration form. After this conversation has ended, this form is handed in at the secretarial office of the institute. Here, the information on the form is stored in the information system and subsequently printed. For new patients, a patient file is created. The registration form as well as the printout from the information system are stored in the patient file. Patient files are kept at the secretarial office and may not leave the building. At the secretarial office, two registration cards are produced for respectively the future first and second intaker of the patient. The registration card contains a set of basic patient data. The new patient is added on the list of new notices.

Fig. 8.8 The intake process
model

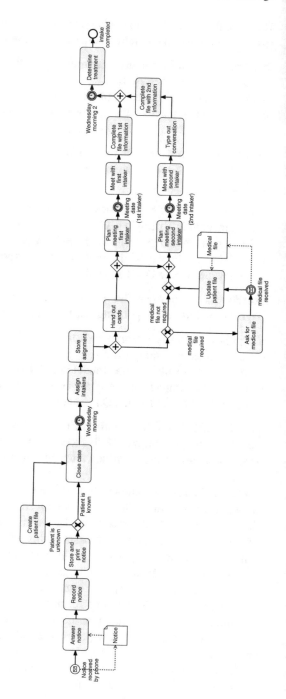

Halfway during each week, on Wednesday, a staff meeting of the entire medical team takes place. The medical team consists of social-medical workers, physicians, and a psychiatrist. During this meeting, the team leader assigns all new patients on the list of new notices to members of the team. Each patient will be assigned to a social-medical worker, who will act as the *first intaker* of the patient. One of the physicians will act as the *second intaker*. In assigning intakers, the team leader takes into account their expertise, the geographical region they are responsible for, earlier contacts they might have had with the patient, and their case load. The assignments are recorded on an assignment list, which is handed to the secretarial office. For each new assignment, it is also determined whether the medical file of the patient is required. This information is added to the assignment list.

The secretarial office stores the assignment of each patient of the assignment list in the information system. It passes the produced registration cards to the first and second intaker of each newly assigned patient. An intaker keeps this registration at times when visiting the patient and being at the office. For each patient for which the medical file is required, the secretarial office prepares and sends a letter to the family doctor of the patient, requesting a copy of the medical file. As soon as this copy is received, the secretarial office will inform the second intaker and add the copy to the patient file.

The first intaker plans a meeting with the patient as soon as this is possible. During the first meeting, the patient is examined using a standard checklist which is filled out. Additional observations are registered in a personal notebook. After a visit, the first intaker puts a copy of these notes in the file of a patient. The standard checklist is also added to the patient's file.

The second intaker plans the first meeting only after the medical information of the physician—if required—has been received. Physicians use dictaphones to record their observations made during meetings with patients. The secretarial office types out these tapes, after which the information is added to the patient file.

As soon as the meetings of the first and second intaker with the patient have taken place, the secretarial office puts the patient on the list of patients that reach this status. For the staff meeting on Wednesday (the same that was mentioned before), they provide the team leader with a list of these patients. For each of these patients, the first and second intaker along with the team leader and the attending psychiatrist formulate a treatment plan. The determination of the treatment plan formally ends the intake procedure.

a Develop two redesign scenarios for the Intake process with the Heuristic Process Redesign method, using the full set as described in Appendix A. For each of the scenarios:

- Clearly define the performance goal;
- List any information beyond that is found in the case description that you assume;
- Specify and motivate which redesign heuristics are part of the scenario.

b For each scenario, model the redesigned process in BPMN.

Exercise 8.22 Consider the booking-to-cash process at Fotof described in Exercise 4.31 (page 155) and the stakeholder analysis and issue register developed in Exercise 6.13. In the spirit of the NESTT method, develop the following:

a A to-be process that can be launched within 20 days.
b A to-be process that can be launched within 20 months.
c A to-be process that can be launched within 3 years.

Apply the redesign heuristics from Appendix A to generate the various scenarios. For each scenario, model the redesigned process in BPMN.

Hint: To get a feel for addressing this exercise in the spirit of the NESTT method, carry it out in cooperation with one or two fellow students. Find consensus on the issues, the way to address these, and the preferred time horizon for doing so.

Exercise 8.23 The following is an excerpt of the stipulations of a Dutch bank concerning medium-length business loans.

> If a medium length loan is made available to a client, the funds that are not fully withdrawn by that client will be temporarily placed on the money market. This temporary placing leads to financial rewards. However, leaving the remaining part of the loan to be available for the client at any time leads to funding costs. If the funding costs are higher than the temporary rewards, then this difference is the basis for a monthly disposal provision, to be paid by the client [..]. The disposal provision amounts to half of the difference between the funding costs and the temporary rewards with a minimum of 1/12% per month [...]. The disposal provision is part of the loan proposal.

Develop a product data model where the "loan proposal" is the top information element and the "disposal provision" is one of the other elements. You may leave out the production rules for this exercise.

8.7   Further Readings

Hammer has written many highly readable books with his co-authors on process redesign, for example [60, 62]. Other management books that deal with the topic are, for example, [30, 101, 161]. In contrast to the topic of process modeling, process redesign has not received as much attention from the scientific community. When BPR is studied, the focus is mostly on case studies or the diffusion of the concept in practice itself, for example in what domains it is applied or in which countries it is most popular. One of the most interesting studies in this category is quite dated [121], but it clearly shows the problems of what was initially considered business process redesign and how it quickly evolved over time into a more incremental approach. A very interesting study into the characteristics of different redesign methods is provided in [77], which has inspired various concepts that were dealt with in this part of the book.

The redesign heuristics that were discussed in this chapter have been described in quite some detail. After their initial presentation as best practices in [135], they have been validated and further analyzed in follow-up studies [102, 103]. More recent efforts by various researchers are aimed at supporting practitioners in making sensible selections of redesign heuristics in specific cases [63, 90]. Also, attempts have been made to extend the set of redesign heuristics to their application in other domains, for example in [119].

How to change organizations by the introduction of ERP systems is a topic that has received broad attention, see for example [57] and [162].

Product-Based Design was developed at Eindhoven University of Technology in cooperation with a Dutch consultancy company. Various case studies are available, which give a better idea of the practical application of this method and its potential benefits [131, 132]. Recently, the emphasis of researchers working on this topic has been moving towards the automatic generation of process designs and the automated support of the execution of such processes [182]. Another way of looking at Product-Based Design is that it is an approach that blends data and process. IBM's artifact-centric approach [27] and the data-driven process structures developed by the University of Ulm [117] are other approaches that go in this direction, but they are process modeling techniques rather than redesign methods.

As mentioned, the NESTT is a very recent redesign method. The interested reader may want to check its description and application in [148]. The book that contains this chapter is a good resource to read about cases of business transformation and process redesign [188].

One of the main open questions in the area of process redesign is to what extent it makes sense to follow industrial reference models or to try and develop company-specific designs. While industrial reference models are offered by many vendors, it is not so obvious that they represent the best possible way to carry out processes.

Chapter 9
Process-Aware Information Systems

> *Besides black art, there is only automation and mechanization.*
> Federico García Lorca (1898–1936)

In the previous chapters, we have learned how to use qualitative and quantitative analysis techniques in order to identify issues of existing business processes. We have also seen that many processes in practice have problems with flow-time efficiency. Various redesign heuristics emphasize the potential of using information systems to improve the performance of processes.

This chapter deals with information systems that support process automation. First, we will briefly explain what an automated business process is, after which we will focus on a specific kind of technology that is particularly suitable to achieve process automation, i.e., Process-Aware Information Systems (PAISs) and Business Process Management Systems (BPMSs). We will present the different variants of these systems and explain their features. Finally, we will discuss some of the advantages and challenges that are involved with introducing a BPMS in an organization.

9.1 Types of Process-Aware Information Systems

Process automation is a subject that may be approached from different angles. In a broad sense, it may refer to the intent to automate *any* conceivable part of routine work that is contained within a business process, from *simple* operations that are part of a *single* process activity up to the automated coordination of *entire*, complex processes.

Take, for example, the order-to-cash process that we modeled in Chapter 3. Automating such a process may imply that every time the seller receives a purchase order, this is automatically dispatched to the ERP systems of the warehouse and distribution department where the availability of the product is checked against the warehouse database. If the product is not in stock, the relevant suppliers are automatically contacted, e.g., via a Web service interface, to manufacture the

© Springer-Verlag GmbH Germany, part of Springer Nature 2018
M. Dumas et al., *Fundamentals of Business Process Management*,
https://doi.org/10.1007/978-3-662-56509-4_9

product. Otherwise, instructions are sent to a warehouse worker, e.g., using an electronic form, to manually retrieve the product from the warehouse. Subsequently, an order clerk from sales receives a notification that a new order needs to be confirmed, e.g., via email. That clerk would then log into the purchase order tracking system within sales, check the order electronically, and confirm it by pressing a button.

In this example the dispatching of the purchase order, the automated check of the product's availability, and the automated Web messages are all manifestations of process automation in its broadest sense: They automate a particular aspect of a process. In this context, we will refer to an *automated business process*, also known as *workflow*: a process that is automated in whole or in part by a software system, which passes information from one participant to another for action, according to the temporal and logical dependencies set in the underlying process model. Let us now consider systems that work with automated business processes. These systems are called *Process-Aware Information Systems* (PAISs).

9.1.1 Domain-Specific Process-Aware Information Systems

A specific kind of process automation, which interests us most in this book, exploits knowledge about how different process activities *relate* to one another. In other words, the type of information systems that we consider are *process-aware*. The overarching group of Process-Aware Information Systems (PAISs) can be subdivided into two major categories: domain-specific PAISs and domain-agnostic PAISs.

There is a plethora of domain-specific PAISs. Here, we briefly describe four prominent types, which are offered as commercial packages from various software vendors such as Microsoft,[1] Oracle,[2] Salesforce,[3] and SAP.[4] These include the following:

Enterprise Resource Planning (ERP) systems: These systems provide essential and generic business functionality, which is required across various industries. The core modules of ERP systems support business processes in accounting and controlling, human resource management, and production management. The two most important processes that most ERP systems fully cover are the procure-to-pay and the order-to-cash process.

Customer Relationship Management (CRM) systems: These systems support marketing and sales processes that directly interact with customers, both on an

---

[1] https://dynamics.microsoft.com/.

[2] https://www.oracle.com/applications/erp.

[3] https://www.salesforce.com.

[4] https://www.sap.com/products/erp.html.

individual and on an aggregated level. On the individual level, CRM systems help to document the interaction with individual customers through various channels, including telephone, email, Internet portal, and personal encounters at brick-and-mortar branches. On the aggregated level, CRM systems support sales and marketing activities related to products, pricing, distribution, and campaigning. At the heart of a CRM system is an extensive database that provides information on existing and prospective customers. Many CRM systems integrate data mining techniques to help with customer segmentation. Important processes supported by CRM systems are campaign-to-leads and lead-to-order.

Supply Chain Management (SCM) systems: These systems focus on the support of logistics operations that integrate with suppliers and customers. On an operational level, SCM systems support the management of freight and transportation, inbound and outbound warehousing, storage and inventory, as well as corresponding planning and calculation processes. On a technical level, SCM systems support electronic data interchange with suppliers and customers, as well as various tracking technologies such as Radio-Frequency Identification (RFID) and barcode scanning. Key supply chain processes are order-to-delivery and return-to-refund.

Product Lifecycle Management (PLM) systems: PLM systems support the various processes of the lifecycle of a product from an engineering perspective. These include the conception and design phase in which the product is specified, designed, and validated. In the realisation phase, the manufacturing system is planned and actual products are built, assembled, and tested. In the service phase, products are sold and delivered, used, maintained, and eventually disposed of. Important processes supported by PLM systems are idea-to-launch and different types of order processes including built-to-order, engineered-to-order, or assembled-to-order.

Although less numerous, there are also several types of domain-agnostic PAISs, chiefly Issue Tracking systems, Document Management Systems (DMSs), and Business Process Management Systems (BPMSs). Issue Tracking Systems, such as JIRA[5] and Pivotal Tracker,[6] have their roots in the field of software development and IT service management. The central concept behind these systems is the notion of an issue, which can be, for example, a bug in a software system, a request to add a feature to a software system, or a request to grant privileges to a given contractor to be able to access an IT system. Each issue goes through different states, including opened, assigned to an employee, suspended, canceled, closed, re-opened, etc. An issue moves from one state to another according to a pre-defined lifecycle. Different tasks may be performed when an issue is in a given state, some of them manually, others automatically. In this way, an Issue Tracking System supports the resolution of an issue, and accordingly, issue trackers are commonly used to support issue-to-

---

[5]https://www.atlassian.com/software/jira.

[6]https://www.pivotaltracker.com.

resolution processes. Nowadays, Issue Tracking Systems are widely used to support issue-to-resolution processes even outside the fields of software development or IT services management.

In line with its name, a DMS supports the management of documents all the way from their creation to their archival or deletion. They provide functions to create, search, access and update documents, but they also provide functions to route a document across multiple stakeholders. Originally, the document routing capabilities of DMSs were rather limited, but over time they became more sophisticated to the point that modern DMSs can support relatively complex processes. Nowadays, many companies employ DMSs to execute employee-initiated processes, such as vacation request approvals and travel requisition approvals. Concretely, an employee starts an instance of a vacation request process by creating a vacation request from a pre-defined template. This template contains rules for routing the request from said employee to his supervisor. Once the supervisor approves, the request is forwarded to the human resources department, where the vacation is recorded and the corresponding rosters are updated.

DMSs have evolved over time to support not only documents, but almost any type of content, whether structured content such as vacation requests or travel requisitions, to unstructured content such as scanned documents, images, and audio recordings (e.g., recordings of telephone conversations with customers). As DMSs grew more sophisticated and their use became widespread in enterprises, they became known as Enterprise Content Management (ECM) systems. Major ECM systems include IBM FileNet,[7] Microsoft SharePoint,[8] and OpenText.[9]

Exercise 9.1 The PAISs mentioned above (ERP, CRM, SCM, PLM, ECM) form a specific category in the market for enterprise software. Enterprise software covers not only PAISs, but also database systems, middleware, office software, and analytical software, which are not directly process-aware. The market for enterprise software is huge. According to a Gartner Report from 2017, it is estimated with a sales volume of almost $ 400 billion (more than € 340 billion). Conduct an Internet search to find the Top 5 vendors of (a) enterprise software in general and (b) ERP systems specifically.

9.1.2   Business Process Management Systems

A Business Process Management System (BPMS) is a system that supports the design, analysis, execution, and monitoring of business processes on the basis of explicit process models. As discussed in Chapter 1, BPMSs originate from an older

---

[7]https://www.ibm.com/us-en/marketplace/filenet-content-manager.
[8]https://products.office.com/en-us/sharepoint.
[9]https://www.opentext.com.

type of PAIS known as *Workflow Management System* (WfMS), which was focused on modeling and execution and did not very well support the other phases of the BPM lifecycle.

The purpose of a BPMS is to coordinate an automated business process in such a way that all work is done at the right time by the right resource. To explain how a BPMS accomplishes that, it is useful to see that a BPMS is in some way similar to a *Database Management System* (DBMS). A DBMS is a standard, *off-the-shelf* software package offered by many vendors in many different flavors, such as Microsoft SQL Server,[10] IBM DB2,[11] and Oracle Database Server.[12] With a DBMS it is possible to capture company-specific data in a structured way, without ever having to consider how the exact retrieval and storage of the involved data takes place. These tasks are taken care of by standard facilities of the system. Of course, at some point it is necessary to configure the DBMS, fill it with data, and it may also be necessary to periodically adapt the system and its content to actual demands.

In a similar manner, a BPMS is also a standard type of software system. Vendors offer different BPMSs with a varying set of features, covering different phases of the BPM lifecycle: from simple systems only catering for the design and automation of business processes, to more complex systems also involving process intelligence functionality (e.g., advanced monitoring and process mining), complex event processing (CEP), service-oriented architecture (SOA) functionality, and integration with third-party applications and social networks.

There are several ways to classify the available BPMSs. Figure 9.1 shows a classification based on two axes: one that captures the *degree of support* that the BPMS delivers, while the other that expresses how these systems differ from each other with respect to their *orientation on process or data*. We describe and illustrate four different types of systems: groupware systems, ad hoc workflow systems, production workflow systems, and case management systems. These systems can be positioned in the spectrum of BPMSs as shown in Figure 9.1.

Groupware systems: The two underlying principles of groupware systems are that the user is enabled to: (i) easily share documents and information and (ii) directly communicate with other users. The best known example of a groupware system is IBM Notes.[13] Groupware systems are widely used and particularly popular for their high operational flexibility. On the downside, Groupware systems traditionally do not directly support business processes in a strict sense; however, several commercial groupware systems offer workflow extensions.

---

[10]https://www.microsoft.com/sql-server.

[11]https://www.ibm.com/analytics/us/en/db2.

[12]https://www.oracle.com/database.

[13]https://www.ibm.com/us-en/marketplace/enterprise-email.

Fig. 9.1 The spectrum of
BPMS types

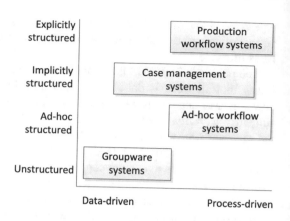

Ad hoc workflow systems: Ad hoc workflow systems, like TIBCO's ActiveMa-
trix BusinessWorks[14] or Comala Workflows,[15] allow on-the-fly process definitions that can be created and modified. Even when there is already a process
defined to deal with a specific case type, it is possible to adapt the process during
the execution, for example by adding steps. On the technical level, these systems
often maintain a private process definition for each case in order to offer this
flexibility. This means that working on a case might even start from a completely
empty process definition, which is extended as it becomes clearer what needs
to happen and in what order. Alternatively, the ad hoc workflow system might
work on the basis of a standard solution or template, which can be modified
during execution. Interestingly, such a modified procedure may be used as the
template for starting the processing of a new case. In general, there are two major
requirements to successfully apply an ad hoc workflow system in an organization.
The first requirement is that end users are aware of the processes in which they
operate. This means that processes should be defined or modified only by people
with a good overview of the process and the consequences of deviating from
usual practice. The second requirement is that users have sophisticated tools at
their disposal to model business processes and that they are capable of modeling.
The combination of these requirements restricts the application of these systems
at this point.

Production workflow systems: The most prominent type of BPMS is the production workflow system. Typical representatives are IBM's Business Process
Manager,[16] Bizagi Studio,[17] and Camunda BPM.[18] Much of what we described
in the previous sections on workflow applies to this class of BPMSs. Work is

---

[14]https://docs.tibco.com/products/tibco-activematrix-businessworks.

[15]https://www.comalatech.com/products/comalaworkflows.

[16]https://www.ibm.com/us-en/marketplace/business-process-manager.

[17]https://www.bizagi.com/en/products/bpm-suite/studio.

[18]https://camunda.com/bpm.

routed strictly on the basis of explicitly defined process descriptions captured in process models. The management of operational data is typically handled by a complementary DBMS. In general, it is not allowed to deviate from a process logic if that has not been explicitly captured in the process model. Sometimes, the two types of *administrative* and *transaction processing* BPMSs are distinguished based on the degree of automation of the work that is coordinated. Administrative BPMSs are used in settings where a large portion of work is performed by people; transaction processing BPMSs support business processes that are almost fully automated.

Case management systems: The idea behind a case management system (or adaptive case management system (ACM)) is to support processes that are neither tightly nor completely specified. Rather, *implicit* process models are used, which capture a conventional flow from which a user can deviate—unless this is explicitly prohibited. A case management system is usually fully aware of the precise details of the data belonging to a case (including customer data, financial or medical data). On the basis of such awareness, the system is able to inform end users about the status and history of a case, as well as the most obvious steps to continue with. Contemporary examples are i-Sight's Case Management Software,[19] Case Management by PEGA,[20] and ISIS Papyrus.[21] The latter also, if desired, supports a production workflow approach and in that sense is a hybrid BPMS.

There are other types of systems that often integrate characteristics and functionality of BPMSs. Document Management Systems primarily take care of the storage and retrieval of documents, like document scans and PDFs, but they often offer workflow automation features as well. An example is Adobe LiveCycle.[22] *Process orchestration servers* focus on process automation but have a specific emphasis on automated processes that require the integration of multiple enterprise applications. An example is Oracle SOA Suite.[23]

9.1.3 Architecture of a BPMS

How does a BPMS work and what are its components? Figure 9.2 shows the main components of a BPMS, namely the execution engine, the process modeling tool, the worklist handler, and the administration and monitoring tools.

---

[19]https://i-sight.com.

[20]https://www.pega.com/de/case-management.

[21]https://www.isis-papyrus.com.

[22]http://www.adobe.com/products/livecycle.html.

[23]www.oracle.com/technetwork/middleware/soasuite.

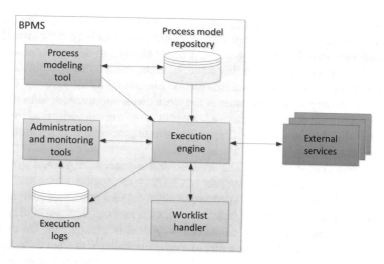

Fig. 9.2 The architecture of a BPMS

Execution Engine: Central to the BPMS is the *execution engine*. The engine
provides different functionalities including: (i) the ability to create executable
process instances (also called cases); (ii) the ability to distribute work to process
participants in order to execute a business process from start to end; (iii) the
ability to automatically retrieve and store data required for the execution of the
process and to delegate automated activities to software applications across the
organization. Altogether, the engine is continuously monitoring the progress of
different cases and coordinating which activities to work on next by generating
work items, i.e., instances of process activities that need to be taken care of
for specific cases. Work items are then allocated to resources which are both
qualified and authorized to work on them. The execution engine also interacts
with the other components, as discussed next.

Process modeling tool: The *process modeling tool* component offers functionality such as (i) the ability for users to create and modify process models; (ii) the
ability to annotate process models with additional data, such as data input and
output, participants, business rules associated with activities, and performance
measures associated with a process or an activity; and (iii) the ability to store,
share and retrieve process models from a *process model repository*. A process
model can be *deployed* to the engine in order to be executed. This can either be
done directly from the modeling tool or from the repository. The engine uses the
process model to determine the temporal and logical order in which the activities
of a process have to be executed. On that basis, it determines which work items
should be generated and to whom they should be allocated or which external

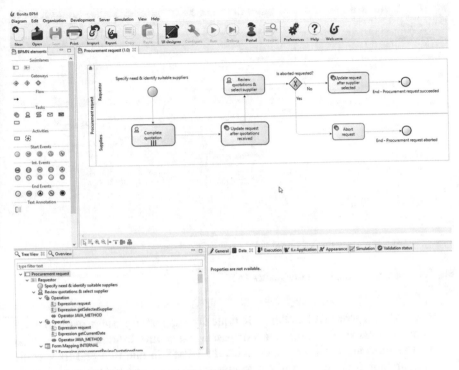

Fig. 9.3 The process modeling tool of Bonita BPM

services should be called. Figure 9.3 shows the process modeling tool of Bonita
BPM.[24]

Worklist handler: A *worklist handler* is the component of a BPMS through
which process participants (i) are offered work items and (ii) commit to these. It
is the execution engine that keeps track of which work items are due and makes
them available through the worklist handlers of individual process participants.
The standard worklist handler of a BPMS can best be imagined as an *inbox*,
similar to that of an email client. Through an inbox, participants can see which
work items are ready to be executed. The worklist handler might use electronic
forms for an activity's input and output data. When a work item of this activity
is selected and started by the participant from the worklist, the corresponding
electronic form is rendered on screen. This step is called *check-out*. Participants
can then enter data into the form and signal completion to the engine. This step
is called *check-in*. Afterwards, the engine determines the next work items that
must be performed for the case in question. Often, participants can to some
extent exert control over the work items in their worklist, e.g., with respect to
the order in which they are displayed and the priority they assign to these work

---

[24]https://www.bonitasoft.com.

Fig. 9.4 The worklist handler of Camunda BPM

items. Also, a worklist handler will typically support a process participant in temporarily suspending work items or passing on control to someone else. What exact features are available depends on the BPMS in question and its specific configuration. It is fairly common to customize worklist handlers, for example according to corporate design, to foster its efficient usage and acceptance within an organization. Figure 9.4 shows the default worklist handler of Camunda BPM.

External services: It may be useful to involve external applications in the execution of a business process. In many business processes, there are activities which are performed fully automatically, such that the execution engine can simply call an external application, for example to assess the creditworthiness of a client. The external application has to expose a service interface with which the engine can interact. We refer to such applications as *external services*. The execution engine provides the invoked service with the necessary data it will need for performing the activity for a specific case. On completion of the request, the service will return the outcome to the engine and signal that the work item is completed. Sometimes too, a BPMS may need to transfer control over cases between different organizational units or organizations. One way of achieving this is by interacting with an external BPMS, which exposes a service interface for this purpose. For example, consider a global insurance company that has offices in three different time zones: Japan, the UK, and California. At the end of the working day in each of these time zones, all work items can be transferred to the execution engine in the next zone where the work day has just started. In this way, the execution of the business process never stops.

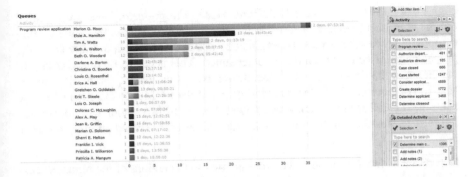

Fig. 9.5 The monitoring tool of Perceptive

Administration and monitoring tools: Administration and monitoring tools are the tools necessary for the administration of all operational matters of a BPMS. Consider the actual availability of specific participants as an example. If someone is unavailable to work because of illness or a vacation, the BPMS has to be made aware of this fact in order to avoid allocating work items to that person. Administration tools are also required to deal with exceptional situations, for example to remove outdated work items from the system. Administration tools are also equipped with process monitoring functionality. One can use these tools to monitor the performance of the running business processes, in particular with respect to the progress of individual cases. These tools can aggregate data from different cases, such as average cycle times of cases or the fraction of cases that are delivered too late. The BPMS records the execution of a process model step-by-step. The execution-related events recorded in this way are stored and can be exported in the form of *execution logs* from which performance dashboards are generated. An example of a dashboard generated by Perceptive[25] is shown in Figure 9.5. The topic of performance dashboards will be discussed in Chapter 11.

Exercise 9.2 The monitoring of user queues provides good transparency of the current workload of the different process participants. However, any sort of chart should be carefully reflected upon before decisions are made. Before interpreting the chart in Figure 9.5, try to answer the following questions.

1. Which important information is not visible in the chart?
2. Does the chart allow you to conclude who are good and bad employees?

The generic BPMS architecture described above is the evolution of a reference model for WfMSs, which was proposed by the Workflow Management Coalition (WfMC) in the 1990s. The box "WfMC Reference Model" expands on this model.

To illustrate how a BPMS works, recall BuildIT's business process for renting equipment from Chapter 1. Let us suppose it is supported by a BPMS. The execution

---

[25]https://www.hyland.com/en/perceptive.

engine can track that for orders #1,220 and #1,230 *site engineers* have already filled out the equipment rental requests. On the basis of a process model of the renting equipment process, the execution engine can detect that for both of these cases the proper piece of equipment must be determined. This needs to be done by any of the clerks at the depot. Therefore, the BPMS passes on the request to all worklist handlers of all clerks for further processing. For order #1,240, on the other hand, the equipment rental request is not available yet. So, the BPMS engine will not pass on a similar request for this order yet. Instead, it will await the completion of this work item.

Exercise 9.3 In which state is the process after all the actions of the rental process of BuildIT have been performed as described above? Which work items can you identify that are under control of the BPMS? Make sure to identify both the case and the activity for each work item.

WfMC REFERENCE MODEL

The Workflow Management Coalition (WfMC) is a standardization organization, founded in 1993, in which BPMS vendors, users, and researchers have a seat. The purpose of the WfMC is to achieve generally accepted standards for terminology and interfaces for the components of a BPMS [68].

The WfMC has produced the so-called *WfMC reference model*, which has become well-established in the world of process automation. The idea behind this reference model is that any supplier of a BPMS can explain the functioning of its specific system on its basis. The original reference model included six components, which resemble the components of the BPMS architecture in Figure 9.2. They are: workflow engine, process modeling tools, administration and monitoring tools, worklist handler, external applications and external BPMSs.

In the reference model, the interactions between its components take place through so-called *interfaces*, which are numbered from 1 to 5. Three of these interfaces can be directly recognized in the BPMS architecture that is discussed in this chapter: *Interface 1* concerns the interaction between the engine and process modeling tools, *Interface 2* concerns the interaction between the engine and the worklist handler, *Interface 5* concerns the interaction between the engine and the administration and monitoring tools. The other interfaces of the WfMC reference model have become obsolete since the introduction of Web services.

Exercise 9.4 Consider the following questions about a BPMS:

- Can you imagine that a BPMS can work on the basis of a business process model without any information on the types of resources that are available to work on the tasks? What problems would the BPMS run into when executing this process?

- In what situation will the execution engine generate multiple work items after the completion of a single work item?
- Can you provide examples of external services that may be useful to be invoked in a loan application process?
- If it is important that a BPMS hands out work items to available resources, can you imagine information on resources that is useful to be captured by an administration tool (apart from whether they are ill or on vacation)?

9.1.4 The Case of ACNS

Building on the explanation of the BPMS architecture in the previous section it is now possible to sketch an example of an operational BPMS. We use a simplified view on a process in which claims are assessed within the ACNS company (*A Claim is No Shame*). The first activity in this process is an assessment of the claim, which is done by a *senior acceptor* or a *regular acceptor*. Regular acceptors are responsible for assessments when the amount of the claim is below € 1,000; more valuable claims are assessed by senior acceptors. In case of a negative assessment, it is the responsibility of the account manager to convey the bad news to the customer. In case of a positive assessment, an electronic invoice is to be generated by a clerk of the financial department, who needs to dispatch it to the client. After these activities, the process is completed. Figure 9.6 shows this process.

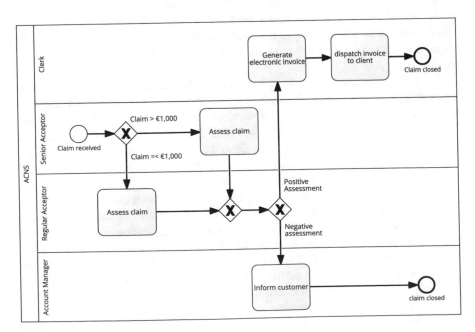

Fig. 9.6 Model of the claims handling process at ANCS

The above description shows that there are two dimensions that must be covered with the process modeling tool of the BPMS: (1) the procedure that specifies the various activities and (2) the various participants who are involved in carrying out the activities. The former part is recorded in a process model; the second is captured in what is often referred to as a *resource classification*. In addition, the relations between these two specifications must be defined, i.e., who is able and qualified to perform what activity. Often, these relations are also specified as part of the process model. These relationships may be dependent on all kinds of business rules. For example, the distinction between the authorization levels of the senior and ordinary acceptor in assessing claims is an example of a dynamic rule, i.e., it is determined by the current value of a variable.

Once these process and resource specifications are defined, the execution engine of a BPMS would generally be able to support the process. Now let us assume that almost simultaneously two claims come in:

1. A car damage of € 12,500, as claimed by Mr. Bouman.
2. A car damage of € 500, as claimed by Mrs. Fillers.

Ms. Senora has been with ACNS for a long time and, for the past years, works as a *senior acceptor*. This month, *Mr. Regulo* has started his training and works as an *regular acceptor*. At the start of his contract, the system administrator has used the administration tool of the BPMS to add Mr. Regulo to the pool of available acceptors.

Based on the process model, the resource classification, and operational data on the availability of the various employees, the enactment service of the BPMS now takes care of forwarding both newly received claims to the worklist handlers of Ms. Senora. After all, she may assess both claims based on her qualifications. Mr Regulo, in his turn, will only see in his worklist handler the damage claim of Mrs. Fillers.

On noting the work item in his worklist, Mr. Regulo starts to work on it immediately. He selects the damage claim of Mrs. Fillers to handle. In response to that action, the execution engine ensures that the corresponding work item *disappears* from the worklist of Ms. Senora. The reason is that this piece of work needs to be carried out only once. Ms. Senora herself is at this point still working on the handling of an earlier case, but shortly thereafter selects the claim of Mr. Bouman through her worklist handler to deal with.

In response to the selection of work items by both Mr. Regulo and Mrs. Senora, the execution engine will ensure that both will see the electronic claim file on their screen of the respective customers. The execution engine does so by using the appropriate parameters in invoking the DMS of ACNS at the workstations of the acceptors. The DMS also displays the scanned version of the claims, which were originally sent in on paper. In addition, the BPMS takes care of displaying to both the acceptors an electronic form that they can use to record their assessment, also through the invocation of a service.

Mr. Regulo decides to reject the claim. The worklist handler notices this, because it monitors the specific field on the electronic form that receives a negative value. Based on the logic captured in the process model, the execution engine can determine that the case must be handed over to the account manager of Ms. Fillers and sends a work item to that participant, requesting to inform the client on the negative assessment.

Ms. Senora arrives at a positive assessment of the claim under her watch and decides to approve it. The execution engine ensures that a service is invoked to determine the new monthly premium for Mr. Bouman, taking into account his no-claim history which is registered in a claim database. The retrieval of the information from this database is also realized through a service. Once this calculation is completed, a work item for the various available financial employees is created to pay the damage. The work item appears in the worklist of each of these financial officers, until one of them selects it for processing. After the payment has been carried out, the process is complete.

As can be seen in the ANCS example, all components of the BPMS architecture play a role in coordinating the work, specifically to ensure that the appropriate work items are created and carried out by the involved participants.

Exercise 9.5 Consider the following developments and indicate which components of the BPMS architecture are affected when they are addressed

1. A new decision support system is developed to support acceptors in making their assessment of claims.
2. Ms. Senora retires.
3. A new distinction between claims becomes relevant: regular acceptors are now also qualified to deal with claims above € 1,000 as long as they worked on previous claims by the same client.
4. Claims that are issued on cars which are over 10 years old need to be continuously monitored by management.

9.2   Advantages of Introducing a BPMS

In this section we reflect on why it would be attractive for organizations to use a BPMS. There are four broad categories of advantages that we will discuss here: workload reduction, flexible system integration, execution transparency, and rule enforcement.

9.2.1   Workload Reduction

A BPMS automates part of the work that is done by people in settings where such a system is not in place. First of all, it will take care of *transporting work* itself. In a paper-based organization, work is usually transported by internal postal services, often delaying processing for one work day at each handoff, or by the participants themselves at the expense of their working time. All such delays are completely eradicated when a BPMS can be used to dispatch work items electronically. In some situations, the BPMS can take care of the entire process by invoking fully automated applications. In such cases, we speak of *Straight-Through-Processing* (STP). Particularly in the financial services, many business processes that used to involve human operations are now in STP mode and coordinated by BPMSs. Also in other domains–think for instance of electronic visa–at least a portion of the cases can be handled in a completely automatic fashion.

The second type of work that is being taken over by the BPMS concerns *coordination*. The BPMS uses the process model for determining which activities need to be performed and in what order. So, every time the BPMS uses this knowledge to route a work item it potentially saves someone the time to even think about what should be done next. Another form of coordination time saved is the signaling of completed work. In a paper-based organization, work will be lying around for quite some time in case of work handoffs. What often happens is that someone takes over work, suspends it for some reason, after which the work package gets stuck in another pile of work. The BPMS will at all times be able to signal the status of all work items and it can take actions to ensure that progress is being made.

The final type of workload reduction by using a BPMS is the *gathering of all relevant information* to carry out a particular task. In a situation without a BPMS, it is the employee who needs to do this collection. Finding the right file in particular—it is never there where you would expect it—can be a time-consuming affair. Note that this type of advantage rests on the assumption that along with the introduction of the BPMS the effort is taken to digitalize the stream of documents in an organization. The implementation of a DMS is actually what is often observed alongside a BPMS implementation. Certain vendors, such as IBM and ISIS Papyrus, offer integrated suites of BPMS and DMS functionality. Other BPMS vendors often have strategic cooperations with companies that offer a DMS, such that it is relatively easy to integrate their joint systems.

9.2.2 Flexible System Integration

Originally, the most popular argument to start with a BPMS was the increased flexibility that organizations achieve with this technology. To explain this best, a short reflection on the history of computer applications is due. There is an interesting trend, as identified by Van der Aalst and Van Hee [176], that generic functionality is split off from applications at some point.

Roughly throughout the 1965–1975 period, computer applications were run directly on the operating systems (OS) of a computer. Each application would take care of its own data management and would be using proprietary techniques to do this efficiently. As a result, it turned out to be difficult to share data among applications and to maintain consistency. Clearly, programmers of different applications would be involved with developing similar routines to solve similar problems. From 1975 onwards, DBMSs as a new type of standard software emerged that took on the generic task of managing data efficiently. As a result, data could be shared rather easily and programmers of new applications would not need to worry anymore about ways to store, query, or retrieve date. Some 10 years later, around 1985, User Interface Management Systems (UIMS) were introduced to provide a very generic interface component to many applications. Through the provision of facilities like drop-down boxes or radio buttons in accessible libraries, each computer programmer would be able to make use of these. By 1995, the first commercial BPMS enters the marketplace. Like DBMSs and UIMSs in their focus area, BPMSs would provide generic support for the area of business process logic.

The introduction of a BPMS is a logical sequel to the separation of generic functionality of what were once monolithic computer programs. Still in the 1990s, it was estimated that 40% of all the lines of code running on the mainframe computers of banks would have to do with business process logic, not with the calculations or data processing themselves. The typical kind of information processing in the context relates to the identification of activities, their order of execution, or the participants responsible for carrying them out. For example, it would be specified that after a mortgage offering was completed, this needed to be signaled to the manager of the department, triggering a signal on her monitor.

The obvious advantage related to this development is that it has become much easier with a BPMS to manage business process logic on its own. This is due to the fact that it is much more convenient to update the description of a business process without having to inspect the application code. Also, the inverse of this scenario would become easier, i.e., modifying an application while not touching on the order of how things on the business process level would need to unfold. BPMSs, in short, would enable organizations to become more flexible in managing and updating their business processes as well as their applications.

BPMSs also provide the means to "glue" together separate systems. Large service organizations typically deploy myriads of IT systems, which more or less all exist independently of each other. Often, such a situation is referred to as *island automation*. A BPMS may be introduced in such a situation as a means of integrating such systems. It will ensure that all the separate systems will play their due role in the business processes they support.

A word of caution is due here. The BPMS itself will offer no direct solution to the problem of redundant storage of information across many different IT systems. In fact, a BPMS will in general have no knowledge of the actual data that end users will manipulate using the various IT systems. If the BPMS is to operate as an integrator between all the existing systems, this will require a thorough information analysis to map which data is used and available.

9.2.3   Execution Transparency

An advantage that is often overlooked is that a BPMS can operate as a treasure trove with respect to the way that business processes are really executed. Sure enough, to have a BPMS operate at all, it must keep track of which work items are. This can only be determined by actively monitoring which work items have been completed by which resources and at what time new cases enter the process. Yet, for a BPMS to function properly, it is not necessary to keep all that data available once the associated cases are completed. The management overseeing such a process, however, may have an entirely different perspective on this issue. There are two types of information that may be useful to generate business insights from BPMS data:

1. *Operational information*, which relates to recent, running cases, and
2. *Historic information*, which relates to completed cases.

Operational information is relevant for the management of individual cases, participants, or specific parts of a business process. A characteristic example is the following. From analyses of various governmental agencies involved with granting permits in the Netherlands it has become clear that determining the exact status of a permit application was one of the most time-consuming activities for the civil servants involved. Through the use of most commercially available BPMSs, retrieving that status is a futility. Such a status may be, for example, that the request of Mr. Benders to extend his house with an extra garden wing has been received, matched with the development plans for the area he is living in, and that further processing is now dependent on the receipt of the advice of an external expert. Another use of operational information would relate to the length of a queue in terms of work items. For example, there are 29 applications for building permits that await the advice of an external expert. From these examples it becomes clear that initiatives to improve customer service, in particular with respect to answering questions about their orders, often relies on the use of a BPMS.

Historic information, in contrast to operational information, is often of interest on a particular level of aggregation, for example covering more cases over an extended period of time. This kind of information is of the utmost importance to determine the performance of a particular process or its conformance to particular rules. With respect to the former, you may think of average cycle times, the number of completed cases over a particular period, and the utilization of resources. The latter category could cover issues like the kind of exceptions that have been generated or the number of cases that violated a particular deadline.

It makes sense to consider the kind of insights that need to be retrieved from a BPMS before it is actually implemented in an organization. Technical issues play a role here, like the period of time that the logs of a BPMS need to be kept and, therefore, how much storage space should be devoted for that. Consider that it becomes problematic if historic information is important on the aggregate level of years if there is only space to save the events of at most a month. There are also conceptual issues. If it is important to monitor a certain milestone within a process, it is essential that it is represented in the model that is used for the execution of the related business process. To use the previous example: If it is important to be able to recognize the stage in which a case has to wait for the advice of an external expert, then that milestone must be part of the process model. In this way, process automation provides the foundation for process intelligence (see Chapter 11).

9.2.4 Rule Enforcement

Except for the obvious advantage that a business process could be executed more efficiently by using a BPMS, such a system will also ensure that the process is carried out in precisely the way that it has been designed. When rules are explicitly enforced, this can be considered as a quality benefit: one does what one promises. In many settings, employees will have considerable freedom to carry out a business process in the way it looks best to them (or most convenient). This individual assessment does not necessarily coincide with the best possible way a business process is executed from the overall perspective of an organization. In this respect, a BPMS can be a means to safeguard that business processes are executed in a pre-defined way, without any concessions.

As an illustration, consider the *separation of duties* control that is well known in the financial services domain. It means that the registration and inspection of a financial transaction will need to be carried out by different individuals. This type of logic is both quite easily implemented and enforced in a BPMS. The BPMS registers which individuals have carried out which work items and can take this information into account when allocating new work items. Note that a BPMS is, in general, sufficiently sophisticated so that employees can alternatively fulfill the registering and inspecting role for different cases.

The capacity of a BPMS to enforce rules is currently of much interest to organizations. Around the year 2000, governmental organizations used BPMSs purely for reasons of enforcement, such that they could prove that they comply with the law. Nowadays, financial and other professional service organizations have become similarly enamored by BPMSs. An important development is the rise of various governance frameworks, which started in 2002 with the *Sarbanes-Oxley Act* as a reaction to misconduct in Enron and Worldcom. The law places a high responsibility with company executives to install management controls and to check their proper execution. Obviously, this is where BPMSs can play an important role.

Exercise 9.6 To which categories would you classify the following incentives to introduce a BPMS in an organization?

- An auditing agency has found out that the written procedures and actual execution of business processes are not aligned. The management of that organization wishes to enforce the written procedures and decides to introduce a BPMS.

- The clients of a company complain that they can only get very shallow updates on the progress of the orders they make. The IT manager of that organization looks into the use of a BPMS to capture and provide status information on all these orders.
- An insurance organization finds out that there is an urgent need to quickly adjust their claims processing to the offerings that its competitors bring to the market. Using a BPMS is considered to address this demand.

9.3   Challenges of Introducing a BPMS

Despite the many advantages, there are some notable obstacles to the introduction of a BPMS in an organization. We distinguish between technical and organizational challenges.

9.3.1   Technical Challenges

What should be one of the strengths of a BPMS is also one of its pitfalls. A BPMS is capable of integrating different types of information systems to support a business process. The challenge is that many applications have not been developed with this coordinated use in mind. The mainframe applications that can still be found within banks and insurance companies today are notorious in this regard. In the most favorable case, such systems are technically documented but it often happens that there is no one of the original development team available anymore who knows exactly how these are structured. In such cases, it is very hard to determine how a BPMS can trigger such systems to make them support the execution of a particular work item, to exchange information between the BPMS and such a system (e.g., case data), and how to determine when an employee has used such a system to complete a particular work item.

A technique that has been used to make interaction at all possible with such legacy systems is *screen scraping*. The interaction between a BPMS and the mainframe application then takes place on the level of the user interface: The key strokes that an end user should make are emulated by the BPMS and the signals sent to the display are tracked to establish the progress of carrying out an activity. It will come as no surprise that such low-level integration solutions bring in its train much rigidity to the overall solution and will, in fact, undermine the flexibility advantages that are normally associated with using a BPMS. Recent systems that provide so-called *Robotic Process Automation* promise a more flexible integration. The following box explains how it works.

ROBOTIC PROCESS AUTOMATION

Robotic Process Automation (RPA) [15] refers to a novel class of software tools that automate tasks, or entire business processes, which are heavily based on clerical work. This includes highly-repetitive tasks or chains of tasks, such as copying data from one screen to another, that are quite time-consuming and error-prone, and can thus benefit from automation. RPA tools are configured by observing what human workers enter in different screens of existing systems, such as a claims management system or a legacy mainframe. For example, an RPA tool can be configured to automate the following human behavior: when a customer fills out a Web form to inquire about the status of an order, an employee copies the order number from this form, uses this number to search for the order status in an ERP system, copies the status from there and pastes it into a reply email. RPA tools can identify, extract, and analyze relevant information from user interfaces that are implemented in a variety of technologies, from Web-based forms and Java applications through to legacy command-prompt interfaces, where screen-scraping is required. As such, RPA constitutes a powerful and versatile technology. RPA can relieve human workers from tedious work on standard cases and it is often set up by organizations to achieve better process scalability and cost savings. However, configuring an RPA tool requires knowledge of the systems in place at an organization, and technical skills to train and test the software robots that will mimic human behavior.

A specific problem that occurs with respect to the integration of existing applications with BPMSs is the lack of process awareness of traditional systems. In a process-aware system, separate cases will be handled separately. In other words, such a system works on a case-by-case basis. In many traditional systems, however, *batch processing* is the dominant paradigm. This means that a particular task is executed for a large set of cases, which does not always align with the philosophy of a BPMS. Note how the "Case-based work" heuristic mentioned in Chapter 8 explicitly targets this situation.

Fortunately, in the area of system integration much progress has been made in the past decade. Many old systems are being phased out and new, open systems with clearly defined interfaces take their places. Technologies that are referred to as *Middleware* and *Enterprise Application Integration* tools are now available that strongly facilitate the communication and management of data in distributed applications. Microsoft's BizTalk Server[26] and IBM's WebSphere[27] are well-known software suites that can be used in this respect. There are open source technologies available as well. The success of *Web services* is another driver behind improved,

---

[26]https://www.microsoft.com/en-us/cloud-platform/biztalk.

[27]https://www.ibm.com/developerworks/downloads/ws/was.

coordinated use of different types of information systems, including BPMSs. A Web service is a piece of functionality, for example the identification of the best possible price for a particular good within a range of providers, which can be invoked over the Internet. Most BPMSs provide good support for integrating specific Web services in executable business processes. This kind of set-up would fit within a popular software architecture paradigm that is commonly referred to as *Service-Oriented Architecture*.

With respect to technical integration capabilities it is fair to say that recent developments are favorable for the use of BPMSs and that technical challenges, at least with respect to this aspect, are likely to further decrease over the next years.

9.3.2 Organizational Challenges

The introduction of an operational BPMS has an impact on extensive parts of an organization. This implies that the introduction of a BPMS can be challenging from an organizational perspective. The interests of different stakeholders have to be balanced, since they usually have diverging performance objectives and vie for the same resources. Getting an insight into how existing processes unfold is an enormous challenge in itself, sometimes taking months of work. Here, not only political motives may play a role—not everyone will be happy to give away how work is done, especially if not much work is done at all—but psychological ones as well: People tend to focus on describing the worst possible exceptions when asked to describe what their role is in a process. One scholar has referred to this tendency as the reason "why modelers wreck workflow innovation".

A factor that adds to this complexity is that organizations are dynamic entities. It it fairly usual that during the introduction of a BPMS, which may span a couple of months, organizational rules change, departments are scrapped or combined, participants get other responsibilities, and new products are introduced or taken off the market. These are all examples of events that may be important to consider when the aim is to make a BPMS function properly in an organizational setting. In practice, this accounts for the insight that the gradual introduction of a BPMS is usually more successful than a "big bang" strategy, in which a BPMS from 1 day to the other is expected to replace the way operations were managed.

The perspective of the users on the introduction of a BPMS should be considered carefully. Most process participants will first need to experience *hands-on* what it is to use a BPMS before they can really appreciate what that means for their job. There may also be concerns and fears. First, there might be a "Big brother is watching you" sentiment. Indeed, a BPMS will record all the events that are involved with executing a process, including who carried out what piece of work and at what time. It makes no use—and from a change management perspective, it could actually be self-defeating—to ignore this concern. Rather it is up to organizations to clarify how this information will be used and that there are positive effects that can be expected of the usage of this information as well.

Another fear that is common with end users of BPMSs is that their work will take on a mechanistic trait, almost as if they are working as a chain gang. This fear is in part genuine. It is true that the BPMS will take care of the allocation and routing of work. What can be argued, though, is that these are not the most exciting or valuable parts of the work that needs to be done (which is precisely the reason that they could be automated in the first place). If you would consider the situation where employees need to spend large parts of their time on finding the right information to do the job properly, the BPMS can be an attractive mechanism to give that time back to the employees. Another line of reasoning is that it highly depends on the configuration of the BPMS whether the mechanization effect will actually occur. Compare, for example, the situation where a BPMS pushes a single work item at a time to an employee to be carried out versus a range of work items such that someone could choose according to his or her own preferences. These options, which result from a configuration decision, can make a huge difference in the perception of the value of the BPMS.

To sum up, the introduction of a BPMS is particularly complex, precisely because it supports entire business processes. It is for a good reason that research into IT projects identifies "strong management commitment" as a major factor that explains implementation success. The introduction of a BPMS is, perhaps even more so than for other types of technologies, not for the faint of heart. The box on "Change Management" points to principles that any project to introduce a BPMS should consider.

CHANGE MANAGEMENT

Introducing a BPMS is often part of larger transformation initiatives, which tend to be far from easy. Some studies have suggested that two out of three transformation initiatives fail. The reason for failure is often poor management: poor planning, monitoring, and control, lack of resources and know-how, and incompatible corporate policies and practices [55]. Change management is the collective term for approaches that deal with change, from the perspective of both an organization and the individual, to make it succeed. Here, we briefly summarize some of the principles that have been identified as being conducive to successful change.

Factors of influence: A popular view on the factors that influence the success of a change management is the following: what truly matters is the **D**uration of the initiative, the **I**ntegrity of the project team, the **C**ommitment of the top management on the one hand and the affected employees on the other, and the **E**ffort that is demanded of employees on top of their usual work. This is referred to as **DICE**. Its maxim is: The shorter the project is, the more capable the project team, the higher

(continued)

the commitment of management and employees, and the lower the excess demand on employees, the bigger the chance on success [165].

Early victory: A phenomenon that has been observed in many process redesign projects is that victory had been declared too soon. After two or three years into the project, the team gets dissolved and the organization is trusted to continue with the fresh new way of working or the technology that had been implemented. But then, within two more years, the seemingly useful changes that had been introduced slowly disappear—even to the extent that sometimes no trace of the original change can be found back. What is killing the momentum is *premature victory celebration.* By contrast, successful efforts focus on short-term wins or small projects to use these as stepping stones for even bigger projects over time [81].

The nature of resistance: One of the most confounding aspects for managers is that skilled and smart employees, highly committed to the organization, and genuinely supporting a change, actually *do nothing* to make that change successful. The reason is that many people are unwittingly applying productive energy toward a hidden *competing commitment.* For example, a professional may have experienced that each time she completes a difficult assignment she ends up being assigned with an even more difficult one. This type of experience may make her less willing, perhaps even unconsciously, to embrace yet another new initiative. The key here is to take the time to truly understand people's behavior and analyze the assumptions they hold [74].

Programmatic change fallacy: Arguably the greatest mistake is to expect that change can only be brought about by company-wide change programs driven by corporate staff teams. This is also called the *fallacy of programmatic change.* A key element in a successful change program is that it spreads to all departments without too much pushing from the top. This means that there must be room for individual units to adopt a modified version of the envisioned change. Only after change has taken root in this way, the formal structure of the organization should change to institutionalize the applied changes [19].

Exercise 9.7 Consider the following issues that come up when introducing a BPMS in a hospital to support preoperative care, i.e., the preparation and management of a patient prior to surgery. Classify them as technical or organizational issues.

1. On hearing about the plans to introduce a BPMS, the surgeons flatly reject to cooperate on this endeavor. Their claim is that each patient is an individual person that cannot be trusted to the care of a one-size-fits-all system.

2. The anesthetists in the hospital use a decision support system that monitors the proper dosage of anesthetics to patients. The system is developed as a stand-

alone system that is difficult to synchronize with the BPMS, which has to feed the decision support system with patient data.
3. The nurses are provided with mobile devices, which they can use to access their worklist handlers. However, they find it difficult to follow up on the automatic notifications, which are signaled to them as gentle vibrations of the device.

9.4   Recap

In this chapter we discussed Process-Aware Information Systems (PAISs) with a specific focus on Business Process Management Systems (BPMSs). We described the architecture of a BPMS and its main components: the *execution engine*, the *process modeling tool* and *the process model repository*, the *administration and monitoring tools* and the *execution logs*, as well as the *external services* that can be invoked.

There are many reasons for considering process automation using a PAIS. First, it provides workload reduction in terms of coordination: work is assigned to process participants or software services as soon as it is available. Second, it offers integration flexibility. Processes can be changed with significantly less effort as compared to legacy systems, provided they are explicitly represented via process models. Third, the execution in a BPMS generates valuable data on how processes are executed, including performance-relevant data. Finally, BPMSs improve the quality of process execution as they directly enforce rules, such as separation of duties.

Introducing BPMSs poses various challenges. Technical challenges arise from the fact that many applications that have to be integrated are typically not designed as open systems with transparent interfaces. Beyond that, organizational challenges are rooted in the fact that BPMSs directly interfere with how people do their job. This fact calls for sensitive change management.

9.5   Solutions to Exercises

Solution 9.1 There are market research reports with different estimates available. For the period of 2016, they often mention Microsoft, Oracle, IBM, SAP, and EMC among the Top 5 enterprise software vendors. The Top 5 ERP vendors often include SAP, Oracle, Microsoft, Infor, and Epicor in the list.

Solution 9.2

1. There are various pieces of information that are not visible in the chart. It is not clear with what allocation strategy work items are assigned to process participants. It is also not clear whether the different participants work full-time or only part-time. It also does not tell in how far the participants have comparable

skills and expertise. Finally, it is not clear whether the activity Program review application is fully homogenous and standardized or whether there are important variations in the characteristics of the applications.

2. Without knowing the details about the matters discussed, it is difficult to interpret the chart in a way that is fair for the process participants. Note in this context that it is often the competent employees that are overloaded, because they help less-skilled colleagues when they do not know the right way to proceed.

Solution 9.3 There are three current work items:

1. Case #1,220: Determine Proper Piece of Equipment
2. Case #1,230: Determine Proper Piece of Equipment
3. Case #1,240: Complete Equipment Rental Request

Solution 9.4

- The execution engine would be unable to allocate work items to resources on the basis of a process model alone, when it would only cover control-flow information.
- One common situation would be that the process model in question specifies that after a certain activity there is a parallel split, enabling the execution of various follow-up activities.
- Other examples of services that can be useful to be invoked: calculation services (e.g., to determine a mortgage rate or to estimate the total cost of a service), information storage and retrieval services (e.g., to register the outcome of a completed work item or to look up client information), scheduling services (e.g., to plan work that is to be done in follow-up or to estimate a delivery date), communication services (e.g., to get in touch with the client or a business partner).
- Most notably, it would be important to specify on which working days particular resources are available and during which hours, e.g., Ms. Senora only works on Mondays and Fridays and then only from 9 a.m. to 4 p.m. In this way, it becomes possible for the execution engine to allocate work items in an efficient manner.

Solution 9.5

1. It should become possible that the new decision support system can be invoked as an external service.
2. If Ms. Senora retires, this must be recorded with the administration tool.
3. The new rule to allocate work items to resources must be captured in an updated process model.
4. The monitoring service must be implemented in a monitoring tool.

Solution 9.6

- Quality
- Transparency
- Flexibility

Solution 9.7

1. Organizational issue: BPMSs can be highly tailored to take patient-specific data into account.
2. Technical issue: The integration of the decision support system may require additional, customized software development.
3. Organizational/technical: The nurses may on the one hand get accustomed to using the BPMS in general and worklist handlers specifically. On the other hand, it may not be a good technical solution to use vibration signals—an alternative would be, for example, to use sound signals.

9.6 Further Exercises

Exercise 9.8 Draw the architecture of one specific commercial or open-source BPMS and identify all its components.

Exercise 9.9 Explain the similarities and differences between production and ad hoc workflow systems. Include in your explanation a reflection on the type of support they provide on the one hand and their orientation in the spectrum of data versus process on the other.

Exercise 9.10 Classify the following objectives of the various organizations described that use a BPMS and use the categories of advantages that were explained in Section 9.2.

- A legal company wishes to track all the participants it has involved in its formalized process for the preparation of litigation cases.
- A governmental agency wishes to reduce the penalties it must pay for late payments of invoices.
- A bank wishes to demonstrate to its external auditor that it strictly enforces the principle that each large loan is approved by two separate clerks.

Exercise 9.11 In a 2009 posting on LinkedIn, the director of Walgreens, an online pharmacy, asks what the common pitfalls are when implementing a workflow management system. A consultant at Microsoft answers as follows:

> It's really all about people buying in to the system. The general tendency of people is that they don't like change, even if they say they do. Even if their current processes are very inefficient, they know how it works. So, when you introduce something that changes their world (with a workflow mgt system), they'll be very apprehensive. Also, the more the system changes how they do their job, the more resistance you'll get. Then it becomes an issue of how you gathered your business requirements. Chances are that due to misunderstandings the requirements will be different than expectations of how things should get done.

Explain whether you think this explanation relates to a technical or an organizational challenge.

9.7 Further Readings

Van der Aalst and van Hee's classic book [176] offers an introduction to workflow management technology as of the early 2000s. The evolution from workflow management systems to BPMSs that took place during the 2000s is discussed at length by Weske [193]. As stated in this chapter, the WfMC reference model was instrumental in shaping the architectures of workflow management systems and later that of BPMSs. Details on the WfMC reference model can be found on the website of the Workflow Management Coalition,[28] while Hollingsworth [69] gives a summary of the development and directions of this reference model.

A frequent critique of BPMSs is that they follow a Fordist paradigm, meaning that the BPMS forces process participants to act in a certain direction, i.e., exactly in the way it is captured in a process model. In the context of processes where unanticipated exceptions are common and where there is no predictable way to perform the process, a BPMS often ends up obstructing the work of process participants rather than supporting them. Approaches to support non-standardized or unpredictable processes are described by Reichert et al. [130]. One of those approaches is case handling. An introduction to this topic is given by Van der Aalst et al. [179], while a more comprehensive treatment of the subject is provided by Swenson [172].

A recent longitudinal study involving ten organizations has shed light into the success of BPMS deployments and their business impact [138]. Half of the organizations in this study abandoned their BPMS deployment efforts due to a variety of organizational reasons, chiefly related to change management. This finding highlights the importance of change management when introducing a BPMS in an organization as discussed in the "Change Management" box in Section 9.3.2 (see page 363). On the other hand, those organizations in the study that managed to deploy a BPMS benefited from substantial process improvements.

BPMSs are mainly focused on the automation of business processes within a given organization (*intra-organizational processes*). Many processes, however, span across organizational boundaries. For example, an order-to-cash process typically involves a purchasing company, a supplying company, and a logistics company. There might also be sub-contractors involved (e.g., a customs broker) as well as insurers and export credit agencies. Traditionally, the coordination of all these parties is done via message exchanges. Dispute resolution is a recurrent problem in these processes, for example when a party claims that goods have not been delivered or when a party does not accept an invoice issued by another party. These problems are particularly acute when there is a lack of trust between the parties. Blockchain is an emerging technology that can be used to coordinate *inter-organizational processes* involving untrusted parties. A blockchain provides a way to record that something has happened in a way that ensures that once something has

---

[28]http://wfmc.org/reference-model.html.

been recorded, it cannot be deleted. Modern blockchains also provide mechanisms to ensure that a given routine (called a *small contract*) is executed every time a given type of transaction is recorded. Instead of exchanging messages, parties involved in an inter-organizational process can execute transactions on a blockchain. This alternative approach ensures that important business rules are always followed (e.g., an accepted delivery is followed by a payment).

Opportunities of applying blockchain technology for BPM are discussed in [113]. Research in this field has demonstrated the feasibility of executing business processes on top of blockchains by taking process models as a starting point [53, 191]. At the time of the writing of this book, BPMS vendors and other PAIS vendors have started to incorporate blockchain-based capabilities into their products. An open-source BPMS running entirely on blockchain has been recently released, namely Caterpillar [95].[29]

---

[29]http://git.io/caterpillar.

Chapter 10
Process Implementation with Executable Models

Check for
updates

> *You don't make progress by standing on the sidelines,*
> *whimpering and complaining. You make progress by*
> *implementing ideas.*
> Shirley Chisholm (1924–2005)

In the previous chapters, we have learned how to create *conceptual process models* and use them for documentation and analysis purposes. Because of their purpose, these models are intentionally abstract in nature, i.e., they do not provide technical implementation details. This means that conceptual process models must be systematically reworked into *executable process models* to be interpreted and automatically executed by a software system, such as a BPMS.

In this chapter, we propose a five-step method to incrementally transform a conceptual process model into an executable one, using the BPMN language. As part of this method, we also show how to make use of two other standards complementary to BPMN: the Case Management Model and Notation (CMMN) and the Decision Model and Notation (DMN). The steps are:

1. Identify the automation boundaries,
2. Review manual tasks,
3. Complete the process model,
4. Bring the process model to an adequate level of granularity, and
5. Specify execution properties.

Through these steps, the conceptual model will incrementally become less abstract and more IT-oriented. These steps should only be carried out on a process model that is syntactically correct. For example, if the model contains behavioral errors like deadlocks, then the BPMS may get stuck while executing an instance of this process model. This may have a negative impact on the operations of the organization (e.g., slowdowns or impediments in the fulfillment of purchase orders). We have already discussed verification in Section 5.4.1. In the following, we assume that the process model is sound.

© Springer-Verlag GmbH Germany, part of Springer Nature 2018
M. Dumas et al., *Fundamentals of Business Process Management*,
https://doi.org/10.1007/978-3-662-56509-4_10

10.1   Identify the Automation Boundaries

A conceptual process model does not typically describe how each process task should be implemented. Depending on its nature, a task may not easily be implemented automatically or it may not be possible to implement it at all via a BPMS. Accordingly, the principle driving this first step is that *not all processes can be automated*. Based on this principle, we start by identifying which parts of our process can be coordinated by the BPMS and which parts cannot. To do so, we distinguish three types of tasks, in line with the BPMN language: *automated*, *manual*, and *user* tasks. Automated tasks are performed by the BPMS itself or by an external service. Manual tasks are performed by process participants without the aid of any software. User tasks sit between automated and manual tasks. A user task is a task that is performed by a participant with the assistance of the worklist handler of the BPMS or an external task list manager.

The differentiation between automated, manual, and user tasks is important: Automated and user tasks can easily be coordinated by a BPMS, while manual tasks cannot. Therefore, we first have to identify the type of each task. In the next step, we review the manual tasks and assess whether we can find a way to hook them up to the BPMS. If this is not possible, we will have to consider whether or not it is convenient to automate the rest of the process without these manual tasks.

Let us consider again the order-to-cash process model that we created in Chapter 3. It is shown in Figure 10.1 for convenience (for the moment, please discard the markers). Let us assume that we obtain this model from a process analyst. Our job is to automate it from the seller's viewpoint. As such, we need to focus on the process in the seller pool and discard the rest. The first task, "Check stock availability", belongs to the ERP lane. This means that it was already identified as an automated task at the conceptual level. ERP systems provide modules to manage inventories, which automatically check the stock levels of a product against a warehouse database. This task is highly repetitive since it is performed for each purchase order received. Performing it manually would be inefficient, because it would keep a process participant busy with a trivial yet time-consuming task. Similar observations can be made for "Check raw materials availability", which is also an automated task. Another example is the "Manufacture product" task. This is performed by the manufacturing plant, which exposes its functionality via an IT service interface. From the perspective of a BPMS, it is also an automated task.

Continuing with our example, there are other tasks, such as "Request raw materials from Supplier 1(2)" and "Get shipping address", that are devoted to sending and receiving messages. These are examples of automated tasks, too. They can be implemented via an automatic email exchange or a Web service invocation. Note that BPMSs typically provide these capabilities. So far, these tasks are not explicitly modeled inside a system lane. Recall that we are looking at a conceptual process model, where it may not be relevant to model all existing systems (in this case an email service or a Web service) via lanes.

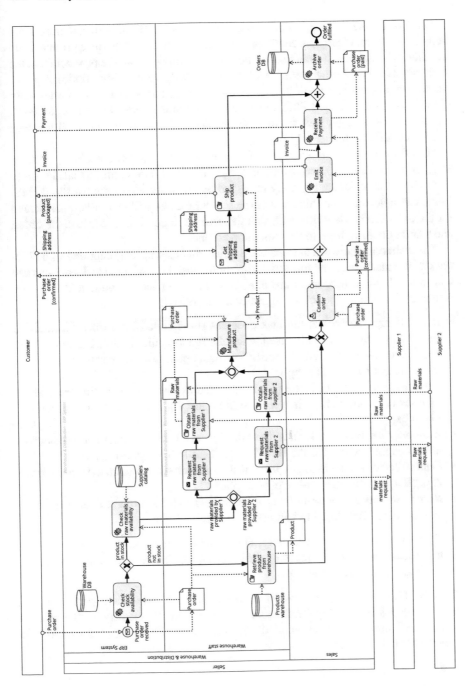

Fig. 10.1 The order-to-cash model that we want to automate

Other tasks like "Retrieve product from warehouse", "Obtain raw materials from Supplier 1(2)", and "Ship product" are manual. For example, "Retrieve product from warehouse" requires a warehouse worker to physically pick up the product from the shelf for shipping. In the presence of a manual task we have two options: (i) we isolate the task and focus on the automation of the process before and after it, or (ii) we find a way for the BPMS to be notified when the manual task has started or completed. We will get back to this point in the second step. For now, all we need to do is identify these manual tasks.

"Confirm order" is an example of a user task: it requires somebody in sales (e.g., an order clerk) to verify the purchase order and then confirm that the order is correct. User tasks are typically managed by the worklist handler of the BPMS. In our example, an electronic form of the purchase order will be rendered on screen for the order clerk, who will verify that the order is in good state, confirm the order, and submit the form back to the execution engine.

The distinction between automated, manual, and user tasks is captured in BPMN via specific markers on the top-left corner of the task box. Manual tasks are marked with a hand, while user tasks are marked with a user icon. Automated tasks are further classified into the following subtypes in BPMN:

- *Script* (script marker), if the task executes some code (the script) internally to the BPMS. This task can be used when the functionality is simple and does not require access to an external application, e.g., opening a file or selecting the best quote from a number of suppliers.
- *Service* (gears marker), if the task is executed by an external application, which exposes its functionality via a service interface, e.g., "Check stock availability" in our example.
- *Business rule* (table marker), if the task triggers a business rule to be executed by a rules engine external to the BPMS, e.g., the rule for approving a loan.
- *Send* (filled envelope marker), if the task sends a message to an external service, e.g., "Request raw materials from Supplier 1".
- *Receive* (empty envelope marker), if the task waits for a message from an external service, e.g., "Get shipping address".

These markers apply to tasks only. They cannot be used on sub-processes, since a sub-process may contain tasks of different types. The relevant markers for our example are shown in Figure 10.1.

Exercise 10.1 Assume you have to automate the loan assessment process model of Solution 3.8 (page 111) for the loan provider. Start by classifying the tasks of this process into manual, automated, and user tasks. Then, represent them with appropriate task markers.

10.2 Review Manual Tasks

Once we have identified the type of each task, in the second step of our method we need to check whether we can link the manual tasks with the BPMS. The principle driving this step is: *if the task cannot be seen by the BPMS, it does not exist.* So, we either find a way to support manual tasks via technology or, alternatively, we need to isolate these tasks and automate the rest of the process. There are two ways of linking a manual task to a BPMS: we implement it either via a user task or via an automated task.

Implement as User Task: If the participant involved in the manual task can notify the BPMS of the task completion using the worklist handler of the BPMS, then the manual task can be turned into a user task. For example, the warehouse worker performing task "Retrieve product from warehouse" could check out a work item from the worklist to indicate that the task is being worked on, manually retrieve the product from the shelf, and then check in the work item back into the BPMS engine. Alternatively, check-out and check-in can be combined in a single step, by which the worker notifies the worklist handler of the completion of the task.

Implement as Automated Task: In some cases, a process participant may use technology that is integrated with the BPMS to notify the engine of a work item completion. For example, the warehouse worker could use a device such as a barcode scanner to scan the barcode of the raw materials that are picked up. If the device is connected to the BPMS, scanning the barcode will automatically signal the completion of task "Obtain raw materials from Supplier 1(2)". In this case, the manual task can be implemented as a receive task, which will be awaiting the notification from the scanner, or as a user task handled by a worklist handler, which in turn is connected to the scanner. If we use a receive task, the BPMS will only be aware of the work item's completion: informing the warehouse worker that a new work item is available will be outside the scope of the BPMS. If we use a user task, the worker will be notified of the new work item by the BPMS and will use the scanner to signal the work item's completion to the BPMS engine. Similar considerations hold for task "Ship order". Since each manual task of our example can be linked with a BPMS, this process can be entirely automated.

Exercise 10.2 Consider the loan assessment model that you analyzed in Exercise 10.1. Review the manual tasks of this model in order to link them to a BPMS.

There are cases in which it is not convenient to link manual tasks to a BPMS.

Example 10.1 Let us consider the university admission process described in Exercise 1.1 (see page 5), with the improvements discussed in Solution 1.5 (page 29). The process can be automated until the point where the application is batched for the admission committee (shown in Figure 10.2a). Once all the applications have been batched, the committee will meet and examine all of them at once. However, this part of the process (shown in Figure 10.2b) is outside the scope of a BPMS.

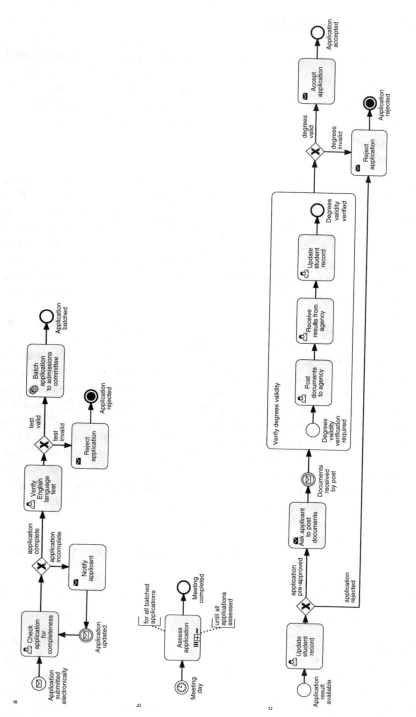

Fig. 10.2 Admission process: the initial (**a**) and final (**c**) assessments can be automated in a BPMS; the assessment by the committee (**b**) is a manual process outside the scope of the BPMS

The tasks required for assessing applications cannot be automated, because they involve various human participants who interact on an ad hoc basis. It would not be convenient to synchronize all these tasks with the BPMS. Eventually, the committee will decide on a list of accepted candidates and transfer it to the admissions office. Then, a clerk at the admissions office will update the various student records, at which time the rest of the process can proceed within the scope of the BPMS (shown in Figure 10.2c).

In this example, we cannot automate the whole process. So, we need to isolate the task "Assess application", an ad hoc task containing various manual tasks, and automate the process before and after this task. An option is to split the model into three fragments as shown in Figure 10.2 and only automate the first and the third fragment. Another option is to keep one model and simply remove the ad hoc task. Some BPMSs are tolerant to the presence of manual tasks and ad hoc tasks in executable models, and will discard them at deployment time (like comments in a programming language). If this is the case, we can keep these elements in.

Observe the use of the untyped event to start the third process model fragment in Figure 10.2. In BPMN, a process that starts with an untyped event indicates that instances of this process are explicitly started by a BPMS user, in our case a clerk at the admissions office. This process initiation is called *explicit instantiation*. *Implicit instantiation* refers to the situation where process instances are triggered automatically by the event type indicated in the start event, e.g., an incoming message or a timer.   □

Exercise 10.3 Consider the final part of the prescription fulfillment process described in Exercise 1.6 (page 30):

Once the prescription passes the insurance check, it is assigned to a technician who collects the drugs from the shelves and puts them in a bag with the prescription stapled to it. After the technician has filled a given prescription, the bag is passed to the pharmacist who double-checks that the prescription has been filled correctly. After this quality check, the pharmacist seals the bag and puts it in the pick-up area. When a customer arrives to pick up a prescription, a technician retrieves thise prescription and asks the customer for the co-payment or for the full payment in case the drugs in the prescription are not covered by the customer's insurance policy.

One way of modeling this fragment is by defining the following tasks: "Check insurance", "Collect drugs from shelves", "Check quality", "Collect payment" (triggered by the arrival of the customer), and finally "Retrieve prescription bag". Assume the pharmacy system automates the prescription fulfillment process. Identify the type of each task and if there are any manual tasks, specify how these can be linked to the pharmacy system.

There are other modeling elements besides manual tasks that are relevant at a conceptual level but cannot be interpreted by a BPMS. These are physical data objects and data stores, messages bearing physical objects, and text annotations. Pools and lanes are only meaningful at the conceptual level, too. In fact, as we have seen, pools and lanes are often used to capture coarse-grained resource assignments, e.g., task "Confirm order" is done within the sales department. When it comes to execution, we need to define resource assignments for each task and capturing this information via dedicated lanes (potentially one for each task) would make the model too cluttered. Electronic data stores are also not directly interpreted by a BPMS, since the BPMS assumes the existence of dedicated services that can access these data stores, e.g., an inventory information service that can access the warehouse database. So, the BPMS will interface with these services rather than directly with the data stores. Also, the state of a data object indicated in the object's label, e.g., "Purchase order [confirmed]", cannot be interpreted as such by a BPMS. Later, we will show how to explicitly represent object states so that they can be interpreted by a BPMS.

Some BPMSs tolerate the presence of non-executable elements in their modeling tool. If this is the case, it is good practice to leave these elements in. Especially pools, lanes, message flows bearing electronic objects, electronic data stores, and annotations will guide us in the specification of some execution properties. For example, the Sales lane in the order-to-cash model indicates that the participant who is to be assigned the "Confirm order" task has to be from the sales department. Other BPMSs do not support these elements, so it is not possible to represent them in the process model.

Exercise 10.4 Consider the loan assessment model that you obtained in Exercise 10.2 (page 375). Identify the modeling elements that cannot be interpreted by a BPMS.

10.3   Complete the Process Model

Once we have established the automation boundaries of the process and reviewed the manual tasks, we need to check that our process model is *complete*. Two principles underlie this step: (i) *exceptions are the rule* and (ii) *no data implies no decisions and no task handoff*. Often, conceptual process models neglect certain information; because modelers deem it as irrelevant for the specific modeling purpose, they assume it is common knowledge, or they are simply not aware of it. Depending on the application scenario, it may be fine to neglect this information in a conceptual model. However, information that is not relevant in a conceptual model may be highly relevant for a process model to be executed.

A typical example is when the process model focuses on the "sunny-day" scenario and neglects all negative situations that may arise during the execution of the process, working under the assumption that everything will work well. As we saw in Chapter 4, there are various exceptions that can occur in the order-to-cash process. For example, this process may be aborted if the materials required to manufacture the product are not available at the suppliers or if the customer cancels the order. So, based on the first principle above, we need to make sure that all exceptions are handled using appropriate exception handlers. For example, if the order cancelation is received after the product has been shipped or after the payment has been received, then we also have to compensate for these tasks by returning the product and reimbursing the customer. Another exception that is commonly neglected is the situation when a task cannot complete correctly. What happens if the customer's address is never received? Or if the ERP module for checking the stock availability does not respond? We cannot assume that the other party will always respond or that a system will always be functional. Similarly, we cannot assume that tasks always lead to a positive outcome. For example, an order may not always be confirmed.

You may be surprised about how rarely exceptions are captured in a conceptual process model in practice. Thus, in the majority of cases, such a model will require to be completed with these aspects before being executed.

Looking at the second principle, in this step we also need to specify all *electronic data objects* that are required as input and output by the tasks of our process. For instance, in Figure 10.1 (see page 373) there is no input data object to task "Request raw materials from Supplier 1(2)", though this task does need the list of raw materials to be ordered. Another example is task "Check stock availability". This task uses the purchase order as input (to obtain the code of the product to be looked up in the Warehouse DB), but does not produce any output data to store the results of the search. However, without this information, the subsequent XOR-split cannot determine which branch to take (we can now better grasp why this is called a *data-based XOR-split*). If you have not noticed the absence of these data objects so far, it is probably because you assumed their existence. This is fine in a conceptual model where only aspects relevant to the specific modeling purpose are documented, but not in an executable model, where a software engine has to run the model. So, make sure each task has the required input and output electronic data objects. The point is that every data object needed by the BPMS engine to pass control between tasks and to take decisions must be modeled.

The completed order-to-cash example, including exception handlers and data objects that are relevant for execution, is shown in Figure 10.3.[1]

Exercise 10.5 Take the loan assessment model that you obtained in Exercise 10.1 (page 374) after incorporating the revisions from Exercise 10.2 (page 375). Complete this model with control-flow and data-flow aspects relevant for automation. For the sake of simplicity, you may disregard the modeling elements that are not interpretable by a BPMS.

---

[1] The content of the sub-processes and some of the elements that cannot be interpreted by a BPMS have been omitted for simplicity.

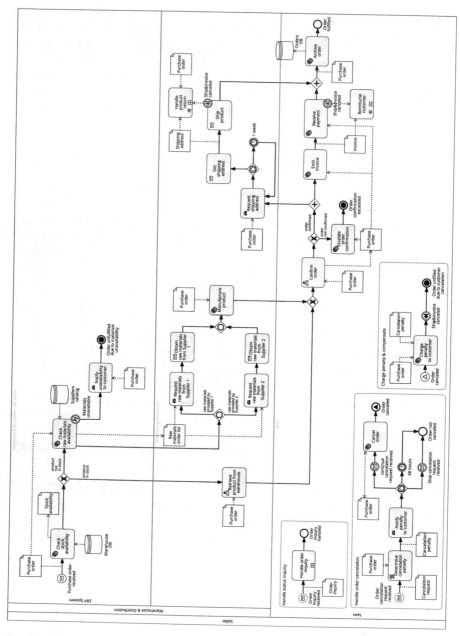

Fig. 10.3 The order-to-cash model of Figure 10.1, completed with control-flow and data-flow aspects relevant for automation

10.4   Bring the Process Model to an Adequate Granularity Level

Tasks in a conceptual model may not be at the right level of granularity for implementation. They may be either too abstract, in which case we need to decompose them, or too detailed, in which case they should be aggregated. For example, two consecutive tasks assigned to the same resource are candidates for *aggregation*. In a similar way, if a task requires more than one resource to be performed, then it is too *coarse-grained*. We should then decompose it into finer-grained tasks such that these can be assigned to different resources. The principle driving these examples is that *a BPMS adds value if it coordinates handoffs of work between resources*. Indeed, we should keep in mind that a BPMS is intended to coordinate and manage handoffs of work between multiple resources (human or non-human). If this were not the case, the BPMS would not add value between tasks.

A special case are ad hoc sub-processes, which are difficult to define in terms of the order of tasks within the sub-process. These sub-processes may be implemented using the Case Management Model and Notation (CMMN), a language complementary to BPMN.

10.4.1   Task Decomposition

If a task requires more than one resource to be performed, we should *decompose* it into more fine-grained tasks, such that these can be assigned to different resources. For example, a task "Enter and approve money transfer" is likely to be performed by two different participants even if they have the same role. In this case, we typically want to enforce a *separation of duties*: first a financial officer enters the order, then a different financial officer approves of it.

Exercise 10.6   Figure 10.4 shows the model for the sales process of a business-to-business (B2B) service provider. The process starts when an application is received

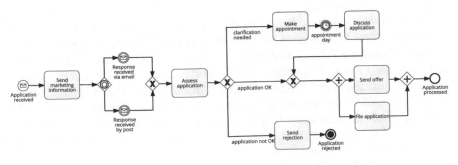

Fig. 10.4   The sales process of a B2B service provider

from a potential client. The client is then sent information about the available services. A response by the client is awaited to arrive via either email or postal mail. When the response is received, the next action is decided upon. Either an appointment can be made with the client to discuss the service options in person or the application is accepted. It could also be rejected right away. If the application is accepted, an offer is sent to the client and at the same time the application is filed. If it is rejected, the client is sent a thank-you note. If an appointment has to be made, this is done and, at the time of the appointment, the application is discussed with the client. Then, the process continues as if the application had been accepted right away.

1. Identify the type of each task and find ways of linking the manual tasks to a BPMS.
2. Remove elements that cannot be interpreted by a BPMS.
3. Complete the model by adding the control-flow and data aspects required for execution.
4. Bring the resulting model to a granularity level that is adequate for execution.

Acknowledgement: This exercise is adapted from a similar exercise developed by Remco Dijkman, Eindhoven University of Technology.

10.4.2   Decomposition of Ad Hoc Sub-Processes with CMMN

Unordered tasks, such as those within an ad hoc sub-process (see Section 4.1.2), are often difficult to implement using a BPMS based on the BPMN language. Take, for example, the model in Figure 4.6 (page 122). This model, which captures the order-to-cash process from the perspective of the customer, has three tasks within an ad hoc sub-process: "Check order status", "Update details", and "Cancel order". These tasks can hardly be coordinated by a BPMS based on BPMN, since there is no strict order for their execution. Also, each of these may potentially be repeated multiple times. As a rule of thumb, a (sub-)process whose tasks are performed in an ad hoc manner, without any predictable order, is not suitable for automation via a BPMN-based BPMS. In this case, a case management system or an ad hoc workflow system is more appropriate.

Several BPMSs, such as Camunda, do not only support the BPMN language, but also the Case Management Model and Notation (CMMN) language. This is another standard by OMG, available in version 1.1. BPMN and CMMN differ in the way they describe processes. BPMN builds on the explicit specification of those execution sequences that are allowed. Thereby, it forbids any other order of processing. CMMN defines which tasks have to be executed, although potentially restricted by certain conditions. In this way, it remains underspecified how the case is to be handled, except for those tasks that are bound to conditions. Therefore, CMMN is often considered as a more flexible way to describe *what* has to be achieved in a process instead of *how* to achieve it. Often, CMMN will be used as a

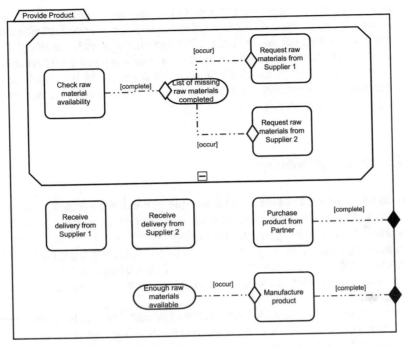

Fig. 10.5 Excerpt of an order-to-cash process model (from out-of-stock product to product provided) captured in CMMN

type of sub-process in a BPMN model, but also vice versa: tasks in a CMMN model can have BPMN sub-processes.

CMMN offers a set of elements for describing processes. This set includes tasks and events with the same graphical symbols as we know them from BPMN. Figure 10.5 shows a simple example including the most important elements. The model was created by a process analyst who felt that the the order-to-cash process within their company was difficult to model in BPMN from the point where the product is out-of-stock to the provisioning of the product. In a CMMN model, everything is organized in a *case*, depicted as a large box with a tab to make it look like a folder. For example, consider the "Provide product" case in our example. A case contains a stage, tasks, milestones, sentries, and connections. The *stage* is a large octagon, which can be used to group other elements. Here, it is used to describe how raw materials are checked for availability as a *task*, how this contributes to arriving at the *milestone* of compiling a list of missing raw materials, and how this milestone must occur before raw materials can be requested from Supplier 1 or 2. This condition is expressed using a *sentry*, which is a small, diamond-shaped symbol on the entry-side of elements. The reason why the process analyst decided to use CMMN is the fact that those requests do not exactly match deliveries. First, the suppliers deliver standard materials on a regular basis, even without an explicit request. Second, it often happens that one request is served by several separate deliveries. In other to express the fact that deliveries can happen at any time, the two "Receive delivery" tasks do not have any sentries. There is another milestone in the lower part of the model, which is called "Enough raw materials available". If this is reached, the product can be manufactured. This leads to a successful completion of the case, as indicated by the black diamond element on the border of the case container. Our example model also includes another option to provide the product, i.e., by purchasing it from a partner.

10.4.3   Task Aggregation

Tasks on a conceptual level can also be too fine-grained. For example, a sequence of user tasks "Enter customer name", "Enter customer policy number", and "Enter damage details" should be aggregated into a single user task "Enter claim" if they are all supposed to be performed by the same claims handler. Otherwise, all the BPMS would do would be to interfere with the work of the claims handler. Accordingly, two or more consecutive tasks assigned to the same resource are candidates for *aggregation*.

There are some cases, though, where we may actually need to keep consecutive tasks separate, despite that they are performed by the same resource. For example, in Figure 10.2c we have three user tasks within the sub-process "Verify degrees validity": "Post documents to agency", "Receive results from agency", and "Update student record". While these may be performed by the same admin clerk, we want to keep track of when each task has been completed for the sake of monitoring the progress of the application and managing potential exceptions. For example, if the results are not received within a given timeframe, we can handle this delay by adding an exception handler to the "Receive results from agency" task.

Exercise 10.7   Are there tasks that can be aggregated in the model as obtained in Exercise 10.5 (page 379)?
Hint: candidate tasks for aggregation may not necessarily be consecutive due to a sub-optimal order of tasks in the conceptual model. In this case, you need to resequence the tasks first.

10.5   Specify Execution Properties

At the end of the fourth step, we obtain a *to-be-executed* process model, i.e., a process model that contains the right elements and is at the right level of granularity to be automated with a BPMS. However, this model is still technology-agnostic. That is to say, it is independent of the specific BPMS technology we will choose for automation. As such, software engineers may be supported by process analysts in the incremental transformation of a conceptual model into a to-be-executed model.

To make the model fully executable, we need to specify in the last step *how* each model element is effectively implemented by our BPMS of choice. For example, take the first service task of our revised order-to-cash example: "Check stock availability". Saying that this task requires the purchase order as input to contact the warehouse ERP system is not enough. We need to specify which specific service provided by the ERP system is to be used to check the stock levels, the location of its interface in the network, the format of its input object (the purchase order), and the format of its output object (the stock availability). These implementation details are called *execution properties*. They are required to obtain a fully-executable process model. More specifically, these properties are:

- Variables, messages, signals, errors, and their data types,
- Data mappings,
- Service details for service, send and receive tasks, and for message and signal events,
- Code snippets for script tasks,
- Participant assignment rules and user interface structure for user tasks,
- Task, event, and sequence flow expressions, and
- Other BPMS-specific properties.

The BPMN language provides the means to specify most of these properties. However, in practice, BPMS vendors often diverge from the standard way of specifying these properties and rather offer alternative, sometimes proprietary, mechanisms. This may be because of legacy reasons or to gain a competitive advantage. In the rest of this section, we will focus on how the above properties can be defined according to the standard BPMN specification and point out to some alternatives, where available.

Execution properties do not have a graphical representation in a BPMN model, but are stored in the BPMN interchange format. The BPMN interchange format is a textual representation of a BPMN model in XML format. It is intended to support the interchange of BPMN models between tools and also serves as input to a BPMN execution engine. BPMN modeling tools provide a visual interface to edit most of these non-graphical properties. So, most of the times you will not need to write XML directly. Still, you will need to at least understand standard Web technology and be familiar with the notion of Web service to be able to implement an executable process model. This section assumes that you have a basic knowledge of technologies such as XML and XML Schema (XSD). We provide pointers to further readings on these technologies at the end of this chapter.

Figure 10.6 shows the structure of the BPMN exchange format. It consists of a list of elements, where some are optional (those with a dashed border) and others are mandatory (those with solid borders). The process element is mandatory. It consists of data objects, events, tasks, and flows. The elements outside the process are reusable components needed by the various process elements, such as message definitions and service interfaces that are used by service, send, and receive tasks, and by message and signal events. With reference to this structure, let us now go through each of the execution properties listed above.

Fig. 10.6 Structure of the
BPMN format

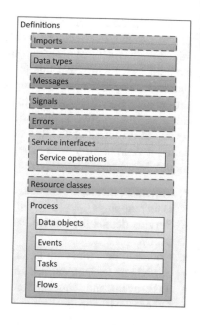

10.5.1   Variables, Messages, Signals, Errors, and Their Data Types

Process variables are managed by the BPMS engine to allow data exchange between process elements. Each electronic data object, e.g., the purchase order in the order-to-cash process, is represented by a process variable. Each of the variables we want to use in the process has to be explicitly defined by assigning a *data type* to it. In BPMN, the type of each variable is specified as an XSD type. However, some BPMSs may use different languages or proprietary definitions. With reference to XSD, the type of a variable can be *simple* or *complex*. The complex types can be either defined directly in the BPMN model or imported from an external document (see Figure 10.6). Simple types are strings, integers, doubles (numbers containing decimals), booleans, dates, times, etc.. These are already defined in the XSD specification. For example, the object "Stock availability" can be represented as a variable of type integer (capturing the number of available units of a product). Complex types are hierarchical compositions of other types. A complex type can be used to represent, for example, a business document, such as a purchase order or an invoice. Figure 10.7a shows the possible format of a purchase order, captured as a complex type called "purchaseOrderType". Figure 10.7b is the XML representation of a particular instance of this purchase order at runtime. From the type definition we can see that a purchase order contains a sequence of two elements:

- "order" to store the order information (order number, order date, status, currency, product code and quantity), and

a)

```
<complexType name="purchaseOrderType">
  <sequence>
    <element name="order">
      <complexType>
        <sequence>
          <element name="orderNumber" type="integer"/>
          <element name="orderDate" type="date"/>
          <element name="status" type="string"/>
          <element name="currency" type="string"/>
          <element name="productCode" type="string"/>
          <element name="quantity" type="integer"/>
        </sequence>
      </complexType>
    </element>
    <element name="customer">
      <complexType>
        <element name="name" type="string"/>
        <element name="surname" type="string"/>
        <element name="address">
          <complexType>
            <sequence>
              <element name="street" type="string"/>
              <element name="city" type="string"/>
              <element name="state" type="string"/>
              <element name="postCode" type="string"/>
              <element name="country" type="string"/>
            </sequence>
          </complexType>
        </element>
        <element name="phone" type="string"/>
        <element name="fax" type="string"/>
      </complexType>
    </element>
  </sequence>
</complexType>
```

b)

```
<purchaseOrder>
  <order>
    <orderNumber>15664</orderNumber>
    <orderDate>2012-10-23</orderDate>
    <status>confirmed</status>
    <currency>EUR</currency>
    <productCode>345-EAR</productCode>
    <quantity>10</quantity>
  </order>
  <customer>
    <name>John</name>
    <surname>Brown</surname>
    <address>
      <street>8 George St</street>
      <city>Brisbane</city>
      <state>Queensland</state>
      <postCode>4000</postCode>
      <country>Australia</country>
    </address>
    <phone>+61 7 3240 0010</phone>
    <fax>+61 7 3221 0412</fax>
  </customer>
</purchaseOrder>
```

Fig. 10.7 The XSD describing the purchase order (**a**) and one of its instances (**b**)

- "customer" to store the customer information (name, surname, address, phone and fax).

The data fields order, customer, and address are complex types that can contain sub-elements. Also, observe the field "status" within order: It is used to capture the state of the purchase order, e.g., "confirmed".

Process variables are assigned a data type and defined to be used within the whole lifetime of a process instance. They are visible at the process level in which they are defined and in all the sub-processes within the process model. This means that a variable defined in a sub-process (i.e., a sub-process variable) is not visible in the parent process. The data objects that we discussed above, like purchase order, are typically defined as process variables.

Similarly to process variables, we also need to assign data types to each message, signal, and error used in the process model. For the *messages*, we can look at the existing message flows in the diagram and define one data type for each uniquely-labeled message flow. So, for example, if we have two message flows labeled "purchase order", then they will obviously take the same type "purchaseOrderType". If message flows are not modeled, we can look at the send, receive, and service tasks, as well at the message events present in the model in order to understand what messages to define.

For *signals* and *errors* we have to look at the signal and error events that we have defined in the diagram. While for a signal the data type describes the content of the signal being broadcasted or listened to, for an error the data type defines what information is carried with the error. For example, if it is a system error, then we can use this to specify the error message returned by the system. In addition, we need to assign an *error code* to each error. This code uniquely identifies an error, so that a catching error event can be related to a throwing error event.

Besides the above data elements, we need to define the *internal variables* of each task, which are called *data inputs* and *data outputs* in BPMN. Data inputs and outputs act as interfaces between a task and the task's input and output data objects. They also need to refer to an XSD type that defines their structure, but, differently from process variables, they are only visible within the task (or sub-process) in which they are defined. Data inputs capture data that is required by the task to be executed. Data outputs capture data that is produced by the task upon completion. Data inputs are populated with the content of input data objects while data outputs are used to populate the content of output data objects. For example, we need a data input for task "Check stock availability" to store the content of the purchase order. Thus, the type of this data input must match that of the input object, i.e., "purchaseOrderType". Similarly, the data output must be of type integer to store the number of items in stock, so that this information can be copied into the output object stock availability upon task completion.

Similarly to tasks, events that transmit or receive data, i.e., message, signal and error events, also have internal variables. Specifically, the catching version of these events has one data output only, which is used to store the content of the event being caught (e.g., an incoming message). The throwing version has one data input only, which is there to store the content of the event being thrown (e.g., an error). Thus, we also need to assign to these data inputs and outputs a type that has to match that of the message, signal, or error associated with the event. For example, the start catching message event "Purchase order received" in the order-to-cash example uses a data output to store the purchase order message once this has been received. So, this data output must match the type of the incoming message, which is precisely "purchaseOrderType". In turn, the output object must have the same type as the output data to contain the purchase order.

10.5.2   Data Mappings

In BPMN, data is manipulated and processed inside tasks and events. The *mapping* between data objects and task (event) data inputs or outputs is defined via the task *data associations*. Data associations can also be used to define complex data assignments beyond one-to-one mappings. For example, consider task "Manufacture product" in our order-to-cash example. The service invoked by this task only requires the order product code and quantity to start the manufacturing of the product. We can use a data association to extract the product code and quantity from the input purchase order and populate a data input containing two sub-elements of type string and integer, respectively. In most cases, the BPMS will automatically create all the tedious data mappings between data objects and tasks. For the case above, for example, all we need to do is to select the sub-elements of the purchase order we want to use as input to "Manufacture product". The BPMS will then create the required data inputs and their mappings for this task. BPMN relies on XPATH 1.0 as the default language for expressing data assignments like the one above. However, other languages can be used like Java Universal Expression Language (UEL) or Groovy. The choice depends on the BPMS adopted. For example, Activiti supports UEL, Bonita and Camunda support Groovy while Bizagi supports its own expression language.

10.5.3 Service Tasks

Once we have defined the types of all data elements and mapped task and event data inputs and outputs to these types, we have to specify how tasks and events have to be implemented. For service tasks, we need to specify how to communicate with the external application that will execute the task. Be it a complex system or a simple application, all that the BPMS needs to know is its *service interface* that the service task can use. A service interface contains one or more *service operations*, each of which describes a particular way of interacting with a given service. For example, a service for retrieving inventory information provides two operations: one to check the current stock levels and one to check the stock forecast for a given product (based on product code or name). An operation can be either *in-out* or *in-only*. In an in-out operation (also called *synchronous* operation), the service expects a request message, then replies with a response message once the operation has been completed or, optionally, provides an error message if something goes wrong. For example, the service invoked by task "Check raw materials availability" receives stock availability information as input message and replies with a list of raw materials to be ordered as output message. Alternatively, if the service experiences an exception (e.g., the suppliers catalog is unreachable), it replies with an error message. The message triggers the boundary error event of this task, such that the related exception handler can be executed.[2] Conversely, in an in-only operation (also called *asynchronous* operation), the service expects a request message but will not

---

[2]Note that there is no throwing end error event inside "Check raw materials availability" since the catching error event is triggered by the receipt of an error message by the service task. The ability to link error messages with error events is a common feature of BPMSs.

reply with a response message. For example, the task "Archive order" notifies an archival service for the purchase order; however, the process does not wait for an archival confirmation.

Each message of a service operation needs to reference a message in the BPMN model, so that it can be assigned a data type. For instance, the request and the response messages to interact with the inventory service have the data type "purchaseOrderType" and XSD integer, respectively. For each interface, we also need to specify how this is concretely implemented, i.e., what communication protocols are used by the service and where the service is located in the network. The BPMN specification recommends the use of Web service technology to implement service interfaces. It relies on WSDL 2.0 to specify this information. In practice, this corresponds to defining one or more external WSDL documents (which specify the interface of the service to be accessed) and importing them into our BPMN model. Once again, other implementations are possible, e.g., one could implement a service interface via a Java remote procedure call or plain XML over HTTP.

Contemporary BPMSs allow the use of Web services designed according to the Representational State Transfer (REST) architectural style, a style that is supported by WSDL 2.0. A *RESTful* service is viewed as a resource or as a source of specific information (data and functionality) and identified with a Uniform Resource Identifier (URI). A service task accesses a RESTful service using the URI and a fixed set of operations. The service returns a representation of the resource. The latter typically takes the form of an XML or JavaScript Object Notation (JSON) file, which is transmitted over HTTP. When HTTP is used as the transport protocol, the operations that can be performed are the creation, retrieval, updating, and deletion of resources. BPMSs such as Camunda or Bonita offer the possibility for service tasks to invoke RESTful services. Additionally, these BPMSs expose their own functionality (e.g., the ability to create new cases of a process or to check the status of a case) via a REST Application Programming Interface (API).

After defining the service interfaces for our process, we need to associate each service task with a service operation as defined in a service interface. Based on the type of the operation (in-out or in-only), we then need to define a single data input that must match the type of the request message in the referenced service operation and, optionally, a single data output that must match the type of the response message in the operation. The BPMS engine will correctly bind the data input of the task to the request message and send it out to the service. Once the response message has been received, it will bind the content of this message to the data output of the task.

10.5.4   Send and Receive Tasks, Message and Signal Events

Send and receive tasks work similarly to service tasks. A send task is a special case of the service task: it sends a message to an external service using its data input, without expecting a reply. An example is the "Notify unavailability to customer" task. A receive task waits for an incoming message and uses its data output to store the message content. The "Get shipping address" task is an example of this. Both task types need to reference an in-only service operation where the message is defined. For the receive, the message being received is seen as a request coming from an external service requester. So, in this case, the process itself acts as the service provider.

A receive task can also be used to receive the response of an asynchronous service, which has previously been invoked with a send task. This is the case for the "Request shipping address" and "Get shipping address" tasks. The asynchronous service is provided by the customer. Accordingly, in the send task the seller's process acts as the service requester sending a request message to the customer. In the receive task, the roles are swapped: the seller acts as the service provider to receive the response message from the customer. This pattern is used for long-running interactions, where the response may arrive after a while. The drawback of using a synchronous service task instead of a pair of send-receive task is that the service task blocks the execution of the process (or the execution of the branch of the process where it is located) until a response is received. This is not the case in Figure 10.3 (page 380). Here, the send and receive tasks are in parallel to "Emit invoice", which may well be performed between these tasks.

Message and signal events work exactly as send and receive tasks. Signal events should be used when the service being consumed has publish-subscribe capabilities, e.g., a Web service for subscribing to RSS feeds. In all other cases, we should either use message events or send and receive tasks.

10.5.5 Script Tasks

For script tasks, we need to provide the snippet of code that will be executed by the BPMS. This code can be written in a scripting or programming language, such as JavaScript or Python. BPMN does not prescribe the use of a specific language, so the choice depends on the BPMS to be used and any organizational preferences. The task's data inputs store the parameters for invoking the script while its data outputs store the results of executing the script. For example, for the "Determine cancelation penalty" task we can define a script that extracts the order date and the cancelation request date from two data inputs. These are mapped to the input objects purchase order and cancelation request. The information is then used to compute a penalty of € 15 for each day past the order date, which is then copied to the data output.

10.5.6 User Tasks

For each user task, we need to specify the rules for allocating work items to process participants at runtime, the technology for communicating with process participants, and the details of the user interface to use. Moreover, like for any other task, we need to define data inputs to pass information to the participant, as well as the data outputs to receive the results.

Process participants that can be assigned user tasks are called *potential owners* in BPMN. A potential owner is a member of a resource class. In the context of user tasks, a resource class identifies a static list of *participants* sharing certain characteristics, e.g., holding the same role or belonging to the same department or unit. An example of a resource class for the order-to-cash process is *order clerk*, which groups all participants holding this role within the sales department of the seller organization. Note that these resource classes are unrelated to pools and lanes, which are only notational elements in a conceptual process model. A resource class can be further characterized by one or more *resource parameters*, where a parameter has a name and a data type. For example, we can define two parameters *product* and *region* of type string to indicate the particular products an order clerk works with, and the region he or she works in.

Once we have defined all required resource classes and, optionally, their parameters, we can assign each user task to one or more resource classes based on an expression. For example, we can express that work items of the "Confirm order" task must be assigned to all participants of type "Order clerk" who deal with the particular product being ordered and work in the same region as the customer. For this, we can define an XPATH expression that selects all members of the order clerk resource class who are responsible for the country specified in the purchase order.

Finally, we need to specify the implementation technology used to offer the work item to the selected participant(s). This entails aspects such as how to reach the participant (e.g., via email or worklist notification), how to render the content of the task data inputs on screen (e.g., via one or more Web forms organized through a particular screenflow), and the strategy to assign the work item to a single participant out of those satisfying the assignment expression (e.g., assign it to the order clerk with the shortest queue). Different allocation strategies for assigning work items to process participants are discussed in the box "Task allocation strategies". The configuration of all these aspects, as well as the association of participants to resource classes is dependent on the specific BPMS being used.

TASK ALLOCATION STRATEGIES

There are different strategies that can be used to allocate tasks to process participants. Research on workflow resource patterns has gathered an extensive set of such strategies. They include patterns for determining the set of participants who are considered for a task (so-called *creation patterns*), including the following ones:

Direct allocation: The participant responsible for a task is defined at design time.

(continued)

Role-based allocation: A task is assigned to a specific role at design time. At runtime, work items are offered to all participants belonging to this role.

Deferred allocation: The participant who will work on a task is only determined at runtime.

Authorization: Work items are made available only to those participants who are authorized to work on them.

Separation of duties: Two given tasks must be executed by different participants.

Case handling: Work items of a case are all allocated to the same resource.

Retain familiar: Two given tasks must be executed by the same participant.

Capability-based allocation: Work items are made available to those participants who possess the right capabilities to work on them.

History-based allocation: Work items are allocated to those participants who have successfully conducted them in the past.

Organizational allocation: Work items are allocated to those participants who hold a specific position in the organizational hierarchy.

Once this set of participants is determined, the BPMS might deliberately choose one specific participant to work on a task. Among others, the following strategies might be used (so-called *push patterns*):

Allocation by offer: A new work item is offered to participants who can check them out, having the effect that these items are no longer available to others.

Random allocation: A new work item is allocated to a randomly selected participant who fulfills the allocation condition.

Round-robin allocation: A new work item is allocated, in a circular way, to the participant who has not received an item for the longest time.

Shortest queue: A new work item is given to that participant with the shortest work item queue.

Other task allocation mechanisms are possible, such as mechanisms where participants can select the work items they wish to work on. In practice, two other mechanisms are important. **Delegation** refers to mechanisms through which participants can hand off work items to other participants. Consider that John is about to close his work day before his annual leave. He delegates all work items that are still in his list to a colleague. **Escalation** refers to mechanisms to monitor progress and automatically trigger counter-measures. Assume John forgot to delegate one of his work items. In the first week of his holidays, the BPMS discovers that an item has been pending without progress for 3 days and escalates it to his boss Mary. Mary re-allocates the work item to a colleague of John.

10.5.7   Task, Event, and Sequence Flow Expressions

Finally, we need to write expressions for the various attributes of tasks and events, as well as for the sequence flows with conditions. For instance, in a loop task we need to write a boolean expression that implements the text annotation indicating the loop condition (e.g., "until response approved"). This boolean expression will determine if the loop task is repeated. This expression can be defined over data elements, e.g., it can be an XPATH expression that extracts the value of the boolean element "approved" from the response object. We can also use *instance attributes* inside these expressions. These are variables that vary by instance at runtime. An example is *loop count*, which counts the number of iterations for a loop task. For the timer event we need to specify an expression to capture the temporal event informally expressed by its label (e.g., "Friday afternoon"). Here, we have three options: we can either provide a temporal expression in the form of a precise date or time, a relative duration, or a repeating interval. Once again, these expressions can be linked to data elements and instance properties so as to be resolved dynamically at runtime. For example, we can set an order confirmation timeout based on the number of line items in an order.

Finally, we need to write a boolean expression to capture the condition attached to each sequence flow following an (X)OR-split. For example, the condition "product in stock" after the first XOR-split in the order-to-cash example can be implemented as an XPATH expression that checks whether the value of variable stock availability is at least equal to the product quantity contained in the purchase order. There is no need to assign an expression to a default sequence flow, since it is taken by the BPMS engine if the expressions assigned to all other arcs emanating from the same (X)OR-split evaluate to false.

10.5.8   Implementing Rules with DMN

Sometimes, the conditions that allow a process instance to be routed towards one or another path in the model can be quite complex. The reason is that the business rules underpinning these conditions are inherently complex, such as the rules for assessing the credit risk of a loan applicant. Business rules may also happen to change over time, for example when a request is approved or an application is accepted. It would be convenient if in such a case only the rules were to be changed, not the whole process model. For these reasons, OMG has developed the Decision Model and Notation (DMN) standard, which at the time of writing is available in version 1.1. Instead of defining complex expressions in the outgoing arcs of (X)OR-splits, DMN allows us to define business rules separately and link these with BPMN business rule tasks or conditional events. Specifically, the rule is defined at design time and evaluated at runtime by a DMN rules engine. This engine is invoked by a business rule task or conditional event whenever an instance of such elements is

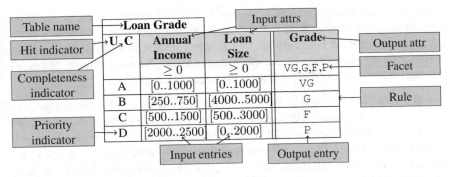

Fig. 10.8 Example of a decision table for loan applications

reached during process execution. Note, however, that the link between BPMN and DMN has not been standardized by OMG yet. Hence, each BPMS vendor offers a proprietary mechanism to link BPMN elements to DMN rules.

In essence, DMN provides three parts for the specification of business rules: the Decision Requirements Graph (DRG) that describes how data is propagated between different decisions, the Simple Expression Language (S-FEEL) to define how values are extracted from variables, and Decision Tables (DMN tables). Here, we briefly introduce DMN tables.

Figure 10.8 shows a DMN table that captures the rules for grading loan applications. The figure provides explanations of the various components of a DMN table. Each table has a name, indicators of hit, completeness and priority, input and output attributes with corresponding entries, facets, and, most importantly, rules. Each row represents a *rule* and the columns its respective *inputs* and *outputs*. Columns have a type (e.g. string, integer, or date) or specifically defined ranges called facets. In our example, a *facet* is defined with values VG (very good), G (good), F (fair), and P (poor). For a particular combination of input attributes, like $AnnualIncome = 500$ and $LoanSize = 4230$, we have to find the row that *matches* in order to identify the output value. The given values match row B and yield the $Grade = G$.

DMN tables have different indicators. The *hit indicator* specifies whether one or many rows are allowed to match a given input. The most prominent hit indicator is U, which indicates that any combination of input values should yield a unique output. If there is more than one match, the *priority indicator* defines which row to choose. In our example, A, B, C, D define an alphabetical order of priority. It is also possible to specify, for example, that the minimum or maximum value should be chosen. The *completeness indicator* specifies whether there must be at least one row for each possible input configuration, or if also no matches are allowed. The most prominent one is C indicating that the table should be complete, meaning that any combination of input values should map to an output. It is a good practice that DMN tables have unique hits and a complete set of rules.

Analysts can make mistakes when creating DMN tables. For example, it is a mistake to specify *overlapping rules* when the hit indicator does not allow it. In this case, there is an input configuration that matches several rows. It is also a mistake to have *missing rules* when the completeness indicator does not allow it. If a rule is missing, there is no row that matches a particular configuration.

Example 10.2 Let us check if the decision table of Figure 10.8 has overlapping and missing rules. Two rules are overlapping if their values on all input columns overlap. We observe the following overlaps for the first column of annual income: A and B, A and C, and B and C. For the column loan size, we observe: B and C, A and C, and A and D. This means that there is an overlap for the values where A and C overlap. This is an annual income between 500 and 1,000 together with a loan size between 500 and 1,000. This means that A and C are overlapping rules.

In order to find missing rules, we have to find values that are not covered by either column. We observe that there are missing rules for an annual income between 1,500 and 2,000, as well as for incomes greater than 2,500. There are also missing rules for a loan size between 3,000 and 4,000, and greater than 5,000. □

Exercise 10.8 Consider the DMN table in Figure 10.9. Identify overlapping and missing rules.

10.5.9 Other BPMS-Specific Properties

Strictly speaking, the only BPMS-specific properties that we have to configure in order to make a process model fully executable are those of user tasks. In practice, however, as we discussed, BPMSs may diverge from the standard way of specifying execution properties. Moreover, we likely need to connect our executable process model with one or more specific enterprise systems that are in use in our company. This is called *system binding*. BPMSs offer a range of predefined service task extensions, called *service adapters* (or *service connectors*), to implement common system binding functions in a convenient way. Examples of such binding functions include: performing a database lookup, sending an email notification, posting a message to Twitter, setting an event in Google Calendar, reading or writing a file, and adding a customer in a CRM system. Each adapter comes with a list

Fig. 10.9 Another decision table

U C	Annual Income	Loan Size	Grade
	≥ 0	≥ 0	VG,G,F,P
A	[0..2000]	[0..3000]	VG
B	[1000..3000]	[2000..5000]	G
C	[4000..6000]	[7000..9000]	F
D	[7000..8000]	[6000..6500]	P

of parameters that we need to configure. Many BPMSs provide *wizards* to auto-discover some of the parameter values. For instance, a database lookup requires the type of the database server (e.g., MySQL, Oracle DB) and the URL where the server can be reached, the schema to be accessed, the SQL query to run, and the credentials of the user authorized to run the query.

In our example, instead of implementing "Check stock availability" as a service task, we could implement it with a generic database lookup adapter, provided we know what to search for and where. Similarly, we could implement the tasks for communicating with the customer, such as "Notify unavailability to customer" and "Request shipping address", as email adapters. In this way, we do not need to implement a dedicated email service in our organization. The number and variety of adapters that a BPMS provides contribute to increasing user productivity with that particular BPMS.

Exercise 10.9 Consider the loan assessment process model that you obtained in Exercise 10.7 (page 384). The loan application contains these data fields:

- Applicant information:

  - Identify information (name, surname...)
  - Contact information (home phone, cell phone...)
  - Current address (street name and number, city...)
  - Previous address (as above plus duration of stay)
  - Financial information (job details, bank details)

- Reference information (identify, contact, address, relation to applicant)
- Property information (property type, address, purchasing price)
- Loan information (amount, number of years, start date, interest type: variable/fixed)
- Application identifier
- Submission date & time
- Revision date & time.
- Administration information (a section to be compiled by the loan provider):

  - Status (a string attribute with pre-defined values: "incomplete", "complete", "assessed", "rejected", "canceled", "approved")
  - Comments on status (optional, e.g., used to explain the reasons for rejection)
  - Eligibility (whether or not the applicant is eligible for a loan)
  - Loan officer identifier
  - Insurance quote required (a boolean to store whether or not a home insurance quote is sought).

The credit history report contains these data fields:

- Report identifier
- Financial officer identifier
- Reference to a loan application

- Applicant's credit information:
  - Loan applications made in the last five years (loan type: household/personal/domestic, amount, duration, interest rate)
  - Overdue credit accounts (credit type, default amount, duration, interest rate)
  - Current credit card information (provider: Visa, Mastercard..., start date, end date, interest rate)
  - Public record information (optional, if any):
    - Court judgements information
    - Bankruptcy information
- Credit assessment (a string with predefined values: AAA, AA, A, BBB, BB, B, unrated).

The risk assessment contains the following data fields:

- Assessment identifier
- Reference to a loan application
- Reference to a credit history report
- Risk weight (an integer from 0 to 100).

The property appraisal contains the following data fields:

- Appraisal identifier
- Reference to a loan application
- Property appraiser identifier
- Property information (property type, address)
- Value of three surrounding properties with similar characteristics
- Estimated property market value
- Comments on property (optional, to note serious flaws the property may have).

The agreement summary contains the following data fields:

- Reference to a loan application
- Conditions agreed (a boolean indicating if the applicant agreed with the loan conditions)
- Repayment agreed (a boolean indicating if the applicant agreed with the repayment schedule)
- Link to digitized copy of the repayment agreement.

The loan provider offers a website where applicants can submit and revise loan applications online, track the progress of their applications, and, if required, cancel applications in progress. This website implements an underlying Web service with which the loan assessment process interacts. In practice, this service acts as the applicant from the perspective of the loan assessment process. For example, if the applicant submits a new loan application through the website, then this service wraps this application into a message and sends it to the BPMS engine of the loan provider. In turn, this starts a new instance of the loan assessment process. If the loan assessment process sends an application for review to this service, then the service presents this information to the applicant via the loan provider's website.

Further, the loan assessment process interacts with an internal service for assessing loan risks. This service determines a risk weight, which is proportional to the credit assessment contained in the credit history report, on the basis of the applicable risk rules. The risk assessment service returns a risk assessment containing an identifier (freshly generated), a reference to the loan application and one to the credit history report (both extracted from the credit history report), and the risk weight.

Based on the above information, we can specify the execution properties for the elements of this process model. It is neither required to define the actual XSD type of each data element, nor to specify the actual Groovy scripts or XPATH expressions. Instead, we identify what properties have to be specified, i.e., what data inputs and outputs, service interfaces, operations, messages, and errors are required, and determine their data type in relation to that of process variables. For example, a data input may map to a process variable or to a data field within this. For scripts, we define via task inputs and outputs what data is required by the script, what data is produced, and how the input data is transformed into the output one. For example, based on the value of a data field in a process variable, a script may write a particular value in the data field of another process variable. Similarly, for each user task, we identify what information is presented to the task performer and how the data output is obtained. Finally, we explain how each expression can be evaluated on the basis of data fields within process variables (e.g., to implement the condition of a sequence flow) or constant values like a date (e.g., to implement a timer event).

10.6   The Last Mile

Now that you have become familiar with what is required to turn a process model into an executable one, the last step for you is to take a process model and implement it using the BPMS of your choice (e.g., Activiti, Bonita, Bizagi, Camunda, IBM, Oracle, YAWL). The landscape of BPMSs and their specificities evolve continuously. We can identify three categories of BPMSs with respect to their support for BPMN:

1. **Pure BPMN:** These systems have been designed from the ground up to support BPMN natively. They follow the specification "to the letter" though they might not fully support it. Examples are Activiti and Camunda.
2. **Adapted BPMN:** These tools use a BPMN skin but rely on an internal representation to execute the process model. They can import and often also export BPMN. They typically predate BPMN and evolved from previous versions to support the specification. Examples are Bizagi and Bonita.

3. **Non BPMN:** There is, lastly, a general category of BPMSs that use their own proprietary language and semantics. These systems do not support BPMN. An example of such a system is YAWL.

Note that a BPMS may not fully cover all aspects of the BPMN specification that are relevant for execution. For example, some systems may not support compensation events or non-interrupting events. In this case, we need to give up on one or more of these elements depending of the BPMS that we adopt.

This section illustrated how to design executable BPMN models in a vendor-independent manner. The book's website[3] provides tutorial notes showing how to perform the last step of our method (the specification of execution properties) for various concrete BPMSs.

Exercise 10.10 Based on the execution properties that you specified in Exercise 10.9, implement the loan assessment process using a BPMS of your choice.

10.7 Recap

In this chapter, we presented a method for transforming conceptual process models into executable models, which can be interpreted by a BPMS. In this method, we first need to identify the type of each task (automated, manual, or user) and review manual tasks to find a way to link them to the BPMS whenever possible. Next, we have to complete the process model by specifying all control-flow and data aspects that are relevant for execution. As part of this step, we need to bridge the diverging level of granularity between conceptual and executable process models. Finally, we need to specify a number of execution properties for each model element. Some of these properties, such as those related to user tasks, are vendor-specific. They are supported in different ways by different BPMS vendors.

10.8 Solutions to Exercises

Solution 10.1 See Figure 10.10.

---

[3]http://fundamentals-of-bpm.org.

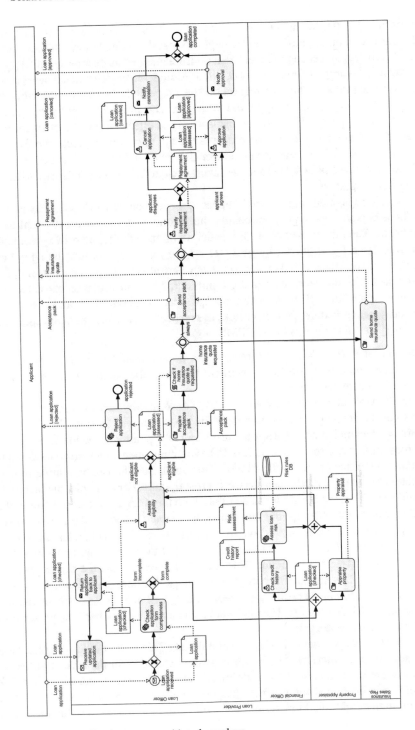

Fig. 10.10 Loan application process with task markers

Solution 10.2 All five manual tasks of this process, namely "Appraise property", "Prepare acceptance pack", "Send acceptance pack", "Send home insurance quote" and "Verify repayment agreement", can be implemented as user tasks. In "Appraise property", the property appraiser is notified through the worklist that a new property has to be appraised. The information on the property is carried by the work item of this task (e.g., property type and address). The property appraiser physically goes to the property address for an inspection and checks the value of surrounding properties. Once done, he or she prepares the appraisal on an electronic form and submits it to the BPMS engine via the worklist handler. "Prepare acceptance pack", "Send acceptance pack", "Send home insurance quote" can be implemented as user tasks in a similar way.

"Verify repayment agreement" appears in the loan officer's worklist as soon as the acceptance pack and, optionally, the insurance quote have been sent to the applicant. The officer checks out this work item once the repayment agreement is received from the applicant by post. He or she manually verifies the agreement, digitizes it and attaches it as a file to the agreement summary—an electronic form associated with this work item and pre-populated with information extracted from the loan application. If the applicant accepted all loan conditions and agreed with the repayment schedule, the officer ticks the respective checkboxes in the agreement summary and submits this to the BPMS engine.

Solution 10.3 Task "Check insurance" can be automated through a service that determines the amount of the co-payment based on the details of the prescription and on the customer's insurance policy.

Tasks "Collect drugs from shelves" and "Check quality" are manual tasks. These tasks can be implemented as user tasks in the automated process. To do so, the pharmacy technician who collects the drugs, and the pharmacist who quality-checks the prescription and seals the bag, should have a convenient mechanism to signal the completion of these tasks to the BPMS. This could be achieved by putting in place a system based on barcode scans to track prescriptions. For example, the technician would see a list of prescriptions to be filled from the worklist. He or she would then pick up one of the prescriptions and the system would associate the prescription to a new barcode which is printed on an adhesive label. The technician would then attach the label to a bag, collect the drugs and put them in a bag, and when done, he or she would scan the barcode from the label to record that the prescription has been fulfilled. This signals the completion of task "Collect drugs from shelves" to the pharmacy system. In turn, it generates a new work item of task "Check quality" in the pharmacist's worklist. The pharmacist can then quality-check the prescription and scan the barcode again.

Task "Collect payment" is also a manual task. This task could be implemented as a service task whereby the pharmacy system would push the task of collecting the payment for a prescription to a Point-of-Sale (POS) system and expect the POS system to indicate that the payment has been collected. The pharmacy technician would interact with the POS system once the customer arrives, but this interaction

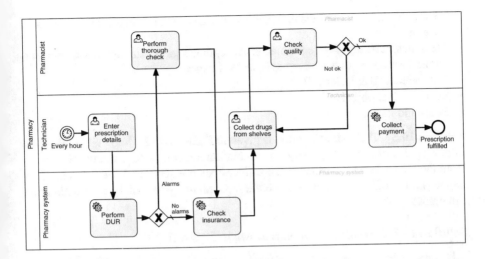

Fig. 10.11 The automated prescription fulfillment process

is outside the scope of the pharmacy system. The pharmacy system merely pushes work to the POS system and waits for completion.

The description of the process implicitly refers to a manual task whereby the pharmacist seals the bag and puts it into the pick-up area. However, this "Seal bag" task is not included in the executable process model. Instead, this task is integrated into the "Check quality" task. In other words, at the end of the quality check, the pharmacist is expected to seal the bag if the prescription is ready and drop the bag in the pick-up area. Task "Retrieve prescription bag" is also manual but there is no value in automating it in any way. So this task is left out of the executable process model, which completes once the payment has been made. The executable model of the entire prescription fulfillment process is illustrated in Figure 10.11.

Solution 10.4 It makes sense for tasks "Prepare acceptance pack" and "Send acceptance pack" to be performed by the same loan officer. However, task "Check if home insurance quote is requested" is meant to be executed between these two tasks. Since there is no temporal dependency between "Check if home insurance is requested" and the other two tasks, we can postpone the former to after "Send acceptance pack" or parallelize it with the other two tasks. This way we can aggregate the two consecutive tasks into "Prepare and send acceptance pack".

Solution 10.5

- Physical data objects: Acceptance pack (this is the loan offer on paper), Repayment agreement (this is signed by the applicant on paper and has been replaced by the Agreement summary, an electronic document containing a link to a digitized copy of the repayment agreement plus a reference to the loan application). We assume all other communications between applicant and loan provider to occur via email

- Messages carrying physical objects: Acceptance pack, Repayment agreement, Home insurance quote (the quote is sent on paper)
- Data stores: Risk Rules DB
- States of data objects
- Pools and lanes.

Solution 10.6   A possible solution is given in Figure 10.12. Note that in this solution, a work item of task "Verify repayment agreement" automatically disappears from the loan officer's worklist if the officer does not start it within 2 weeks. This happens if the officer has not received the repayment agreement by post within that timeframe.

Solution 10.7   A possible solution is shown in Figure 10.13.

1. Task types: the manual task of this process is "Discuss application". This can be implemented as a user task that completes by producing a recommendation.
2. Non-executable elements: all elements can be interpreted by a BPMS. Note that the catching message event "Response received by post" assumes the existence of an internal service at the service provider that notifies the process when the response has been received by post.
3.1. Missing control-flow: task "Create electronic response" is needed to convert the response received by post into an electronic version, which can be consumed by a BPMS. Task "Assess response" may be interrupted by a request to cancel the application, for which the process is aborted. This request may also be received during the acceptance handling, in which case tasks "Send offer" and "File application" need to be compensated. A 1-week timeout is added to receive the response.
3.2. Missing data: all electronic data objects were missing in the conceptual model.
4. Granularity level: task "Make appointment" has been disaggregated to explicitly model the task of notifying the client of the result. Similarly, "Send offer" and "Send rejection" have been disaggregated to model the preparation of the offer and the rejection letter, respectively. Given that "Send offer" has been split into two tasks ("Make offer" and "Send offer") each needs to be compensated if a cancelation request is received.

Solution 10.8   Overlaps in the annual income column are A and B for values between 1,000 and 2,000. A and B also overlap in loan size of 2,000 and 3,000. This means A and B are overlapping rules. Missing rules exist for annual income between 3,000 and 4,000, 6,000 and 7,000 as well as greater than 8,000. There are also missing rules for loan size between 5,000 and 6,000, 6,500 and 7,000 as well as greater than 9,000.

Solution 10.9   We need two service interfaces to interact with the Web service behind the loan provider's website. One interface where the loan provider acts as the service provider and the other where the website service acts as the service

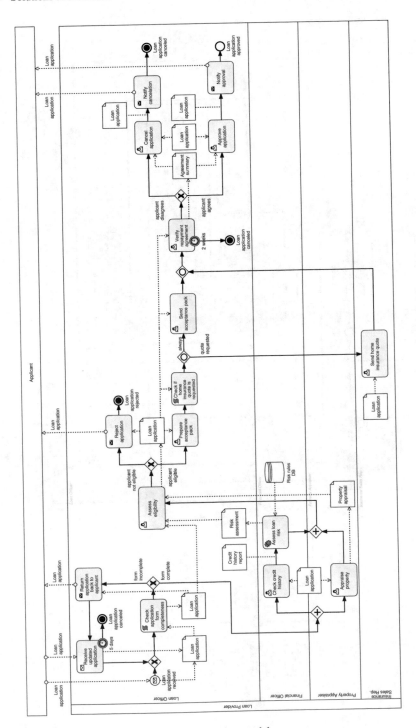

Fig. 10.12 Completed version of the loan application model

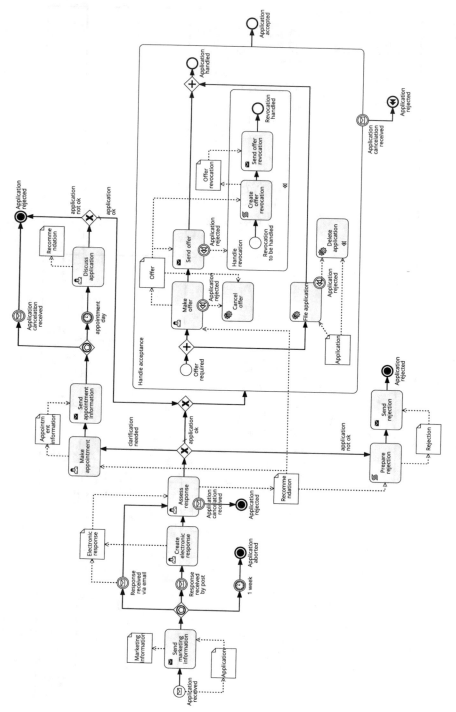

Fig. 10.13 The model for the sales process of a B2B service provider, completed with missing control-flow and data relevant for execution

provider. The former interface contains one in-only operation for the loan provider to receive the initial loan application. The latter interface contains the following four operations for the website service:

- an in-out operation to receive the assessed loan application (containing change requests), and to respond with the revised loan application (where changes have been made)
- an in-only operation to receive the rejected loan application
- an in-only operation to receive the approved or canceled loan application.

The four operations above require five messages in total, all of the same data type as the loan application's. These operations are assigned to the start message event, the four send tasks and the receive task of the process, which need to have suitable data inputs and outputs to contain the loan application. The mapping of these data inputs and outputs to data objects is straightforward, except for the send task "Reject application", which needs to modify the status of the loan application to "rejected" while copying this input data object into the task data input.

A third service interface is required to interact with the service for assessing loan risks in task "Assess loan risk". This interface has an in-out operation with two messages: an input message to contain the credit history report and an output message for the risk assessment.

The script for task "Check application form completeness" takes a loan application as input and checks that all required information is present. Depending on the outcome of the check it changes the application status to either "complete" or "incomplete", assigns a fresh application identifier to the application if empty, writes the submission or revision date and time and, if applicable, fills out the status comments section with pointers to incomplete data fields. The script task "Check if home insurance quote is requested" is actually not needed. While in a conceptual model it is important to explicitly capture each decision with a task as we have illustrated in Chapter 3, in an executable model this can be directly embedded in the conditions of the outgoing arcs of an (X)OR-split if the outcome of the decision can easily be verified. In fact, our example just needs to check the value of a boolean field in the application, which can be achieved with an XPATH expression directly on the arc labeled "quote requested".

All user tasks of this process are implemented via the worklist handler of the loan provider and offered to participants having the required role (e.g., task "Assess eligibility" is offered to a participant with role loan officer). This implementation depends on the BPMS adopted. The mapping between data objects and data inputs and outputs for these tasks is straightforward. In the case of task "Assess eligibility", at runtime the loan officer will see an electronic form for the loan application (editable), and two more forms for the risk assessment and for the property appraisal (non-editable). The officer is required to edit the loan application by entering the identifier, specifying whether or not the applicant is eligible for the loan and adding status comments in case of ineligibility. The other user tasks work similarly.

We have already discussed how to implement the condition of arc "quote requested". The conditions on the other sequence flows can be implemented with an expression that extracts data from a data object in a similar way. The expression for the arc labeled "always" is simply "true" as this arc is always taken. The temporal expression for the two timer events is a relative duration (5 days and 2 weeks).

Solution 10.10 The book's companion website[4] provides tutorials showing how to automate the loan application process in several BPMSs, including Bizagi, Camunda, IBM BPM, and Oracle.

10.9 Further Exercises

Exercise 10.11 Identify the type of the tasks in Figure 4.13 (page 148), and represent them using appropriate BPMN markers.

Exercise 10.12 Consider the following business processes. Identify which of these models can be automated and justify your choice.

1. Recruiting a new soldier.
2. Organizing a court hearing.
3. Buying an item at an auction on eBay.
4. Managing inventory assets disposition.
5. Booking a trip online.
6. Handling an IT-system maintenance job.
7. Servicing a used car at a mechanic.
8. Making online trade customs declarations.
9. Processing employee payrolls.
10. Synchronizing data servers in a distributed environment.

Exercise 10.13 Figure 10.14 shows the process model that FixComp follows when a client files a complaint. Upon receipt of a new complaint from a client, the process starts by sending an automatic reply to the client in order to reassure it that FixComp is following up on its request. A complaints representative then takes the complaint for discussion with people in the department the complaint refers to. Next, the complaints representative sends a personal letter of apology to the client and proposes a solution. The client can either accept or reject the solution. If the client accepts the solution, the solution is executed by the relevant department. If the client rejects the solution, the client is called by phone to discuss possible alternatives by the complaints representative. If one of these alternatives is promising, it is discussed with the department and the process continues. If no agreement can be reached, the case is brought to court.

The company wants to automate this process to deal with complaints in a more efficient manner. Your task is to prepare this model for execution.

---

[4]http://fundamentals-of-bpm.org/supplementary-material.

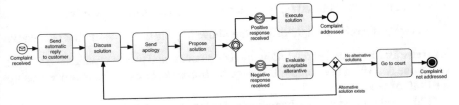

Fig. 10.14 FixComp's process model for handling complaints

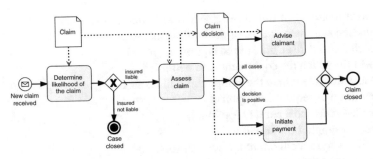

Fig. 10.15 Claims handling process model

Acknowledgement This exercise is adapted from a similar exercise developed by Remco Dijkman, Eindhoven University of Technology.

Exercise 10.14 Consider the claims handling process modeled in Figure 10.15. Implement this business process using a BPMS of your choice.

The process starts when a customer submits a new insurance claim. Each insurance claim goes through a two-stage evaluation process. First of all, the liability of the customer is determined. Secondly, the claim is assessed in order to determine if the insurance company has to cover this liability and to what extent. If the claim is accepted, payment is initiated and the customer is advised of the amount to be paid. All tasks except "Initiate Payment" are performed by claim handlers. There are three claim handlers. The task "Initiate Payment" is performed by a financial officer. There are two financial officers.

As shown in the model, there are two data objects involved in this process: Claim and Claim decision. A claim includes the following data fields:

- Name of claimant
- Policy number (a string with alphanumeric characters)
- Description of the claim
- Amount claimed.

A claim decision consists of the following data fields:

- Reference to a claim
- Decision (positive or negative)
- Explanation

- Amount to be reimbursed (greater than zero if the decision is positive).

You may add other data fields into the above objects if you deem that necessary.

Exercise 10.15 Consider the following equipment rental process, which is a variant of the one described in Example 1.1 (page 3). Implement this business process using a BPMS of your choice.

The rental process starts when a site engineer fills in an equipment rental request containing the following details:

- Name or identifier of the site engineer who initiates the request
- Requested start date & time of the equipment rental
- Expected end date & time of the equipment rental
- Project for which the equipment is to be rented
- Construction site where the equipment will be used
- Description of required equipment
- Expected rental cost per day (optional)
- Preferred supplier (optional)
- Supplier's equipment reference number (optional)
- Comments to the supplier (optional).

The rental request is taken over by one the clerks at the company's depot. The clerk consults the catalogs of the equipment suppliers and calls or sends emails to the supplier(s) in order to find the most cost-effective available equipment that complies with the request. Once the clerk has found a suitable piece of equipment available for rental, he or she recommends that it be rented. At this stage, the clerk must add the following data to the equipment rental request:

- Selected supplier
- Reference number of the selected equipment
- Cost per day.

Equipment rental requests have to be approved by a works engineer (who also works at the depot). In some cases, the works engineer rejects the equipment rental request, meaning that no equipment will be hired. Of course, before rejecting a request in this way, the works engineer should first discuss his or her decision with the site engineer and also add an explanatory note to the equipment rental request. In other cases, the works engineer rejects the recommended equipment (but not the entire request) and asks the clerk to find an alternative equipment. Again, in this case the works engineer should communicate the decision to the clerk and add an explanatory note.

Rental requests where the cost per day is below € 100 are automatically approved, without going through a works engineer.

Once a request is approved, a purchase order is automatically generated from the data contained in the approved rental request. The purchase order includes:

- Supplier's equipment identification
- Cost per day

- Construction site where the plant is to be delivered
- Delivery date & time
- Pick-up date & time
- Comments to the supplier (optional).

The supplier delivers the equipment to the construction site at the required date. The site engineer inspects the equipment. If everything is in order, he or she accepts the equipment, adds the date of delivery to the purchase order and optionally a note to indicate any issues found during the inspection. Similarly, when the equipment is picked up by the supplier at the end of the renting period, another inspection is performed, and the supplier marks the pick-up date in the purchase order (possibly with a pick-up note).

Sometimes, the site engineer asks for an extension of the rental period. In this case, the site engineer writes down the extended pick-up time into the purchase order, and the revised purchase order is automatically resent to the supplier. Prior to doing this change, the site engineer is expected to call the supplier in order to agree on the change of pick-up date.

A few days after the equipment is picked up, the supplier sends an invoice to the clerk by email. The clerk records the following details:

- Supplier's details
- Invoice number
- Purchase order number
- Equipment reference number
- Delivery date & time
- Pick-up date & time
- Total amount to be paid.

Having entered these invoice details, the clerk verifies the invoice details against the purchase order and marks the invoice as accepted or rejected. In case of rejection, the clerk adds an explanatory note (e.g., requesting the supplier to send a revised invoice). Eventually, the supplier may send a revised invoice if needed.

The accepted invoice is forwarded to the financial department for payment, but this part of the process is handled separately and is not part of this exercise.

Exercise 10.16 Define appropriate data types for the sales process shown in Figure 10.13 (page 406) and implement it using a BPMS of your choice.

10.10 Further Readings

A discussion on executable BPMN 2.0 is included in Silver's book [163]. He also wrote a book with Sayles about DMN [164]. A good coverage of the three modeling standards BPMN, CMMN, and DMN, and their usage in making processes executable, is provided in the book by Freund & Rücker [49]. An in-depth coverage of process automation using the YAWL language is given by ter

Hofstede et al. [67]. Weske also extensively discusses the implementation aspects of executable business processes in his book [193]. A classic book on how process execution works inside the process engine is Leymann & Roller [89].

A gentle introduction to XML, XML Schema, and XPath can be found in Møller & Schwartzbach's book [116]. Web services are covered in depth by Erl et al. [45]. This latter book also includes a discussion of WSDL 2.0, the default technology for implementing service interfaces in BPMN 2.0. There are also books on RESTful Web Services, including the one by Richardson & Ruby [141]. A good discussion of technical concerns, but from a technology-independent perspective, is included in the book on workflow patterns [155]. This book also discusses various strategies of allocating work to resources.

Chapter 11
Process Monitoring

> *If you can't measure something, you can't understand it. If you can't understand it, you can't control it. If you can't control it, you can't improve it.*
> H. James Harrington (1929–)

Once we have implemented and deployed a redesigned business process, it may happen that the new process does not meet our expectations. For example, certain types of unforeseen exceptions may arise, the processing time of some tasks may be much higher than expected due to these exceptions, and queues may build up to the extent that process participants start taking shortcuts due to high pressure, while customers become unsatisfied due to long waiting times. A first step to address (and to preempt) these issues is to understand what is actually happening during the execution of the process. This is the overarching goal of the last phase of the BPM lifecycle, namely *process monitoring*.

We start this chapter by discussing the context of process monitoring, i.e., when process monitoring can be done, what classes of techniques exist, what data is required as input, and what output can be produced by these techniques. Next, we introduce common types of process performance dashboards, both for offline and online process monitoring. We then move to process mining techniques, which emphasize the use of process models for process monitoring. We conclude by showing how these techniques provide a bridge from the monitoring phase back to the discovery and analysis phases of the BPM lifecycle.

11.1 The Context of Process Monitoring

Process monitoring is about using the data generated by the execution of a business process in order to extract insights about the actual performance of the process and to verify its conformance with respect to norms, policies, or regulations. The data

© Springer-Verlag GmbH Germany, part of Springer Nature 2018
M. Dumas et al., *Fundamentals of Business Process Management*,
https://doi.org/10.1007/978-3-662-56509-4_11

generated by business process executions generally takes the form of collections of event records. Each event record captures a state change in a process, such as the start or completion of a task, an incoming or outgoing message, or a timeout or escalation. Collections of such event records are called *event logs*.

Business process monitoring techniques take as input event logs and produce a number of artifacts to help process participants, analysts, process owners, and other managers to get a picture of the performance of the process at different levels of detail. Some performance monitoring techniques allow us to detect that the actual execution of the process deviates with respect to the intended execution captured in a process model, e.g., an invoice is paid out before it is approved by a financial officer, whereas normally this should not be the case. Other techniques help analysts to understand how and why the performance of a process varies across different cases or groups of cases, e.g., why some cases take too long to be completed. Or why some cases lead to customer complaints.

Process monitoring techniques can be broadly classified into those that provide a post-mortem view of a process, focused on already completed cases, and those that provide an on-the-fly view, focused on running cases. In this respect, we can classify process monitoring techniques into two categories:

Offline Process Monitoring is concerned with the analysis of historic process executions. The input for offline process monitoring are event logs covering a set of cases completed during a particular period of time, for instance a month, a quarter or a full year. Offline process monitoring techniques provide a picture of the performance of the process, the reasons for poor performance or for undesirable performance variations, and the conformance of the process with respect to certain rules or expected behaviors.

Online Process Monitoring is concerned with the assessment of the performance of currently running process instances. The main input for process monitoring are (incomplete) traces of ongoing cases. Online process monitoring techniques produce real-time pictures of the performance of ongoing cases, and generate alarms or trigger counteractions whenever certain performance objectives or compliance rules are not fulfilled, e.g., when a customer request remains un-replied beyond a given period of time.

Process monitoring techniques can also be classified into *statistics-based* and *model-based* techniques. The former category of techniques relies on statistical analysis of performance measures. This category encompasses descriptive analyses of the distribution of a given performance measure via aggregation functions such as mean, standard deviation, minimum and maximum cycle time, and processing time. It also encompasses visualization techniques allowing us for example to compare the distribution of the cycle time of ongoing cases of a process against that of all cases in the current semester or in the same month of the previous year. Process monitoring tools that emphasize statistics-based techniques are known as *Business Activity Monitoring* (BAM) or *Process Performance Measurement* (PPM) tools. The main output of these tools are *performance dashboards* displaying the performance of a process via a combination of aggregate measures (e.g., mean cycle time, mean processing time) and various types of charts as discussed in the next section.

On the other hand, model-based techniques allow us to analyze the execution of cases based on process models. For example, given an event log containing events related to purchase orders, shipments, deliveries, and invoices, some model-based techniques allow us to discover a process model of an order-to-cash process and to visualize the performance of the process (e.g., waiting times) on top of this automatically discovered model. Other model-based monitoring techniques allow us to detect deviations between an event log and a process model manually constructed by an analyst. For example, the latter techniques allow us to detect that in some cases an invoice has been paid without a required approval. Process monitoring tools that emphasize the use of process models are known as *process mining* tools.

11.2 Process Performance Dashboards

A process performance dashboard is a graphical representation of one or more performance measures or other characteristics of a business process. Depending on their purpose and targeted users, process performance dashboards can be classified into three categories: *operational*, *tactical*, and *strategic*.

11.2.1 Operational Dashboards

Operational process dashboards target process participants and their operational managers (including the process owner). Their purpose is to display the performance of ongoing or recently completed cases in a way that allows process participants and their managers to plan their short-term work. For example, in the context of an order-to-cash process, an operational dashboard might target a financial officer involved in the business process or a dispatcher at a warehouse.

Typical measures displayed in an operational dashboard include the number of ongoing cases (work-in-process) classified by type of cases. For example, a dashboard may display the number of cases that are on time, overdue, and at risk of being overdue. This idea is illustrated in Figure 11.1, which shows a dashboard produced by Bizagi's BAM component. The left-hand side of this dashboard displays the work-in-process by means of a pie chart. The same dashboard contains a histogram (see bar chart on the right) showing the number of cases that will reach their expiry time (deadline) for different periods of time.

Sometimes, operational dashboards are defined at the level of resources or tasks rather than at the level of cases. For example, we saw in Figure 9.5 an operational performance dashboard generated by a BPMS (Perceptive), which displays the number of pending work items per resource.

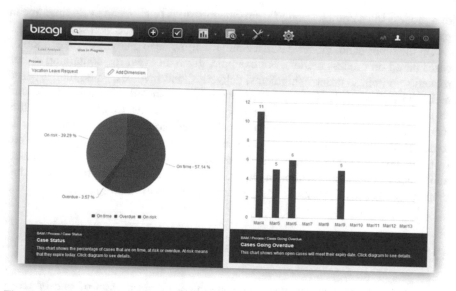

Fig. 11.1 Example of operational dashboard produced by Bizagi's BAM component

Exercise 11.1 We consider the prescription fulfillment process in Exercise 1.6 (page 30). Throughout a working day, the pharmacists and technicians at the pharmacy need to monitor the workload over the coming hours and detect situations where deadlines might be missed. Note that each case (i.e., each prescription) has a designated pick-up time (e.g., some prescriptions will be picked up at 5 p.m., others at 6 p.m., etc.). Also, we can assume that each pharmacist and each technician can handle a number of cases per hour. You can assume that pharmacists can do their part of the work on a given prescription in about 6 min of processing time, while pharmacists need 10 min of processing time per prescription to do their part of the work. You may also assume that a given prescription will always be in one of the following states: unprocessed, entered-and-verified, ready-to-deliver, and delivered. Describe two possible operational process dashboards to fulfill this need.

11.2.2 *Tactical Dashboards*

Tactical process dashboards target process owners, functional managers with oversight over parts of a process, and the analysts upon whom these managers rely. The purpose of tactical dashboards is to give a picture of the performance of a process over a relatively long period of time (e.g., a month or quarter or even a year) in order to put into evidence undesirable performance variations and their possible causes, long-term bottlenecks and deviations, or frequent sources of defects.

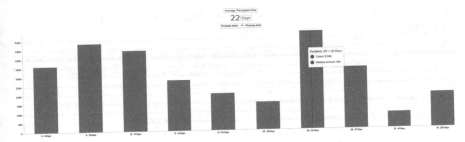

Fig. 11.2 Cycle time histogram of cases completed during a 1-year period

Typical measures displayed in a tactical process dashboard include number of completed cases, cycle time, waiting times, processing times, resource utilization, cost per case, and defect rate. For a given performance measure, a tactical dashboard may display statistics such as the minimum, maximum, mean, and standard deviation of this measure, or the entire distribution of the performance measure in the form of a histogram. For example, Figure 11.2 shows a cycle time (called throughput time) histogram of cases of a business process completed over a period of 1 year. For each bucket in the histogram, the dashboard allows us to inspect the number and the percentage of cases whose cycle time falls within that bucket. Some dashboards would allow us to drill drown and inspect the specific set of cases behind each bar.[1]

Since some of the above performance measures can also be defined at the level of tasks of a process, a tactical dashboard may provide a decomposed view of a performance measure on a per-task basis. For example, a tactical dashboard may display the mean waiting time of each task of a process. Such dashboards allow analysts to identify performance bottlenecks.

Tactical dashboards may also provide *longitudinal* or *cross-sectional* views of the performance of a process. A longitudinal view shows the variation of a given performance measure over time. For example, a longitudinal dashboard may show the mean cycle time of a process on a per-month basis. Such dashboards allow us to observe trends. A cross-sectional view is one that shows the distribution of a performance measure according to a given classification of cases. For example, a tactical dashboard may show the distribution of cases by geographical region (overlaid on a map) and within each region, it may also show the distribution of cases by type of product.

We can also use tactical process dashboards to comparatively analyze the performance of different teams. For example, if a lead-to-order process is performed by multiple sales teams in different geographical locations, a tactical dashboard may display the amount of time that each team spends in each stage of this lead-to-order

---

[1]This histogram was produced by Celonis—a tool we will mention again later in the context of process mining.

process. Such a comparative dashboard allows analysts and managers to understand why some teams perform better than others.

Exercise 11.2 Let us consider again the pharmacy prescription fulfillment process in Exercise 1.6 (page 30). The owner of this process oversees hundreds of pharmacies distributed across multiple regions. Specify what performance measures should be displayed and describe how could they be displayed in order to help the process owner to spot issues related to poor customer service.

11.2.3   Strategic Dashboards

Strategic process dashboards target executive managers. Their purpose is to provide a high-level picture of the performance of groups of processes along multiple performance dimensions. Accordingly, strategic dashboards are typically constructed by aggregating performance measures in two ways: (i) aggregating performance measures defined for individual processes into performance measures defined for entire groups of processes in a process architecture; and (ii) aggregating multiple performance measures related to the same performance dimension (e.g., multiple measures related to efficiency) into a single measure.

Example 11.1 We consider an insurance company with three core groups of processes: service development, sales, and claims handling. For each group of processes, there may be multiple measures related to efficiency, such as cycle time efficiency, resource utilization, and cost-to-revenue ratio per case.[2] Given these performance measures, and assuming that we give them equal weight, we can define a single measure of process efficiency using a weighted average. Let us assume that there are twelve processes related to claims handling (one process per type of service, for example claims handling for personal vehicle insurance, for commercial vehicle insurance, for home insurance, etc.). If we give equal weight to each of these twelve processes, we can define a measure of efficiency for the entire group of claims handling processes in the architecture. If we repeat this procedure for each type of performance dimension (efficiency being only one of them) and for each group of processes (claims handling being one of them), we get a set of performance measures for each group of processes in the architecture. Given this, we can construct a strategic performance dashboard that displays to us a set of aggregated performance measures for each group of processes in a process architecture. This can be achieved, for example, by using balanced scorecards as shown in Figure 2.10 (see page 63). This dashboard can then be used by executives to get a bird's-eye view of the performance of a given business area over a period

---

[2]The performance dimensions of an organization are usually defined in a *balanced scorecard* introduced in Section 2.1. In a balanced scorecard, efficiency is one of the performance dimensions of the *internal business process* perspective.

of time (a month, a quarter, or a year), and to compare it with the performance in previous periods, or in other business areas. □

Exercise 11.3 Consider the process landscape of Vienna's public transport operator Wiener Linien given in Figure 2.6 (page 48). The CFO of this organization has a long-term goal to improve efficiency, mainly by reducing costs. What dashboard could we offer to the CFO (updated every month) to give them an idea of where to focus the attention in terms of process improvement efforts? What data would we need to produce this dashboard?

11.2.4 Tools for Dashboard Creation

Operational and tactical process dashboards are often provided off-the-shelf by almost any BPMS. They can also be created using dedicated dashboarding tools available in other PAISs, e.g., CRM and ERP systems such as Microsoft Dynamics and SAP. Some types of process performance dashboards are also provided off-the-shelf by process mining tools, which we shall discuss next.

It is also a common practice to create process performance dashboards (at all three levels) using business analytics and business data visualization tools, such as Microsoft PowerBI,[3] QlikView,[4] and Tableau.[5] These tools allow one to design customized dashboards by dragging and dropping dashboard components using a visual editor and to import data from files or from databases.

One of the trends in the field of performance dashboards is to incorporate machine learning techniques in order to make predictions about future performance. At the time of writing this book, BPMS and process mining vendors are gradually incorporating predictive capabilities into their products. An example of an open-source tool to create predictive business process performance dashboards is Nirdizati.[6]

11.3 Introduction to Process Mining

Process mining is a family of techniques to analyze the performance and conformance of business processes based on event logs produced during their execution. Process mining techniques complement tactical process monitoring dashboards. Whereas tactical dashboards allow managers and analysts to get an aggregate picture

---

[3] http://powerbi.microsoft.com.

[4] http://www.qlik.com.

[5] https://www.tableau.com.

[6] http://nirdizati.org.

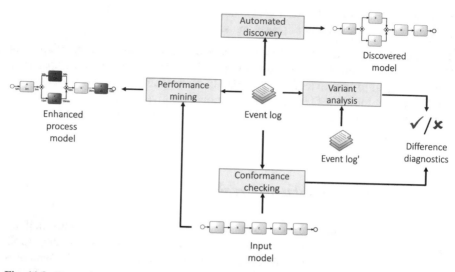

Fig. 11.3 Categories of process mining techniques and their inputs and output

of the health of a process, process mining techniques allow them to dig deeper. Specifically, these techniques allow us to understand how the process is actually being executed and to decorticate the performance of a process down to the level of individual tasks, resources, and handoffs.

In this section, we provide an overview of process mining techniques and we describe the structure of the event logs that are taken as input by these techniques.

11.3.1   Process Mining Techniques

As depicted in Figure 11.3, process mining techniques can be classified according to four use cases: (i) automated process discovery, (ii) conformance checking, (iii) performance mining, and (iv) variants analysis.

Automated process discovery techniques take as input an event log and produce a business process model that closely matches the behavior observed in the event log or implied by the traces in the event log. Automated process discovery can be used as part of a process discovery effort, in conjunction with other discovery methods presented in Chapter 5, or as part of tactical process performance monitoring efforts in conjunction with performance mining techniques as discussed below.

Conformance checking techniques take as input an event log and a process model, and they give us as output a list of differences between the process model and the event log. For example, the process model might tell us that after executing a task called A, we must execute a task called B. But maybe in the event log, sometimes after task A, we do not see task B. This might be because of an error, or more often than not, it is because of an exception that is not captured in the process model. Some conformance checking techniques take as input an event log and a set of business rules instead of a process model. These techniques check if the event log fulfills the business rules, and if not, they show the violations of these rules.

Performance mining techniques take as input a process model and an event log and produce as output an *enhanced process model*. The enhanced process model contains additional elements (e.g., color-coded elements) that can answer questions like: "Why is the process slow?", or "Where do we waste the largest amount of time in a business process?" In other words, they can pinpoint the bottlenecks that slow down the process. Note that the process model used for performance mining might be a process model provided by the analyst or an automatically-discovered one.

Finally, *variants analysis* techniques take as input two event logs (corresponding to two variants of a process) and produce as output a list of differences. Typically, one of the event logs contains all the cases that end up in a positive outcome according to some criterion, while the other log contains all the cases that end up in a negative outcome. For example, the first log may contain all cases where the customer was satisfied, while the second one contains all cases that led to a complaint. Or the first log may contain all cases where the process completed on time, while the second one contains the delayed cases. Variants analysis techniques help their users to diagnose the reasons why an execution of a business process sometimes does not end up in a desirable outcome.

As Figure 11.3 shows, these four categories of process mining techniques take as input event logs. Accordingly, before discussing each category of techniques, we will present the structure of an event log and the challenges that need to be overcome to obtain those event logs in the first place.

11.3.2 Event Logs

When a process is executed on a BPMS, on an enterprise system (CRM, ERP), or on another supporting system, the system usually takes care of coordinating individual cases and informing participants about which tasks they need to work on. Participants often see only those tasks that they are directly responsible for, while the system hides the complexity of the overall process. Each participant typically has a personal *worklist* that shows the set of *work items* that need to be completed. If an explicit process model exists, each work item corresponds to a task in the process model. There might exist multiple work items corresponding to a single task if several cases are currently being worked on. For example, Chuck (as a process participant) might see that four work items are in his worklist, all relating to the "Confirm order" task of the order-to-cash process: one work item relates to an order from customer A, one from customer B, and two from customer C.

The structure of a work item is defined in the executable process model or directly implemented in the software. This means that participants see those data fields that have been declared as input for a task. For each work item they are working on, they are supposed to document at least the completion. In this way, the system can keep track of the state of the process at any point in time. Among others, it is easy to record at what point in time somebody has started working on a work item, what input data was available, what output data was created, and who was the participant working on it. For example, when Chuck has confirmed the order of customer B, he enters the result in the system, and the system can decide if next the invoice should be emitted or the order confirmation should be escalated to someone above Chuck.

Most BPMSs and also other enterprise systems record events corresponding to the execution of work items and other relevant events such as the receipt of a message related to a given case of a process. These event records can be extracted from the database of the BPMS or enterprise system and represented as an *event log*.

An *event log* is a collection of timestamped event records. Each event record tells us something about the execution of a work item (and hence a task) of the process (e.g., that a task has started or has been completed), or it tells us that a given message event, escalation event, or other relevant event has occurred in the context of a given case in the process. For example, an event record in an event log may capture the fact that Chuck has confirmed a given purchase order at a given point in time.

Figure 11.4 illustrates what data is typically stored in an event log. We can see that a single event has a unique event ID. Furthermore, it refers to one individual case, it has a timestamp, and it shows which resources executed which task. These may be participants (e.g., Chuck and Susi) or software systems (SYS1, SYS2, DMS). For most mining techniques discussed in this chapter, it is a minimum requirement that for each event in the log we have three attributes: (i) in which case the event occurred (*case identifier*); (ii) which task the event refers to (herein called the *event class*); and (iii) when the event occurred (i.e., a *timestamp*). In practice, there may be other event attributes, such as for example the resource who performed a given task, the cost, or domain-specific data such as the loan amount in the case of a loan origination process.

The event log of Figure 11.4 is captured as a list in a tabular format.[7] Simple event logs such as this one are commonly represented as tables and stored in a Comma-Separated-Values (CSV) format. However, in more complex event logs, where the events have data attributes (e.g., the amount of a loan application, the shipping address of a purchase order), a flat CSV file is not a suitable representation.

A more versatile file format for storing and exchanging event logs is the *eXtensible Event Stream* (XES) format[8] standardized by the *IEEE Task Force on Process Mining*.[9] The majority of process mining tools can handle event logs in XES. The structure of an XES file is based on a data model, partially depicted in Figure 11.5. An XES file represents an event log. It contains multiple traces, and each trace can contain multiple events. All of them can contain different attributes.

---

[7]For simplicity, we only consider one supplier in this example.

[8]http://www.xes-standard.org.

[9]http://www.win.tue.nl/ieeetfpm.

CaseID	EventID	Timestamp	Activity	Resource
1	Ch-4680555556-1	2012-07-30 11:14	Check stock availability	SYS1
1	Re-5972222222-1	2012-07-30 14:20	Retrieve prod. from warehouse	Rick
1	Co-6319444444-1	2012-07-30 15:10	Confirm order	Chuck
1	Ge-6402777778-1	2012-07-30 15:22	Get shipping address	SYS2
1	Em-6555555556-1	2012-07-30 15:44	Emit invoice	SYS2
1	Re-4180555556-1	2012-08-04 10:02	Receive payment	SYS2
1	Sh-4659722222-1	2012-08-05 11:11	Ship product	Susi
1	Ar-3833333333-1	2012-08-06 09:12	Archive order	DMS
2	Ch-4055555556-2	2012-08-01 09:44	Check stock availability	SYS1
2	Ch-4208333333-2	2012-08-01 10:06	Check materials availability	SYS1
2	Re-4666666667-2	2012-08-01 11:12	Request raw materials	Ringo
2	Ob-3263888889-2	2012-08-03 07:50	Obtain raw materials	Olaf
2	Ma-6131944444-2	2012-08-04 14:43	Manufacture product	SYS1
2	Co-6187615741-2	2012-08-04 14:51	Confirm order	Conny
2	Em-6388888889-2	2012-08-04 15:20	Emit invoice	SYS2
2	Ge-6439814815-2	2012-08-04 15:27	Get shipping address	SYS2
2	Sh-7277777778-2	2012-08-04 17:28	Ship product	Sara
2	Re-3611111111-2	2012-08-07 08:40	Receive payment	SYS2
2	Ar-3680555556-2	2012-08-07 08:50	Archive order	DMS
3	Ch-4208333333-3	2012-08-02 10:06	Check stock availability	SYS1
3	Ch-4243055556-3	2012-08-02 10:11	Check materials availability	SYS1
3	Ma-6694444444-3	2012-08-02 16:04	Manufacture product	SYS1
3	Co-6751157407-3	2012-08-02 16:12	Confirm order	Chuck
3	Em-6895833333-3	2012-08-02 16:33	Emit invoice	SYS2
3	Sh-7013888889-3	2012-08-02 16:50	Get shipping address	SYS2
3	Ge-7069444444-3	2012-08-02 16:58	Ship product	Emil
3	Re-4305555556-3	2012-08-06 10:20	Receive payment	SYS2
3	Ar-4340277778-3	2012-08-06 10:25	Archive order	DMS
4	Ch-3409722222-4	2012-08-04 08:11	Check stock availability	SYS1
4	Re-5000115741-4	2012-08-04 12:00	Retrieve prod. from warehouse	SYS1
4	Co-5041898148-4	2012-08-04 12:06	Confirm order	Hans
4	Ge-5223148148-4	2012-08-04 12:32	Get shipping address	SYS2
4	Em-4034837963-4	2012-08-08 09:41	Emit invoice	SYS2
4	Re-4180555556-4	2012-08-08 10:02	Receive payment	SYS2
4	Sh-5715277778-4	2012-08-08 13:43	Ship product	Susi
4	Ar-5888888889-4	2012-08-08 14:08	Archive order	DMS

Fig. 11.4 Example of an event log for the order-to-cash process

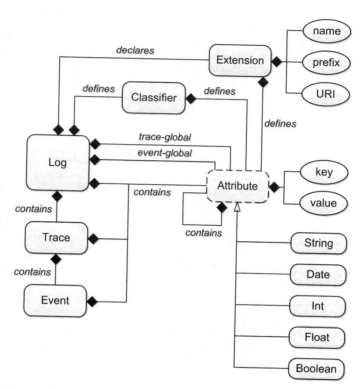

Fig. 11.5 Metamodel of the XES format

An attribute has to be a string, date, int, float, or boolean element as a key-value pair. Attributes have to refer to a global definition. There are two global elements in the XES file: one for defining trace attributes, the other for defining event attributes. Several classifiers can be defined in XES. A classifier maps one of more attributes of an event to a label that is used in the output of a process mining tool. In this way, for instance, events can be associated with tasks.

Figure 11.6 shows an extract of an XES log corresponding to the event log in Figure 11.4. The first global element (scope="trace") in this log tells us that every trace element should have a child element called "concept:name". This sub-element will be used to store the case identifier. In this example, there is one trace that has a value of 1 for this sub-element. At the level of individual events, there are three expected elements (i.e., "global" element with scope="event"): "concept:name", "time:timestamp", and "resource". The "concept:name" sub-element of an event will be used to store the name of the task to which the event refers. The "time:timestamp" and "resource" attributes give us the time of occurrence of the event and who performed it, respectively. The rest of the sample XES log represents one trace with two events. The first one refers to "Check stock availability", which

```
<log xes.version="1.0" xes.features="arbitrary-depth" xmlns="http://.../xes">
    <extension name="Concept" prefix="concept" uri="http://.../xes/concept.xesext"/>
    <extension name="Time" prefix="time" uri="http://.../xes/time.xesext"/>
    <global scope="trace">
        <string key="concept:name" value=""/>
    </global>
    <global scope="event">
        <string key="concept:name" value=""/>
        <date key="time:timestamp" value="1970-01-01T00:00:00.000+00:00"/>
        <string key="resource" value=""/>
    </global>
    <classifier name="Activity" keys="concept:name"/>
    <float key="log attribute" value="2335.23"/>
    <trace>
        <string key="concept:name" value="1"/>
        <event>
            <string key="concept:name" value="Check stock availability"/>
            <date key="time:timestamp" value="2012-07-30T11:14:00:000+01:00"/>
            <string key="resource" value=" SYS1 "/>
        </event>
        <event>
            <string key="concept:name" value="Retrieve product from warehouse"/>
            <date key="time:timestamp" value="2012-07-30T14:20:00:000+01:00"/>
            <string key="resource" value="Rick"/>
        </event>
    </trace>
</log>
```

Fig. 11.6 Example of a file in the XES format

was completed by SYS1 on the 30th of July 2012 at 11:14. The second event captures "Retrieve product from warehouse" conducted by Rick at 14:20.

Event data that is available in tabular format as in Figure 11.4 can be readily converted to XES. In many cases though, the data which is relevant for event logs is not directly accessible in the required format, but has to be extracted from different sources and integrated. This extraction and integration effort is generally not trivial. We can identify four major challenges for log data extraction, potentially requiring considerable effort in a project:

1. **Correlation challenge:** This refers to the problem of identifying the case an event belongs to. Many enterprise systems do not have an explicit notion of process defined. Therefore, we have to investigate which attribute of process-related entities might serve as a case identifier. Often, it is possible to utilize entity identifiers such as order number, invoice number, or shipment number.

2. **Timestamping challenge:** The challenge to work properly with timestamps stems from the fact that many systems do not consider logging as a primary task. This means that logging is often delayed until the system has idle time or little load. Therefore, we might find sequential events with the same timestamp in the log. This problem is worsened when logs from different systems potentially operating in different time zones have to be integrated. Partially, such problems can be resolved with domain knowledge, for example when events are known to always occur in a specific order.

3. **Longevity challenge:** For long running processes (e.g., processes with cycle times in the order of weeks or months), we might not yet have observed all cases that started during a recent time period (e.g., cases that started in the past 6 months) up to their completion. In other words, some cases might still be incomplete. Mixing these incomplete cases with completed cases can lead to a distorted picture of the process. For example, the cycle times or other performance measures calculated over incomplete cases should not be mixed with those of the completed ones, as they have different meaning. In order to avoid such distortions, we should consider the option of excluding incomplete cases from an event log. Also, we should ensure that the time period covered by an event log is significantly longer than the mean cycle time of the process, so that the event log contains samples of both short-lived and long-lived cases.

4. **Granularity challenge:** Typically, we are interested in conducting event log analysis on a conceptual level for which we have process models defined. In general, the granularity of event log recording is much finer such that each task of a process model might map to a set of events. For example, a task like "Retrieve product from warehouse" on the abstraction level of a process model maps to a series of events like "Work item #1,211 assigned", "Work item #1,211 started", "Purchase order form opened", "Product retrieved", and "Work item #1,211 completed". Often, fine-granular events many show up repeatedly in the logs while on an abstract level only a single task is executed. Therefore, it is difficult to define a precise mapping between the two levels of abstraction.

Exercise 11.4 Consider the final assembly process of Airbus for their A380 series. The final assembly of this aircraft series is located at the production site in Toulouse, France. Large parts are brought by ship to Bordeaux and brought to Toulouse by waterway and road transport. What is the challenge when log data of the A380 production process has to be integrated?

Once we have overcome the above data quality challenges, we are able to produce an event log consisting of *traces*, such that each trace contains the perfectly ordered sequence of events observed for a given case, each event refers to a task, and every task in the process is included in the event log. An event log with these properties can be re-written in a simplified representation, called a *workflow log*. A workflow log is a set of distinct traces, such that each trace consists of a sequence of symbols and each symbol represents an execution of a task. For example, given a set of tasks represented by symbols $\{a, b, c, d\}$, a possible workflow log is $\{\langle a, b, c, d \rangle, \langle a, c, b, d \rangle, \langle a, c, d \rangle\}$.

Case ID	Event ID	Timestamp	Activity
1	Ch-468	2012-07-30 11:14	Check stock availability
1	Re-597	2012-07-30 14:20	Retrieve product from warehouse
1	Co-631	2012-07-30 15:10	Confirm order
1	Ge-640	2012-07-30 15:22	Get shipping address
1	Em-655	2012-07-30 15:44	Emit invoice
1	Re-418	2012-08-04 10:02	Receive payment
1	Sh-465	2012-08-05 11:11	Ship product
1	Ar-383	2012-08-06 09:12	Archive order
2	Ch-405	2012-08-01 09:44	Check stock availability
2	Ch-420	2012-08-01 10:06	Check materials availability
2	Re-466	2012-08-01 11:12	Request raw materials
2	Ob-326	2012-08-03 07:50	Obtain raw materials
2	Ma-613	2012-08-04 14:43	Manufacture product
2	Co-618	2012-08-04 14:51	Confirm order
2	Em-638	2012-08-04 15:20	Emit invoice
2	Ge-643	2012-08-04 15:27	Get shipping address
2	Sh-727	2012-08-04 17:28	Ship product
2	Re-361	2012-08-07 08:40	Receive payment
2	Ar-368	2012-08-07 08:50	Archive order

Letter	Actvities
a	Check stock availability
b	Retrieve product from warehouse
c	Check materials availability
d	Request raw materials
e	Obtain raw materials
f	Manufacture product
g	Confirm order
h	Get shipping address
i	Ship product
j	Emit invoice
k	Receive payment
l	Archive order

Workflow Log

a,b,g,h,j,k,i,l

a,c,d,e,f,g,j,h,i,k,l

...

Fig. 11.7 Definition of a workflow log

Figure 11.7 sketches how a workflow log can be constructed from an event log.

Exercise 11.5 Have a look at Figure 11.4 and finish translating this event log into a workflow log by following the mapping rules sketched in Figure 11.7. Note that in this figure we have omitted the delimiters $\langle$ and $\rangle$ at the start and end of each trace.

Sometimes, it is useful to know how many times each *distinct trace* is observed in the event log. This is the case for example for robust process discovery techniques, discussed later in this chapter. When a trace occurs multiple times in a workflow log, we will write the number of occurrences before the contents of the trace. For example, we will write $10 \times \langle a, b, c, g, e, h \rangle$ to refer to a distinct trace $\langle a, b, c, g, e, h \rangle$ occurring 10 times in a log.

11.4   Automated Process Discovery

An automated process discovery technique takes as input an event log and produces as output a process model that captures the behavior of the log in a representative way. By *representative*, we mean that the constructed process model should be able to replay the traces of the event log and that it should not be able to replay traces that are neither in the event log nor implied by the traces found in the event log.

There is a wide range of automated process discovery techniques. Below we present a few of them. We start with a technique that produces a simple albeit rather incomplete representation of how tasks in the process follow each other, namely the so-called *dependency graph*. We then introduce a simple technique to generate a BPMN process model from an event log under very strong assumptions, which often do not hold in practice. This technique gives us an idea of how difficult it is to automatically discover BPMN process models from event logs. Finally, we introduce more sophisticated and robust techniques that are able to generate relatively readable process models from large, real-life event logs.

11.4.1 Dependency Graphs

Dependency graphs are a popular technique to visualize event logs. A *dependency graph* (also known as a *directly-follows graph*) is a graph where each node represents one event class (i.e., a task) and each arc represents a "directly follows" relation. An arc exists between two event classes A and B if there is at least one trace in which B comes immediately after A. The arcs in a dependency graph may be annotated with an integer indicating the number of times that B directly follows A (hereby called the *absolute frequency*). In some process mining tools, it is also possible to annotate each arc with a temporal delay, e.g., the average time between an occurrence of task A and an occurrence of task B, among all occurrences of B that immediately follow an occurrence of A. This temporal delay gives an indication of the waiting time between a given pair of tasks in the process.

Example 11.2 Figure 11.8 shows an event log (left) and a corresponding dependency graph (right). We observe that the arc from task a to task c has an absolute frequency of 20. This is because the event log has two distinct traces where c occurs immediately before a and each of these distinct traces occurs 10 times.   □

Exercise 11.6 Write down the dependency graph corresponding to the workflow log resulting from Exercise 11.5.

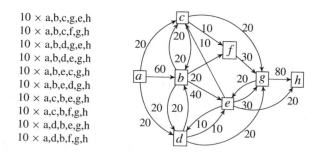

Fig. 11.8 Event log and corresponding dependency graph

Owing to their simplicity, dependency graphs are supported by most commercial process mining tools, such as Celonis,[10] Disco,[11] Minit,[12] myInvenio,[13] and ProcessGold.[14] They are also supported by the so-called *fuzzy miner* plugin of ProM[15] and by Apromore,[16] two open-source process mining toolsets. All these tools provide visual cues to enhance the readability of dependency graphs. For example, the color and the thickness of the arcs may be used to encode how frequently a task in a pair directly follows the other (e.g., a thick and dark-blue arc may represent a frequent directly-follows relation relative to a thin, light-blue arc). These tools also offer visual zoom in operations that allow users to explore specific parts of a dependency graph in detail.

Besides their simplicity, one of the most appealing features of dependency graphs is that they are amenable to *abstraction* operations. In this context, abstraction refers to removing a subset of the nodes or arcs in a dependency graph in order to obtain a smaller dependency graph of a given event log. For example, process mining tools allow us to remove the most infrequent nodes or arcs from a dependency graph in order to obtain a simpler map that is easier to understand. Abstraction is an indispensable feature when we want to explore a real-life event log, as illustrated below.

Example 11.3 We consider the event log of the Business Process Intelligence Challenge 2017 available at https://tinyurl.com/bpic2017. This is an event log of a loan origination process at a Dutch financial institution. The event log covers the application-to-approval and the offer-to-acceptance sub-processes of a loan origination process, meaning that it starts when a loan application is submitted by a customer and it ends when the customer accepts (or refuses) the corresponding loan offer. The full dependency graph produced by the Celonis Web-based tool on this event log is shown in Figure 11.9a. This map is too detailed to be understandable by a user. Even if we visually zoom-in to inspect specific parts of this map, it will be very difficult to understand what is going on in this process. For this reason, Celonis and other tools can abstract away the map by retaining only the most frequent arcs. Figure 11.9b shows the filtered map produced by Celonis when setting the task abstraction slider to 98% and the arc abstraction slider to 90%. □

While abstraction is a useful mechanism when visualizing large event logs, it is not sufficient to handle the full complexity of real-life event logs. Accordingly, process mining tools also offer a second type of simplification operation called *event log filtering*. Filtering an event log means removing a subset of the traces, events or

---

[10]http://www.celonis.com.

[11]https://fluxicon.com/disco.

[12]http://minitlabs.com.

[13]http://www.my-invenio.com.

[14]https://processgold.com/en.

[15]http://www.promtools.org.

[16]http://apromore.org.

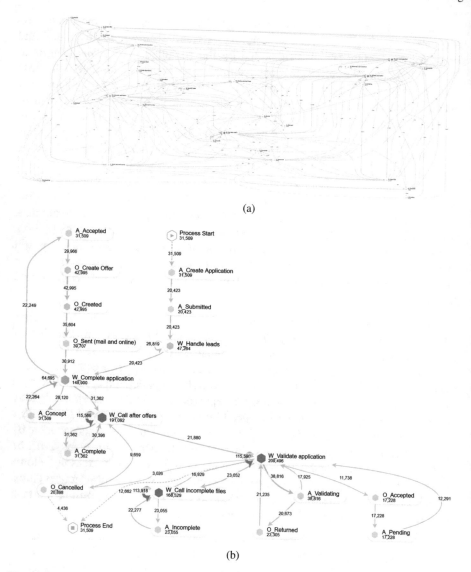

Fig. 11.9 Example of a full dependency graph and an abstracted version thereof. (**a**) Full dependency graph. (**b**) Filtered dependency graph

pairs of events in order to obtain a simpler log. Note that filtering and abstraction have different inputs and outputs. Whereas filtering transforms an event log into a smaller log, abstraction only affects the dependency graph, not the log.

In general, process mining tools provide three types of filters:

- *Event filters*, which allow us to remove all events in a log that fulfill a condition or, conversely, to retain only those events that fulfill a condition. For example, in an event log of a procure-to-pay process, we can define a filter that removes all events that contain an event of event class "Amend purchase requisition". This operation returns a filtered event log that has the same set of traces as the original log, but some of the traces are slightly shorter because any occurrence of "Amend purchase requisition" is removed. The conditions used in a filter can involve multiple sub-conditions. For example, we can define an event filter to remove all occurrences of event "Amend purchase requisition" such that the value of attribute "reason" is equal to "SupplierChanged", meaning all purchase requisition amendments corresponding to a change of supplier. Similarly, we can define a filter that removes all the "Amend purchase requisition" events performed by a given resource (e.g., Rick).
- *Event pair filters*, which allow us to remove all pairs of events in a log that fulfill a condition, or to retain only those pairs of events that fulfill a condition. For example, we can define a filter that only retains event pairs (e1, e2) in each trace, such that e2 appears after e1, and such that e1 corresponds to task "Amend purchase requisition" and e2 corresponds to task "Approve purchase requisition amendment".
- *Trace filters*, which allow us to remove all traces in a log that fulfill a condition, or retain only those traces that fulfill a condition. For example, we can remove all traces where an event corresponding to a given task occurs (e.g., remove all traces where event "Amend purchase requisition" occurs). We can also use temporal conditions here, such as for example removing all traces that have a cycle time of less than 20 days. Note that here we are removing entire traces and not just individual events in a trace.

Exercise 11.7 Using a process mining tool of your choice, answer the following questions with reference to the event log of the Business Process Intelligence Challenge 2017 (https://tinyurl.com/bpic2017):

A. How many cases are represented in this event log in total?
B. What is the mean cycle time of the cases captured in this event log?
C. Let us say that a case is successful if its trace contains at least one occurrence of event O_Accepted, meaning that the customer accepted the loan offer. How many cases are successful? What is the mean cycle time of the successful cases?
D. Let us say that a case is unsuccessful if its trace contains at least one occurrence of event O_Refused. How many cases are unsuccessful? What is the mean cycle time of the unsuccessful cases?
E. Let us say that a case is canceled if the last event in its trace is O_Cancelled. Note that a trace may contain O_Cancelled, but if it contains other events after

O_Cancelled then we will not treat it as canceled because it means that the case continued despite the occurrence of a cancelation event. How many cases were canceled? What is the mean cycle time of the canceled cases?

While dependency graphs are a useful log visualization approach, especially when used in combination with filtering and abstraction operations, they do not allow us to understand in detail what is happening at each point in the process. In particular, they do not allow us to easily distinguish whether two tasks are in parallel, in a loop, or in some other relation, as a BPMN process model would do. If our goal is to understand in detail how the process is executed, we are much better off with a BPMN process model. Fortunately, there are a number of techniques to automatically discover a BPMN process model from an event log. Below, we present first a simple but limited technique, namely the α-algorithm, and we then discuss other more sophisticated techniques that can discover readable process models from large event logs.

11.4.2   The α-Algorithm

The α-algorithm is a basic algorithm for discovering process models from event logs. The algorithm is simple enough that we can easily grasp how it works in detail. However, it makes a strong assumption about the event log, namely behavioral completeness. An event log is behaviorally complete if whenever a task a can be directly followed by a task b in the actual process, then there is at least one case in the event log where we observe ab. In practice, we can hardly assume that we find the complete set of behavioral options in a log. Advanced techniques, which we will discuss later, try to lift this assumption by trying to guess which traces the process might have, which are not present in the event log.

The α-algorithm constructs a process model from a behaviorally complete event log in two phases. In the first phase, a set of order relations between pairs of events are extracted from the workflow log. In the second phase, the process model is constructed in a stepwise fashion from these identified relations. The order relations refer to pairs of tasks which directly follow one another in the log. They provide the basis for the definition of three more specific relations that refer to causality, to potential parallelism and to no-direct-succession. We refer to this set of relations as the α relations.

- The basic directly-follows relation $a > b$ holds if we can observe in the workflow log L that a task a is directly followed by b. This is the same relation as that captured in a dependency graph.
- The causality relation $a \rightarrow b$ is derived from the directly-follows relation. It holds if we observe in L that $a > b$ and that $b \not> a$.
- The relation of potential parallelism $a \| b$ holds if both $a > b$ and $b > a$ are observed in the workflow log L.
- The relation of no-direct-succession $a\#b$ holds if $a \not> b$ and $b \not> a$.

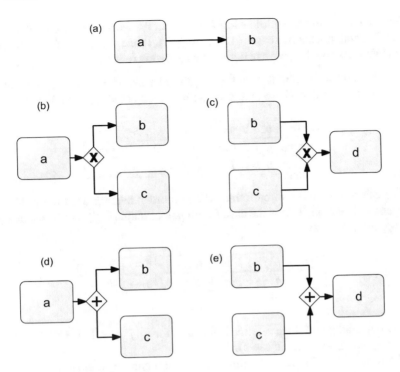

Fig. 11.10 Simple control flow patterns

The reason why exactly these relations are used is illustrated in Figure 11.10. There exist five characteristic combinations of relations between the tasks in a workflow log that can be mapped to simple control flow patterns.

Pattern (a)   depicts a sequence of tasks a and b. If we model them in this way, it should be guaranteed that in a workflow log we will find a followed by b, i.e., $a > b$, but never b followed by a, i.e., $b \not> a$. This means that the causality relation $a \rightarrow b$ should hold.

Pattern (b)   also relates to a characteristic combination of relations. The workflow log should show that $a \rightarrow b$ and $a \rightarrow c$ hold, and that b and c would not be mutual successors, i.e., $b\#c$.

Pattern (c)   also requires that b and c are not mutual successors, i.e., $b\#c$, while both $b \rightarrow d$ and $c \rightarrow d$ have to hold.

Pattern (d)   demands that $a \rightarrow b$ and $a \rightarrow c$ hold, and that b and c show potential parallelism, i.e., $b\|c$.

Pattern (e)   refers to $b \rightarrow d$ and $c \rightarrow d$ while b and c show potential parallelism, i.e., $b\|c$.

The idea of the α-algorithm is to identify the relations between all pairs of tasks from the workflow log in order to reconstruct a process model based on Patterns (a) to (e). Therefore, before applying the α-algorithm, we must extract all basic order relations from the workflow log L. Consider the workflow log depicted in Figure 11.7 containing the two cases $\langle a, b, g, h, j, k, i, l \rangle$ and $\langle a, c, d, e, f, g, j, h, i, k, l \rangle$. From this workflow log, we can derive the following relations.

- The basic order relations $>$ refer to pairs of tasks in which one task directly follows the another. These relations can be directly read from the log:

$a > b$	$h > j$	$i > l$	$d > e$	$g > j$	$i > k$
$b > g$	$j > k$	$a > c$	$e > f$	$j > h$	$k > l$
$g > h$	$k > i$	$c > d$	$f > g$	$h > i$	

- The causal relations can be found when an order relation does not hold in the opposite direction. This is the case for all pairs except (h, j) and (i, k), and their opposites. We get:

$a \rightarrow b$	$j \rightarrow k$	$a \rightarrow c$	$d \rightarrow e$	$f \rightarrow g$	$h \rightarrow i$
$b \rightarrow g$	$i \rightarrow l$	$c \rightarrow d$	$e \rightarrow f$	$g \rightarrow j$	$k \rightarrow l$
$g \rightarrow h$					

- The potential parallelism relation holds true for $h \| j$ as well as for $k \| i$ (and the corresponding symmetric cases).
- The remaining relation of no-direct-succession can be found for all pairs that do not belong to $\rightarrow$ and $\|$. It can be easily derived when we write down the relations in a matrix as shown in Figure 11.11. This matrix is also referred to as the *footprint matrix* of the log.

Exercise 11.8 Have a look at the workflow log you constructed in Exercise 11.5 (page 427). Define the relations $>, \rightarrow, \|, \#$, as well as the footprint matrix of this workflow log.

The α-algorithm takes an event log L and its α relations as a starting point. The essential idea of the algorithm is that whenever a task directly follows another one in the log, the two tasks should be directly connected in the process model. Furthermore, if there is more than one task that can follow another, we have to determine whether the set of succeeding tasks is partially exclusive or concurrent. An exception from the principle that tasks should be connected in the process model is when two tasks are potentially parallel, i.e., those pairs included in $\|$. The details of the α-algorithm are defined according to the following eight steps.[17]

1. Let T_L be the set of all tasks in the log.
2. Let T_I be the set of tasks that appear at least once as first task of a case.

---

[17] Note that the α-algorithm was originally defined for constructing Petri nets. The version shown here is a simplification based on the five simple control-flow patterns of Figure 11.10, in order to construct BPMN models.

	a	b	c	d	e	f	g	h	i	j	k	l
a	#	→	→	#	#	#	#	#	#	#	#	#
b	←	#	#	#	#	#	→	#	#	#	#	#
c	←	#	#	→	#	#	#	#	#	#	#	#
d	#	#	←	#	→	#	#	#	#	#	#	#
e	#	#	#	←	#	→	#	#	#	#	#	#
f	#	#	#	#	←	#	→	#	#	#	#	#
g	#	←	#	#	#	←	#	→	#	→	#	#
h	#	#	#	#	#	#	←	#	→	||	#	#
i	#	#	#	#	#	#	#	←	#	#	||	→
j	#	#	#	#	#	#	←	||	#	#	→	#
k	#	#	#	#	#	#	#	#	||	←	#	→
l	#	#	#	#	#	#	#	#	←	#	←	#

Fig. 11.11 Footprint represented as a matrix of the workflow log $L = [\langle a, b, g, h, j, k, i, l \rangle,$ $\langle a, c, d, e, f, g, j, h, i, k, l \rangle]$

3. Let T_O be the set of tasks that appear at least once as last task in a case.
4. Let X_L be the set of potential task connections. X_L is composed of:

   a. Pattern (a): all pairs for which $a \to b$ holds.
   b. Pattern (b): all triples for which $a \to (b\#c)$ holds.
   c. Pattern (c): all triples for which $(b\#c) \to d$ holds.

Note that triples for which Pattern (d) $a \to (b||c)$ or Pattern (e) $(b||c) \to d$ hold are not included in X_L.

5. Construct the set Y_L as a subset of X_L by:

   a. Eliminating $a \to b$ and $a \to c$ if there exists some $a \to (b\#c)$.
   b. Eliminating $b \to c$ and $b \to d$ if there exists some $(b\#c) \to d$.

6. Connect start and end events in the following way:

   a. If there are multiple tasks in the set T_I of first tasks, then draw a start event leading to an XOR-split, which connects to every task in T_I. Otherwise, directly connect the start event with the first task.
   b. For each task in the set T_O of last tasks, add an end event and draw an arc from the task to the end event.

7. Construct the flow arcs in the following way:

   a. Pattern (a): for each $a \to b$ in Y_L, draw an arc a to b.
   b. Pattern (b): for each $a \to (b\#c)$ in Y_L, draw an arc from a to an XOR-split, and from there to b and c.

   c. Pattern (c): for each $(b\#c) \to d$ in Y_L, draw an arc from b and c to an XOR-join, and from there to d.

   d. Pattern (d) and (e): if a task in the so-constructed process model has multiple incoming or multiple outgoing arcs, bundle these arcs with an AND-join or AND-split, respectively.

8. Return the newly constructed process model.

Let us apply the α-algorithm to $L = [\langle a, b, g, h, j, k, i, l \rangle, \langle a, c, d, e, f, g, j, h, i, k, l \rangle]$. Steps 1–3 identify $T_L = \{a, b, c, d, e, f, g, h, i, j, k, l\}$, $T_I = \{a\}$, and $T_O = \{l\}$. In Step 4a all causal relations are added to X_L including $a \to b, a \to c$, etc. In Step 4b, we work row by row through the footprint matrix of Figure 11.11 and check if there are cells sharing a $\to$ relation while relating to tasks that are pairwise in $\#$. In the row a, we observe both $a \to b$ and $a \to c$. Also, $b\#c$ holds. Therefore, we add $a \to (b\#c)$ to X_L. We also consider row g and its relation to h and j. However, as $h||j$ holds, we do not add them. In Step 4c, we progress column by column through the footprint matrix and see if there are cells sharing a $\to$ relation while relating to tasks that are mutually in $\#$. In column g, we observe two $\to$ relations to b and f. Also, $b\#f$ holds. Accordingly, we add $(b\#f) \to g$ to X_L. We also check i and k that share the same relation to l. However, as $i||k$ holds, we do not add them. There are no further complex combinations found in Step 4d.

In Step 5, we eliminate the basic elements in X_L that are covered by the complex patterns found in Steps 4b and 4c. Accordingly, we delete $a \to b$, $a \to c$, $b \to g$, and $f \to g$. In Step 6a we introduce a start event and connect it with a; in 6b, task l is connected with an end event. In Step 7, arcs and gateways are added for the elements of Y_L. Finally, in Step 8 the resulting process model is returned, as shown in Figure 11.12.

Exercise 11.9 Consider the workflow log and the footprint you constructed in Exercises 11.5 (page 427) and 11.8 (page 434). Show step-by-step how the α-algorithm works on this workflow log, and draw the resulting process model.

11.4.3 Robust Process Discovery

The α-algorithm can reconstruct a process model from a behaviorally complete event log if that log has been generated from a structured process model. There are also limitations to be noted, though. The α-algorithm is not able to distinguish so-called *short loops* from true parallelism. As can be seen in Figure 11.13, all three models can produce a workflow log that yields $b||c$ in the corresponding footprint. Several extensions to the α-algorithm have been proposed. The idea of the α+-algorithm is to define the relation $||$ in a stricter way such that $b||c$ is only included if there is no sequence bcb in the log. In this way, models (b) and (c) in Figure 11.13 can be distinguished from model (a) in their generated logs. Furthermore, we can use pre-processing to extract direct repetitions like aa or bb from a log, note down

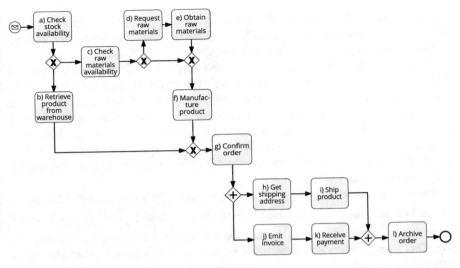

Fig. 11.12 Process model constructed by the α-algorithm from log $L = [\langle a, b, g, h, j, k, i, l \rangle, \langle a, c, d, e, f, g, j, h, i, k, l \rangle]$

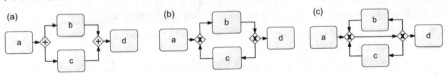

Fig. 11.13 Examples of two short loops, (**b**) and (**c**), that cannot be distinguished from model (**a**) by the α-algorithm

the corresponding tasks, and continue with a log from which such repeated behavior is mapped to a single execution.

Another limitation of the α-algorithm is its inability to deal with *incompleteness* in an event log. The α-algorithm assumes that the $>$ relation (from which the other relations are derived) is complete, meaning that if the process allows task a to be directly followed by task b, then the relation $a > b$ must be observed in at least one trace of the log. This assumption is too strong for processes that have a lot of parallelism. For example, if in a process there is a block of ten concurrent tasks $a_1, \ldots a_{10}$, we need to observe each relation $a_i > a_j$ for each $i, j \in [1..10]$, meaning 100 possible combinations. It suffices that one of these combinations has not been observed in the event log for the α-algorithm to discover the wrong model. This example shows that we need more robust process discovery algorithms, which can smartly infer relations that are not explicitly observed in the event log, but that are somehow implied by what can be observed in the log.

A related limitation is the α-algorithm's inability to deal with *noise*. Event logs often include cases with a missing head, a missing tail, or a missing intermediate episode because some events in a case have not been recorded. For example, a worker might have forgotten to mark an invoice as *paid*, and hence the "Payment received" event is missing in the corresponding trace. Furthermore, there may be logging errors leading to events being recorded in the wrong order (or with wrong timestamps) or recorded twice. Ideally, such noise should not distort the process model produced by a process discovery technique.

Fortunately, there are other more robust algorithms for automated process discovery, such as the *heuristics miner* [192], the *structured heuristics miner* [11], the *inductive miner* [86] and the *split miner* [10]. These techniques generally work as follows. First, they construct the dependency graph from the event log. Second, they remove some of the nodes and arcs in the process dependency graph in order to deal with noise (infrequent behavior). Finally, they apply a set of heuristic rules to discover split gateways and join gateways in order to turn the filtered dependency graph into a (BPMN) process model.

For example, to handle noise, the heuristics miner [192] uses a relative frequency metric between pairs of event labels, defined as $a \Rightarrow b = \left(\frac{|a>b|-|b>a|}{|a>b|+|b>a|+1} \right)$, where $|a > b|$ is the number of times when task a is directly followed by task b in the log. This metric has a value close to +1 when task a is directly followed by task b sometimes and task b is (almost) never directly followed by a. This means that there is a clear direct-precedence relation from a to b. When the value of $a \Rightarrow b$ is not close to 1 (for example when it is less than 0.8), it means that the direct precedence relation is not very clear (it might be noise) and hence it is deleted. Other similar frequency metrics are used to detect self loops and short loops in order to avoid the limitations of the α-algorithm.

Once the dependency graph has been filtered and self and short loops have been identified, the heuristics miner identifies split and join gateways by analyzing both the filtered dependency graph and the traces in the log. Specifically, if task a is directly followed by b and by c, but not by both (i.e., after b we do not observe c or we very rarely observe it), the heuristics miner will put an XOR-split between task a on the one hand, and tasks b and c on the other hand. Meanwhile, if a is generally followed by both b and by c, the heuristics miner will put an AND-split after task a and before b and c. The term *generally* here means that the heuristics miner tolerates some cases where a is not followed by b or by c if this happens infrequently. Join gateways are discovered similarly: An XOR-join is placed between tasks b and c on the one hand, and task d on the other hand, if d is generally preceded by either task b or c but not both, while an AND-join is placed there if d is generally preceded by both b and c.

Unlike the α-algorithm, the heuristics miner is able to detect self-loops and short-loops, and to handle incomplete and noisy event logs. However, when applied to large real-life event logs, the heuristics miner often produces process models that are too large, spaghetti-like and not sound (see Section 5.4.1 for a definition of soundness of process models).

As discussed in Section 5.4.3, a desirable property of process models is that they should be block-structured. Block-structured process models are always sound, and in addition, they are generally easier to understand than unstructured ones. Accordingly, some of the most robust process discovery techniques try to produce block-structured process models. This is the case for example of the inductive miner and the structured heuristics miner. Like the heuristics miner, the inductive miner starts by constructing a dependency graph and filtering out infrequent arcs. But instead of immediately proceeding to identifying gateways from the filtered dependency graph, it first analyzes the filtered dependency graph in order to identify arcs that (if removed) would bisect the dependency graph into two separate parts. By doing this several times, it ends up dividing the dependency graph into blocks. Finally, it discovers the gateways locally within each block, in such a way that each split gateway has a corresponding join gateway of the same type, which is the key characteristic of block-structured process models.

The structured heuristics miner implements an alternative approach. It first applies the heuristics miner in order to discover a process model. This process model might be relatively complex (high number of gateways) and highly unstructured. To improve this model, the structured heuristics miner then applies an algorithm that converts unstructured process models into block-structured ones. In doing so, the algorithm also ensures that the resulting model is sound.

The split miner goes beyond the inductive miner and the structured heuristics miner by discovering process models that are sound, but not always perfectly block-structured. By allowing itself to discover non-block-structured models, the split miner technique discovers higher-quality models as discussed below.

The heuristics and inductive miners can be both found in ProM, while these two algorithms, as well as the structured heuristics miner and the split miner, can all be found in Apromore.

11.4.4 Quality Measures for Automated Process Discovery

Given the availability of several algorithms for automated discovery of process models, one may wonder which algorithm to choose for a given event log. A series of experiments reported in [12] suggests that the inductive miner and the split miner are among the most robust algorithms for automated process discovery. However, their relative performance on a given event log can vary and some tuning is needed. By *tuning*, we mean that the algorithm needs to be applied with different parameter settings. Each parameter setting leads to a different process model. Hence, we then need to select the best of them.

This raises the question of how to assess the quality of a process model discovered from an event log. The quality of automatically-discovered process models is usually evaluated using four criteria: *fitness*, *precision*, *generalization*, and *complexity* [1].

Fitness is the ability of the discovered process model to replay the behavior contained in the log. A fitness equal to 1 means that the model can replay every trace in the log. We will discuss later how traces are replayed against a log in order to compute a fitness measure.

Precision refers to the extent to which the discovered process model generates only the traces found in the log. A precision equal to 1 means that any trace produced by the process model also appears in the log. If a process model can produce a trace that is not in the log, this reduces the precision. A precision of 0 would mean that none of the traces that the model produces is observed in the log.

Generalization refers to the extent to which the discovered process model captures traces that are not present in the log because the log is incomplete, but that are likely to be allowed by the underlying business process. It is tricky to measure generalization, because it is hard to know if a trace T belongs to a process, if all we have is an incomplete event log and trace T does not appear in this log. A standard trick to measure generalization is called k-fold cross-validation. The idea is to divide the log into k parts (for example five parts), to discover the model from $k - 1$ parts (i.e., we hold out one part), and to measure the fitness of the discovered model against the hold-out part, and the precision of the discovered model against the entire log. This operation is repeated for every possible hold-out part, and the measures of fitness and precision obtained for every hold-out operation are averaged, leading to two measures called *k-fold fitness* and *k-fold precision* respectively. A k-fold fitness equal to 1 means that the discovered model produces all traces that are part of the observed process, even if those traces are not in the event log. Similarly, a k-fold precision close to 1 means that the discovered model does not over-generalize the process, i.e., it does not produce traces that are not part of the process.

Finally, the *complexity* of a process model quantifies how difficult it is to understand the model. Complexity can be measured simply in terms of size (number of nodes in a BPMN model). Usually, larger models are more complex and hence difficult to understand. However, two models can have the same size and one of them might be more difficult to understand because it contains too many gateways. Hence, it is common to also measure complexity of a BPMN process model using a metric called *Coefficient of Network Connectivity* (CNC), which is the number of flows in a BPMN model divided by the number of nodes. The higher the CNC is, the higher is the number of gateways relative to nodes, which makes the model more difficult to understand. Also, as discussed in Section 5.4.3, block-structured process models are easier to comprehend than unstructured ones. Accordingly, it is also common to measure the complexity of a process model via a measure called *structuredness*. The structuredness of a process model is the percentage of nodes located directly inside a well-structured single-entry single-exit fragment. A perfectly block-structured process model has a structuredness equal to 1, whereas a spaghetti-like process model (with arcs going all over the place) would have a low structuredness.

Example 11.4 We consider the event log available at: http://tinyurl.com/ sampleSAPLog. The process model discovered using the heuristics miner implementation in ProM version 6 is shown in Figure 11.14a. This process model is not sound. For example, if task D is executed, the next task according to the model should be N. After task N is executed, a token is placed in the flow between task N and the AND gateway. There is no token anywhere else in the model. Hence, the other incoming flow of this AND gateway will never receive a token thereafter.

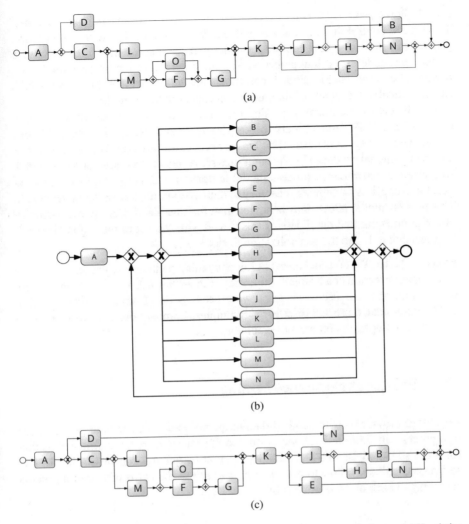

Fig. 11.14 Models discovered from a sample log using three discovery techniques . (**a**) Heuristics miner (ProM v6). (**b**) Inductive miner (ProM v6). (**c**) Structured heuristics miner (Apromore)

The process is hence in a deadlock. Similarly, observe that if after task K, task E is executed, the case ends up in a deadlock for the same reason as above.

The model discovered using the inductive miner (in ProM v6) for this same log is shown in Figure 11.14b. This model is block-structured and sound. However, the model is very unconstrained—it can produce too many traces. After executing task A, from the first XOR-split we can execute any task between B and N, after which the second XOR-split is reached (the one before the end event). Once this gateway has been reached, any of the tasks in the process can be executed, potentially again, via the loopback arc, or the case may end immediately. Therefore, this process model allows tasks B-N to be executed in any order and any number of times. This type of control-flow structure is called a *flower pattern*. Because of this flower pattern, this process model can produce many traces that are not in the event log. Hence, the model has a low precision. On the other hand, the process model has perfect fitness. Indeed, given that it can accept almost any sequence of tasks A-N, it can in particular accept any of the traces that appear in the event log.

Finally, the model discovered using the structured heuristics miner is shown in Figure 11.14c.[18] This model is also block-structured and sound. We note that in this model there are two tasks labelled N. This is because the structured miner transforms the process model produced by the heuristics miner into a structured process model. And when an unstructured process model is transformed into an equivalent block-structured one, it is sometimes necessary to duplicate some of the tasks in the model. This process model allows less behavior than the one discovered by the inductive miner. It turns out that the fitness of this model with respect to the log is almost 1, the precision is 1, and the generalization is close to 1.   □

Exercise 11.10 We consider an event log containing pathways of patients suffering from sepsis infection at a hospital: http://tinyurl.com/SepsisLog. Using one or more process mining tools, discover at least two process models from this event log using different automated process discovery techniques. Compare the discovered models in terms of complexity, fitness and precision.

11.5   Process Performance Mining

Event logs provide us with detailed data to quantify and visualize the performance of a process. In Section 8.1.3, we discussed the four performance dimensions that form the so-called Devil's Quadrangle: time, cost, quality, and flexibility. In this section, we will show how to use event logs to assess the performance of a process according to each of these dimensions.

11.5.1   Time Dimension

Time and its more specific measures *cycle time* and *waiting time* are important general performance measures. Event logs typically show timestamps such that they can be used for time analysis. Time analysis is concerned with the temporal occurrence and probabilities of different types of events. The event logs of a process generally relate each event to the point in time of its occurrence. Therefore, it is straightforward to plot events on the time axis. Furthermore, we can utilize

---

[18]The split miner produces this same model when applied to this log (with a parallelism threshold of 40%).

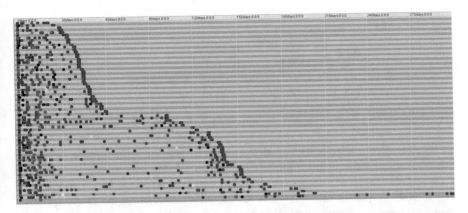

Fig. 11.15 Dotted chart of log data

classifiers to group events on a second axis. A classifier typically refers to one of the attributes of an event, like case ID or participant ID. There are two levels of detail for plotting events in a diagram: *dotted charts* using the timestamp to plot an event and *timeline chart* showing the duration (processing time) of a task and its waiting time.

The dotted chart is a simple, yet powerful visualization tool for event logs. Each event is plotted on a two-dimensional canvas with the first axis representing its occurrence in time and the second axis as its association with a classifier like a case ID. There are different options to organize the first axis. Time can be represented either *relative*, such that the first event is counted as zero, or *absolute* such that later cases with a later start event are further right in comparison to cases that started earlier. The second axis can be sorted according to different criteria. For instance, cases can be shown according to their historical order or their overall cycle time.

Figure 11.15 shows the dotted chart of the event log of a healthcare process. This chart has been produced using the ProM tool. The events are plotted according to their relative time and sorted according to their overall cycle time. It can be seen that there is a considerable variation in terms of cycle time. Furthermore, the chart suggests that there might be three distinct classes of cases: those that take no more than 60 days, those taking 60 to 210 days, and a small class of cases taking longer than 210 days. Such an explorative inspection can provide a good basis for a more detailed analysis of the factors influencing the cycle time.

Exercise 11.11 Draw a dotted chart of the event log in Figure 11.4 (page 423) showing relative cycle time and being sorted by cycle time.

If the event log contains timestamps capturing both the start and the end of each task, we can plot tasks not as dots, but as bars, as shown in Figure 11.16. This type of a visualization is called a *timeline chart*. A timeline chart shows the waiting time (from activation until starting) and the processing time (from starting until completion) for each task. The timeline chart is more informative than the dotted chart, since it shows waiting times and processing times separately, and hence it allows us to pinpoint bottlenecks in the process.

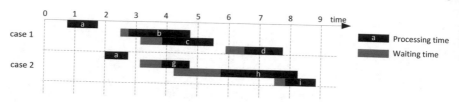

Fig. 11.16 Example of timeline chart

We saw in Section 11.4.1 that dependency graphs are a versatile approach to visualize event logs. In particular, we saw that dependency graphs can give us a picture of the most frequent paths in a process. Another useful property of dependency graphs is that they can be used to visualize temporal delays (e.g., waiting times or processing times) via color-coding or thickness-coding. Concretely, arcs in the dependency graph may be color-coded by the corresponding temporal delay between the source event and the target event of the arc. This visualization allows us to identify the longest waiting times in the process—also known as *bottlenecks*. Meanwhile, the nodes in a dependency graph can be color-coded with the processing times of each task. The latter requires that each task captured in the log have both a start timestamp and an end timestamp so that the processing time can be computed. If the log contains only the completion timestamp of each task, it is only possible to analyze the cycle times of tasks and not the processing times.

Example 11.5 Figure 11.17 shows the *performance view* produced by Disco when applied to the BPI Challenge 2017 log. The most infrequent arcs have been removed to avoid clutter. The task and the arc with the highest times are indicated in red. If we visually zoom in, in the tool, we are able to see that the task with the slowest processing time is "W_Assess Potential Fraud" (3.1 days) and the highest inter-event time is the one between "A_Complete" and "A_Cancelled" (27.4 days).   □

Exercise 11.12 Using a process mining tool, analyze the following event log of a telephone repair process: http://tinyurl.com/repairLogs with the aim of identifying the bottlenecks in this process. Which task has the longest waiting time and which one has the longest processing time?

Dependency graphs can also be used to analyze delays resulting from handoffs between process participants—in addition to delays between consecutive tasks as discussed above. When discussing the structure of event logs, we pointed out that an event record in an event log should have at least a case identifier, a timestamp, and an event class (i.e., a reference to a task in the process), but there can be other event attributes too, like for example the *resource* (process participant) who performed the task in question. The event class is the attribute that is displayed in each node of a dependency graph. When importing an event log into a tool that supports dependency graphs, the tool gives an option to specify which event attribute should

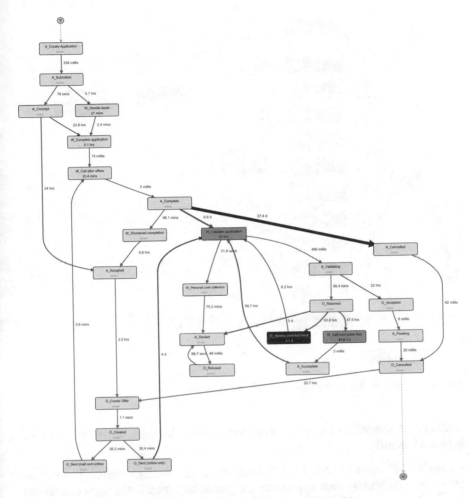

Fig. 11.17 Performance view of the BPI Challenge 2017 event log in Disco

be used as the event class.[19] We can set the tool so as to use the *resource* attribute as the event class.[20] If we do so, the resulting dependency graph will contain one node per resource (process participant) and there will be one arc between nodes A and B if resource B has performed a task immediately after resource A in at least one trace in the log. This map captures all the handoffs that have occurred in the process. We can then apply filters and abstraction operations to this map of handoffs, in the same way as we can apply filters and abstraction operations to dependency graphs where the nodes correspond to tasks. The handoff map can also be color-coded, with the

---

[19]In some tools, the event class is called the "Activity".

[20]In Disco, this option is only available when importing logs in CSV format. In Celonis, Minit and myInvenio it is available also when importing XES files.

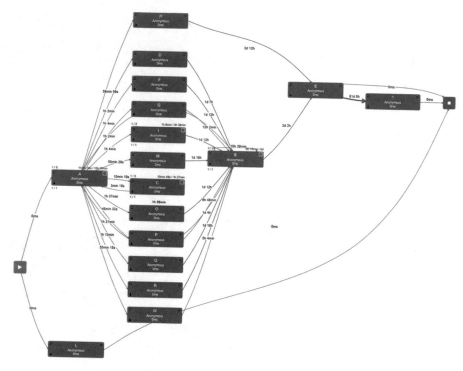

Fig. 11.18 Handoff view of the Sepsis event log in myInvenio

colors corresponding either to the frequency of each handoff, or the waiting time between handoffs.

Example 11.6 Figure 11.18 shows a fragment of the *average duration view* produced by myInvenio when applied to the previously mentioned sepsis treatment log.[21] The map shows that when a case starts (leftmost node), it is first handled by resource A. After a few minutes or about an hour, resource A hands off to resource H or to resources D, F, ..., R. Resource H hands off to E, while F, ..., R hand over to B who later hands off to E. Handoffs that take longer than 1 day are shown in red (this threshold can be configured). For example, the handoff from H to E and from B to E take 2–3 days. Resource E hands off to a resource marked as "?". This last handoff takes the largest amount of time (81 days and 6 h), most likely because

---

[21] We imported the log in CSV format, marked the "org:resource" column as the "Activity" in the import wizard, the "Case ID" column as the "Process Id", and the "Complete timestamp" as the "Start timestamp" because MyInvenio requires a start timestamp column. We filtered the graph so that it shows the 60% most frequent nodes and we placed the *arcs filter* at its minimum value. Finally, we moved to the average duration view, turned on the KPI palette, and set the upper-bound of "activity wait queue threshold" to 1 day so that all arcs with duration of more than a day are shown in red.

cases are left in a pending state until (on average) 81 days and 6 h after the last task, once it is clear that the patient does not need further treatment. In this map, the nodes have a duration of zero, because this event log only has end timestamps (no start timestamps) and hence the processing time cannot be computed.   □

11.5.2 Cost Dimension

When measuring the cost of a business process, we need to take into account both direct and indirect costs. Direct costs, like the purchasing costs of four wheels which are assembled on a car, can be more directly determined on a per-case basis. Indirect labor costs or machine and infrastructure depreciation costs are more difficult to handle. In accounting, the concept of *activity-based costing* (ABC) was developed to assign indirect costs to products and services, and to individual customers. The motivation of ABC is that human resources and machinery are often shared by different products and services, and they are used to serve different customers. For instance, the depot of BuildIT rents out expensive machinery such as bulldozers to different construction sites. On the one hand, that involves costs in terms of working hours of the persons working at the depot. On the other hand, machines like bulldozers lose in value over time and require maintenance. The idea of ABC is to use tasks for distributing the indirect costs, e.g., associated with the depot.

Example 11.7 According to Figure 1.6 in Chapter 1 (see page 19), the rental process of BuildIT contains five major tasks. We observe the following durations in the event logs for the case of a bulldozer rental requested on 21st August:

- "Submit equipment rental request" is conducted by the site engineer. It takes the engineer 20 min to fill in the form on paper. The production of each paper form costs € 1. The site engineer gets an annual salary of € 60,000.
- The clerk receives the form, selects a suitable piece of equipment, and checks its availability. These tasks take altogether 15 min. The clerk has an annual salary of € 40,000.
- The works engineer reviews the rental request (annual salary of € 50,000). This review takes 10 mins.
- The clerk is also responsible for sending a confirmation including a purchase order for renting the equipment, which takes 30 min.

In order to work with these numbers we have to make some assumptions. First, at BuildIT the actual working year contains 250 working days of 8 h. Furthermore, all employees receive health insurance and pension contributions of 20% on top of their salary. Finally, people take on average 10 days of sick leave per year. Given the above, the labor cost of each participant per minute is $\frac{salary \times 120\%}{(250-10) \times 8 \times 60}$. This is for the site engineer € 0.63 per minute, for the clerk € 0.42 per minute, and for the works engineer € 0.52 per minute. Altogether, this case created costs of 20 min × € 0.63

per minute + (15+30) min × € 0.42 per minute + 10 min × € 0.52 per minute, which sums up to € 36.70.

Now consider a case of a street construction process. We observe from the event log the following durations (processing times) for these two tasks:

- "Prepare the foundation" is conducted by four workers. It took one week at a specific construction case. The used excavator costs € 100,000. It is written off in 5 years and has annual maintenance costs of € 5,000. A worker gets an annual salary of € 35,000.
- "Tar the road" is conducted by six workers. It took 2 days in this case. The tarring machine costs € 200,000, is also written off in 5 years and costs € 10,000 in annual maintenance.

For this case, we can also take the costs of the machinery into account. The labor cost per day is € 175 for one worker. The excavator costs € 20,000 + 5,000 per annum for write-off and maintenance, which is € 104.17 per working day. For the preparation of the foundation, this amounts to 4 × 5 × € 175 + 5 × € 104.17 = € 4,020.85. For the taring of the road, the costs are 6 × 2 × € 175 + 2 × € 208.34 = € 2,516.68.

□

Exercise 11.13 Consider that the paper form is printed by the site engineer in the rental process, that the printer costs € 300 written off in 3 years, and that a pile of 500 pieces of paper costs € 10. Why would it make sense to include these costs in the calculation? Or why not?

An inherent problem of ABC is the need to keep track of the duration of tasks like renting out equipment or approving rental requests. Event data stored in process-aware information systems can help to provide such data. Some systems only keep track of task completion. However, ABC also requires the start of tasks to be kept. This means that we need to keep track of the timestamps of the point in time when a resource starts working on a specific task. What is important to take into account here is the cost of achieving additional transparency. There is a trade-off, and once it becomes overly expensive to gain more transparency, it is good to not include those costs in the calculation.

11.5.3   Quality Dimension

The quality of a product created in a process is often not directly visible from execution logs. However, a good indication is to check whether there are repetitions in the execution logs, because they typically occur when a task has not been completed successfully. Repetitions can be found in sequences of task. In Chapter 7, we saw that the loop of a rework pattern increases the cycle time of a task to $CT = \frac{T}{1-r}$ in comparison to T being the time to execute the task only once. The question is now how to determine the repetition probability r from a series of event logs.

The first part of the answer to this question can be given by reformulating the equation such that it is solved for r. By multiplication with $1 - r$, we get $CT - r \times CT = T$. Subtraction of CT yields $-r \times CT = T - CT$, which can be divided by $-CT$ resulting in

$$r = 1 - \frac{T}{CT}.$$

Both CT and T can now be determined using the data of the event logs. Consider the five cases in which we observe the following execution times for task a:

1. 5 min, 10 min;
2. 10 min;
3. 20 min, 6 min, 10 min;
4. 5 min;
5. 10 min, 10 min.

The cycle time CT of a can now be calculated as the average execution time of a per case, while the average execution time T is the average execution time of a per instantiation. Both can be determined based on the sum of all executions of a, which is 86 min here. We have five cases, such that $CT = 86/5 = 17.2$. Altogether, a is executed nine times yielding $T = 86/9 = 9.56$. Hence, we get $r = 1 - \frac{86/9}{86/5} = 1 - \frac{5}{9} = 0.44$. Of course, this calculation is only an approximation of the real value for r. It builds on the assumption that the duration of a task always follows the same distribution, no matter if it is the first, the second or another iteration.

Exercise 11.14 Determine the probability of repetition r for the following execution times of task b:

1. 20 min, 10 min;
2. 30 min;
3. 30 min, 5 min;
4. 20 min;
5. 20 min, 5 min;
6. 25 min.

Also explain why the value is misleading for these logs.

In some software systems it might be easier to track repetition based on the assignment of tasks to resources. One example are *ticketing systems* that record which resource is working on a case. Also, the logs of these systems offer insights into repetition. A typical process supported with ticketing systems is incident resolution. For example, an incident might be a call by a customer who complains that the online banking system does not work. Such an incident is recorded by a dedicated participant, e.g., a call center agent. Then, it is forwarded to a first-level support team that tries to solve the problem. In case the problem turns out to be too specific, it is forwarded to a second-level support team with specialized knowledge in the problem domain. In the best case, the problem is solved and the customer is notified. In the undesirable case, the team identifies that the problem is within the competence area of another team. This has the consequence that the problem is rooted back to the first-level team. Similar to the repetition of tasks, we now see that there is a repeated assignment of the problem to the same team. By analyzing the event log, we can determine how often this repeated assignment occurs and to what extent it is affecting the mean cycle time of the process.

Using a process mining tool, we can apply a filter to an event log so as to retain only those cases where the same task appears (at least) twice. In Disco this is achieved using a so-called "follower" filter while in Celonis it is called a "process flow selection" filter.

Exercise 11.15 With reference to the event log of the Business Process Intelligence Challenge 2017 (https://tinyurl.com/bpic2017), in how many cases was "W_Assess Potential Fraud" completed at least twice in the same case?

11.5.4 Flexibility Dimension

Flexibility refers to the degree of variation that a process permits. This flexibility can be discussed in relation to the event logs the process produces. For the company owning the process, this is important information in order to compare the desired level of flexibility with the actual flexibility. It might turn out that the process is more flexible than what is demanded from a business perspective. This is the case when flexibility can be equated with lack of standardization. Often, the performance of processes suffers when too many options are allowed. Consider again the process for renting equipment at BuildIT. The process requires an equipment rental request form to be sent by email. Some engineers however prefer to call the depot directly instead of filling the form. Since these engineers are highly distinguished, it is not easy for the clerk to turn down these calls. As a result, the clerk fills out the form while being on the phone. Not only does this procedure take more time, but, due to noise at the construction site, it also increases the likelihood of errors. In practice, this means that the rental process has two options to submit a request: by form (the standard procedure) and via the phone.

Partially, such flexibility as described above can be directly observed in an event log. We have seen that the workflow log of a process plays an important role for automated process discovery. It can also be used to assess the flexibility of the process. The workflow log summarizes the essential behavior of the process. As it defines each execution as a sequence of tasks, it abstracts from the temporal distance between them. In this way, the workflow log contains a set of traces that have a unique sequence. This means that if two executions contain the same sequence of tasks, then they only result in a single trace to be included in the workflow log. This abstraction of process executions in terms of a workflow log makes it a good starting point for discussing flexibility. Accordingly, the number of *distinct executions* DE can be defined based on a workflow log L as

$$DE = |L|.$$

Exercise 11.16 Consider the event log of the order-to-cash process in Figure 11.4 (page 423). What is the number of distinct executions DE?

The question arises whether the number of distinct executions always gives a good indication for flexibility. At times, the number of distinct executions might give an overly high quantification of flexibility. This might be the case for processes with concurrency. Such processes can be highly structured, but having only a small set of concurrent tasks results in a rich set of potential execution sequences. Consider the process model constructed by the α-algorithm in Figure 11.12 (page 437). The tasks i and h are concurrent to j and k. Indeed, there are six options to execute them:

1. i, h, j, k,
2. j, k, i, h,
3. i, j, k, h,
4. j, i, h, k,
5. i, j, h, k and
6. j, i, k, h.

While the order is not strict, all of them must be executed. Therefore, it might be a good idea to additionally consider whether a task is optional. If T refers to the number of tasks that appear in the workflow log, then the set T_{opt} contains those tasks that are optional. Optionality according to the log means that for a particular task there exists at least one trace in which the task does not occur. For the log of Figure 11.4, we observe that the tasks b to f depend upon the availability of raw materials. We can quantify the degree of *optionality* OPT as

$$OPT = \frac{T_{opt}}{T}.$$

11.6 Conformance Checking

Conformance checking is concerned with the question whether or not the execution of a process follows predefined rules or constraints. This question can be answered by inspecting the event log. If a particular constraint does not hold, we speak of a *violation*. In particular, conformance checking is concerned with identifying these violations and making statements about the extent of them altogether. Violations might relate to the three process perspectives of control flow, data, and resources, in isolation or in combination. In the following, we describe how they can be specified.

11.6.1   Conformance of Control Flow

From the control-flow perspective, conformance can be analyzed in two ways: based on *constraints* or based on a *normative process model*. Below, we discuss these two approaches in turn.

There are three recurrent types of control-flow constraints: mandatoriness, exclusiveness, and ordering. These three constraint types define how two tasks are allowed to be related in a process. A company might want to define a *mandatoriness* constraint for certain tasks, because these tasks are required from a control perspective. Consider again the case of BuildIT and its equipment rental process. A works engineer is supposed to review the rental request. This task serves as a control for ensuring that only appropriate equipment is rented. This measure might help to keep the rental costs in line. This verification task is a likely candidate for being mandatory. At the level of the event log, violations of mandatory task constraints can be found by searching for traces in which the task in question is not executed.

An *exclusiveness* constraint states that two or more tasks cannot co-occur in the same case. In the case of the equipment rental process, for example, an exclusiveness constraint might state that a rejection of a rental request cannot be followed by its approval. This exclusiveness can be checked by searching for traces in which both tasks appear.

An *ordering* constraint states that two tasks must always occur in a given order. In the equipment rental process, an ordering constraint might state that the availability of the requested equipment must be checked before the request is reviewed. Obviously, it is a waste of effort to review requests that cannot be met because the equipment is not available. Violations to order constraints can be found by searching for traces with the tasks appearing in the wrong order.

Exercise 11.17 Consider the event log in Figure 11.4 (page 423). Which tasks can be considered mandatory, or exclusive with respect to one another?

Conformance of control flow can also be checked by comparing the behavior observed in the log against a process model. In this setting, the purpose of conformance checking is to identify two types of discrepancies:

- Unfitting log behavior: behavior observed in the log that is not allowed by the normative process model.
- Additional model behavior: behavior allowed in the normative process model but never observed in the log.

If some discrepancies are found, a conformance checking technique will tell us where each discrepancy occurs, and what exactly is different between the event log and the process model.

There are broadly three families of techniques for conformance checking between an event log and a process model: replay, trace alignment, and behavioral alignment. In replay techniques [152], each trace is replayed against the process

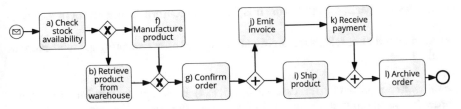

Fig. 11.19 BPMN model with a token on the start event for replaying the case $\langle a, b, g, i, j, k, l \rangle$

model one event at a time starting from the initial state of the process model (i.e., the state where there is a token in the start event). At each step of the replay, we determine if the next event in the event log was allowed to be executed according to the process model. If the next event can be replayed, we advance to the next state in the process model by moving tokens forward in the model. If the next event cannot be replayed, we record a *replay error* and a local correction is made to resume the replay procedure. The local correction may be for example to skip/ignore a task in the process model or to skip an event in the log.

Example 11.8 Using the token rules of BPMN, we can replay the case $\langle a, b, g, i, j, k, l \rangle$ on the model shown in Figure 11.19. In the initial state, the process has a token on the start event. Once the case is started, this token moves to the output arc of the start event. This arc leads to task a ("Check stock availability"), which means that the token enables this task to be executed. The token moves to this task while it is executed, and it is forwarded to the output arc once the task is completed. Now, the XOR-split is activated, which means a decision has to be taken to continue either with b ("Retrieve product from warehouse") or with f ("Manufacture product"). For the considered case, we continue with b. After g ("Confirm order") has been completed, we arrive at an AND-split. An AND-split consumes a token from its input arc and creates one token on each of its output arcs. As a result, we have two tokens afterwards: one enabling i ("Ship product") and one enabling j ("Emit invoice"). In this state we can proceed either with i or j. These tasks are concurrent. In order to replay the case, we first execute i and j afterwards. Once i and later k are completed, the AND-join is allowed to proceed. One token on each of its input arcs is required for that. Both these tokens are consumed and a single token is created on its output arc. As a result, l ("Archive order") can be executed. When a replay error is detected, it is reported and a local correction is made to resume the replay procedure. The local correction may be for example to skip a task in the process model or to skip an event in the log. □

Using token replay, we can also measure the conformance of a trace to a process model by comparing at each step the number of tokens that are required to replay an event versus the tokens that are actually available. Specifically, at each step we can keep track of the following values:

- c: the number of tokens that are correctly consumed,
- p: the number of tokens that are correctly produced,

- m: the number of tokens that are missing for executing the next event in the trace, and
- r: the number of tokens remaining unconsumed after executing the final event in the trace.

Example 11.9 Consider the case $\langle a, b, i, j, k, l \rangle$ in which the confirmation of the order has been omitted. Figure 11.20 first shows the state before replaying b of the case $\langle a, b, i, j, k, l \rangle$. After replaying b, there is a token available to execute g, but it is not consumed. Instead, there is a missing token for firing the AND-split, which would activate i and j. The figure also shows the number of correctly produced and consumed tokens for each step until completion. Using the four values of c, p, m, and r, we can calculate the fitness measure for a complete trace as an indicator of conformance. It is defined based on the fraction of missing tokens to correctly consumed tokens ($\frac{m}{c}$) and the fraction of remaining tokens to produced tokens ($\frac{r}{p}$) as

$$fitness = \frac{1}{2}(1 - \frac{m}{c}) + \frac{1}{2}(1 - \frac{r}{p}).$$

Summing all our values of c, all values of p, of m, and of r, we obtain an overall $c = 12, p = 12, m = 1$, and $r = 1$. From these, we get a fitness of $\frac{1}{2}(1 - \frac{1}{12}) + \frac{1}{2}(1 - \frac{1}{12}) = 0.9166$. When we consider a set of cases, not just a single case, we can easily calculate the fitness in the same way. The idea is to simply continue counting c, p, m, and r by replaying the next case in the process model. Once we have replayed all cases, we get the resulting overall fitness of this set of cases.   □

The results of conformance analysis can be interpreted in two ways. First, we can use the overall fitness measure to get an idea of how accurately the process model matches the actually observed behavior as reflected by the set of cases. While the fitness as an overall measure is useful to this end, it does not help us to analyze the deviations in more detail. Therefore, and secondly, we can inspect at which arcs of the process model we have encountered missing or remaining tokens. Figure 11.21 shows the corresponding numbers from replaying several cases in the process model. It can be seen that apparently most deviations relate to task g and some to task l. This information can be utilized to ask process participants why g has been omitted for some cases. The goal of such an inquiry would be to find out whether this omission is desirable. The question is whether the process participants have found a more efficient way to handle the confirmation, or whether an omission has to be considered bad practice and as such be discouraged. For the case of the archival (task l), the omission is likely to be bad practice.

In replay techniques, the recovery from an error is done locally. Hence, these techniques might not identify the minimum number of errors that can explain the unfitting log behavior. This limitation is addressed by *trace alignment* techniques [4]. These techniques identify, for each trace in the log, the closest corresponding trace that can be parsed by the model. Trace alignment techniques also compute an alignment showing the points of divergence between these two traces.

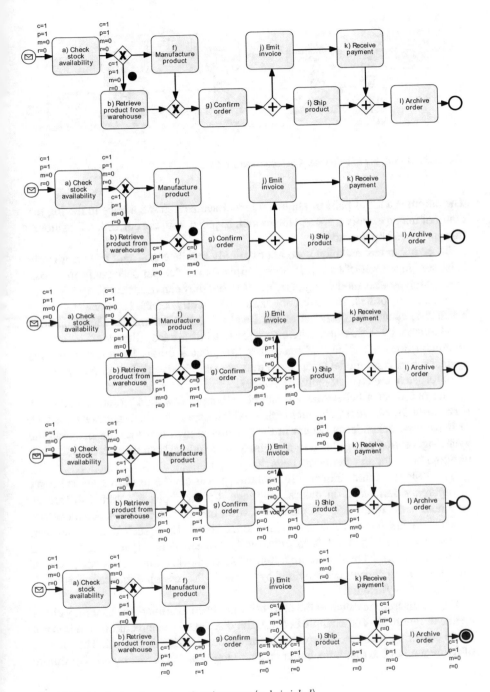

Fig. 11.20 Replaying the non-conforming case $\langle a, b, i, j, k, l \rangle$

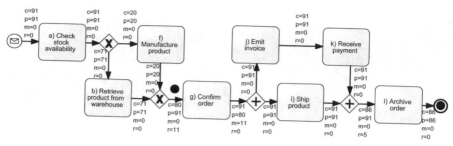

Fig. 11.21 Result of replaying cases in the process model

The output is a set of pairs of aligned traces. Each pair shows a trace in the log that does not match exactly a trace in the model, together with the corresponding closest trace produced by the model.

Trace alignment techniques do not explicitly handle concurrent tasks nor cyclic behavior (repetition of tasks). If for example four tasks can occur only in a fixed order in the process model (e.g., $\langle a, b, c, d \rangle$), but they can occur concurrently in the log (i.e., in any order), this difference cannot be directly detected by trace alignment, because it cannot be observed at the level of individual traces. This limitation is addressed by *behavioral alignment* [54]. Unlike trace alignment, behavioral alignment does not align one trace at a time, but it aligns the entire event log against the process model at once, so that we can observe differences that cannot be observed at the level of individual traces.

The output of a behavioral alignment technique is a data structure known as a *Partially Synchronized Product* (PSP), which captures every state where a task or behavioral dependency occurs in the process model, but does not occur in the event log, or vice versa. Behavioral alignment techniques can therefore detect both unfitting behavior and additional behavior.

The PSP is a rather unreadable structure, but it can be used to generate a set of *difference statements* in natural language. For example, a possible difference statement is the following: "In the model, after task a, task b always occurs before c, while in the log, tasks b and c are concurrent.". Each such discrepancy can be displayed visually in addition to textually. For example, Figure 11.22 shows a discrepancy detected by Apromore's conformance checker. Similar visualizations of model-log discrepancies are provided by Signavio Process Intelligence,[22] LANA,[23] Celonis, and MyInvenio.

Once a discrepancy such as the one above has been identified, the user may either decide to ignore it—for example because the discrepancy occurs rarely and it is not worth capturing such rare exceptions in the model—or decide to fix it. The process of fixing a model so that it fits better an event log is called *model repair*. Apromore

---

[22]https://www.signavio.com.

[23]https://lana-labs.com/en.

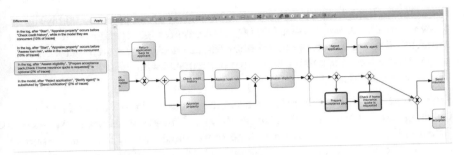

Fig. 11.22 Visualization of a model-log discrepancy in Apromore

provides features for fixing each identified discrepancy automatically. In other tools, this repair can be done manually by updating the model according to the detected difference, and then re-running the conformance checker.

11.6.2   Conformance of Data and Resources

In the above discussion, we have focused on checking conformance along the control-flow perspective, that is, checking that the occurrence of tasks and their relative order in the event log are consistent with a given process model. Equally important though is to check conformance along the data and the resource perspectives of a business process. Consider the situation where an expensive caterpillar is requested for a construction site of BuildIT. Many companies have extra rules for high expenses or risky commitments. In the case of BuildIT, the rental of the caterpillar requires the additional signature of a manager. Similar cases can be found in banks where a loan of more than € 1,000,000 might require the additional sign-off from a director. There might also be a rule stipulating that a loan should not be granted to a black-listed applicant. Such constraints can be checked by searching for cases in the log where a given data field takes a forbidden value.

The example of the additionally required signature already points to a combination of data and resource constraints. If a certain amount is exceeded, then there is a dedicated resource who is required to approve it. However, there are also constraints that purely refer to the resource perspective. Participants usually require *permissions* to execute certain tasks. For instance, the person signing off the caterpillar rent must be a manager, and it is not allowed that this person is a construction worker. Typically, permissions are bundled for specific *roles*. For example, this can be done by explicitly listing what a manager and a construction worker are allowed to do. Violations of permissions can be checked by searching for each task performed by a participant, and verifying if the appropriate role or permission existed. A control rule that requires two different persons to approve a business transaction is called a *separation of duties* constraint. These rules do not necessarily involve supervisors.

For example, it might be ok with a particular bank if a loan of € 100,000 is signed by two bank clerks, while a € 1,000,000 loan requires the signature of a clerk and a director. This separation-of-duties policy can be checked by searching for cases in the log where the same participant or two participants with the same role approved the same transaction.

Exercise 11.18 With reference to the event log of the Business Process Intelligence Challenge 2017 (https://tinyurl.com/bpic2017), in how many cases was "W_Assess Potential Fraud" completed at least twice in the same case by the same resource? Hint: This exercise is similar to Exercise 11.15 (page 450), but it involves an additional constraint: the same resource should be involved in both task occurrences.

11.7 Variants Analysis

The performance of a business process can vary considerably over time (e.g., the performance this month is lower than last month's), geographically (the performance of a prescription fulfillment process across several pharmacies is different), or across business units, product types, or customer types. And even within a given period of time, a given place, a given business unit, type of product, and type of customer, we will often observe significant differences between the cases with the best and with the worst performance. Some cases go smoothly and lead to a positive outcome in a timely manner, while others lead to negative outcomes or they are delayed, leading to customer dissatisfaction. A frequent question in the mouth of a process owner is: "Why is the performance for some cases so much worse than for others?"

Variants analysis techniques allow us to analyze differences across subsets of cases in a process (i.e., two variants). Given two subsets of cases L1 and L2, these techniques allow us to identify characteristics that are commonly found in the cases in L1, and are rare or non-existent in the cases in L2. There might be many such characteristics, and of course, we are interested in finding those that can help us to explain why the cases in L1 might exhibit better or worst performance than those in L2.

We can use any criterion to split the cases in a log into L1 and L2. This criterion could be based on the time when the case started (e.g., all cases that started in the year 2015 go to L1, all those that started in 2016 go to L2). Or it could be based on product type (e.g., all car insurance claims for sports cars go into L1, all other car insurance claims go into L2). It is also common to split the log into cases that have a normal (or satisfactory) performance (L1) vs. those with undesirable performance (L2). This type of analysis is called *deviance mining*, because what we want is to understand why some cases are deviant (i.e., those in L2). Note that deviance can also be seen from a positive perspective. Indeed, we could split the log into those cases that have normal or below-normal performance (L1) and those that have above-normal performance (L2). The cases in log L2 are hence positively deviant.

Variants analysis can be done manually or automatically. In the manual approach, we typically start by discovering a process model for L1, another one for L2, and we compare these two models visually. For example, we can discover a dependency graph for L1 and another for L2, put them side-by-side, and compare them using the frequency view (nodes and arcs are annotated by frequency) and the performance view (nodes and arcs are annotated with times). In this way, we can spot tasks or paths that are more frequent in L1 than L2 or vice versa, or we can spot differences in the cycles times of tasks. We can go further and inspect the data perspective, for example to determine if some data attribute values are more common in L1 than in L2, or if some resources are more active in L1 than in L2.

An alternative is to apply automated *log delta analysis* techniques [175]. These techniques take as input two event logs and produce a set of *patterns* that are common in L1 and uncommon in L2 or vice versa. We then analyze these patterns and determine which ones might be able to explain the observed differences in performance. For example, the log delta analysis technique implemented in the Apromore tool takes as input two event logs and produces a set of *difference statements* similar to those we saw in the context of conformance checking, e.g., "In log L1, task a is sometimes skipped, whereas in log L2, task a is always executed", or "In log L1, task a is sometimes repeated, whereas in log L2, task a is almost never repeated".

Other log delta analysis techniques are based on so-called *association rules*, which are commonly used in the field of data mining. These techniques take as input a log (which they see as a set of sequences) and produce as output patterns of the form "after a, we eventually observe b". Some of these techniques (called *discriminative sequence mining* techniques) take as input two logs and identify association rules such as the one above, which are common in one log but not in the other.

In general, manual comparison is suitable for relatively small event logs, or in cases where we can filter the event log or abstract the dependency graph sufficiently so that the key differences are still visible, yet the dependency graph is not overwhelmingly complex. For more complex scenarios, we can use automated log delta analysis to identify a set of patterns, select a subset of those patterns, and analyze them further by manually inspecting a few cases where these patterns occur, and determining if the occurrence of these patterns might help to explain why those cases exhibit higher or lower performance.

Example 11.10 We consider again the event log of the Business Process Intelligence Challenge 2017 (https://tinyurl.com/bpic2017), used in Example 11.3 (see page 429). We observe that the distribution of the cycle time across cases has a long tail. Specifically, 96% of cases take less than 45 days to complete, but the remaining 4% of cases have cycle times going to 169 days in some cases. One may wonder why do these handful of cases take so long? To answer this question, we split the log into two sub-logs: one log contains the cases that take less than 45 days (we call these the *fast cases*) and the other contains all cases that take 45 days or more (*slow cases*).[24] We then discover a dependency graph for each of these two sub-logs.

By doing a side-by-side inspection of these dependency graphs under the frequency view, we observe that the offer cancelation (event type "O_Cancelled") is very frequent among the slow cases, while not so frequent in the fast cases. Specifically, among the 1,299 slow cases, this event type occurs 2,061 times in 1,035 cases (80% of slow cases), hence about twice per case where it occurs. Meanwile, among the 30,209 fast cases, this event type occurs 18,834 times in 14,466 cases (48% of slow cases), hence about 1.37 times per case.[25]

Also, 994 cases out of 1,299 slow cases end with an "O_Cancelled" event (again about 80% of cases).[26]

Similar remarks can be made regarding event "A_Cancelled" (application cancelation), which occurs in about half of slow cases, but only in about a third of fast cases.

We also observe that the situation where the customer is called due to incomplete files is much more frequent in slow cases. Indeed, task "W_Call Incomplete files" occurs 1,725 times in 793 slow cases (61% of slow cases), while it occurs 21,493 times in 14,210 cases of the fast cases (47% of fast cases). If we look at the performance view, we see that this task is a bottleneck in the slow cases (5.9 days of processing time), but less so in the fast cases (11.4 h), suggesting that in the slow cases, the customer turns out to be more difficult to reach.

In summary, we conclude that cancelations and incomplete files are possible factors explaining why some cases take over 45 days to complete.   □

Exercise 11.19 We consider a process for handling health insurance claims, for which we have extracted two event logs, namely L1 and L2. Log L1 contains all the cases executed in 2011, while L2 contains all cases executed in 2012. The logs are available in the book's companion website or directly at: http://tinyurl.com/ InsuranceLogs.

Based on these logs, answer the following questions using a process mining tool:

1. What is the cycle time of each log?
2. Describe the differences between the frequency of tasks and the order in which tasks are executed in 2011 (L1) versus 2012 (L2). Hint: If you are using dependency graphs, you should consider using the abstraction slider in your tool to hide some of the most infrequent arcs so as to make the maps more readable.

---

[24]This split into sub-logs can be achieved using the filtering operations supported by Celonis, Disco, Minit, myInvenio, and other process mining tools.

[25]These numbers are calculated using Disco. The numbers can slightly differ in other tools. For example, Celonis finds 1,378 slow cases, out of which 1,088 contain "O_Cancelled".

[26]To determine which cases end with a given event type in each log, we can add a second filter to each of them, specifically a filter of type *endpoint* in Disco, an *activity selection* filter with a *case ends with* constraint in Celonis, or a *match at the end of case* filter in myInvenio.

3. Where are the bottlenecks (highest waiting times) in each of the two logs and how do these bottlenecks differ?

11.8 Putting It All Together: Process Mining in Practice

We have seen that the term *process mining* refers to a broad collection of techniques to extract insights from event logs generated during the execution of a business process. Some of these techniques are focused on discovering a model of the process, while others allow us to analyze the process from different perspectives (conformance, performance, variants).

Faced with a business problem, an analyst is likely to use several of these techniques together. In this respect, there are two approaches to apply process mining to a given business process:

1. The *exploratory* approach, which is driven by the curiosity to understand how a business process is executed without any specific question at hand. In this approach, we typically start by discovering a process model or by doing conformance checking against an existing model. This analysis is typically complemented with a general analysis of bottlenecks and by a longitudinal analysis (e.g., comparing the performance of the process in the latest month versus the month before) or a cross-sectional analysis (e.g., comparing the performance of the process for different customer or product types).
2. The *question-driven* approach is driven by a business problem. For example, we may want to find out why certain insurance claims take too long to be resolved. In this case we start by identifying and scoping the problem, formulating questions and then applying process mining techniques to answer these questions.

These two approaches are complementary. Oftentimes we start with an exploratory approach, and as we get a clearer picture of the process and its bottlenecks, we continue the analysis with concrete business-driven questions in mind.

In a question-driven approach, there are typically five phases involved: (1) framing the problem; (2) collecting the data; (3) analyzing the data; (4) interpreting the results; and (5) formulating a process improvement proposal.

Example 11.11 We discuss each of these phases using an example of a process mining project reported in [171].

> With its nine million customers and 16,000 employees, Suncorp is the largest insurer in Australia and second largest in New Zealand. Besides insurance services, it provides wealth management services, banking and superannuation services. As of 2012, the typical value chain for insurance would consist of four core processes: insurance service development, sales, after-sale services, and claims handling, covering all in all around 500 tasks.
> Suncorp provides a wide range of insurance services, for example home insurance, commercial insurance, and motor insurance. The company has acquired over time a number of insurance brands targeting various market segments. As of 2012, Suncorp managed

nine different brands and 30 core value chains. This high degree of variation manifested itself within the organisation into diverging performances in their claim handling processes, particularly the one for commercial insurance. The owner of the process noticed that frequently, claims with low payout (i.e., low-value claims), which should have been resolved in a matter of days, were taking unexpectedly long. In fact, some of these low-value claims were taking longer to be resolved than some of the high-value claims.

By talking to different stakeholders, the process owner formulated various possible reasons for these unexpected delays. For example, she hypothesized that these delays came from the fact that a new system had been recently put in place to manage claims, and maybe the resources using this new system did not have appropriate training. However, acting on this or other hypotheses had not led to any significant process improvement.

It is in this context that a question-driven process mining project was started with the aim of shedding light into the causes behind the observed delays.

$\square$

In the first phase of the question-driven approach, we need to formulate a top-level problem or question for the process mining project. For example, why does the process perform poorly, for example, in terms of cycle time? Or why do we have frequent defects (high error rates)?

In the Suncorp case study, the top-level problem was that oftentimes simple claims take an unexpectedly long time to complete. This problem leads to the following questions: What distinguishes the processing of simple claims completed on time, from simple claims that are not completed on time? And what early predictors can be used to determine that a given simple claim will not be completed on time? The next step was to define what is a *slow simple claim*. After some analysis of the distribution of cycle times, it was decided to define it as a claim with a payout of less then X (for an undisclosed X) that takes more than 5 days to be resolved.

Having framed the problem in this way, the project got on board two part-time business analysts with prior expertise in this business process, a database administrator, and a process mining expert. The process owner acted as the business sponsor of the project. The project took 4 months.

The second phase of the question-driven approach is *data collection*. Here, we need to find relevant data sources, which are typically the databases of the enterprise systems over which the process is executed. As part of this extraction, we need to identify the process-related entities and their identifiers (in particular the case identifier) so as to be able to group different events into traces, which is necessary in order to produce an event log in the XES format. In the Suncorp case, the data was extracted from different tables of a claims handling system.

A time-consuming step within this phase is that of data pre-processing. Once we have the event log, we need to clean the data by filtering irrelevant events, cover gaps that may exist due to recording errors, and combine equivalent events from different tables if the data is scattered across tables (potentially originating from different systems, e.g., a CRM and an ERP system)—recall that we are interested in tracing the end-to-end business process. Often, for example, the control-flow data (events and their timestamps) are available in one table, while the resource data is in another table, and the business objects (containing the data attributes) are in another set of tables. It also happens that different tables may record different variants of the same process, for example one table per product.

The third phase is that of *analysis*. In the Suncorp case, a data analyst took the log consisting of traces of low-value claims and divided it into two sub-logs: fast simple claims and slow simple claims, as defined above. The analyst applied a manual variants analysis technique. Specifically, the log was split into two by applying filtering operations (less than 5 days, more than 5 days) and two dependency graphs were discovered and visually compared. After some effort, it became apparent that there were some relevant differences, specifically two types of unwanted repetitions were occurring frequently in the slow cases, but rarely in the fast cases. These results were backed up by a statistical analysis of the repetitions.

The fourth phase is dedicated to extracting insights from the analysis results and to validating these insights with the domain experts and other stakeholders. In the Suncorp case study, the analysts discussed the findings with several process participants and other stakeholders knowledgeable of the process. They took concrete instances where unwanted repetitions occurred, and showed them to these stakeholders. Based on these focused discussions, they managed to determine the key reasons for the unwanted repetitions.

Using these insights, they put up a business case for process improvement (last phase), which proposed a set of changes to the process in question. The latter project led to a reduction in cycle time (from 30–60 days to 5 days) and a reduction of 30% in resource utilization.

11.9 Recap

We discussed two families of process monitoring techniques: statistics-based techniques and model-based techniques. Given a set of performance measures, statistics-based techniques allow us to analyze the performance of a process by means of aggregation functions (e.g., mean and standard deviation) or by means of data visualization techniques. These statistical aggregates and visualizations are typically grouped into dashboards. We saw three types of dashboards: strategic dashboards (targeted at the top management), tactical dashboards (targeted at analysts, process owners and other managers), and operational dashboards (targeted at process participants and operational managers).

On the other hand, model-based techniques (also known as process mining techniques) use process models as a central instrument. Given an event log capturing a number of executions of the process, these techniques allow us to discover a process model (automated process discovery), to compare a given process model to the event log (conformance checking), to analyze the performance of the process with respect to a process model (performance mining), and to compare the performance of different subsets of cases (variants analysis).

We discussed several automated process discovery techniques, starting with dependency graphs, which give us a zoomable view of an event log, all the way to techniques to automatically discover BPMN process models, such as the split miner.

With respect to conformance checking, we discussed how to check different types of control-flow constraints using an event log. We also saw how to compare a process model and an event log in order to determine if, how, and to what extent the execution of cases recorded in the log deviates with respect to the process model.

We then saw how performance mining techniques allow us to use event logs and process models as a basis to analyze the performance of a process with respect to each of the four dimensions of the Devil's Quadrangle. In particular, we saw how dependency graphs can be enhanced with temporal measures (waiting times, processing times) in order to analyze the performance of a process.

With respect to variants analysis, we saw how a visual comparison of dependency graphs allows us to understand the differences between two variants of a process (e.g., normal and deviant executions). We also discussed an alternative technique known as log delta analysis, which automatically computes a list of differences between two event logs.

11.10   Solutions to Exercises

Solution 11.1 The simplest (but insufficient) solution is to display the histogram of due times of pending cases, i.e., a bar chart showing how many pending prescriptions are due at 3 p.m., 4 p.m., etc., as in the right-hand side of Figure 11.1. This histogram gives us an idea of the work-in-process, but it says nothing about our capacity to handle it nor about the progress of partially-completed cases.

A more complete alternative is a segmented bar chart where each bar shows the amount of prescriptions due in a given 1-h-period (as above) and each bar is decomposed into segments corresponding to states. As illustrated in Figure 11.23a, this bar chart tells us how much work has to be done by each hour of the day. But it does not tell us anything about of our capacity to handle it.

Another approach is to estimate, for each hour of the day h, the amount of *cumulative processing time* required in order to fulfill all prescriptions that are due before h. For example, the 5 p.m. bar in this chart would represent how much processing time is needed to fulfill all prescriptions due before 5 p.m. The *cumulative processing time* can be displayed as a bar chart. Next to each bar, we can then display the *cumulative capacity* available up to each hour of the day, i.e., how much effort the employees of the pharmacy can collectively deliver before each hour of the day. For example, if there are three technicians and one pharmacist, then they can collectively deliver 4 person-hours per calendar hour. So if it is currently 10 a.m. in the morning, they can collectively deliver 4 person-hours by 11 a.m., 8 person-hours by 12 p.m., etc. When the cumulative processing time due at a given hour is close to or exceeds the capacity available before that hour, it means that deadlines are likely to be missed. For example, Figure 11.23b shows a situation where the cumulative processing time due by 6 p.m. is about the same as the cumulative

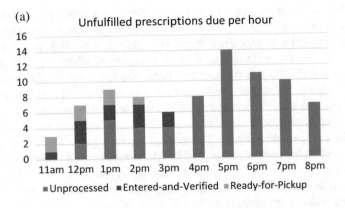

(a) Unfulfilled prescriptions due per hour

■ Unprocessed   ■ Entered-and-Verified   ■ Ready-for-Pickup

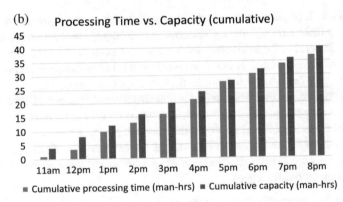

(b) Processing Time vs. Capacity (cumulative)

■ Cumulative processing time (man-hrs)   ■ Cumulative capacity (man-hrs)

Fig. 11.23 Operational dashboard for pharmacy prescription process . (**a**) Segmented bar chart of unfulfilled prescriptions. (**b**) Bar chart of demand (required processing time) vs. capacity

capacity. Hence, it is possible that deadlines will be missed at 5 p.m. due to the small amount of slack. Note that this chart can be drawn separately for pharmacists and for technicians.

Solution 11.2 Given that the focus is on customer service, a natural performance measure could be the defect rate for different types of defects, e.g., percentage of prescriptions not delivered on time, percentage of prescriptions delivered incorrectly, and percentage of prescriptions canceled due to OOS. Since the pharmacies are geographically distributed, we can display these measures on top of a map. For each region, we can display three circles: one per performance measure. The value of a performance measure for a given region can be encoded by the radius of the circle and also the color of the circle. This way, the process owner can visually identify which regions are under-performing with respect to each of the chosen measures.

Solution 11.3 We can use the process landscape as a starting point and assign a color to each process group to encode the change in efficiency with respect to the previous month (blue = efficiency improved, yellow = neutral, red = efficiency increased). To do so, we need to have a measure of efficiency for groups of processes. Since the focus is on cost reduction, one approach would be to define a measure of aggregate cost per month for each process (the cost required to execute the instances of the process during a month). Then, we can aggregate this measure to an entire group of processes via summation. Finally, we can compute the difference between the cost generated by each process group on a given month and calculate the delta between the current month and the previous one (or current month versus same month the previous year to adjust for seasonality). Ideally, it should be possible to drill down in this dashboard and open each process group to see how the cost is decomposed within each process group.

Solution 11.4 It might be the case that parts of the production process are administered using different information systems. Accordingly, the event logs have to be integrated. In terms of correlation, this means that case identifiers from different systems have to be matched. If the timestamps of the events are recorded in different time zones, they have to be harmonized. The shipment might not be arranged by Airbus. Therefore, it might be the case that different snapshots of transportation might not be accessible. Also, information systems might not be directly producing case-related event logs. The data would then have to be extracted from the databases of these systems. Finally, the events might be recorded at diverging levels of granularity, ranging from a detailed record of production steps to coarse-granular records of transportation stages.

Solution 11.5 The workflow log considers the order of events for each case. We use letters a to l for referring to the tasks. The workflow log L contains three traces as the first and the fourth trace are the same. Therefore, we get $L = [\langle a, b, g, h, j, k, i, l \rangle, \langle a, c, d, e, f, g, j, h, i, k, l \rangle, 2 \times \langle a, c, f, g, j, h, i, k, l \rangle]$.

Solution 11.6

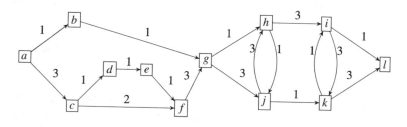

Solution 11.7

A. 31,509 cases.
B. 21.9 days.
C. 17,228 cases, 18.1 days.

D. 3,720 cases, 16.8 days.
E. 4,436 cases, 23 days.

Note that to answer questions C and D, we need to apply a filter that retains only cases where O_Accepted and O_Refused occur, whereas to answer question E we need to apply a filter that retains only those cases that finish with O_Cancelled. The latter can be achieved with an "endpoint" filter in Disco or an *activity selection* filter with a *case ends with* constraint in Celonis.

Solution 11.8 The following basic relations can be observed:

$a > b$	$h > j$	$i > l$	$d > e$	$g > j$	$i > k$
$b > g$	$j > k$	$a > c$	$e > f$	$j > h$	$k > l$
$g > h$	$k > i$	$c > d$	$f > g$	$h > i$	$c > f$

The following matrix shows the resulting relations.

	a	b	c	d	e	f	g	h	i	j	k	l
a	#	→	→	#	#	#	#	#	#	#	#	#
b	←	#	#	#	#	#	→	#	#	#	#	#
c	←	#	#	→	#	→	#	#	#	#	#	#
d	#	#	←	#	→	#	#	#	#	#	#	#
e	#	#	#	←	#	→	#	#	#	#	#	#
f	#	#	←	#	←	#	→	#	#	#	#	#
g	#	←	#	#	#	←	#	→	#	→	#	#
h	#	#	#	#	#	#	←	#	→	‖	#	#
i	#	#	#	#	#	#	#	←	#	#	‖	→
j	#	#	#	#	#	#	←	‖	#	#	→	#
k	#	#	#	#	#	#	#	#	‖	←	#	→
l	#	#	#	#	#	#	#	#	←	#	←	#

Solution 11.9 The α-algorithm stepwise yields the following sets:

1. $T_L = \{a, b, c, d, e, f, g, h, i, j, k, l\}$.
2. $T_I = \{a\}$.
3. $T_O = \{l\}$.
4. $X_L = Z_1 \cup Z_2$ with
   $Z_1 = \{a \to b, a \to c, b \to g, c \to d, c \to f, d \to e, e \to f, f \to g, g \to h, g \to j, h \to i, i \to l, j \to k, k \to l\}$ and
   $Z_2 = \{a \to (b\#c), c \to (d\#f), (c\#e) \to f, (b\#f) \to g\}$
5. $Y_L = Z_2 \cup \{d \to e, g \to h, g \to j, h \to i, j \to k, i \to l, k \to l\}$.
6. Add start event pointing to a and end event following after l.
7. Construct process model based on Y_L with XOR and AND gateways.

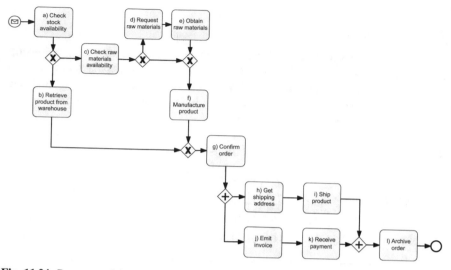

Fig. 11.24 Process model constructed by the α-algorithm

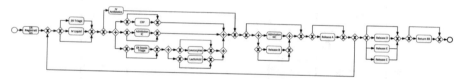

Fig. 11.25 Model discovered by the inductive miner from the Sepsis log

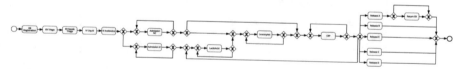

Fig. 11.26 Model discovered by Apromore's split miner from the Sepsis log

8. Return process model, see Figure 11.24.

Solution 11.10 Figures 11.25 and 11.26 show the models discovered from this log using the inductive miner (available in ProM and Apromore) and the split miner (available in Apromore). The model produced by the inductive miner has 50 nodes and is perfectly block-structured as expected. The one produced by the split miner has 31 nodes and it is block-structured except for a cycle with two entry points.

The model produced by the inductive miner exhibits the flower pattern—all but the first task can be skipped or repeated any number of times. Accordingly, it achieves almost perfect fitness (0.99 according to ProM),[27] but at the expense of

---

[27]The fitness was calculated by translating the BPMN model to a Petri net and checking for log conformance using the "Replay a Log on Petri Net for Conformance Analysis" in ProM v6.5.

low precision (0.48). The model produced by the split miner has a fitness of 0.73 and a precision of 0.86.

The structured heuristics miner gives a very large model when applied on this event log (over 200 nodes).

Solution 11.11 First, we have to determine the cycle time. Case 1 takes roughly 2 h less than 7 days, case 2 1 h less than 6 days, case 3 takes 4 days and 20 min, and case 4 takes 4 days and 6 h. Therefore, the relative order must be case 3, case 4, case 2 and case 1. Each event has to be visualized according to the time elapsed since the first event of the case.

Solution 11.12 The longest waiting time is the one between "Analyze defect" and "Inform user" (9.7 days on average). The longest processing time is that of "Repair (complex)" (11.6 days). Note: It might be, however, that in reality this processing time includes some "waiting time" in the sense that a worker might start working on a work item W of this task, then stop and move on to other work items, and then come back to item W.

Solution 11.13 In general, it is preferable to include all expenses in the cost calculation as it provides transparency on what is spent where. In this case, however, this might not be a good idea since the cost per paper is relatively low (€ 0.02). It has to be kept in mind though that the decision whether to record certain costs should not be governed by the unit piece, but by the relative impact on cost calculation. A cost of paper of € 0.02 is small as compared to overall process costs of several thousand Euros. However, it can be relatively high if the overall process produces € 0.30 costs per instance and millions of instances are processed per day. Think of the situation of processing bank transactions using paper forms versus using online banking. The high amount of transactions per day might result in considerable costs per year.

Solution 11.14 The formula yields $r = 1 - \frac{T}{CT} = 1 - \frac{18.3}{27.5} = 0.333$. This result is apparently misleading because every second task required rework. However, the rework time is in general much smaller than the first-try duration. Hence, T appears to be relatively small in comparison to CT, which results in a low value for r.

Solution 11.15 In Celonis, this question can be answered by applying a *rework* filter that retains only cases where event "W_Assess Potential Fraud - complete" occurs at least twice in the same case. The answer given by Celonis is 13 cases. In Disco, this question can be answered by applying a *follower* filter that retains only those cases where an event of type "W_Assess Potential Fraud" is eventually followed by another event of type "W_Assess Potential Fraud". In the version of Disco we tested (version 2.0), this filter retrieved 20 cases. This is because Disco also counts cases where "W_Assess Potential Fraud" was scheduled or started twice or more, but was not completed twice or more (it counts cases where this task was aborted).

Solution 11.16 We have to consider four different cases. However, as the first and the fourth case show the same sequence of tasks, there are three distinct executions.

Solution 11.17 There are several tasks that can be observed in all cases. These mandatory tasks are a, g, h, i, j, k, l. The other tasks b, c, d, e, f are not mandatory. Exclusiveness relationships hold between b and c, d, e, f pairwise.

Solution 11.18 In Disco, this question can be answered by applying an event pair filter ("follower" filter) that retains only those cases where an event of type "W_Assess Potential Fraud" occurs after another event of type "W_Assess Potential Fraud" and such that both events refer to the same resource. In our test using Disco v2.0, the answer is 8 cases. In Celonis, this question can be answered by opening an analysis of type "Case Explorer" on this event log, applying a filter that retains all cases where "W_Assess Potential Fraud - complete" occurs twice, and inspecting each of the 13 cases one by one, to determine which resource performed "W_Assess Potential Fraud - complete". The result is 3 cases. It is also possible in Celonis to textually specify a filter that extracts all cases where at least two distinct resources have performed an event of type "W_Assess potential fraud - complete". This latter approach requires familiarity with the filter specification language of Celonis.

Solution 11.19

1. L1: 54.8 days; L2: 25 days.
2. In log L2, task "Contact Hospital" is executed four times less often than in log L1 (130 times versus 518 times). Also, in log L1, task "Contact Hospital" is executed in parallel with "High Medical History" whereas in log L2, "Contact Hospital" is executed always after "High Medical History".
3. In log L1, there are waiting times of over 30 days between sending the notification and sending the questionnaire. These waiting times are of around 16–19 h in log L2. Also, in L2, there are waiting times of around 21 days before "Receive Questionnaire" and "Archive" (and similar waiting times between "Skip questionnaire" and "Achive"). These waiting times are in the order of 10 days in L2. On the other hand, in log L2, there is a waiting time of around 28 days between "Register" and "Create questionnaire", whereas this waiting time is around 58 min in L1. This bottleneck however only affects about a third of the cases in L2.

11.11 Further Exercises

Exercise 11.20 Consider the following event log. Write the corresponding workflow log using the same approach as in Figure 11.7 (page 427). You may use abbreviations CF, SB, SR, and CC to denote the four tasks in this process.

Exercise 11.21 Draw the dependency graph of the workflow log obtained in Exercise 11.20.

Exercise 11.22 With reference to the event log of the Business Process Intelligence Challenge 2017 (https://tinyurl.com/bpic2017), does it sometimes happen that a

Case ID	Task Label	Timestamp
1	Create Fine	19-04-2017 14:00:00
2	Create Fine	19-04-2017 15:00:00
1	Send Bill	19-04-2017 15:05:00
2	Send Bill	19-04-2017 15:07:00
3	Create Fine	20-04-2017 10:00:00
3	Send Bill	20-04-2017 14:00:00
4	Create Fine	21-04-2017 11:00:00
4	Send Bill	21-04-2017 11:10:00
1	Process Payment	24-04-2017 14:30:00
1	Close Case	24-04-2017 14:32:00
2	Send Reminder	19-04-2017 10:00:00
3	Send Reminder	20-05-2017 10:00:00
2	Process Payment	22-05-2017 09:05:00
2	Close Case	22-05-2017 09:06:00
4	Send Reminder	21-05-2017 15:10:00
4	Send Reminder	21-05-2017 17:10:00
4	Process Payment	26-05-2017 14:30:00
4	Close Case	26-05-2017 14:31:00
3	Send Reminder	20-06-2017 10:00:00
3	Send Reminder	20-07-2017 10:00:00
3	Process Payment	25-07-2017 14:00:00
3	Close Case	25-07-2017 14:01:00

loan offer is canceled (meaning that event "O_Cancelled" occurs), but later the offer is accepted (i.e., "O_Accepted")? If yes, in what percentage of cases does this happen?

Exercise 11.23 Consider the workflow log $[\langle a, b, c, d, e \rangle, \langle a, b, d, c, e \rangle, \langle a, c, d, b, e \rangle, \langle a, d, c, b, e \rangle, \langle a, d, b, c, e \rangle, \langle a, d, c, b, e \rangle]$. Show step-by-step how the α-algorithm works on this workflow log, and draw the resulting process model.

Exercise 11.24 Consider the log in Exercise 11.20 (page 470). Show step-by-step how the α-algorithm works on this log, and draw the resulting process model.

Exercise 11.25 Draw a model in BPMN that can produce every possible execution sequence that includes tasks $\{a, b, c, d, e\}$. Discuss the fitness and precision of this model with respect to the workflow log $\{\langle a, b, c, d, e \rangle, \langle a, c, b, d, e \rangle\}$. Draw a process model that would have perfect fitness and perfect precision with respect to this workflow log (i.e., a model that can produce exactly this log). Would the α-algorithm produce this model with perfect fitness and precision?

Exercise 11.26 Using a process mining tool, discover a BPMN process model from the following event log of an authentication process: http://tinyurl.com/simpleEventLog (also available in the book's companion website).

Note: This log is sufficiently simple that it is possible to manually derive the BPMN process model from a dependency graph.

Exercise 11.27 Using a process mining tool, discover a BPMN process model from the following event log of a telephone repair process: http://tinyurl.com/repairLogs (also available in the book's companion website).
Note: This log is more complex and difficult to manually understand using a dependency graph. Consider using a process mining tool that can discover BPMN process models (e.g., ProM or Apromore).

Exercise 11.28 Consider there is an AND-split in a process model with two subsequent tasks a and b. What kind of pattern do these tasks show on the timeline chart?

Exercise 11.29 Consider the workflow log that you created for Exercise 11.5 (page 427) from the cases shown in Figure 11.4. Replay these logs in the process model of Figure 11.21 (page 456). Note down consumed, produced, missing and remaining tokens for each arc, and calculate the fitness measure. Assume that tasks not shown in the process model do not change the distribution of tokens in the replay.

Exercise 11.30 Do the models you discovered in Exercises 11.26 and 11.27 perfectly fit the corresponding event log? If not, describe to what extent and how the event log differs with respect to the discovered model.

Exercise 11.31 We consider again the health insurance process examined in Exercise 11.19 on page 460 (available at http://tinyurl.com/InsuranceLogs) and specifically the log containing the 2011 cases (log L1). Based on this log, complete the following tasks using a process mining tool:

1. Extract from the log all the cases containing at least one occurrence of high insurance check. The filtered log will be called FilteredHigh.
2. Extract from the log all the cases containing at least one occurrence of low insurance check. The filtered low will be called FilteredLow.
3. Compare the mean cycle time of cases of FilteredHigh and FilteredLow.
4. Describe the main differences between FilteredHigh and FilteredLow in terms of the frequency and relative order of tasks. Hint: You may use a log delta analysis tool or you may derive a dependency graph for FilteredHigh and another for FilteredLow, and abstract away all infrequent behaviors in the dependency graph (i.e., set the task and the arc abstraction sliders to their minimum).

11.12 Further Readings

The question of selecting process performance measures is crucial when setting up a process monitoring system. Leyer et al. [88] propose a procedure for defining performance measures for a given business process. They also show how to use process mining techniques to calculate performance measures from event logs.

Harmon's book [64] gives a broad perspective on how to define process performance measures at the level of an entire organization, and how to set up a governance framework to maintain these performance measures.

There are two complementary questions when designing performance dashboards. The first one is how to go from the definition of the performance objectives down to a sketch of a dashboard. This question is thoroughly covered in Eckerson's book [41]. The second question is how to design a performance dashboard that is understandable and compelling. To this end, we recommend following the guidelines on storytelling with data given in [80] and other data visualization guidebooks.

A comprehensive overview of existing techniques and research challenges in the field of process mining is given in Van der Aalst's book on process mining [1]. A more concise overview can be found in the process mining manifesto [70] composed by the IEEE Task Force on Process Mining. The website of the IEEE Task Force on Process Mining provides datasets (event logs) and case studies that illustrate how process mining is used in a range of industries.[28] A survey and comparative evaluation of automated process discovery techniques is provided in [12], while an overview of conformance checking techniques is given in [118].

In Section 11.8, we discussed a case study in which an insurance company applied a question-driven process mining approach. When applying process mining in a large organization, it is desirable to adopt a systematic approach (i.e., a method). Two methods for conducting process mining projects are presented in [180] and [5].

---

[28]http://www.win.tue.nl/ieeetfpm.

Chapter 12
BPM as an Enterprise Capability

Be not afraid of growing slowly, be afraid only of standing still.
Chinese proverb

In this book we presented a range of methods and related techniques for the identification, discovery, analysis, redesign, implementation, and monitoring of business processes. Along the six phases of the BPM lifecycle, we also discussed software tools and systems that can support us in the application of these methods for the effective management of business processes. In other words, given a business process in need of improvement, we discussed how a *BPM project* can be carried out to achieve the desired improvement goals, regardless of whether these are related to efficiency, quality, or anything else.

Due to the need to improve different business processes, chances are that multiple BPM projects are being conducted at the same time within the same organization. Collectively, we call the set of BPM projects within a company, including its specific management structure, a *BPM program*. Depending on various characteristics, such as the overall performance of an organization, its size, and its context, the number of concurrent projects may be high and the scope of the individual projects themselves may be large. As a result, the coordination of the BPM program may become extremely complex and individual projects may fail altogether because of their decreasing relevance or lack of progress.

This chapter deals with the following question: "What does it take to successfully manage a BPM program?" To answer this question, we consider BPM as an enterprise capability, which places it at the same level as other organizational management disciplines such as risk management and human performance management. After introducing the typical reasons for BPM programs to fail, we introduce transversal aspects of BPM, such as governance and strategic alignment, and discuss how these are critical to avoid the fail reasons. Next, we organize these aspects in a *BPM maturity model* and show how to use this model to assess the BPM maturity of an organization.

© Springer-Verlag GmbH Germany, part of Springer Nature 2018
M. Dumas et al., *Fundamentals of Business Process Management*,
https://doi.org/10.1007/978-3-662-56509-4_12

12.1 Barriers to BPM Success

A common problem among BPM practitioners is how to relate perceived BPM success to actual success. Perceived measures of BPM success that are often mentioned include: the configuration of a modeling tool, the completion of a Six Sigma training course, the delivery of a job description for a process owner, the roll-out of a BPMS, or an update of the process architecture. However, BPM success should not be a function of the quality of an activity (e.g., the quality of a training program) or artifact (e.g., the quality of a process architecture). BPM success should ultimately link to business success, i.e., to the ability to meet or exceed the business performance objectives that are part of the corporate strategy. Accordingly, common reasons for the failure of BPM programs include:

- A sole focus on BPM methods and tools, not on business goals,
- The belief that BPM is the single source of truth,
- BPM projects that are managed as isolated silos, and
- An overall inability to change.

Let us discuss these reasons in a bit more detail. One of the major fail reasons for a BPM program is that the focus is exclusively on methods and tools along the various phases of the BPM lifecycle. The perspective is then lost on what effective value can be derived from their application. For example, an organization may enthusiastically roll out an enterprise-wide Six Sigma training and start using Six Sigma-specific techniques all around. However, that company's strategic objective may not at all be to improve the quality of existing products. If its aim would be, for example, to outsmart competitors through innovative products, the focus on Six Sigma is misplaced. Similarly, another organization may acquire a BPMS thinking that this process automation software will fulfill all its process improvement needs, but the licensing costs could overshadow the corporate aims for cost reduction.

As to the second reason, it should be clear at this point in this book that BPM is a powerful concept to think about how organizations perform and may perform better. Yet, there are two things to keep in mind. First of all, there are other management concepts that can deliver value to organizations. The trick is to see how BPM and other management disciplines can be aligned such that they reinforce each other, rather than that they lead to tribalism and organizational infighting. Secondly, BPM is not something that comes natural to everyone. People are often highly committed to their job and to the activities they perform, but may easily fail to see how their work fits in the bigger picture. It is counterproductive to push BPM down their throats.

Moving to the third reason, BPM is a holistic management concept: it stresses the relevance of looking at the relations between activities, people, and technology to deliver products and services. It is, therefore, slightly ironic when ongoing BPM projects are managed in isolation from each other, which is the third reason in the list above. Such a situation may lead to all kinds of problems. Participants who are active in different processes that undergo process change may get confused by the differences between methods, policies and technologies used across the projects. Something similar may apply to customers that interact with an organization through different processes undergoing change. Finally, a company's top management may not appreciate the loss of efficiency due to bad management of the interrelationships between projects or the outright mistakes that follow from it.

Finally, it is worth stressing again how difficult it is to bring about change. A fantastic to-be process model, even if it is based on a meticulous analysis of the as-is process and incorporates a range of innovative principles, is still a far cry from an improved, operational business process. Clearly, the process implementation phase of the BPM lifecycle is duly concerned with introducing a new process design into an organization. Still, it is well known that organizational changes do not easily stick (see the "Change Management" box in Section 9.3.2 on page 362). This is not different for BPM programs.

The failure reasons we discussed here can be traced back to a lack of strategic alignment, a weak or nonexistent governance structure, or an underestimation of the role that employees and an organization's culture have within the success of applying BPM. We will see how these aspects can be addressed through the notion of BPM maturity, as discussed in the next section.

Exercise 12.1 Indicate to what extent the following activities can be considered a success for a BPM program. For your assessment, try to distinguish between prerequisites and measures of success. *Prerequisites for success* are those activities conducive to or necessary for the eventual success of a BPM program, but are not an end in themselves. In contract, *measures of success* are activities that relate to the achievement of a business goal through BPM.

(a) The BPM team has correctly configured a modeling tool.
(b) A process analyst has completed a Six Sigma training course.
(c) The job description of a process owner has been updated.
(d) The cycle time of the order-to-cash process was reduced by 5%.
(e) A BPMS was installed.
(f) The handling time of over 90% of claims was reduced to up to 5 days.
(g) The process architecture was updated.

12.2   The Six Success Factors of BPM Maturity

Let us consider the case of an insurance company that has a BPM team within each line of business: home, motor, and commercial insurance. Each of these teams may spawn a new BPM project based on the needs of the particular insurance service they manage. For example, there might be a project to improve the home insurance claims handling process for efficiency reasons, or another project, shared between motor and commercial insurance, to improve the quality of the process for validating customer policies. When dealing with multiple projects at a time, to avoid the failure reasons discussed in the previous section, we need to go beyond the application of the methods and tools that we learned in this book.

First of all, we also need to employ methods and tools for managing individual projects and for managing the entire program. These are not specifically related to BPM and can be adapted from current project management practices, such as *PRINCE2* (Projects in Controlled Environments), an ISO standard, or *PMBOK* (Project Management Body of Knowledge) from the Project Management Institute.

A mature BPM organization should thoroughly apply a variety of BPM-specific methods and tools across the various phases of the BPM lifecycle, coordinated by the use of methods and tools for project and program management. As such, *methods* and *information technology* (IT) are two factors critical to the success of a BPM program. This book has put a strong emphasis on these methods and IT. However, we also need to consider other factors that are equally important for BPM success. First of all, we need to put in place a *governance* structure that establishes relevant and transparent accountability, decision making processes, and quality control mechanisms. This includes, for example, the definition of the responsibilities of the various roles involved in a BPM project, such as the process owner or the process analyst, as well as setting appropriate BPM standards, i.e., which methods are to be used in each phase of the lifecycle. A governance structure is especially relevant when moving from a project to a program dimension, when effective coordination becomes indispensable.

A company should also aim to ensure *strategic alignment* in each phase of the lifecycle. This entails the clear definition of desired process outcomes and process performance measures (also called KPIs), which are based on the objectives of process customers and stakeholders. Such definitions can serve as a guide in the choice of what BPM methods and tools to use. As an example, if a company aims to improve process quality, it should focus on value-added analysis rather than on the critical path method, as the latter is more suited to analyze time issues.

Last but not least, people and organizational culture are deeply important for the success of a BPM program. As to the *people*, think of the development of appropriate skills for the employees of the organization, both in terms of BPM knowledge (methods and IT) by those who are expected to apply it (e.g., process owners and process analysts) as well as in terms of process knowledge (procedures, policies) by those who participate in the processes. Without the right skill set, the use of BPM methods and tools will not be effective. *Culture*, in this context, is the set of corporate values and beliefs, which may contribute to shaping the process-thinking mindset of employees. This, in turn, has implications on the extent to which process participants will adhere to new process designs or how much corporate leaders will be interested in and value BPM.

In light of the above, we can identify six orthogonal factors that are critical to the success of a BPM program: (i) strategic alignment, (ii) governance, (iii) methods, (iv) IT, (v) people, and (vi) culture. These *critical success factors* have been organized by Rosemann and de Bruin in the *BPM Maturity Model* [33, 150], as shown in Figure 12.1.[1] This model is intended as an instrument to measure the

---

[1]The original model has been adapted to the terminology of this book.

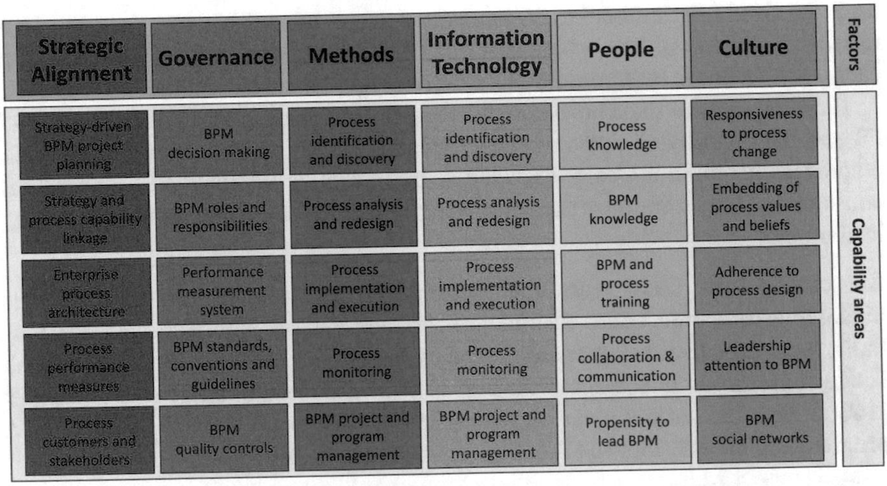

Strategic Alignment	Governance	Methods	Information Technology	People	Culture	Factors
Strategy-driven BPM project planning	BPM decision making	Process identification and discovery	Process identification and discovery	Process knowledge	Responsiveness to process change	
Strategy and process capability linkage	BPM roles and responsibilities	Process analysis and redesign	Process analysis and redesign	BPM knowledge	Embedding of process values and beliefs	
Enterprise process architecture	Performance measurement system	Process implementation and execution	Process implementation and execution	BPM and process training	Adherence to process design	Capability areas
Process performance measures	BPM standards, conventions and guidelines	Process monitoring	Process monitoring	Process collaboration & communication	Leadership attention to BPM	
Process customers and stakeholders	BPM quality controls	BPM project and program management	BPM project and program management	Propensity to lead BPM	BPM social networks	

Fig. 12.1 The BPM Maturity Model, adapted from [33, 150]

maturity of a BPM program within a given organization. The underlying assumption is as follows: a higher BPM maturity will be reflected in higher business process performance; in turn, a higher business process performance will lead to higher organizational performance. In the next section, we will discuss how to use this model to measure the maturity of a BPM program within an organization. For now, let us focus on the six success factors.

Each factor sports five *capability areas*, as illustrated in Figure 12.1. For example, *strategic alignment* includes a capability area for strategy-driven BPM project planning, while *governance* includes a capability area for BPM decision making. Note how the capability areas for both *methods* and *IT* are related to the different phases of the BPM lifecycle, extended with a capability area for the overall management of BPM projects and programs for each of these factors.

Let us now consider how these factors are orthogonal to each other. By way of example, *methods* and *IT* measure the degree of the application of different BPM methods and related tools within the BPM lifecycle. For example, in what way is BPMN (as a process modeling technique) used during process discovery? Do we limit ourselves to capturing simple sequences or do we include elaborate routing and exception handling constructs? Furthermore, how do we discover business processes? Do we only rely on workshops or do we also use document analysis, observations, and interviews? Clearly, the more sophisticated the models we create during process discovery and the more extensive the ways we discover processes, the higher our maturity in process discovery methods will be.

Governance, among others, measures the existence of BPM standards to select which methods and tools to use, as well as the existence of conventions and guidelines to restrict the use of these methods and tools. For example, we model business processes with BPMN and use Signavio as the modeling tool (standards), limit the size of each model to 30 nodes and avoid, where possible, the use of the OR-join (guidelines). Moreover, we organize workshop sessions of maximum 3 h each, each followed by a consolidation activity (guidelines).

People measures the knowledge our employees possess of such methods and IT, and the maturity of corporate BPM training activities. For example, have our employees acquired a strong knowledge of BPMN or do they rely on external consultants? And were they trained internally or did we employ external training institutions?

Exercise 12.2 In recent years, many companies have started initiatives towards digital transformation, better customer experience, and regulatory compliance. Partially, these initiatives are operationalized by the help of BPM programs. Rabobank is one of the largest financial service providers in The Netherlands. In a white paper [166], Pieter van Langen, a senior manager with Rabobank, reports on their BPM program and the way they use ARIS as a process modeling tool.

> The speed and quality of our application development determines how our customers experience the service. [...] Therefore, we can't afford any mistakes in our software. This is all the more true now that the supporting role of employees at local member banks is disappearing. Processes must be fully functional. At the same time, we must make sure that we can promptly anticipate customers' desires and comply with laws and regulations. This requires clear-cut and transparent processes for software development. [...] If we develop an application for an innovative mobile service, it is crucial to know exactly what its impact will be on the environment and other systems and processes. We use models to do this. [...] We wanted to be able to find and maintain all system documentation related to our IT in one central location. [...] Moreover, we wanted everyone, from the business analyst to the architect, to be able to count on the fact that the retrieved system documentation will be correct, and that everybody can feel confident in using it. [...] In this way we have more control over the quality of the applications we develop. These benefits directly translate into a better service for our customers.

Which of the six BPM critical success factors does Van Langen's report refer to?

In the previous chapters of this book, we covered in-depth *methods* and *IT*. In the rest of this section we overview the other four success factors: *strategic alignment*, *governance*, *people*, and *culture*.

12.2.1   Strategic Alignment

Strategic alignment measures the role and impact of business strategy on BPM, as well as the role and impact of BPM on business strategy. It can be broken down into the following capability areas:

1. **Strategy-driven BPM project planning:** How aligned are the methods and tools we choose in each phase of the BPM lifecycle to the particular business goals we want to achieve?

2. **Strategy and process capability linkage:** Does the business strategy directly influence the business processes and vice versa?
3. **Enterprise process architecture:** How well is the enterprise process architecture specified?
4. **Process performance measures:** How well are process outcomes and related process performance measures defined?
5. **Process customers and stakeholders:** How well is the view of customers and other process stakeholders incorporated in BPM projects?

Strategy-driven BPM project planning refers to the level of strategic alignment throughout the BPM lifecycle. This is defined by the choice of which methods and tools we use in each phase of the lifecycle. Strategic alignment already starts in process identification, where strategic importance is one of the criteria we use to drive the selection of which processes to manage. For example, if our business strategy is that of "customer intimacy", we need to prioritize the management of those core processes that have the strongest influence on customer experience. During discovery, we will pay particular attention to modeling all interactions with the customer for the process chosen, given that customer interactions have a strong effect on the overall customer experience. Next, during analysis, we would pick qualitative techniques, such as value-added analysis where the customer perspective is central, and measure primarily external quality through quantitative analysis techniques using metrics such as customer satisfaction or violations of service level agreements. Likewise, during the redesign phase, if we decide to employ redesign heuristics, we will first focus on the application of those heuristics that tend to increase quality, such as *empower* or *triage*.

The next capability area is the *strategy and process capability linkage*, which captures the bi-directional relation between strategy and business processes. This area involves the strategic implications that exist for our business processes (strategy to process) and, vice versa, the process implications that exist for our business strategy (process to strategy). Balanced scorecards (see Section 2.1 on page 35) provide a concrete method to link strategy with processes. Typical questions to ask when studying the strategy-to-process link are:

- *Do we know which processes are impacted by a change of strategy?* For example, as part of a strategy that aims at cost leadership, we realize that the travel insurance service is no longer profitable and, therefore, we decide to discontinue it. As a result, all processes related to this insurance service (development, sales, and claims handling) will have to be decommissioned too.
- *Which processes should we handle in-house as core competency and which ones are candidates for outsourcing or offshoring?* For example, the claims handling process for pet insurance is high-volume and low-value (this process is carried out frequently but the profit generated is limited due to the low value of the related insurance policy). As a result, in pursuit of cost leadership, we decide to outsource this process in order to reduce its operational costs.

The following questions can be used to study the process-to-strategy link:

- *How does process performance influence strategy implementation?* Or in other words: *Which processes could become a bottleneck to the execution of the business strategy?* For example, if our business strategy aims at simplifying business operations through standardization, having different variants of the claims handling process (one per insurance service) will hamper this strategy.
- *Is the strategy designed and continually reviewed in light of current and emerging process capabilities?* Or in other words: *Do new process capabilities enable new strategic options?* For example, we may review our marketing strategy in view of the emergence of digital marketing processes through social media.

Another capability area is the *enterprise process architecture*. As discussed in Chapter 2, an enterprise-wide process architecture can offer a high-level yet comprehensive view on how the organization delivers value to its customers and shareholders via its set of core processes, how these processes are enabled by the support processes, and how they are regulated by the management processes. Given that the process architecture is the starting point of any BPM project, it is important that this artifact is well defined, as complete as possible (enterprise-level versus project-level), and kept up-to-date with regular review cycles for the success of the overall BPM program.

Moving on, the next capability area under strategic alignment is *process performance measures*. In order to measure process performance and, ultimately, to translate business strategy into process objectives, we need to clearly define objectives and related process measures for each business process. This information needs to be shared among all relevant process stakeholders. As illustrated in Chapter 2 (see page 51), a concrete way to achieve this is to equip each process with a *process profile*. In such a profile the following information is included: the process vision in line with the business strategy, the envisaged outcomes, and the success factors. The latter can be complemented with a list of process measures over relevant performance dimensions (e.g., time, cost) and related process performance objectives, so that it becomes clear how the process responds to our business goals. For example, let us consider again our insurance company, which manages a number of insurance services as a result of different mergers. The vision of this company's set of claims handling processes could be that of "generating superior customer advocacy through the provision of simple, timely, low cost delivery on the customer promise." Such an objective incarnates two strategic goals: (i) increasing customer satisfaction (front-office level—quality dimension), and (ii) reducing the number of independent claims handling processes due to previous mergers (back-office level—efficiency dimension). For each goal, we define one or more process performance measures and related performance objectives. For example, we measure customer satisfaction as the average between customer rating and customer loyalty index, both with the objective of exceeding 90%.

It is important that process performance measures are standardized across processes and process variants (e.g., different insurance services) to enable cross-process measurements and hierarchical aggregations. For example, by standardizing the definition of customer rating and customer loyalty index, we can measure these KPIs across all our insurance processes, including different processes (service development, sales, claims handling) and their variants (home, motor, and commercial insurance). Moreover, we can aggregate these into a single measure of customer satisfaction, and in turn, we can aggregate the latter with the rate of customer complaints to obtain a single measure of customer excellence. Balanced scorecards offer a concrete method for the cascading definition and measurement of process performance measures.

For the success of the overall BPM program, we need to consider a last capability area: *process customers and stakeholders*. This last capability area focuses on process stakeholders, such as company shareholders, executives, and government bodies, as well as on customers and other external parties who have an interest or participate in the process. This means taking into account the various priorities that influential individuals or groups have, which are often conflicting. For instance, a change at the executive level (e.g., a new CEO) may have a significant impact on the popularity of the BPM program and, consequently, on its success even though nothing has changed in the way BPM is carried out internally. Likewise, if a BPM project aimed at rectifying the negative opinions that customers have on certain services fails, this may undermine the survival of the overall BPM program. Hence, it is of utmost importance to incorporate the views of the various process stakeholders in a BPM program. When dealing with external parties such as customers, the focus is on the core processes, since these provide the touchpoints to interface directly with external parties. Consider a claims handling process in view of a business strategy aimed at improving customer experience. A BPM project tasked to redesign this process according to this strategic objective will have to pay special attention to the number and quality of the touchpoints with the customer, depending on the particular target audience: An insurance brand that focuses on a young clientele may reduce and digitalize all customer touchpoints (e.g., milestone updates only, via email), while an insurance brand that targets an elderly clientele may decide to increase the number and duration of these touch points (e.g., various progress updates, via phone).

Exercise 12.3 In a case study, Reisert, Zelt, and Wacker report on the corporate strategy of the software vendor SAP and the way how they used BPM to achieve their goals [139].

> In order to produce innovative solutions faster and more simply, SAP started in 2008 to transform its research and development processes. SAP moved away from complex and static project methods toward agile and simple processes, thereby significantly reducing the throughput time of the standard innovation cycle. Based on the experience of this transformation and optimization, [...] SAP decided to increase the emphasis on Business Process Management (BPM). Therefore, BPM initiatives were implemented on a company-wide level in the effort to establish a process infrastructure and a process improvement culture. [...] The key success factor in SAP's journey from BPM concepts and ideas to measurable impact [...] was the strategic alignment of BPM with top management support. [...] The Process Manager is responsible for defining the process improvement goal (with approval from the Business Owner), which is typically derived from the SAP strategy (improvement portfolio, strategic objectives), from a current issue in the process

(impediment, audit finding), or from an idea from the SAP idea management initiative. [...] The effect of the process changes are measured according to Process Performance Indicators (PPIs), which include throughput time, customer satisfaction, and cost per unit output. These PPIs are measured by the Process Manager and compared with previously defined success criteria. [...] Although the triggers for actual process improvement can be numerous, the [...] activities involved in improving a process are standardized and, as such, are documented in the SAP Process Map.

Which capability areas associated with *strategic alignment* are described?

12.2.2 Governance

BPM *governance* is dedicated to the definition of appropriate and transparent accountability in terms of roles and responsibilities for different levels of BPM (program, project, and operations). Furthermore, it is tasked with the design of decision-making and reward processes to guide process-related actions. We can articulate BPM governance according to the following capability areas:

1. **BPM decision making:** What BPM decisions can be taken and when, to handle both expected and unexpected circumstances?
2. **BPM roles and responsibilities:** Is there a clear definition of BPM roles and associated responsibilities?
3. **Process performance measurement system:** What mechanisms are in place to measure process performance and how appropriate are these mechanisms based on the chosen performance measures?
4. **BPM standards, conventions, and guidelines:** How well are BPM standards, conventions, and guidelines defined?
5. **BPM quality controls:** What control measures are in place to review and guarantee quality in all phases of a BPM project?

The first capability area is *BPM decision making*. A critical challenge for BPM governance is the clear definition and consistent execution of related BPM decision-making processes that guide actions in both expected and unexpected circumstances. For example, who can take the decision to start or to stop a BPM project? In addition to who can make which decision, it is important to stipulate the required speed of decision making and the authorization levels to influence resource allocation and organizational responses to process change. This requires alignment with related governance processes, such as IT change management and business continuity management. In BPM decision making, we determine the whole approach to BPM, what decisions to take and when (e.g., the BPM lifecycle and related decisions: when to start each phase, when to start the whole project), while in BPM project planning we ensure alignment in each phase of the lifecycle.

Another capability area of BPM governance is *BPM roles and responsibilities*. This covers the entire range of BPM-related roles, from process analysts, who are e.g., apply BPM methods and IT under the advice of the BPM methodologist, through to process owners, who manage individual BPM projects. In large organizations with a *BPM Center of Excellence*, this also includes the dedicated role of the *BPM Program Manager*, also called the Chief Process Officer (CPO) or the Chief Process and Innovation Officer (CPIO); this role manages the whole BPM initiative and is ultimately accountable for its results. This capability area also includes, when available, BPM decision boards and committees. For example these are the *BPM Steering Committee*, which is made up of the BPM management team and provides overall direction to the development of the BPM program, and the *BPM Advisory Board*, which offers external advice and controls the quality of the BPM program. This capability demands a clear specification of the duties and responsibilities of each role, as well as of their reporting structure. A description of the roles and responsibilities of all involved in the BPM program is provided in the "Stakeholders in the BPM Lifecycle" box on page 24.

A *process performance measurement system* is required for the efficient measurement of process performance. While the actual definition of process performance measures is part of the strategic alignment factor, this capability area specifies who is accountable for measuring process performance, which (cost-effective) procedures are to be followed for performing the measurements, and what supporting tools should be used. Typically, the person accountable for measuring process performance is the process owner, while the definition of the actual measurement procedures is done by the process analysts in consultation with the BPM methodologist.

BPM standards, conventions, and guidelines must be clearly defined and documented to ensure consistency across BPM projects and the sustainability of the overall BPM program. BPM standards define which methods and software tools are to be used across the BPM lifecycle. They also include the standardization of project and program management methods and tools to ensure the effective coordination of different projects within the BPM program. Guidelines and conventions restrict the use of such methods and tools. For example, in Chapter 5 we discussed a series of process modeling guidelines to restrict the vocabulary, structure, and appearance of BPMN models (see page 192). Guidelines and conventions also apply to other phases of the lifecycle beyond discovery. For example, in process identification they can be used to determine the scope of business processes, or the hierarchical levels of the process architecture; in process analysis they can be used to configure the content of an issue register; in process redesign, they can be used to restrict the number and type of heuristics to use. While conventions are hard constraints, guidelines are recommended but not mandatory. It is the role of the BPM methodologist to set standards, guidelines, and conventions and to keep these up-to-date and relevant.

Finally, *BPM quality controls* capture the regular review cycles on BPM projects to maintain the quality and currency of process management principles (e.g., process reuse should prevail over process development, or process automation should only apply to a redesigned process). It also includes mechanisms to monitor the compliance with BPM standards and guidelines, as defined in the previous capability area, as well as with relevant organizational policies.

Exercise 12.4 In their case study, Reisert, Zelt, and Wacker also report on the governance of BPM at SAP [139].

> As the transformation significantly reduced the standard innovation cycle's throughput time, SAP decided to build on this success and founded the Productivity Consulting Group (PCG). [...] PCG was founded as a process office with direct oversight over SAP's corporate functions throughout all regions. The PCG is responsible for establishing a process infrastructure in the company, including process governance, idea management, and improvement services. The PCG is located in the area of SAP's COO [the Chief Operations Officer], which facilitates a direct connection between the PCG's portfolio and the corporate strategy. By grouping PCG with an organizational unit called Business Insight and Technology, the company ensures a close relationship with IT projects and innovations. [...] PCG manages the SAP Process Map and provides SAP-wide BPM standards on how to design, measure, and improve processes. It also manages the BPM community, which entails educating the Process Managers on BPM methodology. Process Managers are responsible for defining, operating, and improving processes, so they pursue the business goals, strategies, and objectives defined by Business Owners. [...] The effect of the process changes are measured according to Process Performance Indicators (PPIs). [...] SAP uses its own process maturity model that has been tailored to the company's needs.

Which capability areas associated with *governance* are described?

12.2.3 People

The *people* factor is about the different individuals and groups that are directly involved in carrying out the various BPM projects but, just as importantly, also about those that are affected by such projects. What needs to be understood is what knowledge people have access to and how the interaction between them takes place to realize an improvement of business process performance. This critical success factor involves the following capability areas:

1. **Process knowledge:** To what level do process participants and related process stakeholders know the processes they participate in?
2. **BPM knowledge:** How much do the people in BPM roles, such as process analysts, know about BPM methods and tools?
3. **BPM and process training:** How developed is the corporate training in BPM and business processes?
4. **Process collaboration and communication:** How do process stakeholders collaborate and communicate with each other for the achievement of process objectives?
5. **Propensity to lead BPM:** How willing is a company's management team to lead BPM projects?

Process knowledge relates to the comprehensiveness and depth of the capabilities of all the involved stakeholders in light of the specific requirements of a process. For people who fulfill a process-oriented role, such as process owners, it is obvious that they need to understand a business process in quite some depth. However, also for regular process participants it may be essential for the success of a BPM program that they understand the overall processes that their work contributes to.

The second capability area, *BPM knowledge*, captures both the explicit and tacit knowledge about BPM principles and practices among people. To what extent is BPM as a management practice generally understood and recognized? A sign that people in an organization have acquired at least a basic understanding of BPM is whether they are familiar with process concepts, such as activities and cases. Specifically for those people who fulfill a BPM role this capability area is also about their knowledge of and skillfulness in existing BPM methods, techniques, and tools. For process analysts, for example, it is important to know how versed they are in the use of different modeling techniques and redesign methods.

The next capability area, *BPM and process training*, captures to what extent an organization invests in the development and maintenance of BPM skills and process knowledge. It relates to the content of educational programs, internal or external, that are available to the employees of the company, the organizational efforts taken to let these people follow such programs (e.g., incentive schemes for participating in training such as reduced workloads), and the certifications that can be acquired by following these. Training is related both to upskilling in knowledge of BPM methods, techniques, and tools for those involved in the BPM program (e.g., training a process analyst on new process mining techniques) and to increasing the knowledge of relevant business processes for those who participate in these processes (e.g., updating a claims handler on the latest insurance procedures and policies). Many large organizations, for example, have set up internal programs to train their employees in the application of Six Sigma techniques; employees can acquire belts of different colors (e.g., Green Belt, Black Belt) as certificates for the programs they have completed. Thus, this capability area does not only focus on the scope and depth of the training offered, but is also concerned with the success of such initiatives.

The *process collaboration and communication* area focuses on the way individuals and groups interact in order to achieve desired process outcomes in a collaborative manner. This area relates to the formal channels that are used in the communication between process stakeholders, such as process participants and process owners, for example, in terms of meetings and briefings that take place. From a more informal perspective, it is important to understand whether people are able to communicate in terms of concepts that make sense in a BPM context: Do they use terms such as "processes", "cases", and "triggers" in a consistent way? A final element worth mentioning is the infrastructure that is available to foster collaboration and communication, such as an intranet or messaging tools.

The final capability area that we discuss in relation to the people factor is *Propensity to lead BPM*. For any organization that desires change, it is crucial that senior management is willing to lead, take responsibility of, and be accountable for change initiatives. This, of course, also applies to BPM projects or programs. Particularly in this area, it is important to distinguish between the formal role that people have on the one hand and the actual role that people perform. The actual advocate of a BPM program may be different than the manager who is formally responsible for it, for example. While such a mismatch may still lead to successful outcomes, no BPM program will succeed without anyone preaching the BPM gospel and steering the projects when they are in turbulence.

Exercise 12.5 Continuing with the case study by Reisert, Zelt, and Wacker, the extract below reports on the activities of the Productivity Consulting Group (PCG), which is in charge of BPM at SAP and of the people in relation to BPM activities [139].

> The PCG supports a series of communication and enablement activities in order to establish a solid relationship with the BPM community.
>
> - SAP Process Excellence Newsletter: Bi-monthly issues that contain training offers, information on upcoming events and success stories on process improvement.
> - Process Manager Information Sessions: Bi-monthly sessions for Process Managers to share best practices and roll out information about BPM standards.
> - Process Management Training: Classroom and virtual training sessions on [SAP's] BPM methodology, tools, and best practices (from Process Managers for Process Managers).
> - SAP Process Summit: Annual event where all Process Managers come together to exchange best practices, get inspiration from external speakers, and learn about new topics related to BPM.
> - SAP Process Excellence Award: Increases the visibility of excellent processes and provides a platform for employees who are working on process improvement by rewarding outstanding processes that accomplish measurable process improvements and have a positive impact on the company.

Which capability areas associated with *people* are described?

12.2.4 Culture

The measures in *culture* quantify the extent to which corporate culture is supportive of BPM. Corporate culture in essence refers to the values and beliefs of the persons working in the organization and, more specifically, how far these stimulate a process-thinking mindset and a positive attitude towards process redesign. *Culture* covers the following capability areas:

1. **Responsiveness to process change:** To what extent does the organization embrace and respond to continuous process change?
2. **Embedding of process values and beliefs:** How deep is process-thinking ingrained in the corporate values and beliefs?
3. **Adherence to process design:** To what degree do process participants adhere to process designs?
4. **Leadership attention to BPM:** How much support do leaders exhibit for BPM?
5. **BPM social networks:** Are social networks in place to shape and disseminate BPM in the organization?

Responsiveness to process change describes how easy it is for process stakeholders to embrace new ways of carrying out processes. One of the key benefits of BPM is the ability of an organization to respond to environmental changes quickly and to drive innovation internally. For this reason, BPM is often described as a *dynamic capability*. A key prerequisite for change is the willingness to change, and this willingness is deeply encoded in the corporate culture. If this is missing, it requires a continuous effort over a longer period of time to foster this responsiveness.

Process values and beliefs are associated with how explicitly members of the organization think in terms of processes and which positive attitudes are related to this. For instance, do employees naturally see themselves as process participants who contribute to the overall objective of a process, or do they perceive themselves as subordinates to a manager in a particular silo of the organization? In those organizations that exhibit a strong BPM culture, we often find processes explicitly mentioned in strategic documents such as the corporate vision, the mission statements, or the description of the value proposition. When processes are often mentioned in that context, it is likely that the key persons in the organization maintain a strongly positive attitude towards BPM and that many employees have a good understanding of BPM concepts.

When such a general, positive attitude towards BPM has been established, it is also observed that the *adherence to process design*, which is the next capability area of culture, is high. This aspect is closely related with the overall acceptance of the BPM principles and ideas as much as the specific process improvements that stem from redesign projects. Process participants who adhere to the process design mostly act in this way, because of a deeper understanding of the dependencies between different tasks in the process and the overall benefits that result from working in a well-organized fashion. Such an attitude is an asset of any BPM project and for the BPM program altogether.

Management support is often mentioned as the most important success factor at all. Such support is not self-evident and requires ongoing *leadership attention to BPM* on different levels. This, in turn, requires the ongoing efforts of all persons involved within the various BPM projects. Management support is quickly gained when substantial benefits can be demonstrated in a monetary way. It is also easily lost when results fail to appear. Therefore, process owners always have to assess the actions of their project members from the perspective of major impact they can deliver in order to foster leadership attention.

Finally, the principles and ideas of BPM should not only be clear to process analysts, but also to any stakeholder group in the organization. *BPM social networks* subsumes all initiatives beyond formally defined projects that stimulate the exchange of experiences in BPM communities of practice or events organized by a BPM Center of Excellence. Such forums are highly important for the dissemination of BPM in the organization and for nurturing its reputation. Often such events and meetings are supported with social media technologies such as Yammer, Facebook, or Twitter.

Exercise 12.6 The last extract from the case study by Reisert, Zelt, and Wacker reports on the results and lessons learned from the way SAP embraced BPM [139].

With the implementation of the SAP Process Map and easy-to-use tools for process documentation, process modeling has become an important part of Process Managers' jobs. Currently, 626 employees have an editor user for process modeling, and more than 1,200 employees are enrolled in internal training that helps them to design and leverage processes at SAP. Today, 92% of all Level 3 processes are documented and published in the SAP Process Map, and 1,023 processes on Level 3 and below are documented. [...] Based on a sample of 100 projects per year, SAP currently achieves a typical result of 20:1 payback and a customer satisfaction that exceeds 75%. In addition, many processes' processing time has been reduced significantly, including a process in the marketing services team that eliminated eleven process steps and reduced processing time by up to 74%. [...] A strong BPM community and a culture that supports BPM initiatives, where every single employee contributes to process improvement, are essential. SAP established the Process Excellence Award, process management events, and other activities that contribute to the creation of a process management culture and a deeper understanding of the value of BPM.

Which results can be related to the capability areas associated with *culture*? Consider also the descriptions for Exercise 12.5 (page 488).

12.3   Measuring Process Maturity and BPM Maturity

Maturity models, such as the BPM Maturity Model presented in the previous section, aim to assess two properties in an integrated way: the *breadth* of how complete a given spectrum of aspects is, and the *depth* with which each aspect is addressed. In the management of business processes, we can distinguish two complementary approaches to maturity assessment: BPM maturity and process maturity. *BPM maturity* is concerned with assessing how broad and deep the spectrum of BPM activities is, within the BPM program of an organization. This can be done, for example, by using the six critical success factors of the BPM Maturity Model that we introduced before. In contrast, *process maturity* is concerned with assessing how broad and deep a given spectrum of business processes is within the organization. In fact, based on the particular business sector in which it operates, an organization is ideally expected to put in place a given set of business processes, so process maturity measures the range and quality of these processes.

First, let us focus on *process maturity* assessment. One of the most widely-used frameworks for process maturity assessment is the *Capability Maturity Model Integration* (CMMI), administered by the CMMI Institute. This framework distinguishes a number of so-called process areas. There are three domain-independent areas: process management, project management, and support, plus various other areas that are specific for a particular domain. The latter are defined in various CMMI specifications, e.g., for product and service development, and for their acquisition.

The coverage of process areas and the degree of their support provide the basis for a process maturity assessment in terms of the five CMMI maturity levels: Level 1 (Initial), Level 2 (Managed), Level 3 (Defined), Level 4 (Quantitatively managed), and Level 5 (Optimizing). The higher the level of maturity, the broader the spectrum of processes the company is engaged in, and the higher the level of sophistication of each individual process, ranging from generic to specific practices. As process maturity increases, also documentation and performance monitoring of the processes in place increases. Note, however, that CMMI focuses on *what* processes should be implemented, rather than on *how* they should be implemented. In fact, different organizations may implement the very same process in a different way and achieve different performance results. This means that, even though successful organizations are associated with high levels of CMMI maturity, applying CMMI alone does not guarantee higher business performance.

Second, we turn to *BPM maturity*. The BPM Maturity Model that we presented in the previous section adopts the nomenclature of the CMMI maturity levels to differentiate between five levels of maturity of a BPM program. These levels are described below.

Level 1 (Initial):   At this level of maturity, BPM is nonexisting or rarely used within the organization. When available, BPM projects are carried out in an ad hoc fashion within individual IT or business divisions. Such initiatives are uncoordinated, and have a limited scope and minimal employee involvement.

Level 2 (Managed):   The organization starts capitalizing on its first BPM experiences to build up BPM capabilities. A process-thinking mindset starts to emerge among its employees. As the awareness of BPM increases, the first processes are documented and analyzed. There is also increasing involvement of the management level, though knowledge of BPM methods and tools remains with external experts.

Level 3 (Defined):   The organization reaps the benefits of the first BPM projects, though the focus is still on the early stages of the BPM lifecycle. The use of methods and tools becomes more sophisticated. In-house BPM training is established to reduce the dependence upon external experts. The first process collaboration and communication forums are set up to facilitate the dissemination of BPM experiences (e.g., using intranets to share process models).

Level 4 (Quantitatively managed):   The focus of BPM projects shifts towards the last phases of the lifecycle: change management accompanies BPM projects to guarantee the acceptance of the redesigned processes; systematic performance monitoring ensures that BPM projects deliver strategic benefits. A *BPM Center of Excellence* is established with well-defined roles to coordinate all BPM efforts. There is process orientation in every project (not only in BPM-specific ones) and the company minimally relies on external expertise.

Level 5 (Optimizing):   BPM is fully-established, on both the operational level and the strategic level, where it has become an integral part of any manager's activities, accountabilities, and performance measurements. BPM methods and tools are widely accepted and a standardized, company-wide approach to BPM is in place. As BPM becomes the way business is done, the *BPM Center of Excellence* reduces in size.

An approach to obtain a single measurement of BPM maturity on a scale from 1 (Initial) to 5 (Optimizing) is to start by measuring the maturity of each

BPM capability area. For example, we may interview the process analysts of our organization to assess their knowledge of discovery methods (maturity of the capability area *BPM knowledge* under *people*) and how far these methods are effectively applied in practice (maturity of *process identification and discovery* under *methods*). For each capability area that we assess, we assign it a maturity level from 1 to 5. This measurement per capability area can be used as feedback information for specific BPM roles, e.g., informing the process methodologist of the quality of the BPM corporate training. Next, we average these results for each success factor to obtain respective maturity assessments. These latter assessments may be reported to the BPM program manager, e.g., the CPO or CPIO. Finally, we average across all success factors to obtain a single measurement of the maturity of the overall BPM program. This can be used by the BPM program manager in discussions with the CEO and other board members.

From the application of the BPM Maturity Model to various organizations, three patterns of adoption have emerged, as shown in Figure 12.2. The blue pattern (high maturity in strategic alignment and governance, low elsewhere) is typical of those organizations where BPM is driven from the top, e.g., the program is sponsored by the CFO or directly by the CEO. There is strong executive support for BPM, often because of a sense of urgency. For example, new regulations demand a large-scale improvement of all the claims handling processes, which are at the core of insurance companies, in order to avoid government fines. As such, the BPM program is strategically aligned; it relies on a well-defined governance structure to maximize standardization and reuse across projects, and to accelerate the achievement of results. However, given the sense of urgency, organizations in this pattern tend to heavily rely on external expertise (consultants) to achieve their BPM results quickly, rather than investing in internal training. Consequently, the use of methods and IT may be ad hoc rather than systematic.

Acknowledgement This figure is adapted from teaching materials of Michael Rosemann, Queensland University of Technology.

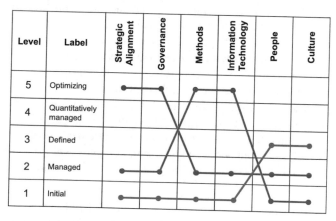

Fig. 12.2 Patterns of BPM maturity

The orange pattern (high maturity in methods and IT, low elsewhere) is typical of those organizations where BPM is driven from within the IT department, under the sponsorship of an IT director or the CIO directly. As such, in this bottom-up approach to BPM, there is a strong emphasis on BPM methods and software solutions, which are applied extensively and in-depth. This leads to high-quality outputs such as sophisticated process models or feature-reach process automation solutions. However, the use of these methods and tools is not necessarily driven by an alignment with corporate priorities. Hence, the outputs produced may be hardly used outside IT. Moreover, organizations in this pattern suffer from an inability to democratize BPM internally, due to the often-introverted personality of the technical experts driving BPM.

Finally, the green pattern (medium maturity in people and culture, low elsewhere) is observed in those organizations that are affected by rule-based governance and heavy unionization, where everyone's buy-in is sought for any redesign decision. For example, this is the case for certain agencies in the public sector. Here, BPM may be democratized across different organizational levels. However, its principles are hardly embedded in the corporate values and beliefs, because there is no strong urgency to change (e.g., the company has the monopoly of the market). In addition, the quest for widespread consensus implies that all key decisions as part of any BPM project have to be scrutinized by different committees, leading to a slowdown in the delivery of BPM results.

Figure 12.3 shows an example of BPM maturity assessment for an insurance company. The assessment is framed in the context of a BPM roadmap, which describes desired levels of maturity over time. The company in this example follows the orange pattern: The driver for BPM is methods and IT, rather than strategy.

Critical Success Factor	Implementation Stages			
	Foundation	Capability	Business Architecture	The Last Mile
Strategic Alignment	Level 1	Level 1	Level 2 *Drive synergies*	Level 3-4 *Group-wide approach*
Governance	Level 1	Level 1	Level 2 *IT-wide approach*	Level 3-4 *Group-wide approach*
Methods	Level 2 *Workshop and observation methods*	Level 3 *Integrate into System Dev Lifecycle*	Level 4 *Integrate into Enterprise Architecture*	Level 5 *Integrate into Service Architecture*
Information Technology	Level 2 *ARIS for modeling*	Level 3 *ARIS for simulation and analytics*	Level 4 *Link to Enterprise Architect*	Level 5 *Link with Enterprise Service Bus and BPMS*
People	Level 1 *Establish BPM Team*	Level 2 *Extend into App Dev Team*	Level 3 *Integrate into Ent Arch Team*	Level 4 *Whole organization*
Culture	Level 1 *Basic process awareness*	Level 2 *Integrate into IT culture*	Level 3 *Become part of Enterprise planning*	Level 4 *Integrate into org culture*

Application focus | Service focus

Fig. 12.3 Example of BPM maturity assessment for an insurance company

Acknowledgement This figure is adapted from teaching materials of Michael Rosemann, Queensland University of Technology.

The assessment of an organization in terms of the various levels of BPM or process maturity leads to a so-called *appraisal*. Appraisals can be conducted internally within the organization (also called self-appraisals) or by external organizations with expertise in BPM or process maturity assessment. For example, different types of appraisals are distinguished for measuring process maturity, as defined in the *Standard CMMI Appraisal Method for Process Improvement* (SCAMPI).

Exercise 12.7 In Exercises 12.3 to 12.6 on pages 483–489, we have learned about the BPM program at SAP. Assess the BPM maturity of SAP from what is reported in the quoted text.

Finally, it has to be emphasized that a maturity assessment captures only the current state of the processes or of the BPM program. Several BPM experts have teamed up to formulate the principles that eventually will make BPM more mature and more successful. The box on "Ten Principles of Good BPM" summarizes them.

TEN PRINCIPLES OF GOOD BPM

The ideas behind BPM maturity are summarized in the Ten Principles of Good Business Process Management [189]:

1. **Principle of Context Awareness**   BPM should fit the organizational context. It should not follow a cookbook approach.
2. **Principle of Continuity**   BPM should be a permanent practice. It should not be a one-off project.
3. **Principle of Enablement**   BPM should develop capabilities. It should not be limited to firefighting.
4. **Principle of Holism**   BPM should be inclusive in scope. It should not have an isolated focus.
5. **Principle of Institutionalization**   BPM should be embedded in the organizational structure. It should not be an ad hoc responsibility.
6. **Principle of Involvement**   BPM should integrate all stakeholder groups. It should not neglect employee participation.
7. **Principle of Joint Understanding**   BPM should create shared meaning. It should not be the language of experts.
8. **Principle of Purpose**   BPM should contribute to strategic value creation. It should not be done for the sake of doing it.
9. **Principle of Simplicity**   BPM should be economical. It should not be over-engineered.
10. **Principle of Technology Appropriation**   BPM should make opportune use of technology. It should not consider technology management as an afterthought.

12.4 Recap

This chapter argued that to achieve sustainable success with BPM, we need to go beyond the application of methods, techniques, and software tools, and consider BPM as an enterprise capability embedded in the corporate structure. Accordingly, BPM should not be seen as a one-off project, but as a coordinated set of projects developed over time, each of these aiming to improve one or more business processes via the BPM lifecycle.

First, we presented typical fail reasons of BPM programs and traced these back to a lack of strategic alignment, a weak or nonexistent governance structure, or an underestimation of the role that employees and corporate culture play for the success of the BPM program. Using these causes, we then introduced the BPM Maturity Model as a tool to measure the success, or maturity, of a BPM program within an organization. This model revolves around six critical success factors: strategic alignment, governance, methods, IT, people, and culture, each sporting five capability areas. The underlying assumption is that BPM success influences business process success, which in turn influences business success.

Finally, we turned to maturity assessment, where we differentiated between BPM maturity and process maturity. The former measures the completeness and quality of the set of processes executed in an organization; the latter measures the maturity of the BPM program that drives the management of these processes. We overviewed the CMMI framework for process maturity assessment, and reused the nomenclature of its maturity levels to discuss five levels of BPM maturity according to the BPM Maturity Model. From this, we delineated three key patterns of BPM adoption within companies.

12.5 Solutions to Exercises

Solution 12.1 Many activities that the BPM team and other BPM stakeholders are responsible for only have an indirect effect on the success of the BPM program. These are prerequisites rather than measures of success.

(a) The BPM team has correctly configured a modeling tool. Without this step, it will be difficult to systematically model processes. This is a prerequisite for success.

(b) A process analyst has completed a Six Sigma training course. Without this step, it will be difficult to systematically analyze various processes. This is a prerequisite for success.

(c) The job description of a process owner has been updated. Without this step, the responsibility for a certain process might not be clear. This is a prerequisite for success.

(d) The cycle time of the order-to-cash process was reduced by 10%. This is likely a measure of success, which might spring from a BPM project to improve the order-to-cash process. Whether it is a true success measure or not depends on the actual business goal set for the organization. For example, if the goal was to improve operational efficiency by at least 5%, then the reduction of cycle time by 10% in the order-to-cash process is probably an indication of the achievement of this goal.

(e) A BPMS was installed. Without this step, we cannot automate business processes with the BPMS. This is a prerequisite for success.

(f) The handling time of over 90% of claims was reduced to up to 5 days. This is likely a measure of success, which might result from a BPM project to improve the claims handling process.

(g) The process architecture was updated. Through this step, we provide the infrastructure for specific BPM projects. This is prerequisite for success.

Solution 12.2

- Strategy: High customer experience, no mistakes in software, functional processes, compliance with law, transparent processes for software development.
- Governance: All documentation in one location, documentation always up-to-date.
- Methods: Use models to trace impact of development on systems and processes.
- Information Technology: In-house development to support customer processes in an innovative way.
- People: Trust in correctness of documentation.
- Culture: Transparency through well-documented processes.

Solution 12.3

1. Strategy-driven BPM project planning: Each process has improvement goals derived from strategic priorities. Selection criteria are not explicitly discussed in the quoted text.
2. Strategy and process capability linkage: Strategy and processes are directly related. On the one hand, strategy is formulated in terms of process performance: "produce innovative solutions faster and more simply". On the other hand, the improvement objectives refer to strategy.
3. Enterprise process architecture: The SAP Process Map described in the text, which we illustrated in Section 2.2.5 (see page 55), is the process landscape model. It plays a central role for the strategic alignment of all BPM projects at SAP.
4. Process performance measures: Each process improvement project at SAP has a clear improvement objective tied to specific process performance measures.
5. Process customers and stakeholders: Strategic objectives are driven by the customer perspective.

Solution 12.4

1. BPM decision making: The Productivity Consulting Group (PCG) in SAP is responsible for decision making related to BPM projects. It closely cooperates with the unit responsible for IT projects and innovation.

2. BPM roles and responsibilities: PCG manages BPM standards and the SAP Process Map. Process managers are responsible for defining, operating, and improving processes, in pursuit of the company's business goals. Business owners define objectives.
3. Performance measurement system: While not explicitly mentioned, it is reasonable to assume that mechanisms are in place for the measurement of process performance measures. At SAP, these mechanisms are part of the BPM standards defined by the PCG.
4. BPM standards, conventions, and guidelines: PCG defines BPM standards for the whole corporation.
5. BPM quality controls: A SAP-specific maturity model is used to assess quality.

Solution 12.5

1. Process knowledge: The newsletter helps to keep stakeholders up-to-date, including process participants.
2. BPM knowledge: The information sessions, trainings, and the process summit disseminate BPM knowledge. Hence, we can assume that the level of BPM knowledge is high with all those involved in BPM initiatives at SAP.
3. BPM and process training: Corporate training on BPM and on business processes is available through SAP's Process Management Training.
4. Process collaboration and communication: Beyond their duties to improve those processes they are responsible for, process managers also have forums like the Process Manager Information Sessions to exchange experiences. While not explicitly mentioned in the text, it is reasonable to assume that this has a positive cascading effect on process participants.
5. Propensity to lead BPM: Business owners and process managers have to agree on the process strategy and drive processes towards improving process performance measures.

Solution 12.6

1. Responsiveness to process change: Several measures promote a culture of continuous improvement.
2. Embedding of process values and beliefs: The overall organizational anchoring of BPM at SAP strongly establishes process values at all levels of the organization. An extensive number of employees have received BPM training and various projects have contributed to tangible improvements in the organization. All this contributes to a strong embedding of process values and beliefs, leading to a high credibility of the overall BPM program.
3. Adherence to process design: Substantial improvements are reported in relation to customer satisfaction and processing times. These numbers indicate that changes to processes have found their way into daily work routines.
4. Leadership attention to BPM: The BPM program has achieved a substantial improvement to various processes. Such success contributes to management attention.

5. BPM social networks: The PCG has established various networking activities, through which people can meet and learn about ways of enhancing their BPM-related skills.

Solution 12.7 The BPM maturity of SAP is high. A BPM Center of Excellence is in place called Productivity Consulting Group. This means that at least Level 4 (Quantitatively managed) is reached. There are also indications that Level 5 could be reached, because BPM is part of the managers' daily work. Corporate BPM standards are also in place and used quite extensively within the company. An appraisal would determine the correct BPM maturity level.

12.6   Further Exercises

Exercise 12.8 In a case study, Kloppenburg, Kettenbohrer, Beimborn, and Bögle report on the BPM approach at Lufthansa Technik, the technical division of the airline Lufthansa [79].

> At its 30 subsidiaries worldwide, more than 20,000 employees perform tasks like aircraft overhaul, component maintenance, and V.I.P. cabin completion. The basis for all aircraft-related tasks are the approvals of the respective aviation authorities from 69 countries. To gain these approvals, Lufthansa Technik must demonstrate to these regulatory authorities its compliance with international laws and standards. The company accomplishes this requirement based on the process-oriented management system called IQ MOVE.
> Since the beginning of the IQ MOVE implementation in 2002, "Finding all relevant procedures quickly and easily" has been the guiding vision of the development and operation of the system. Its acceptance by the employees is the key indicator of the success of the IQ MOVE implementation. [...] An essential step in increasing employees's acceptance was the introduction of a process-management role concept that facilitates clear assignment of management responsibilities to specific roles, such as Process Owner, Process Architect, and Process Manager (for process responsibility) and Line Manager (for disciplinary responsibility). Intensive training and coaching for these roles has helped to improve the operation of processes by, for example, keeping processes up-to-date and providing process training to employees. In addition, the integration of top management into the system development is ensured by regular reporting to and discussion with the organization's senior line managers.

(a) Which of the six BPM capability areas does the quoted text refer to?
(b) On which maturity level is the described organization?

Exercise 12.9 In a case study, Wolinski and Bala report on the BPM approach at Siemens [194].

> Siemens strengthened its process-wise approach and worldwide process standardization by implementing a formalized process policy. As a first step, the Business Process Excellence (BPE) regulation (also referred to as BPE policy) was introduced. It formulated the Siemens Processes for Excellence (SIPEX) process standards, which replaced the previous processes base, referred to as Reference Process House (RPH). At the same time, process roles (sponsor, owner, and manager) and corporate tools with which to visualize the processes, such as ARIS, were introduced. In the Polish organization, the program was formulated as a vehicle with which to implement the process organization. The goal of the initiative, which

was referred to internally as "Streamlining business processes", included Chief Financial Officers (CFOs) as process sponsors and the head of the business process management team as the program manager. [...] From the implementation of the program we learned four primary lessons:

- Complexity in many dimensions (number of processes, number of roles, and number of formal documents and circulars) is not supportive of effective process management.
- Having a strong, dedicated sponsor is one of the most important keys to success.
- Not everyone in the organization will appreciate the effort at first, but they will if an attempt is made to understand their businesses and support their efforts.
- Be flexible: without putting one's best effort into implementing the corporate recommendations and without alignment with the business, no appreciation or cooperation should be expected.

(a) Which of the six BPM capability areas does the quoted text refer to?
(b) On which maturity level is the described organization?

Exercise 12.10 In a case study, Kovačič, Hauc, Buh, and Štemberger report on the BPM approach at Snaga, a public company operating in Slovenia [82].

Snaga is a Slovenian public company that provides a series of waste treatment services for 368,000 citizens of the Municipality of Ljubljana and ten other municipalities. In 2006, prior to adopting BPM and implementing a new information system, the company had obsolete and non-integrated IT solutions that did not provide sufficient support to the business operations. The existing business processes were not well organized, resulting in unnecessary duplication of work and excessive delays. The company also faced new challenges in waste management and new legislation that dictated the development of waste-processing technologies. [...]

The company comprehensively transformed its business operations and adopted BPM in order to undertake the critical examination, rethinking, and then redesigning of current business processes, practices, and rules. The BPM project was conducted in three phases: (1) planning for strategic business transformation, (2) business process restructuring and information architecture development, and (3) information system development and implementation in six interdependent projects. [...]

A key change brought by the BPM adoption was the transition from a functional to a more process-oriented organization with an increased customer focus. The company implemented an ERP solution to support the redesigned business processes, established process ownership and a BPM office, and introduced KPIs to measure the performance and efficiency of processes and business operations using a business intelligence solution. The involvement rather than just [the] support of top management is one of the most important critical success factors in all phases of BPM adoption.

(a) Which of the six BPM capability areas does the quoted text refer to?
(b) On which maturity level is the described organization?

12.7 Further Readings

The BPM Maturity Model presented in this chapter is an adaptation of the original model by Rosemann & de Bruin [33, 150] to the terminology of this book. Rosemann & de Bruin's BPM Maturity Model is the result of a consolidation of existing maturity models from the literature, corroborated with insights obtained from a series of Delphi studies with BPM practitioners and academics [35], and validated with case studies in different business sectors, such as [34, 149, 151]. Further applications of this maturity model are reported in [13, 14] in the form of teaching cases. Recently, a new version of this model has been presented, which specifically focuses on BPM capabilities in the digital age [76].

Another maturity model that we discussed in this chapter is CMMI, which focuses on process maturity as opposed to BPM maturity. CMMI is the evolution of the Capability Maturity Model (CMM) [125], which was originally intended as an instrument to assess the ability of government contractors to deliver on a software project. While it originates from the area of software development, it has been widely applied as a general model of business process maturity, e.g., for IT service management processes. In its version 3.1, there are three official models of CMMI, based on the following areas of interest: product and service development (CMMI for Development) [25], service establishment and management (CMMI for Services) [46], and product and service acquisition (CMMI for Acquisition) [52]. The Standard CMMI Appraisal Method for Process Improvement (SCAMPI) that we mentioned in this chapter is described in [6].

A comprehensive overview of maturity models for BPM and for business processes, including an analysis of their overlap, differences and shortcomings, is provided in the book of Van Looy [94].

In the context of the BPM Maturity Model, we discussed critical success factors such as strategic alignment, governance, people, and culture. A discussion on the relation between these four factors and the various phases of the BPM lifecycle is provided in [98]. This is done in the context of a BPM success assessment framework, which explores the relation between BPM success and business success empirically. Strategic aspects of BPM are discussed in depth by many authors, including Luftman [96] and Burlton [23]; BPM governance aspects are covered, for example, by Spanyi [167], while the role of culture in BPM is explored, among others, by Schmiedel et al. [158]. Such aspects are also discussed from the viewpoint of expert BPM professionals and academics in the book by Harmon & Tregear [66], while many practical tips around these topics are offered by Tregear [174].

In this chapter we related the BPM maturity of an organization to the existence of a dedicated BPM Center of Excellence. However, we did not delve into the operational aspects of how to set up and manage such a Center. The books by Franz & Kirchmer [47] and by Alkharashi et al. [16] discuss such aspects and provide many practical guidelines.

The descriptions of how major companies use BPM that appeared in this chapter are taken from a book on BPM cases [188]. This book includes 31 case studies in different industries. Several of these explicitly discuss BPM as an enterprise capability.

Appendix A
Redesign Heuristics

As part of the explanation of Heuristic Process Design in Chapter 8, a limited number of heuristics were discussed. In this appendix, the full list of 29 heuristics is presented that is part of this method. To further classify these heuristics, we will use the elements that were discussed to delineate business processes, i.e. customers, business process operation, business process behavior, organization, information, technology, and the external environment (see Section 8.1.2, page 300). Note that it is to some extent arbitrary how the heuristics are categorized, since some of these relate to more than one of these characteristics. At the end of this appendix, a table is shown that for each redesign heuristic indicates which of the performance dimensions of the Devil's Quadrangle it primarily targets.

A.1 Customer Heuristics

The three heuristics in this category focus on improving the interaction with customers:

Control relocation: "Move controls towards the customer". Different checks and reconciliation activities may be moved towards the customer. By moving billing controls towards the customer, for example, we may eliminate the bulk of billing errors and improve client satisfaction as a result.

Contact reduction: "Reduce the number of contacts with customers and third parties". The exchange of information with a customer or third party is always time-consuming, especially when it takes place by regular mail. Also, each contact may introduce errors. Imagine a situation where reconciliations are needed, like in the Ford example in Section 1.3.2 on page 11: Reducing the number of contacts in such a case may decrease cycle time and improve quality. Note that it is not always necessary to skip certain information exchanges, but that it is possible to combine them with limited extra cost.

© Springer-Verlag GmbH Germany, part of Springer Nature 2018
M. Dumas et al., *Fundamentals of Business Process Management*,
https://doi.org/10.1007/978-3-662-56509-4

Integration: "Consider the integration with a business process of the customer or a supplier". This heuristic captures the idea of supply chain integration. The actual application of this heuristic may take on different forms. For example, when two parties jointly produce a product, it may be more efficient to perform several intermediate reviews than performing one large review after both parties have completed their parts. In general, integrated business processes should render a more efficient execution, from both a time and cost perspective.

A.2   Business Process Operation Heuristics

A business process operation view considers the implementation of a business process in terms of its activities. There are five heuristics with this focus:

Case types: "Determine whether activities are related to the same type of case and, if necessary, distinguish new business processes". One should be cautious of parts of business processes that are not specific for the business process they are part of. Ignoring this phenomenon may result in a less effective management of such a sub-process and a lower efficiency. Applying this heuristic may result in faster processing times and less cost.

Activity elimination: "Eliminate unnecessary activities from a business process". An activity is superfluous if it adds no value from a customer's point of view. Typically, control activities in a business process are unnecessary from this perspective; they are incorporated in the model to fix problems created (or not elevated) in earlier steps. The redundancy of an activity can also trigger activity elimination. The aims of this heuristic are to increase the speed of processing and to reduce the cost of handling an order.

Case-based work: "Remove batch-processing and periodic activities". Some examples of disturbances in handling a case are (a) that the case becomes piled up in a batch and (b) that the case is slowed down by periodic activities, e.g. because computer systems are only available at specific times. Getting rid of these constraints may significantly speed up individual cases.

Triage: "Split an activity into alternative versions". This heuristic suggests aligning the characteristics of cases with capabilities of resources to increase quality. An alternative is to subdivide activities into sub-categories. For example, a special cash desk may be set up for customers with an expected low processing time.

Activity composition: "Combine small activities into composite activities". Composing larger activities from smaller ones should result in the reduction of setup times, i.e., the time that is spent by a resource to become familiar with the specifics of a case.

A.3   Business Process Behavior Heuristics

A view on the behavior of a business process is concerned with ordering of activities. There are four heuristics within this category:

Resequencing: "Move activities to their appropriate place". In existing business processes, actual activity orderings often do not reveal the necessary dependencies between activities. Sometimes it is better to postpone an activity if it is not required for its immediate follow-up activities. The benefit would be that perhaps its execution may prove to become superfluous, which saves cost. Also, an activity may be moved into the proximity of a similar activity, in this way diminishing set-up times.

Parallelism: "Put activities in parallel". The effect of placing activities in parallel is that throughput time may be considerably reduced. The applicability of this heuristic in business process redesign is large. In practical settings, activities are often ordered sequentially without the existence of hard logical restrictions prescribing such an order.

Knock-out: "Order knock-outs in an increasing order of effort and in a decreasing order of termination probability". A typical element of a business process is the subsequent checking of various conditions that must be satisfied to deliver a positive end result. Any condition that is not met may lead to a termination of that part of the business process: the *knock-out*. If possible, the condition that has the most favorable ratio of (1) expected knock-out probability versus (2) the expected effort to check the condition should be pursued. Next, the second best condition, and so forth. This way of ordering checks yields on average the least costly business process execution.

Exception: "Design business processes for typical cases and isolate exceptional cases from the normal flow". Exceptions may seriously disturb normal operations. By isolating them, precious time may be saved and flexibility of the overall process is improved.

A.4   Organization Heuristics

The organization view refers to two categories of heuristics. The first set relates to the *structure* of the organization, specifically how resources are allocated. There are seven heuristics in this category:

Case assignment: "Let participants perform as many steps as possible". By using case assignment in the most extreme form, a participant will carry out all activities that belong to a particular case. The advantage of this heuristic is that this person will know the case well and will need less set-up time in carrying out subsequent activities. Also, quality of service may be increased.

Flexible assignment: "Keep generic participants free for as long as possible". Suppose that an activity can be executed by either of two available participants. Then, this heuristic suggests assigning it to the most specialized person. In this way, the likelihood of committing the free, more general participant to another work package is maximal. The advantage is that an organization stays flexible with respect to assigning work and that overall queueing time is reduced. Also, the workers with the highest degree of specialization can be expected to take on most of the work, which may result in a higher quality.

Centralization: "Let geographically dispersed participants act as if they are centralized". This heuristic exploits the benefits of a BPMS (see Chapter 9). After all, when a BPMS assigns work to process participants it becomes less relevant where they are located geographically. The specific advantage of this measure is that resources can be committed more flexibly, which yields a better cycle time.

Split responsibilities: "Avoid shared responsibilities for tasks by people from different functional units". The idea is that shared responsibilities are more likely to be a source of neglect and conflict. Reducing the overlap in responsibilities should lead to a better quality of activity execution. Also, a higher responsiveness to available work may be developed, so that customers are served quicker.

Customer teams: "Consider composing work teams of people from different departments that will take care of the complete handling of specific sorts of cases". The heuristic calls for creating dedicated teams that have the time and the commitment to take on particular work. It provides benefits in terms of time and quality. In addition, working as a team may improve the attractiveness of the work, which is another quality aspect.

Numerical involvement: "Minimize the number of departments, groups and persons involved in a business process". This will lead to less coordination problems, which makes more time available for the processing of cases. Reducing the number of departments may also split responsibilities, which has a positive impact on quality.

Case manager: "Appoint one person to be responsible for the handling of each type of case". The person, called *case manager*, is responsible for a specific order or customer. The difference with case assignment is that the emphasis is on management of the process—not its execution. The most important aim is to improve upon the external quality. The business process will become more transparent from the viewpoint of a customer: the case manager provides a single point of contact. This, in general, positively influences customer satisfaction. It may also have a positive effect on the internal quality of the business process, as someone is accountable for and committed to correcting mistakes.

The second set relates to the organizational population and the resources being involved in terms of their type and number. This category includes three heuristics:

Extra resources   "If capacity is insufficient, increase the available number of resources". This heuristic aims at extending capacity to reduce queue time. It may also help to implement a more flexible assignment policy.

Specialize "Consider deepening the skills of participants". Participants in a process may be turned into specialists. They may work quicker and deliver higher quality than less specialized resources due to their experience.

Empower "Give workers decision-making authority instead of relying on middle management". In traditional business processes, substantial time may be spent on authorizing the outcomes of activities that have been performed by others. If workers are empowered to take decisions autonomously, this may result in smoother operations with lower throughput times. The reduction of middle management from the business process also reduces labor cost.

A.5 Information Heuristics

The information category describes redesign heuristics related to the information that is being processed within the business process. It covers two heuristics:

Control addition: "Check the completeness and correctness of incoming materials and check the output before it is sent to customers". This heuristic promotes the addition of controls to a business process in order to increase quality.

Buffering: "Instead of requesting information from an external source, buffer it and subscribe to updates". Obtaining information from other parties is time-consuming. By having information directly available when required, throughput times may be substantially reduced. This heuristic can be compared to the caching principle that microprocessors apply.

A.6 Technology Heuristics

This category describes redesign heuristics related to the technology the business process utilizes. It includes activity automation and integral technology.

Activity automation: "Consider automating activities". Automation improves processing time and provides more predictable results at lower cost. Instead of fully automating an activity, it may also be considered to provide automated support to process participants.

Integral technology: "Elevate physical constraints in a business process by applying new technology". In general, new technology can offer all kinds of positive effects across an entire business process. For example, a BPMS may support the coordination of all its activities; a Document Management System, in its turn, will open up to all participants the same information available on cases. The major effect would be a better quality of service.

A.7 External Environment Heuristics

The external environment category contains heuristics that try to improve upon the collaboration and communication with third parties. There are three heuristics in this category:

Trusted party: "Use the insights of a trusted party". Some decisions are generic and standardized to the extent that other parties will get the same result for the same input data. An example is the creditworthiness of a customer that bank A wants to establish. If a customer can present a recent creditworthiness certificate of bank B, then bank A may be likely to accept it. Relying on a trusted party reduces cost and may cut processing time.

Outsourcing: "Consider outsourcing a business process completely or parts of it". Another party may be more efficient in performing the same work, so it might as well perform it for the business process that is up for redesign. The obvious aim of outsourcing work is that it will generate less cost.

Interfacing: "Consider a standardized interface with customers and partners". A standardized interface diminishes the occurrence of mistakes, incomplete applications, or unintelligible information exchanges. This may yield better quality due to less errors and faster processing time.

The various heuristics are listed in Table A.1, which shows the main performance dimensions of the Devil's Quadrangle that are explicitly being targeted by each (+).

Table A.1 Performance dimensions for the redesign heuristics

	Time	Cost	Quality	Flexibility
Activity automation	+	+	+	.
Activity composition	+	.	.	.
Activity elimination	+	+	.	.
Buffering	+	.	.	.
Case assignment	+	.	+	.
Case manager	.	.	+	.
Case types	+	+	.	.
Case-based work	+	.	.	.
Centralization	+	.	.	+
Control addition	.	.	+	.
Control relocation	.	.	+	.
Contact reduction	+	.	+	.
Customer teams	+	.	+	.
Empower	+	+	.	+
Exception	+	.	.	+
Extra resources	+	.	.	+
Flexible assignment	+	.	+	+
Integral technology	.	.	+	.
Integration	+	+	.	.
Interfacing	+	.	+	.
Knock-out	.	+	.	.
Numerical involvement	+	.	+	.
Outsourcing	.	+	.	.
Parallelism	+	.	.	.
Resequencing	+	+	.	.
Specialize	+	.	+	.
Split responsibilities	+	.	+	.
Triage	.	.	+	.
Trusted party	+	+	.	.

References

1. W.M.P. van der Aalst, *Process Mining: Data Science in Action*, 2nd edn. (Springer, Berlin, 2016)
2. W.M.P. van der Aalst, Verification of Workflow Nets, in *Application and Theory of Petri Nets 1997*, ed. by P. Azéma, G. Balbo. Lecture Notes in Computer Science, vol. 1248 (Springer, Berlin, 1997), pp. 407–426
3. I. Adan, J. Resing, *Queueing Theory* (Eindhoven University of Technology, Eindhoven, 2002)
4. A. Adriansyah, Aligning observed and modeled behavior. PhD thesis, Eindhoven University of Technology (2014)
5. S. Aguirre, C. Parra, M. Sepúlveda, Methodological proposal for process mining projects. Int. J. Bus. Process Integr. Manag. **8**(2), 102–113 (2017)
6. D.M. Ahern, J. Armstrong, A. Clouse, J.R. Ferguson, W. Hayes, K.E. Nidiffer, *CMMI SCAMPI Distilled: Appraisals for Process Improvement* (Addison-Wesley, Reading, 2005)
7. T. Allweyer, *BPMN 2.0: Introduction to the Standard for Business Process Modeling*, 2nd edn. Books on Demands (2016)
8. A. Alves, A. Arkin, S. Askary, C. Barreto, B. Bloch, F. Curbera, M. Ford, Y. Goland, A. Guizar, N. Kartha, C.K. Liu, R. Khalaf, D. Koenig, M. Marin, V. Mehta, S. Thatte, D. van der Rijn, P. Yendluri, A. Yiu, Web services business process execution language version 2.0. Committee specification 31 january 2007, OASIS, 2007
9. R. Anupindi, S. Chopra, S.D. Deshmukh, J.A. van Mieghem, E. Zemel, *Managing Business Process Flows* (Prentice Hall, New York, 1999)
10. A. Augusto, R. Conforti, M. Dumas, M. La Rosa, Split miner: Discovering accurate and simple business process models from event logs, in *Proceedings of the IEEE International Conference on Data Mining (ICDM)* (IEEE Computer Society, 2017)
11. A. Augusto, R. Conforti, M. Dumas, M. La Rosa, G. Bruno, Automated discovery of structured process models: Discover structured vs. discover and structure, in *Proc. of the 35th International Conference on Conceptual Modeling (ER)*, Cham, Switzerland, 2016 (Springer, Berlin, 2016)
12. A. Augusto, R. Conforti, M. Dumas, M. La Rosa, F.M. Maggi, A. Marrella, M. Mecella, A. Soo, Automated discovery of process models from event logs: Review and benchmark. CoRR, abs/1705.02288 (2017)
13. W. Bandara, S. Bailey, P. Mathiesen, J. McCarthy, C. Jones, Enterprise business process management in the public sector: The case of the Department of Human Services (DHS) Australia. J. Inf. Technol. Teaching Cases (2017)
14. W. Bandara, H. Opsahl, Developing organization-wide BPM capabilities in an SME: the approaches used, challenges and outcomes. J. Inf. Technol. Teaching Cases (2017)

© Springer-Verlag GmbH Germany, part of Springer Nature 2018
M. Dumas et al., *Fundamentals of Business Process Management*,
https://doi.org/10.1007/978-3-662-56509-4

15. G. Barnett, Robotic process automation: Adding to the process transformation toolkit. White paper IT0022-0005, Ovum Consulting, 2015

16. A.M. Bassam Alkharashi, L. Jesus, R. Tregear, *Establishing the Office of Business Process Management* (Leonardo Consulting, Brisbane, 2010)

17. J. Becker, M. Kugeler, M. Rosemann, *Process Management: A Guide for the Design of Business Processes* (Springer, Berlin, 2011)

18. J. Becker, M. Rosemann, C. von Uthmann, Guidelines of Business Process Modeling, in *Business Process Management. Models, Techniques, and Empirical Studies*, ed. by W.M.P. van der Aalst, J. Desel, A. Oberweis (Springer, Berlin, 2000), pp. 30–49

19. M. Beer, R.A. Eisenstat, B. Spector, Why change programs don't produce change. Harv. Bus. Rev. (November-December 1990)

20. B.L. Berg, H. Lune, *Qualitative Research Methods for the Social Sciences* (Pearson, Boston, 2004)

21. J.D. Blackburn, Time-based competition: White-collar activities. Bus. Horiz. **35**(4), 96–101 (1992)

22. N. Brand, H. van der Kolk, *Workflow Analysis and Design (In Dutch)* (Kluwer Bedrijfsweten-schappen, Deventer, 1995)

23. R.T. Burlton, Delivery business strategy through process management, in *Handbook on Business Process Management 2*, 2nd edn., ed. by J. vom Brocke, M. Rosemann (Springer, Berlin, 2015)

24. T. Chamorro-Premuzic, Why group brainstorming is a waste of time. Harv. Bus. Rev. (2015)

25. M.B. Chrissis, M. Konrad, S. Shrum, *CMMI for Development: Guidelines for Process Integration and Product Improvement*, 3rd edn. (Addison-Wesley, Reading, 2011)

26. J.G. Clark, D.B. Walz, J.L. Wynekoop, Identifying exceptional application software developers: A comparison of students and professionals. Commun. Assoc. Inf. Syst. **11**(1), 8 (2003)

27. D. Cohn, R. Hull, Business artifacts: A data-centric approach to modeling business operations and processes. IEEE Data Eng. Bull. **32**(3), 3–9 (2009)

28. S. Conger, Six sigma and business process management, in *Handbook of Business Process Management 1*, ed. by J. vom Brocke, M. Rosemann (Springer, Berlin, 2015), pp. 127–146

29. T. Curran, G. Keller, *SAP R/3 Business Blueprint: Understanding the Business Process Reference Model* (Prentice Hall, Upper Saddle River, 1997)

30. T.H. Davenport, *Process Innovation: Reengineering Work Through Information Technology* (Harvard Business School Press, Boston, 1993)

31. T.H. Davenport, J.E. Short, The new industrial engineering: information technology and business process redesign. Sloan Manag. Rev. **31**(4), 11–27 (1990)

32. R.B. Davis, E. Brabander, *ARIS Design Platform: Getting Started with BPM* (Springer, Berlin, 2007)

33. T. de Bruin, Business process management: theory on progression and maturity. PhD thesis, Queensland University of Technology, Brisbane, Australia (2009)

34. T. de Bruin, G. Doebeli, An organizational approach to bpm: The experience of an australian transport provider, in *Handbook on Business Process Management 2*, 2nd edn., ed. by J. vom Brocke, M. Rosemann (Springer, Berlin, 2015)

35. T. de Bruin, M. Rosemann, Using the delphi technique to identify bpm capability areas, in *Proceedings of the 18th Australasian Conference on Information Systems* (Association for Information Systems, 2007)

36. J. Dick, E. Hull, K. Jackson, *Requirements Engineering*, 4th edn. (Springer, Berlin, 2017)

37. J.M. Digman, Personality structure: Emergence of the five-factor model. Annu. Rev. Psychol. **41**(1), 417–440 (1990)

38. R. Dijkman, I. Vanderfeesten, H.A. Reijers, Business process architectures: overview, comparison and framework. Enterp. Inf. Syst. **10**(2), 129–158 (2016)

39. M. Dumas, L. Garcia-Banuelos, M. La Rosa, R. Uba, Fast detection of exact clones in business process model repositories. Inf. Syst. **38**(4), 619–633 (2013)

40. M. Dumas, M. La Rosa, J. Mendling, R. Mäesalu, H.A. Reijers, N. Semenenko, Understanding business process models: the costs and benefits of structuredness, in *International Conference on Advanced Information Systems Engineering* (Springer, Berlin, 2012), pp. 31–46

41. W. Eckerson, *Performance Dashboards: Measuring, Monitoring, and Managing Your Business*, 2nd edn. (Wiley, New York, 2010)

42. C.C. Ekanayake, M. La Rosa, A.H.M. ter Hofstede, M.C. Fauvet, Fragment-based version management for repositories of business process models, in *Proceedings of the International Conference on Cooperative Information Systems (CoopIS)*. Lecture Notes in Computer Science, vol. 7044 (Springer, Berlin, 2011), pp. 20–37

43. D.J. Elzinga, T. Horak, C.Y. Lee, C. Bruner, Business process management: survey and methodology. IEEE Trans. Eng. Manag. **42**(2), 119–128 (1995)

44. G. Engels, A. Forster, E. Heckel, S. Thone, Process Modeling Using UML, in *Process-Aware Information Systems*, chapter 5, ed. by M. Dumas, W.M.P. van der Aalst, A.H.M. ter Hofstede (Wiley, New York, 2005)

45. T. Erl, A. Karmarkar, P. Walmsley, H. Haas, *Web Service Contract Design and Versioning for SOA* (Prentice Hall, New York, 2008)

46. E. Forrester, B. Buteau, S. Shrum (Author), *CMMI for Services: Guidelines for Superior Service*, 2nd edn. (Addison-Wesley, Reading, 2011)

47. P. Franz, M. Kirchmer, *Value-Driven Business Process Management* (McGraw-Hill, New York, 2012)

48. P.J.M. Frederiks, T.P. van der Weide, Information modeling: The process and the required competencies of its participants. Data Knowl. Eng. **58**(1), 4–20 (2006)

49. J. Freund, B. Rücker, *Real-Life BPMN: With introductions to CMMN and DMN*, 3rd edn. (CreateSpace Independent Publishing Platform, 2016)

50. V. Frolov, D. Megel, W. Bandara, Y. Sun, L. Ma, Building an ontology and process architecture for engineering asset management, in *Proceedings of the 4th World Congress on Engineering Asset Management (WCEAM)*, Athens, Greece, September 2009 (Springer, Berlin, 2009)

51. D. Fürstenau, *Process Performance Measurement* (GRIN, Santa Cruz, 2008)

52. B. Gallagher, M. Phillips, K. Richter, S. Shrum, *CMMI for Acquisition: Guidelines for Improving the Acquisition of Products and Services*, 2nd edn. (Addison-Wesley, Reading, 2011)

53. L. García-Bañuelos, A. Ponomarev, M. Dumas, I. Weber, Optimized execution of business processes on blockchain, in *Proceedings of the 15th International Conference on Business Process Management (BPM)*. Lecture Notes in Computer Science, vol. 10445 (2017), pp. 130–146

54. L. García-Bañuelos, N.R.T.P. van Beest, M. Dumas, M. La Rosa, Complete and interpretable conformance checking of business processes. IEEE Trans. Softw. Eng. (2017). https://doi-org.vu-nl.idm.oclc.org/10.1109/TSE.2017.2668418

55. R. Gill, Change management–or change leadership? J. Change Manag. **3**(4), 307–318 (2002)

56. E.M. Goldratt, *The Goal: A Process of Ongoing Improvement* (North River Press, Great Barrington, 1992)

57. B. Grabot, A. Mayère, I. Bazet, *ERP Systems and Organisational Change: A Socio-Technical Insight* (Springer, Berlin, 2008)

58. A. Greasley, A redesign of a road traffic accident reporting system using business process simulation. Bus. Process Manag. J. **10**(6), 635–644 (2004)

59. M. Hammer, Reengineering work: Don't automate, obliterate. Harv. Bus. Rev. **68**(4), 104–112 (1990)

60. M. Hammer, *Beyond Reengineering: How the Process-Centered Organization Is Changing Our Work and Our Lives* (HarperBusiness, New York, 1997)

61. M. Hammer, What is business process management, in *Handbook of Business Process Management 1*, ed. by M. Rosemann, J. vom Brocke (Springer, Berlin, 2015), pp. 3–16

62. M. Hammer, J. Champy, *Reengineering the Corporation: A Manifesto for Business Revolution* (Harpercollins, New York, 1993)
63. P. Hanafizadeh, M. Moosakhani, J. Bakhshi, Selecting the best strategic practices for business process redesign. Bus. Process Manag. J. **15**(4), 609–627 (2009)
64. P. Harmon, Analyzing activities. BPTrends Newsl. **1**(4) (2003). http://www.bptrends.com
65. P. Harmon, *Business Process Change: A Guide for Business Managers and BPM and Six Sigma Professionals*, 2nd edn. (Morgan Kaufmann, San Mateo, 2007)
66. P. Harmon, R. Tregear, *Questioning BPM?* (Meghan-Kiffer Press, Tampa, 2016)
67. A.H.M. ter Hofstede, W.M.P. van der Aalst, M. Adams, N. Russell, (eds.), *Modern Business Process Automation: YAWL and Its Support Environment* (Springer, Berlin, 2010)
68. D. Hollingsworth, The Workflow Reference Model. TC00-1003 Issue 1.1, Workflow Management Coalition, 24 November 1994
69. D. Hollingsworth, The Workflow Reference Model: 10 Years On, in *The Workflow Handbook 2014*, ed. by L. Fischer (Workflow Management Coalition, Cohasset, 2004), pp. 295–312
70. IEEE TaskForce on Process Mining, Process Mining Manifesto. http://www.win.tue.nl/ieeetfpm/doku.php?id=shared:process_mining_manifesto. Accessed October 2017, 2011
71. J. Jeston, J. Nelis, *Business Process Management: Practical Guidelines to Successful Implementations*, 3rd edn. (Routledge, New York, 2014)
72. F. Johannsen, S. Leist, G. Zellner, Implementing six sigma for improving business processes at an automotive bank, in *Handbook of Business Process Management 1*, ed. by J. vom Brocke, M. Rosemann (Springer, Berlin, 2015), pp. 393–416
73. R.S. Kaplan, D.P. Norton, The balanced scorecard - measures that drive performance. Harv. Bus. Rev. **70**(1), 71–79 (1992)
74. R. Kegan, L.L. Lahey, The real reason people won't change. *HBR's 10 Must Reads on Change*, pp. 77 (2001)
75. W.D. Kelton, R.P. Sadowski, N.B. Swets, *Simulation with Arena*, 5th edn. (McGraw-Hill, New York, 2009)
76. G. Kerpedzhiev, U. König, M. Röglinger, M. Rosemann, Business process management in the digital age. BPTrends (July 2017)
77. W.J. Kettinger, J.T.C. Teng, S. Guha, Business process change: a study of methodologies, techniques, and tools. MIS Q., 55–80 (1997)
78. M. Kirchmer, P. Franz, The chief process officer: A role to drive value. White paper, Accenture, 2012
79. M. Kloppenburg, J. Kettenbohrer, D. Beimborn, M. Bögle, Leading 20,000+ employees with a process-oriented management system: Insights into process management at lufthansa technik group, in *Business Process Management Cases*, ed. by J. vom Brocke, J. Mendling (Springer, Berlin, 2018), pp. 505–520
80. C.N. Knaflic, *Storytelling with Data: A Data Visualization Guide for Business Professionals* (Wiley, New York, 2015)
81. J.P. Kofter, Leading change: why transformation efforts fail. Harv. Bus. Rev. **92**, 107 (2007)
82. A. Kovačič, G. Hauc, B. Buh, M.I. Štemberger, Bpm adoption and business transformation at snaga, a public company: Critical success factors for five stages of bpm, in *Business Process Management Cases*, ed. by J. vom Brocke, J. Mendling (Springer, Berlin, 2018), pp. 77–89
83. J. Krogstie, *Quality in Business Process Modeling* (Springer, Berlin, 2016)
84. M. La Rosa, M. Dumas, C.C. Ekanayake, L. Garcia-Banuelos, J. Recker, Detecting approximate clones in business process model repositories. Inf. Syst. **49**, 102–125 (2015)
85. M. Laguna, J. Marklund, *Business Process Modeling, Simulation and Design* (Prentice Hall, New York, 2004)
86. S.J.J. Leemans, D. Fahland, W.M.P. van der Aalst, *Discovering Block-Structured Process Models from Event Logs Containing Infrequent Behaviour* (Springer, Cham, 2014), pp. 66–78
87. H. Leopold, R.-H. Eid-Sabbagh, J. Mendling, L.G. Azevedo, F.A. Baião, Detection of naming convention violations in process models for different languages. Decis. Support Syst. **56**, 310–325 (2013)

88. M. Leyer, D. Heckl, J. Moormann, Process performance measurement. *Handbook on Business Process Management, Volume 2* (2015), pp. 227–241

89. F. Leymann, D. Roller, *Production Workflow - Concepts and Techniques* (Prentice Hall, New York, 2000)

90. S. Limam Mansar, H.A. Reijers, F. Ounnar, Development of a decision-making strategy to improve the efficiency of bpr. Expert Syst. Appl. **36**(2), 3248–3262 (2009)

91. O.I. Lindland, G. Sindre, A. Sølvberg, Understanding quality in conceptual modeling. IEEE Softw. **11**(2), 42–49 (1994)

92. N. Lohmann, Correcting deadlocking service choreographies using a simulation-based graph edit distance, in *International Conference on Business Process Management*, vol. 8 (Springer, Berlin, 2008), pp. 132–147

93. P. Lohmann, M. zur Muehlen, Business process management skills and roles: An investigation of the demand and supply side of BPM professionals, in *Proceedings of the 13th International Conference on Business Process Management (BPM)*. Lecture Notes in Computer Science, vol. 9253 (Springer, Berlin, 2015), pp. 317–332

94. A.V. Looy, *Business Process Maturity. A Comparative Study on a Sample of Business Process Maturity Models* (Springer, Berlin, 2014)

95. O. López-Pintado, L. García-Bañuelos, M. Dumas, I. Weber, Caterpillar: A blockchain-based business process management system, in *Proceedings of the BPM Demo Track and BPM Dissertation Award co-located with 15th International Conference on Business Process Modeling (BPM 2017), Barcelona, Spain, September 13, 2017*, ed. by R. Clarisó, H. Leopold, J. Mendling, W.M.P. van der Aalst, A. Kumar, Br.T. Pentland, M. Weske. CEUR Workshop Proceedings, vol. 1920 (2017). CEUR-WS.org

96. J. Luftman, Strategic alignment maturity, in *Handbook on Business Process Management 2*, 2nd edn., ed. by J. vom Brocke, M. Rosemann (Springer, Berlin, 2015)

97. M. Malinova, A language for designing process maps. PhD thesis, WU Vienna University of Economics and Business (2016)

98. M. Malinova, B. Hribar, J. Mendling, A framework for assessing bpm success, in *Proceedings of the 22nd European Conference on Information Systems* (Association for Information Systems, 2014)

99. M. Malinova, H. Leopold, J. Mendling, An explorative study for process map design, in *Information Systems Engineering in Complex Environments - CAiSE Forum 2014, Thessaloniki, Greece, June 16–20, 2014, Selected Extended Papers*, ed. by S. Nurcan, E. Pimenidis. Lecture Notes in Business Information Processing, vol. 204 (Springer, Berlin, 2015), pp. 36–51

100. M. Malinova, J. Mendling, The effect of process map design quality on process management success, in *21st European Conference on Information Systems, ECIS 2013, Utrecht, The Netherlands, June 5–8, 2013* (2013), p. 160

101. R.L. Manganelli, M.M. Klein, American Management Association, *The Reengineering Handbook: A Step-by-Step Guide to Business Transformation* (Amacom, New York, 1994)

102. S.L. Mansar, H.A. Reijers, Best practices in business process redesign: validation of a redesign framework. Comput. Ind. **56**(5), 457–471 (2005)

103. S.L. Mansar, H.A. Reijers, Best practices in business process redesign: use and impact. Bus. Process Manag. J. **13**(2), 193–213 (2007)

104. N. Martin, B. Depaire, A. Caris, The use of process mining in business process simulation model construction - structuring the field. Bus. Inf. Syst. Eng. **58**(1), 73–87 (2016)

105. N. Martin, M. Swennen, B. Depaire, M. Jans, A. Caris, K. Vanhoof, Retrieving batch organisation of work insights from event logs. Decis. Support Syst. **100**, 119–128 (2017)

106. A. McAfee, Pharmacy service improvement at cvs (a). Harv. Bus. Rev. Case Stud. (2005)

107. K. McCormack, The development of a measure of business process orientation and its relationship to organizational performance, April 1999. Online tutorial available at http://www.prosci.com/mccormack.htm

108. J. Mendling, *Metrics for Process Models: Empirical Foundations of Verification, Error Prediction, and Guidelines for Correctness.* Lecture Notes in Business Information Processing, vol. 6 (Springer, Berlin, 2008)
109. J. Mendling, Empirical studies in process model verification, in *Transactions on Petri Nets and Other Models of Concurrency II, Special Issue on Concurrency in Process-Aware Information Systems*, vol. 5460 (2009), 208–224
110. J. Mendling, H.A. Reijers, W.M.P. van der Aalst, Seven process modeling guidelines (7pmg). Inf. Softw. Technol. **52**(2), 127–136 (2010)
111. J. Mendling, L. Sánchez-González, F. García, M. La Rosa, Thresholds for error probability measures of business process models. J. Syst. Softw. **85**(5), 1188–1197 (2012)
112. J. Mendling, M. Strembeck, J. Recker, Factors of process model comprehension - findings from a series of experiments. Decis. Support Syst. **53**(1), 195–206 (2012)
113. J. Mendling, I. Weber, W.M.P. van der Aalst, J. vom Brocke, C. Cabanillas, F. Daniel, S. Debois, C. Di Ciccio, M. Dumas, S. Dustdar, A. Gal, L. García-Bañuelos, G. Governatori, R. Hull, M. La Rosa, H. Leopold, F. Leymann, J. Recker, M. Reichert, H.A. Reijers, S. Rinderle-Ma, A. Rogge-Solti, M. Rosemann, S. Schulte, M.P. Singh, T. Slaats, M. Staples, B. Weber, M. Weidlich, M. Weske, X. Xu, L. Zhu, Blockchains for business process management - challenges and opportunities. CoRR, abs/1704.03610 (2017)
114. W. Mertens, J. Recker, T.-F. Kummer, T. Kohlborn, S. Viaene, Constructive deviance as a driver for performance in retail. J. Retail. Consum. Serv. **30**, 193–203 (2016)
115. N. Modig, P. Ahlström, *This Is Lean: Resolving the Efficiency Paradox* (Rheologica, Stockholm, 2012)
116. A. Møller, M.I. Schwartzbach, *An Introduction to XML and Web Technologies* (Addison-Wesley, Reading, 2006)
117. D. Müller, M. Reichert, J. Herbst, A new paradigm for the enactment and dynamic adaptation of data-driven process structures, in *Advanced Information Systems Engineering* (Springer, Berlin, 2008), pp. 48–63
118. J. Munoz-Gama, *Conformance Checking and Diagnosis in Process Mining: Comparing Observed and Modeled Processes* (Springer, Berlin, 2016)
119. M. Netjes, R.S. Mans, H.A. Reijers, W.M.P. van der Aalst, R.J.B. Vanwersch, Bpr best practices for the healthcare domain, in *Business Process Management Workshops* (Springer, Berlin, 2010), pp. 605–616
120. Object Management Group, Unified Modeling Language (UML) Version 2.5, 2015
121. P. O'Neill, A.S. Sohal, Business process reengineering a review of recent literature. Technovation **19**(9), 571–581 (1999)
122. A. Osterwalder, Y. Pigneur, *Business Model Generation: A Handbook for Visionaries, Game Changers, and Challengers* (Wiley, New York, 2010)
123. A. Ottensooser, A. Fekete, H.A. Reijers, J. Mendling, C. Menictas, Making sense of business process descriptions: An experimental comparison of graphical and textual notations. J. Syst. Softw. **85**(3), 596–606 (2012)
124. M.A. Ould, *Business Process Management: A Rigorous Approach* (British Informatics Society Ltd., Swindon, 2005)
125. M.C. Paulk, C.V. Weber, B. Curtis, M.B. Chrissis, *The Capability Maturity Model: Guidelines for Improving the Software Process* (Addison-Wesley, Reading, 1994)
126. M. Petre, Why looking isn't always seeing: Readership skills and graphical programming. Commun. ACM **38**(6), 33–44 (1995)
127. K. Pohl, *Requirements Engineering: Fundamentals, Principles, and Techniques* (Springer, Berlin, 2010)
128. M.E. Porter, *Competitive Advantage: Creating and Sustaining Superior Performance* (The Free Press, New York, 1985)
129. G. Redding, M. Dumas, A.H.M. ter Hofstede, A. Iordachescu, A flexible, object-centric approach for business process modelling. SOCA **4**(3), 191–201 (2010)
130. M. Reichert, B. Weber, *Enabling Flexibility in Process-Aware Information Systems* (Springer, Berlin, 2012)

131. H.A. Reijers, Product-based design of business processes applied within the financial services. J. Res. Pract. Inf. Technol. **34**(2), 110–122 (2002)
132. H.A. Reijers, *Design and Control of Workflow Processes: Business Process Management for the Service Industry* (Springer, Berlin, 2003)
133. H.A. Reijers, T. Freytag, J. Mendling, A. Eckleder, Syntax highlighting in business process models. Decis. Support Syst. **51**(3), 339–349 (2011)
134. H.A Reijers, S. Limam, W.M.P. van der Aalst, Product-based workflow design. J. Manag. Inf. Syst. **20**(1), 229–262 (2003)
135. H.A. Reijers, S.L. Mansar, Best practices in business process redesign: an overview and qualitative evaluation of successful redesign heuristics. Omega **33**(4), 283–306 (2005)
136. H.A. Reijers, J. Mendling, A study into the factors that influence the understandability of business process models. IEEE Trans. Syst. Man Cybern. A **41**(3), 449–462 (2011)
137. H.A. Reijers, J. Mendling, R.M. Dijkman, Human and automatic modularizations of process models to enhance their comprehension. Inf. Syst. **36**(5), 881–897 (2011)
138. H.A. Reijers, I.T.P. Vanderfeesten, W.M.P. van der Aalst, The effectiveness of workflow management systems: A longitudinal study. Int. J. Inf. Manag. **36**(1), 126–141 (2016)
139. C. Reisert, S. Zelt, J. Wacker, How to move from paper to impact in business process management: The journey of sap, in *Business Process Management Cases*, ed. by J. vom Brocke, J. Mendling (Springer, Berlin, 2018)
140. S.-H. Rhee, N.W. Cho, H. Bae, Increasing the efficiency of business processes using a theory of constraints. Inf. Syst. Front. **12**(4), 443–455 (2010)
141. L. Richardson, S. Ruby, *RESTful Web Services* (O'Reilly Media, Inc., Sebastopol, 2008)
142. J.J. Rooney, L.N. Vanden Heuvel, Root cause analysis for beginners. Qual. Prog., 45–53 (2004)
143. M. La Rosa, A.H.M. ter Hofstede, P. Wohed, H.A. Reijers, J. Mendling, W.M.P. van der Aalst, Managing process model complexity via concrete syntax modifications. IEEE Trans. Ind. Inf. **7**(2), 255–265 (2011)
144. M. La Rosa, P. Wohed, J. Mendling, A.H.M. ter Hofstede, H.A. Reijers, W.M.P. van der Aalst, Managing process model complexity via abstract syntax modifications. IEEE Trans. Ind. Inf. **7**(4), 614–629 (2011)
145. M. Rosemann, Potential pitfalls of process modeling: part a. Bus. Process Manag. J. **12**(2), 249–254 (2006)
146. M. Rosemann, Potential pitfalls of process modeling: part b. Bus. Process Manag. J. **12**(3), 377–384 (2006)
147. M. Rosemann, A. Hjalmarsson, M. Lind, J. Recker, Four facets of a process modeling facilitator, in *Proceedings of the 32nd International Conference on Information Systems* (Association for Information Systems, 2011)
148. M. Rosemann, The nestt: Rapid process redesign at queensland university of technology, in *Business Process Management Cases* (Springer, Berlin, 2018), pp. 169–185
149. M. Rosemann, T. de Bruin, Application of a holistic model for determining bpm maturity, in *Proceedings of the AIM Pre-ICIS Workshop on Process Management and Information Systems* (Actes du 3e colloque Pre-ICIS de l'AIM, 2004)
150. M. Rosemann, T. de Bruin, Towards a business process management maturity model, in *Proceedings of the 13th European Conference on Information Systems* (Association for Information Systems, 2005)
151. M. Rosemann, T. de Bruin, Towards understanding strategic alignment of business process management, in *Proceedings of the 17th Australasian Conference on Information Systems* (Association for Information Systems, 2006)
152. A. Rozinat, W.M.P. van der Aalst, Conformance checking of processes based on monitoring real behavior. Inf. Syst. **33**(1), 64–95 (2008)
153. G.A. Rummler, A.P. Brache, *Improving Performance: Managing the White Space on the Organizational Chart* (Jossey-Bass, San Francisco, 1990)

154. G.A. Rummler, A.J. Ramias, A framework for defining and designing the structure of work, in *Handbook of Business Process Management 1*, ed. by M. Rosemann, J. vom Brocke (Springer, Berlin, 2015), pp. 81–104

155. N. Russell, W.M.P. van der Aalst, A.H.M. ter Hofstede, *Workflow Patterns: The Definitive Guide* (MIT Press, Cambridge, 2016)

156. A.-W. Scheer, *ARIS Business Process Modelling* (Springer, New York, 2000)

157. K.D. Schenk, N.P. Vitalari, K.S. Davis, Differences between novice and expert systems analysts: What do we know and what do we do? J. Manag. Inf. Syst. **15**(1), 9–50 (1998)

158. T. Schmiedel, J. vom Brocke, J. Recker, Culture in business process management: How cultural values determine bpm success, in *Handbook on Business Process Management 2*, 2nd edn., ed. by J. vom Brocke, M. Rosemann (Springer, Berlin, 2015)

159. A. Schwegmann, M. Laske, As-is modeling and process analysis, in *Process Management: A Guide for the Design of Business Processes*, ed. by J. Becker, M. Kugeler, M. Rosemann (Springer, Berlin, 2011), pp. 133–156

160. I. Seidman, *Interviewing as Qualitative Research: A Guide for Researchers in Education and the Social Sciences* (Teachers College Press, New York, 2006)

161. A. Sharp, P. McDermott, *Workflow Modeling: Tools for Process Improvement and Applications Development*, 2nd edn. (Artech House, Norwood, 2008)

162. A. Shtub, R. Karni, *ERP: The Dynamics of Supply Chain and Process Management* (Springer, Berlin, 2010)

163. B. Silver, *BPMN Method and Style*, 2nd edn. (Cody-Cassidy Press, Aptos, 2011)

164. B. Silver, A. Sayles, *DMN Method and Style: The Practitioner's Guide to Decision Modeling with Business Rules* (Cody-Cassidy Press, Aptos, 2016)

165. H.L. Sirkin, P. Keenan, A. Jackson, The hard side of change management. Harv. Bus. Rev. **83**(10), 108 (2005)

166. Software AG, *Transparent Processes Lead to Improved Customer Service and Regulatory Compliance. Reference Story* (Software AG, 2016). https://tinyurl.com/y8j6lgwh

167. A. Spanyi, The governance of business process management, in *Handbook on Business Process Management 2*, 2nd edn., ed. by J. vom Brocke, M. Rosemann (Springer, Berlin, 2015)

168. G. Steinbauer, M. Ossberger, D. Dorazin, Wiener linien: Infrastruktur für den öffentlichen verkehr bereitstellen: Prozessmanagement mit hoher komplexität, in *Prozessmanagement individuell umgesetzt*, ed. by E.-M. Kern (Springer, Berlin, 2012), pp. 221–236

169. J. Stirna, A. Persson, K. Sandkuhl, Participative Enterprise Modeling: Experiences and Recommendations, in *Proceedings of the 19th Conference on Advanced Information Systems Engineering (CAiSE 2007)*, ed. by J. Krogstie, A.L. Opdahl, G. Sindre. Lecture Notes in Computer Science, vol. 4495, Trondheim, Norway, 2007 (Springer, Berlin, 2007), pp. 546–560

170. D. Straker, *A Toolbook for Quality Improvement and Problem Solving* (Prentice Hall, New York, 1995)

171. S. Suriadi, M.T. Wynn, C. Ouyang, A.H.M. ter Hofstede, N.J. van Dijk, Understanding process behaviours in a large insurance company in australia: A case study, in *Proceedings of the 25th International Conference on Advanced Information Systems Engineering (CAiSE)*. Lecture Notes in Computer Science, vol. 7908 (Springer, Berlin, 2013), pp. 449–464

172. K.D. Swenson, *Mastering the Unpredictable: How Adaptive Case Management Will Revolutionize the Way That Knowledge Workers Get Things Done* (Meghan-Kiffer Press, Tampa, 2010)

173. R. Tregear, *Reimagining Management* (Blurb, San Francisco, 2017)

174. J.M. Utterback, W.J. Abernathy, A dynamic model of process and product innovation. Omega **3**(6), 639–656 (1975)

175. N.R.T.P. van Beest, M. Dumas, L. García-Bañuelos, M. La Rosa, Log delta analysis: Interpretable differencing of business process event logs, in *Proceedings of the 13th International Conference on Business Process Management (BPM)* (Springer, Berlin, 2015), pp. 386–405

176. W.M.P. van der Aalst K. Van Hee, *Workflow Management: Models, Methods, and Systems* (MIT Press, Cambridge, 2004)
177. W.M.P. van der Aalst, Business process simulation survival guide, in *Handbook of Business Process Management 1*, ed. by J. vom Brocke, M. Rosemann (Springer, Berlin, 2015), pp. 337–370
178. W.M.P. van der Aalst, M. Rosemann, M. Dumas, Deadline-based escalation in process-aware information systems. Decis. Support Syst. **43**(2), 492–511 (2007)
179. W.M.P. van der Aalst, M. Weske, D. Grünbauer, Case handling: a new paradigm for business process support. Data Knowl. Eng. **53**(2), 129–162 (2005)
180. M.L. van Eck, X. Lu, S.J.J. Leemans, W.M.P. van der Aalst, PM ^2 : A process mining project methodology, in *Proceedings of the International Conference on Advanced Information Systems Engineering (CAiSE)* (Springer, Berlin, 2015), pp. 297–313
181. A. van Lamsweerde, *Requirements Engineering: From System Goals to UML Models to Software Specifications* (Wiley, New York, 2009)
182. I. Vanderfeesten, H.A. Reijers, W.M.P. van der Aalst, Product-based workflow support. Inf. Syst. **36**(2), 517–535 (2011)
183. R.J.B. Vanwersch, I. Vanderfeesten, E. Rietzschel, H.A. Reijers, Improving business processes: does anybody have an idea? in *International Conference on Business Process Management* (Springer, Berlin, 2015), pp. 3–18
184. R. Verganti, *Design-Driven Innovation* (Harvard Business School Press, Boston, 2009)
185. L. Verner, The challenge of process discovery. BPTrends (May 2004)
186. J. vom Brocke, M. Rosemann, *Handbook on Business Process Management 1: Introduction, Methods, and Information Systems*, 2nd edn., vol. 1 (Springer, Berlin, 2015)
187. J. vom Brocke, M. Rosemann, *Handbook on Business Process Management 2: Strategic Alignment, Governance, People and Culture*, 2nd edn., vol. 2 (Springer, Berlin, 2015)
188. J. vom Brocke, J. Mendling, *Business Process Management Cases: Digital Innovation and Business Transformation in Practice* (Springer, Berlin, 2018)
189. J. Vom Brocke, T. Schmiedel, J. Recker, P. Trkman, W. Mertens, S. Viaene, Ten principles of good business process management. Bus. Process Manag. J. **20**(4), 530–548 (2014)
190. K.W. Wagner, G. Patzak, *Performance Excellence-Der Praxisleitfaden zum effektiven Prozessmanagement* (Carl Hanser Verlag GmbH Co KG, KolbergerstraSSe 5, 2015)
191. I. Weber, X. Xu, R. Riveret, G. Governatori, A. Ponomarev, J. Mendling, Untrusted business process monitoring and execution using blockchain, in *Proceedings of the 14th International Conference on Business Process Management (BPM)*. Lecture Notes in Computer Science, vol. 9850 (Springer, Berlin, 2016), pp. 329–347
192. A. Weijters, J. Ribeiro, Flexible Heuristics Miner (FHM), in *Proceedings of the International Conference on Computational Intelligence and Data Mining (CIDM)* (IEEE Computer Society, 2011)
193. M. Weske, *Business Process Management: Concepts, Languages, Architectures*, 2nd edn. (Springer, Berlin, 2012)
194. B. Woliński, S. Bala, Comprehensive business process management at siemens: Implementing business process excellence, in *Business Process Management Cases*, ed. by J. vom Brocke, J. Mendling (Springer, Berlin, 2018), pp. 111–124
195. Workflow Patterns Initiative, Workflow Patterns Home Page, 2001. http://www.workflowpatterns.com
196. Y. Yang, M. Dumas, L. García-Bañuelos, A. Polyvyanyy, L. Zhang, Generalized aggregate quality of service computation for composite services. J. Syst. Softw. **85**(8), 1818–1830 (2012)
197. J.M. Zaha, A.P. Barros, M. Dumas, A.H.M. ter Hofstede, Let's Dance: A language for service behavior modeling, in *Proceedings of the OTM Conferences (1)*. Lecture Notes in Computer Science, vol. 4275 (Springer, Berlin, 2006), pp. 145–162
198. M. zur Muehlen, D.E. Wisnosky, J. Kindrick, Primitives: design guidelines and architecture for BPMN models, in *Proceedings of the Australasian Conference on Information Systems (ACIS)*, 2010

Index

Symbols
α-algorithm   432, 436, 437, 451, 467, 471
7FE   306, 307, 311–315
7PMG   *see* Seven Process Modeling
         Guidelines

A
ABC   *see* activity-based costing
accountability   54, 478
ACM   *see* adaptive case management system
active branch   88
activity   3, 76, 487
   call   106
   compensation   137
   concurrent   79
   dead   185, 186
   decision   80, 86, 91, 97, 126, 138
   label   77
   multi-instance   119
   mutually exclusive   79
activity-based costing   305, 447
activity-based modeling   211
actor   *see* process actor
ad hoc   *see* sub-process
ad hoc workflow system   345, 382
adaptive case management system   345, 347
allocation
   authorization   393
   by offer   393
   capability-based   393
   case handling   393
   deferred   393
   delegation   393
   direct   392

escalation   393
history-based   393
organizational   393
random   393
retain familiar   393
role-based   393
round-robin   393
separation of duties   359, 381, 393, 457
allocation by offer   *see* allocation
American Productivity and Quality Center
         46, 52, 53, 67
AND gateway   *see* gateway
application model   37
application system design   79
application-to-approval   2, 429
appraisal   494
approval   188
APQC   *see* American Productivity and
             Quality Center
Apromore   86, 194, 456, 459
ArchiMate   72
ARIS   37, 85, 115, 194
arrival rate   266, 270, 274, 276, 282, 286,
             289, 290
artifact   93, 211, 325
artifact-centric modeling   211, 339
as-is   17, 19, 22, 23, 159, 167, 172, 173, 205,
         206, 208, 253, 287, 292, 305, 322,
         477
association   96
   compensation   137
association rule   459
ATAMO procedure   305
authorization   *see* allocation

© Springer-Verlag GmbH Germany, part of Springer Nature 2018
M. Dumas et al., *Fundamentals of Business Process Management*,
https://doi.org/10.1007/978-3-662-56509-4

automated process discovery   166, 175, 420,
        427, 438, 450
automated task   *see* task

B
backoffice   59
balanced scorecard   36, 63, 418, 481, 483
BAM   *see* Business Activity Monitoring
batch   261
behavioral completeness   432
behavioral correctness   187
Benchmarking   309
bill-of-material   326
black box   *see* pool
block structure   187, 189, 272
blockchain   368
bottleneck   270, 444
BPM Advisory Board   485
BPM Center of Excellence   26, 485, 489,
        491, 500
BPM Group   *see* BPM Center of Excellence
BPM lifecycle   1, 6, 8, 16, 22–25, 27, 32, 75,
        79, 345, 413, 475–481, 484, 485,
        491
BPM maturity   475, 477, 479, 490, 491, 498,
        500
    assessment   493
BPM Maturity Model   478, 479, 492, 499
BPM program   232, 312, 475–478, 480, 482,
        483, 487, 489–492, 494, 495, 497
BPM Program Manager   485
BPM Steering Committee   485
BPMN   *see* Business Process Model and
        Notation
BPMS   *see* Business Process Management
        System
BPTrends   33, 311
branching probability   257, 282
Business Activity Monitoring   414
business fault   129
business impact   51
business model   36
Business Model Canvas   320
business object   4, 50, 93
business party   4, 97
Business Process Management System   15,
        263, 341, 343, 344, 371, 476
    architecture   347
    engine   348, 349, 375, 379, 385, 386,
        390, 394, 398, 402
    orchestration   347
    worklist handler   349, 372, 374, 375, 402,
        404

Business Process Model and Notation   18,
        45, 75, 115, 117, 381, 382, 411, 479
    components   92
    tool   85
Business Process Reengineering   319, 323
business strategy   35
Business Value Adding   214–218, 244, 249
BVA   *see* Business Value Adding

C
call center   59
capability area   479
Capability Maturity Model   500
Capability Maturity Model Integration   490,
        500
capability-based allocation   *see* allocation
case   162, 166, 222, 262, 273, 286, 317, 329,
        346–348, 350, 358, 359, 382, 384,
        414, 415, 421, 422, 487, 502
    identifier   422, 424, 425, 444, 462, 466
case handling   *see* allocation
Case Management Model and Notation   371,
        381, 382, 411
case management system   345, 347, 382
case manager   504
causal factor   236
    chart   253
cause-and-effect diagram   236
CEO   *see* Chief Executive Officer
CEP   *see* Complex Event Processing
certification   189
CFO   *see* Chief Financial Officer
change management   363
check-in   *see* work item
check-out   *see* work item
Chief Executive Officer   24, 483, 492
Chief Financial Officer   25, 492
Chief Information Officer   25, 493
Chief Operations Officer   24, 71, 255, 486
Chief Process and Innovation Officer   25,
        485, 492
Chief Process Officer   25, 485, 492
churn rate   61
CIO   *see* Chief Information Officer
CMM   *see* Capability Maturity Model
CMMI   *see* Capability Maturity Model
        Integration
CMMN   *see* Case Management Model and
        Notation
collaboration   *see* diagram
Colored Petri Nets   296
compensation   136
    handler   137

completeness   51, 188
Complex Event Processing   345
compliance   54
conceptual   *see* process
conformance checking   420
consistency   51
contributing factor   236
control step   216
conversation   *see* diagram
COO   *see* Chief Operations Officer
coordination   356
core process   41
cost   17, 29, 36, 59, 60, 255, 271, 303, 308,
      417, 422, 447
   incidental   60
   labor   60
   leadeship   481
   operational   60, 481
   production   59
CPIO   *see* Chief Process and Innovation
      Officer
CPN Tools   296
CPO   *see* Chief Process Officer
Critical Path Method   263
culture   26, 27, 478, 488
customer intimacy   481
customer journey   61
customer relationship   50
Customer Relationship Management system
      342, 396
customer satisfaction   60, 308
customer value proposition   36
cycle time   59, 255, 308, 316, 442
cycle time efficiency   262

D
data
   association   93, 388
   collection   120
   input   388
   object   18, 93–95, 97, 101, 102, 115, 120,
         146, 182, 184, 187, 286, 377–379,
         385–388, 403, 404, 407, 409
      state   94
   output   388
   store   94, 95, 182, 377
   type   386
      complex   386
      simple   386
data mapping   388
data model   37
data-flow diagram   18
database   12, 341

Database Management System   345
DBMS   *see* Database Management System
dead activity   *see* activity
deadlock   89, 91, 127–129, 185, 186, 203,
      371, 441
decision making process   478
Decision Model and Notation   139, 371, 394,
      411
   table   395
decision point   4
decomposition   43
default flow   *see* flow
deferred allocation   *see* allocation
deferred choice   *see* split, XOR, event-based
delegation   *see* allocation
Delphi   305
dependency graph   427, 428
Design-led Innovation   320
deviance mining   458
Devil's Quadrangle   303, 304, 315–317, 319,
      442, 464, 501
diagram
   choreography   157
   collaboration   101
   conversation   157
DICE   363
direct allocation   *see* allocation
division of labor   9, 10, 268
DMN   *see* Decision Model and Notation
DMN table   *see* Decision Model and
      Notation
DMS   *see* Document Management System
document analysis   165
Document Management System   343, 347
domain expert   160

E
ECM system   *see* Enterprise Content
      Management system
EDI   *see* Electronic Data Interchange
Electronic Data Interchange   219
end-to-end process   49
enhanced process model   421
Enterprise Application Integration   361
enterprise architecture   37
Enterprise Content Management system   344
Enterprise Resource Planning system   14,
      342, 372
EPCs   *see* Event-driven Process Chains
equipment   96
ERP system   *see* Enterprise Resource
      Planning system
error code   388

error rate   255
escalation   *see* allocation
event   3, 76, 388, 394
    boundary   130
    catching   124
    compensate   137
    conditional   138
    end   76, 129
    error   130, 387
    intermediate   123
    interrupting   130
    label   77
    message   102, 123, 390
    non-interrupting   133
    signal   134, 387, 390
    terminate   129
    throwing   124
    timer   124
event class   422
event filter   431
event log   166, 414, 415, 422, 463
    filtering   429
event pair filter   431
event-based gateway   *see* split
Event-driven Process Chains   18, 114, 115
evidence-based discovery   175
exception   129, 140, 166, 170, 358, 362, 368,
        378, 413, 421, 503
    complex   134
    external   132
    handler   182, 378
    internal   130
    unsolicited   132
exception flow   *see* flow
executable   *see* process
execution engine   *see* Business Process
        Management System
execution log   273, 282, 351, 358, 365, 448
execution property   385
    BPMS-specific   396
exponential distribution   274
eXtensible Event Stream   422
external service   *see* service

F
facilitator   172–174, 211, 311, 312
factor   236, 237
fallacy of programmatic change   364
feasibility   57
Fishbone diagram   240
Five Factor Model   163
flexibility   17, 59, 61, 303, 356
flow

default   81
exception   130
message   99, 101, 102, 107, 121, 129,
        180, 184
sequence   19, 76, 80, 92–94, 99, 101,
        122, 123, 126, 131, 136, 179, 180,
        183–186, 219, 385, 394, 399, 407
flowchart   18, 305
flower pattern   442
footprint matrix   434
Fordism   368
functional organization   11
fuzzy miner   429

G
gateway   79, 184
    AND   82, 86, 164, 174, 180, 193, 272,
        440
    decision   255, 257, 263, 282
    exclusive   80
    inclusive   87
    OR   87, 88, 184, 190, 193, 259
    parallel   82, 257
    XOR   80, 81, 86, 92, 164, 184, 190, 193,
        272
governance   27, 475, 478, 479, 484
group dynamics   307
groupware system   345

H
handoff   29, 50, 177, 179, 180, 195, 214–
        216, 218–220, 226, 245, 246, 261,
        293, 334, 355, 356, 381, 420, 444,
        446
    internal   180
handoff point   *see* handoff
health   56
Heuristic Process Redesign   307, 315
heuristics miner   438–440
historic information   *see* information
history-based allocation   *see* allocation
HR director   25
HTTP   390
human capital   36

I
IDEF3   *see* Integrated DEFinition for Process
        Description Capture Method
idleness   222
IEEE Task Force on Process Mining   422
implicit termination   84

inductive miner   438, 439, 441, 442, 468
information
    historic   358
    operational   358
Information Technology Infrastructure Library
        45, 114
infrastructure model   37
innovation   36
instantiation
    explicit   377
    implicit   377
Integrated DEFinition for Process Description
        Capture Method   18, 305
inter-arrival time   274, 286
interview-based discovery   168, 170, 175
Ishikawa diagram   240
island automation   357
Issue Tracking system   232, 343
issue-to-resolution   2, 343
IT   479
IT Service Management   343
IT-oriented   see process
ITIL   see Information Technology
        Infrastructure Library

J
JavaScript Object Notation   390
join   80, 184, 185
    AND   82, 83, 87–89, 91, 126, 129, 269
    OR   88, 89, 91, 114
    XOR   80, 81, 84, 87–89, 91, 117, 143,
        259
        event-based   127
JSON   see JavaScript Object Notation

K
Key Performance Indicator   59, 478, 483, 499
KPI   see Key Performance Indicator

L
lack of synchronization   89, 185, 203
lane   97
Lean   7, 310
Lean Six Sigma   8, 311
learning   189
livelock   185, 186, 203
log delta analysis   459
loop count   394

M
M/M/1 queue   275, 276

M/M/c queue   275, 276
maintainability   189
manageability   51
management process   41
Management Team   24
Mannesmann   38
manual task   see task
master vendor list   31
merging   see token
message   387
message flow   see flow
methods   479
middleware   361
model
    abstraction   78, 104, 174, 426
    fully-executable   385
    mapping   78, 160, 426
    purpose   19, 75, 78, 182, 189, 310, 378,
        379
    target audience   78
modeling
    convention   183, 192
        naming   77, 189
    guideline   183, 192
    language   92
    theory   78
    tools   85
monitoring   351

N
negative effect   236
NESTT   306, 321, 338
net promoter score   61
Non-Value Adding   214, 215, 217, 218, 223,
        244, 249
normal distribution   282
normative process model   see process model
notation   92
NVA   see Non-Value Adding

O
object   see business object
observation   166
occupation rate   267
Operating System   356
operational information   see information
operational manager   161
OR gateway   see gateway
order-to-cash   1, 5, 25, 266, 341, 415
organization chart   37
organizational allocation   see allocation
organizational change management   21

organizational design   79
organizational perspective   96

P

PAIS   *see* Process-Aware Information System
Pareto
   analysis   232, 233, 235, 252, 253, 305
   chart   233, 235
passthrough   81
patterns
   creation   392
   push   393
PCF   *see* Process Classification Framework
people   27, 480, 486
performance
   dashboard   414, 415
   objective   62, 225, 326, 362, 414, 473,
      476, 482
   target   62
Performance Framework   46
performance measure   *see* process
      performance measure
performance mining   420, 421
perspective
   control-flow   93
   data   93
   functional   93
   object   93
   resource   96
Petri nets   305
PICK chart   235
PLM system   *see* Product Lifecycle
      Management system
PMBOX   *see* Process Management Body of
      Knowledge
pool   97
   black box   101
   collapsed   101
   white box   101
Positive Deviance   309
potential owner   392
PPM   *see* process performance measurement
pragmatic quality   189
premature victory celebration   364
primary factor   239
PRINCE2   *see* Projects in Controlled
      Environments
private process   *see* process
Process
   maturity   490
process
   actor   4, 6, 13, 15, 28, 30
   customer   6, 13, 30

instance   76
   attribute   394
   state   76
inter-organizational   368
intra-organizational   368
model
   business-oriented   371
   conceptual   79, 371
   connectivity   115
   correctness   184, 187
   deployment   348
   diameter   115
   executable   79, 371
   IT-oriented   79, 371
   normative   452
   size   115
   structuredness   115, 187
   unstructured   272
   validation   170
outcome   4, 6, 13, 17, 31
   negative   4, 17, 20
   positive   4
private   101
public   101
scope   132
value   6, 13, 30
variable   386
process analysis   20, 213, 255
process analyst   25, 160, 163
process architecture   17, 22, 35, 37, 43
process automation   21
process category   41
process checklist   39
Process Classification Framework   46, 67
process discovery   17, 159–163, 175, 177,
      254, 273
process group   48
process identification   17, 35
process implementation   21
process landscape model   42, 43, 48
Process Management Body of Knowledge
      478
process maturity   490
process methodologist   26
process mining   415
process model repository   348
process modeler   172
process modeling tool   348
process monitoring   22, 413
process owner   15, 25, 161
process participant   4, 25, 96, 392
process performance dimension   59
process performance measure   17, 20, 22, 25,
      56, 59, 478, 482

process performance measurement   414
process performance metric   *see* process
          performance measure
process portfolio   64
process profile   51
process redesign phase   21
process simulation   279
    input analysis   282
Process-Aware Information System   15, 19,
          22, 219, 263, 318, 342, 343
    domain-agnostic   342
    domain-specific   342
processing time   60, 226, 261, 262, 264, 266,
          268, 269, 271, 275, 276, 280
procure-to-pay   2, 249, 342, 431
product   325
product and service catalog   37
product data model   326, 327
product lifecycle   50, 56, 67, 343
Product Lifecycle Management system   343
Product-Based Design   325
production rule   328
production workflow system   345, 346
profitability   54
project management   225
Projects in Controlled Environments   478
public process   *see* process
pyramid   44

Q
quality   17, 59, 60, 303
    external   60, 481
    internal   61, 504
quality control mechanism   478
queue   274
queueing system   274
queueing theory   273
queueing time   60
quote-to-order   2

R
random allocation   *see* allocation
redesign heuristics   316
redesign method   297
    ambition   306
    analytical   307
    creative   307
    evolutionary   307
    inward-looking   307
    nature   307
    outward-looking   307
    perspective   307

    revolutionary   307
    transactional   306
    transaformational   306
Redesign Orbit   306
reference model   49
repetition block   91
Representational State Transfer   390
resistance   364
resource   96, 98, 99, 102
    active   96
    class   96, 392
    classification   354
    consumption   308
    contention   273
    parameter   392
    passive   96
    pool   268, 281
    utilization   267, 270, 276, 280
REST   *see* Representational State Transfer
RESTful   *see* service
retain familiar   *see* allocation
rework   222
rework probability   260
Robotic Process Automation   221, 360, 361
role   457
role-based allocation   *see* allocation
role-playing   305
root cause   241
round-robin allocation   *see* allocation
RPA   *see* Robotic Process Automation
rule enforcement   359
rule task   *see* task

S
Sarbanes-Oxley Act   359
SCAMPER   305
SCAMPI   *see* Standard CMMI Appraisal
          Method for Process Improvement
scientific management   10
SCM system   *see* Supply Chain Management
          system
SCOR   *see* Supply Chain Operations
          Reference Model
screen scraping   360
scribe   172
script task   *see* task
secondary factor   239
selection criteria   56
semantical correctness   187
semantics   92
separation of duties   *see* allocation
sequence   42, 76
sequence flow   *see* flow

service 350
   adapter 396
   connector 396
   external 350
   in-only 389
   in-out 389
   interface 389
   operation 389
      asynchronous 389
      synchronous 389
   RESTful 390
service level agreement 60
service task *see* task
service time *see* processing time
Service-Oriented Architecture 345, 362
Seven Process Modeling Guidelines 192,
   193, 210
shortest queue 393
Signavio 86, 194, 286, 456, 479
simulation *see* process simulation, 305
simulation log 279
Six Sigma 7, 60, 308
Six Thinking Hats 305
SLA *see* service level agreement
smart contract 369
social network 167, 345, 488, 498
software development 343
software system 96
soundness 186, 187, 371
specialization 43
speech act modeling 305
split 80, 180, 184
   AND 82–84, 87, 89, 97, 119
   data-based 126
   event-based 180
   OR 87, 89, 255
   XOR 80, 81, 83, 86–89, 91, 117, 126,
      255, 259, 394
      data-based 379
      event-based 126, 127, 140
split miner 438, 439, 442, 464, 468, 469
stakeholder 24
stakeholder analysis 225
Standard CMMI Appraisal Method for Process
   Improvement 500
standardization 450
state *see* process instance
step 213
STP *see* Straight-Through-Processing
Straight-Through-Processing 356
strategic alignment 26, 27, 475, 477–480
strategic goal 37
strategic importance 41, 56
strategy map 36

structural correctness 184
structured heuristics miner 438, 439, 442,
   469
sub-process 102
   ad hoc 122, 382
   collapsed 104
   event 135
   expanded 104
   global 106
success factor 478
supply chain 50
Supply Chain Management system
   343
Supply Chain Operations Reference Model
   46, 114
support process 41
synchronization 83. *see* token
synchronizing merge 88
syntactic quality 183
syntactical correctness 187
syntax 92
system binding 396
system engineer 26

T
task 4, 102, 388, 394
   automated 372
   manual 372
   receive 374, 390, 391
   rule 374
   script 374, 391
   send 374, 390, 391
   service 374, 389
   user 372, 391
task allocation strategy 392
technology fault 129
terminology 49
text annotation 96
The Open Group Architecture Framework
   37, 72
theoretical capacity 267
Theory of Constraints 308
throughput time *see* cycle time
ticketing system 449
time 17, 59, 175
timeline chart 443
timeout 133
timestamp 422
to-be 21–23, 287, 305, 322, 334, 335, 338,
   477
to-be-executed 384
TOC *see* Theory of Constraints

TOGAF   *see* The Open Group Architecture
        Framework
token   76
    merging   83
Total Quality Management   7
touchpoint   483
Toyota Production System   7, 218
TPS   *see* Toyota Production System
trace   426
trace filter   431
transaction processing   347
transaction stage   50
transactional method   *see* redesign method
transformational method   *see* redesign
        method
Transparency   358
tree diagram   241
TRIZ   308
trust   368

U
UIMS   *see* User Interface Management
        System
UML Activity Diagrams   18
understandability   189
unit capacity   269
unit load   268
unrealized value   221
User Interface Management System   357
user task   *see* task

V
VA   *see* Value Adding
validation   187
validity   188
Value Adding   214, 216, 217, 220, 244, 249
value chain   44
value-chain modeling   42
variants analysis   420, 421, 458
verification   187
violation   451
vocabulary   92

W
waiting time   60, 261, 262, 442

waste
    defects   219
    inventory   219, 221, 227, 228, 245
    motion   219, 220
    overprocessing   219, 222, 223, 226, 245
    overproduction   219, 223, 226, 245
    transportation   219, 220
    waiting   219, 221, 227, 245
Web service   15, 114, 341, 352, 361, 372,
        385, 390, 391, 398
Web Services Description Language   390
Web technology   385
WfMC   *see* Workflow Management Coalition
WfMC reference model   *see* Workflow
        Management Coalition
WfMS   *see* Workflow Management System
white box   *see* pool
why-why diagram   236
WIP   *see* Work-In-Process
work item   279, 348, 421
    check-in   349
    check-out   349
Work-In-Process   221, 266, 276
Work-in-Process   266
workflow   342
workflow log   426
Workflow Management Coalition   352
    reference model   352
Workflow Management System   14, 345
worklist   421
workload reduction   355
workshop-based discovery   172, 174–177
WSDL   *see* Web Services Description
        Language

X
XES   *see* eXtensible Event Stream
XML   385, 390
XML Schema   385, 386, 390
XOR gateway   *see* gateway
XSD   *see* XML Schema

Z
Zachman Framework   37, 72

Printed in the United States
By Bookmasters